# CHRISTIAN PERSPECTIVES ON CHURCH SCHOOLS

**a reader**

# CHRISTIAN PERSPECTIVES ON CHURCH SCHOOLS

## a reader

edited by

Leslie J Francis
DJ James Professor of Pastoral Theology
Trinity College, Carmarthen,
and St David's University College, Lampeter, Wales

and

David W Lankshear
Deputy Secretary, National Society, London, England.

First Published in 1993
Gracewing
Fowler Wright Books
Southern Avenue, Leominster
Herefordshire HR6 0QF

*Gracewing Books are distributed*

*In New Zealand by*
Catholic Supplies Ltd
80 Adelaide Rd
Wellington
New Zealand

*In Australia by*
Charles Paine Pty
8 Ferris Street
North Parramatta
NSW 2151 Australia

*In U.S.A. by*
Morehouse Publishing
P.O. Box 1321
Harrisburg
PA 17105
U.S.A.

*In Canada by*
Meakin and Associates
Unit 17, 81 Auriga Drive
Nepean, Ontario, KZE 7Y5
Canada

Compilation and editorial material © David Lankshear and Leslie J. Francis, 1993
Copyright information for individual chapters is given on pages 489–90

The right of the editors and the contributors to be identified as the authors of this work has been asserted in accordance with the Copyright, Designs and Patents Act, 1988

ISBN 0 85244 235 1

Typesetting by Action Typesetting Limited, Gloucester
Printed by The Cromwell Press, Trowbridge, Wiltshire

# Contents

# Preface

*Leslie J Francis and David W Lankshear*

Both editors have a long standing interest in and commitment to the church school debate. We believe that this debate is best advanced in an interdiscplinary, international and ecumenical context.

We have become increasingly aware of the important contributions made to the church school debate during the past decade through seminal articles published in scholarly journals in the USA, Canada, Australia and Europe, as well as within the UK. Our aim in this reader is to re-publish a collection of these articles and thereby to make them more readily accessible to a wider readership. In so doing we hope both to advance the quality of scholarly debate about church schools and to promote good quality practice within them.

Two of our main guiding principles in making the selection have been the twin convictions that the church school debate needs to be both educationally and theologically informed, and that claims about the distinctiveness and effectiveness of church schools need to be subjected to close empirical scrutiny. We have not found it difficult to identify good quality material which addresses the theoretical and practical issues. Here our major problem has been the harder one of deciding what to omit. We have experienced greater difficulty in identifying good quality material which evaluates aspects of church schools from an empirical perspective. Here we have been obliged to rely more heavily on our own published research than ideally we would have wished.

The task of editing this reader has been appropriately located within the Centre for Theology and Education at Trinity College in Carmarthen. The College, originally funded by the National Society in 1846 to train teachers for the developing network of National Society and Church of England schools throughout England and Wales, remains firmly committed to pioneering initiatives in church-related education.

We are grateful to many authors and publishers who have permitted their work to be represented in this reader and to Professor John M Hull for furnishing the foreword. We also wish to record our sincere thanks to the Pantyfedwen Fund of St David's University College, Lampeter, and those who have helped in the processes of collating resources, compiling materials, copy-editing text, proof reading, word-processing, and seeking permissions, especially Anne Rees, Sue Jones and Diane Drayson.

Leslie J Francis
David W Lankshear
June 1993

# Foreword

## John M Hull

A foreword is something to think about before the words start. True, it is also expressed in words, but the words before the real words start invite the reader to prepare to listen by considering the font from which all Christian speech springs.

It is noticeable that the editors of this collection of essays did not think it sufficient to entitle the volume *Perspectives on Church Schools*. After all, there might be various perspectives on church schools, such as those of government planners, or those which represent some other basic commitment such as secularism. These essays, however, represent *Christian* perspectives on church schools. Of course, this could also mean many things, and the reader will soon find that indeed it does, but the overall intention of such a collection is clearly to consider the character and the influence of church schools in so far as they spring from and contribute to the meanings and messages of the Christian faith. Diverse though these may be, they may all be thought of as springing from the baptismal font, where the divine calling first wins a response in the words of confession and commitment, and from a textual and historical perspective they spring from the speech of the New Testament.

These hints about origins may suggest that we return to the Magnificat, the ancient hymn or psalm attributed by St Luke to Mary before the birth of Jesus. Luke intends the Magnificat to be part of his foreword to the gospel and we may consider it in this way as offering a pause before the real words of this book begin. In his two volume work Luke is about to describe the expansion of the mission of the church from Bethlehem to Rome, and the prologue to volume 1 – the Gospel – sets out the broad guidelines for that development. In its content, the Magnificat establishes continuity with the tradition, and in that sense it looks back; in its context it introduces a remarkable new turn of events, since it is a song of expectation. In that sense it looks forward. It makes no reference to education or to church schools, but then it makes no reference to the crucifixion and resurrection of Jesus either, or to the Holy Trinity or to many other themes which became significant in Christianity. From the later Christian point of view it is (to borrow an expression from Emile Durkheim) an elementary form of the religious life.

Such simplicity enables us to grasp again some of the fundamentals of the mission.

> My soul magnifies the Lord and my spirit rejoices in God my Saviour for he has regarded the low estate of his hand maiden.

We magnify God by making him and her greater. Christian education enables children to magnify God when they realise that no pronoun does justice to God, who is greater than our language. No image can contain the greatness of God. Christian education magnifies God when children are enabled to see that God is greater than the church, and that no religious tradition, even the Christian tradition, can contain the one whom heaven and earth themselves cannot contain. Christian education by so magnifying God sets us free for a world-wide vision which embraces all people. God is realised when a comunity of free speech is established in a context of equality and reciprocity. Such a community is based upon the solidarity of all its members, and thus in principle no-one can be excluded. All human beings are to contribute to that world-wide free speech community; it has no human boundary. God is restricted in a restrictive community but magnified in a community which in principle exists in solidarity with all. It is significant that the Magnificat could be equally at home in Judaism, Christianity or Islam. In its fundamental character and in its determination to make God greater, it already directs us towards that which is greater than our tradition and yet that within which the elementary forms of our tradition are retained.

The greatness of God is nurtured and affirmed in worship. The Magnificat is an outburst of praise. Education into worship must always be a central feature of church schools, and that worship will be not only liturgical but prophetic in its character. True worship can never be practised in isolation, and the worship of the church school has a particular responsibility to be connected to the curriculum and to the community and the world. The central logic of biblical worship is that we are to honour the sojourner and the stranger within our gates because we were once sojourners and strangers in the land; we are to honour the widows and the fatherless, the disadvantaged and the disabled, because God rescued us when we were slaves in an alien land. The curriculum of the church school offers worship to the greatness of God when the Holy Spirit of God is seen at work in other cultures and in other faiths. To act out this solidarity is to worship God in spirit and in truth.

> For behold! Henceforth all generations will call me blessed, for he who is mighty has done great things for me, and holy is his name, and his mercy is on them that fear him from generation to generation.

Christian education is mainly concerned with the creation of a future. The question is what our children will called blessed. To what will they attribute blessing? Where will they find blessing? To what will they offer their loyalty? Church schools are not so much carriers of a tradition. Their task is not so much to transmit the past as to empower the past, to release it for the task of future-creation. In church schools the Christian tradition is not so much reflected as rejuvenated.

This is to take place, however, through the processes of learning. These are intergenerational in character. Teachers, parents, pupils both young and old and the community all have a role in rejuvenating the mission. In this process of learning, the identity of each child and each adult is to be affirmed and challenged. The mighty one has done great things for me and holy is his name. Moreover, this learning experience takes place within the context provided by mercy and respect.

> He has shown strength with his arm. He has scattered the proud in the imagination of their hearts. He has put down the mighty from their thrones and has exalted those of low degree. He has filled the hungry with good things and the rich he has sent empty away.

There is an indissoluble connection between Christian education and justice. The world-wide gulf between the rich and the poor is growing wider. The Magnificat calls Christians to adopt a critical stance towards this. We must examine the institutions which cause or perpetuate such an unequal distribution of resources. If church schools are to be measured by the values of the Magnificat, then they are to be judged by that comprehensive standard of solidarity with the weakest and the most impoverished. Too often in education the advantaged attract even greater resources while the disadvantaged finish up with less and less. The Church of England comprehensive school has a unique role to play in redressing this imbalance and in witnessing to a society in which each takes responsibility for all. Thoughtful Christian parents, who seek to find ways in which their family commitment to Kingdom of God values can be expressed through church structures are increasingly drawn towards the comprehensive secondary schools of the Anglican, Catholic and other Christian traditions, and to the primary schools which feed and sustain them. There is no doubt that the spirit of the Magnificat rests upon such schools.

> He has helped his servant Israel in remembrance of his mercy as he spoke to our parents before us, to Abraham and Sarah and to their offspring forever.

The ideals of the Magnificat as a manifesto of Christian education will be actualised in church schools as a result of theological reflection, worship and action in the light of a renewed appropriation of the Bible. The Magnificat offers us a Christian education which is based upon promise and hope. God has remembered his promise.

Great is the faithfulness of God. The Magnificat was not attributed to one of the influential Apostles such as Peter or Paul. It is on the lips of a young woman, possibly a teenager, from a small rural community. We will not be able to enter into its message for church schools unless we who read this book can also stand in solidarity with Mary and those who like her are of a lowly estate. If, however, we can identify with that point of view we will be able to look at Christian education and the mission of the church schools from a very fundamental perspective, that of the font, that of the child, that of the servant.

This has been a word from the font, a reminder from a song which was sung before the speech really starts. I am very happy to be associated in this way with the editors of this collection, and to renew my contact with the contributors, almost all of whom are known to me personally. In many and varied ways they extend and apply and in some cases offer a critique of the values which I have regarded here as those of the Magnificat in Christian education. I believe that their work and the work of this book will contribute to the realisation of that common goal.

John M Hull
School of Education
The University of Birmingham
England

# Introduction

*Leslie J Francis and David W Lankshear*

This reader brings together in an accessible form some of the recent key articles which have made significant contributions to the church school debate. The selection clearly displays the interdisciplinary, international and ecumenical context of the debate. The thirty-three articles chosen for inclusion have been organised within thirteen chapters. These chapters fall into three clear groups.

The first group of chapters identifies four major theoretical perspectives from which the church school issue may be debated. Chapter one opens the reader with an *educational* perspective. Two educational philosophers, Professor Paul H Hirst from the UK and Dr Elmer J Thiessen from Canada, debate whether the churches' concerns with education and catechesis are consistent with the liberal view of education accepted within contemporary secular society.

Chapter two presents three contributions which address the church school debate from a *theological* perspective. The Very Revd Robert M Waddington reflects on the nature of a Christian school in the light of the doctrine of the Trinity. He identifies ten key characteristics of the church school, which he characterises as theology of nurture, theology of service and theology of prophecy. The Revd Peter Marr examines the implications of the Anglican Roman Catholic International Commission for the development of inter-denominational cooperation in church schools.

Chapter three examines the implications of *social* context on church schools. Professor David N Aspin and Dr Nigel P Blake debate the social implications of the proliferation of faith community schools within multi-ethnic, multi-faith and multi-cultural societies. Clearly the case for Christian and denominational schools has to be set in the wider context of schools sponsored by other religious groups. In a third article in the chapter Geoffrey Duncan, the General Secretary of the Church of England General Synod Board of Education, reflects on the response of Church of England schools to being part of a multi-cultural society.

Chapter four addresses the *spiritual* character of church schools. First, the Revd Dr Derek H Webster distinguishes between two ways of understanding the spiritual dimension in current educational and religious thought and argues that church schools have a particular opportunity to address the spiritual dimension. Then the Revd David A Attfield discusses the educational role of the eucharist within the church primary school.

The second group of chapters identifies the five major cultural contexts in which the church school issue is currently debated. Chapter five begins by presenting *British* perspectives. The Revd Professor Leslie J Francis reviews the history of the churches' involvement in education in England and Wales from the beginning of the nineteenth century to the eve of the 1988 Education Reform Act. He gives particular attention to the strengths and weaknesses of the partnership forged between church and state in the 1944 Education Act. Alan Brown assesses the current contribution to the state maintained sector of education in England and Wales by the three religious groups which have a significant investment in voluntary aided and special agreement schools, namely the Church of England, the Roman Catholic Church and the Jewish faith community. Then the Revd David G Attfield and Dr James Arthur discuss the challenge of the 1988 Education Reform Act to church schools from an Anglican and a Catholic perspective respectively.

Chapter six presents three *European* perspectives. Dr Seamas Ó Buachalla examines the relationship between church and state in Irish education throughout the twentieth century. He concludes that the presence and power of the churches have been increased significantly in the course of the present century and have been further consolidated in the expansion of educational provision sine the 1960s. Marjanne de Kwaasteniet describes the place of denominational schools in the Netherlands, setting the present situation within its historical and political contexts. Here the Protestant sector continued to grow in the 1980s while the Catholic sector began to decline. Dr Oliver Boyd-Barrett turns attention to Spain, where he examines the transition from a church-dominated educational system during the Franco dictatorship to a state-dominated system in which the Catholic church has less power.

Chapter seven presents two *Australian* perspectives. First, Professor Brian V Hill distinguishes between the three main forms of Christian schools in Australia: Catholic schools which in statistical terms outweigh the others; traditional 'independent' schools, mostly sponsored by the major Protestant denominations; and the smaller 'alternative' schools, characterised by conservative theology and parental involvement. He addresses the same sharp questions to each of these sectors. Then Dr Patricia Malone scrutinises the language of the religious education curriculum guidelines implemented by the two largest Catholic Education Offices in Australia.

Chapter eight presents two *American* perspectives. Both articles in the chapter scrutinise the growth of the independent Christian school movement in America from different research perspectives. Professor William J Reese examines closely the public statements of those who have promoted the development of independent Christian schools. He discerns the key motives to include the view that schools within the state funded system have betrayed their roots in biblical theology, morality and academic standards, and the belief that parents have the primary responsibility in education. Professor Alan Peshkin draws on the experience of his eighteen month participant obervation with one independent school to evaluate whether fundamentalist Christian schools should be regulated by the state. His response balances the danger of restrictive state control with the danger of such schools engendering harmful divisiveness by their very intolerance towrds the secular system which permits them to flourish.

Chapter nine presents two *Canadian* perspectives. Both articles in this chapter focus on the debate in Canada regarding public funding for private schools. First, Dr Bernard J Shapiro rehearses the arguments and counter-arguments put forward to the Commission on Private Schools in Ontario, which published its findings in 1985 and for which he was commissioner. Then Professor Ralph M Miller argues that, in spite of Canada's long history of public education and considerable effort to distinguish *religious* from *public* education, it is now more than ever difficult to determine whether or not to include religious alternative schools within the public system.

The third group of chapters identifies four major areas of empirical research into the contemporary functioning of church schools. Chapter ten begins by presenting three enquiries into the *distinctiveness* of church schools. In the first study Brenda M Gay analyses the public statements made by independent schools in England about themselves in two major school year books in order to profile independent schools associated with the Church of England. She gives particular attention to the involvement of clergy, religious education and worship. In the second study the Revd Professor Leslie J Francis compares the presence of church-related educational perspectives in Church of England state maintained schools, Roman Catholic state maintained schools and county (or non-denominational) state maintained schools in Gloucestershire.

Chapter eleven presents three enquiries into the curriculum in church schools. In the first study Wendy Ball and Dr Barry Troyna analyse the views of head teachers and departmental or faculty heads to the relevance of multi-cultural education within their church schools. In the second study the Revd Dr Edwin Cox and Dr Martin Skinner set out to uncover the attitudes of teachers in church primary schools to multi-faith religous education and to assess the impact of in-service training on their attitudes. In the third study the Revd John L Higgins analyses the ways in which the syllabuses of religous education developed for use in Church of England voluntary aided schools treat the role of women.

Chapter twelve presents two enquiries into the attitudes of the pupils who attend church schools. In the first study the Revd

Professor Leslie J Francis and Sister Josephine Egan research the attitudes of pupils attending Catholic schools in the USA. Building on their earlier studies in England, Wales and Australia, they pay particular attention to the differences in attitudes between practising Catholic pupils, pupils from non-practising Catholic backgrounds and non-Catholic pupils. In the second study the Revd Dr John E Greer researches the attitudes of pupils attending Catholic and Protestant secondary schools in Northern Ireland. He pays particular attention to the openness with which these pupils view members of the other religious group and to the factors which predict differences in the degrees of openness expressed by pupils.

Chapter thirteen presents two enquiries which explore the effectiveness of church schools from rather different theoretical and empirical persepectives. In the first study Dr Joseph Rhymer and the Revd Professor Leslie J Francis assess the impact of Catholic educational provision in Scotland on the attitudes of Catholic adolescents. In Scotland this means taking into account the effectiveness both of the publicly funded Catholic school system and of the provision of Catholic religious education within non-denominational schools in areas where Catholic schools are not available. In the second study the Revd Professor Leslie J Francis and David W Lankshear assess the impact of Church of England voluntary aided primary schools on village church life in England.

It is the editor's shared hope that this reader will now contribute to raising the level of theologically and educationally informed debate about church schools, to promoting good practice among classroom teachers and church school administrators, and to stimulating educational researchers into undertaking further empirical enquiry into the distinctiveness and effectiveness of church schools.

# 1. Educational perspectives

The existence, purpose and nature of church schools raise crucial questions for educational philosophy. These questions have been shaped most starkly in Britain by Professor Paul H Hirst, writing from the perspective of logical analysis.

In the first article in this section, Paul Hirst develops the view of education as concerned with the promotion of rational autonomy. He contrasts this view of education with the activity of catechesis, where 'the aim is from the stance of faith, the development of faith.' He argues that there are real difficulties in church schools endeavouring both to educate and to catechise, unless the activities of education and catechesis are sharply separated within the school, being self-consciously and deliberately presented to the pupils as clearly different in character and objectives.

At the time of writing Paul Hirst was professor of education in the University of Cambridge. This article was first published in *British Journal of Religious Education* in 1981. An earlier version had been given as the 1978 Wiseman Lecture at Oscott College and published th *The Oscotian.*

In the second article, Dr Elmer J Thiessen subjects Hirst's position to critical analysis. He argues that Hirst is wrong in treating the transmissionist and the rational critical concepts of education as two radically different and opposed concepts of education. He maintains that the transmission of beliefs is an important and necessary preliminary phase to rational critical thought which has been traditionally linked with liberal education.

Elmer Thiessen lectures in the philosophy of education at Medicine Hat College in Alberta. He has written widely on the subject of indoctrination. This article was first published in *Journal of Philosophy of Education* in 1987.

# 1.1 Education, catechesis and the church school

*Paul H Hirst*

## Introduction

I think it can hardly be denied that the two great Christian denominations in this country which are responsible for large numbers of church schools, are both now somewhat at a loss to know what the precise role of their specifically denominational schools should be; if indeed there is now any coherent function that can be found for them.[1] Not *very* long ago the central view of the Catholic church at any rate was quite clear on the matter. Perhaps this can best be seen in the 1929 encyclical letter of Pope Pius XI, *Divini Illius Magistri*.[2] After setting out that

> The specific and immediate purpose of Christian education is to co-operate with divine grace in forming the true and perfect Christian

the letter goes on to state that of its nature a true school must therefore be both subsidiary and complementary to the family and the Catholic church.

> The mere fact that religious teaching ... is imparted in a school does not make it satisfy the rights of the church and the family, nor render it fit to be attended by Catholic pupils. For this the whole of the training and teaching, the whole organisation of the schools − teachers, curriculum, school books on all subjects − must be so impregnated with the Christian spirit under the guidance and motherly vigilance of the church, that religion comes to provide the foundation and the culminating perfection of the whole training. And this applies not only to elementary (or primary) schools but to secondary schools as well.

Indeed the encyclical goes on to forbid Catholic children to attend schools which are not Catholic in nature and curriculum, except by special permission from the local bishop.[3]

This statement seems clear enough about the role and character of the Catholic school almost to the point of denying any validity in Christian terms to the work of all other schools. Following this line it has been said, I think rightly, that in this country, right up to Vatican II, Catholic schooling was marked by first an insistence by the church on its right to operate its own schools, and that with the aid of state finance, and secondly the church's insistence

2

that Catholic parents have a solemn duty to send their children to Catholic schools[4].

> The Catholic child from the Catholic home should continue his education at the hands of Catholic teachers in a Catholic school.

Not that other views have been wanting. Sheer practical necessity long ago led some Catholics to advocate interdenominational schools if perhaps only as a second best. And it is I think most appropriate to this occasion for me to draw attention to the fact that in 1836 the future Cardinal Wiseman gave evidence to a Select Committee on Education in Ireland to the effect that

> it might easily be managed to give Protestants and Catholics a common education, reserving the religious education of their respective classes to their own pastors.

To the perception and good sense of the Cardinal whom we honour on this occasion I shall return in due course. But even before the Second Vatican Council of the 1960s, let alone since then, criticisms of the traditional Catholic position that I have sketched were gaining ground. The religious education church schools give has been accused of being dangerously ghetto-like, in some ways self-destructive of the very values it seeks to teach in the church's mission to the world, and anti-ecumenical. The belief that religion does in fact significantly influence any part of the curriculum in Catholic schools, other than that of specifically religious education, can be seriously doubted. Again it is argued by some that Catholic schools have the effect of encouraging parents to neglect their own duties in matters of religious education, and there is strong evidence that parental influence, not school influence, is much the more significant in determining religious commitment. There is also evidence that there is no significant difference in the moral attitudes of Catholics who have gone to Catholic schools and those who have gone to non-Catholic schools. If serious doubt has thus been cast on the desirability and even the efficacy of Catholic schools, questions also begin to arise as to whether the enormous cost to the church of these institutions is really justifiable. Just think what the church might do with the vast human resources and the money that at present go into these schools. Might it not be the case that the distinctive ends Catholic schools have sought can be better achieved, and at far less cost, by other means?

Yet through all these criticisms the notion of a Catholic school pursuing the distinctive goals of Catholic education, can be considered untouched. Maybe there is here at least an ideal which we should always pursue so far as is practically possible, using all the criticism there may be to improve these institutions whenever they can in fact be maintained. But what if the very concept of Christian education that is the basic premise of this traditional approach is itself questioned and found wanting? Is there some other Christian view of education that might lead to a re-assessment of the Catholic school? I wish to argue that there is another view, which I believe has its roots as firmly within Catholic teaching as the traditional view which I have outlined. This other view I also believe does much more justice than the traditional view to our contemporary understanding of the nature of human knowledge, of man, of society and of its institutions.

## Two concepts of education

In seeking to map out this different approach, it is necessary to distinguish two concepts of education.[6] The first of these I call the primitive concept, for it clearly expresses the view of education a primitive society might have when it seeks to pass on to the next generation its beliefs and values, its rituals, its way of farming and so on. In this situation, whatever is held by the group to be true or valuable, simply because it is held to be true or valuable, is what is passed on so that it comes to be held as true and valuable by others in their turn. On this view, clearly, there can be a Christian concept of education, one based on those things which Christians hold to be true and valuable, things which they wish the next generation to hold in the same way. Similarly there can be a Humanist or a Buddhist concept; indeed, there will be as many concepts of education as there are systems of beliefs and values, concepts overlapping in character in so far as the beliefs and values of the different groups overlap.

But there is a second much more sophisticated view of education I suggest, arising from a recognition that not all the things held to be true or valuable by a group are of the same status. Some of the group's claims and activities will be rationally defensible on objective grounds, whereas others, perhaps held equally tenaciously, may on objective grounds be highly debatable. Some may in fact be matters of nothing but mere custom and tradition. Once it is fully recognised that the belief that something is true, even if that belief is universal, does not of itself make it true, a new principle emerges for carefully assessing what we pass on to others and how we wish them to regard it. That we hold something to be true or valuable is, of itself, no reason why anyone else should so regard it. But that something can, on appropriate objective grounds, be shown to be true or reasonable is a very good basis for everyone's accepting it. What is more we can then seek that others will hold it, not because we hold it, but because there are the objective grounds for it. In that case people can be educated so as to be prepared to reconsider, and where necessary revise, their beliefs and practices when new evidence and better arguments arise.

This second, sophisticated view of education is thus concerned with passing on beliefs and practices according to their objective status and with their appropriate justification. It is dominated by a concern for knowledge, for truth, for reason, distinguishing these clearly from belief, conjecture and subjective preference. On this view, when science is taught, its methods and procedures are seen to be as important as any contemporary scientific beliefs, for these may in significant respects have to be changed. In history, pupils are introduced to examining evidence so that they come to recognise that claims about what happened must satisfy the canons of historical scholarship. Where there is dispute, debate and divergence of opinion, just that fact is taught. Where in any area there do not seem to be agreed objective principles of judgment, exactly that is what is set out. Of course, mistakes will be made in seeking to follow as closely as possible the ideals of objectivity and reason, but education committed to these ends will be very different from education determined by the particular beliefs and values of a specific group.

On this second view, the character of education is in the end determined simply by the canons of objectivity and reason appropriate to the different forms of knowledge and understanding that we have. What is involved in teaching say the sciences, history, the arts, is determined by the nature of these pursuits themselves and not by characteristics that are in any way dependent on any religious presuppositions. Though certain Christians at times try to argue otherwise, I suggest we have now reached a point in our understanding of the nature of the sciences, the arts, mathematics, philosophy and so on, that their autonomy and independence of any specifically Christian presuppositions must be granted. Of course these pursuits have presuppositions, but these are definitive of the nature of the pursuits and are not dependent on the acceptance of particular religious beliefs.

## Education and rational autonomy

But surely, it may be argued, education in this sophisticated sense, devoted to respecting in all the matters it handles the limits of reason and objectivity, cannot begin to teach what the Catholic parent or the Catholic church wishes to teach to children in the interests of their coming to embrace the Catholic faith. Of course that is true, but the point of demarcating a concept of education as tied to objectivity and reason is precisely to draw attention to the very considerable difference between the character and logical status of the matters with which it will then deal and the character and logical status of the matters which are the concern of the church. Education in my second, sophisticated sense is clearly not concerned with the total good of the child as Christians, or many others, would see that. It has, however, I suggest a fundamentally important function that is in the interests of every child, and that certainly from a Christian point of view. But how far can such an education go? Could it in fact include any moral education or would that involve stepping beyond the strict limits of reason into concern with matters of faith? Just as I have insisted on the autonomy over against religion of other areas of human understanding, so I would defend the autonomy of a wide area of morality and see basic moral education as well within the limits of the sophisticated concept I have sketched.

What education in these terms would be aiming at in fact is clearly the basic development of children as autonomous rational beings. Put that way, it may seem an excessively intellectual notion. Yet education in this sense I see not merely as intellectual training, but the development of a rational person in every aspect, for instance his emotions, dispositions and skills as well. It views the development of the person's reason as central to his development in all other aspects. What is more the autonomous rational being that is aimed at is not one who, as it were, starts from scratch making his own judgments and decisions *ab initio* on everything. He is certainly a person who recognises that beliefs and judgments require appropriate evidence and good grounds. But although he regards everything as in principle open to rational questioning, he recognises that he is not individually in a position to make his own judgments on many matters. It is only rational to accept in the first place the judgments of those genuinely in a better position to decide.

Built into the notion of education in these terms however is the belief that, where it is publicly recognised that reason does not lead to general agreement amongst even the informed and knowledgeable, because objective judgment is unattainable, the personal judgment of individuals shall be as fully respected as possible. This means in particular that in matters of genuine controversy, be they in science or history, in religious belief, moral and social practice, or artistic values, the presentation of particular commitments as if they were not radically disputable on rational grounds is seen as anti-educational.

Of special importance in our present context is the status from an objective and rational point of view, of religious claims. From this point of view alone, it seems to me the Christian church has now to accept, as indeed many within it have long accepted, that there are, certainly at present, no publicly agreed objective tests for those claims. No grounds have been found for them that in their logical significance parallel the grounds that exist in say the sciences or mathematics or history. That is not to say that religious beliefs cannot be assessed rationally in a secondary sense wherever those beliefs presuppose understanding of an historical, scientific or moral kind. Indeed a historical faith like Christianity necessarily puts itself in a vulnerable position in this way. But after all such secondary tests have been survived by a religious position, the distinctively religious claims it makes, over and above these other elements, remain unjustified by acceptable public criteria. That we so readily speak of Christian faith and of revelation is witness enough to the widespread recognition of this status of religious claims from a rational point of view. If then education is seen as determined in its limits by the development of reason and objectivity, any attempt to bring about deep understanding of one or more religious faiths and their significance can be fully compatible with that only if those religious claims are presented as, on purely publicly accepted rational grounds, radically controversial. The explicit or implicit advocacy of any one set of beliefs as true, or any attempt to bring about commitment to a particular position, must be seen as an illegitimate objective for education in the sense I have been developing. Education in this sense then pursues rational autonomy, but of its essence must stop short of seeking any particular commitment on matters that are rationally controversial.

## Faith and the limits of reason

Yet human life is no respector of the limits of reason in this sense. We live constantly in a context where decisions and judgments have to be made for which no objectively based arguments provide an answer. What does the rationally autonomous man do then? He will go to the limits that reason can take him. He will seek to be as informed as he can about the possibilities open to him and their implications. As a rational being he recognises that he might be mistaken. He is aware too that his judgment can have very significant consequences not only for his own life but for that of others. He will thus respect to the fullest extent the equal freedom of others to their judgment in this matter. Yet in the end he must follow where he believes the truth or the best judgment lies. He is necessarily involved in acts of faith, faith that goes beyond the limits set by objectivity and reason. Education in this second sense therefore, just because it is bound by the limits of reason, stops short of seeking, to determine the personal development of pupils in terms of belief, action, attitudes, etc., where reason itself stops. It does all it can in terms of reason to prepare for personal commitment and faith, but beyond that it cannot go. It is concerned with all that reason can provide for the rationally autonomous life, on controversial as much as on non-controversial issues. But the life of reason it seeks to develop, it cannot of itself seek to complement by developing the life of faith.

The second sophisticated concept of education I have been articulating is I suggest implicit in a great deal of contemporary education and I have deliberately sought to express it in a stark way over against the more primitive concept. It is, I suggest, marked above all by:

a.   a commitment to the autonomy or independence from religious beliefs of the pursuits of objectivity and reason; and
b.   a commitment to developing a rationally autonomous person whose life is self-directed in the light of what reason determines.

But what is the Christian to make of education in this second sophisticated concept? It is by definition not itself a specifically Christian concept. But it does not follow that there is anything about it which makes it incompatible with Christian belief. Indeed, may it not perhaps be the case that education in natural reason, as I shall henceforth refer to it, is a part, even a necessary part, of a truly Christian life? That is indeed what I hold to be the case and I think there is strong support for that position from within the Catholic church's own teaching.

In the first place there is a long tradition of thought within the church which has recognised the autonomy of vast areas of human knowledge and understanding. Indeed, there is, in the doctrine of natural law, a view that even much moral understanding is not a matter of divine revelation or of faith but a product of natural reason. What is more, history has vindicated the wisdom of acknowledging to the full the autonomy of human knowledge whenever that is recognisable. Whenever, in the history of the church, Christians have sought to deny the autonomy of a branch of learning, as on notorious occasions in the story of the development of the physical and biological sciences, the result has in the end been invariably a triumph for autonomy. Where an understanding of what is perceivable by the senses is at stake, claims based on the use of the senses must in the end take priority over claims on grounds of revelation. The very meaning of what is claimed in science, as in any other area, we now appreciate is tied to an understanding of the appropriate tests for its truth. Where there is a clash, our understanding of revelation has to give way in a process of reinterpretation. Unfortunately, the church learns the lessons of its own history slowly and still seems bent on denying the autonomy of moral and social reasoning on a number of conspicuous issues.

But secondly, there is in keeping with the view of the proper role of natural reason in human affairs that I am emphasising, the longstanding view within the church that religious claims complement the understanding of natural reason. The proper logical relationship between Christian beliefs and autonomous rational beliefs is thus understood as one in which the claims of revelation are seen to presuppose areas of natural knowledge and understanding, revelation going beyond any conclusions that natural reason can itself secure, to make claims calling for the response of faith. In saying this it is not at all that religious claims are seen as irrational or anti-rational. It is rather that they complement other areas of autonomous understanding and that they are thereby different in character. An essential part of that difference is that certainly right now, and perhaps of their very nature, religious beliefs cannot be assessed by agreed objective criteria. There is a third important tradition within the church that lends support to my claim that education in terms of natural reason is part of the development of the Christian life. That is the tradition within the church which recognises that in all matters, including those of religion, the autonomy or freedom of the individual is a value of fundamental importance. What is wanted basically in the Christian life is not uncritical submission to personal or institutional authority in any area. Rather the aim must be intelligent free response to the claims of truth whether that truth is the product of natural reason or presented as revelation. What is sought is someone whose understanding and beliefs in all areas rest as far as possible not on the authority of teachers and tradition as such, but on the validity and significance of what is presented. This is to seek precisely the ideal of the rationally autonomous person whose life is determined by reason, so far as that is appropriate, but for whom the life of reason alone is complemented by the life of faith in which he freely responds as he judges best to religious claims to truth.

For these reasons I consider education in my second sense to be seeking goals which though they are in themselves in no sense distinctively Christian, but autonomous, are a necessary part of the Christian life and can be seen as such in terms of certain longstanding elements in the church's own teaching.

## Education and catechesis

In stressing the limitations that education in terms of natural reason will inevitably have, I have nevertheless been at pains to make it clear that it will certainly include the aim of developing pupils' accurate understanding of religious claims and of their rational status. Religious beliefs and practices will be presented from the stance of reason. But religious belief and practice can also be presented to pupils from the stance of faith. From this point of view the aim is the free response in decision and faith by the pupil, and where that has occurred the development of the committed life. In education in natural reason, the educator seeks from the stance of reason the development of reason in matters concerning religion as in all other matters. In catechesis, as I shall call it, the aim is from the stance of faith, the development of faith.[7] I am of course using the term catechesis in a distinctive way. It is essential to my argument that 'education' and 'catechesis' as I am using those terms, be seen as activities with quite distinct aims conducted by agents operating from within quite distinct positions. To seek to catechise from the basis of natural reason, or to educate from the basis of faith, is to try to engage in necessarily self-defeating activities. Yet education and catechesis, based respectively in reason and faith, are properly to be seen as complementary. And when so understood education is concerned with matters that are presupposed in catechesis. Indeed education can be seen as a form of pre-catechesis. What is more, within catechetical teaching there will be found an appropriate Christian view of the significance of education in natural reason. In education any faith the educator has is irrelevant to his goals. The catechiser on the other hand is properly an educated man but also a man of faith.

Yet in seeing education and catechesis as complementary activities, the sharpness of the divide between them which I have drawn must not be minimised. In particular I have explicitly denied the notion that faith itself can be justified by reason, for reason, as I am using that term, natural reason, I see as necessarily inadequate to settle precisely those matters on which faith is called for. I stress this all the more as my distinction between reason and faith is in practice not easy to apply. Just how far at any one time reason can take us even in matters of science is open to debate near the frontiers of the subject. Certain things believed demonstrably and indisputably true today, might turn out to be false ere long. In moral matters there is much uncertainty on rational grounds on numerous matters of deep importance to us all personally. Just what does reason prescribe? In religious matters, just what natural reason alone can achieve in terms of critical understanding is a matter of dispute. Where a rational presentation of Christian claims steps over into a presentation from faith may be itself a difficult matter of judgment, maybe as hard as determining when exactly a man is to be pronounced bald. Yet the distinction is in no way invalidated simply because it is in fact a distinction to which we can often only approximate in practice. What it does is to mark out sharply the aims and intentions of education and the aims and intentions of catechesis.

From all this analysis and distinction drawing then, I suggest that Christians should reject the idea that there is a distinctively Christian form of education which they wish their young to have, in favour of two distinct yet related concepts, a concept of education as the development of a person within the limits of reason and that of Christian catechesis which seeks to complement education in matters of faith. My reasons are that such a view alone

  a.  does justice to the autonomy of the achievements of natural reason;
  b.  does justice to the logical status of religious beliefs; and

c.  does justice to the distinct forms of free, autonomous response required from men in the face of the achievements of reason on the one hand and claims to religious revelation on the other.

## The role of the school

Armed with these notions which I maintain should be thoroughly acceptable to Christians, what sort of social institutions ought Christians then to seek, for the development of the Christian life? Clearly one theoretically neat solution is to suggest that on the basis of my division, schools should be instituted to look after all matters of education and education only, and that other, distinctly church institutions should look after all matters of catechesis. To repeat a previous point, that would of course mean that the schools would be involved in education in religion but in no way involved in seeking any particular personal commitment or faith from pupils. The church would then by its own institutional means seek to complement the education of the schools. If in the light of that suggestion we look at our existing institutions we certainly do not have anything of that kind right now. Though our society is increasingly pluralist and its state institutions are increasingly uncommitted in matters of religious belief, even our totally state financed schools are not officially at present religiously uncommitted. They do in fact engage in religious activities, especially those of worship, which in terms of my distinction are catechetical rather than educational. These are, however, progressively on the wane and I think there is good reason to argue that our county schools are slowly, in matters of religion as in many other matters, becoming concerned more and more with education in the particular sense I have outlined. With that move I would wholeheartedly agree and in the light of my earlier arguments I see nothing in it to which Christians should object. Christians would simply need to recognise very fully the limitations of such schools from their point of view.

But we have also in our society explicitly denominational schools, Catholic and Anglican in particular, intended for the children of parents who explicitly want the school to provide catechetical activities other than those of the county schools. The denominational schools have in the past been concerned with a form of Christian education, in the traditional sense of that term which I have rejected as primitive and unacceptable. But why should they not in future be seen as institutions seeking to carry out in one place both the two distinct activities of education and catechesis which I have argued together constitute what Christians should now wish for their children? After all, I have maintained that from a Christian point of view education in natural reason is a presupposition of catechesis and a necessary preparation for the Christian life. That being so, Christians have a duty to provide education in this sense and not just to provide catechesis. If the state does not provide education in my sense then Christians must provide it themselves. If society is religiously pluralistic, is it not one way of recognising that to have a variety of religiously committed schools for the children of parents who want these? Is not a variety of committed schools, each combining education with a form of catechesis according to parental wishes, an alternative to purely educational schools with separate institutions looking after catechetical activities? And if so, why not have such schools, perhaps state financed as much as independent?

There are I think real difficulties with this notion however. First a church school in these terms is endeavouring both to educate and to catechise. It is at one and the same time committed to trying to develop commitment to reason and commitment to a particular faith. But whereas the aim of education as I have outlined it must be one of leaving religious commitment open, catechesis is necessarily aimed at a personal response of one and only one kind. In the area of religion then the school as an institution would not be presenting open-ended religious education, but committed religious catechesis. True the outcomes aimed at in these two activities are perfectly compatible. But the two different activities demanded of the teachers seeking these different kinds of response must necessarily be sharply distinguished if confusion is not to result. If matters that should be seen as claims to faith are regarded as the conclusions of reason alone, or if matters that should be seen as the conclusions of reason are seen as claims to faith, the nature of both faith and reason is thereby confused. I see only one way out for the church school to prevent such confusion and that is if the activities of education and catechesis are sharply separated within the school, being self-consciously and deliberately presented to the pupils as clearly different in character and objectives.

Just this conclusion also seems to me to follow from somewhat different considerations. Education in natural reasoning is concerned with children learning matters which we do not regard as in any sense presented for their personal decision. We do not regard it as a proper exercise of their freedom and autonomy that they decide whether to accept or reject the idea that $2 + 3 = 5$, or that metals expand when heated, or that they ought not to steal. Similarly, even in matters of religious education we do not consider that pupils should be free to decide, for instance, whether or not Catholics believe in the deity of Jesus Christ. That is a matter of objective truth. But whether or not pupils themselves are to come to accept the deity of Jesus Christ or to believe in transubstantiation we do think are matters on which pupils must in the end freely exercise their own personal faith. In matters of education, the school has the right to expect intellectual and behavioural acceptance which in matters of catechesis is totally inappropriate. Even in our present maintained school system, all children must attend school from 5 – 16 except for those areas of school life that touch on religious commitment. There we allow a conscience clause. We allow parents to exercise their rights on behalf of their children's interests as they think best. This situation properly reflects, I suggest, the crucial distinction I have been drawing between the necessary universality of reason and the personal particularity of faith. If then we are to have denominational schools, I suggest that the education in natural reason they offer must be marked out from their catechetical activities so that the ultimately essential voluntary character of commitments of faith is plain to parents, and at an appropriate stage plain to pupils.

## Demarcating education and catechesis

But how can education and catechesis be so sharply distinguished in one institution's practice? Education and catechesis differ in their aims, in the forms of response that are sought, the states of mind they seek. They will therefore use the methods of and materials of teaching in distinctive ways. Neither can legitimately use indoctrinatory techniques if it is to respect the developing rational autonomy of the pupil. But whereas education will be dominated by a concern for the justificatory status of beliefs by natural reasoning, and demand response solely on that basis, catechesis will present beliefs so as to challenge pupils to free response. This difference needs to be marked out self-consciously by teachers precisely at the points where the confusion will most occur, in the school's concern for religion. It means, to my mind, the sharpest separation of religious educational activities concerned with reason and denominational catechetical activities. The former will necessarily be religiously pluralistic and open-ended even in a denominational school, the latter clearly will not be that as it is an activity conducted from within one faith, even though it may consider other faiths from that position. The attempt, within one range of activities, labelled say 'religious studies,' to assimilate both religious education and religious catechesis is precisely to undermine all I have argued for in the autonomy of natural reason. It is to my mind to deny the proper development of the Christian life by distorting the proper character of reason and the proper character of faith. It is to return to the primitive concept of Christian education that I argued is inadequate.

But how are we to draw the distinction explicitly, so that it sticks, so that it is significant to the pupils? Perhaps, by the separation in time and place of the two kinds of activity, by the explicit use of denominational labels for catechetical activities only, by the use of quite different personnel to mark out the difference in the roles of the teachers. To ask for this kind of separation within the work of the church school must seem to some rather alarming. And indeed, the means I am suggesting may be inappropriate. I am also very conscious of the fact that a separation of this kind may run counter to the pupils becoming aware of the relationship between reason and faith that is to me at the very heart of the business — faith seen as a complement to reason. Yet the very separation of education and catechesis can be used to promote that relationship. This means that in education the legitimacy of faith is presented, and in catechesis the necessity for reason as a pre-requisite for faith is clearly maintained. It might be argued that somewhere in the church school the spelling out of this relationship that binds faith and reason together is vital to the coherence of its enterprise. And if there is to be such a link established, why the need for the separation I have been insisting on? My reply is simply that, however it is to be achieved, a grasp by pupils of the difference between faith and reason is crucial to their understanding of the proper relationship between them. Somehow the distinction must be got over so that pupils grasp the objective necessity for accepting the conclusions of reason and the voluntary commitment that alone is appropriate in the face of claims on one's faith. In many situations within the total activities of a church school, this distinction can only be properly upheld if those involved in teaching and preaching exercise the most scrupulous care. But without some institutionalisation of the difference I doubt if it can ever be effectively communicated to pupils.

## A future for church schools?

So central is this distinction to all I am suggesting that it might seem as though only the total separation of education and catechesis as the discreet functions of school and church can hope to achieve what I am advocating. That is not however how I regard the matter. We have to recognise that practical decisions can never be satisfactorily made simply on abstract theoretical arguments. Principles have always to be applied to existing practical situations and the likely consequences of particular decisions must be fully considered. We can see quite enough of the results of the separation of school and church in our society to know what some of the consequences of further development along these lines would be for the church. There is good reason to doubt the capacity of the church to respond adequately with new types of activity if it ceased its catechetical work in schools. If the church was to maintain even its present standing as a presenter of the gospel to the young, it would have to establish quite new approaches appropriate to pupils attending purely 'educational' schools. In the USA there has been much relevant experience from which the church here might learn a great deal. But the demands of such an undertaking would be enormous. Again many Christians are perhaps rightly distrustful of the notion of a purely 'educational' school. Such an institution can only too easily become a place where by implication the validity of all religious claims is dismissed. Such an institution is as distorting of the proper place of reason and faith in life as any institution that functions on a false concept of faith. Both these fears are I think serious and are I think justification for cautious development. The church school, I have maintained, is a legitimate institution under certain important conditions. The separation of all catechesis from the school is I think likewise defensible, but only when other conditions hold in the schools – that they do strictly restrict themselves to a respect for the limits of natural reason in all matters, including those of religion. As I have emphasised previously, right now even our county schools are by law committed to certain catechetical activities – activities not acceptable to at least some Catholics.

But the schools of our religiously pluralist society are I am sure moving steadily to a secular position as a result of social forces that are quite beyond the control of the church. The challenge to Christians in that situation is double. First, it is to see that the schools are genuinely religiously open ended and concerned with the limits of education as I have sought to outline that. Secondly, it is to see that the church finds ways in a new range of catechetical work that builds on the education of those schools and matches up to the challenge it will present. The official message of the fifth Synod of Bishops held in Rome in 1977, entitled 'Catechesis in our time'[8] expresses well, at least in terms of general principle, what I have in mind. With all it says about catechesis and its relationship with education I disagree hardly at all. Here, as in other matters, I see ever greater realism and ever greater hope within the Catholic church.

But let me conclude as befits this occasion by recalling my quotation from Cardinal Wiseman.

> It might easily be managed to give Protestants and Catholics a common education reserving religious education of their respective classes to their own pastors.

I think the Cardinal was moving in exactly the right direction in his separation of common education and religious education. But now we must I suggest go one major step further down that same road. My recipe, in my terminology, is that we should indeed seek in our schools a common education for all children (bounded by the limits of natural reason). We should also seek their encounter with Christian faith through the activities of the church in catechesis. Particular institutional arrangements to achieve both these purposes we must approach flexibly, according to our social context. And I see no one clear, simple, institutional answer in our present context. What we need right now is to be clearer about the nature of the education and the catechesis that our institutions should serve. It is to that clarification that I have sought to address myself on this occasion.

**Notes**
1.  This paper is an edited version of the author's 1978 Wiseman Lecture given at Oscott College and published in *The Oscotian*, 1978 – 9 issue.
2.  *Divini Illius Magistri*, Acta Apostolicae Sedis, 20 (22nd February 1930). See also A E C W Spencer, 'An evaluation of Roman Catholic education policy in England and Wales 1900 – 1960,' in P Jebb (ed.), *Religious Education*, London, Darton, Longmann and Todd 1968.
3.  See J M Lee, 'Roman Catholic religious education,' in M J Taylor (ed.), *Foundations for Christian Education in an Era of Change*, Nashville, USA, Abingdon Press, 1976.
4.  See A E C W Spencer, *op. cit.*, to which I am much indebted in the early paragraphs of this paper.
5.  See M Gaine, 'The development of official roman catholic educational policy in England and Wales,' in P Jebb, (ed.), *op. cit.*
6.  This distinction was first made in similar terms in my paper 'Christian education: a contradiction in terms?' *Learning for Living*, 11 (4), 1972, pp. 6 – 11. I also used it for other purposes in chapter 5 of my book *Moral Education in a Secular Society*, London, Hodder and Stoughton, 1974.
7.  For a discussion of many of the complex factors that lie behind different uses of the term 'catechesis' see R M Rummery, *Catechesis and Religious Education in a Pluralist Society*, London, T. Shand, 1975.
8.  'Catechesis in Our Time: official message of the 5th Synod of Bishops, Rome 1977,' published by *The Tablet*, 5th November, 1977.

# 1.2 Two concepts or two phases of liberal education?

*Elmer J Thiessen*

## Introduction

It is common in educational writings to contrast two concepts of education: the one primitive, and the other sophisticated; the first concerned with passing on to children what we believe, the second concerned with the development of critical rationality.[1] When applied to religious education this same distinction is expressed in terms of a contrast between Christian nurture[2] (or Muslim nurture, etc.) and an objective, critical study of world religions. The main thrust of this paper is to critically evaluate the above commonly made distinctions and contrasts.

## The contrast

The distinction between these two concepts of education has been made repeatedly and perhaps most forcefully by Professor Paul H Hirst (1974, 1981, 1985). The primitive or traditionalist concept of education, according to Hirst, 'is concerned with the transmission of a body of specific concepts, beliefs, values, skills and so on within a particular tradition' (1985, pp. 6f). 'Whatever is held by the group to be true or valuable, simply because it is held to be true or valuable, is what is passed on so that it comes to be held as true and valuable by others in their turn' (Hirst, 1974, p. 80). We shall, with Hirst, label this *education I* (1985, pp. 6f).

The second, sophisticated, view of education, according to Hirst, is by contrast 'concerned with passing on beliefs and practices according to their objective status and with their appropriate justification. It is dominated by a concern for knowledge, for truth, for reason, distinguishing these clearly from belief, conjecture and subjective preference' (1981, p. 86). The central aim of this sophisticated concept of education is the development of 'rational autonomy,' characterised particularly by a willingness to assess openly and critically all beliefs held (Hirst, 1981, p. 87; 1985, pp. 12f). Again we shall follow Hirst and label this sophisticated concept of education *education IV* (1985, pp. 12ff).[3]

Hirst goes on to apply this same contrast to the area of religious instruction where Christian nurture or catechesis must be distinguished from religious education in terms of its starting point and its aim (1985, p. 14; 1981, p. 92).[4] In religious education the educator seeks 'from the stance of reason the development of reason in matters concerning religion,' whereas in Christian catechesis 'the aim is from the stance of faith, the development of faith' (Hirst, 1981, p. 89). Whereas religious education will accept the fact of religious pluralism and will seek to understand and critically examine alternative belief systems, Christian nurture 'is likely to favour the procedures of exposition, instruction, catechesis and indoctrination,' and is further 'likely to be ghetto-istic, concerned to preserve the tradition against other possibilities, favouring a large measure of social isolation and possibly indifference, even hostility towards others' (Hirst, 1985, pp. 7, 14).

There are four aspects of Hirst's description of the contrast between *education I* and *education IV* (or between Christian nurture and religious education) which I would like to highlight here for purposes of critical analysis later in this essay.

Hirst argues first of all that these two concepts of education are 'quite different,' operating on 'different principles,' each resting on 'a distinctive view of the foundation of knowledge and belief' (1974, pp. 79, 89; 1985, p. 6), and that therefore they should be kept separate and distinct. Christian catechesis must be 'sharply distinguished' from religious education since these activities have 'quite distinct aims conducted by agents operating from within quite distinct positions' (Hirst, 1985, p. 14; 1981, p. 89).

Second, Hirst is at times concerned to stress that these two concepts of education are opposed to each other. *Education I* starts from within a particular tradition, in contrast to *education IV* which begins with no prior commitment to certain presuppositions or an overall framework (Hirst, 1985, pp. 7, 10, 14). *Education I* is simply not concerned with the rational justification of beliefs taught, as is the case with the sophisticated concept of education (Hirst, 1981, p. 86). *Education IV* is further very much concerned to avoid 'seeking any particular commitment on matters that are rationally controversial,' while *education I* is notorious for its failure to make distinctions concerning the logical status of beliefs taught and hence its procedures are 'anti-educational' (Hirst, 1981, pp. 87f). While *education IV* is committed to a critical appraisal of beliefs taught as well as an openness to alternative beliefs, *Education I* 'contains within itself no challenge by way of deliberately sought alternative beliefs, no self-critical monitoring procedures and no questioning of the overarching framework' (Hirst, 1985, pp. 12, 7). With regard to religious instruction, Hirst maintains that it is simply 'self-defeating' to seek to catechise on the basis of reason, or to seek to educate on the basis of faith (1981, p. 90). Church schools are engaged in 'something quite other than education' (1974, p. 89; cf. p. 90; 1985, p. 16). They 'are not even in principle committed to demands of open, critical, rational education' (1985, p. 15). State-maintained schools, however, are, or at least should be, committed to true education which is open, critical and rational (Hirst, 1985, p. 16).

Third, there is an evaluative component inherent in this contrast. The one concept of education is often described as superior to the other. There is the 'primitive concept' and the 'much more sophisticated view of education' (Hirst, 1974, p. 80; 1981, p. 86). *Education I* is associated with indoctrination and with a ghetto-mentality; it is opposed to rationality and autonomy, and hence must be viewed as 'inadequate,' committed to goals that can only be described as 'improper, even sub-human' (Hirst, 1981, p. 92; 1985, pp. 7, 10, 15). Church-related schools seem to Hirst 'not only to offer an indefensible form of religious education, but to be inconsistent with the principles that should govern an open, critical, rational and religiously pluralistic society' (1985, p. 15).

Finally, Hirst also wants to maintain that the two concepts of education can in fact be seen to complement each other. What Hirst has in mind here are the teaching activities of the home, the church and other religious institutions which he wishes to protect, though as 'private' institutions, separate from and yet in some way complementary to sophisticated secular and state-maintained education (1974, pp. 84, 86, 88, 90). Thus, concerning the home, Hirst maintains that the 'purpose of many family activities is not educational, and the particularity of them, and the attitudes and sentiments involved, are such that, though compatible with education, they are not what education is about' (1974, p. 90). Thus, churches and other religious institutions also, which are concerned primarily with the practice and propagation of faith, and hence are committed to *education I*, can nevertheless conduct their activities in such a way as to 'complement and harmonise with education, rather than run counter to it' (Hirst, 1974, p. 89, cf. 1981, pp. 90, 92). 'Worship, preaching and evangelisation are not incompatible with the aims of religious education, but they certainly cannot be part of it' (Hirst, 1974, p. 89, cf. 1981, p. 91). In fact, Hirst spends a good deal of time trying to show that 'an intelligent Christian' can and should accept Hirst's own secularised concept of autonomous education based on reason alone (1974, p. 85; 1981, pp. 88ff). It should be noted, however, that in pointing to the complementary relationship between education and catechesis, Hirst in no way wants to minimise 'the sharpness of the divide between them' (1981, p. 90).

## Complementary or contradictory?

We are now in a position to evaluate critically the above commonly made distinction between the primitive and the sophisticated concepts of education. This will again be done on two levels, first of all with regard to the contrast between general nurture (*education I*) and the ideal of critical rationalism inherent in *education IV*, and secondly with regard to the contrast between Christian nurture and a critical rational approach to the study of world religions.

I would like to focus, first of all, on the complementary relationship between *education I* and *education IV* and the way in which this seems to contradict Hirst's other claim that these two concepts of education are radically different and opposed to each other. It is difficult to see how *education I* which is described as 'anti-educational' can also be described as complementary to and compatible with *education IV*. In fact, Hirst specifically raises objections against two other concepts of education (*II and III*), both of which involve attempts at integrating and harmonising *education I* and *education IV* (1985, pp. 9–12). Consistency would demand that he should similarly reject any description of *education I* and *education IV* as somehow complementing each other.

One can, of course, understand why Hirst is led to argue for a complementary relationship between *education I* and *education IV*, in that he wants to protect in some way what goes on in the family, the church and other religious institutions. In fact, Hirst is quite explicit in stating that he does not want to criticise the nature of family life. 'A rational society will, of course, have its families and no doubt its churches,' according to Hirst, though these are relegated to the 'private' domain and will exist alongside public and thoroughly secular schools committed to *education IV* (1974, p. 90).

But there is a very fundamental problem with this rather generous attitude towards the family, the church and other religious institutions which is displayed by Hirst and other writers within the liberal education tradition. We have already seen that Hirst characterises *education I* as primitive, inadequate, improper and even subhuman. Consistency would therefore demand that Hirst should likewise condemn the kind of education that goes on in the family, the church and other religious institutions, because these institutions are committed to *education I* according to Hirst's own criteria. It simply will not do to relegate these institutions to the private domain as Hirst tries to do, because we are dealing here with ethical considerations which by their very nature are of universal application. If Christian nurture involves indoctrination, and if indoctrination is immoral, then Christian nurture should be condemned as immoral regardless of where it occurs. Given the moral concerns of liberal educators, they simply cannot adopt a *laissez faire* attitude towards the family and the church, allowing these institutions to do whatever they please in the name of tolerance. Education is not a private matter, regardless of where it occurs and whatever the content might be, because it has to do with persons relating to and influencing other persons and it is therefore subject to ethical evaluation. Hirst's ethical ideals entail that *education I* should be condemned universally, and thus the home, the church and other religious institutions, which according to Hirst are committed to *education I*, cannot be accepted as providing an education which is somehow complementary to those institutions committed to *education IV*.

Hirst would no doubt respond to my criticism by pointing to passages where he does in fact condemn indoctrinative activities 'in any context,' and where he argues for the compatible and complementary relationship between *education IV* and education in the home, the church and other religious institutions, only where the latter institutions are committed to rational nurture (1985, pp. 13f). The basic problem with this response is that, on Hirst's own criteria, there cannot be such a thing as rational nurture, or rational Christian nurture. The central feature of nurture is that it is committed both in terms of its starting point and in terms of its aims, and it is precisely this element of commitment that Hirst finds so objectionable. Thus, there is an inherent contradiction in the very idea of rational nurture or rational Christian nurture. In his later essay, Hirst bluntly states that religiously oriented schools 'are not even in principle committed to the demands of open, critical, rational education' (1985, p. 15). This is entirely in keeping with Hirst's general characterisation and contrast of *education I* and *education IV*, as we have already seen. Hirst, therefore, cannot appeal to the possibility of rational nurture as a means of protecting the family, the church and other religious institutions. These institutions are, by their very nature, committed to *education I*, and therefore the kind of education that goes on in these institutions should be universally condemned by Hirst. This is, of course, a very radical position, and one can appreciate why Hirst tries to avoid such an extreme, even at the expense of an inconsistency within his position. I want to suggest that this inconsistency points to a more basic problem in Hirst's contrast between *education I* and *education IV*, which will be dealt with in the next two sections.

## Is *education* I radically different from *education IV*?

We have seen that Hirst's two concepts of education are described as radically different and opposed to each other. Of central importance is the fact that *education I* is concerned with the transmission of beliefs and values, whereas *education IV* encourages critical appraisal of all beliefs and values. But is not *education IV* also concerned with the transmission of certain beliefs and values, such as the belief in the worthwhileness of rationality and criticism?[5] Hirst is forced to concede that some transmission seems to be 'inescapable,' though he wants to argue that the transmissionist component in *education IV* differs in significant ways from what occurs in *education I* (1974, p. 83). Be that as it may, and we shall return to this difference later, the fact remains that there is a transmissionist component in *education IV*. Like *education I, education IV*, too, is concerned to pass on certain beliefs and values. In fact, Hirst goes so far as to deny the right of students to reject matters of objective truth in *education IV*. 'In matters of education, the school has the right to expect intellectual and behavioural acceptance ...' (1981, p. 91).

*Education I*, according to Hirst, is merely concerned to pass on the beliefs and values that are held by the group to be true and valuable whereas *education IV* is concerned with the transmission of beliefs according to their objective status and with their appropriate justification. But, as anyone acquainted with the history of philosophy will know, the notion of objectivity has had a long and tortuous history. Here we can only note that it would seem to be difficult to define 'objective justification' without some reference to the notion of 'inter-subjective' agreement, as R S Peters has observed (1966, p. 54). Tradition and authority have a very important part to play in science as has been noted by various contemporary philosophers of science.[6] Thus, when science is taught as part of *education IV*, it will be found that 'knowledge and belief from traditional sources are considered justified and valued because of their proven worth across a period of time,' a characterisation which, the reader should note, is taken from Hirst's description of *education I* (1985, p. 7). Philosophers of science have also acknowledged the conservative nature of normal science. The teaching of science will necessarily be 'intellectually conservative' and will also view a 'diversity' of scientific beliefs and practices as 'a weakness,' as something to be overcome in the search for truth, to borrow again from Hirst's description of *education I* (1985, p. 7). Hirst's distinction between knowledge, truth and reason, on the one hand, and belief, conjecture and subjective preference on the other, is philosophically suspect and simply not as neat and tidy as he would have us believe, and since this is the basis of his distinction between *education I* and *education IV*, a sharp distinction between these two concepts of education is thereby called into question.

*Education IV* is described by Hirst as having a monopoly on concern for providing evidence and justification for beliefs transmitted to the young. But surely *education I*, too, always has included, and will include, the providing of evidence for beliefs being transmitted, simply because the most effective way to transmit beliefs to others is *via* providing evidence and justification. Of course, Hirst may not think that the evidence supplied is good evidence, but that is another matter. The key point here is that all education concerns itself with providing reasons for beliefs being transmitted and therefore this too is not a distinguishing feature of *education IV*.

It also needs to be pointed out that *education IV* is not, and cannot be, as committed to rational justification as it pretends to be. For finite human beings, the process of rational justification must necessarily stop somewhere, either by an appeal to authority or by an appeal to unquestioned assumptions or presuppositions. Hirst is himself aware of this problem, and thus qualifies the inevitable appeal to authority with the suggestion that 'there must be a rational acceptance of authorities' (1985, p. 13). But, in the given context, this is to beg the question and, more importantly for our purposes, this concession once again blurs the distinction between *education I* and *education IV*, since both appeal to authority as a necessary step in the process of rational justification.

*Education I* is criticised by Hirst for failing to make any distinctions concerning the logical status of beliefs being passed on, while *education IV* prides itself in making such distinctions, in passing on only those beliefs where there are agreed objective principles of judgment, and in leaving the rest to personal judgment and decision (1974, p. 81, 86f; 1981, pp. 86f). But this fails to recognise that most of our beliefs are controversial to some degree, and Hirst himself is forced to concede that there is 'no clear line of demarcation' between controversial and non-controversial matters (1974, p. 87). Despite Hirst's claim to the contrary (1985, pp. 8–10), there are some basic assumptions underlying his ideal of critical rationalism that are seriously questioned by the 'informed and knowledgeable' (1981, p. 87). There have been some forceful rational criticisms levelled against the principles of individualism, autonomy, etc.[7], that underlie liberalism and the ideal of liberal education, and yet Hirst wants to impose these values on everyone via a system of education. Thus *education IV* does not always 'stop short of seeking any particular commitment on matters that are rationally controversial,' as Hirst maintains it does (1981, p. 88).

## Is *education I* inferior to *education IV*?

I wish finally to consider the evaluative overtones of Hirst's contrast between *education I* and *education IV*. Should *education I* and *IV* really be contrasted as primitive *versus* sophisticated? Here it needs to be pointed out first of all, that in using these descriptions, Hirst commits the fallacy of loaded terms. The use of these loaded terms at the beginning of his analysis further begs the question because Hirst first of all has to prove that the one is indeed superior to the other before he can properly use these labels. The ideals and the presuppositions underlying liberal education are increasingly being called into question by intelligent, informed and well-educated individuals, as has already been pointed out. My earlier argument also undermines the positive attitude expressed towards *education IV*. If *education IV* shares many of the features of *education I*, as I have shown, then *education IV* should similarly be rated inferior. Or, perhaps it would be better to see *education I* as just as sophisticated as *education IV*, which is the position I wish to defend in the final section.

There is, I believe, a fundamental problematic assumption underlying Hirst's evaluative contrast between *education I* and *IV*, which it might be helpful to bring to the fore here. Hirst in fact identifies this assumption when he begins his earlier volume (1974) with a chapter describing the process of secularisation which is such a dominant feature of modern western societies. Hirst is clearly assuming that this process of secularisation is a good thing. But various sociologists such as Greeley (1974) and Berger (1974) have challenged this widely held unexamined prejudice that the process of modernisation and secularisation is necessarily a process from lower to higher forms of social life. Both writers further challenge the widely held liberal assumption that man's search for identity and meaning in his ethnic, cultural and religious heritage is part of man's primal, primitive, pre-rational past out of which he is evolving (Greeley, 1974, p. 14; Berger, 1974, p. 199). It is beyond the scope of this paper to examine critically this assumption concerning the evolution of human society, or to defend my agreement with Greeley and Berger in their rejection of this assumption. My purpose here is merely to suggest that it is this assumption that is at the root of Hirst's distinction between primitive and sophisticated education and that this assumption is at least not self-evident.

## Two concepts or two phases of education

I have been concerned thus far with a critique of a radical distinction between the transmissionist and the critical rationalist concepts of education as advocated by Hirst and other contemporary philosophers of education. There is, however, still a germ of truth hidden within this contrast, which can best be brought to the fore by reinterpreting Hirst's analysis. What I wish to propose is that we look at *education I* and *IV* not as two radically different concepts of education, but rather as two equally important and necessary phases of liberal education.

Hirst himself hints at such a possible reinterpretation when he points out that 'education must start within some system of beliefs' (1985, p. 13). In other words, liberal education must start with a transmissionist phase of education. Hirst even identifies some of the content which must be transmitted when he describes liberal education in terms of an exposure to the seven or eight forms of knowledge, each with its central concepts, distinctive logical structure and unique criteria of truth (1974, pp. 84f). It seems to me, however, that Hirst fails to address sufficiently the question as to how the content within each of the forms of knowledge is transmitted. In fact, Hirst would very likely want to play down the content aspect of the forms of knowledge, and characterise them more in terms of types of rational methodology. But the forms of knowledge clearly do involve some content which must be transmitted in some way.

It seems to me that R S Peters addresses this issue much more carefully than does Hirst: we find Peters putting much emphasis on education as a process of initiation. The term 'initiation' already figures prominently in Peters' 1963 Inaugural Lecture, 'Education as Initiation' (Peters, 1965). The first two chapters of *Ethics and Education* (1966) cover much the same ground, and here education is characterised as involving the development of the mind, and such development is 'the product of the initiation of an individual into public traditions enshrined in the language, concepts, beliefs and rules of a society' (Peters, 1966, p. 49). The child must be initiated into 'a public inheritance' so as to get the barbarian outside the gate inside 'the citadel of civilisation' (Peters, 1966, pp. 50, 53; 1965, p. 107). Peters specifically criticises those who see education as more concerned with critical thinking than with the transmission of a body of knowledge. Critical thought without content is vacuous, argues Peters (1966, pp. 53f).

We see here that education (i.e. liberal education), for Peters, necessarily includes a transmissionist component. Rationality and critical thinking can only be developed *after* there has been initiation into certain content. In other words, *education I* is an essential component of *education IV*. We have here not two radically different concepts of education, but two important and equally necessary phases in the process of liberal education.

These two phases of liberal education can be seen as running parallel to the phases of human development. It is to Peters' credit that he faces the question as to how young children are initiated into the public traditions. He points out that such initiation depends on learning by example, and involves mechanisms of imitation and identification (1977, p. 83, cf. 1966, p. 60). Robin Barrow similarly points out that the lives of young children 'are predominantly taken up with the acquisition of attitudes and beliefs via non-rational influences' (1974, p. 55). Barrow also points out that young children are incapable of distinguishing between differences in the logical status of beliefs (1974, pp. 54f). All the beliefs that a young child is initiated into are received and understood as fixed and absolute and are accepted in an unquestioning manner. In other words, with a very young child education is only possible in terms of what Hirst has labelled *education I*. Nurture is a necessary part of a liberal education.

It is only *after* a child has been initiated into the public traditions of a society that he/she can begin to evaluate them critically. In other words, *education IV* is necessarily parasitic on *education I*. But even here we must not move too quickly. The transition from the *education I* phase to the *education IV* phase is a gradual one.

Thus, after the initiation or nurture phase there will be a gradual opening-up phase where the child is exposed to other influences, other beliefs, though still from the vantage point of the tradition into which he/she was first initiated. Still later in a child's development, he/she will be taught to reflect critically on the tradition he/she was initiated into, as well as the alternative traditions that have been and are continuing to be taught. At a final stage, vigorous critically reflective skills are developed, though even here we must be careful to avoid the extreme of a 'critical scepticism' as Hirst himself realises (1985, p. 13). Liberal education will therefore be seen as moving through a series of phases, starting with a nurture phase (Hirst's *education I*), moving gradually to a phase where nurture and critical rationalism go hand in hand, and ending with a phase where critical rationalism (i.e. Hirst's *education IV*) is dominant. I say 'dominant' because I believe, with Kohlberg, that it is doubtful that even adults ever entirely dispense with a traditionalist approach to learning.

It might be objected that this reinterpretation of Hirst's two concepts of education as two phases of liberal education lands me in a contradiction. Does not the admission of two phases of liberal education entail that there are some differences between them, when earlier I was arguing that Hirst's two concepts were not as different as he would have us believe? In response, I would point out that I have already conceded that there is some truth to Hirst's contrast. There is, however, a big difference between interpreting *educations I* and *IV* as two radically different concepts of education, as Hirst does, and interpreting liberal education as involving two phases of education where the latter gradually evolves out of the former. Most of the time elements of the one are mixed with elements of the other, sometimes one and sometimes the other being predominant. It is only in the very early stages of a child's development that education can be described exclusively in terms of Hirst's *education I*. As soon as the child has acquired language, it begins to probe and question, and parents will be forced to give reasons for what they claim, i.e. elements of *education IV* are already coming to the fore. Clearly this still differs from the kind of critical/rational thought that is possible later in a child's development. Mental maturity obviously transforms child-like thinking, but there are still some similarities between the two phases. Thus, it is quite consistent to say that the two phases of liberal education are both similar and different. It also needs to be stressed that Hirst describes *education I* as primitive and inferior to *education IV*. My reinterpretation clearly rejects this kind of contrast. Both the transmissionist and the critical/rational phases of education are equally legitimate and essential to liberal education.

There is one further objection that can be raised against this reinterpretation of Hirst's two concepts of education as two phases of education, an objection which has been highlighted in a recent essay by T Kazepides (1983). Kazepides is particularly concerned about associating initiation with education, because this will encourage the assimilation of socialisation into education and thus make it easier for those who wish to advocate some form of indoctrination (1983, pp. 304, 314, 316). Kazepides, however, is simply refusing to face the problem of a young child's initial introduction (initiation) into the traditions and beliefs of a society. I heartily concur with Dearden, who in discussing the notion of autonomy makes the astute observation that philosophers 'may have been too apt to overlook or ignore the fact that men have childhoods' (1975, p. 6). Discussions of liberal education invariably assume a school context where children have already matured to some degree. But what does liberal education entail with regard to the pre-school child? This is a central question that needs to be faced by philosophers. It will not do to describe liberal education simply in terms of liberating a person 'beyond the present and the particular,' as has been done recently by Charles Bailey (1984). A theory of liberal education must also address the question of how children arrive at the present and the particular in the first place. It is to Peters' credit that he dares to face the problem of educating young children, and this leads him to acknowledge Hirst's *education I* as an essential element of liberal education. It is in this connection that Peters, in some of his later essays, is led to acknowledge certain 'ambiguities' or 'dilemmas' inherent in the notion of liberal education that still need to be resolved (1977, pp. 46ff, 68ff). Thus Peters points to 'the necessity for much more thought' on the problem of distinguishing liberal from illiberal teaching procedures (1977, pp. 84f). I would suggest that philosophers need to think much more about educating the pre-school child. What is needed is a philosophy of liberal pre-school education. There are some welcome signs that philosophers are beginning to address problems in this area (see, for example, McLaughlin, 1984 and Ackerman, 1980, Chapter 5).

And what about Kazepides' worry that the admission of *Education I* as a phase of liberal education will make it easier for those who wish to advocate some form of indoctrination? But what do we mean by 'indoctrination'? Here again it seems to me that the fundamental problem with the considerable body of literature on indoctrination is that most writers have failed to address the very difficult question as to what it means to educate a pre-school child. Here too we need to distinguish between liberal and illiberal teaching procedures, but we shall have to be careful not to make this distinction in terms of features that only apply to adult learning. Thus it will not do to make this distinction in terms of rational versus non-rational teaching methods because, as has already been pointed out, these categories are not applicable to pre-school education. Nor will it do to define this distinction in terms of intentions or aims, because this is to skirt the issue. We need to stay within the present and the particular. Surely, there is a distinction to be made between acceptable and non-acceptable ways of transmitting beliefs and values to the young child, prior to his/her being able to reflect on them rationally and critically.

I would suggest that what is needed is a developmental analysis of the concept of indoctrination which takes into account the different stages in cognitive development. Thus, what it means to indoctrinate a pre-school child who is at the transmissionist phase of education (Hirst's *Education I*) will be very different from what it means to indoctrinate an adolescent who is capable of rational and critical reflection. At this point in time, however, the most urgent assignment for philosophers of education is to address the pre-school phase of education, and at this early phase of a child's mental development to distinguish between liberal and illiberal education.

## Conclusion

Let me summarise and conclude by drawing some theoretical and practical implications of my argument. I have argued that Hirst and other philosophers of education are wrong in treating the transmissionist and the rational critical concepts of education as two radically different and opposed concepts of education. I have argued, instead, that the non-rational and uncritical transmission of beliefs is an important and necessary preliminary phase to rational critical thought which has been traditionally linked with liberal education. It has been suggested that philosophers specifically need to address the transmissionist phase of liberal education and develop a theory of pre-school education. Philosophers also need to distinguish between indoctrinative and non-indoctrinative initiation or transmission at this pre-school level, and this, I have suggested, will require a new developmental approach to analysing the concept of indoctrination.

A further practical implication follows from the argument of this paper, if we focus more particularly on the question of how children move from one phase to the next. It has been suggested, and I believe psychological considerations would support this suggestion, that the transition from a transmissionist phase to the rational/critical phase of liberal education should be gradual. If we see the family as primarily concerned with the transmissionist phase of education and educational institutions as concerned with the rational/critical phase of liberal education, then it is important to ensure a smooth and gradual transition from family to school education. This point has been well made by Ackerman (1980, p. 157), among others, who, after acknowledging the need for a child first of all to be initiated into a 'primary culture,' argues that schools must be respectful of this primary culture shaped by parental influence.[8] The opening-up process must start from the tradition into which children have been initiated, and only gradually should children be exposed to other traditions. There is no place for an arrogant and condescending attitude towards parents and parental influence on the part of professional educators. Nor is there any place for the rather common practice, especially among philosophy instructors at universities, of using a systematically sceptical approach in teaching which seeks to destroy students' present beliefs, especially religious beliefs, in the hope that they will then be enabled to rationally build a belief system on a solid and certain foundation. The rational/critical phase of education must always start with, and should therefore be respectful of, the transmissionist phase of education.

The above principle would also entail that we should be more sympathetic with those arguing for independent religious schools. One of the fundamental reasons why parents want to send their children to an independent school is that they want a school which reflects the basic values and beliefs that were taught in the home. If the critical/rational phase of education must build from the nurture phase, then clearly the independent school is one way in which to facilitate this transition in a sympathetic manner. This point is used very effectively by Halstead (1986) in his defence of Muslim voluntary-aided schools.

The above implications bring to light a difficult question as to who has the right to determine the transmissionist phase of a child's education, as well as the later choice of an independent school which will facilitate the transition to the critical/rational phase of education. I am assuming that this right is fundamentally a parental right based on parents' responsibilities in bringing up their children and the need for a stable and coherent primary culture (White, 1982, p. 166; McLaughlin, 1984; Halstead, 1986). Much more would need to be said to defend this position, but that is beyond the scope of this paper.

I wish finally to draw some implications of all this for religious education. As has already been pointed out, the contrast between *education I* and *IV* is today also often applied to the area of religious instruction where the objective rational/critical study of religions is sharply contrasted with Christian nurture (or Buddhist nurture, etc.). By extrapolation, my argument would suggest that these two approaches to religious instruction are not so radically different and opposed as is often assumed. Nor should Christian nurture be viewed as inferior to the supposedly more sophisticated approach to religious instruction. What is often forgotten in the debate concerning religious education is that the objective study of world religions is parasitic on there having been religious nurture of some kind in the first place. One can study other religions, only if people have first of all been brought up in various religious traditions. Given the need for a gradual transition from nurture to the rational critical phase of education, I would suggest that we need to be much more sympathetic with the gradual exposure to other religions from within the context of one particular religious tradition.

Here, no doubt, some will object that this approach would pre-empt any later more critical and open consideration of one's own religion and other religious traditions. This objection rests on a failure to appreciate the conditions for the development of critical openness. The intellectual virtue of critical openness can only develop out of a certain context which will necessarily be acquired by the transmissionist phase of liberal education. Critical thought without content is empty, as has already been noted. Various writers have further argued not only that critical openness is compatible with nurture into a religious tradition, but that this intellectual virtue is in fact encouraged by various religious traditions (McLaughlin, 1984; Halstead, 1986; Hull, 1984, chapters 16, 18). More attention also needs to be given to clarifying the notions of critical openness and autonomy.

There is not space here to consider, either, the difficult question concerning the epistemological status of religious beliefs, except to suggest that the alleged contrast between religious beliefs and, for example, scientific beliefs is subject to the same sorts of criticism as have been levelled against the contrast between *educations I* and *IV*. Elsewhere, I have argued that many of the supposed differences between scientific and religious beliefs rest on a caricature of religion and an illegitimate idealisation of science (Thiessen, 1984, 1982). I conclude, therefore, that the central argument of this paper can be applied to all education, including religious education.

The approach to religious education being advocated in this paper has been so delightfully summed up by Ursula King who reminds us of the example of Gandhi 'who spoke of opening the windows of his own house to the winds from the outside world without being swept off his feet. Every individual needs to be deeply rooted in his or her own tradition but also has to learn to grow upwards and outwards like the many branches of a large tree' (King, 1985, p. 97). We shall be able to do justice to the profound truth captured in this imagery only if Hirst's two concepts of education are reinterpreted as two equally important and necessary phases of liberal education.

**Notes**
1.  I wish to express my thanks to Medicine Hat College for a sabbatical leave at Oxford, during which time this article was written.
2.  Although my analysis and argument could equally well apply to a contrast between Muslim nurture (Buddhist nurture, etc.) and an objective, critical study of world religions, I will limit my considerations to Christian nurture.
3.  Hirst considers two further intermediate concepts of education which involve attempted compromises between *education I* and *education IV*. This paper will

have little to say about *education II* and *III* which, according to Hirst, are unsuccessful in achieving a compromise between *education I* and *IV*.

4.  John M Hull is essentially in agreement with Hirst in that he draws the same sharp distinction between Christian nurture and religious education (1984, pp. 38–42). Hull's position is in fact somewhat confusing. Although he seems to be more sympathetic with Christian nurture, there is nevertheless a tendency to view it in a somewhat negative light. For example, Hull is concerned to show 'that between education (a term of approbation) and indoctrination (a pejorative term) there is indeed a middle ground' which involves nurture (1984, p. 39). In other words, on a sliding scale nurture is half-way between education and indoctrination, and one gets the distinct impression that nurture is really closer to indoctrination than to education. In seeming contradiction to this, Hull argues elsewhere that he does not want to suggest that nurture is in 'some way inferior to a critical and exploratory religious education' (1984, p. 197). But in yet another essay, nurture is grouped together with evangelism and indoctrination as being a convergent activity where 'the personal faith of the teacher converges with the content of his lessons and with his hopes for the pupils' (Hull, 1984, pp. 175f). Education, by contrast, is characterised by divergence, which 'is itself a value, or a bundle of values' and which therefore possesses several marks of 'superiority' over convergence (Hull, 1984, pp. 181f). Thus, although Hull does at times defend Christian nurture by showing that it includes some aspects of liberal education such as critical openness (1984, pp. 207ff), I would suggest that the overall thrust of Hull's treatment of Christian nurture is that it is not only radically different from, but also somewhat inferior to, a liberal education in religion. This view is, as Hull suggests, generally accepted among educators concerned with religion (1984, p. 117).

5.  On this, see an excellent recent article by Ieuan Lloyd (1986), where he argues that there is an inescapable confessional approach present in the teaching of all subjects.

6.  See, for example, M. Polanyi (1946, Chapter 2) and T S Kuhn (1962).

7.  See, for example, the communitarian critics of liberalism, MacIntyre (1981) and Hauerwas (1983).

8.  There is abundant research supporting Ackerman's claim regarding the importance of children first of all being raised in a stable and coherent primary culture. See, for example, the research of Urie Bronfenbrenner, who in an article summarising this research, goes on to argue for closer links between home, school and neighborhood (1980). By implication, Bronfenbrenner is arguing for a closer link between *educations I* and *IV*. See also Berger (1974) and Greeley (1974). A similar argument to mine is also developed by Halstead (1986, pp. 27, 42f).

**References**

Ackerman, B A (1980) *Social Justice in the Liberal State*, New Haven, Yale University Press.

Bailey, Charles (1984) *Beyond the Present and Particular: a theory of liberal education*, London, Routledge and Kegan Paul.

Barrow, R (1974) 'Religion in the schools,' *Educational Philosophy and Theory*, 6, pp. 49–57.

Berger, P L (1974) *Pyramids of Sacrifice: political ethics and social change*, New York, Penguin.

Bronfenbrenner, U (1980) 'On making human beings human,' *Character*, 2 (2), pp. 1–7.

Dearden, R F (1975) 'Autonomy as an educational ideal,' in S C Brown (ed.) *Philosophers Discuss Education*, Basingstoke, Macmillan.

Greeley, A M (1974) *Ethnicity in the United States: a preliminary reconnaissance*, New York, Wiley.

Halstead, J M (1986) *The Case For Muslim Voluntary-aided Schools: some philosophical reflections*, Cambridge, The Islamic Academy.

Hauerwas, Stanley (1983) *The Peaceable Kingdom: a primer in Christian ethics*, Notre Dame, University of Notre Dame Press.

Hirst, Paul H (1974) *Moral Education in a Secular Society*, London, University of London Press.

Hirst, Paul H (1981) 'Education, catechesis and the church school,' *British Journal of Religious Education*, 3, pp. 85–93.

Hirst, Paul H (1985) 'Education and diversity of belief,' in M C Felderhof (ed.) *Religious Education in a Pluralistic Society*, London, Hodder and Stoughton.

Hull, J M (1984) *Studies in Religion and Education*, Lewes, Falmer Press.

Kazepides, T (1983) 'Socialisation, initiation and indoctrination,' in *Philosophy of Education 1982: Proceedings of the 38th Annual Meeting of the Philosophy of Education Society*, Normal, Illinois, Philosophy of Education Society, Illinois State University, pp. 309–318

King, U (1985) 'A response to Howard W Marratt,' in M C Felderhof (ed.) *Religious Education in a Pluralistic Society*, London, Hodder and Stoughton.

Kuhn, T S (1962) *The Structure of Scientific Revolutions*, Chicago, University of Chicago Press.

Lloyd, I (1986) 'Confession and reason,' *British Journal of Religious Education*, 8, pp. 140–145.

MacIntyre, A (1981) *After Virtue: a study in moral theory*, Notre Dame, Notre Dame Press.

McLaughlin, T H (1984) 'Parental rights and the religious upbringing of children,' *Journal of Philosophy of Education*, 18, pp. 75–83.

Peters, R S (1965) 'Education as initiation,' in R D Archambault (ed.) *Philosophical Analysis and Education*, London, Routledge and Kegan Paul, pp. 87–110.

Peters, R S (1966) *Ethics and Education*, London, Allen and Unwin.

Peters, R S (1977) *Education and the Education of Teachers*, London, Routledge and Kegan Paul.

Polanyi, Michael (1946) *Science, Faith and Society*, Chicago, University of Chicago Press.

Thiessen, E J (1982) 'Indoctrination and doctrines,' *Journal of Philosophy of Education*, 16. pp. 3–17.

Thiessen, E J (1984) 'Indoctrination and religious education,' *Interchange*, 15 (3), pp. 27–43.

White, J (1982) *The Aims of Education Restated*, London, Routledge and Kegan Paul.

# 2. Theological perspectives

The theology of education is an appropriate activity of practical theology. This section displays three Anglicans reflecting on the distinctive character and function of church schools from a theological perspective.

In the first article, the Very Revd Robert M Waddington reflects on the nature of a Christian school in the light of the doctrine of the Triune God. He identifies ten key characteristics of the church school. These ten characteristics have become an important basis for subsequent Anglican studies on church schools. Throughout Waddington demonstrates that the theology of education is something to be 'done' as well as debated and he sees in church schools an opportunity for the churches to be engaged in the theology of education at a practical level.

At the time of writing Robert Waddington was General Secretary of the Church of England General Synod Board of Education. This article was first published in the General Synod green paper, *A Future in Partnership*, in 1984, which was influential in stimulating a wide ranging debate within the Church of England about its role in the state maintained system of education. Robert Waddington is currently Dean of Manchester Cathedral.

In the second article, the Revd Professor Leslie J Francis scrutinises the bi-partite theological distinction between the church's domestic and general functions in education, advanced by the Durham Report in 1970. He argues that this two-fold distinction between nurture and service no longer provides an adequate theological basis for the church's involvement in the state maintained system of education in England and Wales. To theologies of nurture and service he proposes adding a theology of prophecy.

Leslie Francis is D J James Professor of Pastoral Theology at Trinity College, Carmarthen, and St David's University College, Lampeter. This article was first published under the shorter title 'Theology of education' in *British Journal of Educational Studies* in 1990.

In the third article, the Revd Peter Marr examines the implications of the Anglican Roman Catholic International Commission (ARCIC) for denominational schools. In particular he argues that commitment in dialogue must involve social witness of which shared education forms a part. This article was first published in *One in Christ* in 1989. Peter Marr is parish priest of St Barnabas, Beckenham, in the diocese of Rochester.

# 2.1 No apology for theology
## Robert M Waddington

The real image that falls on the sensitive light-catching cells at the back of the eye is, as in a camera, upside down. It is the brain that learns to right it so that vision matches experience. Seeing is the mind's picture of the world built from component senses, primarily looking, but also touching, hearing, tasting.

Faith which is God's gift, nourishes a vision, a growing apperception of the world seen through the eye of God. It is a vision of the world righted, of evil turned to good, of man's self-aggrandisement transmuted to humility and love, of depressing agonies raised by hope. It is at first seen as through a glass darkly, yet even in that dimness can be perceived the distant grandeur of the final vision — that which will be, face to face, a beatific vision. It is not a sight to numb one's sensibilities for, in that it shows what might be, it activates the mind, stirs the emotions and challenges the will. At the centre of the vision is the turbulent, blinding, initiating love that is God. He it is who invites man's co-operation in achieving his rightful sovereignty and the first step for man in such collaborative action is 'metanoia,' repentance, a willingness to stop in one's track and change direction. Thus the vision provided through God's gift of faith informs newness in individual and corporate action. Through the vision comes rebirth. Theology helps articulate the vision; it authenticates or questions the believing community's version of it. Theology is a bridge between the forms and symbols of everyday living and the inherent truths within the vision itself. So culture can feed theological expression yet never exhaust its possibilities. The disclosure of the vision comes in the gift of faith; man's desire to share it even with those who see nothing of it, demands conversation, image-building, story-telling, proclamation, perhaps plain speaking. These belong to the action of theology which is something that is done.

It seems strange that education, a process which helps to shape the vision humans can have of a particular cultural world and which indicates how personal and communal fulfilment within a particular society might be achieved, has aroused relatively little interest among theologians. In spite of the vigorous contributions that have been made since the 1870s to validate the contribution of the Church of England to the education service of the nation through its schools, there has been little written within the vision of faith as articulated in theology. Arguments in favour are often framed as responses to those who argue against. The need to speak alongside politicians, teachers and administrators seems to entangle the church's education officers, no doubt at times very properly, in a discussion based on benign pragmatism. Immersed in practicalities, theirs is not to reason why! Yet reasoning why is just exactly what is required on the part of all the partners in the education service. Relativism can draw the sinews of a robust and healthily plural society. Is it to be wondered that shallow forms of consensus and purely pragmatic or utilitarian courses of action are likely to follow? The clarity and distinctiveness of the church's voice is important in two respects. First, the education officers of the church must expect to *earn* respect with colleagues by making positive contributions to educational debate and planning in an articulate and responsible manner. That may well require mastering the right 'lingo.' Second, such officers also have a duty to make it plain that their contributions are illuminated by faith and mature theological reflection.

This chapter attempts to initiate such a reflection on the nature of a church school community and the Christian education that should be conducted within it.

It is brief, explorative and very tentative. Those with more mature theological understanding may help to extend the discussion. Two preliminary points need noting. One is the nature of theology as a *selective* activity and this chapter therefore sticks close to the major Christian themes. The other is to point out that what is *not* required is theology *of* education. Indeed, one must seriously wonder whether it is right to speak of a theology of anything. Rather must theological reflection be brought to bear upon individual and social life, and education as a particular slice of social activity cannot be excluded. For the Christian, the objectives, direction and methods as well as the content of education might well need modifying, even radically changing in the light of such reflection.

The shared vision of faith, and its articulation in theology belong to the community of faith, the church. Incorporation into that family is by baptism in the name of the Trinity, the Father, the Son, and the Holy Spirit. It was a natural symbol that Christ adapted from John's baptism, something that in its simplicity needs little explanation; water is the base of life, the cleanser, it becomes the vehicle for spiritual rebirth and incorporation. Immediately one is forced to reflect on the immense size of the Anglican family, for many parents still seek for their children this sacrament of membership. Whatever one may infer about vestigial folk religion, superstition or simply force of family habit, the church has never adopted a policy of rigorism. It has sought to use the contacts with families at times of baptism as pastoral opportunities. However tenuous, therefore, is the subsequent contact with the worshipping congregation, the baptised are in membership. Potentially, they share the vision of faith. Could it be the vocation of Christian teachers to awaken in their pupils a capacity to look and at length the ability to see? Faced with hundreds of thousands of baptised children, far more than could be coped with by all church schools, there is a temptation to propound a new rigorism. The Bishop of Liverpool is unequivocal:[1]

> If the gap (between very large numbers of urban working-class people and the organised church) is to be bridged, there needs to be many stepping stones ...
>
> It follows ... that the church should welcome rather than reject folk religion. Understandably some clergy and congregations want to withdraw from this often frustrating and ambiguous encounter, for example in baptisms. The English people have been encouraged for centuries to bring their children to be baptised. The desire for a clear-cut understanding of Christian commitment leads some clergy to lay down demanding conditions to prove the willingness of parents to come to church before baptising their babies. They do not give much account to the place a believing grandmother may have in a family, or to the inarticulate longings after God of many who cannot think of themselves as churchgoers. Many poor people have to make humiliating requests to officials: if the church insists on parents fitting in to its institutional life before baptising their children, it will make them feel that yet again they are being told to fit in with form filling, behave-like-us institutions. Instead, it can be a helpful stepping stone which brings a family nearer to the Christian experience and to the Christian fellowship.

Last year there was an exchange of letters in *The Times* following a speech by Mr Wedgwood Benn in which he proposed the disestablishment of the Church of England. Speaking of clergy who refuse to baptise children whose families are not members of their congregations, the Revd R N W Elbourne, during the exchange, wrote thus:[2]

> Leaving aside the undeniable fact that they are flying in the face of Christ's teaching and example, they are also failing to take advantage of the opportunities offered by establishment. Baptism is one of the few occasions when young families open their doors to the clergy; an occasion, moreover, when they are particularly receptive to a gospel about a loving creative Father. What a shame not to take this opportunity to introduce them also to a redemptive Son and a sanctifying Spirit, and the other insights presented by the baptismal liturgy.
>
> For if the priest's reaction to a request for baptism is 'No; because ...' any attempt he subseqently makes to explain the gospel is tarnished by his initial refusal to extend Christ's welcome. Far better to do one's duty as a minister of the established Church and say 'Yes;' and then to seize in Christ's name the opportunity to explain the 'because' in terms of his loving and redemptive welcome!

But to whom does the Church of England *school* extend Christ's welcome? Many schools remain undersubscribed and so with places

available must by law accept those children who wish to attend.
Such schools are, perhaps, not sufficient indicators of the church's
intentions; there are, of course, immense problems in manifesting
Christian ethos in such schools. But there are on the other hand
large primary and secondary schools which are seriously *over*subscribed. It is the manner in which the governors deal with the queue
at the door that betrays in many cases a narrow, restrictive policy;
a new rigorism in fact. Vicars' certificates of regular attendance at
church, searching questions directed to parents at interviews asking
about family church attendance, and the publishing in the required
information on the school of a rigorous 'practising Anglicans only'
criterion for admission: all these mirror an image of the church
school as an extension of the *gathered* church. Such schools, in
an age of the great secular slide, might be regarded as a deliberate effort to create solidarity, retrenchment. The governors of
such schools are not behaving illegally, indeed some administrators
would claim from premises other than those that are theological
that the purpose of church schools is indeed to collect together the
children of practising, believing Christian families.

Two things are worth noting at this point. The first is that
such rigorist policies in the selection of pupils are harsher than
the policies of most parishes with regard to baptism, marriage
and burial. At those moments of family or personal life when
people turn to the church, however mixed their motives, however
slight their commitment or however inarticulate their belief, the
church errs on the side of love. It is important that God's love
for mankind is accepted as preceding any response that humanly
speaking we can make; to put it differently, it is worth emphasising
the beneficent graces of God even at the risk of minimising human
commitment in some measure. How strange that in dealing with
children, those who stand most in need of guidance and support,
those from nominally Christian homes, those whose baptism is
the only recognisable point of contact with the believing community can be turned away. Some strange arguments emerge in
rigorist governing bodies. 'We cannot turn children of practising
Anglicans away in favour of other children, can we?' 'After all,
our congregation raises 15% of the capital costs of the school and
a similar amount for external maintenance. Their children have first
claims!'

What kind of congregationalism undergirds such narrowness?
Whatever happened to the Christ of the gospels whose ministry
began with compassionate concern for ostracised lepers, the marginal elements of society, the disenfranchised minorities? What
theological perspective of *mission* is exhibited through such policies?
Where is the innovating spirit of the founders of the National
Society in 1811 whose admittedly somewhat paternal philanthropic
attitude to the education of the poor was nevertheless shot through

with genuine Christian love and care for their eventual well-being in community?

The second point to be emphasised is the way in which rigorist policies separate the undiffentiated twin aims of the Church of England with regard to its schools, and home in upon one strand only, that of Christian education for Christians. The element of service to the nation is neatly sidestepped. Rigorist policies expose Governors to accusations of hidden selection, and they may lead to the 'ghetto-like' huddles of which *The Fourth R*[3] warned. Such evidence as exists does not support the wilder accusations of racism and selection by ability that have been made about church schools, but the danger of either is never far away.

What about large half-empty church schools, small rural church schools serving a whole community, inner-city schools of church foundation which have two-thirds Moslem or Sikh pupils? Whence can they gain inspiration, where look for exemplars of Christian care and ethos? If not to the successful, oversubscribed primary or secondary church schools whose maximum rolls and staffing give them the privilege and opportunity to become examples, to be creative and imaginative and explorative about Christian ethos, then where else can they look? Rigorist policies about admissions, however, may well breed an introversion that stifles the taking of risks, often a very necessary precursor to creative, imaginative working. It must be stated firmly, however, in this theological glance at the ethos of the Christian school, that it seems difficult to square rigorist policies for admitting children to church schools with the more generous policies regarding the use of baptism as the sacrament of membership. Many, many hundreds of parish clergy, often after agonies of prayer and reflection, nevertheless extend to those who seek sacramental graces a generosity that speaks of God's own love. Children of churchgoing families are those who may well not need the support of a Christian ethos at school when home and parish can do so much to sustain nurture in the faith. Nor is there any guarantee that filling a school with such children will of itself create Christian ethos — as there is no certainty that filling a school with only nominal Christians or indeed those of other faiths, will hinder the creation of such an ethos. Other factors come into play.

To return, then, to incorporation into the community of faith by baptism in the name of the Trinity. The God within the Christian vision is himself relational; he is a community of three persons yet a unity of being. This mysterious Almighty God is revealed to Israel, the peculiar people; he is immanent in some measure in the processes of the nation's destiny and the emerging consciousness of its identity as *chosen*. But in the revelation of Jesus the blurred and distant God is disclosed as a Father. He is addressed as such in the pattern prayer, 'Our Father ...' The Spirit who broods over primaeval chaos and breathes life into the created order is disclosed by Jesus as Paraclete, the one who will be called down upon the community of faith. He will generate within that community modes of life that exemplify what it has seen and heard in the vision of faith. The fruits of such a Spirit are love, joy, peace, longsuffering. But it is Jesus who manifests in his incarnate life the being of this God. He speaks of a truth which he actually authenticates by his acceptance of the role of suffering servant. He points to a way which he encapsulates in dispassionate love and care and compassionate discriminative action for the poor, the downtrodden and the handicapped. He opens up new life by recreating from rejection, humiliation, pain and death a limitless love for his fellows.

Yet what he can reveal is limited both by man's capacity to understand and by the human nature he adopted. So he is called *Son* of God. There rests that within his Father's nature with which finite man cannot cope. Mystery lingers, for there is still a cloud of unknowing. But Jesus is also Son of *man* because as friend and brother he is an exemplar of a totally fulfilled humanity. As a teacher he stands in the Rabbinical tradition, a wanderer with a group of disciples. They cannot be simply 'hangers-on,' however. He gives them the challenges of a charge, they are 'the-ones-sent-out,' for the vision he brings and the life it enjoins are not esoteric, the property of an inner group; they are for all.

In the teaching of Jesus the central gospel message helps the community of faith to fill out its vision with belief; it aids the believer in his building of both the content and grammar of faith. It transforms the inner gift of love perceived through the vision of faith to an overt Christian fellowship. It gives direction to Christians in their yearning to serve society by proclaiming the imperative of bringing about God's kingship.

Like all good teachers, Jesus begins where his students stand. Into a thousand simple, everyday images – sowing, weeding, reaping, fishing, building towers, houses on sand or on rock, journeyings, accidents, robberies, improvidences (giggling girls with no paraffin) and incongruities (a camel stuck in the eye of a needle!) – he injects his message about God's sovereignty. Even the fundamental, sacramental signs of the community of faith are natural, earthbound: the way in through water, a rebirth; sustenance by eating bread and drinking wine.

The gathered community of faith, meeting to adore its God, hearing the gospel proclamation and sacramentally sustaining its life is dispersed, thrown back to the world. Scattered, its members have to learn after the pattern of their Master to minister rather than be ministered unto. Service and compassion have down the centuries been the hall-mark of their commitment. When they have sought power for its own sake, they have prostituted the vocation of suffering-servant; though they may sometimes have gained whole kingdoms, yet they stood in danger of losing their own souls. Historically, there has always been a tension between the church's need to operate as an effective power-base and its duty to be in the world, an active exemplar of a selfless, caring Christ.

From Christ stems an inner-drive in the church, powering its mission to share with all humanity the vision of Creator, Redeemer, Sanctifier. So it must keep the vision intact, refining it, burnishing it. To that process the worshipping, learning and listening gathered church is essential. Tiny increments of the vision are manifested in the world in the scattered church by Christians who seek to love their fellow humans. A church, then, which attempts to direct all the energies of its members to itself ceases to be a sign of the kingdom. Indeed in its pride and triumphalism it may falsely assume the guise of the kingdom.

But it is also possible for the vision of the kingdom to be adulterated to a highflown philanthropy − a social gospel can easily become activism stripped of the grammar of faith and doctrine that provides its direction. Doing good to others is indeed subsumed within true Christian love and care, but it is not itself *the* gospel or *the kingdom*. If, therefore, there are criticisms to be levelled against the model of the church school which suggests it exists *for* practising Christians only, equally one must be highly critical of a model that over-emphasises the philanthropic service to the community at the expense of building a truly Christian ethos in the school. The former model, like a mediaeval wall-picture portraying the church as a ship, is self-contained. It does not spill its contents nor can water leak in. The latter model prostitutes the image of suffering-servant and turns it into mere subservience. For the Christian, philanthropic effort must be informed by the vision of faith. Perhaps the leaven-in-the-lump is a more appropriate image. The distinctiveness of the leaven is not in doubt but it transforms the form of the lump and is itself also transformed.

When T S Eliot tried in an essay to delineate *The Idea of a Christian Society*[4], he described it as a society in which 'well-being in community' would be available for everyone and the beatific vision for 'those with eyes to see it.' Perhaps this almost encapsulates the task of a church school, echoing as it does the undifferentiated twin objectives of the Victorian founders of schools − serving in the general education of the nation, and education in the Christian faith.

The church school standing within the maintained sector shares in the task of creating 'well-being in community,' an objective it helps colour from the Christian vision. It also has a reponsibility for training its pupils by helping them to know what to look for in the Christian vision and to set them on the arduous quest for its ultimate apperception. So the Christian vision can inform and be expressed within the whole ethos of the school; it also forms an important part of what is taught. It is style and content; it is experience and tradition. The difficulty is to translate the theological formulation of the vision into *educational* practice.

There are two temptations here. One is to borrow from the ecclesiastical treasury practices or imagery which it is assumed will not only reinforce the Christian nature of the school community but may create it. The other is the assumption that a great deal of good teaching is enough; Christian ethos will spring from it. It is the thoughtful translation of fundamental elements of the vision of faith into educational aims and practices that is the difficult and challenging task.

'Every activity of the school shall be informed with the Christian spirit' states one church school brochure. This is seen by a secular writer as indoctrination, something quite opposed to modern educational practice. Children must be presented with information on a variety of viewpoints, says the writer. But the impossibility of a value-free education has already been alluded to as well as the false choices offered to children by relativising viewpoints. If Christian values are to be allowed a place within a maintained system alongside a secular humanist (and largely) agnostic set of values, *both* must be capable of translation into educational practices which keep children's options alive. Indoctrination, which is taken to mean pressing on pupils only one view of an area of knowledge when controversy in fact exists about it, cannot form part of such translation.

The problem for the Christian can be stated baldly: how do the theological models which interpret God's revelation as Father, Son and Holy Spirit, relate to the activities of a school?

First, the life of the school *as a whole* must provide sufficient signals to children so that they may begin to piece together the elements of the vision for themselves.

Second, the fundamentals of the vision of faith must be taught in such a way that as children get older the controversies and divided opinions about the theological models among Christians themselves are faced honestly. The vision of faith creates room for genuine enquiry.

The God whom Christians call 'Abba,' Father, enshrines elements of mystery for though the Father is revealed he remains transcendent. Signalling this transcendence in the life of the school is of immense importance. The art that is displayed on its walls speaks of man's urge to probe and interpret. It observes the world using the language of line, form and colour but it is a visually organised reflection often signalling a world outside itself. Music hints at realms beyond its own sounds. Literature narrates and probes, it questions and analyses, it arouses a sensibility in man that is never mere emotion. It tells the human story which, only partly anecdotal, becomes a vehicle for framing questions about destiny, suffering and hope. However implicitly a school curriculum signals the mystery that is God, at length a recognition of transcendence generates wonder and awe and leads man to worship. The various signals of the transcendent from the life of the school can be concentrated a few at a time in relevant, understandable and yet mysterious acts of worship. Such acts draw upon the contributions of staff and pupils and not only are they vehicles for corporate prayer and praise, they also provide an arena in which the basic skills of such worship can be learnt. How to be still, how to create a silence, the art of listening, saying or singing words together, moving in unison or in patterns of dance, reading effectively, recognising within oneself affective responses that lead to wonder, adoration, penitence, intercession − all these are vital skills that enable an articulate adult to find worship full of meaning and relevance. They are almost totally alien to contemporary secular man, for whom silence is largely associated with spectatorship and whose aesthetic experiences are almost entirely second-hand. Too much is expected of schools by the terms of the 1944 Education Act which requires an assembly for worship *every day*. More emphasis should be placed on cultivating the skills associated with worship in *fewer* and *better* acts of worship, some of which in a church school will quite clearly introduce children to the church's liturgy, calendar and sacraments. It is at this point that collaborative action by teachers and clergy needs much greater emphasis and school worship should be a regular matter for discussion in governing bodies.

In spite of the randomness endemic to the universe, man senses that order is basic to creation; it is an aspect of the Father as creator. Humanly speaking, order relates to structure and function both in the way knowledge is organised and communicated and in the social organisations man creates. Order offers a framework for discovery and progress; it protects man from the dangers of anarchy, it undergirds the laws which constrain him, yet provide his basic freedom.

For the Christian the order inherent in organised knowledge and social forms is symbolic of God's righteousness and justice as well as his truth. How a school is ordered, how its experience relate to areas of knowledge, all of which reflect something of truth, will signal to children a sense of rightness about the world which can speak of God. Ritual which is an imposed, dull routine will stifle individual initiative and can even breed fear. Good ritual and the structures within the school create an inherent *safety* since, by means of them, both the community and the child's place in it are held sacred. Young children in particular develop a lively creativity of their own within a structured environment. What are popularly known as 'child-centred' methods of teaching require more skill in the teacher, more organisation and careful goal-setting if the spontaneity and individual initiative of the child are to be capitalised upon.

Order clearly impinges upon curriculum, its balance, rigour and content. Ordering the process whereby children can increase in understanding and develop particular competences can signal man's essentially contingent place in the universe which circumscribes boundaries to his knowledge and experience yet allows new discoveries. This contingency is an aspect of man's finitude and sensing it is the first step on the road to humility before God.

Mystery (or the sense of transcendence) and order essential in the life of a Christian school will not just happen, for all educational experiences need careful thought and planning. The Christian teacher seeks to set a balance between both the activities of questioning, searching and musing that skirt around and dig into the element of mystery in life, and the careful induction into ordered areas of human knowledge that testify to man's successful discoveries of truths. Get the balance wrong and induction into knowledge may breed an arrogant self-sufficiency, while too much musing and questioning will feed mere bewilderment. The acknowledgement and explicit awakening of a sense of transcendence through the curriculum can help emphasise the partial nature of all forms of human knowledge. It will help to keep children's minds open and foster a critical openness that later in life will enable mature views to be taken.

But views about what? Proper questions and real choices will emerge only when disciplined and structured intitiation into forms of knowledge has taken place. Such knowledge may well point beyond itself to a vision for man and the society in which he lives, and to that vision the theological reflection of Christians will make a significant contribution. A brave and thoughtful sixteen-year old once said to his hyperactive headmaster, 'Don't get so busy, sir, that you can't stand back and ask what it is all about.'

Christ was both teacher and suffering-servant. In his life and teaching he disclosed truths about God. The Father is one with whom, he avers, a filial relationship is possible. Through Jesus, such a relationship can be forged. The mode of Christ's revelation sets a pattern that is understandable, for he develops situations of disclosure related to familiar human experiences or to landmarks in the culture of his time. It reveals a care and love, but an *unqualified* care, a *limitless* love. It reveals truths but often embeds them in parable, ellipse, hyperbole, though in himself he embodies truth. Jesus exhibits the qualities of the Son living under the sovereignty of the Father, yet he speaks of an age in which God's rule is yet to come.

For the teacher, all classroom situations are places and times of disclosure. Slowly, proceeding from what is already understood or has been experienced, using images and words accessible to the pupil, the teacher edges the child into unknown territory. 'Miss, I've got it!' shouts the excited child as the penny drops. Many children are eager to explore, test, absorb. Others need leading, cajoling, enabling. All require the challenge to go a great deal further than they thought they could. This fragmentary, incremental, little by little contact with human knowledge and skills is itself a parable of revelation. In the situation of disclosure which *is* learning, no one is passive for there is a shared testing of boundaries, a co-operative venture into new territory. The quality of active learning in a school speaks of God's mode of disclosure. This is not nonsense. The teacher who 'goes through the motions' or whose prime concern is peace at any price, or the teacher whose irritations, frustrations and insecurities surface in the lesson with relentless monotony, or the teacher who wields his expertise as some sort of weapon to crush the initiative and questioning of the class, is failing in his responsibility to construct a safe atmosphere in which effective mutual learning is possible. The teacher has become manipulative and the acted parable of disclosure lost. Of course there will be drudgery at times (schools would not mirror life if there were not), of course teachers flag, lose their tempers occasionally and shout from time to time. But it is the sensitive handling of the encounter of the child and the teacher with either new knowledge or a fresh skill that is ultimately the ground for successful or unsuccessful teaching. Life may be easier if one panders to the 'jug and bottle' theory, the teacher portrayed as pouring information into empty heads, or if one accepts the limited psychological model of learning as fundamentally based on 'stimulus and response' and little else.

The Christian teacher, however, will reflect upon and test the success of the teaching situation not only with educational criteria or yardsticks but by constant recourse to the model of Christ as teacher — the one who enabled disclosures. Christ's reference to the hidden processes of growth of seeds hidden in dark, deep moist soil, might lead to reflections on education's obsession with measurement, management by achievable objectives, its preoccupation with certified academic success. The Son of Man, the carpenter, might challenge the teacher to question the underrating of manual skill and technical competences in today's schools. The oblique method Christ often used, the way in which he sometimes saw that the best answer to a question was another question, the acted parable, all these might help the teacher gauge the quality and inherently unselfish aim of his teaching. The professionalism of his pedagogy can be truly set against the vision of faith, and judged.

Christ as suffering-servant exemplifies the selfless love that should be at the heart of all human relationships. The quality of all the pastoral relationships within the school, staff with pupils, staff with staff, pupil with pupil, the motivation and effectiveness of relationships between those in the school and those who visit from the community, especially parents, will have to be measured against the daunting standard of the Christ figure. The ethos of the school requires constant assessment by governors and staff.

Above all there is the challenge of Christ's attitude to the marginal elements of society, to the physically and spiritually impoverished, for example. The power of his love to create newness, fresh hope, revivified purpose began with such people. Does that suggest to church schools a guiding principle in admissions policies, encapsulated in the title of David Sheppard's book *Bias to the Poor*[5]?

Christ's pattern of disclosure also sets standards, it points up those human motives and drives that under the grace of God will lead to what is good, what can in the end be perfect. Morals and values will not be created in a school by accident, nor should their fount be peremptory edicts from on high. They must be reflected in the life of the school in the simplest of activities – how people speak to each other, degrees of courtesy and help-fulness, how property is handled and resources shared, how to avoid the abuse of power or the use of hierarchies in selfish or restrictive ways, how deficiencies or handicaps are acknowledged and dealt with, how talent and success is accredited without further belittling those who feel they have failed, how those who serve the school as caretakers, cleaners, groundsmen, cooks etc. are made part of the community, how free time and meals are organised, how language is chosen on occasions of kindly judgment or honest recon-ciliation, how the offender is treated both in the justice meted out and the efforts made at rehabilitation – all these reveal the under-lying values held by the school community. Christian reflection will assist in the establishment of sound moral criteria which enable the community to develop good attitudes; these will be caught long before they may be taught. Because a great deal of this ethos is implicit in the life of the school, educationalists sometimes refer to it as the 'hidden agenda' or 'hidden curriculum' of the school. A Christian school through governor/staff discussion and with the involvement of pupils themselves, can shape that agenda or cur-riculum in the light of their theological reflection without letting it become too hidden from view and without it all becoming too solemn. Purposeful, happy schools where occasional kicking-over-the-traces is not regarded as the end of the world, where laughter can be heard and where morality is not the community's dull grey strait-jacket designed to produce a compliant, unthinking obedience are the schools that may well echo the mind of Christ. Ethos cannot be left to chance; it must be thought about and patterns of action tried and assessed.

The Spirit breathes life into all creation and sustains a particular quality of life within the community of faith. As breath of life he is both inspiration and inspirer. He is the fire that both warms and consumes. The images of the Spirit are lively, dynamic and it may appear to be relatively easy to relate this theological language to school practice. Schools attempt to be lively, creative places. The searching, unfolding and striving at the heart of teaching is dynamic.

Creativity is a word often on the lips of educationalists. But caution is required. A child can create nothing unless he is able to draw upon a reservoir of skills and knowledge. Creativity may involve the development of an individual's talents, it may be concerned with shifts in cultural patterns, even violent aesthetic or social change but it depends upon a prior induction into cultural tradition. Without that there will be no language, no conceptual frameworks, no symbols or artistic forms, no myths, no rituals, no faith; without such things individuals and cultures collapse. Education enables man to learn his past, draw upon it as a repository of knowledge and skill, and it leaves him free to be an agent in shaping the future. States which wish to maintain the fiction of progress through revolution are forced to curtail that individual freedom, even to validate the aesthetic elements of culture as suitable reinforcements of ideology. The Christian theological tradition helps to undergird the insistence in western democratic countries on a balance between tradition and personal freedom and so in education between socialisation and individual development. Yet because of the sacred nature of the biblical and credal tradition for the Christian as enshrining a particular revelation of God, there is always the danger that Christian institutions may become conserving, unchanging places lacking in adventure. They must learn to face a paradox and live with it: how to induct pupils into the knowledge and skills that are basic to cultural awareness and yet allow for the development of true individual freedom and creativity so that pupils may fashion tools for shaping the future.

Creativity may mean learning to shift resources, to sit lightly to regimentation in curriculum. Creativity will involve casting aside meanness about aesthetic areas of curriculum. Creativity demands that the teacher is still learner, that on occasions the pupil becomes teacher. Creativity generates a striving after links between areas of knowledge, a discovering of ways of integrating elements of curriculum. Creativity implies that somewhere within the school, as has been suggested, there is some thoughtful talk about values and style — 'What is this school saying by its life and ethos?' At present church schools may be creative about the nature of Christian presence in the school, about the development of the well-rounded curriculum, about reinforcing the Christian core of religious education in such a way that pupils are sensitive to other faiths, and those of other faiths feel strengthened and supported in their own faiths.

Perhaps there is a particular challenge to the Christian in education to express the process of learning as a gradual realisation of human potential and so be prepared to criticise what is mean, narrowing or restrictively utilitarian. Nowhere is this more vital than in the renewal and refurbishing that is required in the education of the 16–19s. The primary school provides a rich educational mix – basic skills, knowledge, a bursting forth of art and music, environmental social and religious studies, a safe moral and supportive community. At 16 the pupil's experiences are severely narrowed by vocational considerations and academic pretensions which only suit some. A real Christian creative adventure would be to challenge the assumptions of the current secondary scene and offer for the non-examination pupils a wide base of practical skill and study that would prepare them for a world in which activity will not necessarily be paid work. Could some church schools take the risk of bias to the academic 'poor' and be of practical service to members of a generation which feels trapped by the guilt that stems from the protestant work ethic and betrayed by an exam-dominated secondary curriculum?

The Spirit of God is the one who can change persons, communities, nations perhaps. What is mean, shallow, base and ungenerous will be turned to what is generous, deep, beautiful, of good report. Christians, therefore, are those who can live with change and who seek some signals of the transcendent even in secular change. Someone recently suggested that Erasmus was the last man who in his time knew everything there was to know. Now, no adult can know everything, nor can he know with certainty the kind of world in which his children will be adult. He teaches them but as he speaks there are changes. Children may assimilate some of these changes faster than adults. Christians must be careful not to shun or belittle the creative potential of current technological change. It opens up immense possibilities in the use of information and the development of new processes of thinking. Some children are quickly gaining skills that parents may never acquire. Greater human interdependence may flow from the increasing use of the 'chip' technology. Further, in a situation where unpaid activity is likely to increase as a result of technological innovation, Christians must offer a rich Christian humanism that helps men and women to develop skills and capacities over wider areas of human knowledge and experience.

Christians do not claim merely to *cope* with change, they interpret it and give it meaning within their vision of faith.

This brief reflection on the nature of a Christian school in the light of the doctrine of the Triune God, in whose name Christians are baptised, is a short and perhaps naïve attempt to illustrate an activity that must form part of the discussions at governor and staff level.

The church school can be summarised as being:

1.  *a safe place* where there is no ideological pressure and yet Christian inferences are built into the ethos and teaching as signals for children to detect;

2.  *an ecumenical nursery* which builds from children's funda-
    mental unity a sensitivity to difference, and the faiths of
    others;
3.  *a place of distinctive exellence* in which excellence is not just
    tied to what is academic but plainly linked to all aspects of
    the the life of the school including the manual, technical, aes-
    thetic and non-verbal;
4.  *stepping stones to and from the community*, for children,
    staff, parents and local interests. The school learns to be part
    of a local community, to share its concerns and to be open
    to those who seek help, support and resources;
5.  *a house of the gospel* in which, starting at governor and staff
    level, there is a deliberate attempt to link the concerns of
    Christ's gospel with the life of the school, but to do this in
    educational terms;
6.  *a place of revelation and disclosure* in which the rigour of
    learning and the art of acquiring skill are seen as parables
    of the revelation of God and his continuous involvement in
    his creation;
7.  *a foster home of enduring values and relationships* in which
    the selfless care and unlimited love of the Suffering Servant
    is the model for the life of the community;
8.  *a beacon signalling the transcendent* by the development of
    awe, mystery and wonder through the curriculum, exemplified
    in acts of corporate worship including contact with the
    Christian calendar and sacraments;
9.  *a place where you can see the wood for the trees*, for there
    are attempts to develop an integrated view of knowledge
    alongside sensitivity to the interests and specialisms of others,
    as well as to cross traditional subject boundaries and carry
    out integrated projects in learning;
10. *a creative workshop* which facilitates a thorough induction
    into cultural tradition and skills yet allows pupils to practice
    initiative, change and new direction as they shape their
    future.

But by now one can hear the protestation of one's secular humanist
colleagues and also Christian teachers working within county schools,
pointing out that with much of this analysis of school activity they
would want to agree. The secular colleagues would, justifiably, argue
that Christians cannot claim to monopolise the sorts of educational
ethos and activities that have been described here. A number of
points must be made in this connection.

First, what is important for Christians is that worship and mature
theological reflection *must* inform all they do. If resulting practice
corresponds closely to the practices of secular colleagues, the
Christian teacher must be profoundly thankful that he is able to

share common ground and he will resist the temptation to claim for his own practice a Christian distinctiveness in which secular colleagues cannot share.

Second, the existence of considerable areas of common ground with secular teachers has enabled a vast number of Christians to work in county schools allowing their own Christian reflection to be carried quietly and unobtrusively into the planning and activities of the school. It has also enabled non-Christians to work in church schools. What is the nature of such common ground? In some sense it is embodied in that gentle humanist tradition already referred to in connection with Erasmus. It is based on tolerance and personal freedom, the latter only curtailed when the well-being of the community is at risk. It is anti-reductionist, that is, it does not believe that the models man builds of himself or of society can completely explain his potential or destiny. It believes in evolutionary changes in society rather than change by revolution. It can share with Christians the cardinal virtues and much of what is natural justice and believes that it is right for faith of whatever kind to be allowed expression, personally and socially. So in education it is right for teachers to reveal their own convictions, yet essential that from the pupils' point of view learning is 'open-ended,' that is, options are not closed before mature choices can be made. It is right for Christians to rejoice in the amount of common ground that can be so shared with secular counterparts, but it is essential not to claim for it more than it deserves. It is not Christian faith; it cannot for many involve worship, prayer, the sacramental Grace of God, the ultimacy of a beatific vision. Its propriety as *common* ground, however, is enhanced when the secular humanist and the Christian both respect and acknowledge the dignity of divergent views and beliefs. The fact that many staff rooms in all kinds of schools epitomise a sharing of common ground and a tolerance of differing faiths suggests that some schools are already cradles of a healthy pluralism. In others where abrasive or bitter political or religious activists spurn any common ground and turn zeal into bigotry, it is plain that much work needs yet to be done before a tolerant sharing is possible.

This article has attempted to suggest that reflection on education in the light of the vision of faith as articulated in Christian theology enables the church school to develop good educational practice consonant with the Christian tradition, in three particular areas: first, the nature of the Christian community in the school, who can comprise it and the possible effects this will have on admissions policies; second, the content of the formal curriculum of the school and in particular a rigorous attention to the grammar of faith in the Christian core of religious education; third, the *style* of the school, its ethos, underlying values and corporate life particularly as expressed in worship.

It has become apparent, however, that church schools can claim no monopoly of Christian endeavour in education. The witness of the Christian working in the county school, the ethos of many a county school, the shared assumptions from which many sensitive and professional Christian and secular humanists can together build sound educational practice, are vital elements within the partnership that this paper is at pains to emphasise. The special responsibility that the aided church school may have to bear is to signal in its worship and life the vision of faith which clearly nourishes its distinctiveness and informs the 'common ground' which has been tentatively outlined above.

**Notes**
1. David Sheppard, *Bias to the Poor*, London, Hodder and Stoughton, 1983, p. 218.
2. Letter to the editor, *The Times*, 2 April, 1983.
3. *The Fourth R: the report of the commission on religion education in schools*, London, National Society and SPCK, 1970.
4. T S Eliot, *The Idea of a Christian Society*, London, Faber, 1982.
5. See note 1 above.

# 2.2 Theology of education and the church school
*Leslie J Francis*

## Introduction

The publication of the first reader in the theology of education[1] was designed to stimulate new interest in this form of enquiry, since at present the concept of 'theology of education' sounds comparatively strange both to educationalists, who are familiar with such areas of discourse as 'psychology of education,'[2] 'philosophy of education'[3] and 'sociology of education,'[4] and to theologians, who are familiar with the application of their discipline to many other applied areas of social and personal life. For the theology of education to be taken seriously, theologians need to be convinced that the subject matter of education is worthy of theological scrutiny and educationalists need to be convinced that the methods of theology are worthy of serious consideration within the educational arena. In his paper in *The Scottish Journal of Theology* in 1977,[5] John Hull set out to convince the theologian of the former case, while Leslie Francis set out in his paper in *The Oxford Review of Education* in 1983[6] to convince the educationalist of the latter case. The question of the place of church schools within the state maintained sector of education provides a good testing ground for the development of the theology of education.[7]

Just as there is no one simple answer to the question 'what is theology?',[8] so there can be no one simple answer to the question 'what is the theology of education?' Different theological methods will be reflected in different approaches to the theology of education, as exampled by William Andersen's perspective from biblical theology,[9] Barbara Mitrano's from feminist theology,[10] Gerard Capaldi's from liberation theology[11] or Randolph Crump-Miller's from process theology.[12] Nevertheless, as a branch of applied or practical theology, the theology of education needs to operate within certain clearly defined parameters. The constraints on the interface between theology and education are not dissimilar from those on the interface between theology and sociology described by Robin Gill.[13] The theology of education must begin by taking its educational context seriously and must conclude by subjecting its empirical claims to appropriate methods of investigation. According to these criteria, the theology of education when applied to church schools must take into account the historical context through which the church school system evolved, the contemporary philosophical climate of educational debate, and empirical research data about the current functioning of church schools.

## Historical context

Church schools are an integral part of the state maintained system of education in England and Wales as a direct consequence of the accidents of history.[14] Long before the state established the machinery to build Board Schools through the 1870 Education Act,[15] the churches had taken their own major initiatives through the National Society and the British and Foreign School Society. The Butler Education Act of 1944[16] secured the future of church schools within the context of post-war educational reconstruction and this future remained unchallenged by the 1988 Education Reform Act.[17] Today in England and Wales Anglican schools provide places for 16.8% of primary and 4.3% of secondary pupils, while Catholic schools provide places for 9.5% of primary and 8.8% of secondary pupils.[18]

Historically the developments of the Anglican and Catholic contributions to the nation's stock of schools have followed very different lines. In the nineteenth century the Church of England developed a strong lead, as the established national church, in the building of new schools, while the Catholic church experienced a much harder struggle. Since the late 1940s the Anglican contribution has dropped from providing 17.8% to 10.8% of state maintained places,[19] while the Catholic contribution has continued to rise from 7.0% to 9.1%.[20]

Historically the aim of Catholic schools in England and Wales was to provide an alternative educational system to make it possible for 'every Catholic child from a Catholic home to be taught by Catholic teachers in a Catholic school.'[21] While the 1981 report to the Bishops of England and Wales, *Signposts and Homecomings*,[22] recognised that Catholic education should be confined neither to the years of compulsory schooling nor to the Catholic school, it continues to reaffirm the identity of the Catholic school as 'a believing and integrated Christian community.'

Historically the aim of Anglican schools in England and Wales has been more complex. Back in 1811 the National Society formulated the objective of its schools to promote 'the education of the poor in the principles of the established church.'[23] In 1970 the Durham Report, *The Fourth R*,[24] teased out two distinct strands from this objective.

> It is extremely important to recognise at the outset that the Church of England voluntary school of today is an institution whose roots go back into a past where its role was seen as two-fold. It was

general, to serve the nation through its children, and domestic, to equip the children of the church to take their places in the Christian community.

This distinction continued to play an important part in the National Society's green paper in 1984, *A Future in Partnership.*[25]

The Durham Report recognises that historically these two roles were 'indistinguishable, for nation and church were, theoretically, one, and the domestic task was seen as including the general.' The Durham Report then recognises that 'nowadays no one would pretend to claim that nation and church are co-extensive' and draws the logical conclusion that the domestic and general functions of church schools can no longer be confused. The report's recommendation is that the Anglican church should:

> see its continued involvement in the dual system principally as a way of expressing its concern for the general education of all children and young people rather than as a means for giving 'denominational instruction.'

This pattern of historical development means that, especially at the primary level, the Catholic and Anglican churches understand their theological involvement in church schools today in very different terms. In theory, Catholic schools exist primarily to serve the domestic purposes of the Catholic community, while Anglican schools exist primarily to serve the general educational needs of specific local neighbourhoods. In practice, however, some Catholic schools find that they are increasingly serving non-Catholic and non-practising Catholic families within their immediate neighbourhood, while some Anglican schools find that they are continuing to serve the domestic needs of Anglican families from a wider geographical area. The need today, therefore, is for a theology of education which is both able to work with the reality of the church school system as it is, and also shape that system to meet the religious and educational challenges of the next decade.

## Educational context

The educational context within which the theological discussion of church schools in England and Wales must operate is characterised by five key areas of debate. These areas are complex, involve many strands of thought and assume no necessary consensus.

First, the emergence of the academic study of education as an autonomous discipline began to question, on grounds of logic, the right of the churches to determine educational theory and practice. This view reached its strongest expression in two papers by Paul Hirst, until recently Professor of Education within the University of Cambridge, 'Christian education: a contradiction in terms,'[26] and 'Education, catechesis and the church school.'[27] Hirst argues[28] that:

> Just as intelligent Christians have come to recognise that justifiable scientific claims are autonomous and do not, and logically cannot, rest on religious beliefs, so also, it seems to me, justifiable educational principles are autonomous. That is to say that any attempt to justify educational principles by an appeal to religious claims is invalid.

While the cogency of Hirst's case has been challenged by reviewers like John Hull,[29] Leslie Francis[30] and Elmer Thiessen,[31] theologians can no longer necessarily assume that the language of theology will be heard in the educational arena.

Second, professional debate regarding the nature and purpose of religious education within the state maintained sector has drawn a sharp distinction between the churches' function in catechesis or Christian nurture to engender faith, and the schools' function in religious education to teach about religious phenomena. This view reached clear expression in the formative Schools Council Working Paper 36, *Religious Education in the Secondary School*,[32] which was heavily influenced by Ninian Smart's phenomenological approach to the study of religion.[33] The influence of this approach is clearly reflected in agreed syllabuses like Hampshire, which argues[34] that:

> The principal aim of religious education in schools within the public sector is to enable pupils to understand the nature of religious belief and practices and the importance and influence of these in the lives of believers.

While the cogency of this distinction between the secular study of religion in schools and the religious transmission of faith in churches has been questioned from a number of perspectives by commentators like Adrian Thatcher[35] and Nicola Slee,[36] theologians can no longer necessarily assume continuity between their concerns and the concerns of the secular religious educator.

Third, professional debate regarding school worship has drawn a sharp distinction between the nature of education, which is committed to a critical enquiry, and the nature of worship, which is committed to and pre-supposes belief. This view reached clear expression in John Hull's seminal book, *School Worship: an obituary*,[37] where he argues that:

> Nurture prepares for belief, evangelisation summons belief, instruction implies belief, catechesis strengthens belief and worship assumes belief.

But education scrutinises belief. It is clear, then, that worship and education cannot take place concurrently.

While other commentators have reasserted the educational value of worship from educational,[38] Christian[39] and Islamic[40] perspectives, theologians can no longer necessarily assume that school assemblies and church services hold much in common.

Fourth, a main strand in secularisation theory argues that the social significance of the Christian churches has declined significantly in England and Wales during the past decades. This view is clearly expressed by Bryan Wilson in his two books, *Religion and Secular Society*[41] and *Religion in Sociological Perspective*[42] and finds a starker exposition in Alan Gilbert's *The Making of Post-Christian Britain*,[43] where he argues that:

> A post-Christian society is not one from which Christianity has departed, but one in which it has become marginal. It is a society where to be irreligious is to be normal, to think and to act in secular terms is to be conventional, where neither status nor responsibility depends on the practice or profession of religious faith.

While a number of commentators on the sociological scene, like David Hay,[44] John Habgood[45] and Edward Bailey[46] warn against underestimating the strength of residual religious experience, feeling or commitment, theologians can no longer necessarily assume that secular society will welcome their intervention in educational debate.

Fifth, since the establishment of the church school system in the nineteenth century, cultural and religious pluralism have developed significantly in England and Wales.[47] The educational implications of these developments are brought into particularly sharp perspective by the Swann Report, *Education for All*,[48] the findings of the committee of inquiry into the education of children from ethnic minority groups. The majority recommendation of this report against the desirability of state funded schools for other faith groups has important implications for the future status of church schools. The majority recommendation reports:

> Our conclusions about the desirability of denominational voluntary aided schools for Muslims or other groups, by extension seriously calls into question the long established dual system of educational provision in this country and particularly the role of the churches in the provision of education.

While other studies have continued to justify denominational schools within a pluralist society from philosophical,[49] Anglican[50] and

Catholic[51] perspectives, theologians can no longer assume that the status of church schools remains unchallenged.

## Research context

While a body of international data is now informing debate about the character and effectiveness of Catholic secondary schools, through research conducted in England,[52] Wales,[53] Scotland,[54] Australia,[55] Canada[56] and the USA,[57] comparatively little is known about the functioning of Church of England secondary schools, apart from Bernadette O'Keeffe's comparative study of church and county schools.[58] Slightly more is known, however, about the functioning of Church of England primary schools as a consequence of six recent research studies.

First, a detailed study of the attitudes of teachers in Church of England schools in Suffolk[59] found that younger teachers were holding a significantly less positive view of the church school system than older teachers. The report concludes that the whole ethos of Church of England schools is likely to change as older teachers are replaced by a younger generation. When theologians speculate about the ethos of church schools, they need to take into account the changes already under way as a consequence of a new generation of teachers.

Second, a detailed study of the attitudes of the governors of Church of England voluntary aided schools in the diocese of Oxford,[60] demonstrated that the foundation governors were committed 'to preserve the ethos of the voluntary aided school,' while 'in contrast parents of children in the school tend to value the Christian ethos of the school less.' The report concludes that as parental involvement in school governing bodies 'is a group that we can expect to see increasing in numbers and influence, this is potentially a worrying situation for those who value the distinctiveness of the church school.' When theologians speculate about local parental support for church schools, they need to take into account the less sympathetic views already being expressed by some parents on the governing bodies of these schools.

Third, a detailed comparative study of the Christian character of county, Church of England voluntary aided and Church of England voluntary controlled schools in Gloucestershire[61] found that, although these church schools were serving specific local neigbourhoods in the same way as county schools, they continued to express more signs of church-relatedness than county schools. Church of England schools in Gloucestershire encourage more contact with the clergy and with the local church. They hold more explicitly Christian assemblies and give more emphasis to the church-related aspects of religious education. When theologians speculate about the ways in which church schools serve the local community, they need to take into account the fact that many church schools currently interpret their brief of service as an opportunity to provide the areas which they serve with a more overtly Christian approach to education than would be provided by county schools.

Fourth, a detailed study of the impact of church schools on a range of indices of village church life,[62] in a sample of 1,637 communities ranging in size from 250 to 1,250 inhabitants, found that the presence of a church school augments slightly the village churches' usual Sunday contact both with six to nine year olds and with adults, although not with other age groups. This suggests that children who attend village church schools are more likely to go to church on Sunday and to take their parents with them. The presence of a church school was also shown to have some positive influence on the number of infant baptisms, the number of six to thirteen year olds in village church choirs, and the number of young confirmands under the age of fourteen years. When theologians speculate about the implications of church schools for local church life, they need to take into account the fact that local churches are currently benefitting in attendances and other membership statistics as a consequence of maintaining a church school.

Fifth, detailed studies of the contribution of church schools to the religious development of eleven year old children in Gloucestershire[63] and in East Anglia[64] found that church schools do exert a measurable impact on the religious attitudes of their pupils, in comparison with county schools and after controlling for the influence of home and church. While Roman Catholic schools were found in both studies to have a small positive influence on pupil attitudes, Church of England voluntary controlled schools in Gloucestershire and Church of England voluntary aided schools in East Anglia were found to have a slight negative influence. When theologians speculate about the contribution of church schools towards their pupils' religious development, they need to take into account the current situation which suggests that, overall, Church of England schools are not contributing positively to their pupils' religious attitudes, but are, in some situations, contributing negatively.

## Theology for the future

Having considered the historical, educational and research contexts within which contemporary theological reflection on church schools must operate, the way has now been cleared to identify some key theological pointers for the future. In place of the Durham Report's bi-partite theological distinction between the church's domestic and general functions in education,[65] I plan to propose a tripartite distinction between nurture, service and prophecy. Just as the Durham

Report recognised an intrinsic conflict between the ideals of the church's domestic and general functions, so I recognise an intrinsic conflict between the ideals of a theology of nurture and those of a theology of service. While the Durham Report resolved its tension by emphasising the general function and eclipsing the domestic function, I shall suggest that the tension between nurture and service needs to be retained and that it is precisely this tension which generates and authenticates a distinctive theology of prophecy addressed to education.

## Theology of nurture

Nurture is concerned with the nature of Christian upbringing. It is the concern expressed by Christian parents who wish their children to grow and to develop within the overall context of the Christian faith. Like catechesis[66] nurture is a much broader concept than religious education and like catechesis it has the potential for integrating the perspectives of church, home and school. Today practical theology has a responsibility both to scrutinise the concept of nurture and to evaluate the contexts in which it is appropriate.

John Hull's careful analysis of the concept of nurture[67] has linked the Christian perspective on nurture with the fundamental notion of critical openness. In so doing he has developed a vocabulary which is able to discuss and to hold in balance respect for both commitment and autonomy on the part of teacher and pupil. Through the notion of critical autonomy, Hull demonstrates how Christian nurture can be distinguished from good education on the one hand and from indoctrination on the other. He argues that because the 'Christian faith is constantly critical of itself' it is able to generate an understanding both of general eduction as open and enquiring, and of Christian nurture as being other than indoctrination. The important defence of Christian nurture against the accusation of indoctrination is given further support by the discussion of Elmer Thiessen in Canada[68] and M A B Degenhardt in Tasmania.[69] Against this background, practical theology seems to have little reason to be nervous of commending Christian nurture.

The next question concerns the contexts in which Christian nurture should take place. Historically three main approaches have been advanced to this question and in very real ways all three answers are now wearing thin. First, at the time of the 1944 Education Act a strong Free Church line, supported by many Anglicans, argued that the churches should give priority to training Christian teachers for staffing county schools.[70] My foregoing analysis of the contemporary climate in educational theory and practice, shaped for a multicultural and secular society, suggests that this view is now irretrievably anachronistic. Second, as many

Free Church and Anglican[71] thinkers have accepted the changing relationship between Christian nurture and the country school, so they have increasingly located the work of nurture within the home and church congregation. This is the view advocated by the British Council of Churches report, *The Child in the Church,*[72] and the Anglican report *Children in the Way.*[73] Empirically this view may both overestimate the potential of the church congregation in fulfilling the requirements of Christian nurture and underestimate the all pervading influence of the secular school on the child's personal and religious development. Third, at the time of the 1944 Education Act, the Roman Catholic view took the clear line that the role of family and church was inadequate without the firm support of a distinctive system of church schools. At great cost the system was put in place, but now fifty years later key weaknesses are apparent with the system. Empirically large tracts of the country, where the Catholic population is sparse, have been unable to maintain Catholic schools. In other areas, demographic changes in the Catholic population mean that some existing Catholic schools increasingly need to recruit non-Catholic pupils and non-Catholic staff. This is changing the whole ethos and functioning of some Catholic schools.[74] Meanwhile, the changing ecumenical climate is encouraging some Catholic schools to seek a more overtly inter-denominational basis.[75]

The logic of this analysis gives three important pointers for a theology of Christian nurture appropriate for the present social context. The first pointer is that the churches should abandon, at least for the time being, the notion that county schools are necessarily working in partnership with the churches to promote a Christian future, in spite of the rhetoric of the 1988 Education Act.[76] The second pointer is that the churches should abandon, at least for the time being, the notion that it is possible to fulfil the function of Christian nurture adequately outside the framework of statutory schooling. The third pointer is that the churches should abandon, at least for the time being, the notion that it is possible, or even desirable, to operate in education within the context of historic denominational rivalry. The implication of these three pointers is to look afresh at the possibilities and problems inherent in a system of ecumenical church schools operated as a distinctive Christian alternative to a predominantly secular system of county schools. Here is an opportunity for the theology of Christian nurture to re-shape the present provision of denominational voluntary aided schools.

## Theology of service

Service is concerned with the churches' perceived responsibility for the needs of those who are not members, as much as those who are members.[77] Historically, in response to basic human needs, the churches have taken pioneering initiatives in key social areas, like housing and health care, as well as education. Today practical theology has a responsibility both to scrutinise the educational needs of all children and young people and to evaluate the appropriateness of the churches' responses to these needs.

Historically the churches' understanding of service in education seemed able to include a theology of religious mission alongside a theology of educational service. Following the analysis of the Durham Report, mission and evangelism are now generally seen as inappropriate aspects of the churches' theology of service in education. Instead of being there to save souls, convert lives or to recruit members, church schools are seen as an enduring symbol of the churches' dedication and commitment to serving the general educational needs of the nation. Historically the churches took the initiative to build schools because the state was failing in this initiative. Now the churches continue to put their decreasing stock of schools at the nation's disposal as a way of witnessing to their radical commitment to altruistic service.

Such a theology of service raises sharp questions about the extent to which church schools, intended to reflect this notion of service rather than the notion of nurture, can or should be distinctive. Especially in single school areas, where the church provides the only accessible school, it may well become increasingly important for the church to insist that these schools should in no way be distinctive from a county school. The educational excellence for which they strive, inspired as it may be by radical commitment to the gospel of Christ, should not be fundamentally different from the educational excellence equally desired and achieved within county schools. A church committed to a theology of service in education should be able to operate within an educational system in which key educational decisions on the purpose and character of schools are made on educational and not on theological grounds.

The commitment to a theology of nurture, seeking expression in the development of an ecumenical network of distinctive Christian schools, as described in the previous section, does not preclude an equal commitment to a theology of service. This analysis, however, makes it clear that these two commitments should operate separately and cannot be confused within the one school. While the current provision of voluntary aided status offers an appropriate framework within which to fulfil a theology of nurture for those Christian parents who seek such an education for their children, the provision of voluntary controlled status offers an appropriate framework within which to fulfil a theology of service, without confusing such service with evangelisation or nurture. The existing provision of educational legislation already provides the churches in England and Wales with an appropriate distinction between two types of church schools, through which two rather different theological perspectives on education could be promoted.

## Theology of prophecy

Prophecy is concerned with testing current social reality against an understanding of God's declared purposes for his creation. The prophetic tradition in theology has always claimed the right to stand outside social practice, to draw attention to the implications and consequences of certain lines of action and to bring to the surface implicit values and beliefs underlying these lines of action. Today practical theology has a responsibility to scrutinise and to evaluate secular educational theory and practice in the light of the Christian gospel and to do so not only in relationship to church schools but to the whole of the state maintained system.

At the same time, the prophetic function of theology has seen its voice as directed both towards those within the household of faith and those without the household of faith. The problem in addressing those on the outside of the household of faith is two-fold. First, there is the problem of engaging their interest in a language form which they can understand and which they deem to be valid. Second, there is the problem of authenticating and validating the prophetic point of view among those for whom the traditional imagery 'thus says the Lord' carries no weight.

The problem of identifying the appropriate language form means listening carefully to educationalists themselves. When theology was the queen of sciences, the language of theology could be spoken across disciplinary frontiers; now dethroned theology needs to learn to speak the languages evolved by other disciplines. If prophetic theology is to make a sensible contribution to contemporary educational debate and if this contribution is to be heeded by educationalists, this will only be achieved when the churches develop a theological critique of education expressed in forms understandable by and acceptable to the language of secular educationalists. This demands the rigorous training of theologians within the thought-forms of educational theory.

The range of educational issues on which the theologian has a prophetic contribution to make is wide. For example, Paul Hirst's secular analysis of the concept of education[78] involves, among other matters, raising questions about the nature of mind, the nature of knowledge and the nature of reality. He raises questions about the relationship between mind and knowledge and the relationship between knowledge and reality. He reviews value judgments about developing the mind in desirable ways and promoting the good life. He deals with ultimate principles and the final court of appeal in human affairs. He discusses the moral life and the freeing of human conduct from wrong. He talks in terms of ultimate justification. He comes close to dealing with issues like what it means to be human and the goals of human life. Not only are these properly educational questions, they are also essentially theological questions. Theology has no one answer to these questions and no one method for dealing with them. Theology has no sole prerogative to handle these questions, nor would the theologian necessarily come to different educational conclusions from the secular educationalists in analysing these questions. What the prophetic voice of theology should be equipped to do, however, is to bring into the open the assumptions and values involved in these questions and to subject them to public scrutiny. Without this perspective of prophetic theology, educational analysis itself is surely incomplete. At the same time, unless theology attempts to bring educational concerns within the professional competence of its scrutiny and analysis, it fails in its *raison d'etre* to witness to its belief in ultimate values at the point where those values can be most influential in shaping the lives of young people and in influencing society itself.

The problem of authenticating and validating the voice of prophetic theology goes deeper, however, than the need to demonstrate the appropriate linguistic and theoretical skills. The churches' prophetic voice in education will be ultimately authenticated by empirical evidence of its practical involvement. It is precisely at this level that the churches' institutional investment through church schools remains so crucial, since through its voluntary aided and voluntary controlled schools the church is able to test and to implement its prophetic voice in direct relationship with its theology of nurture and theology of service.

## Tension and challenge

The previous sections have developed and refined a distinction between the three theological perspectives of nurture, service and prophecy. It has to be recognised now, however, that at key points sharp conflict may emerge between the practical implications and expressions of a theology of nurture on the one hand and a theology of service on the other. The very values represented by the development of a network of ecumenical and distinctively Christian schools may well not only contradict the values most cherished by schools committed to radical Christian service to the community, but also conflict with certain Christian expectations and hopes for the state maintained system of education as a whole. It is precisely in these areas of conflict that the role of prophetic theology comes into its own. The adequacy of prophetic theology to meet this challenge must be tested against the five main objections generally raised against the development of a separatist system of Christian schools. These objections suggest that church schools are divisive, that they tend to be elitist, that they are unfair to the rest of the educational system, that they are guilty of indoctrinating their pupils and that they take Christian teachers and Christian pupils out of the rest of the school system. All five of these objections accuse the church of promoting through its theology of nurture values which its theology of service should be quick to criticise and condemn. While there is no easy solution to these problems, it is precisely in these areas of controversial debate that the churches' true commitment to a theology of education will be tested and either authenticated or invalidated.

**Notes**
1.  L J Francis and A Thatcher (eds), *Christian Perspectives for Education: a reader in the theology of education*, Leominster, Gracewing, 1990.
2.  See, for example, G A Davis and T F Warren (eds), *Psychology of Education*, Lexington, Massachusetts, D C Heath, 1974.
3.  See, for example, J E McClellan, *Philosophy of Education*, Englewood Cliffs, New Jersey, Prentice-Hall, 1976.
4.  See, for example, W B Brookover and E L Erickson, *Sociology of Education*, Homewood, Illinois, Dorsey Press, 1975.
5.  J M Hull, 'What is the theology of education?' *Scottish Journal of Theology*, 30, 1977, pp. 3–29.
6.  L J Francis, 'The logic of education, theology and the church school,' *Oxford Review of Education*, 9, 1983, pp. 147–162.
7.  See, for example, S Sutherland, 'Education and theology,' in G Leonard (ed.), *Faith for the Future*, London, National Society and Church House Publishing, 1986, pp. 35–41, and S Sutherland, 'Theological reflections,' in B O'Keeffe (ed.), *Schools for Tomorrow*, Barcombe, Falmer Press, 1988, pp. 182–190.
8.  M Wiles, *What is Theology?*, London, Oxford University Press, 1976.
9.  W E Andersen, 'A biblical view of education,' *Journal of Christian Education*, 77, 1983, pp. 15–30.
10. B Mitrano, 'Feminist theology and curriculum theory,' *Curriculum Studies*, 11, 1979, pp. 211–220.
11. G I Capaldi, 'Christian faith and religious education: a perspective from the theology of liberation,' *British Journal of Religious Education*, 6, 1983, pp. 31–40.
12. R Crump-Miller, 'Theology and the future of religious education,' *Religious Education*, 72, 1, 1977, 46–60.
13. R Gill, *Social Context of Theology*, London, Mowbrays, 1975.
14. J Murphy, *Church, State and Schools in Britain 1800–1970*, London, Routledge and Kegan Paul, 1971.
15. E E Rich, *The Education Act 1870*, London, Longmans, 1970.
16. H C Dent, *The Education Act 1944: provisions, possibilities and some problems*, London, University of London Press, 1947.
17. M Flude and M Hammer (eds), *The Education Reform Act 1988*, Basingstoke, Falmer Press, 1990.
18. From statistics provided by the Department of Education and Science and the Welsh Office.
19. See, for example, S E Kelly, 'The schools of the established church in England: a study of diocesan involvement since 1944,' unpublished PhD dissertation, University of Keele, 1978.
20. See, for example, M P Hornsby-Smith, *Catholic Education: the unobtrusive partner*, London, Sheed and Ward, 1978.
21. Pope Pius IX's encyclical letter 'Divini Illius Magistri,' 1929.
22. *Signposts and Homecomings: the educative task of the Catholic community*, Middlegreen, St Paul Publications, 1981.
23. H J Burgess, *Enterprise in Education*, London, National Society and SPCK, 1958.
24. *The Fourth R: the report of the commission on religious education in schools*, London, National Society and SPCK, 1970.

25. *A Future in Partnership*, London, National Society, 1984.
26. P H Hirst, 'Christian education: a contradiction in terms?' *Learning for Living*, 11, 4, 1972, pp. 6–11.
27. P H Hirst, 'Education, catechesis and the church school,' *British Journal of Religious Education*, 3, 1981, pp. 85–93.
28. P H Hirst, 'Religious beliefs and educational principles,' *Learning for Living*, 5, 1976, pp. 155–157.
29. J M Hull, 'Christian theology and educational theory: can there be connections?' *British Journal of Educational Studies*, 24, 1976, pp. 127–143.
30. L J Francis, 'The logic of education, theology and the church school,' *Oxford Review of Education*, 9, 1983, pp. 147–162.
31. E J Thiessen, 'A defense of a distinctively Christian curriculum,' *Religious Education*, 80, 1985, pp. 37–50.
32. Schools Council, London, Evans Brothers and Methuen Educational, 1971.
33. N Smart, *Secular Education and the Logic of Religion*, London, Faber, 1968.
34. *Religious Education in Hampshire Schools*, Winchester, Hampshire Education Committee, 1978.
35. A Thatcher, 'The recovery of Christian education,' *Scottish Journal of Theology*, 40, 1987, pp. 437–450.
36. N Slee, 'Conflict and reconciliation between competing models of religious education: some reflections on the British scene,' *British Journal of Religious Education*, 11, 1989, pp. 126–135.
37. J M Hull, *School Worship: an obituary*, London, SCM, 1975.
38. B Watson, *Education and Belief*, London, Basil Blackwell, 1987.
39. D G Kibble, 'Teaching about Christian worship,' *British Journal of Religious Education*, 8, 1985, pp. 26–29.
40. J M Halstead and A Khan-Cheema, 'Muslims and worship in maintained schools,' *Westminster Studies in Education*, 10, 1987, pp. 21–36.
41. B Wilson, *Religion in Secular Society*, London, Watts, 1966.
42. B Wilson, *Religion in Sociological Perspective*, Oxford, Oxford University Press, 1982.
43. A D Gilbert, *The Making of Post-Christian Britain*, London, Longman, 1986.
44. D Hay, *Exploring Inner Space*, Harmondsworth, Penguin, 1982.
45. J Habgood, *Church and Nation in a Secular Age*, London, Darton, Longman and Todd, 1983.
46. E Bailey, 'The religion of the people,' in T Moss (ed.), *In Search of Christianity*, London, Firethorn Press, 1986, pp. 178–188.
47. See H A Halsey (ed.), *British Social Trends since 1900*, Basingstoke, Macmillan, 1988.
48. *Education for All*, London, HMSO, 1985.
49. J Haldane, 'Religious education in a pluralist society: a philosophical examination,' *British Journal of Educational Studies*, 34, 1986, 161–181.
50. General Synod of the Church of England Board of Education, *Schools and Multicultural Education*, London, Church House, 1984.
51. Catholic Commission for Racial Justice, *Learning from Diversity*, London, Catholic Media Office, 1984.
52. See, for example, R G Burgess, *Experiencing Comprehensive Education: a study of Bishop McGregor School*, London, Methuen, 1983.
53. See, for example, J Egan, *Opting Out: Catholic schools today*, Leominster, Gracewing, 1988.
54. See, for example, J Rhymer and L J Francis, 'Roman Catholic secondary schools in Scotland and pupil attitude towards religion,' *Lumen Vitae*, 40, 1985, pp. 103–110.
55. See, for example, M F Flynn, *The Effectiveness of Catholic Schools*, Homebush, NSW, St Paul Publications, 1985.
56. See, for example, P McLaren, *Schooling as a Ritual Performance*, London, Routledge and Kegan Paul, 1986.
57. See, for example, A M Greeley, *Catholic High Schools and Minority Students*, New Brunswick, Transaction Books, 1982.
58. B O'Keeffe, *Faith, Culture and the Dual System: a comparative study of church and county schools*, Barcombe, Falmer Press, 1986.
59. L J Francis, *Partnership in Rural Education*, London, Collins, 1986.

60. B W Kay, H S Piper and J D Gay, *Managing Church Schools*, Abingdon, Culham College Institute Occasional Paper number 10, 1988.
61. L J Francis, *Religion in the Primary School*, London, Collins, 1987.
62. L J Francis and D W Lankshear, 'The impact of church schools on village church life,' *Educational Studies*, 16, 1990, pp. 117–129.
63. See note 61 above.
64. L J Francis, 'Denominational schools and pupils attitude towards Christianity,' *British Educational Research Journal*, 12, 1986, pp. 145–152.
65. See note 24 above.
66. See, for example, G M Rossiter, 'The need for a "creative divorce" between catechesis and religious education in Catholic schools,' *Religious Education*, 77, 1982, pp. 21–40.
67. J M Hull, 'Christian nurture and critical openness,' *Scottish Journal of Theology*, 34, 1981, pp. 17–37.
68. E J Thiessen, 'Indoctrination and religious education,' *Interchange*, 15, 3, 1984, pp. 27–43.
69. M A B Degenhardt, 'The "ethics of belief" and education in science and morals,' *Journal of Moral Education*, 15, 1986, pp. 109–118.
70. See, for example, J D Gay, 'The churches and the training of teachers in England and Wales,' in V A McClelland (ed.), *Christian Education in a Pluralist Society*, London, Routledge, 1988, pp. 207–233.
71. See, for example, A Chesters, 'Where is the child to be nurtured: church, home or school?' *Educational Viewpoint*, 6, 1988, pp. 2–15.
72. *The Child in the Church*, London, British Council of Churches, 1976.
73. *Children in the Way*, London, National Society and Church House Publishing, 1988.
74. See, for example, L J Francis, 'Roman Catholic secondary schools: falling rolls and pupil attitudes,' *Educational Studies*, 12, 1986, pp. 119–127.
75. See P Chadwick and M Gladwell, *Joint Schools*, Norwich, Canterbury Press and Fowler Wright Books, 1987.
76. See, for example, J M Hull, *The Act Unpacked*, London, Christian Education Movement, 1989.
77. G Duncan, 'Church schools in service to the community,' in B O'Keeffe (ed.), *Schools for Tomorrow: building walls or building bridges*, Barcombe, Falmer Press, 1988, pp. 145–161.
78. P H Hirst, 'Liberal education and the nature of knowledge,' in R D Archambault (ed.), *Philosophical Analysis and Education*, London, Routledge and Kegan Paul, 1965, pp. 113–138.

# 2.3 Denominational schools: some implications from ARCIC-I

*Peter Marr*

## Introduction

This article examines an aspect of the Anglican-Roman Catholic International Commission (ARCIC) dialogue that has a social concern: some of the implications for primary and secondary education, especially the nature of joint church schools for Anglicans and Roman Catholics. The issue is an essential part of the concept of *koinonia*.

Aspects of the historical structure of denominational education in England are briefly examined in the light of the country's dual martyr tradition. Alongside, the different ecclesiologies are noted as another area of difficulty in this debate. It is argued that commitment in dialogue must involve social witness of which shared education forms a part.

Finally, models are presented to indicate ways of entering into the quest for the attainment of the fullness of the *koinonia*, ultimately a self-regulating expression of man's relationship to his creator by the living out of the eucharistic life.

## Initiatives from below

Is the church's attitude to the ordinary person a relevant dimension in the ecumenical scenario? The *Final Report* of ARCIC-I seems to imply that basic change is involved:[1]

> We are convinced, therefore, that our degree of agreement, which argues for greater communion between our churches, can make a profound contribution to the witness of Christianity in our contemporary society.

At first, this suggests that such witness is a means to ecclesial unity for which the desire for agreement strives. But the 'united mission' has to be seen as an end. The reason for this derives from the nature of the church. The *mysterion* (that which in its essence is hidden) has, in its sacramental life (that which constitutes the outward form of the church) the enfolding of the whole sweep of grace, and thus of society. It is not merely a one-way channel of grace but an encompassing of man's reaching outward to God and of man to fellow-man. It is valid to ask what social implications there are.

The church, the visual embodiment of the *koinonia*,[2] is in its complete and perfect form self-regulating.[3] It will be impossible to separate out the constituent parts of the perfect *koinonia*. Thus it is mandatory to see the living out of ecumenism as integral to the churches today and to know what perspectives have to be adjusted so as to approach the perfect embodiment of the *koinonia*.

Baptism establishes a person within a eucharistic family, giving him a right to catholic communion under three conditions:

a.   a common eucharistic faith;
b.   a common identity in life and mission;
c.   a common authority (implicitly a recognition of orders and all that that implies).

Clearly we need to separate out the processes by which this works.

Bishops are primary witnesses and guardians of the faith as is, in respect of them, the pope, as the successor of the chief of the apostles.[4] That authority is distinct; it is the casting-vote, and we have to take it into account when we look at the inter-relating of the constituent parts of Christian communities. But authority, when understood by those to whom it is directed,[5] has a gestation time. The consensus of the faithful, through which authority in part works, provides a reflection of perceived (and unperceived) implications of Christian social and spiritual life *as it is experienced*. That is not to say that authority derives from the faithful, but that it must not be isolated from the *koinonia*.

## Values and absolutes

Different traditions have different forms of authority: for instance, the synodical government of the Church of England has allowed a degree of public 'weighing-up' which the Roman Catholic Church has yet to develop. It is the differing styles, rather than the content, of authority which the various traditions find difficult,[6] although it is not the case that common decision-making structures are essential for ecumenical progress. Nevertheless, concepts of authority must exist within the body of Christ. The perfecting of the *koinonia* is a task spread among all its members (the 'ordinary people'); but, at the same time, it is not merely the collective of believers. The *koinonia* is more than the simple sum of its members.

As far as the unity of the *koinonia* is concerned, there must be not only an 'undeniable and irreplaceable local quality, having its own resources and its own initiatives in response to local circumstances,' but it has also to look at the whole *oikoumene*, else it will fall short of its true aim.[7] Furthermore, the truth of Christ does not dwell in a secret tradition possessed exclusively by the hierarchy, but in the *sensus* of the Church as a whole, all of whose members are, by baptism, characterised by priestly discipleship and ministerial responsibility. It surely follows that, whilst being wary of a new form of triumphalism:[8]

> what is really needed in the ecumenical debate ... is that the churches should shake off their hang-ups, their turning of values into theological absolutes and be free: free to structure the Church's ministry of men and women so as to fulfil the mission entrusted to them by Christ, namely, of so nurturing the people of God that they may effectively proclaim the gospel of salvation by word and deed in the world.

Nowhere in England have values been turned into theological absolutes more than in concepts of denominational schools. In them, the immense progress in ecumenical discussion is often unacknowledged, and the present possibilities of living out, in a prophetic way, the 'thoughts of theologians' are untapped. We recall Duquoc's views on the 'provisional' nature of the church: that structures are unimportant as long as authentic concepts of authority, word and sacrament provide the link between the provisional and the kingdom.[9]

## Schools, societies and martyrs

The Church of England's role in the Education Act of 1944 implicitly resulted in the projection of a continuing state church: citizenship couched avowedly in Anglican terms.[10] The struggle of the Roman Catholic community to retain and expand its own system of schools meant that these had to be free to assert the identity of that community. Current debate relating to the 1988 Education Act and diocesan policy over 'opting out' reaffirms that. It was therefore inevitable that the Catholic schools should be predominantly voluntary aided.[11] Although the financial contribution required of the religious bodies to establish and maintain such schools has decreased sharply,[12] the vigorous expansion of both primary and secondary Catholic education resources in the 1950s and 1960s caused a considerable drain on Catholic diocesan and parochial resources. By the late 1970s, the resulting problems were severe, because of a decline in the school population.

As the effects of Vatican II were being felt, there was in the Church of England an intensive period of rationalisation which included the Paul and Sheffield Reports,[13,14] the development of synodical government, and attempts at the redistribution of historic resources.[15] All of this coincided with the growth of dialogue between the two churches. Meanwhile, the breaking down of the fortress mentality of English Roman Catholicism reflected some small convergence of Catholic life as a whole with that prevailing generally in the country.[16] The slow integration of the Irish communities and the emergence of a Catholic activist middle class are further indication of this.[17] Yet, within an educational context, there remains a polarisation of attitudes not entirely explained by the varying speeds of progress of ecumenical understanding and agreement in the different strata of church society. The way in which the ARCIC statements are being received and considered locally reflects this.

In spite of a considerable broadening of religious education syllabuses, Catholic schools have continued to emphasise catechesis (which non-Catholics have interpreted as introversion) and Church of England schools, both controlled and aided, have emphasised citizenship of one kind or another (which Catholics have interpreted as a lack of spiritual concern). These values, of the social and cultural unity of church-based education, have become theological absolutes with, ironically, a negative effect on religious attitudes within Anglican schools.[18]

What has partly overshadowed denominational education, even since 1944, is a mythic and largely unconscious projection of the past. Certain events retained crucial significance for the survival of the groups concerned and, to an extent, for the defeat or wished-for 'defeat of their enemies.' It is thus significant that the English Martyrs still play a large part in the present self-imagery of Catholics in England: that 'our fathers suffered at your hands.' This has been brought to the surface in the canonisation of the Forty Martyrs of England and Wales (1970) and in the comments of Pope Paul VI at the time,[19] a pope who understood Anglicanism in a way that no other pope had before or has since.

In these dimensions, suffering and endurance are seen as ways of sharing in or commemorating painful and self-giving actions. The development of devotions and dedications to the Sacred Heart (and indeed to the Precious Blood) among Catholics in this country is related to this. It is understandable that English Catholics would wish to make reparation for perceived outrages in their country against Divine Love in the church, from the reformation through to relatively recent years.

The reformation struggle in England saw the papacy being treated by the emergent national church as a political rather than an ecclesiastical tyranny. The Church of England survived the onslaught of those of a Calvinistic turn of mind because it was possessed of a unique blend of national identity, scriptural authority, tradition and ecclesiastical discipline. The relationship between monarch and church must be no more unacceptable than the Byzantine relationship between patriarch and emperor. However, it is the Catholic martyrs who had lived and died in the setting of a pre-divided England who are the significant national figures. To them, the English Catholic community owes its identity. In contrast, the Protestant martyr tradition was, and still is, experienced in a different way if only because the emergent dominant church was its outcome. Where that tradition is still active, there is the lingering stubbornness of sixteenth century polemic, of its liturgical and scriptural literature, and a suspicion of Rome that many see as obsessive.

## Intransigence as a reflection of the weight of tradition

There are other aspects of the Roman Catholic martyr tradition existing one step away. We might include the Act of Succession, or add that the Catholic Emancipation Act is not much more than a century-and-a-half old.[20] The loss of buildings and titles at the reformation is still painful to the Catholic community. And in particular there is the relationship of Northern Ireland to a church closely linked with the Protestant cause. Residual elements of the Protestant martyr tradition include the seeming inroads to the authority of the Thirty-Nine Articles of Religion by the ecumenical movement, the loss of influence of the Book of Common Prayer, and the encouragement of dialogue with one whom some see as a foreign bishop, from whose clutches the Church of England paid dearly to release itself. In both traditions, the price of all these somehow has to be measured in suffering.

Understandably, the 'ordinary person' on either side is unwilling to acknowledge the martyr tradition of the other. The shape of its institutional relationships is surely influenced by spiritualities dependent upon such myths: to see the myths of the other side is a basic part of the self-examination that ecumenism must be.[21]

The nature of the martyr tradition suggests that it is essential to separate the present method of Anglican thought from its image as a sixteenth and seventeenth century isolationist phenomenon. What distinguishes Anglicanism is a manner of thought which favours a specific spirit in which theological questions are handled, over and against 'systematic theology,' whose absence from Anglicanism has been deliberate.[22] Through this, reason, scripture and tradition wed together society and church. It is therefore perhaps significant that in the Church of England ritual, the reflector of myth tradition, still finds its clearest expression in affairs of church-and-state, and not in spiritual dimensions. Anglican religious ritualism as developed through the Oxford Movement is often perceived by many Catholics in England as having little integrity.

It is, then, an ecclesiological issue. Anglicanism has been characterised by weaknesses in perception of the church. Among them,
there is not only merely an occasional disposition to go to public
worship but also a defective understanding and a misconceived view
of ecclesiastical autonomy. The term 'provincial congregationalism'
is not unfairly applied to the Anglican Communion. The cultural conceptions of the ministers in both churches (Catholic and
Anglican) have been, at least in part, very different, and therefore
the social and cultural place of local churches has likewise been disparate. It follows that the fear of Catholics towards the Anglican
tradition, inexplicable as it may seem in ecclesial terms, has to be
countered on this basis. The size, weight and the near-arrogance of
the Anglican tradition in England, particularly in social terms, must
continue to affect the impact of dialogue between the two churches.
This is why objections by the Anglican Bishop of London to the
intended administrative centralisation of education has such a firm
foundation on ecumenical grounds.[23]

The task of education must be to look ahead 15–20 years.[24] The
massive shortfall on adult catechesis will perhaps be beginning to be
overcome[25] by an urgency on both sides. In the Church of England,
assuming it retains some corporate identity, the spiritual maturity
of the Christian message, expressed through the church, will be perceived directly by adults, rather than: 'As an Anglican I learnt all
about God as a child.' For the Catholic community, there will be a
richer and fuller involvement in an increasingly pluralistic society.
But the moving of the weight of mythic consciousness and of false
images is a task scarcely begun even now.

## Educational structures seen in an ecumenical context

Some form of shared or ecumenical education[26] strikes at the
heart of this. Shared schools involving the Church of England
with either the Roman Catholic Church or the Free Churches are
slowly emerging.[27] Ecumenical schools involving all Christian traditions (still less inter-faith schools) are much more difficult to
establish structurally (i.e. 'from above') if there is to be representative interests in the decision-making processes. However, we
shall see that it does not follow that a shared school 'from above'
is necessarily or exclusively the way forward; more importantly,
the Christian school is a community living out 'from below' the
eucharistic faith. The diffuseness of this aspect of Anglican schools
causes Catholics to hesitate in ecumenical collaboration. Where it is
sharply defined, this produces a feeling of intimidation because an
Anglican school has seemingly taken upon it some of the characteristics of a Catholic school as the latter perceives itself.

Catholic schools are integral to the Catholic parish system which
is bound both to the hierarchical nature of the church and to the

Catholic subculture. To alter the distinctiveness of such schools is seen as more than diluting their aims: it is perceived as re-directing them. The Catholic answer is often a shrinkage of the system to accommodate decreased numbers. The Anglican answer has often been a weak pluralism. In the independent sector, Catholic schools have long been happy to receive non-Catholics if only to produce financial viability. The shared school is entirely another dimension.[28] But some Catholics perceive shared education as failing to provide a 'proper Catholic education' (cer-tainly a theologising of a value); and some Anglicans in the Church of England see the shared school as an indication that the Spanish Armada is on the horizon.

Inevitably, the emerging pattern of joint Catholic-Anglican schools is one of great variety. Such schools have often been brought about by falling rolls and the joint school has been the only way to maintain a Christian presence in education in an area.[29] Thus, a school has to lose its identity, its name and its exclusive ethos to gain something which, though previously not experienced, should be greater than that which was present before.[30] Such an apparent loss of identity is keenly felt by those Catholics whose model of the church pre-dates Vatican II.

The continuing ARCIC dialogue indicates that the relationship already experienced by Anglicans and Catholics alike is based on something mutually acceptable: a commonly-recognised baptism and an expanding middle ground concerning eucharistic teaching (the latter until recently a possible 'new context' for the recog-nition of Anglican orders) and of a revised but long-term view of authority in the church. The aim of Catholic education must also share this inclusiveness and inclusivity in Christ with those in Anglican schools. The reciprocal action has the same imperative. This is not easily achieved at the local level. The real difficulty is social, because of desires to preserve existing groups. Although previous distinctions between the recusant Catholic families on the one hand and the (largely Irish) immigrant Catholic popu-lation is now fuzzy at the edges, the Catholic subculture still exists to preserve a national Catholic identity. In the same way, the difficulties with ecclesiology and authority in the Church of England is bound up with maintaining a parallel identity. Con-sequently, although the Roman Catholic community in England is seemingly in a minority, the character of its ecclesiology and its past history produce behaviour patterns akin to a dominant group, particularly over educational issues: the feeling of superi-ority over the other group; that the other group is alien; that one's own group possesses a natural right to certain areas of power; and the feeling that the other group harbours designs upon those areas. These become distinct issues where Catholic involvement in shared education is concerned.

## Problems in collaboration

In many places only shared schools will be feasible in years to come. With smaller school rolls, a shared school will often be the only means of having a Christian school at all. On ecumenical grounds, it is difficult to see how Anglican·and Roman Catholics can be serious about the approach of their respective churches to reconciliation unless they are both prepared to share education, and certainly secondary education. The difficulties are no more than those experienced in running any Christian school in a secular age when many of the pupils have, at best, a tenuous attachment to their church.

Shared schools develop according to the varying ways in which the feeling of denominational reconciliation is experienced and lived out. The character of that reconciliation is the relative notions of denominational, political and social identity versus Christian identity. It is in part dependent on how one tradition can see through the myths of the other. If the problem is approached 'from above,' that is, structurally, the sacrifice of the denominational identities seems considerable unless the will for unity is extraordinarily strong. If it is tackled 'from below,' then some or all of that identity is retained. Pluralism within and between institutions is inevitable if the idea of sister-churches[31] is to be developed.

Religious formation is for the future, which puts a special onus on those involved with its planning. For young people to see some unity with those of other traditions, whatever the odds against easy success, this surely must be fostered.

## Some areas of specific difficulty regarding shared schools

Religious education and instruction in a shared school will normally be completely shared, not segregated by denomination. There seems some justification for denominational religious education so as to reflect more fully a specific tradition, but, at a school level, this seems only an expedient. Acceptance of common doctrine and ministry must demand common teaching. It therefore follows that no new mono-denominational schools, whether Roman Catholic or Church of England, should be built.

Daily worship must be in common, for praying together is the authentic ecumenical activity. Sacramental provision is, of course, entirely different whilst the present discipline of the two churches remains as it is, although a common Liturgy of the Word and Thanksgiving would be a desirable step, without eucharistic sharing. What should not happen is for the 'host' school to prohibit eucharistic celebrations by other traditions when the eucharistic discipline of the respective churches forbids eucharistic sharing. No restriction should be placed either on attendance at a eucharist of another tradition; grace can proceed without the fulness of sacramental recognition.

Pastoral care, by definition, should transcend denominational and cultural boundaries. This co-ordination of spiritual and personal development is a lived-out ecumenism which must encompass ecclesial discipline rather than be inhibited by it.

The relationship between church and state may appear to be far removed from shared schools and their growth. A shared school is the church working in that place. The community nature of the shared school is thus emphasised, not the national or political identity of its members. This brings into relief the necessity of developing shared schools in urban areas where religious education in general is at risk.[32] The majority of presently existing shared schools are in suburban districts. This suggests that initially such schools have to consider carefully their obligation to non-Christian religious groups and this may well affect their location.

The role of parents is crucial. The image of the new school must match up to or exceed the image of what it supplants. There is therefore a fear, sufficient to prevent a scheme from coming to fruition, when group pressures by parents from either tradition cannot accept the image of another tradition as it seems to be presented by a shared school.

The role of chaplains includes relating the expression of ecumenism to the eucharistic communities outside the school. The chaplaincy team of a shared school is its initial point of credibility within the community. It gives the institution its Christian ethos, serves as its conscience and, most importantly, exists as its prophetic voice.[33]

## Manifestation: breaking the egg

A shared school 'from above' derives its authority and structure from the respective traditions. One might have expected the concept to have developed more vigorously, but it should be clear that it is not primarily for theological but for cultural reasons. In the light of what has been said, the slogan, 'every Catholic child from a Catholic home to be educated by Catholic teachers in a Catholic school' is a subconscious ensuring of the social unity and solidarity of the Catholic subculture, to counter an imagined (and perhaps real) lack of status in the national community. Not that even now, as Dr Hornsby Smith has pointed out,[34] the emancipated Catholics will provide a recognisable subversive threat to English society. Alongside this, the complacency of the Church of England had promoted a loose-fitting garment of Anglicanism. Thus, when cracks have appeared in the internal social structure of English Catholicism, we find increased vitality in catechetical activity; and the recent vagaries of Anglican doctrinal thought have in turn found accompaniment in increasing concern with ecclesial re-ordering.

Shared schools 'from above' may well be the right answer in some places. But as we have seen, the other answer which offers more opportunity for organic growth is sharing 'from below.' The implications of such sharing rests on the conscious acceptance of cultural identities in the two churches, that is, a positive attitude towards plurality within Christian tradition. Dialogue must become less confessional but developed further between sister-churches, each separately rooted. Instead of structures that are new or based on an overhead merge of existing ones, we can conceive of shared schools being developed (supplanting others, even) by this ecclesial hospitality. This will enable, for example, Catholics to be freely educated in Church of England schools (and vice versa), each school integrating worship and instruction at a level appropriate to its circumstances. One can envisage Anglican chaplaincies in Catholic schools as a result of this until such times as the communities felt happy enough to exist without such an arrangement. But an unrealistic 'sharing from below' is the absorption of, say, Anglican pupils into a Catholic school without proper provision for them.

Ultimately, people have to grow together. This middle ground created by 'keeping one's head down' starts silently. It establishes integrity. It starts an invisible monastery whose end must be the coming of the kingdom and whose manifestation shines, ultimately for all to see. Creativity, the prophetic utterance, is crucial in this. There are indeed differences in the rate of assimilation of the 'grand design,' and suffering in the living out of the process is inevitable. But in that living out, it is the embracing of people which constitutes the embracing of the churches.

## Will and congruity

Such 'living out' is only made possible by the will to do so.[35] The identification with a specific culture, as opposed to the kingdom, is a basic restriction in the exercise of this will. Distinguishing these values at a local level is not easy when the community itself feels vulnerable. This once more emphasises the dangers of turning values into theological absolutes. The common faith leading to the common life in the Body of Christ[36] has as its authentic expression that community which seeks consciously to submit to Christ.[37] This must surely have implications for maintaining barriers which exclude insights into such a quest.[38]

A school 'in the ecumenical tradition' cannot find its identity exclusively within either tradition. Shared schools, whether 'from above' (having joint representation built into their legal framework) or 'from below' (using a policy of ecclesial hospitality) build on common ground and avoid those theological areas and issues where there is active disagreement. Such schools exist to continue the dialogue rather than the culture they represent. Many of the reservations concerning joint schools are based on those cultural values. Consequently it may be helpful to look at some of the social underlay of this.

A built-in ambiguity exists, inhibiting the common social witness which is the outcome of certain statements in the ARCIC Final Report. The ambiguity is a matter of conflicting attitudes whose roots go far into history. The model of mythic-subconscious will only go some way to explaining why there is some real reluctance for shared schools to be developed. The model of congruity offers an explanation as to how the present situation is perpetuated and how attitudes might begin to be changed.

The underlying premise is that 'When a change in evaluation or attitude occurs, it always occurs in the direction of increased congruity.'[39] There is an additional element in the model called 'bonds'. These are of two kinds associative and disassociative: expressions of approval and disapproval respectively.

If A is evaluated positively and makes a statement of which you are in favour, then *congruity* is said to exist. If A reversed his view (and therefore you disagreed with it), there is a state of *incongruity*. Again, if you evaluate B negatively but he has a view with which you agree, this is an *incongruous* position. Entrenched or immutable positions of two traditions are *congruous* unless initiative is taken on one side.

We can place the proponents of exclusive traditions on each end of an axis with a neutral position in between (see figure 1), using additional material about denominational and shared schools. Associative bonds are horizontal between the columns.

No change of attitude can take place when there are similar degrees of agreement or disagreement. Initiative has to be associative or disassociative. There is no change of attitude when bonds are created between objects at the same level of congruity or when bonds are disassociative.

The middle ground tells the significant story. An initiative from a Catholic independent school ($-2$) to make a positive provision for Anglicans in the way that the Anglicans are making provision for Roman Catholics ($+1$) will result, via an attitude change of the participants, in a shared school run by Roman Catholics ($-1$). The initiative for this shift has originally come from an attitude change from the 'exclusive' Roman Catholic position ($-3$) towards the more tolerant Church of England position ($+2$). This leads to a re-establishment of equilibrium (at $-1$).

We can now see that initiative must come from authoritative sources in any tradition, enabling those with whom they have a congruous relationship to fall into line with the changed attitude. 'Non-congruous' leadership (across, for instance, denominational boundaries) will thus ultimately be unsuccessful. This model seems

*Figure 1*

| Column one | | Column two |
|---|---|---|
| exclusive, totally committed Church of England community | + 3 | Church of England independent schools* |
| Church of England community tolerating Roman Catholics | + 2 | Church of England voluntary schools |
| Church of England community making provision for Roman Catholics | + 1 | shared schools 'from below' run by Anglicans |
| **the koinonia position** | 0 | **a unified ecclesiology** |
| Roman Catholic community making provision for Anglicans | − 1 | shared school 'from below' run by Roman Catholics |
| Roman Catholic community tolerating Anglicans | − 2 | Roman Catholic independent schools |
| exclusive, totally committed Roman Catholic community | − 3 | Roman Catholic voluntary aided schools |

The signs + and − have no significance except differentiation.

* This seems to be a reflection of practice.

to reflect the 1966 initiative,[40] and the possible outcome of the ARCIC dialogue as far as schools are concerned.

## The will to act: avoiding cold feet

It is sometimes said that joint Roman Catholic and Anglican schools are either impossible to conceive (because a Roman Catholic school cannot be 'compromised') or undesirable (because the result is likened to being brought up within a mixed marriage). However, a number of such schools do exist jointly under the aegis of the respective dioceses, the oldest dating from 1970.

The more specific problems of their management are beyond the scope of this paper which has been essentially concerned with the will to act. To do so creatively is crucial in the implementation of change. To constitute a successful outcome of a shared school, a situation I have argued to be normative, one has to suggest six points for successful collaboration:

These involve the willingness:

a.   to see through the images, rituals and myths of the other tradition so that suspicion makes way for brotherhood and sisterhood in Christ;[41]

b.  to share in pastoral responsibility;
c.  to see denominational religious education as a temporary expediency on both sides so ecclesial and eucharistic communities will deal with problems of change through grace rather than local power politics;
d.  to pray together and to realise that sacramental worship will grow from this, not be a pre-requisite for it;
e.  to see that social structures affect the pace of absorption of ecumenical innovation;
f.  to accept ecclesial hospitality before organic union or structural innovation 'from above.'

One may well argue that all this side-steps important issues relating to the role of Christian schools within a society, particularly a society with an increasing element of non-Christian cultures.[42] But one has to begin the Christian ecumenical educational debate somewhere and not postpone it in terms of action simply because there are other pressing concerns. The report of one shared school scheme includes the following, which seems to be a fair reflection of reality generally in these matters:

It took eighteen months of debate to accomplish an agreement ...
The plan was not without opposition, not least from the parents at the Anglican school who imagined that there was something sinister about it. Even open-minded people had doubts as to the wisdom of such a merger. Much lip-service is paid to Christian unity, but when decisions are required, many suffer from cold feet.

And from a Roman Catholic nun at whose school the many Anglican pupils are completely absorbed:

I am sorry that your services (Anglican services outside the school) are so like ours. We are not united yet.

Shared schools, whether 'from above' or 'from below' suffer from considerable problems of internal management and of creating a special form of inclusivity. The concept demands confidence from clergy, teachers, families, not to say school governors. Above all, it demands episcopal understanding so that, whilst the universal tradition is being expressed at the local level, the local initiative may, as occasion requires, become part of the universal tradition. The growth process in this area is difficult, complex and at times delicate, but ultimately it must be seen as an essential component in the long-term rapprochement of the two communions.

The level of agreement reached in the ARCIC statements indicates that the development of shared facilities for Christian formation cannot merely be the outcome of ecumenical dialogue. The willingness to take initiatives creates that common ground upon which Christian witness effectively rests. Such common ground will form part of the witness of the churches both sociologically and theologically. This necessitates identifying values that are peculiar to the two traditions, especially when those involve social groupings. Both within and beyond those values lies the concept of *koinonia*. Shared education between the churches, it has been argued, does not compromise that *koinonia*.

**Notes**

1.  *Final Report of the Anglican/Roman Catholic International Commission*, 1982, p. 50.
2.  Cf *Final Report*, Introduction and p. 68.
3.  *Final Report*, p. 52.
4.  *Final Report*, p. 58.
5.  *Final Report*, pp. 54 and 60.
6.  *Final Report*, p. 77.
7.  Pope John Paul II to British Church Leaders, 29 April 1983, *Information Service of Secretariat for Promoting Christian Unity*, 51, 1983, p. 42; *One in Christ*, 1983, no. 3. p. 299.
8.  John Coventry, S J, in review of Max Thurian's *Priesthood and Ministry: ecumenical research* in *Heythrop Journal*, 27, 1986, p. 353.
9.  C Duquoc, *Provisional Churches*, 1986.
10. Cf *A Future in Partnership*, London, National Society for Promoting Christian Education, 1984.
11. *Ibid.*, pp. 38–41.
12. *Ibid.*, p. 12.
13. L Paul, *The Deployment and Payment of the Clergy*, London, Church Information Office. 1964.
14. *Sheffield Report*, 1983.
15. *Historic Resources of the Church of England*, 1983.
16. M Hornsby Smith, *Roman Catholics in England*, Cambridge, Cambridge University Press, 1987, p. 216.
17. *Ibid.*, 133–156.
18. L J Francis, 'Denominational schools and pupil attitudes towards Christianity,' *British Educational Research Journal*, 12, 1986, pp. 145–151.
19. Homily at Canonisation of the Forty Martyrs of England and Wales, 1970.
20. Cf J Bossy, *The English Catholic Community, 1570–1850*, London, Darton, Longman and Todd, 1976.
21. See also M Santer (ed.), 'The reconciliation of memories' in *Their Lord and Ours*, 1982, London, SPCK, 1982, pp. 149–160. Also A D Falconer (ed.), *Reconciling Memories*, Dublin, 1988.
22. H McAdoo, *The Spirit of Anglicanism*, London, A&C Black, 1965, pp. v–vi. Paul Avis in his *Ecumenical Theology and the Elusiveness of Doctrine*, London, SPCK, 1986, draws out this aspect of Anglicanism within the context of ecumenical dialogue.
23. *Church Times*, 8 May 1987.
24. Cf Michael Hurley, S J, 'Christian Unity by 2000' in *One in Christ*, 1983, no. 1, pp. 2–13.
25. For example by schemes such as *The Rite for the Christian Initiation of Adults*, provided that is by other churches as well as the Roman Catholic Church.
26. Schools having admission arrangements involving more than one church are also termed joint schools, although at least one essentially Anglican/RC has the word 'ecumenical' in its title. Generally, for practical reasons, I have used the term 'shared school.'
27. Cf P Chadwick and M Gladwell, *Shared Schools*, English ARC, 1987, which is an important study of the practicalities of this whole subject.

28. There seems to be some argument for such a shrinkage in terms of 'results.' The presence of non-Roman Catholics in Catholic schools does, according to at least one scholar, present distinct problems of attitude formation under the present arrangement of such schools. See L J Francis, 'Roman Catholic secondary schools: falling rolls and pupil attitudes,' *Educational Studies*, 12, 1986, pp. 119–127.
29. The existence of shared schools *alongside* denominational schools, particularly Catholic schools, presents special problems, especially over clergy and parental attitudes.
30. Most shared schools change their name to a more neutral one, particularly if a Catholic title would otherwise have to be used. Cuthbert Mayne School in Torquay, Devon, is one of the few exceptions.
31. This model, derived from Pope Paul's homily on the Forty Martyrs (1970) is discussed sympathetically in Robert Hale, *Canterbury and Rome: sister churches*, London, Darton, Longman and Todd, 1982.
32. Cf *Faith in the City*, London, Church House Publishing, 1985, p. 315, sect. 13.91 (iii) pleads for more shared schools in inner-city areas, including suitable arrangements for non-Christian pupils.
33. Cf *Final Report*, p. 59.
34. *Op. cit.*, p. 216.
35. Cf *Final Report*, p. 63.
36. Cf *Final Report*, pp. 52, 53.
37. *Final Report*, p. 53.
38. *Final Report*, p. 54.
39. See C E Osgood and P H Tannenbaum, 'The principle of congruity in the prediction of attitude change,' *Psychological Review*, 62, 1955, pp. 42–45; also Roger Brown, *Social Psychology*, New York, Collier-Macmillan 1965, pp. 558–573.
40. The first of the Joint Declarations between the Pope and the Archbishop of Canterbury.
41. The position in Northern Ireland, so different from that in England, owes much to this pre-requisite. For a useful series of observations on the Republic of Ireland see Kurt Bowen, *Protestants in a Catholic State: Ireland's privileged minority*, Montreal, McGill-Queens University Press, 1983, pp. 134–165.
42. For example *Swann Report*, London, HMSO, 1985, and *Learning from Diversity*, London, Catholic Media Office, 1984. The earlier *Signposts and Homecomings: the educative task of the Catholic community*, Middlegreen, St Paul Publications, of David Konstant marked the beginning of revised thinking in this direction.

# 3. Social perspectives

The debate about the place of church schools is given a wider focus and a greater urgency by the recognition of the multi-cultural context of contemporary society. The first two articles in this section rehearse the debate in England prior to the publication of the report of the Swann Commission in 1985, *Education For All*, which advised against state funding for Islamic schools and called into question the long term future of state funding for church schools.

In the first article, Professor David N Aspin characterises the Christian churches and other religious faiths as significant minority voices in today's multi-ethnic society. He recognises that such groups will wish to make use of the rights and opportunities available to them in a pluralist society and to perpetuate their cultural identity through schools. He attempts to establish criteria which such schools need to meet in order to justify public funding, including a commitment to the values necessary for the maintenance of a multi-cultural society. In the second article, Dr Nigel P Blake replies to David Aspin by highlighting the difficulties involved in promoting a sectarian education consistent with the values promoted by a multi-cultural society.

Both articles were first published in the same volume of *Journal of Philosophy of Education* in 1983. At the time of writing David Aspin was in the Faculty of Education at King's College, London, and Nigel Blake was in the Institute of Educational Technology at the Open University.

In the third article, Geoffrey S Duncan reflects on the response of the Church of England to shaping its church schools for a future in multi-cultural England. He argues that church schools display both commitment and openness.

Geoffrey Duncan is General Secretary of the National Society and the General Synod Board of Education of the Church of England. This article was first published by the InterEuropean Commission on Church and School in the pamphlet, *Commitment and Neutrality: a useful opposition* in 1989.

# 3.1 Church schools, religious education and the multi-ethnic community

## David N Aspin

In 1980 a discussion took place between representatives of the London Diocesan Board of Education and the faculties of education and of theology and religious studies at King's College London on the nature of religious education and the role of denominational schools in promoting the aims of religious education, as a result of the disquiet about the role and function of church-funded schools in a multi-ethnic inner-city environment that had begun to be expressed and the reservations about it being entertained by many in the education service. Some clergymen thought it odd that in some cases the only practising Christian in a Church of England school was the headmaster, all the children being of the Muslim or other faiths; and some politicians were claiming that church schools were turning out to be highly selective and, in their emphasis on behaviour, dress and the idea of an education for academic excellence, replacing the now largely-extinct grammar schools as bastions of élitism and privilege.

Clearly it was important for providing bodies to know if such claims could in fact be sustained and as a result of this a research project was set up. It was obvious that, at some stage in the investigation, attention would have to be given to the important questions of the nature and function of church schools in a multi-faith society, and the possibility of their providing a 'religious' education – whatever that was – in circumstances in which they now found themselves functioning as providers – sometimes the only one in some places – of any kind of education service.

There are, of course, very many topics raised by this undertaking, any one of which is in itself an area of considerable complexity. What, it might be asked, is the nature and purpose of education in church schools – if indeed it is with education that they are centrally concerned; or is it here that the distinctions between education and schooling get their point of purchase? What, in a word, differentiates the activities of a church school from those of a 'county' school, if anything? Should answer be made in terms of the overt commitment of the former to the idea of a 'religious' education, we have then to go on and seek to establish what talk of such an 'education' might mean and in what ways such an education could be characterised: whether, for instance, it is possible and conceivable to talk of 'education' in respect of 'religion' (whatever that might be) or whether any teaching in such an area of concern will not amount to indoctrination in the final analysis. We must also establish what kind of entity we have in mind when we talk about a 'multi-ethnic, inner-city "community"': whether, for instance, we are talking about some sort of social grouping in which there is a sense of identity and cohesion or whether we merely mean some accidental agglomeration of individuals of disparate colours, countries, classes or creeds.

It is at this point that one of the major problems of the enquiry emerges: presumably the introduction of a reference to a 'multi-ethnic' community into the title of the project by the funding body betokens a concern for that kind of education that we call 'multi-racial' or 'multi-cultural.' What the London Diocesan Board of Education *inter alios* wants to know, we may assume, is whether it should accept and work with the differences in religious beliefs that some of its 'clients' will bear, not seeing its own views as being in any way superior to them but merely of equal value; or whether it has good grounds for seeking to demonstrate the superiority of its own version of such fundamental matters as a person's questions about the meaning of life and relationships with God and his creatures on earth and to endeavour to secure acceptance of that view on the part of all pupils attending its educational institutions. And this is, of course, always assuming complete clarity or agreement on what might count as 'multi-cultural' education and what its aims ought to be.[1]

So, in that respect too, the project will have philosophical work to do, in axiology and meta-ethics, probably involving an excursus into social and political philosophy, while such goals as 'working for equality' and 'harmony and mutual acceptance among different ethnic groups' are elevated as educational *desiderata*.

The claim that church schools do have roles in a multi-faith society is not without its problems; we need not only some attempt at elucidating the nature of 'church schools' and 'education' in an inner-city 'community' (a concept of which, as Raymond Plant has remarked,[2] there are many conceptions) but also some consideration of the question of the kind of society in which such different faiths might see themselves as having claim to a separate identity. It might be thought, for instance, that a polyglot and pluralist society, in which different cultural groups continued to maintain a relatively distinct form of life, is something to be praised and worked for[3] and thus constituting an educational environment in which the churches would have a distinctive part to play; it might be maintained that, notwithstanding the different cultural traditions that members of the various ethnic groups brought to it, all educational efforts should be directed at the development of a unified and integrated national consciousness in which some over-arching norms and beliefs were seen as determinative of the ethos of a community's institutions.[4] But this will bring up some of the most difficult questions of all: those to do with the possibility of agreement in opinions on doctrinal and cultural matters; of there being an agreed set of principles on the idea of 'religious education;' and, the most difficult question, whether there can be a complete inter-cultural understanding. For if we conclude that the idea of inter-faith communication is impossible, then at least one version of the multi-cultural education with which church schools might see it as their role to be concerned will have to be abandoned – and with that, in some cases, the argument for a distinctive role for church schools in a multi-ethnic inner-city community beyond that of merely providing for the upbringing of children of its own members and adherents. Beneath all these questions there lies one fundamental issue – the problem of relativism.

This is a problem germane to previous philosophical approaches to this question,[5] in some of which it has been raised explicitly.[6] This is perhaps the major central issue in attempts to characterise 'multi-cultural' or 'multi-ethnic' education; upon our answers to it much of our thinking on and policies for the structure and organisation of educating institutions and for their program of instruction will be based. Those we might call 'absolutists' may see no problem in justifying the endeavours of a church school in an innercity multi-ethnic environment; the revelation of recent 'official thinking' on the support to be given to schools with 'a clear moral base (perhaps denominational schools),'[7] suggests that plenty of people hold such a view of the nature and function of schooling. Equally some representatives of other public institutions[8] suggest that relativism as to the aims and curricular content of schools is the only tenable account of schools as 'interest-serving' institutions. The advice that either of these groups would give to us is not only confusing; it is in direct conflict. In such a situation, church schools might be forgiven for asking, what shall we do to be saved?

Perhaps we may note that nothing has been said to exclude the possibility of our discerning and choosing a middle way between these two extremes. As Partington remarks:[9]

A moderate and limited form of contingent relativism can be both a corrective to ethnocentrism and naive cultural absolutism and a valuable reminder that ideas and relationships arose in specific contexts.

In other words we should be on good ground in eschewing the dogmatism of both extremes and in seeking a rational basis for our schools' endeavours that will both avoid the charge of cultural imperialism and the *reductio ad absurdum* of an unconditional relativism 'in which the concept of education is inoperative.' Part of that undertaking must include the point that, as it appears in some sources at any rate, there is an ambiguity in the idea of cultural relativism that allows its proponents to elide two versions of it and to slide from one to the other under attack. For in some hands and some places, the idea of relativism relates to the notion of intelligibility, whereas, in others, it has to do with notions of value.

The intelligibility thesis is one with which much modern meta-linguistics and philosophy of language has been concerned. It is derived from and rests upon considerations from a number of sources – the views of structural-functionalist sociologists, such as Malinowski and Talcott Parsons, of the later Wittgenstein and neo-Wittgensteinians, of Kuhnian paradigm theory, of phenomenologists such as Goffmann and Garfinkel, of social anthropologists such as Sapir and Whorf. According to this view rationality is not an all-embracing concept; rather it is only made manifest in particular sets of socially-constructed beliefs and shared endogenous representations of what is taken to be reality, in which the constituent members can only operate in accordance with canons of correctness and admissibility that are internally determined. These canons constitute the logic of the form of discourse and they inevitably structure and define a view of reality of which all entrants to that particular 'paradigm' become bearers. Instead of 'rationality' as an account of such a system of thinking and communicating we do better to think in terms of ideology; this enables us to show that all language is of an idiosyncratic kind and thus all knowledge transmitted in and by it is relative to the norms of the community from which such communications are generated and proceed and to which all claims as to the truth of the propositions in which its knowledge claims are articulated must be referred. There are thus, on this view, no absolute, over-arching, non-contextual truth criteria; there are, simply, competing paradigms of what is to count as the truth, that are radically incommensurable. It follows from this that canons of what Dewey would have called 'warranted assertability' will be context-specific, such that, in the final analysis, propositions uttered in one form of language will only be intelligible to those operating from within it; any attempt to make complete sense of an utterance from inside another language is, on this view, ultimately doomed to failure. Thus there can be no complete inter-linguistic comprehension; there will be, as Quine maintained, a radical indeterminacy of translation between them.[10]

It will also follow from this that one set of truth claims will be as good as the next. It is here where the point about values comes in; for, given that the logic of a system can only be appraised internally, all systems will have equal claims to consideration. There will be no non-contextual criteria of value that will enable outsiders to adjudicate between the versions of reality advanced by competing systems; each of them will have equal, though different merits and standing as explanations of any phenomenon, be it an approach to a picture, the formulation of a policy for social action or a cure for the common cold. The views of the 'bearers of different structured representations of reality' (whether Western medicine, acupuncture or the witch-doctor, for instance) will all have the same right to consideration, acceptance and implementation.

The holding of such a view has particular implications for education; for, if it be true, then the account of education put forward by MacDonald, for example − that,[11]

> within the educational system there is a particular form of social order resulting from and dependent upon historical and social conditions external to it ... (we should understand) the structure of school organisation and its form rather than the content of the curriculum ... much of what is transmitted is implicit or hidden ...

is substantially correct. And of the role and function of church schools we can, *mutatis mutandis*, make the same sort of appraisal as Gintis and Bowles and Katz in their analysis of contemporary American school systems, in which the interests of the capitalist system predominate so that:[12]

> the children of managers and professionals are taught self-reliance with a broad set of constraints; the children of production workers are taught obedience ...;

schools determine the emergence of future workers who are so shaped that:[14]

> their preferences are endogenous to the production process ...;

that, in sum, the principal concern with schools in America:[14]

> has been basically the inculcation of attitudes that reflect dominant and industrial values ... the result has been school systems that treat children as units to be processed ...

For 'industrial' here read 'cultural' or 'religious' and we see what sort of account of the activity of church schools might be offered as an offensive against them by proponents of this sort of thinking. Since there are no non-contextual criteria of value, the only valid account, for such people, of the base underlying the project has less to do with reasons and more to do with motives, less to do with such impartial principles as liberty, tolerance and altruism and more to do with the notion of self- or class-interest and the preservation and maintenance of the *status quo* in a class society. On the basis advanced by such people and their followers in educational circles, ethics is out; the only point of theoretical enquiry is to be found in psychologistic speculation and/or historicist explanation.

A good deal of time and energy has been devoted to the refutation of both forms of relativism adumbrated above. A telling rebuttal of that version of it that maintains the mutual incomprehensibility of independent and mutually competing thought- and language-systems has been suggested by Gellner.[15] Formally, the problem of relativism has no solution: any thinking subject, he notes, can only cognise in terms of a given framework; but, given the multiplicity of such frameworks in the world and the ways in which they differ, there can be no canon for correctness for judging between them. We cannot, therefore, judge the internal criteria of a framework by the use of external criteria; but then, if the only criteria by which we can adjudicate correctness are internal to the system in which cognitions are articulated, each system becomes self-authenticating. As soon as one endeavours to move outside the constraints of the paradigm, one falls into vicious circularity.

Now, if it were true that the only communications that could be conceived and uttered had to conform to the norms of radically discrete paradigms, then no translation between any two paradigms would be possible; but the *reductio ad absurdum* of that position is the incorrigible solipsism to which the theories of the proto-ethnomethodologists finally commit them. The whole point of the 'public language' argument of Wittgenstein has been to demonstrate the untenability of such a view; for if it were true, then we should not even *have* the language in which we could consider the possibility it proposes, much less be able to communicate to other language-users in it. That argument establishes, to my satisfaction at any rate, that common conditions have to be presupposed for any kind of linguistic interchange to take place — that there will be at least some rules (of which we might possibly pick out the requirements of 'well-formedness,' 'consistency,' 'orderly sequence' or 'non-contradiction' as examples — at any rate, the sort of principles that Lukes has called 'criteria of rationality I'),[16] that define and make possible any kind of understanding for participants in any public tradition; and these conditions, though conventional in character rather than natural, will constitute the objective criteria for intelligibility in any and every linguistic code. It is in the very notion of the objectivity of language that we can find a bulwark of interpersonal signification and sense against the irredeemable privacy to which extreme relativism would inevitably consign us — and, incidentally, render any kind of educational action otiose.

This point was well made by Brent,[17] who pointed out that there is a good deal less to be said for the 'indeterminacy' thesis than many have supposed. Noting Yudkin's objection against Quine on the grounds of the 'folly of introducing an alien exactness of ideas by probing inappropriately,' he now concludes:[18]

> Because new possible instances can be added to general classes in either language's conceptual scheme due to the very open character of such classes, then mutual understanding and the mutual translation of languages becomes possible ... This special kind of imprecision, therefore, allowing new discoveries to be incorporated into existing schemes (or open classes) is that which arguably enables cross-cultural understanding and rules out the problem which Quine holds that there is about radical translation.

In other words, as we might say, an Aborigine might not have the concept of an electron or a Cadillac, but he would soon know if he came into contact with one or were affected by it; the language in which he might express his fear or pain or rage would doubtless be different from ours in many respects but language it would be nonetheless and it would be at least minimally intelligible as such and for that reason amenable to translation − a point implicit in Cooper's[19] deft rebuttal of the kind of linguistic relativism exemplified in Sapir and Whorf's account of different cultures' representations of kinship-relations or time. It is illegitimate to infer from a culture's different idiomatic expressions that the cultural differences are absolute or unintelligible. Just because an Eskimo predicates the length of a journey in terms of the number and difficulty of operations to be gone through rather than in hours or days there is no reason to suppose that his language is radically alien to ours in respect of time; for common to both − and indeed, one may suppose, to all − are the presuppositions of not attempting to cure people before they fall sick[20] or to build or buy a cradle before a pregnancy is diagnosed or obvious − that of the categorisation of our linguistic communications about such matters in terms of temporal sequence. It is in consideration of such objectivities that the 'intelligibility' relativist thesis may be decisively rejected.

The same might be said to hold in the case of the 'values' relativity thesis. For the argument against cognitive relativism on the grounds of the interpersonal-objectivity requirements of any form of public communication has normative implications too; as Hare has claimed[21] language itself is predicated upon presuppositions of impartiality and universality that enable any element in it to have public acceptance and application by all employers of it. Of such normative requirements there would be at least one − that of truthfulness − that must be presumed to operate in any of the various forms of linguistic interchange. No form of discourse can be indifferent as to the importance, not to say indispensability of such an institution. So there will be some formal criteria of significance that will be prescriptions for all language users, to which our various kinds of speech activities will have to conform. It might reasonably be claimed that some fundamental procedural principles, such as truth-telling and respect for persons, are presupposed in all occasions of conversation between parties to any linguistic institution or set of conventions.

And that is only at the formal level. Partington rightly draws our attention to the deficiencies of 'values' relativism with respect to our talk on matters of public policy.[22] In his excoriation of the claim of Bourdieu that 'the school is required to perpetuate and transmit the capital of consecrated cultural signs' he notes that the logical conclusion of such a view would be a *memorandum* to us on the lines of:

> Do not ask crude and uncomprehending questions as to who makes the demands on behalf of society, what criteria shaped the demands or how it is ensured that the demands are met.

Dismissing Bourdieu's assertion that 'all pedagogic action is, objectively, symbolic violence, in so far as it is the imposition of a cultural arbitrariness by an arbitrary power Partington rejoins:

> ... the 'in so far as' does not restrict or qualify, but merely paraphrases. If there were a genuinely restrictive 'in so far as' then Bourdieu would have to admit an independent or non-arbitrary concept of education into consideration.

The point is that matters of educational discourse rest upon clearly-admitted judgments of value; and in our attempt to justify such judgments we are required to vindicate our choices and preferences, not merely to speak of our motives or of the causes of people's behaving in the way they do. This brings in the further requirement that such grounds as we advance for our actions be public and impartial, such that any person could, in principle at any rate, make them his or her own.

The opposition of Quine's pragmatism to crude relativism was rejected by Gellner as being simply inaccurate as a picture of the real nature of the cognitive growth of mankind. As a more effective and plausible alternative to that approach, we may consider the evolutionary serialism of Popper to be more suitable to show how a non-arbitrary criterion of the preferability of one paradigm over another could be developed, though this view too is not without its difficulties. The balance may now have been restored to the credit of evolutionary epistemology by the modifications to Popper's fallibilism proposed by Lakatos in his distinction between competing 'research programs' as 'degenerating' and 'progressive' on the grounds that the latter are more fertile of ideas, possess greater explanatory power and enable greater accuracy of prediction and over a longer term, while the former are everything to the contrary of these functions.[23] In such a proposal, it might be thought, we seem to have found a criterion that can function as a non-arbitrary device for adjudicating between the claims of rival systems as to their value, utility and acceptability.

This consideration enables us not only to make sense, in some minimal way and to howsoever limited a degree, of such systems as those of astrology and acupuncture, but also to rate them alongside other such systems as meteorology and medical science and show grounds as to why the latter are to be preferred. It will also *eo ipso* enable us to justify our claim that educational institutions do have aims and purposes that we can discuss in terms more impersonal than those that the rhetoric of 'cultural imperialism' or 'interest-serving economic exploitation' would permit. It is possible, we should be saying, to apply objective criteria of intelligibility to various public institutions and practices, of a kind to which a value can be attached that transcends the private pre-occupations or sectional interests of those who are already on the inside of them. And among those symbolic codes of intersubjective communication and significance from which an educating agency might make a selection for the content of its curriculum, we may place some to which the churches ascribe importance and with which the undertakings of their schools might most reasonably be thought to be concerned, perhaps chief among them, we may presume, being that mode of discourse and cognitive style that we may discern as being central to their religious beliefs.

That this form of discourse and the beliefs expressed in it have equal objectivity and significance with other forms of communication and cognition such as science is a contention on which its claims to be included on the curricula of educating institutions may, at least in part, be based. This case is argued by Laura against opposition to the inclusion of religious education in the curricula of 'state-maintained' schools, that rested upon epistemic foundations that were too shaky to bear the weight assigned to them.[24] He maintains that in science as well as religion the fundamental ground-rules that are presupposed in all attempts at communication in them are not arrived at on the basis of anything that positivists would describe as 'evidence': they are the basic conditions of such communications being articulated — what Laura calls 'the propositional fragments of the distinctive conceptual frameworks within which theistic and scientific enquiry respectively proceed.'[25] The result of this argument is that objections to religion on the grounds of its subjectivity or the untestability of its propositions are not only 'myopic' − they are radically misconceived. For the ground-rules of science, as those of theism, we may infer from his argument, belong to that category of *prima data* of which we recall Wittgenstein's aphorism that:[26]

What has to be accepted, the given is − so one could say − *forms of life.*

And on this basis, or something like it, Laura concludes that:

The epistemic difference between religion and science is a difference of degree, not of logical kind.

This consideration licences us to call into question some of the claims that because religious discourse is replete with utterances that are held to be epistemically degenerate, and since educating institutions are centrally concerned with the transmission of knowledge or the initiation of pupils into the various forms that characterise and indeed constitute public knowledge,[27] the claims of religion for inclusion on the curricula of schools cannot be sustained. Such a contention would, of course, carry conviction if (a) verificationist critiques against religion on epistemological grounds were sound and (b) schools as educating institutions were indeed *centrally* concerned with the imparting of knowledge. But the first claim cannot be considered as other than contentious, while the second needs further consideration. It would be perverse to deny that parents send their children to schools in order for them to acquire knowledge or that schools do not see themselves as being under some sort of obligation so to transmit it. But it is at least open to question whether the transmission of knowledge should be the central concern of schools as educating institutions; there can be other aims of education and to concentrate emphasis upon this one only is to risk falling into the fallacy of mistaking the part for the whole. It might be thought at least as important an aim for educational undertakings to:[28]

suggest that the fabric of society could well be improved by doing far less to ensure initiation into the so-called domains of knowledge and far more by way of instructing children in the art of living with themselves and with each other.

That would be one of Laura's suggestions; another might be found in the concern of Mary Warnock that schools should prepare children for 'the life of the imagination' in all its various forms,[29] at least one of which might be thought to be well-promoted by their being shown the possibility and value of thinking about things from a religious point of view.

In this way we may seek to justify the inclusion of an introduction to religion on to that part of the curriculum of a state-maintained school that is compulsory for all pupils in it. The aims of religious education teachers in such schools should be, Laura maintains, to 'nurture the capacity to *think religiously*' (his emphasis), by which he means:[30]

> to be possessed of the power to see one's experience of the world in religious terms. The weakness of the initiation model is that religious educators aim to do their job so well that their students end up being able to think about the world *only* in religious terms. They lose the power to ask themselves why they are religious or even whether they should be ... Religious education stimulates an expansion of the mind, not a closing of the mind.

The trouble with this view, unfortunately, is that it fails to give us any account of what it means 'to see one's experience of the world in religious terms.' Such a view, it might be argued, differs little from the characterisation of cognising experience from the religious point of view put forward by Hirst, against whom Laura inveighs; neither of them make reference to the sort of 'commitment' which some believers would hold to be a prime feature of such cognitions. An attempt was made to remedy such a deficiency by Hudson,[31] who argued that religious education was concerned with introducing young people to theology and to devotion – to understand, in some way from the inside, what it means to look at our experience from the point of view of a committed believer. But the trouble with that argument is that it appears to fall foul of the counter implicit in Flew's objection to religious education as at least potentially indoctrinatory;[32] for once having become 'committed' and knowing what it means to be 'devoted,' how could one then choose to abandon such a commitment or come to know when one has had sufficient of it to know what its satisfactions consist in without the need to take it any further?

It is this, I suspect, that makes the continued inclusion of religious education in maintained schools a problem; 'devotion' implies 'commitment' and that idea is in conflict with the kind of 'open-mindedness' and the ability to discuss one's belief in rational terms, that is held to be an aim of publicly-funded educating institutions. No such problem faces the proponents of religious education in church schools.

While county schools might have problems with the idea of getting children to know what it is to be 'devoted,' denominational schools and colleges are *prima facie* interested in that end, maybe above all others. It is for that reason, for instance, that orthodox Jews or Jehovah's Witnesses have their children excluded from religous education lessons and the daily 'Act of Worship' in maintained schools, and various religious groups make provision for the education of their young in schools that they have specially constructed and staffed for the purpose of giving public expression to their desire to confine their rearing of their children within the framework of their own view of the world. This has long been true of Roman Catholics, the Church of England and the Society of Friends; it is now becoming true of local schools founded by more recently arrived religions such as Islam. And one can see the sense of religious groups seeking through the medium of such schools to make use of the rights and opportunities available to them in a pluralist and multi-faith society and to stabilise and endeavour to perpetuate their cultural identities and *Weltanschauungen* in them.

There is no special problem about this so long as society at large values that kind of educational opportunity and is willing to accord equal right to establish and maintain such schools to those minority groups that consider it sufficiently important to have them and, in that way, to discharge the obligation incumbent upon all its members to have their young educated in some way or other, subject to their being recognised as 'efficient' for that purpose. The problem arises when it comes to the question of provision; for some schools have conflated the requirement for recognition as efficient with the entitlement to public support in the form of financial subsidy. Schools claiming 'voluntary-aided' status receive very large subventions from the public purse: in the United Kingdom all running costs including teachers' salaries are met by local education authorities, who also pay 85% of capital costs, i.e. external repairs, new buildings; elsewhere the figure is 90%. Since the aims of such schools are at least in part private, clearly some justificatory argument has to be mounted to vindicate the claims of such schools to such a large measure of public support.

Some arguments come readily to mind. Some church schools serve the needs of areas in which no other form of schooling has ever existed and in which, in the current financial climate, it is unlikely that the state will ever be able to make them available. It would not be unreasonable to claim that such schools should have assistance from public funds: the provision of programs of instruction or of boarding facilities in a village, town, or a part of a city where, but for the activities of a church providing body, they simply would not exist, might be thought to be very properly a charge on the exchequer.

Similarly, some voluntary-aided institutions have resources or courses that state-maintained schools in their vicinity do not possess, or value much less than other facilities or courses: the voluntary-aided school might have certain sporting facilities or might have expertise in particular areas of the curriculum, such as modern languages or the creative and performing arts, while the maintained schools might have a computer centre and expertise in technical and industrial subjects. In such a case to allow parents in an area the right to choose certain kinds of provision or areas of expertise that they value more highly and to do so with a very large measure of financial support would not seem to me to be at all unreasonable.

The only qualification that might be made in respect of such arguments as the foregoing arises from the public character of the claims they make for aid on such grounds. For one supposes that, where 85% or more of the income for such institutions is going to come from the state, an equal amount of openness to other sources of state assistance ought also to be incumbent upon them. In this connection it must be remarked that there is something *prima facie* odd in the idea of certain schools claiming subventions of that order from the state while at the same time placing restrictions of a far-reaching kind on the qualifications for employment by them of those staff members who are going to serve the community in these ways and with such a large measure of public support. The exclusion of all teachers other than its own adherents from appointments to senior positions in its schools on the part of at least one denomination seems to me to lie ill with claiming 100% of their salaries from the state.

It is perhaps at such a point as this that a proponent of the kind of 'open' education policy that is thought by some to be a feature of education for a multi-cultural, multi-faith society might begin to pause. For, one might argue, the only other reason that could be put forward for the endowing of church schools with considerable subsidies from public sources lies in the commitment of the community to the values that are embodied in the idea of multi-cultural education. We might well maintain that a community committed to such values of multi-culturalism as equality and tolerance ought to be willing to give financial assistance and legal support to those groups that are concerned to accept and fulfil their obligations as citizens, while at the same time preserving their independence and sense of cultural identity, and believe that one of the best ways of bringing this about is in schools seeking to operate within such groups but committed both to its principles and those of the wider community in which it functions. If we were to come to think, for any reason, that the activities of the educating institutions of such groups were not consonant with such values as say, openness and religious tolerance, or were primarily, not to say exclusively, devoted to ends that had more to do with sectional interests and less to do with the wider concerns common to all constituent cultures in the community, we might be forgiven for concluding that the public funding of such activities was not in the public interest and that further financial support ought to be denied or withdrawn, leaving the entire burden of such expense on that particular section of society that established such schooling for such purposes.

It is, of course, not inconceivable that some schools normally funded in this way might relish being relieved of the thraldom of being subordinate, at least in part, to aims that it was not their primary or original concern to serve; one doubts whether, for instance, A S Neill would have been willing to sacrifice something of his own *ethos* or approach for something that he might have regarded as a 'mess of pottage.' Sufficient unto him was the evil of 'recognition.'

The conclusion seems clear: only where church or any other kind of 'private' schools conform to the kind of criteria advanced above will it be normally accepted as legitimate for them to claim support from public funds. In all other cases, we may think, bodies pre-eminently concerned with the promotion of ends that could be described as promoting their own sectional interests ought properly to be required to bear the entire costs of establishing and maintaining institutions devoted to such purposes themselves. Unfortunately, that leaves us with further problems, some for such sectional groups and some for the wider community.

First, so far as the particular interest groups will be concerned, they will have to be clear about the nature and purpose of the activities which they wish to incorporate in the curriculum program of a school, if there is to be any question of their seeking to attract support from public funding agencies. If they fail to meet with the criteria adumbrated above, or others like them that can be generally commended, then they must be content to support the other preoccupations of their schools themselves. This will, one supposes, be relatively easy in the case of an Islamic school solely interested in teaching its pupils to read and remember the teachings of the prophet in the Q'ran; it is something that is much less easy to be clear about in the case of some schools established and governed by the Church of England's Diocesan Boards of Education. Is such a school run in order to serve the various needs of children of its members only; is it to see itself as having an evangelistic responsibility in some of the grimmer areas of our inner-city environments; is it to consider that, merely by providing a curriculum composed of what we call the 'standard' subjects, it is doing sufficient to carry out its mission of witness and service to the community generally? With at least one of these aims we cannot doubt that proponents of the 'open' view of education would find it difficult to identify and might want to question further funding of such activities from public purses. So church schools and their providing and governing bodies have to be clear as to what it is that they see themselves as doing and to be willing to admit it if partiality can be justifiably urged against them.

Secondly, as far as the wider community is concerned, there will be at least two further problems arising from the presence in their midst of what we have termed schools of special interest

groups. The problems arise in respect of those schools that, while
serving sectional interests predominantly, nevertheless conform
to the 'efficiency' criterion and can therefore stand in the stead
of state-maintained schools for the young of a group to go to
for its full-time 'education' within the meaning of the Acts. The
problem is this: subject to the satisfying of such a demand, should
any and every special interest group be allowed the right to establish
and maintain its own schools? We may think this reasonable for
such bodies as the Church of England, the Roman Catholic church
or the Society of Friends; but if they may, then why not any
group – such as Hindus or Buddhists; Seventh Day Adventists or
Jehovah's Witnesses; Scientologists or Moonies; Rastafarians or
the Socialist Workers' Party? What grounds in general could we
advance for allowing one of the above groups to maintain a separate
set of educational *milieux* but being unwilling to give such permission in the case of another? The underlying paradox of our
granting to some of these groups a licence that we withhold in
the case of others has been pointed up with especial sharpness
recently by Harris,[33] who sees as self-contradictory a view of multi-
cultural society in which practices are tolerated that are quite at
variance with the values that underpin the social fabric in which
such a view is one of the principal strands – a paradox that, for
example, the Amish communities in certain parts of the United
States have been quick to note and, in their educating institutions,
to exploit.

The appreciation of this possibility has led some proponents of
particular values in a community dominated by a pluralism of
practices and different cultural traditions to conclude that there
is only one way in which this paradox can be resolved. To the
question of whether such a licence should be extended to different
groups and sectional interests in such a society as one in which
the primary social values are those of equality and fraternal regard
as to allow them to educate their young in any setting they liked,
some politicians unhesitatingly answer in the negative. The freedom
that some parents enjoy to send their children to private, non-
state-maintained schools is one that, for all its outcomes, in the
view of some defenders of a form of society in which all groups
and faiths are to have equal rights, ought to be removed from
them, if necessary by legislation. But here is the second problem:
such bodies and such politicians cannot, in the final analysis, have
it both ways; politicians, whether of an egalitarian or a libertarian
persuasion, must be content ultimately to let the *demos* decide,
unless they can find an argument to justify them in making their
own particular principles over-riding. Can such arguments be found?
And special interest groups who seek to take advantage of the
freedoms guaranteed them by the commitment of the state to a
form of society in which pluralism of values and beliefs is tolerated

and accepted, can have no cause to complain when those who have doubts about their purposes and achievements marshal evidence against them in the attempt to show that their continued operation in that manner — in some cases, their very existence — is inconsistent with the views of man and his flourishing that are more widely held in the host society and possibly even inimical to them, unless such groups can find ways of vindicating what they are doing that will make their view of human being and his best welfare at least as acceptable as those to which it is held to be inferior or inimical. Can such an argument be constructed?

It is upon the resolution of such problems that the possibility of providing answers to the quest for an unambiguous elucidation of the role and function of church schools in a multifaith inner-city environment will depend. Perhaps I should end by making the very diffident suggestion as to one way of making progress in such an enquiry and one way in which church funding bodies might seek to defend their special role in a multi-cultural society. To quote Walkling:[34]

> The possibility of a pluralistic society depends upon the possibility of understanding people and their beliefs. It must, if it is to be worth anything at all, provide a dynamic context in which people's beliefs are exchanged, defended, argued about, converted, retained, assessed, ignored ostentatiously and so on: all the reactions people have to the beliefs of other people whom they take seriously.

If church schools can produce that kind of serious-mindedness or provide the conditions in which it might develop, they will not have gone far wrong. But the question is, *can* they, of their nature, provide them?

**Notes**

1.  It is often difficult in reading the literature on 'multi-cultural education' to be clear about which of several senses of 'culture' the adjective is being employed. For a good discussion of some of these difficulties, cf. chapter 3, 'The Arts and culture' in P Brinson (ed.), *The Arts in Schools*, London, Calouste Gulbenkian Foundation, 1982. Similar difficulty arises with respect to the concept of 'education' employed in this particular formulation. Both difficulties are not eased by the ways in which such other terms as 'multi-ethnic' are also employed in the debate, sometimes, so it would seem, interchangeably. Our particular concern with a 'multi-faith' society adds to those difficulties.
2.  Raymond Plant, *Community and Ideology*, London, Routledge and Kegan Paul, 1973.
3.  So J J Smolicz, *Culture and Education in a Plural Society*, Canberra, Curriculum Development Centre, 1979. See also his 'Cultural pluralism and education policy,' *The Australian Journal of Education*, 25, 1981, pp. 121–145.
4.  So Bryan S Crittenden, *Cultural Pluralism and Common Curriculum*, Melbourne, Melbourne University Press, 1982.
5.  So Paul Zec, 'Multicultural education: what kind of relativism is possible?'; see also Philip H Walking, 'The idea of a multicultural curriculum,' both in *Journal*

*of Philosophy of Education*, 14, 1980, pp. 77–86 and pp. 87–95 respectively. Cf. M Philip-Bell, 'Multicultural education: a critique of Walkling and Zec, *Journal of Philosophy of Education*, 15, 1981, pp. 97–105.

6.  Cf. Zec, *Loc. cit.* p. 9.
7.  *The Guardian*, 17 February, 1983.
8.  See Madeleine MacDonald, *The Curriculum and Cultural Reproduction*, Open University, 1977, quoted in Partington *vid. inf.*
9.  Geoffrey Partington, 'Cultural relativism and education,' *ACES Review*, 9, 1982, pp. 9–11.
10. W V O Quine, *Word and Object*, Cambridge, Massachusetts, MIT Press, 1960.
11. Madeleine MacDonald, *loc. cit.*, p. 9.
12. S Bowles, 'Unequal education and the social division of labour' in M Carnoy (ed.), *Schooling in a Corporate Society*, 2nd edn, New York, McKay, 1975.
13. H Gintis, 'Towards a political economy of education,' *Harvard Educational Review*, 42, 1972, p. 271.
14. M B Katz, *Class Bureaucracy and Schools*, p. xviii (Praeger Series), New York, Holt Rinehart and Winston 1975.
15. E Gellner, 'The overcoming of relativism,' unpublished lecture at the *Royal Institute of Philosophy*, 25 February 1983.
16. Steven Lukes, 'Some problems about rationality,' in Bryan R Wilson (ed.), *Rationality*, Oxford, Blackwell, 1970. See also his 'Relativism in its place' in Martin Hollis and Steven Lukes (eds), *Rationality and Relativism*, Oxford, Blackwell, 1982.
17. Allen Brent, *Philosophical Foundations for the Curriculum*, esp. pp. 153–6, London, Allen and Unwin, 1978.
18. Allen Brent, 'Multicultural education and relativism: a reply to Phillips-Bell,' *Journal of Philosophy of Education*, 16, 1982, pp. 125–130.
19. David E Cooper, *Philosophy and the Nature of Language*, chapter 5, London, Longmans, 1973.
20. Cooper, *ibid.*, p. 116.
21. R M Hare, *Freedom and Reason*, chapter 2, Oxford, Clarendon Press, 1963; see also his 'Language and moral education,' in Glenn Langford and D J O'Connor (eds), *New Essays in Philosophy of Education*, part 3, chapter 9, London, Routledge and Kegan Paul.
22. Partington, *loc. cit.*, p. 10.
23. see Imre Lakatos, 'Falsification and the methodology of scientific research programs,' in I Lakatos and A Musgrave (eds), *Criticism and the Growth of Knowledge*, Cambridge, Cambridge University Press; also his 'Popper on demarcation and induction,' in P A Schilpp (ed.), *The Philosophy of Karl Popper*, La Salle, Open Court, 1974 both reproduced in his *Collected Works*, Vol. I, J Worrall and G Curtis (eds), Cambridge, Cambridge University Press.
24. So P H Hirst, 'Morals, religion and the maintained school,' *British Journal of Educational Studies*, XIV, 1965, p. 15 ff.; also A G N Flew, 'Indoctrination and doctrines,' chapter 6 in I A Snook (ed.), *Concepts of Indoctrination*, London, Routledge and Kegan Paul, 1972. Laura points to 'the persistence of Flew's enmity to religion' elsewhere in his writings. *Vid.* Laura, *inf. loc. cit.* no. 2.
25. Ronald S Laura, 'Philosophical foundations of religious education,' *Educational Theory*, 28, 1978, pp. 310–317.
26. L Wittgenstein, *Philosophical Investigations* (Trans. G E M Anscombe), p. 226e, Oxford, Blackwell, 1953, 1978.
27. P H Hirst, 'Liberal education and the nature of knowledge,' in R D Archambault (ed.), *Philosophical Analysis and Education*, London, Routledge and Kegan Paul, 1965. So also Kevin Harris, *Education and Knowledge*, Introduction, London, Routledge and Kegan Paul, 1978.
28. Ronald S Laura, 'Rejoinder to Losito: on returning the patches for his own use,' *Educational Theory*, 29, 1979, p. 341.
29. Mary Warnock, *Schools of Thought*, chapter 4, 'The good life,' section III, London, Faber.
30. Laura, *ibid.* p. 343.
31. W D Hudson, 'Is religious education possible?' in Glenn Langford and D J O'Connor (eds), *op. cit.*, part 3, 1973, chapter 10.
32. A G N Flew, 'Indoctrination and doctrines,' in I A Snook (ed.), 1972, *op. cit.*

33. John Harris, 'A paradox of multicultural societies,' *Journal of Philosophy of Education*, 16, 1982, pp. 223–233 and esp. p. 224.
34. Philip H Walkling, 'The idea of a multicultural curriculum,' 1980, *loc. cit.* p. 94.

## 3.2 Church schools, religious education and the multi-ethnic community: a reply to David Aspin

*Nigel P Blake*

David Aspin[1] does well to raise the problem of the relation between non-Christian ethnic groups and Christian church schools in our inner cities, since it is an obvious flashpoint for grievance during troubled times. But if an answer to such problems has to wait on solutions to such enormous questions as the validity of cultural relativism or the objective validity of education in the religious way of life, then it is likely to convince few people, even when it is eventually formulated. Thinking about the many issues Professor Aspin has raised in his paper has led me to conclude that epistemological and religious considerations are irrelevant to a solution of his problems. This is a happy result, if correct, since the problem seems also to be of much wider scope than Aspin recognises, involving not just problems about sectarian schools in general, but also about the teaching of comparative religion to all pupils in the maintained schools.

Let me begin then by making good the following claim; that if there is a problem about giving a distinctively Anglican education to Muslim or Hindu children, then similar problems arise about the religious education of any child in any school who is also being brought up (either inside or outside school) as an adherent of a particular faith.

Why is this? In Aspin's original case, there seemed reason to doubt whether the Church of England could in principle educate young Muslims as Anglicans because the faith in which they are already growing up is ultimately incompatible with Christianity. To a person who already has the central beliefs of one creed, an incompatible creed seems likely to appear at best interesting, deserving of respect but wrong. Young Muslims in church schools can learn a lot about Christianity but seem unlikely to learn to be Christians. It seems equally unlikely that the comparative study of world religions in a maintained school might alter the religious affiliation (or resistance to religious affiliation) of any child who is being brought up outside the school with a particular set of religious or anti-religious beliefs. Thus there seems to be a more general problem embracing the one which currently taxes Aspin.

Now it might be thought that whether this were a real problem would depend on the logical nature of the alleged incompatibility of religions. Cultural relativists would say that the incompatibility is radical; that from within the intellectual framework which supports one religion, the claims of other religions cannot even be understood. It is impossible for a Muslim child to come to understand Christianity or for one reared in an anti-religious manner ever to come to understand any religion – not in any worthwhile sense of understanding, anyway. By contrast, others of us might simply claim that different religions contradict each other – something which one could not even notice unless one could understand equally well what different religions said. And since there is nothing intrinsically difficult about rejecting previously held ideas as wrong and coming to hold new beliefs incompatible with one's prior beliefs, there seems to be no reason why a Muslim couldn't learn to be an Anglican instead. Nonetheless, problems which arise about the religious education of children who already have religious beliefs arise equally urgently no matter how the incompatibility of religions is interpreted.

The problems are clear enough if cultural relativism is true. Relativism says that a person can only understand claims which can be expressed within the conceptual framework of his own culture. Yet if one religious group relies on a framework of concepts different from that of another religious group, and therefore impenetrable to them, then the beliefs of the one religion cannot be communicated to adherents of the other. The very words used to communicate the beliefs will mean different things to the two groups. But in that case none of their members can achieve an objectively true understanding of both religions, and none of them can be described as genuinely studying comparative religion at all. Some relativists might want to try to escape this conclusion without relinquishing their relativism. Can they not follow Phillips-Bell[2] and suggest that individuals can be socialised into several mutually hermetic conceptual frameworks? This would be no help to the relativist even if such were possible. Comparative religion does have to be (as I shall argue) genuinely comparative; 'comparative' is not just an adventitious feature of the name of the study. But if relativism were correct, no one could have a single embracing conceptual framework within which *valid* comparison would be possible. If cultural relativism is true, then, the study of comparative religion is simply impossible for those who have a faith. This applies whether they are taught either as a group at a sectarian school or at their local comprehensive as isolated individuals within a multi-racial, multi-faith class. What they are taught about religions rooted within a different culture from their own means nothing to them at all, or something quite different from what is intended.

But difficulties remain even if cultural relativism is false. Why there should be difficulties is not obvious. After all, the most devout believers in one faith are often remarkably well informed on points of doctrine and history regarding other faiths, and if relativism is false, their understanding may in principle be correct. Now such a person is in a position to evaluate religions other than his own in respect of various kinds of sophistication – the subtlety of the theology, the vitality of the ethic, the philosophical sophistication of the ontological commitments, the strength of the institutional arrangements. Yet he is in no position to evaluate his own religion as though it were on all fours with these others. In contrast to the way he views them, he cannot see his own religion as any more than marginally corrigible, otherwise he would not be a believer. I am not denying that he may occasionally doubt his own faith. But it is one thing to experience moments of religious doubt; quite another to hold one's claimed religious beliefs constantly open to radical revision. In Christianity, for instance, to believe is to fear the loss of faith. That is the difference between a committed Christian or Muslim and someone who simply suspects that Christianity or Islam is true. A true believer chooses the very direction of his life in the light of his faith. Religious beliefs are of their very nature more deep-rooted than other kinds of belief. They are not available for disinterested reexamination and revision in the sense in which economic or historical or scientific beliefs are.

Clearly it is possible for a devout adherent of a faith to study comparative religion seriously and to do the job well. So why is it *not* possible for such a person to engage in such study as a means to revising his own religious beliefs? Holding a faith is a matter of holding its central tenets to be exempt from or invulnerable to rational criticism. I am not saying that clinging to a faith against the testimony of argument is irrational; rather the contrary. It would be a particular kind of irrationality for someone who has a religious faith already, to hold it open to a radical critique on grounds external to that faith. For one thing that religious beliefs seem to me to hold in common is an acute awareness of the fallibility of human powers, powers of reason included. So the believer who thinks himself possessed of insights into a reality far greater and more potent than he, would certainly see it as irrational to let the puny and fallible reservations of the human intellect weigh heavily against those insights. None of this, of course, goes to show that holding religious beliefs is rational in the first place; only that once one has those beliefs, it is not obviously irrational to cling to them against the weight of argument.

But the serious study of comparative religion involves accepting the validity of taking a rationally critical attitude to the tenets of a religion without supposing them to be invulnerable to such criticism – an attitude quite incompatible with the attitude a believer takes to his own faith. If the study of comparative religion is to have any point at all, then it must at least mean introducing students to the central dogmas of the major religions in such a way that they are understood by them and seen as potentially important by them. Yet for students to fail to grasp those points in which the major world religions contradict each other would be for them to understand so little of them as to be worthless. To understand the dogmas of different religions is precisely to understand that they cannot all be true. And to understand the contradictions yet also to see the beliefs as possibly important is to accept the possibility of rational criticism of any of them. There are no epistemic grounds for exempting any one religion from this implicit business of criticism. Yet in default of any empirical means of testing the validity of a religious belief, or any logical means of checking for anything more than meaningfulness and self-consistency, the study of comparative religion could not possibly incline a student to the rational rejection of one faith for another. It would either induce a certain scepticism about all faiths or have no impact on a student's religious faith whatsoever.

Now this might at first blush look like a strong reason for supposing that whatever point there might be to teaching comparative religion, it could not be that one were aiming to enhance children's freedom of religious choice. The likely upshots seem to be either that their religious commitments are untouched or that they are put in limbo. But while these are the likely effects, it does not follow that study of world religions is educationally pointless. The limbo of scepticism is arguably a necessary way-stage on any route to an ultimate autonomous religious commitment on a person's part. Certainly, once the limbo of scepticism has been reached one cannot look to yet further study of world religions for guidance. Perhaps what is needed at that point is some kind of existential leap on the part of the individual person. Yet the existential leap is not open to anyone who does not at least see that the alternative is scepticism (even if he at no point actually lives in scepticism). Study of world religions is obviously not a necessary means to reaching the point where a free autonomous religious commitment could be made; yet it is probably an effective means to that end, and one which is arguably incumbent on educators to use if they take seriously the quality of religious life open to their students.

It seems clear enough, then, that a child who both attends church or Sunday school, for instance, and yet also receives instruction in comparative religion in a maintained school, will be being taught, by different sets of people, attitudes to Christianity which are not merely different but incompatible. If the school's teaching succeeds, he becomes a sceptic with regard to all religions, his own included; if it fails, his religious commitment is untouched. Teaching in comparative religion cannot try to hide the fact that comparative valuations of religions are possible and important; the very activity implies that all religions stand *prima facie* equally open to rational critique. Yet to receive instruction in a faith, to be for instance not just taught about Christianity but taught to be a Christian, is to be taught to see that faith is beyond rational critique in any but peripheral details.

The more general upshot of this seems to be that if a child is being successfully taught to be a Christian, Muslim or Hindu, then from a religious point of view, his study of comparative religion or of any single religion not his own will be pointless. On the one hand it tries to encourage him to see his own religion as problematic, which he cannot do, and on the other to see other religions as no more problematic, which he cannot do either. Of course, this is not to say there would be no point at all in such a child studying comparative religion. On the contrary, it would afford him major insights into other cultures than his own. But there would be no point in pretending that instruction in comparative religion might seriously modify his own religious perceptions. Furthermore, if the rationale of comparative religious study were simply to promote cross-cultural understanding, then it would at most be one element in a constellation of cultural studies, including anthropological, economic and aesthetic studies; and not always necessarily a particularly important element.

Now *prima facie*, all this presents us with a problem. If there are educational reasons for teaching comparative religion which have to do with securing the possibility of autonomous religious choice for educated adults, and not just cross-cultural understanding, then to allow sectarian teaching of any kind, i.e. teaching children to be Christians, Muslims, Hindus, etc. is to frustrate, or let others frustrate one's educational aim. Yet *ex hypothesi*, there will be some kind of moral justification for this aim. Thus everything will be aligned for a clash of moral principles. There are, I think, only two ways to sidestep this problem. One is to deny that there really are any educational reasons for teaching comparative religion with an eye to religious freedom. The other is to line up with the cultural relativist and deny the very possibility of genuine study of comparative religion at all.

I am going to argue now that neither of these ways of avoiding the problem actually works and that the problem is real and needs an answer. Lastly I shall examine how the problem might be solved. First, the cultural relativism position.

While I am broadly in agreement with David Aspin's complaints against relativism, the point I want to raise is not whether relativism is true but whether it has any remote relevance to our own multi-cultural society. Evidently there is indeed some sense in which British society deserves the name multi-cultural; but is British society multi-cultural in the sense required by cultural relativism? I say no.

If cultural relativism has any application at all (and I think it has none), it is to difficulties of relationship between representatives of societies which have been and remain mutually unknown, and which do not share a language. This is obviously not the situation which applies between ethnic groups in Britain. Even in those groups where, for instance, women are sequestered and know no English, nonetheless the group does contain some members (some males, that is) who speak some English and interact with native-born Britons.

It is clearly inadequate, however, simply to point to linguistic interchanges and draw the immediate conclusion that such interchanges are evidence of some communality of culture. For the relativist is sceptical about the very nature of those interchanges. Are they really instances of people communicating meaningfully with each other across a cultural divide; or are my understanding of Mr Patel and his understanding of me deeply flawed? Well, why should the relativist think the latter?

The relativist is used to thinking about people trying to communicate in situations where supposedly everything is different on the two sides of the divide. Not only is the language different, in the elementary sense of different word-stocks and grammar, but also the physical conditions and the material culture are different, i.e. the technologies of food, shelter, transport and communication and the institutions which sustain the use of these technologies. Hence too it must seem that the forms of life are different − the activities people engage in and their point and purpose. And from this the relativist concludes that the word-stock and grammar of the different languages are not different ways of encoding the same stock of concepts but ways of encoding quite different sets of concepts altogether. He then makes one of two assumptions: either that words and phrases in a language cannot be interdefinable if they are learnt as elements of different language games belonging to distinct forms of life; or that every form of life in an alien society is distinct from every form of life in one's own culture. In the first case, he concludes that there are some aspects of alien cultures that we can never understand except by 'getting on the inside of' the relevant form of life; by becoming, that is, a participant observer. In the second case, he is driven to conclude that not even this is possible, because to try to share another group's form of life requires a mutual recognition that that is what one is trying to do; but this is impossible where people from different cultures have no forms of life or concepts in common at all.

Now the second stronger form of relativism simply fails to apply to the situation between cultures in Britain, while the first, if it does apply, presents no problems of communication of a specifically cross-cultural kind. First, it is beyond question that the different ethnic groups in our society share much in terms of material and economic culture and hence also in forms of life. Perhaps not every-thing is shared by all groups, and forms of life which may look superficially the same may conceal subtle differences; nonetheless all groups have something to do with, for instance, cars and buses, post offices, pubs (even if they understand that they are to avoid them), television and the press, housing estates and so on. Thus, everyone in British society shares some forms of life with members of other ethnic/cultural groups. And in sharing a form of life with someone, one shares not only those concepts peculiar to that form of life, but a number of other concepts involved in sharing any form of life – the concepts of an external world, of time and place, of persons, of co-operation between persons, of linguistic meaning and of the difference between a correct and incorrect use of language in a language game related to that form of life. Given the communality of these general concepts, people can learn and be taught forms of life and their attendant language games, even if the forms of life are discrete and the language used in dif-ferent language games mutually irreducible. They can learn and be taught because they and their teachers can know that that is just what they are trying to do and they can both know how to recognise success in such learning and teaching when it happens. Thus secondly there is no epistemological barrier to cross-cultural understanding if there are at least some shared forms of life in the community. If some are shared, we have the wherewithal to come to share them all. But this possibility is in principle no different from bringing a white English child to a grasp of a form of knowledge new to him, like mathematics, ethics or physical science. We take it that forms of knowledge are indeed mutually irreducible, yet do not suppose that familiarity with one hampers a grasp of any other. Thus, to repeat, there are no problems of a novel epistemological kind in coming to 'crosscultural' understanding, at least between subcultural groups in a society such as Britain.

My next step is to argue that if there is a *prima facie* case for including comparative religion on the curriculum, for reasons to do with religious freedom, then we face a dilemma concerning sectarian schools. But first an aside; some may complain that I could have got to this point more quickly simply by pointing to the arguments Aspin deploys against relativism on grounds of internal incoherence. I want to reassert that the reason I have argued to the irrelevance rather than the falsehood of relativism is to show that, complex as the curricular problems before us may be, they do not await our agreement on even more complex problems in epistemology. This is, I suspect, more often true in educational theory than we tend to think.

To return to the main thread; if cultural relativism does not impede 'cross-cultural' communication within British society, no-one can have good grounds for denying that comparative religion can in principle be taught and moreover taught to members of each and every culture in our society, bar the impediments of faith already noted. The sharper question is whether the curricular justification for comparative study of religion is sufficiently strong to override the right of religious people to bring up their own children as members of their own faith. I am thinking of white people no less than coloured or black, and of the various Christian sects no less than any non-Christian sect. The problem is this; that if there is an educational (and *ipso facto*, at some level moral) case for teaching comparative religion, and if the raising of children in a particular faith is likely to frustrate that aim, then there is a *prima facie* moral case against allowing sectarian teaching in schools. Such a case may be answerable, but it cannot be merely ignored.

If there is some kind of educational case for the inclusion of comparative religion in the curriculum on religious grounds, it will rest on:

a.  claims about the nature of the subject — its cognitive richness, the importance of religion to mankind and the claim that comparative religion can indeed be taught notwithstanding superficial difficulties of 'cross-cultural' communication; and also
b.  quite general principles for including activities, subjects or disciplines in the curriculum which justify teaching not only comparative religion but other things as well.

Now of the kinds of claim one might make under (a), i.e. the 'factual' claims, the only one that might at first look controversial is the claim that comparative religion *can* actually be taught, a claim which presupposes that cultural relativism is either false or irrelevant. But this is precisely the claim which a moment ago I argued to be true; cultural relativism is indeed irrelevant. Thus any group which wanted to deny that there was an educational case for teaching comparative religion would have to query the claims made under (b), claims about general principles of curriculum and the values that subtend such claims. This is the only way in which a sectarian school could claim both academic acceptability and curricular consistency. Now this seems to me illuminating *vis-a-vis* one of the problems which vex David Aspin. Some schools which seem up to the academic mark nonetheless also give a strong sectarian education (that is, teach children to *be* Christians, Muslims and so on), and perhaps also infringe other educational principles which the State supports, by fostering elitism, for instance. Now one of three things must be true of any such school:

i   it is simply inconsistent, operating according to widely accepted curricular principles except with regard to religious education; or

ii    it believes there to be some special principle of a non-educational kind which overrides those principles and might justify comparative religion as part of curriculum; or

iii    it might be that the school actually is consistent in its disregard of educational principles, since many other curricular elements are also missing from its syllabus and many educational principles are disregarded by it, so that the school does not actually come up to the mark.

If these are the possibilities, the state will have two options in its dealings with sectarian schools. (That they are defensible will presently become clearer.) These are either:

a.    to oblige the school to stake out a case for its existence as a sectarian school or otherwise cease to be one; or

b.    simply to close the school, on the grounds of being educationally inadequate or objectionable.

The kind of hypothetical case I envisage falling under the second rubric might be that of a school for extremist Shi'ite Muslim supporters of Ayatollah Khomeini, a group which might quite consistently reject not only the teaching of comparative religion but also teaching of non-Islamic art and science and most Western ethical principles along with it. (It is pertinent though, and not facetious, to point out that their attitude to religious education would certainly be one of the least of our worries if such a school were established.)

These two courses of action seem to me more defensible than any derived from David Aspin's principle. Aspin argues that we have a right to require schools to ensure that what they teach is compatible with a commitment to the values necessary to the maintenance of a multi-cultural society. There seem to me to be a number of difficulties in such an approach. First of all, it is far from clear what the values necessary to the maintenance of such a society actually are, or that they are necessarily particularly worthy of respect on purely moral grounds. I fear that Aspin might be unduly idealistic in supposing that equality and fraternal regard really are necessary for the maintenance of a stable multi-cultural society. It can hardly be maintained that our society actually is egalitarian; or that successive governments have done very much more than to smooth over a few of its more tractable inequalities; or that the present government is sympathetic to egalitarian reform.

As to fraternal regard, or respect for persons, how much, one might ask, is truly necessary to the maintenance of our society and how would such respect be made manifest? May we not suggest, world-wearily but plausibly, that the maintenance of a stable multi-cultural society actually requires no more than a grudging tolerance of members of other cultures (and indeed of white sub-cultures) —

that they be recognised as more or less necessary collaborators in economic undertakings? What more is necessary, *for the mere maintenance of stability*, than the satisfaction of their economic and moral needs at a not very extravagant level? A stable multi-cultural society is not of necessity happy, merely quiescent. Respect for persons is clearly a good, but we do well not to pretend to ourselves that it is a political necessity. Danger would lie in the temptation to reason. 'Our society appears to be stable, so it seems there is adequate respect for persons around.' Perhaps we do not treat people with *complete* lack of respect. But many people are treated with *scant* respect; and racism is by no means the sole embodiment of such disdain.

Now of course there is a moral case for asking any group of people to honour such values as egalitarianism and respect for persons. But there are also countervailing reasons against requiring a minority group to do so when it appears that they would be a comparatively saintly group if they did, in contrast to so much of society at large. David Aspin's prudential argument − that the stability of society requires it − would not wash and would appear so hypocritical as virtually to constitute a new form of repression for minorities. If on the other hand we accept the purely formal part of Aspin's argument, and merely require that sectarian schools act in consonance with those shabbier values which arguably do subtend the stability of our society, then I suspect we shall find that almost any school which is academically up to the mark passes *that* unstringent test, whatever other supposedly divisive doctrines it may teach.

In what way, then, are my criteria for the acceptability of sectarian schools preferable − the requirements of acceptability in academic and other educational respects and of rational consistency in curricular planning? It is worth mentioning that one could be equally hypocritical in the application of these criteria, enforcing them on sectarian schools more stringently than on others. But there is less danger of this. It is precisely because it is not really clear what the values integral to the stability of a multi-cultural society actually are, that it is easy for the hypocrite to pretend to be involving them impartially. The criteria I propose rest on less tendentious foundations, I believe. (Of course, that does not show them to be correct.)

Nonetheless, my criteria still need more defence than they have yet received. A major objection against them would be that the actions the state might have to take if a school failed to meet these criteria would be morally indefensible. These would be the acts of either forcing the school to relinquish its sectarian aims or to close. The objection would be founded on the following principle; that to respect a person is necessarily to respect his culture also. Phil Walkling[3] glossed this point very vividly when he wrote ' ... to require a man crassly to accept the unimportance or worthlessness of the things he holds most dear is, in extreme cases, to threaten his very existence as a moral being.' But Walkling also went on to say:

> ... to deny him the right to pass on these things to his children through the medium of formal education with the authority of the wider society behind it is to suggest that they, too (the children), are of little importance unless they become assimilated into the 'host culture' ...

The objection to my criteria might be that the actions they seem to enjoin would be offensive in the way that Walkling describes in the second quoted sentence.

I do not think that is actually the case, though. First, and informally, Walkling's second point has to do with denying people the right to hand on *any* of their culture to their children through formal education and what is more, denying them this either without appeal to any moral reasons or by exclusive appeal to reasons accepted only in the host culture. What I am suggesting is much more circumspect; that one might make a particular case against formal teaching in a religion on particular moral grounds, and grounds which *ex hypothesi* are otherwise accepted by the ethnic group – grounds which they accept in as much as they agree with their host community's broad curricular requirements. In as far as the ethnic group do agree with us in these ways, then in querying their right to give their children a sectarian education, we are not pitching our values against theirs so much as pitching some of their (and our) values against some other of their (and our) values. Indeed in such cases, the requirement to treat persons with respect is not unequivocal. It is not clear that one respects a child's personal rights by letting the requirements of his cultural group override his own right to adult freedom of religious choice. Nor is it clear that one respects his parents the better by waiving, in respect of their children, rights held by other children.

I think this informal answer is probably good enough to justify our applying the criterion of consistency to schools which, narrow sectarian teaching apart, do otherwise conform to our current educational standards. It does not deal, however, with cases like my hypothetical pro-Khomeini Shi'ite school, for here there appears to be very little communality of values. How could one defend simply closing down such a school?

If such action seems unquestionable at first sight, this may be because we sometimes fail to note an ambiguity in the notion of respect. 'Respect for persons' means taking people seriously as people who have their own consciousness and their own conscience, a perspective on life which we cannot, without overbearing arrogance, dismiss out of hand as wrong or inadequate. Practically, such respect involves for instance that we treat people as equally important ends of our moral action. In particular, people are to be granted equal rights in our society, including equal rights to political participation and social influence.

There is, however, another more everyday sense of 'respect' which gets confused with the first. In this sense, to respect someone is roughly equivalent to holding them in esteem. This in turn involves seeing the respected person as worthy of emulation by others, and perhaps more worthy of emulation than many others. (This sense of 'respect' itself encompasses ambiguities.)

Now it seems clear to me that it is only in the first of these senses that we require the state to respect its citizens. Indeed, arguably there is something very disturbing about a democratic state expressing respect in the second, everyday sense for particular groups or individuals, since it seems to imply a comparative lack of respect for 'lesser mortals,' which might in turn also signal a lack of respect for these latter in the *first* sense of respect.

Now if it is only respect in the first sense that a state should hold for its citizens, what kind of respect should it have for their cultures? Surely it need only respect these in the first sense as well. For it is surely possible for someone to treat an individual in the manner required by the virtue of respect for persons even though they actually feel no esteem for that person's culture. Indeed, isn't that the whole point of respect for persons as a virtue − that it enjoins certain decencies of conduct on us even with regard to people whom we hold in low regard?

Now what follows from the state's obligation to treat ethnic cultures with respect in the first and narrower sense? Does it entail accession to any requirement members of the group might make on grounds which are agreed upon *only* by members of that group? If, for instance, a Shi'ite community demanded the right to train its children in the military techniques of insurgence and the moral probity of torture of the enemies of Islam, would the state show a lack of respect of Islamic cultures if it refused to accede to these demands?

Well, surely not. To suppose otherwise would be to suppose that the state had no right to restrain those it designates as criminal if criminals actually have a 'distinctive point of view' from which their activities seem perfectly OK. To treat someone with respect is not necessarily to let them do what they like, for this could well involve a breach of respect for the rights of others. Thus for one group to expect society to suspend its normal moral judgments with respect to their particular activities is for it to demand not equality of respect but superiority of esteem.

Now there are three other objections to my criteria of a quite general kind which I must address. The first would appeal to the principle of religious freedom. It might be alleged that either to close a sectarian school on any grounds at all or to require a school to cease to give sectarian teaching would be to infringe rights of free religious practice. I agree with this — yes, it would be such an infringement. But that does not in itself show such actions to be wrong, because in these cases, there would be no arbitrary abrogation of freedoms but rather a conflict of freedoms and rights; in particular a conflict between the parents' or group's right to teach in conformity with its faith and children's rights to learn in such a way that their adult freedom is maximised. The conflict is not merely a conflict between different rights and freedoms but between the rights and freedoms of different people; and there is no obvious reason why the religious rights of the elders should supervene against the educational rights of their offspring.

A second objection would be that we were opening the door to, indeed indulging in, cultural imperialism. But this could not be so. For the values and principles appealed to are *ex hypothesi* shared by the generality of cultural and sub-cultural groups in the society. The preponderant size and power of the host culture may obscure this fact; but it would be even more senseless to require that the values and principles appealed to be radically different from those of the host culture merely because it is larger and more powerful. (Of course, abuse of power is to be guarded against.)

A third objection might simply be 'Where does it all end?' If an ethnic group's schools are to have their freedom of religious teaching put in question, what may not be thus put in question? But this, I think, is a misplaced fear. The conflict of values and practice between sectarian teaching and comparative religion springs from quite particular considerations concerning the nature of religious faith. They do not apply, surely, with regard to the value and practice of cross-cultural studies of say music, medicine or politics.

If there is, then, a *prima facie* case against allowing formal sectarian education in schools — schools of any kind, I think we must say to — to what special claims might members of an ethnic group appeal to defeat this *prima facie* case? Not, clearly enough, any appeal to the rights of individual children. For even if it is urged that a person has a right to enter fully into the culture of family and community, we have equally been urging that he has other conflicting rights as well. And we have not been denying people the right to enter the faith of their parents at all, but have merely urged that such entry be delayed. I cannot conceal that there are problems lurking here, though. A religious person may feel that their child is not in a state of grace until ritually accepted into the faith by baptism or some other form of initiation; and that should their lives be at risk, then so too would their souls be. Yet it is not clear whether the state should give more weight to religious fears of this sort than it gives, say, to the fears of parents for their child's academic progress in a non-selective school.

An appeal to the rights of parents would be problematic too. There is no abstract right of parents to have a say in their child's education which absolves them from *producing reasons* for their objections or demands. Otherwise, any parent could bar their child from any subject or insist on absolutely any curricular provision by mere appeal to his rights as a parent. What his parental rights amount to is the right to have his point of view taken as a serious, but not a sole consideration. But were we to implement my criteria, that is exactly what we would be doing. The problem would be; in what kind of cases should parental demands for sectarian education be acceded to?

The answer I think is that only considerations of the happiness and integrity of a particular ethnic community could count. It might be the case – though not necessarily – that the religious practices of an ethnic community were so absolutely central to its culture that the culture would wither and die without it; and that that would entail disorientation, anomie and distress for members of that community. In cases such as these, the state might decide to waive certain educational rights of children in order to sustain the greater good of their communities. This, I think, is the solution to the problem. Yet it comes with two caveats. First, it is not enough to say that a group's religious practices are somehow more important to it than any other of its cultural mores. What has to be shown is the stricter claim that almost everything else that is important in their way of life is somehow sustained by their religious practices. Secondly, one would also need to consider carefully whether the well-being of the children (in a very broad sense) were better served by the existence or the disappearance of the culture which sustains their parents; and claims of parent and child might need to be balanced against each other.

But last, let me note what I believe to be a positive virtue of this way of tackling the problem; it only appeals to and balances the educational rights of individual children and the political rights of minority cultural groups. The real or supposed requirements of their host community are not brought to bear on them at all. This must be conducive to the health of all cultural groups and to the health of the multi-cultural ideal itself.

**Notes**
1.   D Aspin, 'Church schools, religious education and the multi-ethnic community,' *Journal of Philosophy of Education*, 17, 1983, pp. 229–240.
2.   M Phillips-Bell, 'Multi-cultural education; a critique of Walkling and Zec,' *Journal of Philosophy of Education*, 15, 1981, pp. 97–105.
3.   P Walkling, 'The idea of a multi-cultural curriculum,' *Journal of Philosophy of Education*, 14, 1980, pp. 87–95.

# 3.3 The church school: commitment and openness

*Geoffrey S Duncan*

## Introduction

Schools both reflect and help to form the wider society. One British study has observed that 'the learning that goes on in school is inextricably bound in with the economic and political reality of the society in which the school educates;'[1] we might want to add 'religious reality.' But in accepting the point of substance here we shall come across the difficulty that there are different and apparently contradictory perceptions of what constitutes the 'reality' of society, particularly the religious reality. In Britain we come across studies that refer to our society as 'secular,' 'post-Christian,' even 'anti-Christian,' unduly still influenced by the Enlightenment; at the same time other studies continue to query the secular hypothesis and increasingly attention is drawn to the 'multi-faith' nature of society. It is perhaps important for us to remember the complexity of the context within which both institutions (such as schools) and individual professionals (such as teachers) are having to face up to the issue of commitment and neutrality.

Perhaps it is possible for all these views of society to have at the same time both some validity and some limitation.

The concerns of this paper are not, of course, exclusively British; although the paper is set very much in the British context.

## A pluralist society?

As far as schools are concerned, in England there are church schools within the state maintained sector whose pupils are almost entirely Muslim. Some, of course, due either to their admissions policy or to the neighbourhood in which they are located, have at least a nominally Christian school population; others serve an incredibly wide range of cultures/faiths/ethnic groups with over twenty languages represented among the homes of the pupils. Perhaps as a starting point the most promising view of our respective societies is to perceive them as 'pluralist' (though recognising that there will be various and differing implications drawn from it).

As we approach the end of this century this shrinking world of the 'global village' will require preparation for 'difference' to assume increasing importance as one of the functions of schools. This was the line taken by a major British report known as the Swann Report[2] which put forward a view of the role 'education can and must play in laying the foundations for a society based on genuinely pluralistic principles.'[3] In developing the concept of pluralism the report explained:[4]

> We consider that a multi-racial society such as ours would in fact function most effectively and harmoniously on the basis of pluralism which enables, expects and encourages members of all ethnic groups, both minority and majority, to participate fully in shaping the society as a whole within a framework of commonly accepted values, practices and procedures, while also allowing and, where necessary, assisting the ethnic minority communities in maintaining their distinct ethnic identities within this common framework.

Later the same report concludes that:[5]

> We would.... regard a democratic pluralist society as seeking to achieve a balance between, on the one hand, the maintenance and active support of the essential elements of the cultures and lifestyles of all the ethnic groups within it and, on the other, the acceptance by all groups of a set of shared values distinctive of the society as a whole.

Another recent study presents the challenge thus:[6]

> It is not always easy to recognise when one is caught up in a revolution. Yet only the most careless and reluctant of educationalists will not have observed the revolutionary thrust of educational thought and practice both internationaly and in recognising the true nature of the composition of the world's population.

Before pursuing this theme, however, and concentrating on the role of the school, I have to observe that even this starting point of Britain being a pluralist society has not been universally accepted. For example a survey reported in *The Times Educational Supplement*[7] quotes one British headteacher as denying that Britain is a multicultural society and arguing that the best way schools can serve the interest of ethnic minorities is to help them fit in with the British way of life, supporting the largely discredited but still prevalent concept of assimilation. Indeed, at the time of writing there has appeared a book that very much takes this line, a book written by a former headteacher who gained some notoriety which ultimately led to his retirement, from his writings on mulicultural education.[8] The author attacks the Swann report particularly for its utopian vision of imposed 'cultural pluralism' and, interestingly, with the use of one of the words being explored in the subject of our study, avers that the Swann committee's commitment to the pursuit of the truth was less important to it than the confirming of ideological presuppositions.

Even when the pluralist nature of society and the fact of difference is accepted, many difficulties and matters for debate remain. For example, a head of a Church of England school recently wrote in his diocesan newsletter that among his reasons for not allowing any religion other than Christianity to be taught in his school is the fact that he could not teach other faiths uncritically.

## Christian and other faiths

Of course, in so far as one is caught up in a revolution, as claimed in the passage quoted above, so questions impinging on commitment and neutrality become unavoidable and increasingly insistent, particularly, in the world of education for teachers and school governors. The head of the school quoted above, for example, obviously sees his commitment to him who is 'the way, the truth and the life,' to him who is reported to have said 'No one comes to the Father but by me' (John 14:6), as being compromised if he was other than critical about faiths other than Christianity. Others, in their commitment to the search for truth, particularly in an academic setting, take the position that texts such as that quoted above should not be taken at their face value or that negative inferences do not have to be drawn from it regarding other faiths. This approach is illustrated by a recent book *Jesus: the unanswered questions* whose author observes that:[9]

> One of the most serious problems raised by and for Christianity in a multicultural, pluralistic world is its inbuilt claim to superiority and finality as a religion.

Later on the author challengingly asserts:[10]

> there are still many ... theologians and church leaders whose attitudes, when it comes to considering those of other faiths, tend to be at best condescending, reluctant to contemplate change and blind to the consequences of their position ... and at worst bigoted and intolerant; and there are 'ordinary' Christians who just do not want to think about the issues now facing them.

People are not, of course, ever likely to think the same about this issue: there will always be a variety of theological background and expression, and hence commitment. I use the term 'commitment' to refer to, at the very least, the giving of assent and support to a proposition, a principle, a belief-statement, with a willingness to express that assent and support defensively and/or in a commending way (in 'thought, word and deed'), the ultimate expression being a willingness to die for it.

But perhaps over and above this sort of commitment at the very least we could do more to encourage those involved in education to become committed to 'think about the issues,' to sort out precisely what their commitments are, the various means of witnessing to them and the implication both of the commitments themselves and the means adopted to put them into effect. I have elsewhere expressed the view,[11] an impressionistic one, that the great majority of teachers in Britain fall between the very 'conservative' and very 'liberal' position and occupy a broad middle spectrum, feeling unhappy with a 'hard' line on both practical and moral grounds but also fearful of betraying their Christian foundation.

## Religious education

It is interesting that the Swann report[12] ascribes an important role to religious education in the attainment of the aims it advocates. Not suprisingly the report soon finds itself grapling with our major concern, namely the inter-play of commitment and neutrality. Its answer is to advocate 'the phenomenological or undogmatic approach,' which is described as one that:

> sees the aim of religious education as the promotion of understanding. It uses the tools of scholarship in order to enter into an empathic experience of the faith of individuals and groups. It does not seek to promote any one religious viewpoint but it recognises that the study of religion must transcend the merely informative....

The report proceeds to explain that the phenomenological approach:

> draws a clear distinction between what can strictly speaking be termed 'religious instruction' i.e. instruction in a religion and 'religion' and in the range of belief systems which exists. It is seen as the function of the home and of the religious community to nurture and instruct a child in a particular faith (or not), and the function of the school to assist pupils to understand the nature of religion and to know something of the diversity of belief systems, their significance for individuals and how these bear on the community.

Although it does not actually use the term the implication that comes through this chapter of the report is that religious education in schools should be 'neutral;' the chapter does, however, interestingly use the term 'commitment' when it calls in aid a seminal Church of England report *The Fourth R* (also known as the Durham Report):[13]

> the press for acceptance of a particular faith or belief system is the duty and privilege of the churches and other similar religious bodies. It is certainly not the task of a teacher in a county school. If the

teacher is to press for any conversion, it is conversion from a shallow and unreflective attitude of life. If he is to press for commitment, it is the commitment to the religious quest, to that search for meaning, purpose, and value which is open to all men.

This quotation refers only to county schools but the Swann report, in calling for a review of the English (and Welsh) system of education that allows for church schools as part of the maintained system, possibly implies that such an approach should apply to all schools. The Swann Report offers nine recommendations concerning religious education, three of which give the flavour suggested in this paragraph:[14]

We are in favour of a non-denominational and undogmatic approach ... (to enable) all pupils ... to understand the nature of religious belief, the religious dimension of human experience and the plurality of the faiths in modern Britain ...

It is important that by the time all children leave their primary schools they should be aware that there are a range of different 'living' faiths in this society ...

We believe that religious education can play a central role in preparing all pupils for life in today's multi-racial Britain, and can also lead them to a greater understanding of the diversity of the global community.

Although many Church of England educationalists would still stand by the above quotation from the Durham Report, many would probably want to question if the inference has to be drawn from it that even in a county school the teacher can or should be 'neutral.' Back in 1970 there was considerable support for the view that neutrality should indeed be the aim of a teacher of integrity.[15]

## Commitment and neutrality — or commitment and openness?

But teachers and others in education who jealously guard their commitments should be reassured by the prevailing overwhelming philosophical view that not only is neutrality impossible but also undesirable. I prefer to refer to the 'commitment/openness' tension rather than the 'commitment/neutrality' polarisation. As a recent Farmington pamphlet concisely states:[16]

Commitment, whether of a religious or a non-religious nature, and whether in a strong conscious form or a largely unconscious and vague form, affects all teaching. Furthermore, the spirit of neutrality offends against the enthusiasm which good teaching needs just as much as against concern for truth and for the values behind education as we see it, such as respect for persons. As for objectivity, even in the sciences this is now regarded as only possible in part, and for arts subjects personal involvement and intuition is accepted as unavoidable and indeed essential and desirable.

As I have quoted from the Farmington pamphlet it is only fair to point out that its main concern is to question the concept of 'openness' particularly when it is allied to 'critical' and to suggest that something like 'critical affirmation' would be a more appropriate concept.

Perhaps there is a time and a place for both approaches; in other words perhaps they are complementary rather than opposed.

Brenda Watson, who is closely associated with the Farmington Institute, has written elsewhere on this issue:[17]

> True openness is paradoxically only possible on the basis of firm convictions.

I could concur with this view, although I am less ready to accept her opinion that

> the more a person is sustained by a certainty in convictions, the more he or she is capable of seeing truth wherever he or she looks.

My reservations over this are illustrated by a current piece of British news concerning the Lord Chancellor, an elder of the strictly Calvinistic Free Presbyterian Church of Scotland, who is being disciplined by his church for attending the funeral of a close friend in a Roman Catholic church. The Free Presbyterians are definitely not short of a certainty in convictions, the core of which is the Calvinistic doctrine of the predestination of the elect, but no way does it appear that such certainty will make them capable of seeing any truth in the Roman Catholic for their very certainty depicts the Pope as Anti-Christ. This little anecdote does, I suggest, provide a very sharp example of a possible implication of having a commitment. However, as Brenda Watson again asserts:[18]

> The opposite of firm commitment is not no commitment but a confusion of weakly-held or conditioned commitments, mostly unarticulated and imprecise.

## The dilemmas facing church schools

The dilemmas for those involved with county schools are real enough. For church schools with their explicit religious foundation, in England and Wales at any rate committed to honouring a trust deed, the dilemmas can be more acute and for the rest of this paper I should like to concentrate on them.

In England and Wales there are at least three broad categories of opinion about the place of religious education in particular and on the school ethos in general. What I shall for convenience call the 'liberal' view would apply the approach in the quotation given earlier from the Durham Report to church schools in virtually the same way as to county schools. The 'conservative' stance would advocate the 'nurture' or 'religious instruction' approach to church schools. Another group would not think it has to be 'either/or,' but that the overall spirit and approach in the quotation could apply, with church schools having something 'extra.' By this I mean that many church schools are happy to follow the agreed syllabus for religious education constructed mainly for county schools but also supplement such an approach with explicit confessional material.

The difficulty with much that I have written so far is that I could have given the impression that religious education can consistently be considered separately from the whole school, but this is far from what I would wish to imply.

A recent government consultative document on the idea of a national curriculum spoke about 'religious education' and 'the secular curriculum,' but after receiving responses from the churches, amongst others, the resulting bill has modified such a position and refers to the spiritual area of experience in a way that seems to accept that there are cross-curricular relationships. This is so in county schools as well as in church schools, but in church schools particularly the claim is made that the whole offering of the school should in subtle and overt ways be a testimony to the religious education of the school, to the values of its foundation, to the foundation's commitments.

Of course when answering the question concerning what church schools do, spokespersons are liable often to confuse descriptive statements with prescriptive statements. Moreover, in the context of what is perceived as an increasingly secular and/or multi-faith environment, Christians and Christian institutions will as ever react in a variety of ways. Church of England schools have historically generally come to serve two roles: a 'general' or service to the community role, and a 'domestic' or nurture in the faith role. There has always been some tension in trying to live with or reconcile the two (the conservative headteacher I quote earlier describes it as unbiblically trying to serve two masters!) and this has become more so when the pupil population consists of few even nominal, let alone practising, Anglicans or even Christians.

Leslie Francis has recently argued that Church of England schools might have to reduce their 'service to the community' function and become increasingly schools for Christians with a definite Christian nurture orientation.[19]

There are other Church of England schools, particularly those of a conservative evangelical background, that welcome children of other faiths but are not willing to make any concessions to other faiths in their religious education or worship even when there is not a single Christian child in the school. Other Church of England schools take a very different approach, for example, the church school in the Earls Court district of London featured in a *Times Educational Supplement* article.[20] It was this school that I had in mind at the beginning of my article. The *Times Educational Supplement* explains that out of 160 children only 38 speak English as a first language and there are no fewer than 24 mother tongues and concludes with the observation that the headteacher

> has found that religious instruction is less of a worry to parents than food. And that is easily solved. If they don't want pork, it will not be forced down their throats. That, too, is the essence of the approach to religion. The ethos of Christianity pervades the school, but its dogma is notably absent.

By contrast a later article in the *Times Educational Supplement* was devoted to an independent school for which 'committed parents' in a fairly wide area 'stump up £1000 a year' to send their children there, parents for whom the Earls Court would be far too diluted. They prefer the PACE regimen (Packet of Accelerated Christian Education); for them 'the biblical account of the Creation is a literal story, and Darwinism a mischievous theory. British history dates from the Flood ...'[21] Such people would have little time for the scenario I outlined in an essay I recently wrote:[22]

> I can best describe my vision of a church school fulfilling a service to the community role by means of an anecdote. A few years ago I visited a Church of England aided middle school serving a mainly Muslim population, a school going through the early stages of wondering just what it, as a Christian foundation, was doing in such a situation. The headmaster invited me to meet one of his former pupils, a girl who had gone on to high school where she had acquired several 'O' levels but whose conservative Muslim parents had decided that she was to go no further with her education but wait until they arranged her marriage. In the meantime the girl returned to her old Church of England school where she acted as a sort of unofficial liaison officer between the school and Muslim parents. From the meeting I gained some idea of the internal struggle that some Muslim girls experience: part of them feeling they could and should take their education further, the other part of them not wanting to be disloyal to their parents. My other reflection was based on the thought that I would like that girl and other children of non-Christian faiths to think back on their Church of England school as a place where they received a good education in a place provided by and largely staffed by Christians who appeared to have no other motive than to serve the children in their charge, certainly with no proselytising motive and no denigrating of the children's faith. Or is this vision too sentimental?

## A future for church schools?

Looking ahead to the twenty-first century the question will, I think, be increasingly posed whether church schools, at least within the state system, are an anachronism. In the essay quoted above I have tried to present one general model for Church of England schools where the challenge of preparing the children to cope with and as far as possible to affirm and rejoice in difference is accepted in a spirit of sincere Christian altruistic service, where, as the *Times Educational Supplement* article concludes 'the ethos of Christianity pervades the school, but its dogma is notably absent.' This will not be the only model for a church school and not all Christians would be happy to work with it, but I believe it is a sustainable one in areas where Christian pupils are in the minority. Even those church schools serving a more Christian, monocultural area will increasingly have to face up to preparing their children for the fact of difference in the wider society. As I wrote in my recent essay:[23]

> No category of school will gain unanimous support from all Christians, secularists, members of other faiths, but it is a tenable vision to see Church of England schools as naving the potential with others to hold together people of many of the philosophical and faith sections into which society forms itself. A church school can, although it involves a tension, both promote a liberal education (liberal in the sense that it practises critical openness and abjures indoctrination) and to that extent satisfy many of the humanist disposition, and at the same time affirm the faiths of those who eschew a secular humanist stance. Of course there will be some atheists/agnostics for whom the religious element will be too strong and who will only be satisfied by a completely secular foundation. There will also be people for whom the religious element will be too watered down. So be it, but there are grounds for believing that many parents see a place for a school that strives to retain a place for worship and religious education other than in a dispassionate phenomenological way, that has one of its main aims to affirm the children's respective faiths but also to help them see beyond their own faith, that in its practice witnesses to the view that 'in a society which generally preaches a secular materialistic ethic particularly through the media and commercial activity, some form of positive discrimination in favour of the religious dimension of life is required in curricular provision in schools.'

I personally believe that in the main within all our respective churches the conservative and liberal elements need each other and can and should complement each other (so long as no one element gets out of hand and so long as they are able and willing to listen to each other). There will properly continue to be church schools that will lean very heavily towards the commitment side of the tension we have been exploring and perceive and express their role in a conservative way. However, I see little hope for or justification for having an educational system that makes provision for church schools if none of those schools show they can be capable of experimental, innovatory and pioneering work in the ever-shrinking world of the 'global village.' Difference is becoming increasingly obvious and challenging and, not least in the context of religion, a theology of other faiths is becoming an increasingly pressing concern, that is to say, a theological rationale for the various stances a person committed to one particular faith can adopt vis-a-vis other faiths, and for the possibilities (or otherwise) for reconciling the different truth claims made by the respective religions. There is the theological and also the practical imperative to engage in such activity. The challenge has been highlighted in a recent WCC publication:[24]

> The question of how to live as religiously committed people in a multi-religious society is of urgent importance in many parts of the world today. It was this question that was discussed from various perspectives in the multi-lateral dialogue on 'Religious Identity in a Multi-Religious society' convened in New Delhi in November 1987. On one side the wide emergence of secularism moves some people away from religious identity of any sort. On the other side, the wide emergence of fundamentalism, communalism, and group chauvinism moves others toward an extreme identification with their own religious tradition. Between the secularist absence of commitment and the communalist excess of commitment, where lies the future of a 'multi-religious society'?

The resolution of such dilemmas, as I have tried to indicate, has to be faced by schools as well as in the wider society, and particularly by church schools. I was heartened to read in the same publication an echo of my own attempt to advocate an approach of 'altruistic service.' In an article tellingly headed 'Dialogue: witness or treason,' the writer argues in the following way:[25]

> Mission, I believe, is sharing God's love, with individuals, with communities, with institutions ... My concept of mission embraces, too, 'diakonia' or 'service' — including the many service activities associated with missionary endeavour, hospitals and schools, development and aid programs. All these are ways of sharing God's love but to be genuine such service must be offered with no strings attached.

As Professor Hoedemaker has recently written, whatever mission implies[26]

> it will never eliminate the question 'who do you say that I am?'; it will never diminish the necessity to name the name of Jesus Christ and to explicate it in contemporary contexts. To be sure, when this is done too soon, too defensively, too much in isolation of what actually goes on in human beings, it may lead to illegitimate alienation, and to a distortion of the missionary nature of the Church.

## Conclusion

Commitment and neutrality? Or commitment and openness? Or commitment and witness? In other words, we are in the familiar territory of means and ends, of distinguishing between first-order and secondary 'commitments.' Far too many people still assert in their actions not only 'My commitments are the only true ones' but also 'The ways I honour them are the only ways.' The Bishop of London perceived this during the debate in the House of Lords on the Education Reform Bill, when a group of parliamentarians succeeded (albeit in a form modified by the bishop) to have Christianity on the face of the Bill, now the Education Reform Act. At one stage in the debate, late at night, the bishop felt moved to exclaim:[27]

> I really feel rather desperate at the moment. What I am being told frankly is that I am barely a Christian because I will not support one particular way of going about this. . . . I give not an inch to anybody in my concern that our children should be given a truly Christian upbringing in every way: but I do not believe that I must be forced into a position where I have to say: 'This is the only way, and if we do not go down this way then we are letting the side down.' It seemes to me that this is what is being said.

The pressure specifically to mention Christianity in the Act in the context of religious education and worship was an example of what some people saw as expressing their commitment. A whole article could be written on the illustrations of the dilemmas relating to commitment and neutrality provided by the debates on the Bill's progress through Parliament.

**Notes**
1. A James and R Jeffcoate, *The School in the Multicultural Society*, New York, Harper and Row, 1981.
2. *Education for All*, London, HMSO, 1985.
3. *Ibid.*, p. xi.
4. *Ibid.*, p. 5.
5. *Ibid.*, p. 6.
6. Ranjit Arora and Carlton Duncan (eds), *Multicultural Education Towards Good Practice*, London, Routledge and Kegan Paul, 1986, p. 1.
7. *The Times Educational Supplement*, 9 October, 1987.
8. Ray Honeyford, *Integration or Disintegration*, Oxford, The Claridge Press, 1988.
9. J Bowden, *Jesus: the unanswered questions*, London, SCM, 1988, p. 165.
10. *Ibid.*, p. 175.
11. Bernadette O'Keeffe (ed.), *Schools for Tomorrow*, Barcombe, The Falmer Press, 1988, p. 147.
12. See note 2 above.
13. *The Fourth R: the report of the commission on religious studies*, London, National Society and SPCK, 1970, p. 471.
14. See note 2 above, p. 518.
15. As epitomised by the *Humanities Project: an introduction*, London, Schools Council, 1970. Lawrence Stenhouse was the Project Director.
16. *Critical Openness*, The Farmington Institute for Christian Studies, 1987, p. 5.
17. Brenda Watson, *Education and Belief*, Oxford, Blackwell, 1987, p. 48.

18. *Ibid.*
19. Leslie J Francis, *Church and School: a future for Christian Education*, Abingdon, Culham College Institute, 1985.
20. See note 7 above.
21. *Times Educational Supplement*, 19 February, 1988.
22. *Op. cit.*, Bernadette O'Keeffe (ed.).
23. *Op. cit.*, Bernadette O'Keeffe (ed.), page 157, quoting from *A Future in Partnership*, London, The National Society, 1984, page 81.
24. *Current Dialogue*, WCC, June 1988, article by Diana Eck, page 3.
25. *Ibid.*, article by Clinton Bennet, page 34.
26. *The Ecumenical Review*, vol 41, no 1, January 1989, article by L A Hoedemaker, page 49.
27. *Hansard*, vol 4076, no 126, column 1350.

# 4. Spiritual perspectives

In view of their religious foundation, church schools have a particular responsibility to think through and to articulate their approach to religious education, school worship and spirituality.

In the first article in this section, the Revd Dr Derek H Webster explores the concepts of 'spirituality' and 'spiritual' in education. He distinguishes between two ways of understanding the spiritual dimension within current usage. The first has a wide reference and concerns the quality of human experience, speaking of its fullness and its totality. The second sets the word 'spiritual' within the boundaries of one of the religions.

Derek Webster is an Anglican priest. He lectures in religious education in the Department of Educational Studies at the University of Hull. This article was first published in *Westminster Studies in Education* in 1987.

In the second article, the Revd David G Attfield illustrates one way in which the eucharist is being presented to children in a Church of England voluntary aided primary school. He provides a picture of the school eucharist and describes the part children play in it. Then he discusses the educational justification for this practice and the limitations on what can be sensibly attempted at the primary stage.

David Attfield is an Anglican parish priest working in a major conurbation. He is currently rector of All Saints, Newton Heath, Manchester. His previous experience includes lecturing at an Anglican College of Education. This paper was first published in *British Journal of Religious Education* in 1990.

# 4.1 Being aflame: spirituality in county and church schools

*Derek H Webster*

## Introduction

Early in his academic career, invited to lecture at a German university, Martin Buber was offered hospitality by a distinguished elderly scholar.[1] Whilst in this house, proofs arrived of the preface of a book on which he had been working. He rose very early one morning to correct them but, on going into the study, found the old man already at his desk. He asked Buber to read the preface to him, which he was happy to do for it amounted to a statement of faith. As he finished he saw that his host was concerned, even astonished, at what he was saying. The old scholar asked how he could bring himself to say 'God' time after time. No word was so abused or desecrated as this one: no word had features which were so effaced by injustice and bloodshed. He accused Buber of taking what was beyond all grasp or understanding and degrading it into human conceptualisation. Buber replied that just because this word had been so soiled and bore the weight of the deaths of so many, because it lay in the dust mutilated by the lives of generations, he could not and must not give it up. There was no other word.

For the last decade the notion of the spiritual has been in vogue in religious education. Like the word 'God,' 'spiritual' carries with it such extensive baggage, such a weight of historical and theological meaning that it may seem unsuitable.[2] Yet, like the word 'God,' there is no other that can be used. To abandon it is to deprive educational discourse of a word which conveys rich layers of understanding. If it disappeared, many teachers would be condemned to starve in the cramped cells of positivist theoreticians. Yet the re-emergence of the word should not serve either to introduce again the ancient controversies surrounding the ideas of the spirit and the flesh, the natural and the supernatural or to re-affirm a piety which is otherworldly and an understanding which stems from secret gnosis.[3] Contemporary educationalists are not the architects of these problems and it would be pitiable if they condemned teachers to tenant them.

## Spirituality and county schools

Within current usage, two ways of understanding the spiritual dimension offer helpful means to those working in schools. The first has a wide reference and is exemplified in Ursula King's view that 'rightly understood, all education is a spiritual activity.'[4] Here 'spiritual' concerns the quality of human experience, speaking of its fullness and its totality. Finding human persons mysterious and unexplained, it encourages a recognition of their depth. It seeks to locate that which most profoundly animates men and women and which they enshrine in their beliefs and behaviour. Her Majesty's Inspectorate puts it like this:[5]

> The spiritual area is concerned with the awareness a person has of those elements in existence and experience which may be defined in terms of inner feelings and beliefs; they affect the way people see themselves and throw light for them on the purposes and meaning of life itself. Often these feelings and beliefs lead people to claim to know God and to glimpse the transcendent: sometimes they represent that striving and longing for perfection which characterises human beings but always they are concerned with matters at the heart and root of existence.

Such a view, sympathetic to the significance of this area in human endeavour and hope, understanding of its depth and personal meaning, has found some favour in the educational literature. Certainly 'official' documents have emphasised the significance of the spiritual in a balanced and contemporary education.[6]

Although all education may be suffused by the spiritual, its dynamic is especially evident in four areas. These concern the reflections teachers have on themselves, their understanding of the teaching relationship, the methodologies they evolve and their perception of their children.

In the first of these, it can be that the self-reflection of teachers helps them pose to themselves R S Thomas' question:[7]

> And homo sapiens, that cracked mirror, mending himself again and again like a pool?

Despite their expertise, their absorption in a school's activities and their concern for the serious issues besetting their profession, teachers may not push into forgetfulness David Jones' words that 'existence is altogether in parenthesis.'[8] For they, too, are driven to quest for the meaning of their lives in an unending labyrinth. They have their own journey to hell and ascent to the seventh heaven. They share with joy and pain the rites of passage of their society and are ringed by the delights and disasters of their sexuality. They have to stand at that abyss which lies at the fiftieth gate and choose between emptiness or faith.[9] They too, as Iris Murdoch puts it, need to perceive that the point is that 'one will never get to the end of it, never, never, never.'[10]

With respect to the second area, it is helpful to affirm that the axis of education is in the relationship forged between teachers and their young people. Only this truly educates. The unending cavalcade of fresh curricular ideas, the imaginative nature of contemporary educational thinking and the sheer inventiveness behind recent technological advances need not obscure this. Teachers educate not as they transmit information, leaning down to the uninitiated with their wisdom, but as they stand with their pupils, one human being before another in creative tension. The persons of teachers more than their knowledge, their being present more than their objectives and organisation, educate – for these confer dignity upon and confirm the value of students. Here the young and the older stand together, neither having unlearned what it is to begin afresh. Thus behind all education stands a meeting of persons, which meeting raises the mystery of both. To forget this is to forfeit awe and to disregard the strangeness of the whole educational venture. The Hasidic tradition puts this shard of truth within the parable of Rabbi Nahum. At the close of the Sabbath, his disciples examined their souls and were overwhelmed by the holiness of God. In their humility they felt that they were without hope. The devotion that they showed to their teacher seemed to them to be their only merit. Therefore they set out for his house straightaway so that he could uplift them. Rabbi Nahum, meanwhile, examining his soul felt that he had sinned greatly. In his holy fear he felt that his only hope lay in the comfort his disciples, men who were good and earnest in prayer, might offer him. So he opened his door to go to them. He saw them coming to him – and at that instant two separate arcs fused into a single ring.[11] Thus the teaching relationship can be a means of hallowing being – in however simple a manner; it can be a way of penetrating existence – in however ordinary a fashion.

Concerning the third area, teachers seem to work within the spiritual dimension when their methods of teaching encourage within their young people an openness to those parts of knowledge which question them as persons, which astonish and prompt a pondering of being. Such methods bring sparks to dry thoughts, leading pupils to wonder at the thousand contingencies of life and fostering a response to what is ultimate for them. They loose intuition and imagination and enable a correlation to be made between those symbols, visions and icons – both old and new – and what is unutterably mysterious. Especially do they offer an approach to those parts of life which lie in bewildering shadows, where loss, hurt and death are to be found.

These methods are seen in approaches to teaching which refocus for children their reality that it may be perceived at greater depth; which provoke radical amazement at the commonplace things of the environment; and which press the questions which are at the heart of reasoning and explanation.

They occur in classroom practices which revere life-forms, refusing to treat them as trivial or needlessly expendable; which encourage a rich symbolic language to express what is beyond present experience; and which introduce what is ineffable, what is sublime and what holds glory, into the curriculum. Behind such methods stand teachers who can marvel in living, who continue to engage in reflective reasoning and whose lives are wonder journeys, parts of which are made with their young people. It can be for both 'an adventure of the heart that is always become an adventure of the mind.'[12]

In the fourth area, there is a movement of ideas beyond too limiting categories. The perceptions teachers have of their young people cannot be fully systematised within the co-ordinates of any of the human sciences. The abstract structures through which these sciences formalise the question of human beings, dissolve the particularity of children and the uniqueness of their specific natures. The personal is diminished to the sub-personal: elementary biological organisms or inadequate material artefacts are pressed as analogies for persons. Teachers can see that, beyond the theories of the academics, their pupils need to respond to the dynamics of who they are. Here the teachers are more radical than the academics, for in their work they have grasped that education is in the last analysis an initiation into what is finally incomprehensible. For theoreticians too easily objectify children in thought forms: teachers set them within personal relationships. Theoreticians tend to intellectualise the human to locate its universal elements: teachers prefer to meet the human in its concrete individuality. Theoreticians too often present persons as passive objects: teachers usually engage with them as seeking subjects. Above all, the one tries to explain existence in the timeless absence of personal experience, while the other celebrates the paradox of the human in the immediacy of a present knowing. Where young people can say:[13]

> ... my soul lay out of sight,
> Untun'd, unstrung:
> ... Like a nipt blossome ...

then teachers have failed and the academics have won.

Within this first and broad usage of the word 'spiritual,' there is a place for a religious education which becomes neither traditional nurture nor partisan catechetics, which is not distinctive of any of the great world faiths and which does not presume on the integrity of those without a religious commitment. This use has appeared in a wide range of agreed syllabuses during the last decade. Such syllabuses hope that the religious education offered by schools will prompt young people to explore the 'spiritual dimension of life'[14] so that they can begin to perceive a fragment of 'what is always and finally mysterious.'[15] This may occur as they achieve an 'imaginative transcendence'[16] and approach with sensitivity 'other people's experiences and attitudes.'[17] Many handbooks on the syllabuses, as well as school texts, suggest the means of translating this into classroom practice. It has, however, to be frankly admitted that few teachers of religious education seem to feel that they succeed in provoking spiritual insight or penetrating to the point where their pupils are helped to 'the experience of what it is like to have a religious commitment.'[18] There is a painful vulnerability in attempting to create out of the very things of which one is oneself made. Nevertheless the challenge needs to be accepted. There is a 'beyond' phenomenology in religious education. It can move to an area where there is a concentration 'on alerting young people to the possibility of a cosmological awareness which is one of transcendent order and value.'[19]

## Spirituality and church schools

The second way of understanding the word 'spiritual' in the present educational context is to set it within the boundaries of one of the religions. Each is an argosy whose richness of experience can contribute to the understanding of all. Within Christianity Karl Rahner finds that 'the personal experience of God ... is the very heart of all spirituality.'[20] This experience does not involve choking the barns of consciousness with torrents of abstract theologising or affirming a zealous allegiance to a particular ecclesiastical establishment. It implies setting aside 'tangible assurances' and moving 'towards the inconceivable where there are no longer paths.'[21] Here spirituality is stamped by the decision of faith. For Christians there would be broad agreement that their spirituality sprang from a faith in that experience of the triune God given in the Bible and history, in the contemporary church and world as well as in their own lives. Where they are prepared to accept a particular relationship with the state they are enabled to foster this spirituality as they educate children in their schools. These church schools however, besides offering opportunities for faith development, give rise to difficult problems, the most pressing of which are writ large in the schools of the Anglicans.

It is curious that that understanding of Christian spirituality widely accepted among Anglicans is itself a model which sharply questions the theories and practices of their own schools. It is an understanding which bids Anglicans reflect further on the role of their schools in the context of contemporary education and which summons them to face strange and rather bewildering problems.

Thus at the centre of Christian spirituality lies that insight into God which is revealed by Jesus Christ and which is interpreted by the Holy Spirit. The truths which emerge from this insight are ultimate and give to Anglicans a particular understanding of reality which cannot be treated as private and about which it is impossible to be neutral. Their implication so far as Anglican schools are concerned is that these exist in the first place to maintain and foster the practices and beliefs of the Christian community. There is no other justification as fundamental as this for the continuance of church schools, though this does not prevent them from fulfilling other important roles. Traditionally Anglican schools contribute to the general educational well-being of the nation. This broader service has grown from roots which are well set in English history and which are particularly evident in the nineteenth century. The National Society's Green Paper *A Future in Partnership* suggests that church schools have then 'undifferentiated twin aims' of service to the church and service to the community.[22] Yet such a view is not as helpful as it was intended to be. Without a priority given to Christian nurture and the maintenance of Christian witness, without a strong faith base, there is no distinctive contribution at the broader level. The danger in setting these two too closely together is that a religious aim will be confused with a social one and that a secondary historical consequence will be confounded with a primary theological principle.

This spirituality which highlights the commitment of believers to a particular pattern of truth has important practical effects in the admission policies of church schools. A priority for the growth of the faith community does not imply a rejection of those outside it. The Christian is committed to promoting love within the family of God wherever it is to be found, in whatever religious tradition, social class or racial background it is situated. So governors will respond to the particular contexts in which their schools are placed with differing solutions. That schools strengthen the Christian community does not mean that they need be uniform in the balance of their intakes. Those placed within a thriving Christian tradition and situation will need to ensure that a proportion of places is available for children outside that tradition. The temptation to exclusivism is attractive but to yield to it is to diminish the possibility of religious and cultural diversity. Those schools placed in areas where the Christian presence is weaker and where there is a large non-Christian intake have a special opportunity and a particular task. Their opportunity is to commence a search for those means whereby Christianity may move in understanding and caring towards those of other faiths and none. They have the task of discerning those missionary strategies which are appropriate for Christian schools in a pluralist society. Such work is founded on the active interest of the local Christian community in a school. It assumes that selection procedures for the appointment of staff take seriously the need for theologically literate teachers in church schools. It presupposes that governors are sympathetic to the role of the church in education, that they receive relevant training and that a proportion of those who serve in a secondary school also serve in linked primary schools. Above all it is based on a diocesan strategy which has the confidence of wider Christian and educational circles.

Christian spirituality is rooted in a profound faith conviction which, as it is interpreted within the framework of history, has changing consequences. The faith which is professed is one which is open, which moves out to others and which accepts that its statements and understanding are provisional.[23] This has its practical effects. They occur especially in the schools' responses to a multicultural curriculum and to world faiths in both worship and religious education. The first of these necessitates a re-thinking of the aims and objectives of education and an identification of those means by which racism and sexual bias may be combatted in schooling. It cannot be acceptable that church primary and secondary schools 'lag behind county schools in the multicultural area;'[24] that their worship is an observance for Christian children and an observation for non-Christian;[25] and that their curricular content in religious education shows no change in response to the multicultural situation.[26] The practices of schools will only be as good as the theology informing them. What is happening in many schools suggests that a deeper consideration of the educational implications of a contemporary understanding of justice and community, of equality and peace as well as the doctrines of creation, election and incarnation, could be helpful.

The second of these, the response of church schools to world faiths, rests on the interim results of that theological enquiry which Christianity makes as it moves from its own isolationism to an acceptance of the truths and realities of other religions. The point from which this enquiry is undertaken is crucial: it can only be a properly ecumenical one. Genuinely Christian spirituality echoes Edmund Campion's prayer, 'Set us in accord before the day of payment, to the end that we may at last be friends in heaven.'[27] The immediate and most practical implication of this is an integration of the schools of the various Christian groupings. In particular there need to be more urgent and enthusiastic discussions between Anglicans and Roman Catholics concerning the means of achieving integration. Present efforts to work together offer valuable frameworks which have to be more widely known. Neither side has to surrender its distinctive understandings in a co-operation which is mutually strengthening and enriching. Both sides must, however, seize the initiatives if their schools are not to be increasingly marginalised in the national educational venture and if Christian conversation with other faiths is not to limp badly. Hans Küng puts it clearly:[28]

Ecumenism *ad intra*, concentrated on the Christian world, and ecumenism *ad extra*, oriented towards the whole inhabited earth, are interdependent.

There are good social as well as political reasons for church schools becoming part of the meeting of Christianity with world faiths. For Christians there are also three important theological reasons. First, God's dialogue with humanity in the incarnation is continued in the dialogue of Christians with believers from other traditions. Church schools offer a natural base for this activity. Secondly, the household of faith is pressed through its love of Christ towards a fellowship with those who are strangers. Church schools provide the occasions for this outreach. Finally the promise that the Holy Spirit will lead to all truth commends that living converse of peoples seeking a deepening of their faiths. Biblical truth is relational, so presence in dialogue is an important instrument of quest. The context within which contemporary church schools function already prompts and encourages this exploration and searching.[29]

Dialogue can actually begin as those from several traditions come to know each other, share part of their living together and witness to the practice of their faith. They may even engage in communal activities. Certainly the preliminary steps of friendly recognition, interest and mutual trust are entirely congruent with the purposes of church schools.

Dialogue occurs at several levels with insights emerging from each which are fruitful for all.[30] Those involved in Christian education have a particular concern for three insights which are deeply rooted in Christian spirituality. They relate to that position which takes seriously the fact of world religions and interprets them with a sympathy which recognises their value; that approach which is honest enough to realise that in dialogue beliefs may change; and that awareness which grasps that the original faith commitment can be deepened in dialogue.

The first of these emphasises the importance of the inclusive stance in the theology of religions. It is a position which acknowledges an authentic presence of God in non-Christian faiths, and which draws those who hold it to locate the Christ who is hidden but latent in the various religions.[31] Such a view takes seriously the idea of a history of revelation and the doctrine of God's universal salvific will. It rejects that exclusivism which regards religions other than Christianity as distorted, in error or inadequate. And it is cautious about that pluralism which presents the different religions as vehicles which embody the same divine life, though each is rooted in its own singular history and conditioned by a particular culture. The life of a church school in its curriculum, relationships, organisation and neighbourhood activities can demonstrate the practical implications of inclusivism. A good motto for its life is the vision in St Matthew chapter 8, verse 4:

And I say unto you, that many shall come from the east and west, and shall sit down with Abraham, and Isaac, and Jacob, in the kingdom of heaven.

The second insight stresses the honesty with which dialogue needs to be undertaken. There are profound implications here, for the question of the truth claims of religions cannot be evaded nor the possibility of change in the participants of dialogue be ignored. Initially, consequences can be startling as when, for example, John Hick questions the extent to which the Christian doctrines of the trinity and the incarnation are 'cultural packaging' which can be discarded by the followers of Jesus.[32] Putting aside traditional intellectual constructions which are sanctified through history and perhaps personal experience, is painful. Yet if participants are not willing for their faith to be called into question then they are only playing, and they are not properly available to others. Perhaps the prime prerequisite for dialogue is 'the freedom to be committed and open.'[33] The church schools are creative workshops where ideas can be tested, where critical judgment is prized and where freedom to experiment is encouraged. At all levels and to all its members, parents, staff, governors and children, it can be an ecumenical nursery, persuasive in its insistence on sensitivity to the faiths of all.[34]

The third insight recognises that to engage in dialogue is to become involved in the on-going process of deepening one's faith. At key points understandings may change. For example, the covenant of God with Israel, so often seen as the separation of a holy people, may be regarded as a vocation of that people to bring blessing to all nations. The election of Israel, implying that she is the centre of God's concern and activity, may also point to the fact that she holds her experience in trust for the whole world. Johannine Logos theology, whilst affirming the manifestation of the Logos in Palestine in the first half century of the common era, also witnesses to other appearances at other times.[35] It is the common experience of those in dialogue that the stories of different faiths can be a ready means to deepen understanding in one's own faith. The pattern of religious education and worship in church schools, as well as a wider reading, friendly contact and serious study among those associated with them, all provide opportunities to listen and reflect on such stories.[36]

## Conclusion

The diversity of church and county schools is very rich and the allegiances of those connected with them are manifold. So often do the two understandings of spirituality sketched here overlap — teachers from many religious backgrounds teach in county schools, pupils from no religious backgrounds abound in church schools — that the question of a common source can be raised. A generation ago Paul Tillich found it answered in the notion of ultimate concern:[37]

> In the depth of every living religion there is a point at which the religion itself loses its particularity, elevating it to spiritual freedom

and with it to a vision of the spiritual presence in other expressions of the ultimate meaning of man's existence.

Contemporary Christians may wonder if love also offers that point of non-particularity. The old insight that it is the essence of love to communicate itself is demonstrated sometimes in words, often in deeds and frequently in artefacts. Perhaps too it is a ground from which that spirituality springs which embraces those of many faiths and none in dialogue. Perhaps it is also the source which sets adancing with its fire what is shaped in schools by intellect and judgment, that it may become imaginative learning and creative searching.

Kazantzakis' myth of St Francis reminds those in education of the cruciality of the spiritual dimension in their work. Speaking to a novice who desired a book to guide him to the truth, Francis told him of his Easter experience. It was his practice to gather with the faithful each Easter around the tomb of Christ to watch the resurrection. In the midst of the weeping each year the tombstone crumbled and Christ sprang from the earth to heaven. There was one year however, when a distinguished theologian from the University of Bologna guided their thoughts. For hours he analysed and elucidated the resurrection:[38]

> He explained and explained until our heads began to swim: and that year the tombstone did not crumble, and, I swear to you, no one saw the resurrection.

Such is the difference that being aflame may make.

**Notes**

1. M Buber, *Eclipse of God*, London, Gollancz, 1953, pp. 16–18.
2. K Rahner (ed.), *Encyclopedia of Theology*, London, Burns and Oates, 1975, pp. 1623–1641.
3. A Richardson and J Bowden (eds), *A New Dictionary of Christian Theology*, London, SCM Press, 1983, p. 549.
4. U King, 'Religious education: transcendence and liberation,' *Celebration and Challenge*, London, CEM, 1984, p. 16
5. H.M. Inspectorate, *Supplementary Note: what the spiritual area is concerned with*, London, DES, 1978.
6. H.M. Inspectorate, *Curriculum 11–16*, London, DES, 1977, p. 6; H.M.I. Series, *A View of the Curriculum*, London, 1980, p. 3; *The School Curriculum*, London, DES (Welsh Office), 1981, p. 8.
7. R S Thomas, 'Pardon' in *Experimenting With An Amen*, Basingstoke, Macmillan, 1986, p. 29.
8. D Jones, *In Parenthesis*, London, Faber, 1982, p. xv.
9. Rabbi Nachmax, *Outpouring of the Soul*, New York, The Breslov Research Institute, 1980, p. 17.
10. I Murdoch, *Henry and Cato*, New York, Viking Press, 1977, p. 270.
11. M Buber, *Tales of the Hasidim: the early masters*, New York, Schocken, 1961, p. 76.
12. J S Dunne, *The Reasons of the Heart*, London, SCM Press, 1978, p. 152.
13. Deniall, *The Poems of George Herbert*, London, Oxford University Press, 1961, p. 71.
14. *The Durham County Agreed Syllabus of Religious Education*, 1982, p. 7.
15. *Humberside Agreed Syllabus of Religious Education*, 1981, p. 5.

16. *Religious Education in Secondary Schools* (Schools Council Working Paper 36), London, Evans/Methuen Educational, 1971, p. 22.
17. *Avon Agreed Syllabus of Religious Education*, 1976 p. 6.
18. *A Framework for Religious Education in Cambridgeshire*, 1982, p. 3.
19. P Holley, *Religious Education and Religious Understanding*, London, Routledge and Kegan Paul, 1978, p. 56.
20. K Rahner, *Theological Investigations*, vol. 20, London, Darton Longman and Todd, 1981, p. 150.
21. K Rahner, *Ignatius Loyola*, London, Collins, 1979, p. 14.
22. *A Future in Partnership*, London, The National Society, 1984, p. 97.
23. See, for example, *Christian Believing* (a report by the Doctrine Commission of the Church of England), London, SPCK, 1976; *The Nature of Christian Belief* (a statement and exposition by the House of Bishops of the General Synod of the Church of England), London, Church House, 1986; *We Believe in God* (a report by the Doctrine Commission of the Church of England), London, Church House, 1987.
24. B O'Keeffe, *Faith, Culture and the Dual System*, Lewes, Falmer Press, 1986, p. 148.
25. *Ibid.*, p. 85.
26. *Ibid.*, p. 107.
27. Quoted in M Santer (ed.), *Their Lord and Ours*, London, SPCK, p. 160.
28. H Küng, *Christianity and the World Religions*, London, Collins, 1987, p. 443.
29. S J Samartha, *Courage for Dialogue*, Geneva World Council of Churches, 1981, p. 11.
30. G D'Costa, *Theology and Religious Pluralism*, Oxford, Blackwell, 1986, p. 118.
31. See especially: K Rahner, *Theological Investigations*, vol. 18, 1984, chapter 17, London, Darton, Longman and Todd; *Ibid.*, vol. 17, 1981 chapter 5.
32. J Hick, *God has Many Names*, Basingstoke, Macmillan, 1980, p. 87.
33. S J Samartha, *op. cit.*, p. 43.
34. *A Future in Partnership*, London, The National Society, 1984, p. 71.
35. *Towards a Theology for Inter-Faith Dialogue*, London, Church House, 1986, chapter 6.
36. W J Bausch, *Storytelling: imagination and faith*, Connecticut, Twenty-Third Publications, 1985.
37. P Tillich, *Christianity and the Encounter of World Religions*, Columbia, Columbia University Press, 1963, p. 95.
38. N Kazantzakis, *Saint Francis*, New York, Simon and Schuster, 1962, p. 231, quoted in J Shea, *Stories of God*, Chicago, Thomas More Press, 1978, p. 69.

# 4.2 Presenting the eucharist in a primary school
*David G Attfield*

## Introduction

I write as rector of an inner-city Anglican parish in Manchester. In the parish is a Church of England voluntary aided school (though, as I shall later contend, what is done in it could in principle properly be attempted in a county school). The practice to be described is what I inherited from my predecessor but I have subsequently developed it in new directions. Responsibility for what is done, as for this article, rests with the incumbent alone, but any credit is to be shared with assistant clergy, governors, headteacher and staff, parents, pupils and congregation, all of whom show a keen interest in what we attempt.

## The school eucharist

We present the eucharist to the whole of our primary school, from the nursery up, at a monthly celebration of holy communion at the school assembly. Every Friday morning an assembly for the whole school is held. Parents are invited to attend and have tea and toast afterwards. Each week one class takes the assembly and is responsible for sharing some aspect of its work with the rest of the school community. Whatever is important, interesting and exciting is offered to God as material for worship. On the last Friday of every month, into this setting at assembly is inserted a eucharist.

The rite is necessarily abbreviated, the whole assembly taking no more than half an hour. The one lesson is read by a child; children read the intercessions, either composed by them or from a suitable source. The celebrant says a few words to point up the theme for the occasion and its connection with eucharistic worship. Sometimes a story is acted out and drama replaces or supplements the gospel. A children's music group accompanies carefully chosen children's hymns or plays a piece for all to listen to. The liturgy used is a modified form of 'the eucharistic prayer for use with the sick' from the *Alternative Service Book 1980*. Communicants are some of the teachers, parents and governors present, who are confirmed and committed Anglicans. (As in the Church of England generally nowadays, members in good standing of other Christian communions, if present, would be welcome to communicate.) The remainder of the school community, teachers, governors, parents and pupils, observe the eucharist, as they do any act of worship at assembly, which they do not or cannot take part in.

## In church

The second aspect of our way of presenting the eucharist to the pupils in our primary school is by inviting children to attend a Wednesday morning said celebration of holy communion in church. The service follows the Anglican *Alternative Service Book* Rite A form of holy communion. There is a normal, adult congregation with a priest presiding at the altar.

Each term, two fourth year Juniors attend every Wednesday. They read the set Old Testament and New Testament lessons and learn to serve at the altar. Thus out of perhaps twenty five children in the top class of the school, six pupils gain actual experience of helping to perform the rite. The whole class (or sometimes subsets of it to ease numbers) attend for a four-week course on the eucharist.

As well as observing the whole service of a holy communion with vestments worn by the celebrant and with moderate ceremonial used, the pupils are also given brief talks on those items of the eucharist that seem appropriate at the upper-primary stage. Briefly these are:

a.　names by which this service is identified (holy communion, eucharist, mass, Lord's supper, etc.);
b.　origins – Jesus' meal with his friends, feeding the multitude, the last supper (and passover, when there has been recent work on this in religious education in the school);
c.　robes (vestments worn, how they are put on and the liturgical colours of the church calendar);
d.　the actual manual acts of the celebrant (the wafer-box, wine- and water-cruets, the various cloths and vessels used are shown and explained as the rite proceeds, with commentary).

It is also important to notice that in this exposure of primary pupils to eucharistic worship, no explanation is given of the meaning of the service, beyond that of compliance with Christ's command to his followers. Nothing is said about anamnesis, the eucharistic sacrifice or the eucharistic presence in the bread and wine.

## Aims and objectives

Given the practice as portrayed above, why do we do it? I begin with the immediate educational aims and objectives. It is hoped that the school eucharist will familiarise children with the fact that this rite is the heart of normal Christian worship in most of the Anglican communion. This is important in an urban working-class culture where many adults have never heard of what one man recently termed 'your bread and wine business.' In an area where, among the actively religious, Roman Catholics are in a substantial majority, everyone knows that in their church they have mass. Often there is complete ignorance that other churches have an equivalent service based on the Last Supper.

It is also crucial for pupils to come to regard eucharists (for Christians) as a normal part of life, to be brought into connection with any theme or topic a class may be working on. The children then discover by repeated and varying experiences that, in the churches' view, anything of significance we do or undergo – whether harvest or road safety or number work or whatever – can be offered to God in bread and wine. Thus familiarity with holy communion and its liaison with everything that matters in our lives are the two background items of knowledge about the Christian faith that we intend pupils to acquire.

As many pupils as is convenient and practicable are given the chance to act as servers and readers. Our equal opportunities' policy means it is specially important to encourage boys, as well as girls, to take up this option in a culture where, from the infant stage onwards, religion is popularly regarded as a female preserve and not for a really masculine male! These children learn by doing what is actually involved in performing the sacrament. Should they ever later want to become communicant servers at the altar, they will also have acquired the appropriate skills.

By reading, furthermore, even difficult lessons, as well as by serving at the altar, pupils are motivated by the encouragement of the adult congregation to regard eucharistic worship as a pleasant and worthwhile part of life; and they may come to think that at least this liturgical practice might be *prima facie* worth exploring when they are mature enough to be able to grapple with what is really at stake in this rite.

As for the mini-course on the eucharist which the top junior class receives in the context of attending and observing an actual celebration, our aim is that the children shall learn about those externals of holy communion (names, origins, vestments, vessels, etc.) which these pupils may be thought capable of grasping at their age. A foundation of factual knowledge is thus laid to inform observation of the actual rite and to provide a springboard for later exploration of its inner meaning.

## Justification by nurture

When I have discussed our eucharistic presentation with professional religious educators, they have seen no justificatory problem, since our school is aided. A rationale can be argued that in a church school, nurture of young Anglicans in knowledge of and acquaintance with the holy communion is perfectly appropriate and educationally sound.

But this argument does not convince. Although nearly all our pupils have been baptised in the Church of England, being in a primary school they are unconfirmed and therefore unqualified to receive communion. Few of the children come from practising and committed Anglican homes. The majority of the parents at a school eucharist are not themselves confirmed and cannot receive the consecrated bread and wine. An Anglican church school in practice largely serves a constituency of nominal Christians who probably just want a good general education and nothing specifically religious or Anglican for their children, beyond a very vague moralism.

Moreover, the argument from nurture assumes our children are already Christians and members of the church. For to nurture, as distinct from to educate, is to deepen in a faith someone already an adherent of it.[1] Now it may be doubted how far any of the key identifying descriptions of a Christian make sense in being predicated of children of primary age: despite their baptism can they significantly be regarded as saved sinners, members of Christ's body, filled with the Holy Spirit?

It may also be questioned how much of the Christian faith and of its key conceptual and belief structure primary pupils can grasp. If religious education must aim for the autonomous commitment of a pupil, when adult, to some faith or none, it seems premature to assume any commitment on the part of young children. Their thinking is not yet advanced far enough to make possible the kind of intention a communicant should have to make reception of communion appropriate. Such considerations make a nurture defence of our eucharistic practice in our schools not very plausible.

## An educational justification

Does an argument from a purely educational treatment of religion fare any better? It is generally agreed today that it is legitimate in religious education to present Christianity as a world faith. Now, clearly, religious education can occur not only in the classroom but in any enterprise in school that communicates religious data in an educationally acceptable manner. It will be granted that the eucharist is the central and distinctive act of Christian worship in the Catholic and Orthodox traditions of Christianity and is important to Protestantism. It is probably the case that our children will not encounter the eucharist outside school. Sunday schools and other church children's organisations will hardly touch on holy communion and pupils from nonchurch-going homes are hardly likely to come across the Lord's supper in their culture. Hence, any adequate educational presentation of the Christian religion must include holy communion.

The practice described above may, therefore, be accepted educationally, simply as descriptive and informative, by presenting the eucharist as it is actually performed in a middle-of-the-road Anglican way. Clearly, a great deal of further teaching is required, both to show the variety of eucharistic traditions in the contemporary church and to introduce the themes that make the sacrament meaningful and define its character: eucharistic anamnesis, sacrifice and presence.

These further ideas are crucial to an educational portrayal of the eucharist but are hardly appropriate to teach at the primary stage. Partly these concepts are too abstract and abstruse, too theoretical and involve figurative, symbolic and metaphorical uses of language: 'This is my body, this is my blood.' Although the educational researches of Goldman *et al.* and the theories of Piaget lying behind his work have been seriously criticised in recent years,[2] commonsense observation of children suggests that to move far beyond literal and concrete fact is not easy for primary pupils; nor is it profitable to teach what involves symbolism and analogy.

Partly also the eucharist is controversial and there is a wide range of interpretation of it in the church, quite apart from the controversial character of Christianity in itself. Primary children are not yet in a position to evaluate these controversies for themselves, even if they could understand what is involved. Hence what can be taught has to be confined to externals.

## The kernel and the husk

In discussing my approach to presenting the eucharist, I therefore employ Harnack's famous distinction between the kernel and the husk.[3] In our primary school we try to communicate the husk of the sacrament, the externals, while reserving the kernel of theory, holy communion's meaning, to a later stage in the children's development. The question then arises, 'Is it sound practice in education to teach the husk without the kernel and prior to it?'

Clearly in many religious topics (as in much else in the curriculum) that involve symbolism and theory, if the husk cannot be depicted alone, there is not much scope for primary education. Perhaps if we were sure the eucharist would be properly treated in the secondary school, we might not trouble with trying to present it in the primary. But given the time-constraints on secondary education, especially with an extensive national curriculum to cover, it may be doubted whether much time will be available within a world-religions' syllabus for teaching about holy communion or for visits to churches for direct encounters with it.

What is obvious is that if children by the secondary stage already have a positive attitude to the eucharist as an interesting and important Christian practice, and if they are not totally ignorant of its names, artefacts and the vessels, etc., used in this rite, there is a foundation for the teacher to build on and the possibility of successful and effective further enquiry in depth into this sacrament. At worst, if no further treatment of the eucharist follows what we attempt in our primary school, the children's natural curiosity, once aroused, about what they have observed in our holy communion service, may lead them as they grow older to find out more for themselves.

## Two concluding observations

If in a county or grant maintained primary school some such presentation of the eucharist, as was outlined above, were to be attempted, it is clear that parental consent would need to be sought, especially for visits to churches to observe holy communion services. Again, lest it be thought that such a portrayal would offend against the Cowper-Temple clause, forbidding the teaching of anything distinctive of any denomination,[4] we must stress that what is shown of the eucharist in our approach is common to a broad spread of Christian tradition. Ideally, visits to the local (Anglican) church should be balanced by visits to other Christian churches, Roman Catholic and Free Church. Facts about Christian denominations which do not celebrate the eucharist, such as the Society of Friends or the Salvation Army, also need emphasis if a rounded picture of Christianity as a world-faith is to be given and a treatment secured that is both fully educational and fully legal.

It may seem contingently unlikely that any county school could attempt, or be allowed by its Local Education Authority to attempt, a program such as that outlined above. Nonetheless in theory such an enterprise is unobjectionable. That it is actually feasible in an aided school is perhaps an educational argument for retaining such schools for the present in the state system!

A second assumption must be that, in so far as other faiths enter primary religious education, similar scope must be afforded for children to observe actual rites and ceremonies in these traditions and to participate in them, while reserving for a later date explorations of their distinctive theologies. It should be noted that such participation, as a server or reader or equivalent in other rites, is educationally harmless, since the child only assists in the external acts – like helping turn over the music for a pianist. The pupil does not have and cannot have an intention to worship at his or her level of comprehension.

My conclusion is that at the primary stage it is possible to prepare the ground for later enquiry into the eucharist and for gaining understanding of its place in Christianity as a world faith. And if perchance some pupils come ultimately to accept the claims made for the holy communion in a denomination, they may penetrate from husk to kernel and may find in it the bread of life. This possible outcome the Christian educator may privately hope for, however little he or she can properly plan and intend it within the open-ended character of contemporary religious education.

## Notes

1. Article on 'Nurture' in J M Sutcliffe (ed.), *A Dictionary of Religious Education*, London, SCM Press, 1984, p. 248.
2. N Slee, 'Goldman yet again,' *British Journal of Religious Education*, 8, 1986, p. 84 and N Slee, 'A note on Goldman's methods of data analysis with special reference to scalogram analysis,' *British Journal of Religious Education*, 8, 1986, p. 168.
3. A Harnack, *What is Christianity?*, translated by T B Saunders, 2nd ed., London, Williams and Norgate, 1901 pp. 12–15.
4. A case for the legality of a eucharist in a county school can perhaps be argued from the *Education Reform Act* (1988), c 40, s 7 (1)(2)(3); for the Cowper-Temple clause as now modified v. schedule 1 (1). Presumably an act of worship is not a catechism or formulary: alternatively a school eucharist might be considered as part of religious education and not as the statutory act of daily collective worship (v. also DES Circular, 3/89 p. 11§34).

# 5. British perspectives

The relationship between church schools and the state maintained sector of education varies considerably from one country to another. This section illustrates some of the advantages and frustrations experienced by church schools in England and Wales where church schools are fully part of the state maintained system.

In the first article, the Revd Professor Leslie J Francis reviews the history of the churches' involvement in education in England and Wales from the beginning of the nineteenth century. He illustrates how the churches pioneered a system of schools before the state entered this field and how, as a consequence, the churches were still able to exert a major influence over the key Education Act of 1944. This article identifies the religious assumptions underlying the 1944 Education Act.

Written before the 1988 Education Reform Act, this article was first printed in *Religion in the Primary School*, published by Collins in 1987. Leslie Francis is D J James Professor of Pastoral Theology at Trinity College, Carmarthen, and St David's University College, Lampeter.

In the second article, written at the time of the 1988 Education Reform Act, Alan Brown assesses the current contribution to state maintained education in England and Wales made by the three religious groups which have a significant investment in voluntary aided or special agreement schools, namely the Church of England, the Roman Catholic Church and the Jewish faith community.

Alan Brown is Director of the National Society Religious Education Resource Centre in London. This article was first published in *Common Ground*, the Journal of the Council of Christians and Jews, in 1988.

In the third article, the Revd David G Attfield discusses his perception of the challenge of the 1988 Education Reform Act to church schools. He identifies two main current conceptions of a church school, which he calls 'the nurture theory' and 'the special value theory,' and shows that both of these theories are open to serious criticism. He concludes by outlining a new kind of church school which, he argues, fully reflects current approaches to religious education and collective worship, appropriate in light of the religious provisions of the 1988 Education Reform Act.

David Attfield writes from the perspective of an Anglican parish priest working in a major conurbation. He is currently rector of All Saints, Newton Heath, Manchester. His previous experience includes lecturing at an Anglican College of Education. This paper was first published in *British Journal of Religious Education* in 1991.

In the fourth article, Dr James Arthur discusses the responses of the Catholic church to the 1988 Education Reform Act. He explores the tensions which arise for a church seeking to work in partnership with the state in the provision of schooling. He identifies examples where he believes that the Roman Catholic hierarchy were unable to protect key aspects of Catholic schooling from additional control by government ministers.

James Arthur writes from the perspective of a Catholic lay person who has taught in the Catholic secondary school sector. Currently he is concerned with Christian education and church schools at Christ Church College, Canterbury. This article was first published in *British Journal of Religious Education* in 1991.

# 5.1 Church and state
*Leslie J Francis*

## Church initiative

The main antecedents of the present system of primary schools in England and Wales were two voluntary societies founded at the beginning of the nineteenth century, the British and Foreign School Society and the National Society. Both were inspired by religious principles and it was religion which kept them apart (Cruickshank, 1963; Murphy, 1971).

The British and Foreign School Society emerged in 1814 from the Royal Lancasterian Society and was supported primarily by non-conformists and liberal Anglicans. British schools were established to promote 'the education of the labouring and manufacturing classes of society of every religious persuasion.' Religious instruction in British schools was confined to scripture and 'general Christian principles.' It was one of the society's original rules that:

> The lessons for reading shall consist of extracts from the holy scriptures; no catechism or peculiar religious tenets shall be taught in the schools, but every child shall be enjoined to attend regularly the place of worship to which its parents belong.

The National Society was founded in 1811 as a direct response to the Royal Lancasterian Society and had the backing of the great body of Anglicans. National schools were established to promote 'the education of the poor in the principles of the established church.' Religious instruction in National schools was to include the doctrines, catechism and liturgy of the established church (Burgess, 1958).

In its early days the National Society was willing to be liberal in its outlook and made allowances for children whose parents objected to the religious instruction given in the schools. The Royal Commission of 1818 made it clear that at this stage that:

> The church catechism is only taught and attendance at the established place of worship only required of those whose parents belong to the establishment.

Later, however, National schools generally took a harder line and insisted on attendance for religious instruction and attendance at an Anglican church on Sunday as conditions of entry to the school.

151

Very soon the greater resources of the National Society, in association with the parochial clergy, enabled it to draw ahead of the British and Foreign School Society. By 1830 the National Society had established 3,678 schools, educating approximately 346,000 children.

During this early period school provision for Catholic children was particularly inadequate, due largely to the relatively small number of middle class subscribers and the large number of poor immigrants from Ireland. Catholic children were forbidden to attend schools where the Authorised Version of the Bible was used.

The state did not enter the field of public education until 1833, and then it did so not by establishing state schools, but by distributing public funds to the National Society and the British and Foreign School Society. A government grant of £20,000 was distributed between the two societies to assist with school building. The government grant was essentially in 'aid of private subscription,' being available only to those voluntary bodies which could raise the first half of building costs and guarantee to meet all future running costs. Because of the greater voluntary resources available to the Church of England, by 1839 about 80% of the state grant went to Anglican schools.

In 1839 a committee of the Privy Council was set up 'to superintend the allocation of any sums voted by Parliament for the purpose of promoting education.' Between 1833 and 1870 the state continued to contribute to public education solely through the administrative system provided by voluntary societies. In 1847 the state was spending £100,000 on education; a decade later it was spending £500,000. In 1847 it was spending public money only on school buildings; a decade later it was contributing towards teachers salaries, the provision of apparatus and, by means of capitation grants, towards the annual income of the schools.

With the provision of state grants, the number of schools established under the sponsorship of the two societies continued to grow. By 1851 there were 17,015 Church of England schools with nearly 956,000 pupils, and 1,500 non-conformist schools with 225,000 pupils. When other church groups saw that these public funds were available for church related schools, they began to establish administrative machinery to claim their share of the state's beneficence.

In 1843 the Methodist Conference decided to enter the field of providing voluntary day schools and accepted its first state grant in 1847, on being assured that this acceptance would not preclude them opposing similar assistance for Catholic schools. Wesleyan policy was midway between that of the two existing societies. Unlike the National Society, the Wesleyan Society found no difficulty in accepting a conscience clause to accommodate children of other denominations; unlike the British and Foreign School Society, the Wesleyan Society insisted on including denominational instruction.

When the Catholic authorities applied for state aid in 1846, this was refused. However, in 1847 the Catholic Poor School Committee was established and after some delay, was recognised as an authority able to receive grants from the state. The Catholic church was now ready to promote the principle of establishing a separate school system. The Westminster Synod, meeting in 1852, declared:

No congregation should be allowed to remain without its schools, one for each sex. Where the poverty of the people is extreme, we earnestly exhort you, beloved children, whom God has blessed with riches ... to take upon yourselves lovingly this burden ... Indeed, wherever there may seem to be an opening for a new mission, we should prefer the erection of a school, so arranged as to serve temporarily for a chapel, to that of a church without one.

In urban areas it was possible for different denominations to establish their own schools, provided that they could afford to do so. In rural districts, however, the National Society often had a form of monopoly, when the Anglican school was the only one available. Nonconformist parents, understandably, often objected to their children being forced to attend lessons on the prayer book and catechism. In her book, *Church and State in English Education*, Marjorie Cruickshank (1963) comments on this problem:

Perhaps nothing in the educational controversies of the nineteenth century did more to inflame denominational bitterness than the Anglican refusal to concede rights of conscience, for it bred deep resentment and distrust which were to rankle in dissenting hearts for many years to come. Herein lay the problem of the single school area, where there was only one school and that a church school.

By 1860 the Committee of Council on Education had taken one important step towards meeting this denominational problem by beginning to refuse grants for proposed schools in what would become single school areas unless a conscience clause were included in the constitution of the school.

During the 1850s and 1860s there was widespread discussion about future educational developments and a wide disparity of views about the relationship of church and state initiative. The *voluntaryists*, consisting mainly of nonconformists, advocated the non-intervention of the state in education: all should be left to voluntary enterprise. They objected strongly to paying for the support of Anglican or Catholic religious instruction. The *radicals* advocated a wholly secular system of education: religious instruction should be left to the churches. Anglican opinion was already divided. One Anglican group supported the voluntaryist view and advocated that education was entirely the responsibility of the church; another Anglican group advocated continued co-operation between church and state. One

Anglican group supported the radical view and advocated that secular education and religious instruction should be kept quite separate; another Anglican group maintained that the two could not be separated out. The Catholic church became even more strongly convinced of the evils of 'united education.'

## 1870 Education Act

The problem with leaving the development of a national system of schools to voluntary initiative was that provision was erratic over the country as a whole. Despite the increased state grants, many children were still not being taught. According to the Newcastle Commission, published in 1861, 'one of the chief failures' of the existing system was that it 'did not touch the districts which required most assistance.' The poor areas which could least well raise voluntary subscriptions also least qualified for government grants.

The 1870 Elementary Education Act recognised that compromise was essential and made provision for two different types of school (Rich, 1970; Murphy, 1972). On the one hand, the schools founded by the voluntary societies were permitted to continue and given official entitlement to grants-in-aid. On the other hand, local school boards were established to build schools in areas where voluntary provision was inadequate. Board schools were intended to make good the gaps in the voluntary system, not to replace that system.

The possibility of the establishment of board schools spurred the voluntary bodies to increase their share in the national provision of schools. The act gave the voluntary societies a period of grace 'not exceeding six months,' to present plans for making good the deficiencies with the help of the existing state building grants. After the completion of those schools for which plans were approved, such grants would cease.

According to the act, voluntary schools could continue to provide denominational religious teaching. Board schools could decide whether or not to include religious teaching, but when they decided to do so it was to be in accordance with the 'Cowper-Temple clause', which stated that:

> No religious catechism or religious formulary which is distinctive of any particular denomination shall be taught in any school provided by a school board.

The Cross Commission in 1888 revealed that very few board schools took advantage of their right to exclude all religious instruction. The Birmingham school board tried to do this in 1873 and for six years permitted religious instruction to be given only outside school hours, by clergymen or others who were not concerned with the secular instruction, and who paid to use the classroom. This situation produced such opposition that from 1879 Bible reading by the headteacher, without note or comment, was permitted.

Different school boards interpreted the Cowper-Temple clause in a variety of ways. Many boards opted for undenominational teaching of one kind or another, explicitly going beyond the Cowper-Temple requirements. The Sheffield board instructed its teachers:

> Not only to adhere strictly to the terms of the fourteenth section of the Education Act which provides that no 'religious formulary which is distinctive of any religious denomination shall be taught in the school,' but also to abstain from all denominational teaching.

On the other hand, the Manchester board argued that denominational instruction could indeed be given in board schools as in voluntary schools, the difference being merely that in board schools 'you must not use a catechism or formulary.'

Anglican views on the acceptability of board schools as an adequate alternative to church schools varied widely. Bishop Fraser of Manchester was reported in 1875 as prepared to transfer his church schools to the public authority. Archdeacon Denison refused even to accept the conditions of state aid for a church school and continued for almost half a century to run his own village school efficiently, without a grant, without a conscience clause and without the interference of Her Majesty's Inspectors.

While the 1870 Education Act enabled voluntary schools and board schools to develop side by side, the financial provisions of the act favoured the board schools. The churches found it increasingly difficult to keep pace with the school boards and to maintain educational standards. According to Murphy (1971), in 1880 the average expenditure in board schools was forty-two shillings for each child, compared with thirty-five shillings in Anglican, Wesleyan and British schools and thirty shillings and six pence in Catholic schools. During the thirty years after the 1870 Education Act nearly 14,000 voluntary schools were transferred to school boards and by the end of the nineteenth century voluntary schools were closing at the rate of 60 a year, while many more were struggling for survival. Nevertheless, voluntary provision still accounted for 71% of the nation's schools and provided 52.5% of the school places.

The 1902 Education Act established greater parity between voluntary and board schools. Under the 1902 Education Act the councils of the counties and county boroughs became local education authorities, as also did some of the larger borough and urban district councils, though with restricted powers. Education thus became one of the local services for which the councils were responsible, rather than the responsibility of a body outside the main system of local government. The new local education authorities took over the educational administration of the board schools; they were also given control over secular education in voluntary schools. Board schools were renamed 'provided' schools; voluntary schools were renamed 'non-provided' schools. The significant feature of this act is that both provided and non-provided schools were to receive rate aid. It was this rate aid for Catholic as well as Anglican schools which provoked a violent opposition from Free Churchmen.

Between 1902 and 1944 the dual system continued, in spite of the churches' increasing financial difficulty in maintaining their commitment to schools and in spite of the Fisher Education Bill's abortive attempt to introduce a unitary system in 1921. By the time of the 1936 Education Act, the partnership between the church and state had become so much part of the English educational system that local education authorities were empowered to enter further into agreements with the churches to assist financially towards the erection of church senior schools.

## 1944 Education Act

The partnership between church and state in state maintained education as we know it today is a direct result of the 1944 Education Act, which set out to reconstitute the educational system after the Second World War (Dent, 1947). At the heart of its thinking was provision of secondary education for all. To make this possible a large number of schools required extension, modernisation and re-equipment; new senior schools were needed. On the one hand, the churches could not afford to maintain their voluntary schools and to bring them up to the new standards required. On the other hand, the state could not afford to buy up the church schools and was reluctant to annex them. In short, the denominational schools presented a major political problem (Butler, 1971).

The fact that the churches owned a high proportion of the nation's schools placed them in a strong position to influence the 1944 Education Act. At the same time, the churches were divided on their understanding of the future of voluntary schools. Catholic opinion insisted on retaining the full denominational character of their schools and remained clearly in favour of separate Catholic schools for Catholic children (Hornsby-Smith, 1978). The main body of Free Church opinion advocated the replacement of the dual system by a unified state system. They argued that the Christian presence in education could best be preserved through non-denominational religious education in state schools. Some Anglicans also took this line. Bishop Brook of St Edmundsbury and Ipswich (Francis, 1986), for example, argued that:

> It is my conviction that so far as religious education is concerned it is neither buildings, syllabuses, nor timetables that matter most. What

matters is that the teachers in all the schools whether voluntary or county shall be Christian men and women.

Others, like Bishop Kirk of Oxford (Kemp, 1959), took a completely different line:

Undenominationalism is the first step on the road to complete irreligion, and ... true religion is only possible by virtue of active and loyal membership in a worshipping community. Our church schools are essential means towards making our witness effective; we must not let them go.

Prolonged negotiations resulted in another compromise between church and state, affecting both the future of church schools and the place of religion in county schools.

As far as the place of religion in county schools is concerned, the 1944 Education Act made three very important points (Dent, 1947). First, the act made religious instruction obligatory in all county schools and specified that this religious instruction shall be:

In accordance with an agreed syllabus ... and shall not include any catechisms or formulary which is distinctive of any particular religious denomination.

Second, the act made school worship obligatory by specifying that:

The school day in every county school and in every voluntary school shall begin with collective worship on the part of all pupils in attendance.

In the case of county schools the collective worship 'shall not ... be distinctive of any particular denomination.' Although religious instruction and collective acts of worship had been a major feature of the English educational scene, they had never previously been made a statutory obligation.

Third, the fifth schedule of the act defined the procedure for preparing and bringing into operation an agreed syllabus of religious instruction. It lays down that the local education authority must convene a conference to bring together representatives from the churches, the local education authority and teachers. This procedure, therefore, gives the churches a key role in agreeing the form of religious instruction to be provided in county schools.

At the same time, the act reaffirmed the legal provision for parents to withdraw their children from worship and religious instruction:

If the parent of any pupil in attendance at any county school or any voluntary school requests that he be wholly or partly excused from attendance at religious worship in the school, or from attendance at religious instruction in the school, or from attendance at both religious worship and religious instruction in the school, then, until the request is withdrawn, the pupil shall be excused such attendance accordingly.

The act also made provision for parents to withdraw their children from school, under certain conditions, to receive denominational religious instruction, if this can be appropriately arranged.

As far as church schools are concerned, the 1944 Education Act continued the dual system and strengthened it. Voluntary schools were individually given the choice between 'aided' or 'controlled' status. This choice enabled schools which could afford to retain a high level of independence to do so, while those that either could not afford or did not desire to retain such a high level of independence could nevertheless retain something of their church-related character.

The aided school approximated the status of the non-provided school, and involved the churches in continued financial liability. The managers or governors of an aided school were responsible for the capital expenditure on alterations required by the local education authority to keep the premises up to standard, for external repairs to the school building, improvements and extensions to existing school buildings. Government grant aid was made available to meet 50% of these costs. Subsequent legislation raised the grant to 75% in 1959, 80% in 1967 and 85% in 1974. Under the 1944 Education Act government grants were also available for providing new aided schools under certain conditions. The local education authority is responsible for all other running costs of the aided school, including teachers salaries, repairs to the interior of the building, the playground and playing fields, and for the erection and maintenance of buildings used exclusively for the school medical and meals services. In return for their continued financial involvement, the churches retained the right to appoint a majority of the school managers or governors[1] and to provide denominational religious instruction and denominational worship. If the managers or governors of an aided school decide that they no longer wish or can afford to maintain aided status, the school may become controlled.

The controlled school gave the churches reduced rights, but involved no ongoing financial liability. In this case, the churches retain the right to appoint a minority of the school managers or governors. Religious instruction is given according to the agreed syllabus, but parents may ask for denominational teaching 'during not more than two periods each week.' Provided the teaching staff of the controlled school exceeds two, up to one fifth of the staff can be 'selected for their fitness and competence to give such religious instruction.' These are called 'reserved teachers.' The daily act of worship can also be denominational in character. Once a voluntary school has accepted controlled status, the act makes no provision whereby the school could become aided. It was only in 1986 that it become possible for a controlled school to acquire aided status.

A third category of voluntary school provided for in the 1944 Education Act is the 'special agreement' school. This category continued to honour the arrangements negotiated between local education authorities and the churches as a result of the 1936 Education Act, the implementation of which had been interrupted by the war. For most practical purposes the provisions regarding religious instruction, worship, finance and school management are basically the same as for aided status, except in relation to the appointment of staff.

The Catholics in 1944 rejected controlled status completely. Just two small Catholic schools accepted the irreversible designation of controlled status. Murphy (1971) accounts for these two anomalies 'as the result of an administrative oversight.' While the Catholic community continued to feel that the financial arrangements of aided status were unfair to a religious minority who, in conscience, could not accept the implications of controlled status, the Catholic church worked hard to finance a national network of aided schools.

As far as Church of England schools were concerned, the choice between aided and controlled status was left in the hands of the governors or managers of each church school. They needed to weigh up the advantages of aided status against the cost and their ability to meet that cost. While Church of England schools are autonomous, the diocese is in the position to offer advice, guidance and financial aid. In the absence of an agreed central policy on the comparable merits of aided and controlled status, each diocese formulated its own recommendations, which the school governors within its area could choose to follow or to ignore, at least as far as their independent sources of finance would permit. Some dioceses, like London, Southwark and Blackburn, opted heavily for aided status; other dioceses, like Bristol, York, Coventry and Lichfield, opted mainly for controlled status.

## Religious consensus

The 1944 Education Act designed an educational system appropriate for a Christian or church-related society. While some of the denominational controversies which had beset the 1870 and the 1902 Education Acts still survived, there was also a new feeling of religious consensus. What made sense of the 1944 Education Act were the key ideas that England was a Christian country and that the churches had a particular right and responsibility to share with the state in shaping the education of the nation's children.

The specific provisions of the 1944 Education Act highlight nine key religious assumptions. These assumptions have looked different from different denominational perspectives and at different times during the intervening years since 1944. They are, however, worth spelling out in some detail, since they are at the heart of the idea of the educational partnership between church and state as conceived in 1944 and now their current interpretation determines precisely what that partnership is like in practice.

First, the act made obligatory a daily act of collective worship in all county and voluntary schools. The churches' assumption was that religious worship is not only compatible with, but an essential component of, the school's educational task. When schools promote religious worship, even undenominational worship, they are helping to prepare their pupils for a place in the worshipping congregations of the churches. Schools and churches share the same hymns, the same language of prayer and the same tradition of reading from scripture.

Second, the act made religious instruction a compulsory subject in all county and voluntary schools. The churches' assumption was that all state maintained schools have a responsibility to teach religion. At the time of the act no sophisticated distinction existed between the churches' confessional teaching and the schools' non-confessional teaching of religion. Many Anglicans, therefore, felt that the rationale behind teaching religion in county schools was so close to their own objectives that there was less need to retain church schools.

Third, the act gave the churches a key role in preparing the agreed syllabuses of religious instruction. The churches' assumption was that religious instruction in county schools was as much a theological question as an educational question. The churches wanted a significant hand in determining what religious instruction should look like in county schools and the opportunity to make sure that denominational interests did not infiltrate what was supposed to be a non-sectarian program. Many Anglicans felt that agreed syllabus teaching was an appropriate foundation on which they could build denominational teaching through church and Sunday school.

Fourth, the act safeguarded parents rights to withdraw their children from religious instruction, from religious worship or from both, whether they attended a county or a voluntary school. The churches' assumption was that these withdrawal clauses protected the rights of a minority. The majority of parents would want to accept the religious worship and the religious instruction which the churches' helped to shape. The minority who desired the protection of the withdrawal clauses were more likely to do so because of sectarian interests, rather than secularist persuasion.

Fifth, the churches felt secure in their continued involvement in training teachers to staff county and church schools. The churches' assumption was that they should influence the teachers who in turn would influence the pupils in school. Many Anglicans felt that church money was better invested in training colleges than schools. Some, indeed, expressed this view with missionary fervour and zeal.

Sixth, the act enabled the churches to maintain controlled schools without continuing financial liability. A number of Church of England schools welcomed controlled status. In controlled schools the church appoints some of the managers, the daily worship can be denominational in character and the clergy continue to have contact. By accepting controlled status in many neighbourhood single-school areas, the Church of England was assuming that it was still appropriate for denominational worship to take place in schools which exist primarily to serve all the children of an area, whatever the religious persuasion of their homes.

Seventh, the act enabled the churches to choose which of their schools they wished to maintain as more distinctively church-related through aided status. Aided status gives the churches control over the majority of the managing body and the right to provide denominational religious instruction throughout the school, in addition to the daily denominational act of worship. A number of Church of England schools in single school areas opted for aided status. By accepting aided status for schools which it proposed to run on a neighbourhood model the Church of England was assuming that it was still appropriate for the church to determine the church-related character of local area schools. Unless parents deliberately withdrew their children from religious instruction and religious worship, the clergy could assume the right to teach them denominational doctrine and to lead them in denominational worship, whatever the religious persuasion of their homes.

Eighth, the act enabled the churches to develop a distinctive system of denominational aided schools, to serve the needs of religious communities, rather than neighbourhoods. In this situation parents were only likely to send their children to the school if they accepted the religious emphasis of the school. The Catholic church opted exclusively to develop schools of this nature; the Anglican church also developed a few schools along these lines, as did the Jewish community. The churches' assumptions here are of a completely different order. Instead of trying to influence the religious formation of the nation's children, they are seeking to serve the needs of their own particular religious community and making the assumption that the general educational system is unable to meet these needs adequately. This assumption is in accord with religious minorities, rather than religious majorities.

Ninth, provisions under the 1944 Education Act gave parents the opportunity to ask for free transport for a reasonable distance to enable their children to attend a school of the denomination they desired. The churches' assumption was that a variety of religious provisions would exist within different schools and that parents should be able to choose the school that would best suit their religious needs.

This assumption, like the previous one, concerns the churches' protection of the rights of their own members, not their intention to influence the rest of the nation.

Since 1944, both educational and church-related thinking in the specific areas of religious education, school worship and church schools, and more generally about the relationship between religion and education, have changed and developed.

**Notes**

1.  The 1944 Education Act distinguished between the *managers* of primary schools and the *governors* of secondary schools. The 1980 Education Act replaced the managers of primary schools by governors, thus providing equality of status to all those who govern schools.

**References**

Burgess, H J (1958) *Enterprise in Education*, London, National Society and SPCK.

Butler, R A (1971) *The Art of the Possible*, London, Hamish Hamilton.

Cruickshank, M (1963) *Church and State in English Education*, London, Macmillan.

Dent, H J (1947) *The Education Act 1944: provisions, possibilities and some problems*, London, University of London Press.

Francis, L J (1986) *Partnership in Rural Education: church schools and teacher attitudes*, London, Collins Liturgical Publications.

Hornsby-Smith, M P (1978) *Catholic Education: the unobtrusive partner*, London, Sheed and Ward.

Kemp, E W (1959) *Kenneth Escot Kirk*, London, Hodder and Stoughton.

Murphy, J (1971) *Church, State and Schools in Britain 1800–1970*, London, Routledge and Kegan Paul.

Murphy, J (1972) *The Education Act 1870*, Newton Abbot, David and Charles.

Rich, E E (1970) *The Education Act 1870*, London, Longmans.

# 5.2 Aided schools: help, hindrance, anachronism or trailblazer?

*Alan Brown*

## Introduction

So much has been made in the past few months of the effect of the Great Reform Bill and the major changes it will create that it is easy to overlook how much legislation passed in the 1944 Education Act still holds good today. For instance, the mechanism for creating Agreed Syllabuses for Religious Education has creaked and groaned over the years but is still able to produce thoughtful and stimulating syllabuses in the late 1980s. Similarly the legislation regarding voluntary schools, although amended over the years, created a situation which, in general terms, remains the same. What is especially remarkable concerning the voluntary schools is that although numbers of schools have declined they are still in demand and represent a wide diversity of approach even within one religion.

After this brief paragraph, all references to 'religious schools' should be taken as referring specifically to 'voluntary aided' or 'special agreement' schools unless otherwise mentioned. In a sense this is unfortunate for the controlled school (almost totally the preserve of the Church of England) in its theoretical model, i.e. a school controlled by the Local Education Authority (LEA) with strong Church of England representation on the governing body with specific responsibility for collective worship, is not a dissimilar pattern to the role of the Church of England vis-à-vis the state.

## How many

There are about 4,000 voluntary aided schools in England and Wales. There are a small number of Jewish schools (about 35) with virtually all the remainder being split almost equally between the Roman Catholic Church and the Church of England. However of the Jewish schools, five are secondary schools; of the 2,000 plus Roman Catholic schools about 500 are secondary; whereas of the 2,000 Church of England schools only about 130 are secondary schools. In themselves the figures mean little but, in very general terms, a pupil who attends a Roman Catholic or Jewish primary school could normally expect to complete his or her education in a Catholic or Jewish secondary school. This is not the case for a pupil of a Church of England primary school.

In any general reflection on aided schools it is really necessary to bear in mind this important numerical distinctiveness. Jewish schools are fairly small in number but are concentrated in a few urban areas; the larger number of Roman Catholic schools also cluster in areas of traditional Roman Catholic practice; but the Church of England schools are frequently village (or 'old village') schools with about a third of the 2,000 schools having under 100 pupils. This spread of provision provides a clue as to the distinctive educational philosophies which underlie the three types of religious provision. For Jews and Roman Catholics it is supremely important that as far as possible pupils should grow up in a strong religious atmosphere with close links between school and family (and synagogue and church also). The Church of England, particularly in its primary schools, tends to encourage and adopt a policy of 'neighbourhood' schools which means that some pupils will not be from Church of England families – indeed there are one or two celebrated cases where the pupils at Church of England primary schools are all from Muslim families. The governors of Church of England primary schools undertake to ensure that the religious education is in accord with the rites, principles and practices of the Church of England but these can be widely and liberally interpreted. On these grounds alone one can make the case that Jewish and Roman Catholic educational policies appear to demonstrate a greater cohesiveness than the Church of England – but then the particular position of the Church of England as the state church may well indicate that it never sought that type of cohesiveness so essential to Jews and Roman Catholics.

One further complication to this already complex situation is that the governors of each aided school have a measure of autonomy. Thus, in principle and occasionally in practice, governors of such schools may not act in concert with each other or with any religious authorities/representatives. In practice many Roman Catholic schools follow a diocesan religious education syllabus while relatively few Anglican dioceses produce one and schools follow it or not as they will. It is this type of situation which is no doubt shared by Jewish schools which makes it so difficult to generalise about religious state schools even within a particular religious tradition.

## A religious ethos

All religious state schools lay great store on the ethos created within the school and the importance of pupils living and working within the ambience of the particular religion. This has at least two areas of importance. We have already noted that in most Roman Catholic schools most of the pupils will be from Roman Catholic families but there are schools where up to 40% of pupils are not from Roman Catholic homes. Pupils in Jewish schools are, in virtually every case, from Jewish families though the King David High School, Liverpool, has up to 40% non-Jewish pupils. The case of the Church of England schools has already been dealt with.

There are a small number of Anglican/Roman Catholic schools (mainly secondary) which, though perhaps born out of pragmatism rather than idealism, provide both churches with an opportunity to develop a deeper understanding. For those who look for a greater ecumenical awareness these may well act as a beacon. Indeed they could well provide a model on which joint or multi-faith schools could be developed in the latter years of the century. What begins with expediency can end in a vision of what might be − a willingness to work together and to respect − even rejoice − in difference.

It is important that if an ethos or an ambience is to be created then there are sufficient pupils of that ethos or ambience to support the staff. And it is the staff who are equally important. Certainly staff in religious state schools would be expected to be in sympathy with the aims of the school even if they were not of the particular religion. It is virtually impossible to staff secondary schools with staff from the particular religious group and Roman Catholic schools have been estimated to have 40% of staff from outside Roman Catholicism. This is likely to be a smaller percentage than in Church of England secondary schools but figures are not available for Jewish schools.

The difficulty of creating a Jewish or Christian ethos is under-lined in both religions by the diversity that exists within. There are those parents, and clergy, who argue that the schools are not religious enough, they do not reinforce the religious tradition sufficiently rigorously, and they will opt to send their children to independent religious schools. In every religious state school there are pupils from families of varying levels of commitment or none so it can be extremely difficult to bind these diverse (and often argumentative) factors together. Perhaps endemic in all such schools is the will to create and maintain a system of religious values which can be absorbed by the pupils so that they will come to recognise the importance of a religious heritage, the beliefs, practices and traditions which they, in their turn, will to hand on to the next generation. Before turning to the subject of religious education one should make some comment on the desire of the Muslim community to have aided schools. There is certainly a strong undercurrent, as I understand, in Muslim educational circles which regards the creation of some, a small number, of Muslim aided schools as a mark of recognition by the British educational establishment. There are further issues involved which are not totally relevant here though much of the debate seems to focus on how much of the curriculum in a Muslim school would be able to cope with the requirements of a British education. In principle there seems to be no reason why there should not be a Muslim aided school but then rolls are falling with aided, controlled and county schools being closed – so to create new schools at this time could be politically difficult.

## Religious education

As regards religious education it could be helpful to return to the 1944 Education Act definition which said, in effect 'religious instruction and collective school worship = religious education.' Many religious schools, certainly the majority, would argue that religious education in their school does not take place solely in the religious education lessons, and we are back again to the importance of religious ethos. However, at a superficial glance it does appear that Roman Catholic and Jewish schools are prepared to give much more time to religious education and its related aspects than are Church of England schools. Perhaps this investment of time and resources and status reflect an attitudinal difference in that the Church of England as the state church adopts a paternalistic approach to religious education in the sense that everyone who is not anything else is Church of England; Catholics are aware of what it is to feel a minority and how difficult it can be (and has been) to fight for one's rights to achieve equality of opportunity. The twin aims of education endorsed by the Church of England's Synod in 1985 – those of service and teaching the principles of the Church of England – create a tension which is not that tension which creates Jewish and Roman Catholic principles in education – or indeed Muslim.

Virtually every Jewish school would surely consider its main *raison d'être* as the re-inforcement of the importance of Jewish tradition and practice with much of the total curriculum supporting this overtly religious aim. For the Muslim educator Islam is central and every aspect of the curriculum would have a specifically Islamic dimension. The threefold link of church, school and home is the foundation stone of Roman Catholic education which probably has a less direct effect upon the curriculum. Many Church of England schools would have an approach to the curriculum more akin to a county school with religious education slotted in where appropriate.

So how can we gather these strands together? In a sense it is impossible, for the 1944 Education Act allowed for such diversity and, who knows, may even have encouraged it. A less benign opinion might be that the state chose to opt out of the religions issue. By so doing it allowed the Church of England to continue and develop the paternalistic attitude it had maintained for a century or more. As the Church of England refused to define itself as a denomination and, quite correctly in the opinion of the writer, continued to open its doors to the neighbourhood children, it fell into the trap of not taking education seriously enough. Somehow, it seemed to say these schools will produce the Anglicans of the future – and they have not. Yet it still continues in its paternalism fostered to large extent, no doubt, by an independent school tradition which produces 40% of its clergy and 70% of its bishops.

The Roman Catholics were encouraged (or allowed) to develop a protectionist policy – what we have, we hold – though there are signs that this may be weakening in some parts of the Roman Catholic Church. Children were sent to Roman Catholic schools and as such learned little of non-Roman Catholic religious practices. Skilfully using the religious orders the Roman Catholic schools were able to develop high education standards but at the price of not looking over the high protective wall they had built.

The Jewish schools, again perhaps because of history, or perhaps because of the different language at the root of its religious expression, run the risk of becoming isolated. Filled almost exclusively with Jewish children with little being taught to them of the Christian, or any other religion, it can be too easy for the Jewish schools to turn inwards and become introspective; to look away from contact and development with the non-Jewish world.

## Isolationism?

The issue of isolation knocks at the door of all religious state schools – for some it knocks louder than others. Here there is a responsibility on the inter-faith groups like the Council of Christians and Jews to increase knowledge and understanding of each other's faith. The great test of trust, of course, is what we allow our young people to be taught and how it is to be taught. The retreat into the religious state can be the blinkered insecurity of a threatened faith or it can be the refusal to recognise the nature of the world in which we live. It would be disappointing indeed if government legislation inadvertently encouraged such a mentality, but equally it is an indictment of all religious traditions if they do not feel able to respond to each other by helping their young people to recognise the integrity of another religion than their own. For those who support the principle of religious schools one has to draw their attention to the many county schools, particularly those in the large urban concentrations, which are full of children whose religious commitment is Christian, Jewish, Muslim, Buddhist, Hindu, Sikh etc. In an ironical turnabout the multi-faith schools are not the religious state schools but the state schools. It is in the 'secular' school that the creative tension of religious inter-action is at its most vivid and vital. We must beware that the aided schools do not appear monochrome and anachronistic when compared with the technicolour religious diversity in many of our county state schools.

These are harsh, if somewhat arbitrary, judgments and they are not fully argued because they represent an anxiety present in the current situation rather than a definitive view. It is a view beginning with the 1944 Education Act where religious state schools were allowed an enormous amount of freedom which has not necessarily been to the best advantage of the religion itself. Ironically the 1988 Education Reform Act could witness the end of aided schools if the Secretary of State gives approval to aided school governing bodies who seek grant maintained status. The implications of this act are, as yet, not fully teased out but it could be the case in some areas that county schools could to all intents and purposes become religious schools with their pupils coming from the same religious tradition. Why should aided school governors have to find 15% of capital costs when grant maintained schools will have the full costs? Will aided school governing bodies want freedom from the local authority? And if so what will be the cost of that freedom?

Perhaps the aided school provision needed a shake-up but how many of the 4,000 aided schools will exist at the turn of the century? Have they become the dinosaurs of the late twentieth century? Should the religious educationalists − from all religions − get together to decide how best they can support the education of their children's children and not allow the government solely to dictate how the young are religiously educated?

# 5.3 The challenge of the Education Reform Act to church schools

## David G Attfield

### Voluntary schools and the new law

The Education Reform Act applies to all maintained schools and its notorious National Curriculum is required of church as much as of county schools. The basic curriculum of the new Act, a legal category wider than the National Curriculum, differs in its content for church schools as contrasted with county schools.[1] The religious education component of the basic curriculum in church schools still follows the 1944 Education Act.[2] In aided schools religious education has to accord with the school's Trust Deed or tradition[3] and in practice is determined by diocesan or other local syllabi, as opposed to the statutory agreed syllabus used in county schools.[4] In controlled schools the archaic and little employed provision for reserved teachers giving up to two periods a week of Trust Deed or traditional (to the school) teaching remains.[5]

Worship in county schools is henceforward to be governed by the extensive and important new provisions of the Education Reform Act[6] and arrangements for collective worship are to be made in the case of the county school by the head teacher after consultation with the governing body. In church schools the converse applies and such arrangements are now to be made by the governing body after consultation with the head teacher.[7] Hence it is possible in this latter circumstance for the head or an educational professional to be overriden by governors representing the local religious community sponsoring a church school and for extra-educational authorities to have the last word!

The important upshot of these recent legal changes is that, while in respect of religious education and worship the Education Reform Act introduces important reforms for county schools, the church school is left largely untouched and it is legally perfectly possible for the traditional church school to stay in business. Church schools can carry on as before, even as they were before 1944, in respect of worship and religious education! But our question is whether it is educationally desirable and ethical that this should happen in the light of those great changes in society and in thinking about schools which are reflected in the 1988 Act.

## The nurture theory

There are two main conceptions current of a church school which we shall call the nurture theory and the special value theory.

The nurture theory of the church school assumes its pupils are largely and predominantly children of parents who are practising members of the faith-community in question and that it is right to nurture them in its belief and practice. School should reinforce home in ensuring that faith is handed down the generations and that the religious aspect of the pupil's identity, both communal and sectarian, is preserved.

The special value theory holds that certain values — that the school should be a caring community, should respect every child as an individual, should give extra help to the less able and deprived — should govern the running of schools and that schools sponsored by a particular faith community, for example the Christian church, will live by these values and thus make a significant contribution to the education system. The claim is that such values are uniquely fostered by the religion of the teachers, pupils, governors and sponsoring-body and will therefore penetrate the school community.

In the remainder of this article we shall criticise these two conceptions and then try to draw out what of positive value can be salvaged from them to justify a future for church schools beyond the legal and practical possibility of continuing to operate them. The nurture theory is open to many criticisms. Some are practical and empirical. Not all or even the majority of pupils in many Anglican schools come from practising Christian homes. The Church of England has long since recognised a dual role for its schools.[8] Their 'general' role is to provide secular education for the whole local community of the village or parish. The church here believes it should take a part in the practical task of resourcing schooling in order that its voice may be taken seriously in educational councils. Church schools also have another, a 'domestic' role of nurturing the children of practising Anglicans.

Now granted the 1944 Education Act's provisions for agreed syllabus religious education in aided schools and for denominational religious education in controlled schools[9] are rarely used, in general no serious differentiation of approach to pupils is made to provide nurture for some, as opposed to a more open-ended, multi-faith program for others. If nurture is taken seriously, it is hard to see how schools could proceed without children being separated into special classes, streams or groups for it. Hence it would seem, *either* little nurturing goes on in an atmosphere of undifferentiated religious education teaching; *or* if nurture dominates the religious education lesson, the school's practice is ethically and educationally objectionable, even on traditional assumptions, since Anglican 'socialisation' of a large number of pupils of only nominal Church of England background, or from other religious backgrounds altogether, is obviously inappropriate.

Another pedagogical objection to the nurture theory is that most church schools of the Anglican variety are primary and it is questionable how much distinctive denominational or even Christian (or other faith) teaching is appropriate for young pupils. Consideration, for instance, of sacrament and ministry and liturgy involves much in the way of background and concepts not suitable for children who have not yet reached powers of abstract thought and the capacity to handle symbols and non-literal language. However, we must concede that this difficulty with nurturing only applies to some church schools. In schools sponsored by the Roman Catholic church and by other faiths there may be majorities of pupils from believing homes; there is no reason in principle why church schools should not be secondary; hence these schools are perfectly able to give the kind of denominational or distinctively Christian or other faith instruction that nurture requires.

The more serious difficulties with the nurture theory are educational and philosophical. The first question that needs raising is whether children can be members of a faith community. It may be traditional and conventional to assume that the offspring of a religious family or group should share its faith but this assumption is not above criticism. With young children does it make sense to say a child can believe a doctrine it does not understand because he or she has not grasped the relevant concepts? If, further, a child can only doubtfully be claimed to have the characteristic beliefs of his or her alleged faith, can he or she properly intend to participate in good faith and meaningfully in its ritual worship? Even if much religion is practical in following rite and custom, without some minimum of belief, can anyone be really said to adhere to the faith in question?

Again, certain characterising descriptions should hold of members of a faith: for example Christians are spoken of as forgiven sinners, members of the body of Christ, being filled with the Holy Spirit. One might ask whether such descriptions make sense in the case of younger children. Are they sinners needing forgiveness, in the light of modern theories of moral development? In what sense are they church members before the years of discretion? Can they really be conscious agents of Christ in the world as his limbs and organs? Does possession by the Holy Spirit make sense of behaviour and is it morally acceptable, except in believers with religious perspectives? Not any kind of love, joy or peace exhibited by a child can be regarded as the Spirit's fruit, unless the emotion concerned is surrounded by a whole web of other concepts and beliefs not found in the young.

Clearly it would be foolish to deny that secondary-age pupils can be believers. Nurture could begin in adolescence but the question then is, 'Is such an approach ethical, before teenagers are mature enough to decide for themselves whether they want to be nurtured in their parents', as opposed to any other, faith or none?' Hence it is doubtful whether pupils are proper objects of nurture and whether schools should be run for this purpose.

A second question that should be raised is whether a child should follow in the faith of his or her parents. Beyond dogmatism, what good reasons can be urged in favour of this age-old assumption? In our culture in Britain today several religions co-exist. The central claims of these faiths are objects of serious study. It emerges that none of these claims is above question and is so certain that all informed students agree in accepting or rejecting them as parts of any particular faith or as a general religious world view. In an age where the elders disagree, is it right to bring up a child to believe the doctrines that happen to be those his or her parents believe in? To do this implies that the older generation is wiser than the younger one will be when they grow up, that the set of human beings born earlier are better, with a greater right to judge in spiritual matters, than those born later!

One reason given for the traditional postulate of the right to induct children into the family faith is the psychological welfare and security of the child. Part of his or her identity is to share the faith of father, mother and other relatives, while there is also said to be the need to maintain the wider cultural identity of the ethnic group or tradition the child belongs to. Home and school should have a unified approach to religion; pupils require a spiritually homogenous 'primary culture.'[10]

Such considerations may have some validity in other ages and societies. Now, apart from the priority which should be given to objectivity and the pupil's autonomy in education, we may ask whether these reasons of security and identity for predetermining the child's faith are cogent in our culture as it is presently evolving. Today in liberal Christian homes of various denominations, faith in childhood plays no part in identity and children are no worse for this in psychological terms, nor is their relationship with parents and relatives impaired. It can also be argued that if parents see that their offspring encounter an educational approach to religion, the young through force of example will still freely opt for the family faith when adult.

If children, on reaching years of discretion, then most probably choose their parents' faith, this should be sufficient for the continuity of that faith and the cultural identity of an ethnic group. It is enough for the common culture of home and school if the religion of the family is sensitively portrayed and the children conform to its customs, without commitment to the beliefs which underlie them. Further, part of the wider culture into which young children should be initiated today is a non-threatening awareness of other faiths among their friends and hopefully their co-pupils. Hence the personal and communal identity argument for nurture fails because such nurture is unnecessary.

Of course some religious communities will in fact make the doubtful assumption of the exclusive and absolute truth of their faith and will claim the right to teach it to the young as true, but it is quite wrong for such principles to govern education. Schools in a pluralist society, pursuing education with its inbuilt concern for truth and reason, have to treat beliefs and belief-systems according to their publicly acknowledged logical and epistemological status. Hence all religious claims of a non-empirical sort, on account of their controversial character, have to be presented descriptively and as open for exploration. Thus there is an educational necessity for the open-ended enquiry into world faiths that typifies current trends in religious education.

Can any school worthy of the name treat religion in any other way and still be considered in this respect a place of *education*? Even if children can be regarded as members of a faith-community, nurture is seen to be improper in education and is therefore no aim for a school, whether church or county. All maintained schools whatever ought then to embrace the kind of new agreed syllabus the 1988 Act requires to be drawn up for county schools, if a Standing Advisory Council on Religious Education embarks on producing a new syllabus which 'shall reflect the fact that the religious traditions in Great Britain are in the main Christian whilst taking account of the teaching and practices of the other principal religions represented in Great Britain.'[11] It is also doubtful, on similar grounds concerning the status of faith and the autonomy of pupils, if nurture is excluded from schooling, whether the worship of a church school, whatever the law permits, should be other than the 'educational' variety of collective worship prescribed for state schools by the Education Reform Act.[12]

## The special value theory

The special value theory of the justification of church schools may be dealt with more briefly. However the content of these special values may be specified, it is simply a fact that they will be upheld not only by Christians but by adherents of other faiths, by humanists and by teachers, governors and parents of no explicit religious standpoint who regard such values as inherent in education or as arising from their professional commitment. This point is more than a matter of sociological fact about education; it is also a question of logic.

The special values in question seem no more to follow logically from any one theology or religious metaphysic than any other. Indeed were such values, as they bear on the schooling of children, not supported by a faith or philosophy, that very fact would give teachers of the young just cause to criticise such a philosophy or faith. Hence it is hard to see what a church school can offer that is unique in this sphere.

## Nurture reconsidered

Though it is legally possible for church schools to continue to nurture children and to offer to embody special values in their life, there seems a powerful case, as we have set out above, against their going on doing so. Are there any arguments left in favour of church schools in the new era after the 1988 Education Reform Act?

It is no longer possible to use the non-religious argument in favour of church schools, that they can set county schools an example and give a lead in the matter of local autonomy, being free in important respects of Local Education Authority control, with a governing body really representing the local community. The reforms of the 1986 Education Act as to the composition of governing bodies, and especially the coming of Local Management of Schools in the 1988 Act, have ensured that all maintained schools, church and county (not to mention grant-maintained schools), possess substantial independence today of local education authorities.

Is it possible to restate the nurture theory? Suppose church schools choose to have the same kind of worship and religious education as county schools are required to have under the Education Reform Act — as is perfectly possible. Their pupils, we hope, become interested in religion, learn about world faiths, explore them as they grow older and reach some rational verdict on religious commitment when they reach years of discretion. What faith and life stance will they choose? Empirically it is highly probable that they will choose the faith of their fathers! Provided the children come from a good home and have had a close relation with their parents, they are likely to adopt their families' religion, because the young model themselves on those they love and respect. If you want to communicate your faith to anyone in a morally proper way, it is necessary to teach about that faith descriptively and to motivate exploration; to wait for the other's unhurried decision; and above all and behind all, to witness to your own commitment in a way that attracts the other to you as a person and to what you stand for.

Now if the example of parents is powerful, when the influence of admired and respected teachers is added, it would seem highly probable that at the end of the day the pupils will come to adopt the faith of school and home. But it may still be asked, 'Should a school, as a place of education, try to attract its pupils toward one religion by the magnetism of believing teachers, governors, sponsoring-community and parents?' We may certainly argue that children will only receive a coherent witness if they meet religion in the particular form of one great faith.

During the primary stage it is probably desirable that younger children should be immersed in a unified and unconfused religious culture, a single 'primary culture,'[13] springing from home, school and community, so that they meet faith in one form to introduce the spiritual domain. But as pupils pass into the secondary stage in a church comprehensive school it could perhaps be arranged that they encounter here the living witness of several great faiths.

Perhaps only in such a church school system can the educational ideals of modern religious education be fully met. First, in both primary and secondary stages, pupils meet a communal climate and the role models of adults who take the spiritual dimension seriously. This encounter is necessary as a counterpoise to the secularist atmosphere in which children today are socialised in their informal culture. Thus they are enabled to take the possibility of faith seriously and become sufficiently interested to want to investigate it. It is doubtful if a county school can provide such a climate in terms of its staff, except accidentally.

Secondly, if in a church secondary school several of the great world faiths are involved in the administration and governing of the school and are exhibited in the lives of the staff, real choice of religions becomes a practical possibility for the pupils, while the extra-influence of parents remains in favour of their family faith. In this way parents can evangelise their own children in a way that is ethical and permitted in education, while a plurality of faith-communities can contribute to the school's religious education at the secondary stage in such a fashion as to satisfy the moral restrictions imposed by the child's need for autonomy in a pluralist culture.

It may be doubted whether the 'educationally appropriate worship'[14] required by the 1988 Act will give a sufficient introduction to real worship as this happens in any one religion. Certainly county schools can offer a propaedeutic to worship, celebrations of beauty and goodness, a consciousness-raising which brings pupils to the threshold of the true worship of God or of meditation as practised in eastern faiths. But even leaving aside those schools that successfully apply to their Standing Advisory Council on Religious Education to opt out of the wholly or mainly Christian character of collective acts of worship prescribed for most occasions in a term, the legally required worship of a school can only reflect the broad traditions of Christian worship without being denominational. As such, 'educationally appropriate' collective worship may become so vague and uncertain as to its object and focus that it fails to present real worship as found in the great faiths of the world.

Of course it may be possible to interpret the new law to include in collective school worship what, for example many Christian denominations have in common in terms of general theme and structure in their worship (the Office-type service or the Protestant service of the word). It could even be argued that a eucharist would be permitted in a county school[15] since most Christian denominations have such an act of worship and even use common forms (the International Consultation on English Texts version of the Creed, Gloria etc.)! Yet it is unlikely many schools will have the courage or independent insight and initiative to interpret the law so generously as to include sometimes at assembly representative acts of distinctive worship in the great traditions of Christianity and of other faiths. Hence the church school may fill a gap by ensuring that the actual types of worship of its own (or of other faith) communities can enrich the collective worship of pupils, so that they see the real thing. In this way the church school may actually achieve one ideal of modern enlightened education in the spiritual sphere that is in practice (and possibly in law?) closed to the county school.

## The special value theory reconsidered

Can anything positive be salvaged from the special value theory of church schools? We have claimed that any special values likely to be named as desirable in education will find theoretical support in various religious, humanist and other standpoints of teachers and governors. Whether schools are actually run in the light of such values is another matter. If the premise is accepted that faith does in fact make a difference to behaviour, it is at least possible that church schools will to some extent embody the values that should inspire their life. When it is so hard to educate in accordance with our ideals, in the face of all the practical problems and the limitations of human nature in pupils and staff, it seems worthwhile to encourage church schools in case they do succeed in living up to their principles in some measure.

Of course this argument extends to schools sponsored by any faith community, provided its belief and practice promote in schools values that should obtain if true education is to take place. Indeed, were experiments made with establishing multifaith or inter-denominational church secondary schools, inspired by values respected by several of the world's great religions or confessions and mediated via their adherents among the staff, governors, pupils and parents of such schools, not only would the open-ended multifaith character of religious education be supported by the multifaith models set before the children but also the school ethos would have a comparable inspiration and theological grounding from many diverse spiritual standpoints.

## Conclusion

Our conclusion is that the educational thinking that lies behind, and is in part embodied in the Education Reform Act, does indeed challenge the church school. It can legally now carry on as before, as a nurturing institution and as an alleged exemplar of the special values its faith claims to support. But, as we have seen, both theories of what a church school should be are open to serious criticism. However, we have also sketched the outlines of a new kind of church school which fully reflects current approaches to religious education and collective worship. Such a school might challenge more effectively than a county school the prevailing secularist climate of our culture. Working from a one faith standpoint as an example of real religion at the primary stage, and at the secondary from a multifaith foundation and inspiration, a school could be created that would promote true openness and rational choice between faiths for pupils and in which the special values any good school needs as a place of education would flourish. As in the nineteenth century, so in the twenty-first century such a new variety of church school could give a lead to the state system and better exemplify educational ideals than may be possible in a county school.

**Notes**

1. *Education Reform Act 1988*, c40, Sect. 2(1).
2. Sect. 8(2).
3. *Education Act 1944*, c31, Sect. 28(1).
4. Sect. 26.
5. Sect. 27.
6. Sects 6 & 7.
7. Sect. 6(3).
8. L J Francis, *Partnership in Rural Education*, London, Collins, 1986, pp. 18–19 and reference therein.
9. Sect. 28(1 & 27).
10. B Ackerman, *Social Justice in the Liberal State*, New Haven, Yale University Press, 1980, pp. 141–149.
11. *1988 Act*, Sect. 8(3).
12. Sect. 7.
13. See note 10 above.
14. J M Hull, *The Act Unpacked*, Birmingham, University of Birmingham School of Education and the Christian Education Movement, 1989, pp. 19–21.
15. D G Attfield, 'Presenting the eucharist in a primary school,' *British Journal of Religious Education*, 12, 1990, p. 171(4).

# 5.4 Catholic responses to the 1988 Education Reform Act: problems of authority and ethos

## James Arthur

### Introduction

The Catholic church in England and Wales is no stranger to educational controversy; before and after each of the crucial acts of 1870, 1902 and 1944 it conducted a campaign for its own vision of education. It is interesting that the 1988 controversies, which it can be argued are far more crucial for this sector, representing ten per cent of schools, have not been absorbed outside the ranks of the Catholic community. The issues which they raise are of importance to all Christians in education, and indeed, to those who hold any philosophy of education apart from the purely utilitarian.

There are three areas of supreme importance in the future policy of the Catholic church which the legislation of the past decade directly threatens. They are, firstly, the provision of a distinctly Catholic education which is articulated by an appropriate philosophy of the curriculum. Secondly, to safeguard the character of the schools by control over admissions. Thirdly, the key to all three, the control of Catholic schools within a clear statutory framework in which there is an amicable division of powers, responsibilities and functions between the state and the church.

### The curriculum

Vital to the existence of Catholic voluntary schools is that:[1]

> they continue to offer a genuine and needed form of education containing appropriate and significant differences from that offered in county schools.

Statements on Catholic schools would indicate that their aim is no less than the creation of a Christian *milieu* through which the philosophy of the curriculum and the ethos of the school are harmonised. As the Sacred Congregation for Catholic Education argues:[2]

> Catholic schools need to have a set of educational goals which are 'distinctive' in the sense that the school has a specific objective in mind and all the goals are related to this objective.

178

Consequently any slide towards secularism through exclusive emphasis on monetary gain, productivity, training for skills and market values do not accord with Catholic teaching or values in education. From a Catholic position a materialistic philosophy of the curriculum ignores the personal, social and spiritual development of the child. Therefore, it was inevitable that the bishops had wider objections to the Education Reform Bill than the non-inclusion of religious education in its provisions for the core curriculum.

The Education Reform Act has defined the curriculum in secular terms with definite instrumental goals as the ultimate objective. Preparation for working life was an avowed aim as was the total development of the child which includes the firm inclusion of spiritual and moral issues in the curriculum. However, little substance has been given to these 'spiritual' and 'moral' aims in the act. The erosion of the right of governors in aided schools to determine the curriculum best suited to the character of their school was completed with the passage of the Education Reform Act. The bishops had fought hard against this and stated that Catholic schools had hitherto[3]

> enjoyed the right to determine the complete school curriculum in the light of their understanding that the educational process should serve and nurture the whole person. The proposed Bill takes away the right ... In practice this means that the Secretary of State and his advisers have the last word on what shall be taught in Catholic schools even if this conflicts with the ideals and practice of Catholic education ... Secular authorities with no professional competence in the matter ... have ultimate control of the curriculum in Church schools.

This has left the church asking itself how it is to respond to an increasingly secular curriculum which will be nationally determined outside its control.

Safeguards under section 17 of the act, which allow for 'exception clauses' to be made on the curriculum, have been added. Consequently, the 'technology of contraception' aspect of the national science curriculum will not apply to Catholic schools. The Secretary of State has said that generally the 'exception clause' will be used in cases where aspects of the national curriculum are unacceptable on religious grounds to Catholic schools.[4] However, since the Act removes from governors this right and places it in the hands of the Secretary of State, it is he and his successors who will have the last word on the curriculum in Catholic schools, even if this conflicts with Catholic teaching. There are no longer any guarantees in statute with regard to the curriculum in aided schools. The bishops had proposed an amendment to place aided schools on the same basis as City Technology Colleges, which are exempt from the national curriculum and simply have to provide 'a broadly based curriculum with an emphasis on science and technology.' The bishops proposed that Catholic schools should likewise have a broad curriculum but with 'an emphasis on the spiritual and moral development of pupils.' Failing this, the bishops argued for a 'Standing Curriculum Committee for Voluntary Aided Schools' to make recommendations to the Secretary of State which they claimed was needed as a safeguard.[5] All these proposals were rejected by the government and the bishops are now calling for representation on the all-powerful National Curriculum Council and School Examinations and Assessment Council which were set up by the Act. They still believe that the Secretary of State has excessive control over what is taught in their schools and over future curriculum development.

In September 1989, governors in all Catholic schools began to ensure that all pupils were taught core and foundation subjects specified by the government 'for a reasonable time.' This has been imposed on a group of schools which Catholic educationalists have argued were already in advance of this narrow and restrictive model of the curriculum.[6]

In practice, Maclure states, governors of aided schools have never exercised their powers over the curriculum, leaving the responsibility to the headteacher and teachers.[7] Major curricular developments such as Technical and Vocational Education Initiative continue to affect Catholic as well as county schools. However, it would be misleading to suggest that therefore the secular curriculum is unrelated to the policies of the school governors in Catholic schools. The model of the school they work on is an all-embracing one of faith, and so as one bishop put it:[8]

> We do not accept that we can include religious education in any curriculum and be content that our duties are fulfilled. Nor can we be satisfied with a situation where a teacher is competent in a particular discipline but does not share in an agreed vision of the whole task.

Religious education in Catholic schools is conducted in accordance with the rites and practices of the Roman Catholic church as stated in the trust deed and articles of government in each school. The initial fears over the position of religious education in the Education Reform Bill caused the bishops to make objections despite the assurances of both section 25(2) of the 1944 Education Act which made religious instruction compulsory and the trust deeds of Catholic schools which ensure its denominational content. Marginalisation of religious education in the school curriculum was the root of these objections since the bishops argued that for them religious education was the foundation of the entire educational process and that:[8]

> It should provide the context for, and substantially shape, the school curriculum

in Catholic schools. Pope John Paul referred to religious education as the 'core of the core curriculum.'[10] In Catholic schools approximately ten per cent of time is given over to religious education on the timetable as opposed to only two-and-a-half per cent in many county schools – four periods as opposed to one.[11]

## Admissions

A school's distinctive identity is often defined by the values and norms that prevail amongst its members. To maintain these values, policy-makers must incorporate them into their policies and actions, which ultimately give a sense of direction and purpose to the school community. Catholic educationalists emphasise the shared nature of these values within a Catholic school and it is for this reason that the bishops, in their campaign over the Education Reform Bill, argued that if schools had to admit non-Catholic pupils up to the limit of the available capacity then the character of the school could be seriously threatened or even totally changed.[12] In other words, admissions have to be controlled in order to safeguard identity.

This same principle is applied to staff appointments, and therefore both admissions and staffing are of outstanding importance because together they make a clear statement about the nature and character of the school. Hitherto, voluntary-aided schools could and did set their own admissions criteria and admitted whom they wished. Catholic schools in particular were not generally open to the wider community. The 1980 Education Act (section 6) was intended to enhance the scope of parental choice by allowing them to 'express a preference' with which it was the duty of governors to comply. However, Catholic schools could make an arrangement with the local authority in respect of admissions which would effectively limit any preference. Indeed, the Catholic Education Council issued guidelines which stated that Catholic schools offer their services first to Catholic families and that these children have a prior claim, which should be reflected in admissions policies. It also warned Catholic schools not to encourage applications of a kind which would not be possible to accept, but did not specify the nature of such applications.[13] The important consequence of this piece of legislation was that governors had now a legally-defined responsibility to publish an admissions policy. The 1986 (no. 2) Education Act section 33 imposed a duty on schools to have regard to the views of the local education authority, but the final judgment remained with the governors.

Since the Education Reform Act 1988, there are no statutory guarantees which allow governors of Catholic schools to refuse to comply with 'parental preference' on the basis of protecting the religious ethos or climate of their school. Instead, there is a provision incorporated into the Act which merely allows governors to refer the matter of admissions to the Secretary of State if they had unsuccessfully sought an agreement with an LEA. Again the issue is left for ultimate determination by the Secretary of State and his successors, rather than the decision of governors which should be in accordance with Catholic philosophy and practice in education. The 1980 and 1988 Education Acts have eroded the discretion once allowed governors in aided schools to operate their own admissions policy.

The whole process on admissions is uncertain and depends on the partial decision of the Secretary of State when all else fails. The 1988 Act gives no more than a mention to the preservation of a school's character in the question of admissions. The bishops failed to convince the government of the need for their amendments which would have explicitly included a safeguard in the act, and in the event none exist.

## The control of Catholic schools

The relative failure of the Catholic negotiations and the campaign surrounding the Education Reform Bill in 1988 needs to be fully assessed in order to evaluate the extent of continued Catholic influence in the shaping of government education policy. The 1988 campaign did expose differences within the Catholic community about the role of the Church in education. Since no consensus was forthcoming, the government has largely imposed its own policies from which the Catholic church has not been able to escape. At the centre of the problem is the failure of the government to distinguish between schools run by an LEA and those of a charitable trust. Cardinal Hume believes this to be exemplified in the provisions of the Education Reform Act 1988 over which he has stated that there has 'not been a true meeting of minds'[14] with the Government. In particular the Catholic church disliked the proposals in the original Bill for Grant Maintained Schools (GMS), open enrolment and the place of religious education in the curriculum. Whilst minor concessions were made on the latter two, the former passed into law largely unchanged. The highly sensitive nature of the situation is acute, since the Act provides the potential for much conflict between parents and governors or between trustees and governing bodies, who all might have different priorities. The Catholic campaign surrounding the passage of the Bill through Parliament provides us with a unique insight into the role of authority within the Catholic Church; in particular, the distribution of rights, obligations and duties in the field of education.

## The role of governors

About the time of the publication of the Education Reform Bill, Cardinal Baum, Prefect of the Sacred Congregation for Catholic

Education in Rome, wrote to Cardinal Hume on the subject of school governors. He wrote:[15]

Individual Catholics who are 'governors' of Catholic schools in the 'dual system' must not only know and fulfil their statutory obligations but must also know their ecclesial rights and obligations. In other words they are to respond to the state's and the church's legitimate expectations of them in such a way as to fulfil their responsibilities both as citizens and as Catholics. The management of one Catholic school should be conducted with due regard for the needs of other Catholic schools and for the interests of Catholic education in general as determined by the bishop of the diocese.

The case being made was that the bishop is the leader of the community and in its name holds most of the Catholic schools in trust, apart from those operated and owned by a religious order. The bishop as trustee is responsible for implementing the trust deed and appointing the foundation governors, who are entrusted with the carrying out of this responsibility in the case of individual schools. Between them they have 'oversight' of the Catholic character of these schools which goes beyond their legal responsibilities − sometimes referred to as a 'duty in conscience.'[16] Nevertheless, the letter from Cardinal Baum had a more direct relevance as in the previous month Cardinal Hume, as trustee of the Cardinal Vaughan Memorial School in London, had dismissed two governors, Mr Mars and Mrs Flynn. They had opposed his policy to reorganise the school which included the loss of the sixth form. Consequently, they were replaced with others who were prepared to implement the policy of the trustee, but the aggrieved governors took the unprecedented step of applying for a judicial review to quash the decision to dismiss them. Their claim was that the trustee had usurped the function of the governors, placed on them by law. The judge accepted that:[17]

the role of the foundation governors was an independent statutory one to arrive in conscience at their own individual conclusion upon the best interests of the school, although taking into account the wider context of Catholic education in the community and with full regard to the trustee's views and advice.

He also accepted that the trustee was not entitled to 'require' the governors to comply with his wishes. However, the judge did not accept that the trustees were bound to leave governors in office since the trustee can have his own policy and may use his statutory powers to dismiss and appoint governors to secure its implementation. This case was significant since it appeared to confirm the power of trustees to dismiss governors who refuse to implement their policy. Subsequent developments have disappointed the hopes placed in this decision by the bishops. The final decision of the courts in the ILEA vs. Haberdashers' Aske's Governors has nullified the effect of the original decision and it is now plain that a bishop cannot prevent a determined governing body from taking its own line and frustrating diocesan plans. To date only three Catholic schools have 'opted out' although there have been other ballots. One 'opting out' approved by the local bishop in Grantham was rejected by the Secretary of State on the grounds of viability. The interest shown in 'opting out' in the Catholic sector is roughly proportionate to that shown overall. The governors in question of the Cardinal Vaughan school challenged the action of the trustees at a time when the bishops were challenging the government proposals, which they believed would undermine their authority.

## The reponse to the Education Reform Bill

In November 1987, the bishops set up an Advisory Committee under the Chairmanship of the Rt. Rev. David Konstant, Bishop of Leeds, to press for amendments to the Bill.[18] In particular, the attacks focused on the most radical aspects of the Bill — the establishment of GM schools. At first sight there appeared to be certain advantages to the 2,400 Catholic schools in England and Wales since by 'opting out' and becoming GM schools they would have ended the financial burden on the Catholic community of providing fifteen per cent of future capital expenditure. However, the CEC pointed out that it has not been the policy of the church to look for one hundred per cent capital grant for Catholic schools.[19] Also the proposals in the Bill, confirmed in the Act, stated that any liabilities in respect of the principal or interest on any loans are not transferred to the GMS. Consequently the trustee, who would remain owner of the school premises, would still be required to pay any debt costs on any loans taken out on behalf of the school previous to it becoming a GMS If the school then proposed its own discontinuance at some future date the Secretary of State would be able to secure compensation for any capital work for which he had paid grant and there would be a charge on any sale of premises to meet redundancy costs or other debts. These debts would fall on the trustee even though he might not have shared in the original move to seek GM status. These serious reservations about the financial implications of the act are however second only to those regarding the position under the act of the trustee himself.

## The role of the bishops

The bishops took severe exception to the 'opting out' provisions, especially the clause that governing bodies had merely to consult trustees about their own desire to seek GM status. Also, the Secretary of State had simply to consider any objections made by the trustee and more importantly could modify a trust deed if it appeared to him to be necessary. These provisions allow parents and governors to remove a school from diocesan control, to become a semi-autonomous concern maintained fully by central government without the express agreement of the trustees. Indeed the bishops noted that 'opting out:[20]

favours the interests of a minority of parents and children at the expense of the majority. Such a general principle is difficult to reconcile with Catholic ideals.

Cardinal Hume in a letter to *The Times* of 13th January 1988 stated that:

The so-called process as now presented offers a serious threat to the balance and very provision of Catholic voluntary education.

He proposed that the bishop should have a veto over any application of a Catholic school for GM status. In the campaign booklet, issued by the bishops against the bill, it was argued that the bishops themselves bear a special responsibility for the education of the Catholic community. This is a point they have consistently maintained and which their statement of 1975 confirmed:[21]

In the area of Catholic education the recognised teachers are the bishops. Hence all matters relating to education are in a peculiar way reserved to the bishops, who have ultimate responsibility for decisions regarding policy.

Consequently, the 1988 statement warned:[22]

the bill in its present form could seriously impede the fulfilment of that responsibility.

During the debates on the bill, and subsequently, the bishops have insisted that Catholic schools have no meaning except in relation to the church. They cannot be viewed in isolation and it is the bishop who must come to a final decision, particularly in matters of controversy within the Catholic community such as the reorganisation of schools. The bishops claim that Catholic schools have a common interest in the success of each other and that the act makes overall planning impossible since transient groups of parents could 'opt-out' harming the interests of the wider Catholic community.[23] Catholics could find, admittedly under extreme circumstances, that the local Catholic GMS was no longer open to them except under the school's own admission procedures. Whilst the Secretary of

State gave verbal assurances to the bishops during the passage of the Education Reform Bill, their attempt to have safeguards explicitly placed in the Bill failed. The governnment's view is that the bishops should be responsible for keeping their own governors in line but, as Cardinal Hume remarks, the reliance on the bishops' powers to dismiss governors will produce 'endless conflict and litigation.'[24] So whilst the option of GM status is now available to most Catholic schools the bishops emphasise that it will do harm:[25]

> without prior consultation and the consent of the community expressed through the trustee.

Nevertheless, the trustees would still appoint the majority of governors to potential GM schools:[26]

> for the purpose of securing, so far as is practicable, that the established character of the school, at the time when it becomes a grant-maintained school, is preserved and developed and, in particular, that the school is conducted in accordance with the provisions of any trust deed relating to it.

However, this does not prevent the parents or governors having different priorities from the diocesan authorities which inevitably place greater emphasis on the wording of the trust deed. Diocesan trust deeds normally provide for:[27]

> property to be held in trust of advancing the Roman Catholic religion in the diocese by such means as the Ordinary (bishop) may think it fit and proper.

Therefore, planning for educational provision is an essential part of this duty which the bishop fulfils in partnership with the people. The workings of this 'partnership' are not however formally constituted since the bishop is normally the focus of unity in a diocese for, as Mgr Vincent Nicholls puts it:[28]

> As partners with the state in the dual system, Catholic authorities certainly accept that the Secretary of State must approve plans, or, if he so desires, veto them. But it is important that the proposals to be put to him be drawn up by the Catholic partner in a manner consistent with Catholic procedures, i.e. with and under the authority of the bishop. In other words, with regard to Catholic schools, which are part of church life, it is for the church to propose and for the state to merely accept or reject, but not to arbitrate between dissenting voices in the church.

Mgr Nicholls emphasises that the functions of the bishop are not simply administrative but that they are responsible for Catholic schools which are rooted in communities with shared convictions and values. However, in the controversy over the Bill and Act there have emerged some serious differences within the Catholic body. The bishops have not received the same full support they enjoyed at the time of the 1944 Education Act.

## Divisions within the Catholic community

According to the bishops, the Education Reform Act poses a major threat to Catholic schools especially since they represent over half of the voluntary schools eligible for GM status.[29] Consequently, during the campaign against the bill, the bishops wrote to all Catholic MPs in an attempt to enlist their support. However, the reaction of some MPs, in particular members of the governing party, contrasts sharply with previous campaigns. Not much support was forthcoming from prominent Catholics in 1988, with James Pawsey, Chairman of the Backbench Education Committee and a member of the Parliamentary Committee which considered the Bill, stating that the Bill extended parental rights and responsibilities. In a letter to the *Catholic Herald* of 12th February 1988, Mr Pawsey insisted that the Bill was 'not devoid of spiritual awareness' even though Cardinal Hume had condemned the Bill previously for its 'spiritual emptiness.' Sheila Lawlor, deputy director of studies at the Centre for Policy Studies, in an article in the *Tablet* of 20th February 1988 argued that diocesan authorities were fearful of parental power and added:

the hierarchy reject the prospect of parents exercising a voice, unless that voice happens to echo its own ... The danger to church schools lies not in 'opting-out' but in a refusal of diocesan planners to respect the wishes of those for whom they plan.

Even among the seventy-one Catholic peers there was little support to be had, with the Duke of Norfolk opposing the whole thrust of the bishops' arguments. This is in spite of the admission by the bishops that they were not against 'opting-out' in principle. Political and secular determinants of values and attitudes had certainly triumphed here.

## Structure of Catholic education after ERA

The powers of the bishops, despite the 1988 Act, are still more substantial and effective than those at the disposal of other denominational figures, though they are not satisfactory to the bishops. These powers are surprising considering there was practically no central fund of manpower or financial resources which could be deployed on the basis of centralised decision-making in and before the campaign over the Education Reform Bill. The situation was clearly unsatisfactory and exposed certain weaknesses in national administrative structures. There also was the problem of representation of essentially lay educational concerns on national bodies which needed to be clarified. A small working party to review national and local structures was established in March 1987 by the bishops and reported in November 1988. Its recommendations included the abolition of the CEC and the creation of a new body, the Department of Catholic Education, as part of the Bishops' Conference of England and Wales. This proposed body would have a number of committees each with a bishop as Chairman and would include representation from all those involved with Catholic education. There would be created a second body, called the Catholic Education Service, whose membership would be more restricted and include a number of bishops and their appointees to provide them with professional advice. It would be this body, dominated by the bishops, which will be responsible for presenting Catholic policies to the government.

## Conclusion

Since the 1988 Act many centrally determined educational policies are no longer based on statute but on the considerable and unprecedented powers awarded to the Secretary of State. Catholic schools have not, despite vigorous opposition, been able to escape the effects of these policies, which some believe undermine the very reason for their existence. The government's avowed policy during the decade has been the extension of parental choice of school in the belief that the distribution, size and character of schools can thus be more efficiently determined. In addition, the government believes that through competition between schools the quality of education will improve; hence the promotion of increasingly differentiated types of schools. Parents are viewed as 'consumers' in this model, with schools as 'producers' and the education offered emphasising the utility value of knowledge. The whole thrust of this policy directly challenges the fundamental principles and values of Catholic education and the ability of the bishops to influence them.[30]

On all the crucial areas, the Catholic bishops have seen a marked erosion of their privileges and rights, and in this light their 1988 campaign against ERA must be viewed as a failure. No significant concessions were made by the Secretary of State. In addition, the support given to the government by prominent Catholic MPs and peers demonstrates that a united Catholic position no longer exists.

The survival of the partnership, on which the 'dual system' was based, now appears doubtful. Ten years of Conservative government, culminating in the Education Reform Act, have eroded the statutory rights built up since 1870. Further moves in this direction will have to be resisted by the bishops if anything significant is to be left of the Catholic schools system in England and Wales.[31]

**Notes**
1. Roehampton Group, 'Maintaining the Catholicity of Catholic schools,' *The Month,* April, 1986.
2. 'The Religious Dimension of Catholic Education,' Congregation for Catholic Education, Rome, 1988.
3. 'Education Reform Bill: a commentary for Catholics,' 1987, p. 11, Bishops' Conference of England and Wales.
4. 'Education Reform Act and Catholic Schools,' 1988, p. 7, Catholic Education Council; see also *The Times*, 13 January, 1988.
5. 'Education Reform Bill − A Commentary for Catholics,' 1987, p. 7.
6. *The Universe*, 1 January, 1988.
7. S Maclure, *Education Re-Formed*, 1988, p. 8.
8. P Kelly, *Catholic Schools*, Diocese of Salford, 1987, p. 10.
9. 'Education Reform Bill: a commentary for Catholics,' 1987, p. 5.
10. Catholic Information Services, *Briefing*, March 1988.
11. 'Education Reform Act and Catholic Schools,' Catholic Education Council, 1988, p. 6.
12. 'Education Reform Bill: a commentary for Catholics,' 1987, p. 8.
13. 'The Education Act 1980 and Catholic Schools,' Catholic Education Council, 1981.
14. B Hume, *Towards a Civilisation of Love*, London, Hodder and Stoughton, 1989, p. 105.
15. *Ibid.*, p. 116.
16. 'Your School: guidelines for governors,' Archdiocese of Birmingham, 1987.
17. *The Guardian* − Legal Report, 17 December, 1987.
18. Catholic Information Services − *Briefing*, December 1987.
19. 'Education Reform Act and Catholic Schools,' 1988, p. 35.
20. Catholic Information Services − *Briefing*, May 1988.
21. Bishops Conference of England and Wales Education Statement of 1975.
22. 'Education Reform Bill: a commentary for Catholics,' 1987.
23. *Ibid.*
24. Catholic Information Services − *Briefing*, May 1988.
25. B Hume, *op. cit.*, p. 116.
26. M Leonard, *The 1988 Education Reform Act*, Blackwells, Oxford, 1988, p. 140.
27. B Hume, *op. cit.*, p. 116.
28. 'Education Reform Act and Catholic Schools,' 1988, p. 37.
29. Catholic Information Services − *Briefing*, July 1988.
30. See speech to the National Conference of Catholic Priests given on 5th September 1989 at Newman College, Birmingham by Cardinal Hume − reported in Catholic Information Services − *Briefing*, September 1989.
31. Some of the material for this article is drawn from the author's unpublished MSc thesis entitled 'A consideration of certain aspects of Catholic educational policy in action,' 1989, University of Oxford Department of Educational Studies.

# 6. European perspectives

This chapter illustrates the contribution made by the churches to educational provision in three very different parts of Europe.

In the first article, Dr Seamas Ó Buachalla argues that the relationship between the churches and the state and their respective roles in the educational system have been central and sensitive issues in Irish political life in this century and the centre of sustained controversy in the last century. He refers in turn to the historical legacy and the present position, to the educational policy of the churches and the response of the political system. He concludes that the presence and power of the churches have been increased significantly in the course of the present century and have been further consolidated in the expansion of educational provision since the 1960s.

Seamas Ó Buachalla is in the School of Education at Trinity College, Dublin. This article was first published in *European Journal of Education* in 1985.

In the second article, Marjanne de Kwaasteniet describes the place of denominational schools in the Netherlands, setting the present situation within its historical and political contexts. The school struggle, lasting between 1840 and 1920, in which the Liberals and the Orthodox Protestants were the main conflicting parties, secured the existence of a significant denominational sector alongside the state schools. Since 1920 this sector in the Netherlands is paid exclusively by the state, like the state sector itself. In the period 1920–1960 a sharp decline in the state sector was accompanied by increases in both the Protestant and Catholic sector. The Protestant sector continued to grow into the 1980s.

At the time of writing Marjanne de Kwaasteniet was in the University of Amsterdam. This article was also first published in *European Journal of Education* in 1985.

In the third article, Dr Oliver Boyd-Barrett turns attention to Spain. He examines the transition from a church-dominated educational system during the forty year period of Franco's dictatorship to a state-dominated system, and identifies the mechanisms by which this transition was achieved. He concludes that it should not be thought that the Catholic church is now a weak force in the Spanish educational system, although it is significantly less strong than used to be the case.

Oliver Boyd-Barrett is Sub-Dean in the School of Education at the Open University. This article was first published in *Compare* in 1991.

# 6.1 Church and state in Irish education in this century
*Seamas Ó Buachalla*

## Introduction

The relationship of the churches and the state and the role which both play in the educational system have been central and sensitive issues in Irish political life in this century and the centre of sustained controversy in the last century. In examining the pattern of the relationship in this century it will prove useful to refer in turn to the historical legacy and the present position, the educational policy of the churches and the response of the political system; some concrete policy issues will then be analysed in an attempt to describe a model of the policy process and the place of the churches in it.

## The present position and the historical legacy

The Irish educational system is best characterised as an 'aided' system, in which the state assists other agencies mainly by means of funding, to provide educational services at all three levels. At both first and second levels, with the sole exception of the vocational system, the majority of the aided agencies are churches, church bodies or trusts, or corporate bodies in which the churches exercise a large influence. This applies equally to the churches of both main denominations, Catholic and Protestant; in the vocational system the aided agency is the local authority or its specialist sub-committee. At third level the state funds universities and colleges of technology either directly, through the Higher Education Authority, or by means of the appropriate local authority.

Thus throughout the formal educational system the churches or their agencies occupy a prominent structural position, both proprietorial and managerial. Practically all of the national schools are managed by boards which are chaired *ex officio* by clergymen and whose other membership is influenced largely by church decision; in addition the legal trustees of the school property also come from the ranks of senior diocesan clergymen and church parochial officers. In the second level the vast majority of secondary schools are owned and managed by church bodies, religious orders or trusts; in the more recently constituted comprehensive and community schools diocesan authorities and religious orders have been given a share in the management and trusteeship. Of the 548 secondary schools, 494 are owned and conducted by Catholic agencies and 26 by Protestant boards or governing bodies; the balance, 28 schools, are owned and managed by lay persons, the majority of whom are Catholic. In the vocational system which conducts 246 schools, the churches have not played a dominant role, yet they are involved, mainly through membership of the controlling Vocational Education Committees.[1]

In addition to the strong quantitative presence of the churches at all levels of the present educational system, the educational controversies of the last century and the signal victories achieved had vested the educational question with a special significance for both churches.[2] Compared to the educational structures in other european states where the churches were losing ground to public initiative, the system obtaining in Ireland by the turn of the century gave economic relief, political power and ideological satisfaction to the churches. In other states where the churches rejected public education, the main price of rejection was the creation out of church funds of an alternative autonomous system; in Ireland the churches had secured a system which was acceptable to and controlled by them, but was funded mainly by the state. The acceptability of such a system to the Catholic church and its satisfaction with the outcome of the educational struggles of the 19th century were clearly indicated by Cardinal Logue in 1900. His pastoral letter issued following the National Synod, expressed satisfaction that the national school system was *de facto* as denominational as could be desired and that there was very little mixed education whatsoever.[3] This satisfaction with the structure of the system was on the whole shared by the Protestant churches; the denominationalisation of the system had produced at first and second level an effective partitioned structure in which each denomination exercised control over its own sector.

Educational policy and provision throughout the 19th century was never far from fundamental controversies, which divided not only the churches one from the other, but frequently occasioned a rift between them and the state and for a period even precipitated a sharp division within the ranks of the Catholic hierarchy. Such controversy, however, should not occlude the very substantial advances made in the elaboration of a national school system providing elementary education for close on a million children by the century's end and a secondary system which offered further education to a growing minority. The Queen's Colleges at Cork, Belfast and Galway, though unsupported generally by the Catholics, and the older Dublin University had established the nucleus of a higher education system whose continuation and wider acceptance would be guaranteed by the creation of the National University in 1908. By the last decade of the century, teacher education was provided in well-endowed training colleges and the position of trained qualified teachers was rising rapidly. Technical education was available in the larger urban areas in institutions funded and managed by local authorities.

These various advances constitute in aggregate a significant achievement and denoted a growing *rapprochement* between the churches and government which effectively removed education from the arena of state/church conflict. The churches had, especially after 1870, assumed a dominant role in educational policy and provision; the Catholic church especially had enhanced its public and national status considerably by means of the educational policies it pursued from 1850 onwards.[4] The structures for the provision and management of education which had evolved in the course of the century had been consolidated by 1900 in a manner which explicitly recognised the dominant role of the churches; these structures would re-emerge as an early controversial issue but would prove resistant to substantial modification for most of the new century.

In examining educational developments in 19th-century Ireland the interaction between the churches and the state is of central importance. The outcome of the various educational controversies surrounding that interaction had by the century's end significantly influenced the status and power of the churches. Furthermore the mechanisms and strategies by which that power had been achieved would in turn directly shape educational policy and provision throughout most of the following century. The Roman Catholic church in the early decades of the 19th century enjoyed none of the overt power and patronage attaching to the Church of Ireland. As an established state church, the church of the minority exercised a major influence in the cultural, political and educational spheres, an influence which was resented and envied by the leaders and members of the majority church. By the end of the century those positions of power and disadvantage had virtually been reversed. While the Catholic Emancipation Act of 1829 and the 1869 Act of Disestablishment removed some of the legal disabilities, it was mainly in and by the educational system that the Roman Catholic Church extended its sphere of power and influence throughout the century, especially after the arrival of Cardinal Cullen from Rome.[5] That church's position of weakness in the early decades, a residual legacy of the penal laws, was transformed by the 1870s into a niche of considerable strength and influence in Irish life. The process of transformation was promoted and catalysed mainly by a prolonged campaign involving a series of resounding victories on educational issues carried by the church against various governments. This strategy of church enlargement and power brokerage in the education system was presided over by a succession of able prelates, notably by Murray, Crolly, Cullen and Walsh, all of whom placed the educational question high on their list of priorities.[6]

The internal structures and the related power patterns which emerged from the educational controversies of the last century proved remarkably resilient and their preservation and defence became central factors in the determination of policy in this century. The dominant role of the churches and their relationship to the state in the organisation and management of the educational system remained as major influences on policy throughout this century. Nevertheless some modifications and evolution can be observed in the power structure, perhaps as early as the 1940s and certainly from the mid-1960s. The simple binary power structure which operated at the turn of the century excluded all but the state and the churches from the process of policy-making. In the course of this century that simple model was extended to encompass in turn the political parties from 1922, the local authorities from 1930, the national teachers from 1946 and other teachers later; the quantitative and qualitative expansion of the system in the last two decades has been accompanied by the partial and gradual inclusion in the power structure of industrial and socio-economic interests and eventually of parents and students.[7] However these inclusions do not represent a serious or significant departure from the reality of the old binary model; the major portion of the system at first and second levels still lies within the direct sphere of influence and managerial direction of the churches and is funded mainly by the state, a situation which yields dominant roles to the state and the churches.

The historical significance of education for the churches was considerably reinforced by the controversies of the last century; in addition, the central role of education in their dogmatic teaching has fashioned church policies which have been coherent and demanding since 1900.

## Church policies on education

Church policy in general throughout this century has been mainly concerned with defence and consolidation of the structural *status quo*; the *ex officio* managerial role of the clergy and church trusteeship at primary level, the private status of secondary schools and the absence of a local public authority presence; these were features which the Catholic church had secured in the last century and intended to defend. Such a policy generated a high sensitivity to structural reforms and especially to those which would diminish the clerical managerial role or dilute it by sharing administration with popular elected representatives. Throughout the two decades prior to independence (1900–22) some attempts were made to reform the structures; the church responses were emphatic as can be seen in the various episcopal statements, almost exclusively concerned with structural aspects.[8] The basic strategy of the Catholic church, which was employed effectively against Wyndham's reform of 1904, as against the Devolution Bill of 1907 and McPherson's Bill of 1919–20, was enunciated in a major statement on education in

1904.[9] The bishops defended the clerical managerial system, claimed that any structural changes would be unacceptable to the Irish people and themselves, and asserted that any changes involving reduced clerical control would be so injurious to the religious interests of the people that it would be imperative for the church to resist them. The central significance of the defeat of the McPherson Bill, lies not in the total victory of the bishops but in the manner in which it was accomplished and in the long-term influence which it exercised on educational policy in the new Irish state. The sharp controversy surrounding the reform measure and the denominational divide characterising it, carried a clear message for the political leaders of the new Irish state; if the independence movement wished to secure the blessing and support of the church, then church and state would need to be *ad idem* on such basic issues as educational policy; this inevitably meant among other things, that the state would accept the church's specification of the respective roles of state and church in the provision and management of education. The political sensitivity attaching to the question is clearly evident in the proceedings of the First Dáil where a resolution supportive of the church stand was unanimously adopted by the cabinet in 1920 and Mr De Valera 'had some definite reason' for not appointing a Minister for Education in the first cabinet.[10]

In the period to the early 1960s, church policy was overtly influenced by the papal teaching contained in the encyclical, *Divini Illius Magistri* of 1929, in which Pius XI specified the functions of the church, the family and the state in education. The church's role was derived from 'a supernatural title conferred by God upon her alone, transcending in authority and validity any title of the natural order;' therefore education is supereminently the function of the church and her rights are independent of any earthly power and universal in scope. The family's rights and responsibilities in education are God-given, inviolate and prior to those of the state, whose rights and duty in education, according to the encyclical, are to protect the prior rights of the parents, respect the rights of the church, to promote and assist the work of the church and the family, to supplement that work where deficient and to build its own schools and institutions.[11]

The encyclical of 1929 was most influential in moulding Irish Catholic educational opinion and policy; its promulgation between the establishment of the Free State and the adoption of the Constitution of 1937, increased Catholic dissatisfaction with the former and influenced significantly the contents of the latter. It also exercised a profound influence on the main Catholic writings in the 1930s and 1940s; this was especially so in relation to a major work[12] which was particularly influential and whose contribution to the framing of the 1937 constitution was significant. In his work, Edward Cahill condemned the principles involved in the slogan 'Free education for all,' as being under the influence of liberalism and socialism and as being 'full of danger to the interests of family life, especially where the free education is to be given at public expense in state schools.' One of those who was instrumental in moulding state policy in the 1920s, the Rev. Professor TJ Corcoran, SJ, expressed the essence of Catholic policy on education to be 'Catholic education in Catholic schools for all Catholic youth.'[13] Quite early in the life of the new Irish State, church leaders would appear to have been quite satisfied; according to an episcopal pastoral letter of 1927 the bishops 'had no ground for complaint.' In 1950 the first chairman of the Council for Education, the Rev. Professor O'Keeffe, identified one feature on which the system was superior to any other he knew of: 'an exact appreciation of what is and what is not the legitimate function of the state. On this there is almost universal agreement.'[14]

Church policy on education throughout the century has been remarkably coherent and consistent; clerical dissent from the official position has been rare and, when it did arise, was disregarded or swept aside by disciplinary action.

The educational policy of the Protestant churches, expressed usually through yearly formal synods, would with some important exceptions correspond closely to that of the majority church; however Protestant churches generally would have favoured local popular control and would have given lay teachers and lay people a larger role in church education structures. On the basic issue of the existing clerical managerial system and the private status of secondary schools, Protestant policy would not have differed from the state position of the Catholic church.[15]

## The response of the political system

The reaction of the political system to the promulgated position of the churches on education and particularly to the policy of the Catholic church, can be observed in published party policies, in the choice of Ministers for Education and the perception which they have of their role and in the outcome of policy issues where church and state hold conflicting views or objectives.

Only one party, the Irish Labour Party, has been consistent over the century in the preparation and publication of education policy documents; the two other main parties, Fine Gael and Fianna Fáil did not do so until the 1960s and, even then, Fianna Fáil's enthusiasm for such exercises was never great. Labour's policies, from its earliest days of 1925, have been progressively, structurally reformist and egalitarian, retaining strong ideological links with its pre-independence phase.[16] Fine Gael and Fianna Fáil have been extremely cautious in their policies, seldom until the recent decades espousing any policies in the *access* or *structure* dimensions which would inevitably raise questions concerning the existing structure. Labour's effective contribution to policy has been diminished considerably by the fact that no Labour deputy has ever occupied the Ministry of Education; all of the 20 ministers from 1922 to date have been from Fine Gael or Fianna Fáil and in the early decades were usually senior party ministers who were acceptable to the church. Until the 1960s, education was not seen as a high profile portfolio and, given the general supervision exercised by the *Taoiseach* (Premier), was unlikely to enhance the political career of the holder.

Ministers reflected this sensitivity in the manner in which they defined their own role. Among the early occupants, MacNeill (1922–25) and O'Sullivan (1926–32) were distinguished by a pronounced distrust of state initiative in education.[17] Deirg, who served for sixteen years in De Valera's governments, saw his role in a more active mode and raised the level of ministerial and departmental initiative. Nevertheless both he and his immediate successors in the late 1940s and 1950s, Mulcahy (1948–51, 1954–57) and Moylan (1954–57) were at pains to assert their full commitment to the preservation of the system's existing structures.[18] The 1960s generated strong popular demand for extended educational opportunity which the politicians responded to by re-defining the State's role in education. For the younger aspiring ministers who have filled the position from 1957 to date, especially for Colley (1965–66) and O'Malley (1966–68), the older received dogma and the associated rhetoric were no longer acceptable.[19] Colley and O'Malley perceived and asserted that the centre of initiative in formulating and implementing policy must be the government and the minister and further that, if the system were dependent on private secondary schools which could select pupils, then equality of opportunity could not be assured by the minister. By the early 1980s, when policy focus had shifted to higher education, the larger question of regionalisation and the creation of local education authorities had again been raised. The ever rising demands for education, the high participation rates and escalating public expenditure have generated a common awareness of the need to rationalise and to raise efficiency, which ultimately may well seek a solution in a localised integrated system.

In general, politicians of all parties have been extremely sensitive to church opinion on all topics, and have seldom adopted a political stance at variance with known church policies. Where conflicts have occurred, as in 1951 and 1985, they have been a major political phenomena leading, in the 1951 instance, to the downfall of the government.[20] Conflict in education between church and state has never been on a major scale or, where it has occurred, it has never been conducted *coram populo*. There have been some limited conflicts surrounding policy initiatives launched by the government and the minister. That these have been few in number and seldom of major proportions is due mainly to the government and departmental practice of submitting all major policy proposals in education to the hierarchy for consideration. In most, if not all, cases where the hierarchy have reacted negatively, in the period from 1922 to 1954, the proposals have been dropped by the government, or were modified to meet the wishes of the church.[21]

## Policy issues

The churches have been consulted formally on a wide variety of policy issues, from extending educational opportunity in the Gaeltacht areas (peripheral, Irish-speaking districts) to the exclusion of married women teachers from employment and measures proposed to overcome unemployment among teachers. The most frequent and continuous topic for consultation revolves around the policies which raise structural or managerial questions; chief among these is the issue of access to the system, equality of opportunity and the publicly-managed vocational system.

In 1930 the vocational educational system was created by act of parliament under which a network of second-level schools was established under county education authorities. The bishops sought an assurance that the vocational schools would not provide general education for those aged between 14–16; this assurance was given by the Minister in October 1930.[22] Consequently, these schools, usually serving remote areas and the less advantaged pupils, were prevented from teaching academic subjects and from entering their pupils for state examinations giving access to higher education; these restrictions were lifted in the reforms of the 1960s.

When submitted to the hierarchy, Mr De Valera's proposal of 1934 to build 20 senior schools in the Gaeltacht and to provide school transport for their pupils, was criticised as involving 'a further extension of state control' and was not proceeded with.

Throughout the 1940s and 1950s the church secondary managerial bodies were strongly of the opinion that the vocational system should be abolished and be started again on new and thoroughly Catholic lines.'[23] This pressure was maintained on the minister and the department during the 1950s so that the minister was simultaneously attempting to satisfy the demands of the bishops and to reassure the threatened local authorities whose schools he was funding from public funds.[24]

In the 1960s some of the various policy measures introduced to extend educational opportunity and plan the expansion of the system were interpreted as being a threat to the 'private' status of the secondary schools. The overwhelming popular support for the 'free' education scheme however gave the Catholic bishops little or no room for manoeuvre on these issues; when the minister's scheme of 1967 was criticised by the school managers, he was quick to inform them that he had been in consultation with the bishops for over two years and that they had agreed to his policy.

## A policy mechanism and consultative model

It is difficult, in the absence of free access to all the relevant archives, to chart with great accuracy the mechanism of policy formulation and the model which best describes the consultative process between church and state. However an attempt can be made based upon the following assumptions which can be justified from available evidence:

a.  all the contributors to education policy and all the contributions are not of equal weight;
b.  the government observes an established sequence of stages in the consultative process;
c.  a policy or policy measure which encounters conflict or criticism in the early stages is seldom persevered with unmodified;
d.  consultation with church leaders, formal or informal, is usually the first stage in the sequence.

The consultative process is complicated by the multiplicity of managerial bodies, divided by sex, denomination and level, with which the minister has to negotiate. In some sectors of policy some groups or contributors have a virtual veto of limited scope; thus teachers and school managerial bodies can effectively exercise such a veto on salary or working conditions and the Department of Finance can effectively control a policy which involves additional expenditure. The churches however enjoy a much more extensive power in policy formation; they can veto measures over a wide range of policy dimensions in a process which is conducted privately between themselves and the state.

In response to the state policy initiatives of the 1960s the churches and the managerial bodies created umbrella groups at various levels to increase their efficacy in negotiations with the state. On the Catholic side these developments have increased the direct input of the bishops in policy formulation. The power structure has consequently assumed a more orderly and systematic form; it has also become symmetrical with corresponding elements on both sides of the denominational divide and a central Joint Managerial Body representing all denominations and interests.

On questions of a routine administrative nature, a low-level process occurs where the Joint Managerial Body interacts with the different administrative divisions of the Department. When central questions of policy are concerned, however, or important initiatives are planned, the minister or senior officers of the department consult with the bishops. This higher level process effectively sets the agenda for the lower level interaction between the government and the school bodies. The churches not only control and manage the major portion of the educational system at first and second level, funded by the state, but they also delimit the dimensions of the educational debate conducted in the state.

The churches, Catholic and Protestant, have been a major element of the educational system throughout this century. Their presence and power have been increased significantly in the course of this century and have been further consolidated in the expansion of educational provision in the last two decades which was achieved mainly by a growing state initiative in education.

**Notes**

1. *Administration Yearbook and Diary, 1982–83*, pp. 99–103.
2. D H Akenson, *The Irish Education Experiment*, London Routledge and Kegan Paul, 1970; E Brian Titley, *Church, State and the Control of Schooling in Ireland, 1900–1944*, Kingston and Dublin, Gill and Macmillan, 1983.
3. *The Irish Ecclesiastical Record*, XX, 1900.
4. E R Norman, *The Catholic Church and Ireland in the Age of Rebellion 1859–73*, New York, Cornell University Press, 1965.
5. Desmond Bowen, *Paul Cardinal Cullen*, Dublin, Gill and Macmillan, 1983; D A Kerr, *Peel Priests and Politics*, Oxford, Clarendon Press, 1982.
6. P J Walsh, *William J Walsh, Archbishop of Dublin*, London, Longmans, 1928.
7. T J O'Connell, *A Hundred Years of Progress*, Dublin, Irish Nation Teachers Organisation, 1970.
8. J H Whyte, *Church and State in Modern Ireland 1923–1970*, Dublin, Gill and Macmillan, 1971; *The Irish Ecclesiastical Record, 1898*, p. 83; *Ibid.*, 1900, p. 553.
9. David W Miller, *Church, Nation and State in Ireland 1898–1921*, Dublin, Gill and Macmillan, pp. 447–452; E Strauss, *Irish Nationalism and British Democracy*, London, Methuen, 1951.
10. S Ó Buachalla, 'Education as an issue in the first and second Dáil,' *Administration*, 2S, 1, 1977, pp. 57–75.
11. *Divini Illius Magistri*, 10, 11, 14, 20, 22, London, 1929.
12. E J Cahill, SJ, *The Framework of a Christian State*; Dublin, M H Gill and Son; see also T P O'Neill, and P Ó Fiannachta, *deValera*, 11, p. 328; and Desmond M Clarke, *Church and State*, Cork, Cork University Press, 1984, Chapters 7 and 8.
13. T J Corcoran, SJ 'The Catholic philosophy of education,' *Studies*, XIX, 1930 p. 206.
14. *The Irish Times*, 1950, May 6th.
15. *Journal of Proceedings of General Synod of the Church of Ireland* from 1908 to date, which includes the *Annual Report* of the Board of Education.
16. A Mitchell, *Labour in Irish Politics, 1890–1930*, Dublin, Irish University Press, 1974; The Irish Labour Party, *Labour's Policy on Education*, 1925; *Challenge and Change in Education*, 1963; *Labour Party Outline Policy – Education*, 1969.
17. MacNeill papers, UCD Archives, LAI/E/76; 'The control of Irish education,' *An Claidheamh Soluis*, May 23rd, 1903; 'The unity of education,' *The Freeman's Journal*, March 23rd, 1906.
18. *Dáil Debates*, 110, 1093; *Dáil Debates*, 126, 1697.
19. 'Changes in Irish education,' Address by Mr G Colley, TD, Minister for Education, November 15th 1965; 'Free education and after?', Address by Mr D O'Malley, TD, Minister for Education, February 16th 1967.
20. J H Whyte, *Op. cit.*, chapters V–IX inclusive.
21. State Paper Office, Cabinet papers, 56506, D 9409, Dublin; Department of Finance Archives, S20/I/34, Dublin.

22. Letter from J M O'Sullivan, TD, Minister for Education to Dr Keane, Bishop of Limerick, October 31st 1930.
23. *Annual Report*, Conference of Convent Secondary Schools, 1949, p. 52.
24. Mulcahy papers, UCD Archives, P7/C/161, note signed T Ó R, June 5th 1956.

# 6.2 Denominational education and contemporary education policy in the Netherlands

*Marjanne de Kwaasteniet*

## Introduction

All Western European societies experienced in the 19th century a struggle between church and state for control of their educational systems. National states, going through a phase of consolidation, tried to turn educational systems into instruments of nation-building, reducing the power of the church, which had held a virtual monopoly with regard to education until then.

Education by the church had served mainly to control its following and to train future clergy. In the era of the secular nation-state however, the aim of education was no longer regarded as religious teaching, but training for loyal citizenship. Depending on the relative strength of both actors, the churches retained influence on educational matters to a greater or lesser extent.

In the Netherlands, a religiously heterogeneous country, denominational, privately owned schools were given an important position next to secular state schools. The resultant school struggle was waged mainly between orthodox Protestant groups and the Liberals; and motives different from the religious one played a part in the conflict. Central, however, was the wish to send children to religious schools, since the religious training still organised by the church was considered to be insufficient to transmit the norms and values of the group. Formal teaching was to be a continuation and extension of education at home. The school system which evolved in the second half of the last century was designed to accommodate that need.

Throughout the 20th century the structure of the school system has essentially remained the same. The demographic expansion caused a strong growth of both the state and the non-state (Protestant and Catholic) sectors of the education system.[1] But the importance of education did not grow only quantitatively (participation rates, expenditure). After the second world war education became increasingly subject to state intervention.

Peculiar to the Dutch educational system is that with regard to a large number of issues, the education policy of the state concerns both the state and the non-state sectors. This situation makes it necessary to develop and to implement every policy in close consultation and co-operation with representatives of the non-state sector. The interests of the non-state sector are catered for, both in the electoral arena, where the confessional political parties are its mouthpiece, and in the corporatist arena, where the state negotiates with education interest organisations. The importance the confessional political parties attach to educational policy can be measured from the increasingly extensive paragraph on education in their party programs. The interesting paradox has developed that although religious groups originally fought for non-state schools, which would give them sovereignty in educational matters, the development of an educational policy by the state and their participation in state power have resulted in their taking up responsibility for the educational system as a whole.

The fact that the religious groups on the one hand participate in state responsibility for education and, on the other, wish to restrict state influence on non-state education has not facilitated education policy making. The paradoxical situation of non-state sector representatives with regard to education policy making, and their political stand on contemporary education issues, will be the focus of the second part of this article. It will become clear that, although many of the principles of the religious parties in the school struggle of the last century are still significant contemporary debate, the dividing line in recent discussions is no longer always between the religious parties on one side and the Liberals plus Socil Democrats on the other. Other divisions, for example that between employers (the school boards) and employees (teachers), or between pedagogical innovators and traditionalists, influence the outcome of debate just as much. On one point, however, the religious parties have remained united, namely in their wish to keep control over part of the school system through the continued existence of denominational schools under the authority of private school boards. I will focus on the historical struggle for this 'pluralistic' school system in the first part of this article.

## Origins of the system

Although the result of the school struggle, which lasted from about 1840 to 1920, was the existence of denominational, privately-owned schools beside neutral state schools, the initial demand did not concern the juridical form of schoolboards. When the first disputes about education arose, between 1840 and 1850, the main issue was the alleged weak religious character of the state schools. This complaint was an expression of the widening gap between the latitudinarian protestantism of the aristocracy and the orthodox protestantism of mainly agricultural, lower income groups. The Orthodox Protestants asked for a *truly* christian national (state) school. Only when they realised that they were fighting a lost battle, with the state schools more neutral under the influence of the Liberals, did they reformulate their demands. With the slogan 'freedom of education' they began to ask for privately-owned denominational schools. The Education Law of 1857 marked the end of the period in which the legal aspect of the demand for freedom of education was central. From that moment onwards founding of privately-owned schools was free, and the number of non-state schools slowly increased, as demonstrated in Table 1.

In the subsequent decades the struggle focused on realisation of the achieved freedom of education by means of state subsidies for non-state schools.

The conflict aroused so many emotions that it almost paralysed the political process. In 1913 the so-called Pacification Committee was established to settle this and two other disputes. Eventually the religious parties were victorious on the issue. The constitution of 1917 stipulated that education was free and that non-state schools in future would be paid from the public purse.

In the school struggle the Liberals and the Orthodox Protestants were the main conflicting parties. The strategies they adopted and the alliances they formed to reach their aims were adapted to new developments in the struggle and to the changes taking place in the political system. The Catholics supported the Orthodox Protestants but generally stayed somewhat in the background, due to organisational weakness. The socialists did not play an important part as they became a relevant political force only around 1890 when the school struggle had already passed its culmination point.

The opposition between the Orthodox Protestants position and that of the Liberals was clearest in the conflict around the Education Act proposed by the liberal statesman Kappeyne. He belonged to the radical wing of the Liberal party, which favoured extension of state intervention both in education and elsewhere. The wish to extend intervention resulted from growing concern among the Liberals about the deteriorating social situation of large groups in society, as a result of industrialisation. The feeling was that, while education should increase social mobility among the middle class, it should also create a workforce for new industries and keep the labourers away from the socialist ideas starting to gain ground. Good education was seen as an instrument for disciplining the working class.

The proposed Act aroused enormous resistance among the Orthodox Protestants. Firstly because of the rationalistic, anti-clerical character of the law, which sought only to improve the knowledge and skills of the people without paying attention to religious teaching. Secondly because it was seen as contributing to the financial difficulties of non-state schools, which would have to improve the quality of teaching without any financial help from the state.

*Table 1: Percentage of children attending state and non-state elementary schools in the Netherlands, 1850–1910*

|      | State schools | Non-state schools |
|------|---------------|-------------------|
| 1850 | 77            | 23                |
| 1860 | 79            | 21                |
| 1870 | 77            | 23                |
| 1880 | 75            | 25                |
| 1890 | 71            | 29                |
| 1900 | 69            | 31                |
| 1910 | 62            | 38                |

Source: P J Idenburg, *Schets van het
Nederlandse schoolwezen*, Groningen,
Wolters, 1960, p. 112.

The mass protest against the liberal education policy of the 1870s and the Kappeyne Law was not only important because of its scale, but also because it formed the transition from a situation in which politics was the realm of the aristocracy and the bourgeoisie to the age of mass politics. As early as 1861 the *Vereeniging van Christelijk Nationaal Schoolonderwijs* (Society for Christian National School Education) was founded and transformed into the *Anti Schoolwet Verbond* (Anti-Education Law League) in 1872. In the parliamentary elections of 1874 this league functioned as a modern political party. The first mass political party in the Netherlands, the Orthodox Protestant (Anti-Revolutionary) party, was founded in 1879. Abraham Kuyper was the driving force behind the organisational activities of the Orthodox Protestants, with whom his success in creating a lasting social organisation depended on two insights. First, his awareness of the importance of organisational skills led him to study the organisational principles of the Anti Corn Law League. Secondly, he realised that to strengthen the political impact of Orthodox Protestant ideas he had to mobilise what he called 'the people behind the voters,' i.e. the lower income groups not yet enfranchised. Central in Kuyper's efforts to organise the Orthodox Protestants was the idea of the anti-these, according to which religious people (the Protestants and the Catholics) were fundamentally opposed to non-believers (the Liberals and Social Democrats).

As already noted, the Liberals sought, by means of the Kappeyne law, to increase the responsibility of the state with regard to the neutral non-religious state schools. The Orthodox Protestants opposed this with the notion of freedom of education. As Wendrich pointed out, the notion of freedom had a double meaning here. It meant 'free from state intervention,' but it also referred to the freedom of parents to give their children the education they thought best. In the Orthodox Protestant ideology people were thus addressed as parents and as members of a particular group (the Orthodox Protestant section of the population) at the same time. This ideology found expression in the two phrases 'sovereignty in one's own group' and 'school to the parents.'[2] Hence what had started as a movement for national christian education was transformed into a protest against state intervention in religious education and, thus, a demand for privatisation of denominational education. It was not merely accepted that religious schools should be privately owned, but the particular juridical basis of denominational schools, namely private administrative bodies, became something important to defend.

The notion of 'sovereignty in one's own group' expressed a particular idea, namely that the community of believers had its own responsibility vis-a-vis God. Its homologue in the Catholic ideology was the principle that the state should only provide what could not be taken care of by the community. Both notions, although weakened by the rapid expansion of the welfare state, are still adhered to in Orthodox Protestant and Catholic circles.

The Orthodox Protestants could not prevent the passing of the Kappeyne Education Act. However, the 1887 elections brought them to power and the Education Act of McKay (1889) established the principle of state subsidised but non-state schools. In the subsequent 30 years, financial aid provision for denominational schools were slowly improved. The major changes took place when the Elementary Education Act of 1920 obliged the state to finance fully both state and denominational schools. The non-state sector soon developed into the largest within the school system.

The expansion of denominational education was not, however, an isolated phenomenon. It was embedded in an overall segmentation of society along ideological lines. I have already mentioned that from 1870 onwards religious groups started to get organised. The aim of this activity was twofold. On the one hand, group cohesion was reinforced (internally) while, on the other, groups were segregated from people with another ideology. Between 1870 and 1920 religious groups, the Orthodox Protestants and somewhat later the Catholics, founded their political parties, unions and social organisations such as those concerned with welfare, sports associations etc. The Social Democrats did the same from 1890 onwards. Hence the Orthodox Protestant section of the population came to live side by side with but separated from the Catholic section, and both religious groups separated from Social Democrats and Liberals. The ideological pluralism, characteristic of Netherlands society, had become a rigid social structure, in which membership of one group excluded membership of another. In sociological literature this structure is called, in Dutch, *verzuiling*. The plural school system was crucial to the *verzuiling* since, by transmitting group values, the structure remained for long unimpaired.

## The quantitative development of the system

Table 2 is the continuation of Table 1, but the non-state sector is now divided into a Protestant, a Catholic and a 'remaining' part (including schools based on a particular pedagogical principle).

In the period 1920–1960 the trend characterising the 1850–1910 period was continued. A sharp decline in the state sector was accompanied by increases in both the Protestant and Catholic sectors. In the second half of the 1960s, however, the trend was reversed. The state sector started to grow slowly, with the decline in the non-state sector reflecting essentially the drop in Catholic school enrolment.

The changing relation between the sectors was due to a number of factors, including, in particular, the (relatively) more marked decline in the Catholic birthrate. The principal explanatory factor, however, is unquestionably related to the process of secularisation and the concomitant decline in support for religious organisations. This development was faster and more widespread among Catholics than among Orthodox Protestants, perhaps precisely because the latter have a more 'orthodox' faith. From about 1960 onwards Catholic organisations quickly lost support and some were even dissolved, like the Catholic unions which merged with the socialist ones. At the political level the three former religious parties (one Catholic and two Protestant) merged, to form a single Christian Democratic Party, still based on religious principles but functioning in the political system as a conservative party.

The recent decline in the Catholic sector of education and the growth in the state sector must be seen in the context of the above-mentioned process. Indeed, taking into account the extensive social and political changes, it is surprising that the shifts in the educational structure have been so small. The relative stability of the *verzuiling* is due to two factors: first, the importance parents still attach to religious education even if they themselves have adopted a secularised value system; and secondly, the positions of power attained by the Catholic and Protestant education interest organisations. Table 3 gives the same type of data for general secondary education.

Here we find a slightly different pattern. The size of both the state and the Catholic sector has been reduced since the mid-1960s. The Protestant sector, on the contrary, has strengthened its position in that period, and seems to be the main group to benefit from the reform of the pedagogical structure at secondary level which took place from 1968 onwards. Does the first half of

*Table 2: Percentage of children attending elementary schools, by education-sector. 1920–1983*

| | | Non-state schools | | |
| | State schools | Protestant | Catholic | Other |
|---|---|---|---|---|
| 1920 | 55 | 22 | 21 | 2 |
| 1930 | 38 | 25 | 36 | 2 |
| 1950 | 27 | 27 | 44 | 2 |
| 1965 | 26 | 28 | 44 | 2 |
| 1970 | 28 | 28 | 42 | 2 |
| 1975 | 30 | 28 | 40 | 2 |
| 1983* | 32 | 28 | 36 | 4 |

* Figures for elementary and pre-elementary education are here taken together.

Sources: Centraal Bureau voor de Statistiek, *De ontwikkeling van het onderwijs in Nederland*, Utrecht, 1951; Centraal Bureau voor de Statistiek, *Statistiek van het gewoon lager onderwijs*, The Hague, Staatsuitgeverji, 1966, 1971, 1977; Centraal Bureau voor de Statistiek, *Statistiek van het Basisonderwijs*, The Hague, Staatsuitgeverji, 1985.

*Table 3: Percentage of children attending general secondary schools by education sector, 1920–1983\**

| | | Non-state schools | | |
| | State schools | Protestant | Catholic | Other |
|---|---|---|---|---|
| 1920 | 75 | | 25 | |
| 1930 | 61 | 13 | 18 | 8 |
| 1950 | 43 | 19 | 29 | 9 |
| 1963 | 34 | 22 | 37 | 6 |
| 1967 | 31 | 23 | 40 | 6 |
| 1980 | 27 | 30 | 37 | 7 |
| 1983 | 26 | 30 | 37 | 7 |

* Types of school represented in the figures up to and including 1967 are the Gymnasium, HBS Lyceum, MMS, and Handelsdag-school. Figures for 1980 and 1983 relate to the Gymnasium, Atheneum, HAVO and MAVO.

Sources: Centraal Bureau voor de Statistiek, *De ontwikkeling van het onderwijs in Nederland*, Utrecht, 1951; Centraal Bureau voor de Statistiek, *Statistiek van het voorbereidend hoger en middelbaar onderwijs*, Zeist, Staatsuitgeverij, 1964; Centraal Bureau voor de Statistiek, *Statistiek van het voorbereidend hoger en middlebaar onderwijs*, The Hague, Staatsuitgeverij, 1968; Ministerie van Onderwijs en Wetenschappen, *Verslag van de staat van het onderwijs in Nederland*, The Hague, Staatsuitgeverij, 1984.

the 1980s, in which relations between the sectors have been stable, form a turning point for changes in the same direction as at elementary level?

## The contemporary role of the non-state sector

It has often been said that the *verzuiling* of the school system has formed an obstacle to education policy-making. The Elementary Education Act of 1920, subsequent ministerial circulars, and jurisprudence have settled the financial relation between the state and the non-state sector and the relation between central government and the non-state sector in a very detailed way. For example, in exchange for subventions to the non-state sector, the central government came to have a considerable say as regards the curriculum and examinations. Proposals for educational change easily ran up against suspicion on the side of Catholics and Protestants that the former would imply a weakening of the position of the non-state sector.

In the period following the Second World War, government education policy has slowly developed from being merely distributive (in which the state finances but implementation is left to private initiative) to constructive (in which the state both influences and stimulates innovation). This has been accepted by the non-state sector as long as it has not altered the basic freedoms, namely the freedom to found schools, the freedom to teach according to any ideology not threatening fundamental democratic rights, and the freedom of teaching (methods). But whenever a proposed policy was seen as a threat to the continued existence of non-state schools there was a strong adverse reaction.

Non-state interests are defended at two points. In parliament and government denominational education is supported by the Christian Democratic Party. The fact that the Department of Education has often been led by a Christian Democrat has been of special importance in this respect. Just as important as the parliamentarian support, however, has been the participation of interest groups from the non-state sector in consultation and negotiation with senior officials in the department.

Conflicts over educational issues have been solved in the Netherlands through negotiation and consensus wherever possible. In fact no laws are considered by government and parliament, and no decisions are taken, without the consultation and consent of the main education interest organisations. Rather than taking place on an *ad hoc* basis, consultation and negotiation have been within a more permanent structure since the beginning of the 1970s. Here, the most important body has been the *Centrale Commissie voor Onderwijs Overleg* (Central Committee for Consultation concerning

Education or CCOO) which reviews virtually all key educational issues. Partners of the government in the CCOO are the leading organisations of the four education sectors, namely the Catholic, Protestant, and general non-state sectors, and the state sector represented by the Association of Netherlands municipalities.[3] It is remarkable that in this and other consultative bodies the 'social partners' (employers and employees) are absent. Apart from the main task of giving all parties the chance to express their views with regard to a specific issue, the CCOO also has an important legitimising function for ministerial policies.

The education issues of the last 10 years fall into two categories. Firstly, there are those which concern the structure of education, the *verzuiling* of the school system. Conflicts may arise about the conditions for opening a school, methods of financing the non-state sector, planning of the school system, or the composition of administrative bodies of non-state schools. Secondly there are the issues which concern the pedagogical structure of education, like the creation of new types of schools, or their homogeneity or heterogeneity. In the following section, I shall examine in turn the reform of the constitution and decentralisation, the Participation Act, planning and rationalisation of the school system, and the middle-school.

## Constitutional reform and decentralisation

In 1976, the Social Democrats (including the Minister of Education) produced a more modern revised draft of the education paragraph in the constitution. One of the proposed modifications concerned partial decentralisation of policy-making power. Conditions for public payment of schools, said the Social Democrats, should not only be stipulated by law, but also by royal decree, while provincial and municipal authorities should be entitled to formulate such conditions. It was argued that the possibility for local authorities to develop an education policy was desirable in particular with regard to education of cultural minorities and school-planning. However, it had to be remembered that if local government was given such powers, it would equally obtain control over the conditions for payment of the non-state sector!

Non-state sector representatives, meanwhile, thought this move conflicted with educational freedom and thus strongly opposed such a reform, handing in what they regarded as an acceptable amendment. Subsequently a Social Democrat tried to make a compromise by representing a sub-amendment. Yet both proposals were rejected, while the Liberals voted twice against them, which typifies their position in the Netherlands political system. Although they principally give preference to state education, they do not go against the Christian Democrats, without whom they would not be in office. In 1981, reform of the constitution figured in the negotiations around the formation of a centre-left government. In exchange for the Department of Education, the Social Democrats were this time prepared to give up their position. They agreed with the Christian Democrats that reform of the constitution would neither reduce freedom of education nor give lower authorities policy-making power with regard to the non-state sector.

## The Participation Act

The issue of the Participation Act is another good example of opposition to changes liable to influence the *verzuiling* of the school-system.

In 1978, three parliamentarians of the Social Democratic Party presented a Bill concerning participation in the education sector. The Bill proposed sharing of decision-making power of parents, management and teachers with the school boards. As was rightly pointed out,[4] the proposal not only implied power-sharing in teaching matters, but also the sharing of freedom of education, since it was intended to give all three parties a say in the identity of the school, a matter hitherto defined by the school boards. The issues with regard to which the boards needed consent of the so-called Participation Council were also to be stipulated by law.

The non-state sector was divided in its opinion on the matter. Catholic, Protestant and the other teachers associations were in favour of the Bill, but the organisations of school boards in the non-state sector (i.e. the employers) were strongly against, since they saw it as a threat to their position as the 'standard-bearers' of educational freedom. They feared that participation of parents, teachers and management in school government might result in a change in the identity of non-state schools.

The Social Democrat Bill was followed in 1979 by a second put forward by the (then) liberal Minister of Education, which immediately received support from the Christian Democrats, because it recognised that the identity of schools was the concern of the school boards alone. The second Bill left the organisation of participation more to the school boards themselves, and did not permit the Participation Council to influence the identity of denominational schools.

On the other hand, the Social Democrats believed that the identity of the school was the concern of all those involved in the education process. It is remarkable that the notion of 'school to the parents,' originally part of the Christian ideology, now forms an important element in Social Democratic ideas about education.

The Social Democrat Bill was ultimately rejected in 1981, with the Liberals and Christian Democrats voting against it. The same majority passed the government proposal somewhat later.

## Planning and rationalisation of the school system

The state has no instrument for the planning of the elementary school network. This is the result of an article in the Law on Basic Education[5] which states that every group of people is free to found an elementary school. Such a group has only to prove that a certain number of pupils, not to be 'creamed' from nearby schools, will attend the new school to be allowed to found and claim public money for it. In residential development areas a quite common procedure for determining the need for schools of a particular denomination is to examine the breakdown of the local population by religion. This procedure has demonstrated that in areas which are traditionally homogeneous from the religious standpoint, like the Catholic southern provinces, it has often proved extremely difficult for parents to open a state school or a school of a denomination other than the dominant one. In many cases, the identity of a new school has already been decided on the basis of statistical evidence, before people even come to live in the area.

In the period of declining enrolment marked by the first half of the 1970s, the aim of the Catholic and Protestant educational sectors was to retain as many schools as possible. Several strategies were open to them: one was to merge with another school of the same denomination; another was to enrol as many children of (Moslem) migrant parents as possible. For some years the creation of an oecumenical (Catholic-Protestant) school was a third option, but under pressure from the Catholic church schools, this strategy has been abandoned. It is difficult to say how successful the non-state sector has been in applying these strategies. Although table 2 shows a decline in the non-state sector, it is impossible to determine to what extent each of the two factors, *ontzuiling* and ineffective 'survival policies' have contributed to this. Moreover, it is known that the state sector too has attracted many 'imigrant' children.

At secondary level the state does dispose of a planning instrument. This is the so-called Procedure for Planning, included in the Law on Secondary Education.[6] The procedure leaves little or no room for 'consumer' influence in education, as is still the case at elementary level, assigning all power instead to the top organisations of the four education sectors. Consequently, the existing relations between the four sections are continuously 'reproduced.' It is virtually out of the question for a school of a particular identity to be present if it has not been incorporated in the plan of the organisation concerned. Each of these organisations annually prepares for its own sector a list of new schools, which is then presented to the minister.

In a special consultative body the sub-plans are negotiated with the minister and a final plan of schools is drawn up.

The Procedure for Planning has given rise to many criticisms, especially from the state sector. The foremost of these concerns the *ad hoc* character of decisions and the lack of a real policy which gives guidelines for long-range planning. Apart from this, there are complaints about the political character of decisions. Successive Christian Democratic ministers and secretaries of state, it is maintained, should have favoured the requests of the Catholic and Protestant organisations, rather than extending the network of schools unnecessarily in this way.

The Procedure for Planning is basically designed to function in a period in which the education system is expanding, losing its relevance in a period of contraction. As a result of the falling birth-rate, a number of schools have been closed, while many more, in which enrolment has dropped below the required minimum, have until recently been kept open with ministerial consent. The economic crisis and pressure on the state budget have persuaded the minister to rationalise the school system, and two operations, for elementary and secondary schools respectively, have been developed to this end. The first was implemented between 1983 and 1985, and the second will take effect between 1986 and 1988. Intended to adapt the size of the schools networks, both are only temporary solutions to current problems, as they do not provide an instrument for continued 'planning for decline.'

An interesting question concerns the effectiveness of a rationalisation program in a pluralist education system in which the rights of private groups are embedded in law, and in which education interest groups have a strong influence on policy-making. In the Netherlands at least two conditions have to be met for such a program to succeed. First, the main education interest groups have to be involved in both development and implementation of the program, for reasons of legitimation and efficiency. Secondly, rationalisation has to be intra-sectoral. Both conditions have been fulfilled in the rationalisation of the elementary education system. The program has been successful in the sense that no major conflict has occurred. Although the Catholics have defended their schools slightly better, the balance between the four sectors has been maintained overall.

However, whether the program has been successful from the point of view of public finance is far from certain. The number of schools closed is very small, owing partly to extra evaluation to prevent Catholic and Protestant sectors losing more than the state sectors. From the economic standpoint, the operation has apparently been only a first step on the road to a rationally planned school system. The minister has already announced a second series of rationalised measures, to which the interest organisations have not yet reacted. In the event, it will be interesting to see whether the power of Catholic and Protestant education sectors will again remain unimpaired.

## The middle school

The final issue I want to discuss is the debate on the reform of secondary education, and the stand the Christian parties have taken thereon. No doubt because pedagogical views are of considerable influence, the non-state sector has not been united on this issue. Moreover the major political division here is not that between Christian Democrats and the rest, but between Liberals and Social Democrats.

Discussion on reform of the secondary education system started after the Second World War. The idea was to abolish the sharp division between different types of schools, each of which was designed to serve a particular social class, and to create a school system that did not force children to make a choice between vocational and general education at the age of twelve. The new Law on Secondary Education did not end the discussions. Many Social Democrats thought that the 1968 reforms had not gone far enough, and launched the idea of a comprehensive school, the so-called Middle School, in which all children aged between 12 and 15 would receive the same education.

The idea of the middle school received a strong impetus from the transfer of the Department of Education to the Social Democrats in 1973.[7] Two memoranda were published in which the idea was further developed.[8] From the outset the Liberal Party opposed the notion, because it left too little room for differentiation between pupils (and therefore disfavoured both highly intelligent children and those with low intellectual capabilities), and because it was not selective (the proposals made no mention of a final examination). Another argument against the middle school was that it would result in too general an education for the demands of working life. However, the Social Democrats were in favour of the idea, believing that it would give children equal educational opportunities, postpone choice of a vocation, and stimulate the development of social abilities. Meanwhile, a variety of interested parties took one side or the other. While the *Nederlands Genootschap voor leraren* (Netherlands Association of Teachers), composed of teachers from 'higher' types of secondary schools like the *Gymnasium and Athenea*, consistently opposed the Middle School, the *Algemene Bond voor Onderwijzend Personeel* (General Union of Teaching Staff) viewed any development towards comprehensive education as positive.

The Christian Democratic Party and the national organisations of school boards did not want a comprehensive-type school. Their arguments were basically the same as those of the Liberals, both arguing that the middle school would reduce freedom of education. It was maintained, first, that it would take from pupils and parents the right to choose a specific type of education and, secondly, that it would restrict freedom as regards methods of teaching. The meaning of freedom of education was thus extended here from free choice between schools of a different identity to free choice between different types of schools. A similarity is also to be noticed in the ideological terms in which the debate between Liberals and Christian Democrats was expressed. When the Social Democrats lost the Department of Education, the middle school disappeared for some time from the agenda to reappear as Continued Basic Education[9] when Van Kemenade began his second term as Minister of Education. The proposed reforms in the Bill concerned are less fundamental than those of the former middle school, which explains why the Christian Democratic Party and Catholic and Protestant education organisations on the whole agree with it. They argue that the type of education proposed should not exclude the existence of different types of schools, as long as the final qualifications are the same. Yet the Liberals and the *Nederlands Genootschap voor leraren* (NGL) still remain opposed to any form of comprehensive education.

Opposition to the 'middle school' has clearly diminished, but consultations between ministerial staff and education interest organisations about the Bill for Continued Basic Education have demonstrated that consensus is still far away. Nevertheless the question seems no longer to be whether some sort of comprehensive school will be introduced, but to what extent the notion of freedom of education will dilute the notion of equality.

## Conclusion

Discussion of contemporary education policies prompts the following conclusions concerning the position of the non-state sector in education policy-making.

First, in their wish to avoid any basic challenge to the structure of education, the different religious parties (the Christian Democrats, and the various Catholic and Protestant education interest organisations) are united in their defence of denominational education, which all regard as vital. Secondly, in situations such as those described above, there is no antagonism between the Catholic and the Protestant sectors of education. Competition between them occurs rather in matters related to school planning.

Thirdly, when there is a debate on the pedagogical structure of education it is by no means certain how the religious parties will react. On the whole, the organisations of school boards (the employers) have taken a more conservative line than the employee organisations (the teachers), but this division is not clearcut. Moreover, within each organisation, whether a political party or an interest group (like a teacher association), one invariably finds a conspicuous demarcation between innovators on the one hand and traditionalists on the other. Next, of the two expressions 'sovereignty in one's own group' and 'school to the parents' used in the 19th century school struggle, the first has clearly gained in importance, at the expense of the second. Each reduction, however minimal, in the power of religious interest groups over 'their' education has been experienced as a threat to freedom of education. Here, 'freedom' is used in the sense of 'free from state intervention,' while the second meaning of the word has lost its former relevance: freedom of education is no longer the freedom of its 'consumers' but of its 'suppliers' (the school boards).

Furthermore, the expression 'school to the parents' seems now an essential part of Social Democratic ideas about education. Social Democrats ask that parents, pupils and all those directly involved in the educational process exert greater influence, either through direct participation in decision-making or a new juridical form of state school management allowing for parents and teachers to be members of school boards.

Finally, the position of the Liberals with regard to state versus non-state education is ambiguous. In the last century, it was they who asked for neutral state education. Since the pacification of the school-struggle in 1917, however, they have never contested the existence of denominational education. Indeed, the Liberal party has been so careful not to evoke conflicts about education with the Catholics and the Protestants that it has, since then, never even claimed to prefer state education to denominational education. From the beginning of this century the state-school has slowly become the school of the Social Democrats. As long as the Liberals are the coalition partner of the Christian Democrats the latter will have nothing to fear as regards autonomy of denominational education. The control of the education interest organisations over the non-state sector may be weakened only if the Liberals seek closer co-operation with the Social Democrats − at present an unlikely development.

**Notes**

1. I use here the concepts of state and non-state education as developed by Guy Neave in his article (mimeograph) 'The non-state sector in the Education Provision of Member-States of the European Communities,' Brussels, 1984. His definition of the non-state sector consists of two elements, for he points out, first, that the sector does not rely exclusively on the public purse; and, secondly, that the administrative bodies of schools within the sector are composed, in part at least, of members nominated by interests other than the public authorities, teachers and parent representatives. A peculiarity of the sector in the Netherlands is that, since 1920, it is paid (like the state sector itself) exclusively by the state. Since I consider this a quantitative, not a qualitative, difference from the non-state sector as defined by Neave I have adopted this concept in writing

about the education system in the Netherlands. As the large majority (95%) of the non-state schools are denominational both terms, 'non-state schools' and 'denominational schools,' are alternatively used in the text.

2.  E Wendrich, 'Liberaal-christelijke ideologie, onderwijs en de sociaal-demokratie,' *Comenius*, 14, 1984 p. 151.

3.  The interests of elementary state schools are defended by the top organisation of Netherlands municipalities, since it is local public authorities that act as administrative bodies for such schools.

4.  F van Schoten, and W Wansink, *De nieuwe schoolstrijd*, Utrecht/Antwerp, Bohn, Scheltema and Holkema, 1984, p. 31.

5.  This law (known as the *Wet op het Basis onderwijs*) became operative on August 1st, 1985. It replaces the Elementary Education Law of 1920 and the Law on Pre-elementary Education of 1955, and brings together both levels of education into a new single type of basic education for all children aged from 4 to 12.

6.  This law (the *Wet op het Voortgezet Onderwijs*) was passed in 1963 and became operative in 1968.

7.  The Social Democrat J A van Kemenade was Minister of Education from 1973 to 1977 and from 1981 to 1982.

8.  Ministerie van Onderwijs, *Contouren van een toekomstig onderwijsbestel I*, The Hague, Staatsuitgeverij, 1975; and Ministerie van Onderwijs, *Contouren van een toekomstig onderwijsbestel II*, The Hague, Staatsuitgeverij, 1977.

9.  Ministerie van Onderwijs en Wetenschappen, *Verder na de Basis-school*, The Hague, Staatsuitgeverij, 1982.

# 6.3 State and church in Spanish education
*Oliver Boyd-Barrett*

## Introduction

Tension between private and public provision for education exists in many countries of Europe. Spain is one of those countries in which this tension has also been exacerbated by a religious dimension. During the 40-year period of Franco's dictatorship, the role of the Catholic church as educational provider was greatly strengthened, especially in voluntary secondary education, serving as the basis for entry to university and professional training. Its role as major provider thus placed the church in a key position in the reinforcement of a socially stratified system of education. Parents had to pay for their children's secondary education. Those who could afford to start their children on the *bachillerato* track at the age of 10 had the advantage over those whose children continued in obligatory primary education before making the transition to *bachillerato* at the age of 12 (later 14), within an overlapping but dual-track *bachillerato* structure which mostly benefited the rich. (From 1964 secondary education started at 14. During the 1990s, secondary education will become compulsory, starting at 12 and continuing at least to 16.) Most children never even proceeded to secondary education. Up to the early 1970s, moreover, more than a million children of primary school age went without education, largely because of inadequate state provision. My purpose in this article is to look at the transition in Spain from a church-dominated educational system to a state-dominated system, and to identify the mechanisms by which this transition was achieved.

## The doctrine of 'subsidiariedad'

Under Franco, the state took only a reluctant interest in educational provision, catering mainly for primary education and for those areas which were too poor to offer a market for the church schools. The state actively transferred a large measure of responsibility for education to the church, and claimed moral virtue for so doing. The relationship of '*subsidiariedad*' of state to church in matters of education helped greatly to identify Francoism with Catholicism. The effect was to place Spain further behind the rest of Europe in its willingness or ability to provide for the educational needs of rural and urban working classes. What progress towards europeanisation in standards of mass education that had been achieved up to and during the Second Republic was largely abandoned. When placed alongside the manifest Catholic indoctrination which permeated both private and public provision, this was a heritage now viewed with indignation by many politicians of the centre and left parties.

The church had been given the right of inspection not only of church schools, but of all schools in matters that concerned religion, doctrinal orthodoxy and customary morality. The 1945 law of primary education established religion as the first and most fundamental guiding principle. The church was able to develop its education network, much of it in valuable inner-city properties, with the support of important tax exemptions, grants, judicial immunity for clergy, and exemption of religious staff from military service. In 1931, 29% of secondary pupils studied in private schools: by 1943 this had risen to 71% (Benitez, 1987). In the period 1940–50, the number of pupils attending state secondary schools fell from 25% to only 9% of the secondary total (climbing only slowly back to 12% in 1960 and 25% in 1974), while between 1953 and 1959 alone the number of Catholic secondary schools increased from 572 to 706 while the number of state schools remained static at 119 and the number of other secular schools fell by 361 (O'Malley, 1990).

Within a decade of the death of Franco, however, the state had become by far the most important source of funding for both public and 'private' grant-aided schools. Private schooling now accounts for roughly only one-third of all schooling in both primary and secondary sectors. The powers of the church have been subordinated to the requirements of democratic involvement in school management of parents, pupils and teachers, and of freedom of conscience of pupils and of teachers. While state schools are obliged to offer religious education as a subject, children are free to decide whether to take that subject. If they do not take religion, they will no longer be required to take ethics as an alternative. If they do take religion, this will not count towards graduation. The total body of private and grant-aided schools now includes a much more substantial number of institutions controlled by bodies other than the Catholic church, such as schools co-operatively owned by teachers and parents, or by other groups. That this transformation occurred peaceably is both a measure of and a contributing factor to the survival of Spanish democracy thus far, despite Catholic protest against what is seen as the reduced status of religious education in the new National Curriculum to be implemented from 1991.

The period of power of José Maria Maravall as Education Minister (*Partida Socialista de Obreros Espanoles* [PSOE]) 1982–88, was particularly significant for this transformation. A controlled bitterness characterises his account of the education legacy bequeathed by Franco and the Catholic church, both in his book *La Reforma de le Ensenaza* (1984) and in his preface to the publication of

*Ley Organica del Derecho a la Education* (LODE) (1985). Under the 'national-Catholic' State of Franco, he charges, thousands of children remained without school, especially in the rural areas. Construction of state schools was paralysed and the ranks of the teaching profession were decimated (either purged or fleeing on their own account). Maltreatment of the public sector accentuated inequality between schools and among students. There was a wholesale retreat to out-dated pedagogy. Teaching became a battlefield of ideological confrontation and clashes of interest.

> In effect, profoundly conservative interests established in Spanish education always responded very toughly to all liberal and progressive attempts to overcome the barriers of scarcity, injustice and inequality in the educational system; a system characterised by secular slovenliness at primary level, very early discrimination at the conclusion of primary education and by the dominance of private interests in secondary education, an educational system to which many children had no access and from which the immense majority were ejected as soon as possible. (LODE, 1985, p. 15)

Maravall recalls earlier Ministers of Education who in their public utterances summed up the spirit of Francoism: like Menéndez Reigarda for whom the 'worst enemies of the state are liberalism, democracy and Judaism;' like Ripalda, who asks scornfully 'Are there other pernicious liberties? Yes, sir, the liberty of education, the liberty of propaganda and meeting. Why are these liberties pernicious? Because they serve to teach error and propaganda.' Maravall struggles to balance his acknowledgment of some of the worthwhile contributions of the church schools against his anger with national-Catholicism and its consequences for public schooling. Those circumstances should never be forgotten, he admonishes, that allowed the church to build up its network of schools during the 1940s, 1950s and 1960s, to grow rich and influential with the full acquiescence of the State and without fear of meaningful competition from a pathetically under-resourced public school system.

> The splendour of private education was built, therefore, not only on the elimination of all previous liberal experiments but also on the deterioration and abandonment of state teaching. (*Reforma*, 1984, p. 18)
>
> It serves no purpose here to record the brutal manifestations of these historical controversies and their lamentable consequences for education in Spain. But nevertheless it should not be forgotten what a heritage was received: a heritage in which the great loser was the humanist, liberal and reformist tradition. Until very recent times the consequences were the paralysis of public education, the fomenting of an unequal educational system, the indoctrination of students and, under the dictatorship, the persecution of all pluralism. Education

was the creature of a monopoly that has been labelled 'national Catholicism.' In the space created by state indifference the private religious schools flourished. (LODE, 1985, p. 12)

## Waning of church power

In *La Reforma*, Maravall gives his account of the waning of church power in education. The process began with the ascendancy of the 'Technocrats' in Franco's administration of the 1960s, committed to the modernisation of Spain. The technocrats were impressed with the 'human capital' theory of economic growth, which attributed differences of growth between countries to differences in their levels of investment in people, and in particular, investments in their education. This was a period of sharply accelerated industrialisation and massive migration from poor rural areas to the margins of the industrial cities, areas never well-served by the educational system of the church. With industrialisation, the usefulness of basic accomplishments in literacy and numeracy became more apparent to both bosses and workers. There was a surge in demand for education as more and more families came to view it as the critical gateway to social mobility, to getting a foot on the city ladder, first of all, and then to climbing that ladder. There was greater encouragement for girls to continue with their education. For the ruling classes, education offered a means of social control, something they could deploy to help them cope with a general increase of population and with new concentrations of population in the cities. It would keep youngsters off the streets, prepare them for urban living while their mothers could go to work. These were the circumstances which led eventually to the *Ley General de Educación* of 1970 which introduced a unified system of free, obligatory, basic education from 6 to 14.

The same forces that denuded the countryside and crowded the cities also struck at the base of church recruitment. The church had depended disproportionately on the lower middle classes of the rural areas for its priests and nuns. But now there were fewer young people, and those who had left with their families for the cities were less likely to keep up the old religion. Urbanisation correlated with secularisation. The influences of secularisation crept back to the countryside: boys and girls who would once have gone into the church were now more likely to study for university and then, ironically, join the burgeoning state school sector as teachers. The religious orders increasingly resorted to employing secular teachers, a process that has continued into the 1980s (the number of religious in church *Bachillerato Unificado Polivalante* [BUP], i.e. secondary schools, declined from 54% in 1969 to 35% in 1981, an absolute fall from 30,000 to 23,419 [González-Anleo 1985]), but to attract these they had to offer salaries more generous than the allowances customarily offered their own members. Just when their costs were going up, they had to face the beginning of real competition from the public sector. Here, the state authorities now committed themselves to making up the 'deficit' in the number of school places, estimated to affect about 1,000,000 children, including both those children of school age who simply had no school to go to, as well as those who occupied very sub-standard places.

## State support for the private schools

Expansion of the public sector was an expensive option. The burden was lightened, and relations with the church sweetened, by grants to the private schools to encourage them to respond to growing demand. State subsidisation of the private sector flourished spectacularly during the 1970s, both before Franco died and then under the succeeding administration of the *Union Central Democrático* (UCD). Grant totals increased from 1385 million pesetas in 1973 to 70,000 million in 1982, an increase of 4954%, seven times the rate of increase of the Ministry's overall budget in the same period and 16 times the rate of increase in expenditure on the public sector. In 1973 the number of grant-aided *Educación General Básica* (EGB) i.e. primary classes was 750. This had risen to 50,000 in 1983. It was this growing flood of money into the hands of private providers, most notably the church, that the socialists found so repugnant about the educational liberalism of the UCD. In UCD's defence it may be argued (González-Anleo, 1985) that in a period of rapidly increasing *Ministerio de Educación y Ciencia* (MEC) educational budgets, grants to private schools did not exceed 15% of the total and actually fell from 15% to 12% in 1983, while private initiative continued to provide for nearly half of pre-school, half of *Formación Profesional* (FP) (i.e. technical secondary education), one-third of EGB and one-third of BUP/*Curso de Orientación Universitaria* (COU) education.

The ruling socialist party, PSOE, from 1982, continued a policy of grants to the private sector, to the extent that by the mid-1980s the state contributed 90% of the combined costs of private and public EGB education and by 1988, 91% of all private schools were subsidised – covering 100% of costs (*Comunidad Escolar*, 6 July 1988). Of the schools which had previously been subsidised (under less stringent conditions), 80% continued to receive '*concierto general*,' while only 5% were altogether excluded. Only 4% of children of compulsory school age now studied at private schools which were not in receipt of public funding. Even in the period of Maravall's holding of office (1982–88), grants to private schools increased by 110.56%. Funding for these grant-aided schools worked out at 2,959,274 pesetas (£14,786) per class in 1987–1988 of which 2,033,642 (£10,168) covered salary costs. Basic salaries ranged from 631,776 (£3108) to 1,337,784 (£6688) pesetas.

But more than its predecessors, the PSOE has exacted its price. Firstly, it has furthered the expansion of the public network, intensifying competition with the private sector. Secondly, it claims to have been more effective than its predecessor in making grants conditional upon the private schools honouring commitments to certain mutually agreed policies, such as siting of schools in rural or poor urban areas, taking students from homes in the immediate vicinity of the school, and ensuring compatibility of teacher qualifications, salaries, class sizes and equipment with the state sector. Thirdly, it has abolished fee-paying for the provision of obligatory education in wholly maintained schools and fixed fees at very low rates in the other grant-aided schools. Additional fees are still demanded with dubious legality in some areas, such as Catalonia, where the private schools allege that state grants are insufficient to cover real costs. Grant-aided education for obligatory education must be non-profit. Such schools cannot discriminate in their policies of admission of students, or in hire (or fire) of teachers. In return for state capital, fourthly, the state also requires democracy in management through the appointment of a governing body, parity with state education norms governing minimum standards of provision, pupil-teacher ratios and the curriculum, and freedom of conscience for both teachers and students. Yet by continuing with subsidies to the private schools, the government has saved itself heavy capital expenditure.

## Stagnation of the private sector

While the number of children going to private schools has remained very constant in absolute terms, the number going to state schools has increased considerably. This is because there are more children, and more children are being educated, especially at secondary levels. From 1939 to 1964 a fairly constant 2,500,000 children attended pre-school and primary school, rising to 3,000,000 by the end of the 1970s. Numbers attending *Institutos de Bachillerato* increased from 82,000 in 1960−61 to 530,000 in 1970−71, and then to 700,000 by 1980−81. While the population of the primary sector rose 20% in this 20-year period, therefore, the academic stream of secondary education rose by over 850%! But the rate of increase was higher in the state than in the private sector, especially at secondary level. In the period 1975−76 to 1982−83, for example, the increase in numbers of *Bachillerato* students was only 30,000 in the private sector, but 450,000 in the state sector. The overall rate of increase was accentuated by greater gender quality of participation in secondary education: the rate of increase in female participation in FP (i.e. secondary technical education) in the period 1975−76 to 1982−83 was 198% as against 78% for men although the totals for the latter year still favoured 388,246 men to 262,683 women.

In BUP/COU the rate of increase for women was 50% as against 23% for men: in 1982–83 there were 405,083 female BUP students and a further 110,535 studied for COU, while there were 470,644 male BUP students and 131,338 studying the COU.

## State of balance in the mid-1980s

Publication in 1989 by the ME of a concise fact digest, *El Sistema Educativo Espanol*, and of the 1989 *Libro Blanco*, provide relevant figures for the years up to 1985/6. These are the main source for the statistics that follow in this section and the next, although they have been supplemented, for the earlier 1980s, by the 1987 *Proyecto para reforma*, the work of González-Anleo (1985), *El Pais Anuario*, and articles from the educational weekly, *Comunidad Escolar*.

In 1970–71, private sector pre-school facilities provided for 456,974 children as against 362,940 attending state centres. By 1985–86 this situation had reversed itself, with 702,057 children attending state centres, 425,291 attending private. The state sector accounted for 64.6% of pre-school classes. Whereas pre-school education is free when provided in state schools, private pre-school education is not. More than half the private classes were categorised as '*iniciativa privada*', a category which indicates their non-confessional character. The Catholic church controlled approximately a third. The remainder was accounted for by other confessional groupings and a miscellaneous category. At the level of EGB, in 1970–71, of a total of nearly 4,000,000 pupils, just under 3,000,000 were educated in state schools and just over 1,000,000 in private. By 1985–86, out of a total of 5,594,285 pupils, 3,621,238 were educated by the state, and 1,973,047 attended private schools. Whereas in 1970–71 private education accounted for approximately 28% of all pupils, its share had risen over the period as a whole to 35% by 1985–86. However, the rate of increase peaked in the later 1970s at 38% in 1977–78 and had fallen consistently since then. While private schools in 1985–86 catered for 35% of all EGB pupils, they supplied only 30.3% of EGB classes.

There were more schools classified as '*iniciativa privada*' (13.97% of the total) at EGB level in 1985–86 than Catholic schools (10.38% of the total). But the Catholic schools catered for 17.32% of all pupils, only fractionally less than the 17.95% of pupils attending all other forms of private education. Of the total numbers of students attending private schools, 49.1% attended Catholic schools, 48% attended schools classified as '*iniciativa privada*', 0.4% attended non-Catholic confessional schools, and 2.5% attended a miscellaneous range of other private establishments. Most private schools were grant-aided, and Catholic schools were more likely than other private schools to be grant-aided: 87.5% of all private schools were grant-aided as against 97.6% of all Catholic schools. Whereas only

46.4% of all pupils at State EGB schools were girls, some 52% of all pupils at private schools were girls. This was thought to reflect, at least in part, the prevalence of feminine religious orders among the Catholic providers: whereas there were more girls than boys in the Catholic schools, there were fewer girls than boys in the total of other private schools. Of all Catholic schools providing EGB education in 1982 (González-Anleo, 1985), 35% were run by masculine orders, 62% by feminine, while at BUP/COU levels there was more even 50–50 balance.

At the secondary level of BUP/COU, private providers accounted for 52.71% of all schools in 1986–86, but only 35.12% of all places and 31% of actual pupils. Of the total number of pupils, the Catholic schools catered for 16.92%, rather more than the 14.03% accounted for by other categories of private provider. There were rather fewer women in private secondary schools of this type than in state schools: 54.9% of all BUP/COU state pupils were women as against 50.1% of private pupils. State provision was notably more pronounced in certain regions of the country than others: for example Andalucia, Cantabria, Castilla-La Mancha, Ceuta and Melilla, Murcia.

At the secondary level of vocational education, FP, private provision accounted for 54.7% of all schools, 41.9% of all places and 41.3% of all actual pupils at this level in 1985–86. Women accounted for only 35.5% of all students in this level of education, but 51.8% of all students attending private schools. Private FP colleges concentrate more on specialisms which traditionally tend to attract high female participation, such as administration, health, cuisine, or hairdressing.

The percentages of BUP students educated in state BUP colleges rose from 59% in 1977–78 to 68% in 1985–86: but of COU students it fell from 87% to 71%; while of FP students it rose from 43% to 59%. In the case of COU, however, there was a dramatic reduction in the percentage of students attending state schools from 87% in 1977–78 to 67% in 1978–89, but from that position there has since been a modest increase in state provision.

In 1988–89, a total of 9,300,000 pupils were registered in private and public schools. There were 15,968 state schools, and 6471 private schools at pre-school and EGB levels: 1347 state and 1345 private schools at BUP/COU levels: and 1078 state and 1121 private schools at FP levels. Of a total of 409,527 teachers, 298,099 taught in the state sector. There were 277,117 teachers at pre-school and EGB levels (of whom 204.345 taught at state schools), 82,135 at BUP/COU level (of whom 58.595 taught in state schools), and 50,095 at FP level (of whom 35,195 taught in state schools) (*Communidad Escolar*, 21 September 1988). In the previous academic year, there had been 6065 schools with grant-aided (*concierto*) status with a total of 61,904 classes catering for 7,564,440 children receiving free education (*Communidad Escolar*,

13 July 1988). From this we can deduce that grant-aided schools accounted for approximately 94% of all private schools.

## Comparative advantages of state and private sectors

In the early 1980s it appeared that overall, private schools were better-endowed than public. In 1983, for example, 45% of state schools had a laboratory as against 94% of private schools; 68% of state schools had a library compared with 95% of private schools; 51% of state schools had sports facilities compared with 78% of private.

The salaries of teachers in the private schools have lagged behind those of the public sector, reflecting the low remuneration traditionally paid to members of the religious orders who in recent years have accounted for a diminishing proportion of the total number of teaching staff in church schools. LODE set in motion a process of homogenisation between teacher salaries in the two sectors, and by the late 1980s there was significant pressure on the government from the teacher unions for homogenisation between teachers and middle-range civil servants (which point was conceded in principle in an agreement with the unions reached in 1988). While the trend to homogenisation is established, disparities between state and private teachers salaries still persist at secondary (non-obligatory) levels, and while they are not directly comparable, state teachers in 1987–88 could earn up to a third more than private teachers. Progress towards complete homogenisation of conditions of employment between employers and unions in the early 1990s was delayed by divisions in the employers ranks between Catholic and other private providers and between the unions. Major points of contention included the length of the working day, holidays, salary increases for non-teaching personnel and for teachers of children at the non-obligatory education levels.

Differences in salary have partly reflected differences of qualification. A higher proportion (84%) of BUP teachers working in state schools in the early 1980s were graduates (*licenciados*) than were teachers in the private sector (73%) (González-Anleo). But all teachers at this level are now required to be graduates, while in the state sector, but not in the private, they are also required to possess a teaching certificate (*Certificado de Aptitud Pedagogica*). At the level of EGB, some 6.1% of all teachers are graduates in state schools, but 13.1% in private schools. At this level the minimum qualification required is the *Diplomado Universitario*. Some 75% of teachers in State EGB schools are now *diplomados*. In 1985–86, a total of 167,441 EGB teachers were either *licenciados, diplomados* or held other specialist qualifications. Of these, 127,187 were teaching in state schools. The remaining 40,254 were teachers in the private sector. As the total number of teachers in the private sector that year was 61,495, it appears that 21,241 or 34.5% were unqualified. The total number of teachers in the state sector was 131,950. The numbers of unqualified teachers in the state sector, therefore, was a mere 3%. It follows that while a higher proportion of private teachers are *licenciados* in EGB than of State teachers, a much higher proportion of private teachers at this level are still unqualified.

There are few teachers in EGB in either private or state schools who teach their specialist subject, but the numbers are even fewer in state that in private schools. In 1981–82, 50% of teachers qualified to teach english, for example, actually did so, but the figure was 72% for private schools; for french, the rates were 45% in state schools as against 63% in private schools. Teachers in private schools also teach longer hours: 27 hours of actual teaching time in 1989, while in state schools this was 25 hours in EGB and 18 hours in BUP.

The staff-student ratio in private schools has been less advantageous than in the state sector, overall. But this is largely because the private sector accounts for a lower percentage of those mainly rural 'incomplete' schools with less than eight classes, reflecting the traditional emphasis of the private sector on serving the wealthier urban and suburb areas. The overall pupil-teacher ratio was 28.9%, but 27.4% for state schools as against 32.8% for private schools. Grant-aided schools had higher ratios overall than non-aided private schools: with 34.21 pupils to the class in grant-aided schools, and 25.67 in the non-aided schools. Catholic grant-aided schools had an average of 37.31 to the class, as against 32.09 in the non-aided church schools. There were considerable variations between regions, with a low of 23.4 in Castilla-Leon among state schools and 23.3 in Pais Vasco for private schools to a high of 30.01 in Madrid for state schools and of 38.03 in Ceuta-Melilla for private schools.

There has been an overall improvement in ratios. In the period 1975–76 to 1982–83, the number of students per class in EGB fell from 32.4 to 30.1 in the state sector and 36.4 to 35.6 in the private sector, and the number of students per teacher fell from 31.8 to 28.7 in the state sector and 33.5 to 31 in the private sector. The number of students per teacher at BUP/COU level dropped from 17 to 15.3 in the state sector and from 16.6 to 16 in the private sector (González-Anleo). In Galicia, 1988, the staff-student ratio was 22 for state schools, yet 35 for private schools. The total numbers of students to a class in BUP/COU in 1985–86 was 27.2, but the pupil-teacher ratio was 16.4%.

Fewer children repeat years in private than in state schools, although this is likely to be due, at EGB level, to the fact that a higher proportion of pupils at private schools are girls and fewer girls than boys repeat years overall. The proportion of 'repeaters' in EGB was 11% in state schools in 1980–81, but only 4% in the private schools. In 1985–86 the proportion of 'repeater' was 8.4% in state schools and 4.1% in private schools, suggesting an overall improvement in state schools during the 1980s, but with private schools still enjoying 'repeater' rates of about half those of state schools. The overall number of students studying *con retraso*, for example 'over age' for their class, was 19% of the overall EGB total in 1985–86, but 22.6 in state schools as against 12.4 in private.

The same pattern is found in BUP/COU although private schools at this level do not benefit from a higher proportion of girls. The proportion of students repeating the first year of BUP was 14.6% in state schools, rising to 17.2% in the second year and falling back to 16% in the third year, while at private school it was 6.7% rising to 7.9% and falling back to 6.2% in the third year. Figures for the proportion of students who abandon their studies at each stage of the *Bachillerato* would very likely show similar trends. Available figures for the abandoning of studies in FP show that between the first and second year of FP, 28% of pupils abandon their studies in state schools, but only 21% in private.

It is a paradox, therefore, that while private schools appear to have better success rates (or lower 'failure' rates), better facilities, deploy their teachers more effectively, and are generally smaller in size, they also have had less well paid staff, less well-qualified staff overall, and higher pupil-teacher ratios. Unfortunately the available figures do not reveal as many of the differences between Catholic and other private providers as one would like, but the indications are that Catholic provision is less generously resourced than other private provision. There appeared to be a fall in public esteem for religious education during the 1970s, foreshadowing a steep fall in the numbers actually attending church schools. González-Anleo (1985) reports surveys showing that the proportion of people saying they believe religious education is best fell from 48% to 38% in the period 1969–75, with a corresponding rise in preference for state education from 29% to 47%. It is perhaps surprising that the distinction between state and grant-aided schools continues to be significant, given that compulsory education in both is now free. In Benissa, Valencia, for example, there are two state EGB schools which are generally well-regarded in the area. Yet many of the wealthier parents prefer to bus their children the 20-mile journey to Denia to attend a private grant-aided school there, with no noticeably superior facilities, and with the cost of travel and added expense. What is being bought, seemingly, at a cost of travel, children's time and parental inconvenience, is a 'better' social-class mix. From an alternative point of view, however, it may be argued that state pressure on private education through LODE has created a more equitable social class mix in these schools than before, with many more working-class and lower-middle class children joining the ranks of the upper-middle-class children.

A continuing urban bias was still evident in the distribution of private schools in the early 1980s. González-Anleo notes that 'the private schools have traditionally concentrated in the urban centres and for many years this preference has given rise to a polemic and to an accusation: why should the religious orders, proceeding by and large from rural zones, desert these and concentrate their educational efforts in the big cities?' According to López Pintor (1987) only 22% of families in rural areas with populations under 10,000 had children studying in private schools, whereas in towns of more than 50,000 the proportion was as high as 51%, and higher still in the largest towns. This is why some of the more industrial regions have very high percentages of private or grant-maintained schools. In 1975, private schools accounted for 83% of schools in Catalonia, 72% in Madrid and 72% in Pais Vasco. In 1982 some 15% of all religious EGB, BUP and FP schools were located in rural zones, 19.5% in urban zones, 12.6% in suburbs, 20.4% in industrial urban zones, and 32.2% in urban zones (González-Anleo, 1985). The predominance of private schools in the industrial zones had declined. In Catalonia, for example, where private schooling was still 20% higher than in the rest of the country in 1988 (*Comunidad Escolar*, 25 May 1988) the consciousness of an 'inherited deficit' of public schooling has inspired considerable new public construction with 193 new schools started in 1985–1988 alone, and the integration into the public system, without loss of their identity as centres of pedagogic innovation, of 60 private schools which had formed the progressive *Federación de Movimientos de Renovación Pedagógica de Catalûna*.

González-Anleo neatly summarises the basis of (debatable) claims to educational superiority that may be advanced by private schools: better resources; more effective deployment of teachers; better diagnosis of student difficulties and more resolute efforts to help the slower students; greater range of complementary or extra-curricular activities (for which parents may be required to pay). Private schools are less likely to make children repeat years – there are fewer such schools in rural zones and they take more clients from the higher classes, thus giving them a 'better' initial intake; they take a higher proportion of girls, who perform better anyway, and because they have more incentive perhaps not to upset parents.

## Implications of the constitution and LODE

Up to the 1978 Constitution, PSOE policy had favoured the dissolution of private schools. Formulation of a constitution in a democratic society presupposes the possibility of inter-party negotiations and the willingness of the political parties to be constrained for some considerable period of time, if not for ever, by the compromises they must reach. The PSOE agreed to modify its policy on private schooling in the interest of securing a lasting foundation for the future of democracy in Spain. Articles 16, 20, 27 and 44 of the constitution provide for the coexistence of public and private education, establish the right to create private schools and allow the provision of public funds to private schools where such schools comply with certain requirements. There are also several measures which in practice have tended to restrain the powers of private educators: namely the right of all citizens to an education, the right of parents to secure for their children the religious or moral education which accords with their convictions, the liberty of teaching and of the teacher, the right of all groups directly involved with education to participate both in its general planning, and in the management and control of all schools supported with public funds. Under the ministry of Maravall, those responsible for PSOE educational policy complained that their predecessors, the UCD, had not complied with the spirit of the Constitution. In its legislative plans for education, the UCD had interpreted 'liberty of teaching,' for example, in the sense of the freedom of private interests to establish new schools and for the owners of any such school to formulate and uphold its particular ideology. The PSOE considered that this relegated the state once more to a somewhat secondary role as the treasurer of funds for grants to private schools.

The socialists' own definition of educational freedom was to be enshrined in the 1984 *Ley Organica del Derecho a la Educación y Reglamiento que la Desarrola* (LODE). It should be noted that much of LODE was actually foreshadowed by the 1970 *Ley Géneral de Educación*. Many secondary and some principal features of that law, however, were never implemented or enforced. Progress on implementing LODE, on the other hand, was able to benefit from the powerful pressure of a formal constitution, together with a governing party which had a clear idea of where it wanted to take the educational system, and a more promising economic climate within which to do so, coupled with falling primary school rolls. The law provoked outraged protest among the opposition who referred it to the constitutional tribunal (which produced little change).

LODE sought to balance the freedom to establish and run private schools against the party's priority of guaranteeing the rights of teachers and clients to participate in school management in all publicly-funded schools, liberty of conscience and of the teacher, together with more rigorous specification and control of the conditions under which grants would be paid to a private school. So under LODE for example, exercise of the right of a private school supported by public funds to establish its own *ideario* (ideology, philosophy) is balanced against the freedom of conscience and of teaching, and participation of the whole school community in its planning and management. So while all grant-aided schools have the right to define their own character, all confessional practice must be voluntary. Teachers' liberty of teaching is itself subject to the general educational goals specified in article 2 of LODE.

Parents have the right to an education for their children, and to a moral or religious formation which accords with their own convictions and they have a right to choose a school among those made available by public funds. Parents are guaranteed the right to form parent associations whose purpose is to assist them in all that concerns the education of their children, including collaboration in the educational activities of schools, and promotion of parent participation in school management.

Among the various rights of students specified in LODE (article 6) are the right to respect for their personal integrity and dignity; and to participation in the life and functioning of their school. It is not difficult to see the potential for conflict between such rights, derived from the constitution and enshrined by law, and the degree of educational sovereignty once enjoyed by religious orders both within the public and private sectors. Students do however have a duty to study and to respect school rules of *'convivencia'* – living together. In this context, students, like their teachers and parents, must also take account of the school's *'cáracter propria'* – its particular character which, in the case of a church school, will involve a religious orientation. LODE guarantees students the right of association. Students' associations may legitimately facilitate the expression of student opinion on school affairs, collaborate in education and extra-curricular activities, promote the participation of students in collegiate bodies of the school, and form federations and confederations. Towards the end of the 1980s, the Ministry of Education gave added force to the specifications of LODE with the formulation of a charter of students' rights and duties, first of its kind in the world. This guarantees students the right of respect for their liberty of conscience, religious, moral and ideological convictions, also of their physical and moral integrity and personal dignity. A basic duty is to study, attend class and participate in activities oriented to the development of study plans.

All private schools in receipt of public funds are designated as *'centros concertados.'* All schools, whether public or private are required to conform to certain minimum standards established by the government with respect to teacher qualifications, teacher-pupil ratios, teaching and supporting facilities and equipment, and numbers of pupil places. Within these constraints and within the law generally, and provided there is no discrimination against any member of the educational community, schools enjoy autonomy in their use of time for optional activities, organising extra-curricular activities and adapting the curriculum and pedagogy to their particular environment.

Private schools which do not receive public funds can freely manage their finances, establish their own school rules, select teachers in accordance with qualifications specified by central government, and determine admission procedures. All private schools, whether grant-aided or not, are represented on the national *Consejo del Estado* (State Educational Council), a national educational advisory committee. Of the 20 teacher representatives on this committee, eight are from private schools, the other 12 from the public sector. Each sector has four management representatives. This council also comprises four representatives of employers' organisations, eight from the Ministry, four from the universities, and 12 individuals of established prestige in the field of education. Of a total of 80 representatives therefore, private schools control 12 or 15%. They may also enjoy indirect representation through some of the other categories.

LODE establishes the criteria by which an application from a private school for grant-aided status is assessed. Preference is to be given to applicants who can show they satisfy certain educational needs and attend to populations in unfavourable socio-economic circumstances or who, having satisfied some of the conditions, conduct educational experiments of general pedagogic interest. *Concierto* or grant-aided status is given for periods of four years, renewable. It is a condition of the receipt of grant that basic education for 4–16 year olds is delivered free of charge, without profit motive, paying due regard to plans of study as laid down by central government, and subject to academic, *'normas de ordenación'* in force. The owners agree to constitute the governing body as the organ of management and control, not to discriminate in the admission of students nor in the selection and dismissal of staff, to fulfil the necessities of schooling, and to meet certain minimum academic requirements established by law.

The overall sum of money for such grants is established in the general state budget or the budgets of the autonomous communities. The budgets specify the amount which is to be spent on teacher salaries (which from 1987 have been paid direct from the MEC to teachers, in an effort to by-pass industrial relations difficulties between teacher unions and staff managements), and paragraph four of article 40 of LODE states that there will be a gradual homogenisation of salaries between private and state schools. Grant-aided schools are recognised as charities for fiscal and non-fiscal purposes. Neither their main teaching nor their complementary or extra-curricular activities can be organised to make profit. Any charge made for complementary activities such as meals or transport has to be authorised by the appropriate educational administration. Any complementary service or extra-curricular activity must have a voluntary character and cannot form part of the main timetable. However there are considerable ambiguities about the bases of educational costing and the real costs of educational provision, and some grant-aided schools have attempted to supplement their income by additional charges to parents, on the grounds that the grants are insufficient to cover expenses. Admission of students to grant-aided schools is to be adjusted, according to LODE, to the overall planning of school places having regard for the need to guarantee the right to an education and the right to choose a school. This seems to suggest therefore that authorities have flexibility in their control of how many places they are prepared to fund in the grant-aided sector. In a period of falling rolls, this can be a source of vulnerability to grant-aided schools in the face of hostile or financially-pressed authorities, in addition to the more general insecurity occasioned by the necessity for these schools to seek renewal of their grant status every four years.

## Internal management

The internal management of grant-aided schools is regulated by LODE to the extent that it is established that such schools must have, at the very least, a *'consejo escolar del centro'* (governing body) and a *'claustro'* of teachers, similar to those of the state schools. The *'consejo escolar'* is described by González-Anleo (1985) as a pseudo-democratic Trojan horse in the grant-aided schools. This comment may be interpreted in various ways: for example, that the governing body represents lay values which undermine the traditional values of private education or that it in fact has little real power. The charge of non-effectiveness with respect to parent and student representatives is argued by Enguita (1987) who points out that the governing body has little say in day-to-day academic and pedagogic issues which are, after all, the main function of schooling and of most importance to students and parents. It may also be argued that parents and students often lack the necessary confidence, knowledge and experience to constitute a forceful influence on school governing bodies. But it could also be said, in full support for González-Anleo that while the governing body may not be very effective as a specifically representative body, it is an instrument which the state can use directly and indirectly to mould the process of change in the grant-aided schools. The *Consejo Escolar* also represents a shift in power away from the teachers' body (the *claustro*).

There are small but significant differences between the regulations governing grant-aided schools and those governing state schools. There is no specified requirement as there is in the case of public schools that there should also be a school secretary and a chief of studies. The role of director is also a little more restricted in the case of private schools, in deference no doubt to the rights of proprietors. The director of a grant-aided school is not called upon to be the official representative of the school. Nor is he required to submit an annual report to the administration. Teachers, parents and students participate in the control and management of grant-aided schools, as they do in the case of state schools, through the governing body, and through any other bodies provided for the purpose by the internal school regulations. The governing body comprises the director, three representatives of the proprietor ('*titular*'), four teachers and four parent representatives, two students and one representative of the administrative and service personnel. In the case of public schools, by contrast, LODE establishes that there should be a place on the governing body for the chief of studies and a representative of the local town hall ('*ayuntamiento*').

It is required that teacher representatives be elected by the *claustro* and that their number should not be less than one-third of the total of governing body members. In grant-aided schools the teachers other than the director account for only 26% of the governing body. Whereas parent representatives in the state schools should account for at least one-third of the governing body, in the grant-aided schools the proportion is again 26%. But *Real Decreto* 2376/1985 lays down that in public schools there should be eight teacher representatives on public school governing bodies where the school has 16 or more classes but only four where there are 8–15 classes. There should be eight representatives to cover both parents and students in schools of 16 or more classes, but only five in schools with 8–15 classes. Of these combined totals, three must be students in schools of 16 or more classes, but only 2 in schools of 8–15 classes.

All this means that the combined number of parent and student representatives can be one greater in grant-aided than in the smaller state schools, but four fewer than in the larger state schools. There would be four fewer teacher representatives in grant-aided schools than in the larger state schools, but only one fewer than in the smaller state schools. It appears that the will to participate is less strong in the private than in the public sector. In Madrid, 1988, 45% of state *bachillerato* institutes had student associations but only 16.6% of grant-aided schools and as few as 3.5% of non-aided private schools. The percentages were even lower in EGB and FP schools (*Comunidad Escolar*, 28 September 1988).

Do the governing bodies of grant-aided schools function as democratically as those of state-owned schools? This question relates to differences between state and grant-aided schools in the powers of the governing bodies. In state schools, for example, the board elects the school director, whereas in grant-maintained schools the director is designated by agreement between the owner and the board; in both cases the director must be chosen from among the permanent teachers of more than one year's teaching experience in the school. In grant-aided schools the board approves only that part of the budget that draws upon public funds, and the budget is first of all proposed by the owner. The owner also initiates the internal school rules for the board to approve. There is no specific requirement under LODE, as in the case of state schools, that the board should meet at least once a term. The board determines criteria for the appointment of teachers, in agreement with the owner but must give priority to the principle of merit and ability. The board sets up an appointment committee which comprises the director, two teachers and two parents. Any vacancies must be advertised publicly. The local administration must verify that procedures for selection and dismissal are in accordance with the law. (For state schools there is no mention in LODE of staff appointments other than for the director or for the management team.) It is the duty of the owner to formalise contracts of employment. Disagreement between the owner and the board may be resolved by recourse to the establishment of a conciliation committee on which sit a representative of the local administration, the owner and a representative of the board. In the case of continuing disagreement the administration can intervene.

The educational weekly newspaper *Comunidad Escolar* (9 November 1988) conducted a survey of union opinion about the operation of governing bodies. Several union spokesmen detected differences between the two sectors in the operation of the governing bodies. *La Federatión de Enseñanza de Comisiones Obreras* considered that there had been only minimal advances in the grant-aid sector towards real participation and control of funds. *Federatión Estatal de Trabajadores de la Enseñanza de la Union General de Trabajadores* (FETE-UGT) thought that governing bodies in this sector tended to be more consultative in character than decision-making. *Union Confederal de Sindicatos de Trabajadores de la Enseñanza* (UCSTE) opined that in the case of grant-aided schools there were no detailed rules governing the electoral process, and that this allowed the owners to influence decisively the arrangement of the electoral lists and to get governors they could manipulate. *Federación de Enseñanza de la Union Sindical Obrera* (USO) pointed out that while the state school governing bodies are responsible for designating the management teams, this privilege was reserved to the owner in the case of grant-aided schools. And whereas state school bodies *decided* on student admissions, grant-aided bodies only *guaranteed* the fulfilment of general norms on student admission. National bodies representing the owners of grant-aided schools, such as *Confederación Expañola de Centros de Enseñanza* (CECE) and *Federación Española de Religiosas de Enseñanza* (FERE), seemed happier with the operations of governing bodies than might be supposed in the light of their opposition to them on first publication of LODE, but cynics might argue that this only confirms that they find them no threat in practice. These comments on the governing bodies of grant-aided schools also need to be placed in the context of a more general concern that regardless of sector, the governing bodies had not lived up to initial expectations.

## Evaluation

Spain has managed a very significant transition away from an education system run essentially for the church and by the church and with poor reach into rural and deprived urban areas and to the industrial working and agricultural labour classes. In its place there is a system mainly financed by the state, largely controlled by, or under, close state supervision, which has achieved significant improvements in quantity of places and resources, and quality and range of content. There has been considerable battle between the state and the political right – hardly surprising in a country sharply divided in its view of the role of the state in education: a 1982 ME survey found that 51% believed that education should be exclusively a state service, while 47% believed that it should be private (González-Anleo, 1985). Nevertheless, the transition has been accomplished in terms which nailed its objectives in relation to the constitution and which have claimed the support of the courts and probably now of the majority of the people. The religious orders are free to preserve their traditions, and they still exercise significant influence. Nevertheless, this influence is subject increasingly to state regulation, to the participation of parents, teachers and students in the running of schools, and to guarantees of liberty of teaching and liberty of conscience which should ensure that the days of unquestioning and unquestioned indoctrinations are now on the decline. The Catholic hierarchy has been upset by the reduced status of religious education in the state curriculum and has argued without effect that this contravenes the constitution and Spain's 'Concordat' with the Vatican.

José Maravall writes in the preface of LODE that this legislation still represents a major concession to private education, despite the conditions which it imposes. It could have been, he says, a 'party' law centering on state education, granting only occasional funds to private schools. In practice, the financing of private education goes beyond anything required by the constitution, the Declaration of Human Rights, or international pacts on civil, political or economic rights. The model of financing of private education which the Spanish system represents does not exist in the majority of the western democracies – indeed, in Italy it is expressly forbidden by the constitution of that country. By means of the *'regimen de conciertos'* LODE gives financial stability to the grant-aided schools, within the constraint of four-yearly periods of approval, and allows them to define their own character, provided they attend to the requirements governing participation of parents, teachers and students. More recently, Maravall is recorded as having said LODE presupposed 'a reduction in the powers of the *titular* only in so far as the *titular* believes that the school community which supports his school is not in sympathy with the school's objectives' (*Comunidad Escolar*, 9 November 1988).

## Vulnerability of private sector

The great danger of the grant-aid system for the private schools is that the government at central or at regional level determines the level of grant and renewal of grant-aided status. At a time of falling rolls or where local authorities are hostile, this can represent a grave worry. In Catalonia the government announced in 1987 that it would not be extending full grants to grant-aided schools in future, given the falling birth-rate and shortages of funds (*Comunidad Escolar*, 23 September 1980). But only two schools were thought likely to close as a result. In the Basque country where grant-aided schools were receiving subsidies at a level of 3,211,494 pesetas for each class (approximately £16,057) in 1988, the regional government has publicised the continuing practice of many grant-aided schools of charging unapproved monthly fees of between 1000 and 4000 pesetas (£5–20) for 'supplementary' activities. While the government could bring action against these schools it has so far confined itself to a campaign of information to parents reminding them that their children are entitled to free EGB education. The government also requires that the invoices which schools send to parents must show that the money is for complementary activities or voluntary charitable help. Annual accounts will have to show receipts from the administration and detail of expenses (*Comunidad Escolar*, 17 February 1988). The schools, primarily Catholic, have responded by saying that the government grant is insufficient to cover the real cost per student place. Wholesale consideration of the renewal of grant-aided status to private schools across Spain was due throughout 1989, and proprietors were quick to complain that they were being subjected to criteria more severe than those applied to state schools. FERE, for example, was moved to manifest its profound disgust and disagreement with the administration's criteria (*Comunidad Escolar*, 1 March 1989). By the end of the process of reconsideration of grant-aided status in 1989, renewal had been given to 1895 schools (21,264 places) within the areas covered by the MEC (i.e. excluding the six, now seven, autonomous areas which enjoy 'full competency' in education). This represented an overall reduction of 7.6%, due mainly to 'lack of necessary requisites' and to a lesser extent, to a low pupil-teacher ratio relative to other schools in the area. But falling rolls were also thought by the unions to be a relevant factor. Exceptionally, some schools were given renewal for a period of one year, either to give them time to bring their facilities up to scratch, or to give the administration time to secure alternative places. The administration guarantees alternative places for displaced students and teachers. (*Comunidad Escolar*, 26 April 1989)

There are two different kinds of grant-aided status: *General* and *Singular*. *General* grants are meant to cover 100% of the cost of providing obligatory education which the beneficiary must provide free; while *singular* grants are meant to be supported in part by fees from parents. Where fees are payable, the ministry fixes the maximum level at which they can be charged, and which in 1987 could not exceed 2000 pesetas (£10) a month. The ministry pays the difference between fee income (which is low) and the amount that would be given on the basis of *general* grant. The majority of grant-aided schools at EGB receive *general* aid. But many query the adequacy of grant levels.

The issues raised by the procedures for the award of grant-aided status underline the significance of a dispute over the criteria by which grant levels are determined. This is discussed by Bosch and Diaz (1988). There are those who interpret the constitutional obligation laid down upon the public authorities to give economic assistance to those private schools which meet certain prerequisites as meaning that such economic help should cover the entire cost for all such schools. Others, supported by a judgment or the constitutional tribunal in 1985 consider there is no such duty to cover entire costs, that the constitution does *not* refer to grants to cover the cost of school places, but only to support of a wide range (for example, loans at low interest). LODE referred to an 'economic model of school class' as a basis for calculation that would differentiate between teaching salaries, other personnel costs and other related expenses. She argued that 'other related expenses' could include opportunity costs of invested capital. A 1985 decree (*reglamiento de normas básicas sobre conciertos educativos*, RD 13.77/85), interprets 'other expenses' to refer to administrative and service personnel, maintenance, conservation and replacement, *not* including amortisation nor interest on private capital. It adds that these quantities are to be fixed on the basis of criteria analogous to those applied in state schools. But this decree has not put an end to the dispute. There is continuing concern, in particular about opportunity costs. The proponents of total grants applaud the view of the constitutional tribunal that the system of *conciertos* should cover 'total costs of these activities,' while their opponents quote LODE to the effect that in grant-aided schools, scholarly activities 'should not be for profit'. Bosch and Diaz argue that a satisfactory resolution of the controversy would require more information concerning the material means, the quality and quantity of fixtures, management efficiency, student results, the minimum results which it is considered students should obtain – considerations which might well reveal the desirability of directing more money to some schools than to others.

In 1988 MEC announced it was setting aside 300 million pesetas for capital investment grants to private schools. The criteria for the disbursement of such grants were: high teaching quality; participation in the reform process; status of co-operative school ownership in the hands of a group of teachers, a *'sociedad anómima laboral,'* a mixed parent-teacher co-operative or a parents' co-operative, in that order, situation in priority areas; having been without access to official funds in the previous five years. (*Comunidad Escolar*, 6 July 1988)

Two test cases developing in 1987 suggested that at least with respect to teachers' freedom to teach, the grant-aided schools were more restricted under LODE than before it. In the first case a lay teacher in Zaragoza was dismissed from a Salesian college after 16 years' service on the ground that he had demonstrated against the *ideario* (philosophy) of the college, and for having spoken against the community. LODE does require teachers to 'respect' the *ideario* of their institutions. In this case the teacher publicly denied the accusations brought against him. It also appeared that the main concern of the college had been to reduce staff. In any case, the *Magistratura de Trabajo* had declared null and void an earlier attempt to dismiss the teacher in question, and the teacher had attracted a wide range of support from left to centre political groups and unions, also from the future *Justicia de Aragón*. Similar support was shown another teacher in the second case, also in Zaragoza. In this case the teacher had worked 12 years for an Augustinian order. She was accused of demonstrating against the *ideario* of the school and of having refused to pray at the beginning of class. The lawyer representing the college had advised his client that the procedure for dismissal which it had adopted was inappropriate, and had negotiated an offer of indemnity of 4,000,000 pesetas (double the legal requirement) if she did not return to work at the college. Instances of this kind may serve to support the judgment of those sympathetic to the private sector that LODE has made direct battle against the *ideario* of non-state schools (González-Anleo, 1985).

It should not be thought that the Catholic church is now a weak force, only that it is less strong. Catholic education has been described as the 'largest private business in the country' with 2,000,000 clients and more than 100,000 employees (González-Anleo, 1985), and as the most effective lobbyist in the political system. This source has counted 61 occasions in which the clergy have 'intervened' in the political process between 1969–1983. Education is the greatest preoccupation of the clergy. Most recently, the church contributed its own note of protest in the debate leading up to reform legislation (*Ley Organica de Ordenación General del Sistema Educativo* [LOGSE]) in 1990, arguing that not enough had been done to secure the place of religion and non-materialistic values. Not all clergy are conservative however: there are socialist sympathisers and groupings within the church but these are in a minority and have less influence. Inevitably this places a strain on church-state relations under a socialist government.

## Conclusion

In the space of little over 20 years, education in Spain has moved from one of church-domination, especially in the secondary sector and in the central urban areas, to a system of secular state control. A key characteristic of this system is that while the church still retains considerable influence in the private sphere, its control over pupils and teachers has been muted through the manipulation of grant-aid which now supports all but 6% of all private schools, and the conditions imposed by LODE for the control and management of grant-aided schools. A further striking feature of the range of private provision in contemporary Spain is the multiplicity of providers. While the Catholic church is still by far the largest single grouping among the total body of private providers, it does not control the majority of private schools, nor even cater for the majority of pupils attending private schools (except at BUP/COU level). There is growing evidence of an awareness of distinctive church interests. In 1988 church grant-aided schools established their own representative body Educación y Gesción distinct from CECE, hitherto the main representative body for all private schools. In 1988 EG represented 6320 colleges catering for 1,850,000 students. In the study of the politics of Spanish education, further research would be desirable to explore the diverging as well as converging interests of Catholic and other private providers. A great deal more needs to be known about these other private providers.

### References

Benitez, Manuel de Puelles (1987) *Educación e Idealogia en La España Contemporanea (1967–1975)*, Barcelona, Editorial Labor, Politeia.

Bosch, F and Diaz, J (1988) *La Educación en España. Una Prespectiva Económica*, Barcelona, Editorial Ariel, SA.

Carabaña, Julio (1988) 'Comprehensive educational reforms in Spain: past and present,' *European Journal of Education*, 23(3), pp. 213–228.

Enguita, Mariano Fernandez (1987) *Reforma educativa, desigualdad social, e inercia institucional (La enseñenza secondaria en España)*, Barcelona, Editoria Laia.

Gonzalez-Anleo (1985) *El sistema educativ espanañol*, Madrid, Instituto de Etudios Económicos.

Lopez Pintor, R (1987) 'Enseñanza religiosa y enseñanza de la religion,' *La opinion publica española*, Sal Terrae, March.

Maravall, Jose Maria (1984) *La Reforma de la Enseñana*, Barcelona Laia/Divergencias, Cuadernos de pedagógia.

Maravall, Jose Maria (1985) 'Discurso del Ministro de Educación y Ciencia en Defensa del Proyecto de Ley Organica del Derecho a La Educación,' in *LODE*, Madrid, Ministerio de Educación y Ciercia, pp. 9–28.

Ministerio de Educación y Ciencia (1987) *Proyecto para la reforma de la Ensenañza*, Madrid, MEC.

Ministerio de Educación y Ciencia (1989a) *Libro Blanca para la reforma del sistema educativo*, Madrid, MEC.

Ministerio de Educación y Ciencia (1989b) *El Sistema Educativo Español*, Madrid, Mec.

O'Mally, Pam (1990) 'Reservoirs of Dignity and Pride; Schoolteachers and the Creation of an Educational Alternative in Franco's Spain,' unpublished Ph D dissertation, Open University School of Education.

El País (1986) *Añuario*, Madrid, El País.

# 7. Australian perspectives

This chapter addresses key issues regarding the future and distinctiveness of Christian schools in the Australian context.

In the first article, Professor Brian V Hill distinguishes between the three main forms of Christian schools in Australia: Catholic schools which in statistical terms outweigh the others; traditional 'independent' schools, mostly sponsored by the major Protestant denominations; and the smaller 'alternative' schools, united by their conservative theology and strong commitment to local control and parental involvement. To each of these sectors Brian Hill addresses four sharp questions. Who are you aiming to provide for? What do you expect schooling to achieve? Are your procedures ethical and Christian? Where do your resources come from?

Brian Hill is Professor of Education at Murdoch University, Western Australia, and sometime editor of *Journal of Christian Education*, where this article was first published in 1982.

In the second article, Dr Patricia Malone examines the language of the religious education curriculum guidelines prepared and implemented by the two largest Catholic Education Offices in Australia. She argues that future guidelines will require close collaboration between people who have a good knowledge of the theory and process of curriculum development and implementation, with those who understand the nature and purpose of religious education and with practising teachers who are aware of the needs of the students in the reality of today.

Dr Patricia Malone is Head of the School of Religion and Philosophy at the Australian Catholic University in New South Wales. This article, based on a paper delivered to the fifth session of the International Seminar on Religious Education and Values, was first published in *British Journal of Religious Education* in 1987.

# 7.1 Christian schools: issues to be resolved
*Brian V Hill*

## Introduction

It was, I think, Walter Murdoch who once adapted the title of a famous war novel and said: 'All's Quiet on the Western Front; no new religion has come out of America in the past fortnight.' Recent developments in education prompt the thought that this should now be adapted to read: 'No new Christian school has come out ... in the past fortnight!'

It is now common knowledge that in both the USA and Australia there has been a remarkable upsurge in the number of small alternative Christian schools. Their emergence implies dissatisfaction with two existing approaches to schooling. One is the government-sponsored school. The other is the older wave of church-sponsored schools in each country.

Where do Christians who have received professional teacher training stand in all this? The answer depends to some extent on where you find them. Interestingly, I think, it is a reasonable guess that the majority work in state school systems. It is, I suppose, faintly possible that they have not thought about their position there, especially if they have children of their own, from a Christian point of view. That, at least, is the belief of one Victorian clergyman, Revd Bob Payne, recently quoted as saying: 'Here is a challenge to all Christian teachers who are still working in Egypt to heed the call of God and move out into the new promised land.'[1] Revd Payne is, I suspect, confusing the call of God with a cry of Payne. His use of Exodus imagery lends a certain air of biblical legitimation to his opinion, but it would be truer to the sense of the Bible to appeal to our Lord's imagery, of moving out into Samaria and the ends of the earth, and becoming salt and light in the world.[2]

As a matter of plain fact, there are convinced, Bible-centred Christians teaching in all three sectors: state, older church school, and newer Christian school. They are not there by accident. Many can give a prayerfully considered explanation of why they have taken up their present respective teaching positions. Admittedly there are some who have drifted into their present employment mainly as the result of an unreflective response to social pressures and traditions. It is these people who are the ones most vulnerable to guilt feelings when challenged by enthusiasts for the more recent pattern of small alternative Christian schools. These enthusiasts, in turn, often lack a balanced theology of witness in the world, and jump to judgmental conclusions about the commitment of fellow Christians who think differently.

There is a need, therefore, to get a dialogue going between Christian teachers in these different sectors: a dialogue characterised not by defensive criticism but by mutual respect. It was to this end that I wrote an article three years ago in the *Journal of Christian Education*.[3] In it, I pointed out that there is no direct biblical command to set up Christian schools, nor any prohibition. What we do find in scripture are various principles of action, such as parental responsibility and the call to be salt in the community, which have to be weighed up in the light of one's own cultural situation at a particular time.

I did not expect readers of this article to come out of Christian schools in droves, nor to leave state systems, for I mentioned problems and opportunities in both patterns. I indicated the pattern to which I presently felt most committed, while conceding that I could imagine not unlikely cultural conditions where I would be motivated to decide differently. The aim of the article was to prompt colleagues in all sectors to re-examine their educational commitments to improve the grounds for doing what they felt called to do, and to have more respect for deeply Christian colleagues who have interpreted their call differently. In the event I heard of one school which rejected subscription to the journal in question because of my article, deeming me to be an enemy of Christian schools simply because I had pointed out flaws in some of the arguments advanced to justify them.

As it happened, the same journal at my suggestion ran a later issue devoted to responses to the article, drawn from a variety of alternative viewpoints.[4] I would hope this dialogue will continue. At various points in the present paper I will refer to some of the arguments advanced in these rejoinders.

But I must now clarify what my role is in this present context. It is not, as it was in the earlier paper, to debate whether Christians should be teaching in public or private schools. This time I am assuming that many Christians after reflection on this question will re-affirm their call to teach in church- or parent-sponsored Christian schools. I respect them for so deciding, and now wish to be of some help to them by discussing some of the questions to which they must be able to provide better answers, if the educational options they represent are to be seen as biblically valid and credible in today's culture. For better answers they must be able to provide. I see a future in which they will be subject to increasing public scrutiny and criticism. Already, public grants are being withdrawn.

My strategy is suggested by something in Catholic tradition. The devil's advocate, as he is popularly known, is a church officer charged with seeking flaws in the characters of persons nominated for Catholic recognition as saints. His real title is 'promoter of the faith,'[5] because it is believed that only by searching self-criticism will the Christian proclamation remain credible to the outside world. I am not about to nominate anyone for sainthood, but I do propose to provoke self-examination by raising, as my title puts it: some 'issues to be resolved.'

One more preliminary. We need some kind of shorthand description to identify the different types of religiously sponsored school. It is hard to invent labels without implying value judgments. The obvious contrast is between Protestant and Catholic, but within the latter it is necessary to distinguish between the top echelon of schools in the grammar tradition and the great number of parochial or parish-based schools. There are also important philosophical differences between the various teaching orders which run Catholic schools. The second obvious contrast is between *all* the types I have so far mentioned and the newer wave of small alternative Christian schools, mostly Protestant. But these in turn may be sub-divided into

a.    individual schools each controlled by a local church, in this case mostly Baptist;
b.    a few instances of individual schools controlled by a local inter-denominational consortium of churches;
c.    a number of parent-controlled schools.

These in turn may be sub-divided according to the educational theory they exemplify, the most numerous types being those promoting a presbyterian-reformed view of curriculum, and those using materials of an American fundamentalist type such as the Accelerated Christian Education and Life Pack Schools.

It would be distracting to try to preserve all these variant classifications in our discussion. In sheerly statistical terms, Catholic schools outweigh the others, and the similarities in their theology of education are far greater than the differences. Second, statistically, are the traditional 'independent' schools, mostly sponsored by the major Protestant denominations. Well behind them, statistically, come the small alternative schools, united by their conservative theology and strong commitment to local control and parental involvement. I will therefore refer, for the most part, to these three groupings collectively, using the terms 'Catholic,' 'independent,' and 'alternative.' But I ask you to keep in mind that there is a diversity of philosophy and practice within all three categories. When referring to all three together, I will call them 'Christian schools.'

As regards this tripartite division, I will be posing four questions:

a.    'who are you aiming to provide for?' which bears on needs-assessment;

b.  'What do you expect schooling to achieve?' which asks for educational aims;
c.  'Are your procedures ethical and Christian?' which concerns content and methods;
d.  'Where do your resources come from?' which concerns funding and sponsorship.

## Needs assessment

Firstly, then, who are you aiming to provide for? In contrast to the private school, the government school is committed to providing for everyone, including the drop-outs from private schools! In theory the motto of the state school is reminiscent of the gospel's 'whosoever will may come.'[6] In practice, one of the most justified criticisms of state schooling is that the individual tends to be submerged in the mass education machine, and there is too much discrimination in favour of the intellectual and sporting elites in the school. How do matters stand with Christian schools?

The answers vary. Catholic schools, while they will usually accept non-Catholic students, are seen as extensions of the church's nurture program for those infused with faith at baptism. As such, they are theoretically suitable only for Catholics, or those in a state of grace. It is my impression, however, that recent Catholic writers have found the doctrine of baptismal regeneration less helpful to an understanding of where their pupils are at than assumptions that have more in common with modern secular views, of education as a process of developing awareness, with explicit evangelism becoming a priority to be met in ways beyond the classroom.[7] Under these circumstances, the needs of all kinds of pupil can be met by a Catholic education.

Independent schools have ineluctably evolved into schools for a social elite. Their traditions were laid down in the nineteenth century, despite the more democratic protestations of some, by the English grammar and public school models they copied. The ability to keep fees down was lost when state assistance was withdrawn, and they became the preserve of the educated and the well-to-do. Since the second world war they have been challenged to foreswear their sub-Christian bias towards the rich by the revival of government subsidies on a very generous scale and by the rival ethos of the state comprehensive high school. There is little evidence that either has had much impact. 'Old boy' and 'old girl' influences have tended to negate the aspirations of more Christianly-minded principals and staff members, and the public is bemused by the continuing fee spiral which, for whatever reasons, keeps them out of the reach of the common people. How does the Christian teacher in this sector come to terms with such condemnations of favouritism towards the rich as we find in the Epistle of James?[8]

Alternative schools tend on the whole to orient their program to the assumed spiritual perception and needs of the children of Christian parents. While some publicise their curriculum in a way which they hope will appeal also to parents who, though not Christian, nevertheless prefer the Christian ethic and a tightly-knit school community to the pluralism of the average state school, generally speaking few concessions are made to the sensibilities of the unsaved. The school attempts to generate an authoritatively Christian environment which in itself will have a faith-enculturating effect on all the children who attend. As one would expect, non-Christians are usually discouraged, if not excluded, from patronising such schools. One must ask what provision there is in the educational theory of such schools for teaching the law of God to other people's children. As Dr Hogg points out in her response to my earlier article, this is a responsibility as strongly enjoined upon us in scripture as the complementary duty to teach our own children.[9]

One area of need which in general is inadequately catered for in state systems is the child retarded by special learning difficulties, physical or mental handicaps, or cultural differences. In the latter category are to be included the children of migrants. How sensitive are Catholic, independent, and alternative schools to such children? The answers vary greatly. The reason given by many people for turning to the non-government sector is often that their children have learning difficulties which call for more individualised attention. If they have the money, smaller class-sizes in independent schools may help. If not, the capacity of alternative schools to draw on parents as teacher-aides in the classroom may substitute. But small schools and non-systemic independent schools cannot necessarily provide the range of facilities and specialist teachers available in the public sector. So the wise parent will investigate all avenues and not just generalise that a religiously-sponsored school will necessarily be better. I suspect that, overall, the provision in both the state *and* non-state sectors is inadequate. There is a clear biblical injunction to help the weak and helpless which should prompt Christian teachers in both sectors to press for better services in this area.

## Educational aims

The second question I want to ask is: what do you expect schooling to achieve? The possibilities may be represented as training, awareness, Christian nurture and conversion. By *training* I mean a concentration on facts and skills, with a view to fitting the individual into existing society. No educational theorist is satisfied to settle merely for this, but there is no doubt that many state schools in fact operate mainly on this level. The result is indoctrination of the shallow, hedonistic consumerism of the affluent society. Conversely, there are Christian schools which aim to fit individuals into the small community of their particular denomination or sect without allowing them to question the values and beliefs pressed into them.

The goal of *awareness* is highly favoured by secular theorists, because it widens the individual's understanding of his or her environment, enabling more intelligent choices to be made with regard to career, faith and friends. It ought also to be highly favoured by Christians attentive to biblical norms, for both Testaments resound with appeals to develop a self-critical understanding. Secular theorists have argued for 'rational autonomy' as an educational goal, and I used this term in my earlier article. Many Christian school theorists, however, react violently when they encounter the term, because they think immediately of 'autonomy' as referring to the sinful human tendency to refuse obedience to God. Predictably, Dr Blomberg, a respondent involved with an alternative school, took me up in this sense.[10] While I agree that some writers can be interpreted in this way, it is wrong to assume that all do. In the context of *my* article, it referred only to the desirable and biblically endorsed goal of helping people to reach the point where they can think for themselves and critically examine the belief claims pressed upon them by others, whether in the church or in the world.

Christian schools in the recent past as well as the present have often given the impression that they fear to give their students too much information or latitude in case they reject the Christian faith. If it is only by shielding people from criticisms or alternative viewpoints that we can prevent the decline of the faith we profess, then perhaps *that* faith deserves to decline. The Bible clearly affirms that the message of Christ is not just a psychological security blanket but a set of truth-claims about the world. As Francis Schaeffer exclaimed to his wife after a night of discussion with thoughtful enquirers: 'It really *is* the answer, Edith; it fits, it really fits. It really *is* truth, and because it is true it fits what is really there.'[11] Our students deserve to see how the Christian faith stands up against other belief-stances, both so that their own acceptance or rejection will be fully their own responsibility, and so that they will understand the mind-sets of others whom they seek to evangelise.

But many writers want to proceed beyond the awareness aim into *Christian nurture* as the objective of the school. I have expressed concerns about such an aim in connection with compulsory classroom instruction in a number of places.[12] Just now I would simply raise the question of the accuracy and the ethics of regarding every student under compulsory instruction as a consenting Christian person. Many Christian schools of all three kinds, for example, invite students either to commit perjury or to view religion as empty ritual by making corporate worship in class or chapel compulsory, when the essence of Christian commitment is the voluntary love of God.[13]

It has been my consistent contention over the years that education is more than school, and that many of the goals we cherish for persons are bigger than education. 'Nurture' is a notion which embraces teaching for deeper Christian commitment, but this by its very nature must occur in voluntary settings where the teacher has no power over the learner save that of friendly persuasion. The same applies to 'evangelism.' We may do much to prepare the ground in the classroom by making children aware of the Christian evidences and implicitly exemplifying Christ in our relationships with them. But the foundation stones of evangelism and nurture must be laid in freer and more equal encounter.

It is quite possible that this may occur on school premises, state or private, in extra-curricular time. It also occurs in youth groups and camps, social occasions in each other's homes, and in moments of personal conversation and counselling. But the essence of the interaction is that it must be without duress or formal assessment, neither of which is ever totally absent from what Westerhoff calls 'the schooling-instructional paradigm.'[14]

But there is a fifth possibility, beyond training or awareness, not identical with Christian nurture or evangelism, which I implied in my earlier paper when I said it is the teacher's task 'to encourage rational autonomy and human sensitivity.' We cannot stop at awareness as if this were a neutral goal. It is not. Already it implies a commitment to a certain view of human persons. Rational autonomy and humane sensitivity go even further. They imply that critical intelligence and compassionate regard for our fellows are both commitments without which the joint enterprise of teaching and learning which is the school cannot go forward. In this sense the school, even the state school, *is* educating for commitment.[15] No school can function without such agreements. That is why state school theorists who argue that the school *should* be value-neutral are talking nonsense, since it *cannot* be.

In short, when I ask you what you hope to achieve by schooling, I want to know in what sense you mean to offer Christian nurture, and what price you put on a critical rational awareness. The community tends to see Catholic and alternative schools as, in the main, agencies for religious proselytisation, whereas independent schools are seen to be so nominal in their contemporary religious ties that their main achievement is a status-enhancing training. Are you satisfied with these images?

## Content and methods

My third question has already been touched on by implication. Are your procedures ethical and Christian? It may seem odd that I mention 'ethical' and 'Christian' separately. Surely any procedure that is Christian must at the least be ethical? The Christian believes that morality ultimately derives from commitment to the God who planted the moral law in the created order. Yet I find many Christian school advocates writing as though they believed it was sometimes Christian to be unethical, particularly when it comes to the issue of evangelism in the formal classroom setting.

The crucial point at issue is: what are the limits of the persuasion we seek to exercise on others? Everyone is fairly clear that physical and psychological coercion are violations of personal rights, especially if used in an attempt to control thoughts as well as behaviour. It is part of my personal agony to have met relatives of my wife behind the Iron Curtain who are under constant pressure to give up their Christian faith. But psychological pressure can be more subtle. We can agree that it is bad when it involves bullying and blatant domination. But people seem less worried when, by conditioning, indoctrination or undisguised group pressure, the individual is benevolently manipulated to accept beliefs and loyalties he has not really had the chance to inspect for himself.

Some Christians seem willing to bend the ethical rules because they have a very commendable sense of urgency about the evangelistic task. I hope we all have; it *is* urgent. They may appeal to Paul's plea to Timothy to preach the word 'in season and out of season'[16] or his willingness to win others 'by all possible means.'[17] But they ignore the fact that in the same passage from which the second of these verses was quoted Paul also says 'though I am not free from God's law but am under Christ's law.'[18] He is saying that what is possible is limited not only by circumstances but by moral rightness. There is a time and a place for explicit evangelism, and a captive audience under formal instruction and assessment is not one of those times.

There is a significant amount of evidence that children and youth placed under pressure to conform to, and profess belief in, Christianity, in situations where they can't get away and are subject to disciplinary action, become either unable to think for themselves or actively resistant to the gospel. So it appears that what is unethical may also in fact be ineffectual.

It is more difficult to argue against indoctrination. The word literally means putting doctrines into the learner. It is not the same as conditioning or brain-washing, for it requires that the learner be conscious and consenting to what is being done to him. So what is so wrong about indoctrination? The word has only become a term of disapproval in the last century or so, since society became more pluralistic in its religious composition, and people became more sensitive to their children being taught as *fact*, things that were matters of disputed belief.

There has been a lot of useful clarifying discussion of the modern notion of indoctrination,[19] to pinpoint what it is that people find offensive. The general objection seems to be that it involves producing people who haven't really been allowed to make up their own minds about things on the best evidence available. The effect has been to guarantee conforming behaviour or repetition of belief statements without the individual being fully aware (or as fully aware as possible) of how they are regarded in the world at large.

It is no defence of indoctrination to say that it is better to have blinkered believers than well-informed unbelievers. The blinkers cannot be kept on forever, and many indoctrinated Christians have crashed when they encountered persuasive critics of the faith or alluring counter-lifestyles after a protectionist schooling. Others, as we said earlier, have proved useless in evangelising and salting society because they lacked any real understanding of how their neighbours thought and lived. But whether or not these are the practical results, the higher question is whether such treatment of learners, if deliberate, is ethical. What rights has the individual to know his situation and to be free to choose amongst available options, including the ones of which I might not happen to approve? Ultimately my answer is given in the conduct of Christ towards enquirers.[20]

It is very clear that Jesus discouraged cheap discipleship, and obliged his enquirers to count the cost, especially in terms of how they would be regarded in the society they lived in. From psalmists and prophets to Christ and the apostles, the call to understand what we are doing and to have reasons for our faith is constantly reiterated. The opposite of indoctrination is making people aware both of the truth as we perceive it and the critique to which the world constantly subjects that truth. This process is also compatible with what modern secular theorists define as 'education.'

We should note, by the way, that some of the critics of indoctrination impose unrealistic demands on schools, forgetting the developmental factor. One cannot bring a young child to a state of mind that is both committed and critically objective. The charge of indoctrination cannot be proved until the whole curriculum for the compulsory years of schooling is examined. That is when the test should ultimately be applied.

Some alternative schools writers toy with the idea that perhaps indoctrination isn't necessarily all that bad.[21] I do not think they realise what they are saying, perhaps because they do not fully grasp the meaning the term has acquired. It is clear to me from the curriculum recommendations they actually make that *they* at least are not aiming to produce blinkered believers, though one concedes that there are some alternative schools that do.[22]

It is interesting that in at least three Australian states questions have been raised about whether schools using Accelerated Christian Education materials should be refused registration. The verdict of many secular authorities is that some of these materials are indoctrinative rather than educative, and the fact that they refuse to allow their pupils seriously to examine the evolutionary theory in biology is not the only reason. I find it even more interesting that so many Christian educationists agree with the states' estimation of these materials. The point at issue is exactly the one I have been discussing, and educational and biblical grounds come together in outlawing the way these materials set out to manipulate young persons.

Of the three types of Christian school I am considering, the independent school has generally been considered least prone to religious indoctrination and compulsory evangelism. But it must disprove another allegation, that it has a tendency to engage in political and social class indoctrination. This charge is made by Marxist theorists but, if true, would have to concern Christian analysts also.

One last word on indoctrination. Some Christians argue that state schools indoctrinate the humanistic view of life, so why should we not counter this by indoctrinating the Christian view? There are several things that could be said about this argument. Firstly, it implies that indoctrination occurs in state schools. I have argued constantly that state schools must come clean on the values they are promoting, negotiate a consensus acceptable to their wider local communities, and at the same time encourage critical thought.[23] Only thus will they avoid indoctrination.

The only other point to be made here about the argument that 'they indoctrinate, so why shouldn't we?' is that it is unworthy of a Christian. It is as though we were to say that since communists use electric shocks to assist in securing personality change, so should we. If a method is unethical, then it can never be justified by Christians in terms of a desired end. Wrong is wrong.

## Funding and sponsorship

The final question I set out to pose was: 'Where do your resources come from?' The question appears straightforward. Approved non-state schools can expect to cover up to sixty percent of their recurrent costs through federal and state subsidies. But it is the other forty percent I am concerned with. This is made up, in varying proportions, of endowments, student fees and the outcomes of local fund-raising.

The hidden agenda is the extent to which this ties up resources that the Christian church needs for other ministries. Independent schools have tended to draw back from making financial claims on their sponsoring denominations, relying instead on consultant fund-raising and high fees. The concealed cost to the church lies in the fact that Christian parents who patronise these schools are unable to give as generously to their church's ministries in other areas because of the extent to which they have mortgaged the family budget to their own children's education.[24]

So far as the Catholic church is concerned, its people have for decades been called upon for sacrificial effort. Even though costs have been lowered by the cheerful dedication of teaching orders willing to embrace the vow of poverty, people in the parishes have laboured continuously to raise funds. Similarly, alternative schools are now repeating this pattern as they invite teachers to accept below-award salaries and draw parents into fund-raising and teaching-aide duties. Community involvement does, of course, have other values besides helping to meet funding needs. It is a good thing in its own right on both biblical and educational grounds, and I have argued strongly in other circles for more parental participation in state schooling.[25] But the fact remains that this can be overdone to the point where no time, energy or money are left for other priorities of witness in the world.

I ask, in my role of friendly critic, are you satisfied with the demands you are making for resources from the Body of Christ? Does this promote or inhibit the investment of its energies in the wider community, in expressions of social ministry and reform, and in evangelism?

The independent school, as I have said, imposes little drain on the financial and human resources of the church, but is that because it has, in general, ceased to be an effective servant of the church's purposes? I well remember a headmaster lecturing to my students years ago. One question after his talk was: 'How much influence does your denomination exercise on the school council and school policies?' He replied with obvious satisfaction: 'Effectively none.' Is this typical? And is it desirable?

## Conclusion

In conclusion, I have posed four questions which, I believe, place the onus of proof on Christian schools of whatever type. If their educational theories are to be seen as adequate, they will have to be able to supply answers that satisfy at two levels. The first level is that of biblical principle, and represents a demand within the Christian community that what is done reflect the principles and priorities of a biblical witness and lifestyle. The second level is that of public accountability. This requires that such schools be shown to be genuinely educational institutions, not liable to charges of indoctrination or the infringement of personal liberties.

**Notes**
1.    Revd Bob Payne of Frankston, quoted in *On Being*, 3, 1982, p. 55.
2.    Acts 1:8 and Matthew 5:13–16.
3.    Brian V Hill, 'Is it time we deschooled Christianity?,' *Journal of Christian Education*, 63, 1978, pp. 5–21.
4.    *Journal of Christian Education*, 67, 1980. Dr Doug Blomberg and Dr Noel Weeks spoke, from slightly variant stances, for parent-controlled Christian schools; Dr Carmel Leavey presented a Catholic view; and Dr Anna C Hogg developed a

theology of Christian education validating state school Christian involvement.

5. See John L McKenzie, *The Roman Catholic Church*, New York, Holt, Rinehart and Winston, 1969, p. 227.
6. Romans 10:11 – 13.
7. Thus Graham Rossiter, in chapter 6 of his *Religious Education in Australian Schools*, Canberra, Curriculum Development Centre, 1981.
8. James 2:1 – 13.
9. Anna C Hogg, 'Christians and schools?' *Journal of Christian Education*, 67, 1980, pp. 48 – 51.
10. Doug Blomberg, 'If life is religion, can schools be neutral?' *Journal of Christian Education*, 67, 1980, p. 20.
11. Edith Schaeffer, *L'Abri*, London, Norfolk Press, 1969, p. 227.
12. See for example Brian V Hill, *Teaching and the Christian Mind*, Grand Rapids, Michigan, Wm B Eerdmans, 1982, chapter 2.
13. See John M Hull, *School Worship: an obituary*, London, SCM Press, 1975.
14. John Westerhoff III, *Will Our Children Have Faith?* Melbourne, Dove Communications, 1976, p. 11.
15. Dr Weeks has misinterpreted me at this point, for I did not myself argue for neutrality in the state school but for a negotiated consensus in which the Christian sought fair representation, and in which critical rationality and humane sensitivity were minimal agreements. See Noel Weeks, 'In defence of Christian schools,' *Journal of Christian Education*, 67, 1980, p. 25.
16. 2 Timothy 4:2. Those who use the verse in this sense are misquoting. Both the Authorised Version and more recent translations have two distinct phrases; 'Preach the word' and 'be instant (or be prepared, *NIV*) in season, out of season.' It does not imply ignoring the ethical propriety of the moment chosen for explicit evangelism.
17. 1 Corinthians 9:22.
18. 1 Corinthians 9:21.
19. See, for example, T A Snook (ed.), *Concepts of Indoctrination*, London, Routledge and Kegan Paul, 1972.
20. I quoted examples of his dealings with people in the earlier article. Hill, 'Is it time we deschooled Christianity,' *Journal of Christian Education*, 163, 1978, pp. 5 – 21. p. 15 and fn. 13.
21. Blomberg, *op. cit.*, p. 14 and Weeks, *op. cit.*, pp. 26 – 27.
22. Weeks, *op. cit.*
23. Both Dr Blomberg and Dr Weeks feel that they have deflected the force of my argument by pointing this out. But I have never denied this, nor supported the claim that state schools can be neutral. But I deny that they necessarily promote a unified humanistic view of life, which is also implied by the line of argument we are looking at. Dr Weeks says I believe in the religious neutrality of the state school, and that proves I am culturally conditioned. But what I believe to be both possible and desirable is recognition of the religious dimension in life, and the study of religious traditions with, in Australia, special emphasis on the Judaeo-Christian heritage. That is not being religiously neutral, but it is a stance commended in several state reports on religious instruction. Dr Blomberg claims that state systems seek to impose one religious view on all students. Given the wide diversity within the *Christian* school spectrum, it is implausible to suggest that state schools can do any better in unifying their stance. Both colleagues are inhibited in their understanding of the kind of education required in a multi-faith society by the presuppositions of reformation social theory devised for the sixteenth century – another kind of cultural conditioning.
24. The author recalls a recent response from a parent invited to give financial support for a worker serving student Christian groups in schools. 'We are very concerned about the Christian presence in schools,' she said, 'that is why we're sending our children to Christian schools. Unfortunately with their fees and the mortgage on our house we can't spare any donation to this work. We do pray that others will be able to support this important ministry.'
25. For example Brian V Hill, 'Community involvement in schools,' *The Western Teacher*, 31st Oct., 1974, p. 7; and 'Community involvement: a practical ideal?' *The Educational Magazine*, Victorian Education Department, 1979.

## 7.2 The language of religious education curriculum in Australian Catholic schools
*Patricia Malone*

### Introduction

In order to consider the language of the religious education curriculum in Australian Catholic schools this paper will focus on two recent sets of curriculum guidelines that have been prepared and implemented by the two largest Catholic Education Offices in Australia, namely Sydney and Melbourne. It will focus in particular on the documents prepared for the secondary school which spans years 7–12 of the schooling period where the students range in age from twelve to eighteen years.

The writer of this paper was responsible in 1977–78 for preparing the Melbourne documents, *Guidelines for Religious Education for Secondary Students in the Archdiocese of Melbourne*, and although they were revised in 1984 they retained much of the language and structure of the original documents. The writer was also a member of the committee in 1984–85 that prepared the Sydney document *Faithful to God, Faithful to People*. This paper focuses on the language questions of these specific examples since the involvement of the writer in these processes provides an insight into some of the reasons for the language chosen. This paper is also an introductory stage in the writer's research on teachers' needs in the process of planning so it proposes a model to describe the stages in this process and considers some language questions in each category.

A review of the literature has not produced any writings on the language of curriculum documents in religious education. The papers of the symposium 'How Can Written Curriculum Guides Guide Teaching?', which were published in the *Journal of Curriculum Studies*, 1983, did provide some general points for consideration. Some of the writings of Schwab (1969), Barnes (1976), Newfield and McElyea (1984), Crismore (1984), Eisner (1979) and Valance (1985) helped in terms of language in the curriculum and in the learning process itself as well as in text-books and curriculum guides; Halliday (1978) provided some basic framework for the study of language.

In the area of language and the various models of religious education the writings of Australians such as Rummery (1975), Rossiter (1981), Elliott and Rossiter (1982), Crawford and Rossiter (1985), Hill (1985) and Elliott (1986) provided good documentation of the on-going debate about the nature and purpose of religious education which has been taking place for the past ten years and which is reflected in the diversity of approaches to religious education that are apparent in Australia. One of the difficulties faced by curriculum developers in Australia is the range of understanding of basic terms such as religious education and both documents under discussion attempted to define these terms and the definitions themselves provide an insight into the language of the documents.

The curriculum documents being considered were prepared at a particular point in time for a specific group of people. Some of the implications of the people and their context will be examined since this raises a number of questions about the language and its appropriateness. This in turn could lead to some questions that need to be considered with respect to other curriculum documents. This paper will at least try and raise some general questions about the type of language that is appropriate for curriculum guides in religious education and some issues about the process involved in enabling change and development in the religious education curriculum.

## Terminology

The following is the meaning of some key terms as they will be used in this paper. Religious education will include all forms of education in, for and about religion; education in faith or religious studies are seen as particular sub-sets of this broader phenomenon of religious education. Catechesis is the peculiarly Catholic term for education in faith and involves some level of dialogue and a systematic exposition of faith within the support of a believing community. In Australia the term catechist is generally reserved for those who teach religion outside the Catholic school system in parish or government school settings.

Although there are many understandings of the term curriculum, when this paper speaks about curriculum and curriculum documents it is referring to the formal school program in religious education which is mainly classroom based. Guidelines is the term used to describe the curriculum documents. Although they are officially prepared and are presented as the basis for the schools to develop their own programs, they do not have the same level of prescription as a syllabus of content.

## Context

In Australia there are Catholic Education Offices (CEOs) in each diocese (Sydney and Melbourne are the two largest urban archdioceses) and the director of religious education in each office is appointed by the Bishop. The directors are assisted by a team of consultants who prepare material and organise and present in-service training for the teachers in the schools. Most schools have a religious education co-ordinator (REC) who has the role of co-ordinating the school's religious education program. These people usually have close links with the CEO and are consulted in the development of Guidelines.

Both the Sydney and Melbourne documents reflect their ecclesial setting as each is prefaced and to a certain extent authenticated by a letter from the respective archbishop. Both state that the documents are being provided as a help for teachers, catechists and co-ordinators in planning religious education. The Melbourne document uses this term with the particular meaning of education in faith; it speaks of young people's 'growth in faith' and in 'the life of the church' and describes the role of the teachers as being a 'ministry in the church'. The Sydney document does speak of the task of the school 'to assist the faith development of Catholic youth' yet it expresses the hope that the 'document will help develop a style of religious education in the Archdiocese that is fruitful and suited to the times in which we live.' There is a stated awareness in both that the documents are being offered for use in a multi-cultural, multi-ethnic, pluralist society.

A recent survey (CEO Victoria [1984] 2) in Victoria (the state of which Melbourne is the capital city) showed that 42.9% of pupils in Catholic secondary schools in Melbourne were classified as having a non-English speaking background, that is either they or their parents were born in a non-English speaking overseas country. This has many implications for education in general and particularly for religious education as there are the many differences of cultural experiences and rites of the Catholic and other religious traditions that these numbers reflect. Another important statistic is that 52.9% of all the teachers in Catholic secondary schools in Victoria (total number − 4,323) were under thirty-five years of age. Of this same population 9.4% were religious, 64.7% lay Catholics and 25.9% lay non-Catholics (CEO Victoria [1984], 1). These figure have very many implications for the type of language, especially church language, that will be understood and considered relevant by the teachers. The corresponding Sydney figures (1985) show that only 6.4% of the teachers are religious; these statistics do not separate the lay teachers according to religious denomination but a similar proportion would exist.

## Melbourne guidelines: process of development

The 1977−78 Guidelines process was itself a review of previous guidelines that had been developed during the decade and was a response to the changes in religious education and the needs of co-ordinators, most of whom had no specialised religious education training and many of whom were lay teachers. The author was fairly new to Melbourne at the time and had found that people were speaking about religious education in a variety of languages. The 'religion as a subject' group were mainly quoting English sources; those who saw 'religion as a way of life' tended to speak from a catechetical point of view. In order to resolve this conflict about the nature and purpose of religious education, the first document that was prepared, The Overview, had two sections. The first, the Pastoral Overview, described the context and the second half, the Curriculum Overview, set out a model and an outline of content for the total program that was consistent with the proposed model.

The language to be used in the various sections was seen as an important issue and the co-ordinators were consulted about the type of language and format that would assist them in their planning. At their annual conference in Easter 1977, they were presented with samples of several religious education curriculum guides from the United Kingdom, United States, Canada and Australia and asked to rate them and comment on the format and language. As a result of this and other consultations a series of language decisions were made.

First, the content was expressed in concept — rather than fact — statements to emphasise the reality that all learning in religious education is of a cumulative nature and that aspects, dimensions, of the concept considered appropriate for different age groups in various settings would become the content of specific learning processes. For example, the third concept read:

In the mystery of Christ man is already caught up in the final realities of the history of salvation which will become known and perfect in the *Parousia*. Believers explicitly participate in this mystery (p 16).

Secondly, the concepts were written in 'church' language. This was to highlight the reality that the teachers had the task of helping their students appreciate and understand the heritage of the Catholic expression of the Christian tradition. It was also thought that some of the 'church phrases' would resonate with the lived church experience of the teachers. The reality of these teachers in terms of age, religious affiliation and experience has posed problems in this area which will be considered later. The one set of concept statements were to be used for the topics at each level of the secondary school to allow for sequential development of content. The concept quoted above was organised into nine topics — New Beginnings; Jesus, the New Creation, the New Way; Celebration of Lent and Easter; Christ sets us Free; Easter Liturgy; Songs of Hope; The Future; Death/Life after Death; *Parousia*. The first three were for the junior secondary, the next three for middle secondary and the final three for senior secondary classes. The Guidelines were divided into three sections to reflect the organisation of many secondary schools – Junior, Middle and Senior Secondary – with two years in each grouping.

Third, educational language was used to translate the concepts into teaching segments. Learning objectives and suggested learning approaches were set out for each concept at each level. An introductory statement prefaced each set of objectives and stated 'In the development of this concept it is envisaged that the students will be given appropriate learning experiences so that they will be able;' the stem of each objective which completed this introduction had a process type verb and an area of content specified, for example, for the above concept at Senior level, 'to reflect on the life/death theme in nature and in literature.' A short descriptive statement was provided for each suggested resource so that teachers would have sufficient information to help them in their selection of material.

Fourth, the language of the model was a hybrid product. Berard Marthaler (1976, 464) had suggested a correlation model for catechetics in which interaction was to take place between the life experience of the learner and the heritage of the tradition. This seemed an important development to the writer since much of the argument about the nature of religious education was expressed in either/or type of language, experience centred or knowledge, subject centred approach. This model proposed a new process and experience was defined as being broader than just the experience of the young person. Indeed the first section of the learning process for each concept read:

> Students' experience reflected on, deepened and extended to knowledge and understanding of the wider human experience as described in literature, art, music, film, etc. Correlation of the above with the experience of the people of God as revealed in Scripture, tradition, liturgy and the life of the church.

The model also specified areas of knowledge and skills and values and these in turn were drawn from the language of moral education and social sciences.

Fifth, various understandings of religious education were presented in the Guidelines but a definite option was made that the approach was to be one of 'education in faith.'

> We are opting for that process of religious education which respects the person's particular stage of development in faith. We are concerned with the development of the person in faith (Overview, p 6).

Some points about the process of faith development were included to emphasise that the model was educational in thrust and that it was not concerned with indoctrination and did not assume that all the students were practising, committed Catholics. This option caused difficulty for some teachers who interpreted it as imposing a catechetical thrust.

## Implementation and revision of Melbourne Guidelines

During 1978 the Overview Document was used as the basis of general in-service at the same time as it was being developed into three separate volumes for the three levels of the secondary school. A rationale statement was written for each topic which tried to establish links between the 'church' language of the concept and the experiential language of the suggested learning approaches for each of the topics.

It was apparent from the first in-service with the co-ordinators in December 1977 that many co-ordinators, and even more of the teachers, were not interested in considering the model or the sequentially developed program. They only wanted ideas, suggestions for their actual lessons. The three volumes that were produced in 1978 contained these practical strategies and many teachers only looked at these without even considering the concept which was expressed in slightly foreign church language. Some simply divided the topics into years and used these as the basis for their school program though the topics had been developed from the concepts so that teachers could organise themes/units that might be appropriate for their own setting.

The 1984 revision of the Melbourne Guidelines had some significant changes which responded to some of the difficulties that teachers had experienced. The Overview was not reprinted as a separate book but the main sections of the Pastoral and Curriculum Overview were included in the front of the volume for each of the three levels of the secondary school. The chart showing all the topics was not included so that teachers could not interpret this as their two-year program. The rationale statement was not included. Instead the revised topics were more sequentially presented. In many cases the first was related to the students' own experience, the second to a development in Scripture or church teaching and often the third was in the area of application to Christian living in terms of service or liturgy. The number of strategies was increased and these were written in slightly more detail to help teachers use them effectively.

The concepts were retained in the same church language – though one was divided into two to allow for more development of sacramental topics and sexist language was removed. The main addition was two pages of Teacher Reflection after each concept statement. This recognised the difficulty teachers were having in interpreting church language and gave the teachers a number of references to Scripture and church documents for further reading and discussion so that they could develop their understanding of the concept. All of this, however, was still in church language.

The basic structure and language of the original documents were maintained in the revision because teachers were only just becoming familiar with this and were feeling more able to use the document in their planning and teaching. The language of the planning process, of assessment and of the overall evaluation of religious education, was repeated without any further development as if these areas were still just being introduced in the area of religious education curriculum. The same option for education in faith was retained. In fact the following statement was given under the heading 'What is Religious Education?':

> When it is initiated by the church, Religious Education is one form of this (catechetical) ecclesial action which aims at leading communities and individual members of the faithful to maturity of faith' (p 9).

The photographs used in the revised documents seem to highlight this strong ecclesial emphasis. Instead of the photographs of secondary age students and their world that had been in the earlier documents, the revised editions contain photographs of sculpture mainly of a religious kind which emphasises the religious – the 'church' language of the document.

## Sydney Guidelines

There are a number of significant differences in the Sydney document. It is only a preliminary document which deals with the nature, the goals of religious education and its place in the Catholic Secondary School. Unlike the Melbourne document, it does not deal with religious education for youth in other settings and as yet the support documents which will contain some expansion of suggested content into practical learning strategies have not been produced. It was not a development from a series of previous Guidelines as had been the case in Melbourne. In fact the last statement on religious education for secondary schools in Sydney was published in 1972. A statement on primary religious education, *Journey in Faith*, was published in 1982 and the secondary document was presented as an extension to this.

The process used, like the Melbourne one, involved a large amount of consultation. There was a core committee comprised of CEO consultants, RECs and college lecturers under the chairmanship of the Director of religious education and a much larger group who responded to questions and drafts that were prepared during the two-year process. Much of this process was concerned with establishing an approach to religious education that was valid in compulsory classes in secondary schools and which respected the diversity of the student population and the range of approaches being used in the schools. The document was an attempt to set out the principles for developing religious education curriculum in Catholic secondary schools.

The option was taken to use educational language and religious education was defined in broad rather than ecclesial terms. It was described as 'an umbrella term covering all forms of education in or about faith and religion' (p 22). In a later section it was slightly limited by the statement:

> Religious education, as a formal part of the school curriculum, is concerned with the presentation of the Christian heritage in an educational manner (p 24).

The content suggested certainly went beyond the Christian heritage and the following statement about religious education in the classroom was made:

> Knowledge about the Catholic tradition, the broader Christian tradition, and other religious traditions, as well as the interaction of religion and society, has the potential to develop students' values, attitudes and beliefs (p 33).

The title of the document *Faithful to God: Faithful to People* is drawn from the fundamental law of catechetical method that is stated in the official Australian directory *The Renewal of the Education of Faith* (Australian Episcopal Conference, 1970), namely the need to be faithful to the tradition as well as to respect the needs of the students themselves.

The image of the religious educator that this highlights is of a person who stands with a foot in two cultures, that of the religious tradition and that of the world of the student. The teacher needs to know, understand and appreciate the language, life and teachings of the heritage as well as the language and life of the students. The teacher is acting as an interpreter, a bridge between two cultures, two languages, and usually needs help in the religious education process to understand each of these languages and to bring about points of contact so that each may speak to the other.

The Sydney Guidelines made the option of speaking directly to the teachers in everyday language about both of these worlds. There is a section about the sources that teachers need to use for their understanding of the tradition and a section about the needs and the world of the students at each stage of the secondary school. There are also sections dealing with the planning, teaching and evaluating phases of the process and of the structure of the school and the roles played by different levels of the school administration. The document offers only a summary list of topics, expressed in everyday terms and grouped in themes for the various stages of the secondary school. The photographs in the document highlight the diverse reality of secondary students in Sydney and some dimensions of that religious search for meaning which is part of the religious education program.

The Sydney CEO prepared a video to support the written document because of the limitations of the written word to bring about a basic change in attitude, in understanding of the religious education process. In Australia, and particularly in Sydney, there are some quite strong groups that oppose any approach to religious education that does not emphasise a transmission model of Catholic teachings and traditional Catholic devotions and moral practices. The aim of the video and indeed of the written documents was to try and identify the educational thrust of the formal religious education program in the school and stress the faith development support role of the total Catholic school and the links with the faith development role of family and parish. The introduction stated:

> The task that schools undertake best is that of teaching. While the schools can assist in the development of faith communities, the growth in faith and the development of faith communities are primarily the concern of families and parishes.

The video attempts to clarify the interrelationship between the faith and religious goals of the total Catholic school and the educational purpose of the religious education program. It offers in visual form some aspects of the language and world of the adolescent but it is addressed to the teacher and parent and contains segments of input about the nature of religious education, of the curriculum process, of the relationship between school and family and the role of teachers and parents in the complex task of religious education in its various facets.

## Planning process in religious education

The Guidelines just discussed were published to help schools develop their own school-based religious education programs. Many schools have had difficulty in translating the guidelines into practice and although some of the problems have been related to the language of the documents and the newness of the ideas they contain, some are related to an inadequate appreciation of the process of planning and of the decisions that need to be made. The following diagram sets out the various phases that are proposed as being part of the planning of religious education in secondary schools. This scheme attempts to analyse the areas about which decisions need to be made so that the overall process may be accomplished.

| Category | Areas for Decision and Action |
|---|---|
| **Overview** | Rationale, assumptions that will underpin the program — overall goals. |
| **Context** | Link with the total school curriculum; information to be gathered about student needs, interests; size, time and type of class groupings; organisation of planning process — roles to be assumed. |
| **Content** | Criteria for selection; sources of content; organisation into topics and themes; sequenced development taking into account student readiness. |
| **Unit Development** | Preparation of teaching/learning strategies, suitable resources; range of approaches to suit various groups and various teachers; possible conflict between need for co-ordination and teacher autonomy. |
| **Language** | Purpose of the school program, its visual and verbal language; consistency of language; practical value for teachers, especially new teachers. |
| **Evaluation** | Records to be kept; times for analysing data and reviewing program; people involved; links with on-going school evaluation. |

These categories could be applied to various models of curriculum development and would suit a program developed from behavioural objectives or one developed in terms of problem solving, or reflection on experience or other processes. The categories would seem to emphasise the need for the school team to consider the following:

- what they are attempting to achieve in religious education classes;
- why it is appropriate for their situation;
- what material they will cover and when;
- how they will present this to the students;
- how they will express their plan for teachers to use;
- how they will be able to check on what happens.

## Language of curriculum guides

Effective curriculum guides should be organised and expressed so as to assist schools in these various areas. The Melbourne Guidelines offered some material for all of these areas. It gave more detail in the Overview, Content and Unit Development categories. It was in the latter area that teachers most valued the material, partly because it provided direct help for their immediate problem, namely what to do in their next lesson, and partly because the language in this section was active in style, actually suggesting what students and teachers might do and how they could interact with various resources. The popularity of this section could also be due to the fact that teachers could adapt the suggested approaches to their own style of teaching and were not necessarily challenged in their basic approach or its underlying assumptions. Some teachers who operated out of an extreme catechetical model used some of the suggested approaches but with very different objectives and results than the ones envisaged.

As Anderson (1983, 9) states, 'teachers have to translate project ideas into lesson language;' the Melbourne Guidelines helped teachers by writing sections of the document in language that was close to lesson language. They used more technical language, indeed a Church language for much of the discussion of the purpose of religious education as well as to describe the content to be taught. Some teachers saw these areas as theoretical and of very little practical value. Schwab (1969, 1) defines the practical as 'the discipline concerned with choice and action.' Vallance (1982, 4) suggests that the 'process of theorising ... is one of the most valuable activities available to us in understanding the practical.' The difficulty is in expressing the theories without using technical language and in religious education there are two sets of jargon to avoid, ecclesial and educational. Eisner (1979, 155) suggests that 'theories ... help us focus attention on aspects of classroom life that we might otherwise neglect. They are tools that help us bracket the world so that we can bring it into focus.'

Writers of curriculum guides need to consider what types of focus they are trying to provide for teachers and to write for this purpose. The Sydney Guidelines tried to help teachers focus on their context and to present an Overview and Content that were appropriate for the school model. Since they were concerned with the teachers who were to make decisions, they used a format with many sub-headings and with lists of points for teachers to consider.

Westbury (1983, 2) raised the question: 'Is it possible to encode "information" about something that is as action-orientated as is teaching within the limitations that are inherent in the static conventions of a written medium?' It was concern for this that led the Sydney CEO to complement their written document with a video and this does seem to be an important step in the process. The Melbourne Guidelines were originally conceived as a tool for in-service, as a focus for the various presentations and discussions that would take place on a school, regional and diocesan level. This has certainly been the case in Melbourne but with the rapid changeover of teachers there are many using the written documents who have not participated in any in-service. This is even more the case in other parts of Australia where the documents are being used on an individual or school level without the formal support of a CEO team.

Both documents made some general comments about the process of assessment and evaluation but they are not described in sufficient practical detail so as to help teachers adapt these skills to religious education. Since the introduction of the 1978 edition of the Melbourne Guidelines there has been some development in the process of ongoing evaluation and some consideration of the records that need to be kept for effective evaluation but the revised edition makes no statement about such practical developments.

Both documents acknowledge the cultural and ethnic diversity of the students and in the content there is some evidence of material that would be appropriate for different groups. There is no real discussion, however, of the issue of language, of resources, and of methodology that is appropriate in such diverse situations. These practical issues are important for effective religious education teaching and need to be addressed specifically in curriculum guides.

## Conclusion

The first language question that needs to be considered by writers of religious education curriculum guides is whether they use religious or educational language. This involves an appreciation of the purpose of the documents and of the people for whom they are written.

In Australia these documents are used by RECs and teachers to develop school-based programs which in turn provide the direction for the actual learning experiences that the teachers implement. The theory and the examples studied would seem to suggest that teachers are seeking practical guides. The language, therefore, needs to be clear and easily understood by teachers so that they can apply it. This would seem to suggest that the language should be both educational and practical. Religious language, although it may be most closely linked to the content to be studied, needs some form of translation, interpretation into topics or units that can be presented in the school setting.

Within the curriculum documents there could be reflections on explanations of the church's doctrine, terminology and symbols so that teachers are helped in their task of interpreting the religious heritage/tradition for students of today. The type of discourse that this would require should still be addressed to teachers and should therefore be written by the expert in language that can be understood by teachers with only a basic knowledge, experience of the subject.

In considering the areas for decision and action that are proposed in the planning model it would seem appropriate that the curriculum documents address all these areas, not necessarily under these headings but in language that will affirm or challenge teachers in their practice. The findings of theory and research could be included but only if they help clarify the process for teachers and they should be expressed with a minimum of technical language and jargon.

Language needs to be considered in terms of all available media. The format, illustrations and lay-out of the printed material are important as the visual language emphasises the approach and the underlying assumptions of the document. Where appropriate, audio-visual language should be used as this enables direct communication about the real world of the classroom.

## Future directions

There would seem to be some value in examining the language used in other curriculum guides for religious education to try and ascertain the most effective for helping teachers with the planning process. There could be some value in trying to test out the proposed set of categories as a check-list in establishing what teachers actually do and what they need at each stage of the planning process. More research on teacher needs and on the language that teachers seem able to understand and use could provide the sort of data that would enable future writers of curriculum guides to produce more effective documents. This will require close collaboration between people who have a good knowledge of the theory and process of curriculum development and implementation, with those who understand the nature and purpose of religious education and with practising teachers who are aware of the needs of the students in the reality of today.

Olson (1983, 23) suggests that we:

> don't need new language, we need new formulations of the old. The guide writer must be a speaker of the practical language of teachers and be able to express the new intentions in such a way that new meanings are possible, but with a maximum of shared meaning.

Part of the task ahead would seem to require that guide-writers seek to broaden the spectrum from which they draw their understandings so that the language used may have the richness of many types of thinking without the technical jargon of any one. Newfield and McElyea (1984, 100–102) suggest the use of 'case rhetoric in curriculum guides which actually provide examples of the theoretical statements and this may be a new direction for curriculum writers but some research is needed. The effect of books like Crawford and Rossiter (1985) and Elliott (1986) which combine a reflection on theory with a detailed program that has been developed from the theory could perhaps be studied to try and ascertain how they affect the understanding and practice of teachers in other situations.

In all these areas researchers will need to pay attention to the needs of teachers in their actual planning and teaching and to particularly note the language that seems appropriate for the specific situations and the teachers involved.

**References**

Anderson, D C (1983) 'Educational Eldorado: the claim to have produced a practical curriculum text,' *Journal of Curriculum Studies*, 15, pp. 5–16.

Barnes, D (1976) *From Communication to Curriculum*, Hammondsworth, Penguin.

Barone, T (1982) 'Insinuated theory from curricula-in-use,' *Theory Into Practice*, XXI, 1, pp. 38–43.

Berryman, J W (1985) 'Children's spirituality and religious language,' *British Journal of Religious Education*, 7, pp. 120–127.

Catholic Education Office, Melbourne (1977, 78, 84) *Guidelines for Religious Education for Secondary Students*, Sydney.

Catholic Education Office; (1982) *A Journey in Faith*; (1984) *Faithful to God: Faithful to People*; (1985) *Faithfully Yours*, Greenwich Video Production.

Catholic Education Office, Victoria (1984) *Statistical Bulletin*, Vol. 4, 1 and 2.

Crawford, M and Rossiter, G (1985) *Teaching Religion in the Secondary School*, Strathfield, Province Resource Group.

Crismore, A (1984) 'The rhetoric of textbooks: metadiscourse,' *Journal of Curriculum Studies*, 16, pp. 279–296.

Elliott, R H (1986) *Exploring Religions and Faith at School*, South Australia, AARE.

Elliott, R H and Rossiter, G M (eds) (1982) *Towards Critical Dialogue in Religious Education*, Sydney, AARE.

Halliday, M A K (1978) *Language as Social Semiotic*, London, Edward Arnold.

Harris, I B (1983) 'Forms of discourse and their possibilities for guiding practice: towards an effective rhetoric,' *Journal of Curriculum Studies*, 15, pp. 27–42.

Hill, B (1985) 'New wine in gumnuts: religion and self-realization,' *Religious Education Journal of Australia*, 1, 1, pp. 4–11.

Hill, B (1985) 'Australian culture and religious education,' *Religious Education Journal of Australia*, 1, 2, pp. 4–9.

Marthaler, B (1976) 'Towards a revisionist model in catechetics,' *The Living Light*, 13, pp. 458–469.

Newfield, J W and McElyea, V B (1984) 'Affective outcomes, indoctrination, and the use of case rhetoric in curriculum studies,' *Journal of Curriculum Studies*, 16, pp. 100–102.

Olson, J K (1983) 'Guide writing as advice giving: learning the classroom language,' *Journal of Curriculum Studies*, 15, pp. 17–25.

Rossiter, G M (1981) *Religious Education in Australian Schools*, Canberra Curriculum Development Centre.

Rossiter, G M (1982) 'Diversity in curriculum in religious education in Catholic schools in Australia,' *British Journal of Religious Education*, 4, pp. 88–98.

Rummery, R M (1975) *Catechesis and Religious Education in a Pluralist Society*, Sydney, E J Dwyer.

Schwabb, J (1969) 'The practical: a language for curriculum,' *School Review*, 78, pp. 1–23.

Valance, E (1982) 'The practical uses of curriculum theory,' *Theory Into Practice*, XXI, 1, pp. 4–10.

Westbury, I (1983) 'Introduction to symposium: how can written curriculum guides guide teaching,' *Journal of Curriculum Studies*, 15, pp. 5–16.

# 8. American perspectives

This chapter turns attention to the growth of the independent Christian school movement in America.

In the first article, Professor William J Reese examines the public statements of those who have promoted the development of independent Christian schools. He argues that key motivations include the perception that schools within the state funded system have betrayed their roots in biblical theology, morality and academic standards, and the belief that parents have the primary responsibility in education. Against this background he discusses issues of state regulation, racial integration and tax exemptions. Then he sets out to review what is known about the nature and characteristics of independent Christian schools.

William Reese is professor in the School of Education at Indiana University. This article was first published in *Educational Theory* in 1985.

In the second article, Professor Alan Peshkin addresses the specific issue as to whether fundamental Christian schools should be regulated by the state. His response is a cautious one balancing the dangers of restrictive state control alongside the dangers of Christian schools engendering harmful divisiveness by their very intolerance towards the secular system which permits them the freedom to flourish. This response is informed by the author's eighteen month participant observation research within one such school and reported more fully in his book, *God's Choice: the total world of the fundamentalist Christian school*, published by University of Chicago Press in 1986.

Alan Peshkin is professor in the Department of Educational Psychology at the University of Illinois at Urbana-Champaign. This article was first published in *Educational Policy* in 1989.

# 8.1 Soldiers for Christ in the army of God: The Christian school movement in America
*William J Reese*

## Introduction

America's public schools have been criticised from the early years of the Republic to the present. Modern-day criticisms, however, have reached such heights that one scarcely hears a word of praise for any aspect of public education. Whether one studies the national press, reads local letters-to-the-editor, or examines the findings of the lastest blue-ribbon educational commission, the conclusion is the same, and it is grim: the nation's schools are in serious trouble.[1] Drug abuse among youth, declining academic standards, incompetent teachers, a preoccupation with fads and frills – these now reportedly characterise public education. But there is one school movement flourishing today that views itself in very positive terms, a rarity amid the cultural malaise that infects American education. Its main supporters speak of growth and progress, not decline and retrogression. At a time when the public schools are condemned at every turn, this school movement literally promises to save the Republic.

'You are the Pilgrims of the 1900s,' proclaimed a leader of the Christian day school movement to an audience in Indianapolis in 1978.[2] Indeed, in small towns and rural areas, in bustling cities and suburban refuges, Christian day schools have enjoyed incredible growth since the early 1960s. Prior to that time, most Protestant day schools were operated by the Lutherans, Episcopalians, Seventh-Day Adventists, and smaller denominations. Over the last two decades, however, enrolments at independent Christian day schools, affiliated mainly with fundamentalist Baptist churches, have soared. There are now approximately five to six thousand such schools in America with a total enrolment of roughly one million pupils.[3] Christian day schools constitute a tiny proportion of the total private, sectarian schooling in the nation, being far overshadowed by Catholic parochial education. Still, their evolution and potential encourages partisans such as Moral Majority leader Jerry Falwell to see them as serious rivals to public education in the future and 'the hope of this Republic.'[4]

This article explores the evolution, ideology, characteristics, and public policy implications of the Christian school movement. Because early Southern Christian schools in the 1960s were often no more than segregationist havens, a response to racial integration in the public schools, the entire movement was once simply dismissed as a product of regional bigotry. It could be explained away simply by reference to the actions of backwoodsmen and proverbial southern rednecks.[5] But the nation-wide popularity of Christian schools can hardly be explained fully by some amorphous white backlash, and the growing popularity of private schools generally constitutes a fascinating and complex chapter in recent cultural and educational history. In an age of advanced technology and an expanded governmental bureaucracy, parents in many fundamentalist Protestant congregations have taken control over their children's education, have reasserted their faith in Bible-based education, and have threatened to undermine state-sponsored public schooling.

Like the early Pilgrims, Christian school activists are imbued with a definite sense of religious mission. This is revealed not only in the writings and sermons of national figures such as Jerry Falwell and other television evangelists, but also in the thoughts and actions of ordinary citizens at the grass-roots level. The zeal of Christian school activists was well illuminated by Josie Zachary, a senior at a Fairfield, Iowa, Baptist church school in 1981. As in many other states, Iowa was then trying to enforce additional state controls over fundamentalist schools, but she characteristically explained to a news reporter that Bible-believing Christians must resist state encroachment. 'The Bible,' she noted, 'says we're soldiers for Christ and part of the army of God.'[6] Whereas fundamentalist Protestants historically have almost universally supported public over private education, the state was now perceived as an enemy, and only a biblically inspired crusade in the name of Jesus could win the day. In the Fairfields of America, 'Onward Christian Soldiers' might well have been revived as the new battle cry.

## The origins of Christian day schools

When the specter and then the reality of public school desegregation occurred in the south in the 1960s, Christian academies and private day schools without explicit religious orientation proliferated in response to the imperatives of the civil rights movement. Many of these segregationist academies withered, while others flourished and were joined by thousands of new fundamentalist schools formed in the past decade. Christian school leaders today are embarrassed by the actions of the small percentage of fellow religious activists who operate all-white schools and preach racial separatism. The still prevalent image of modern Christian schools as purely segregationist havens is, as will be seen, both inaccurate and unwarranted. The cultural roots of fundamentalist schooling are many and varied. Christian day schools are still attended mainly by white children, but racism alone is a poor explanatory device in analysing their historical origins.

In some respects, the hostility of Christian school leaders toward public education today is part of the larger popular dissatisfaction with mass schooling.[7] Public schools have become everyone's scapegoat. At the same time, the alienation of many fundamentalist Protestants from public education during the past twenty years is a complicated historical phenomenon, one that may have far-reaching public policy implications. What is remarkable from the standpoint of history is the hostility that conservative, fundamentalist Protestants began to direct toward state education in the early 1960s. From the nineteenth century to the recent past, many historians note, Protestants helped build, instructed in, controlled, and shaped the policies and practices of public education in America. When Catholics, for example, demanded tax relief for parochial education in the 1840s, Protestants of all persuasions railed against private school interests, which they saw as harmful to public schooling and hence to the public interest.[8] Now Protestants often join with Catholics in entertaining financial reforms such as tuition tax credits, which would enhance the role of private schools in American life. What caused this momentous political change? Because of changes in American culture and in the nature of public schooling, noted two writers in *Christianity Today* in 1967, a 'rapid and significant expansion of the Protestant school movement' almost became 'inevitable.'[9]

A wholesale rejection of liberal social policy helped fuel evangelical opposition toward public education in the last two decades. Busing for racial integration, for example, was a liberal ideal and hence was never very popular with conservative fundamentalists. But dissatisfaction with that particular public school policy accounts for only part of the allure of private education. New 'Christian' schools, as well as other forms of private education, generally assemble when school busing plans are implemented. Busing, therefore, stimulates and accelerates Christian school development.[10] Nevertheless, modern fundamentalist opposition to public schooling is more general and complex. Like many other critics of public schools, fundamentalists active in the Christian school movement complain about declining academic standards, drug abuse, school violence, teacher unions, and bureaucracy. In particular, given their religious orientation, they bitterly oppose values clarification and point to the US Supreme Court banning of state-sponsored prayer and devotional readings in 1962 and 1963 as part of the larger separation of the public schools from their Protestant roots. 'This nation was built on God and the Bible,' argued a Baptist minister in Sioux Falls, South Dakota, in 1979. 'Public schools are getting away from what the nation is all about.'[11]

Modern conservative fundamentalists believe that contemporary public schools do not even remotely resemble the schools of their childhood. Indeed, many Christian school activists view contemporary public education as hostile to 'American' values and, therefore, as beyond redemption. In his well-publicised interview in *Penthouse* magazine, Moral Majority executive Revd Greg Dixon of Indianapolis asserted that the public school system basically 'is atheistic, politically it is socialistic, and philosophically it is relativistic.'[12] When asked why his congregation formed its own Christian school, a leading Baptist leader in Ohio also remarked: 'We felt the need was so great because of the moral pollution, drugs, crime, and perverted sex philosophies in the local schools.' When 'modernism, socialism, and humanism' infected public education, he continued, parents could no longer entrust their children to the state.[13] In response to criticisms that private education deprives public schools of tax monies and community support, one Lansing, Michigan, activist recently responded: 'The private schools aren't destroying the public schools. They're destroying themselves.'[14]

Once self-appointed guardians of mass education, conservative Protestant fundamentalists now routinely attack public schools for undermining traditional values such as hard work, respect for authority, old-fashioned patriotism, and faith in God. The Revd James E Lowden Jr, Executive Director for the Alabama Christian Education Association, testified before a 1979 congressional hearing on tax exemptions for Christian schools and made statements that would have been rejected by evangelical Protestants throughout most of American history. 'I stand before you today,' he argued, 'and say that I believe that, given the philosophy of public school education today, it is a sin for a true believer in the lordship of Jesus Christ to send their [sic] children to a public school.'[15] Even more extreme statements, though hardly common in Christian school circles, were provided by an activist in Louisville, Kentucky, in 1975. 'We want public schools abolished,' he asserted. 'We believe public schools are immoral. . . . The public schools breed criminals. They teach [children] they're animals, that they evolved from animals. Christianity has been replaced by humanism in the public schools. It's disgusting.'[16]

'Secular humanism' has overwhelmed public education, according to many Christian school enthusiasts. That view is popularised by national leaders like the Revd Tim LaHaye and the Revd Jerry Falwell and those countless common folk at the grass roots who form the backbone of this private school revival. As John Ward, principal of the Calvary Christian Academy in Montgomery, Alabama, recently asserted, 'Public schools as a whole have a humanistic philosophy that does not include God.'[17] One Christian activist from Peoria, Illinois, has argued that a 'pagan philosophy' now rules public education.[18] 'A curriculum has to be based on a philosophy,' claimed a Nebraska fundamentalist in 1981, 'and the public schools are now based on humanism.'[19] Humanism, notes a fellow Nebraskan, has 'turned our public schools into a jungle in which any kind of animal can do anything it wants.'[20]

The argument that schools were once heavily Protestant and God-centered, but now are more humanistic, if not atheistic, pervades the ideology of the Christian school movement. Fundamentalist Christians are well aware that Protestants formed the vanguard of the public school movement in the nineteenth century and that the church was once a powerful educational force in American life. Some point to the elimination of school prayer as symbolic of the loss of Protestant influence and of the triumph of secularism; others point vaguely to 'progressive education' and John Dewey as the forces behind low standards and cultural relativism in the schools; but virtually all Christian school activists view modern public education as hostile to religion.[21] As a result, many fundamentalist Christians attracted to private schooling claim only to be reviving past educational ideals and practices, not subverting the social order. As one Christian leader from Oregon recently commented, 'In Colonial times, that's the way it was – the church was the schoolhouse as well as the church.' Since modern Christian schools are integrally bound to local churches, he added, 'We've come full circle.'[22]

Whereas nineteenth-century Protestants believed that state-controlled education reinforced mainstream religious and moral values, Christian school reformers see modern schools as godless, atheistic, immoral, and just plain out of step with decent religious values. The chance to avoid racial integration in the public schools may continue to attract some parents to particular private schools. But the decision to drop out of public education is more complicated than the issue of desegregation. When asked in 1975 why parents chose to patronise Christian schools, one Indianapolis church school administrator responded: 'They express a need felt for an old-fashioned school that teaches basic things and from a Christ-centered point of view.'[23] Old fashioned schools were never integrated, of course, and the Indianapolis schools were then engaged in a civil rights battle that recently led to busing to achieve integration. Still, parents in Indianapolis and elsewhere who are attracted to fundamentalist schools commonly speak of the attractiveness of a Bible-based school, one which is closely tied to parents, a local congregation, and a narrow community of believers. This attitude can hardly promote racial integration, but more is at work than racial bigotry. Indeed, in the minds of many fundamentalists, state-controlled public education cannot provide the larger spiritual training needed for their children's salvation.

## Parents, the state, and Christian schools

The Christian school movement, which remains the fastest-growing segment of private education in America, is squarely opposed to the general secular and humanistic trends of the last half century. Fundamentalist ministers – whether Baptist, Assembly of God, Church of God, or representing smaller denominations – believe that America has reached a turning point in its educational history. Like many modern secular critics, they stereotype public schools as havens of moral confusion and indict them for low academic standards. Indeed, fundamentalist support for separate schools may help balkanise America's educational state, even though Protestants had led the way toward a monopolistic public school system in the nineteenth century. These activists believe that parents form a key element in their children's educational and religious training, two inseparable goals. Moreover, they not only reject state-sponsored education as harmful to sound morals and academic training, but also oppose any real state regulation of their rapidly growing network of schools.

Citing the biblical charge to train children properly in order to form sturdy adults, many born-again Christian fundamentalists have revived the age-old question of whether children's education should be controlled by parents or by the state. Their resolution is clear: parents above all are responsible for their children's education. Throughout the nation, Christian fundamentalists in favor of private education have argued that parental control over schooling is the only way to protect youth from a secular, godless social order. The Bible, they believe, gives them this ultimate responsibility to control the education of youth, whose salvation is their primary concern.[24]

Repeatedly, conservative fundamentalists proclaim the significance of parents in the educational process. While public schools, in their eyes, have grown too bureaucratic, centralised, and professionalised, Christian schools provide a basic way to have input into children's formal education. 'We feel God gives parents the right to choose the kind of education they want their children to have,' argues the Revd Ivan White, principal of the Billings Baptist Temple School in Montana.[25] He would assuredly agree with the South Carolina fundamentalist school official who told listeners: 'You own nothing as important as the children God has entrusted into your care. God holds mothers and fathers responsible for their children. He does not hold the church responsible, he does not hold government responsible.'[26] Many fundamentalists concur. One father from Syracuse, New York, when asked why he sacrificed his money to provide his children with a Christian education, responded directly: 'They're not sacrifices. It's more an investment in our children, an investment that will have eternal value. When I stand before God, I'll wish I had spent more.'[27]

Parental involvement is basic to the life of Christian day schools. The very existence of the schools, after all, comes from the willingness of parents to pay tuition for this alternative to the public schools, and fundamentalist ministers try to unite church, home, and school as closely as possible. Christian schools often require proof that at least one of the parents is born again before children are permitted to enrol, thus enhancing a small community of parental interests.[28] Given the biblical imperative that parents must control their children's education, these fundamentalists believe that accusations that they are closet segregationists overlook the complex origins of Christian school formation. They vigorously argue that control, not race, is the central policy question at the heart of their private schooling revival.

The President of Religious Roundtable, a conservative religious organisation, expressed this perspective clearly in testimony before a congressional committee studying tuition tax credits in 1982. Since the Bible demands that children be trained properly, he asserted, 'The question is, who should do that training? the state? the NEA? the ACLU? the Utopians? the Behaviourists? or the parents?'[29] Like activists elsewhere, a Christian school advocate from Kanawha County, West Virginia, agreed. Kanawha County was the site of public school bombings in the early 1970s when working-class fundamentalists clashed with school officials over textbooks deemed too secular and humanistic. Many analysts tried to reduce the complex struggle to the notion that hayseeds simply opposed 'dirty' school materials. In reality, according to this private school activist, 'The real issue here is not busing, or integration, or dirty textbooks. The issue is who is going to control the education of your child. Is it going to be the state, or the parents? The battle is over freedom of choice, something Americans have cherished for 200 years.'[30]

Because of the primacy placed on parental control and the separatist religious tradition of these mostly Baptist reformers, state regulation is one of the most controversial aspects of public policy concerning fundamentalist education. Many states are very lenient about the operation of private schools and impose few restrictions on Christian schools, except the enforcement of fire and safety codes. But other states have departments of public instruction that historically have enforced additional regulations on private schools, especially in the area of accreditation and standards of teacher certification. Catholics, Lutherans, and Seventh-Day Adventists for the most part have long accepted minimal state standards as reasonable and hardly inimical to their schools. As a result, these groups rarely join Protestant fundamentalists in lawsuits or boy-cotts against state regulation. Conservative Baptist fundamentalists, on the other hand, have supported a strict separation of church and state since the colonial period of American history.[31]

To state departments of public instruction, regulation enhances the likelihood of quality education. To Christian fundamentalists, state intervention must be opposed at every turn. Literally dozens of court battles have been waged between Christian schools and the various states, and many more will undoubtedly be fought in the future. The main objection of Christian school activists is based on their view of the doctrine of separation of church and state. Funda-mentalist Christians see their schools as extensions of their church ministry, and they therefore reject viewing school and church as dis-tinct spheres. Since church and school are virtually indistinguishable in their minds, the state has no constitutional or moral claim on the operation of church-related schools. State interference can only undermine parental and church control.

The idea of state regulation is interpreted by many Christian school partisans as attempts by a godless state to license their churches and undermine religious freedom. 'The state of Alabama is not interested in registering my Sunday school, and I don't think they should register my Monday school,' argued W R Whiddon, President of the Alabama Association of Christian Education in 1981.[32] As one Indiana activist cogently asserted a few years ago, 'We don't think of our school as being anything separate from our church.... We have Sunday school, Monday school, Tuesday school, Wednesday school, and so on. To us it's all the same.'[33] Standing in a cold drizzle in Louisville, Nebraska, in 1981, where he joined a local Christian school's nationally publicised fight against state accreditation. Jerry Falwell warned his listeners that 'to submit to certification is to submit to licensure and the right of the state to license a church and its Christian ministry. We believe the church and the church school are all the church.'[34]

Christian fundamentalists have successfully countered movements for increased state control in Ohio, Kentucky, North Carolina, Indiana, and Colorado, while they have been less successful in Nebraska.[35] There the defiance of one school that refused to submit to state accreditation led to a three-month prison sentence for a fun-damentalist pastor who was viewed as a martyr by fellow religious leaders across the nation. When a local judge reluctantly padlocked the church door, since 'school' was being held within the building in defiance of a court order, it only deepened the fears and hostility of many conservative fundamentalists toward public regulation of sectarian schools.[36] In state after state, Christian fundamentalists have staged impressive protests and have lobbied to turn back all types of legislation they interpret as harmful to their schools. Many state Christian school associations have united their members against efforts to require state teacher certification, have refused to supply basic data on enrolment to state educational officials, and have thereby translated their philosophy of separatism into political resistance.

Accreditation and licensure of fundamentalist schools, Christian proponents believe, ultimately came from God. The state, already contaminated by a bloated bureaucracy that is secular, if not socialistic, is the enemy of all true Christian education, and its serpentine arms must never be allowed to encircle Christian day schools. 'We feel we're accredited by the Lord,' noted one Baptist preacher in Illinois in 1977.[37] Texas evangelist Lester Roloff joined hundreds of fundamentalists in Iowa in 1981 to denounce what they viewed as state harassment of Christian schools. God's rule is far superior to that of the state, he thundered to a receptive audience. Bureaucrats and humanists may control the state and its schools, but 'The Bible is our book of standards, rules, and regulations....'[38] An Iowa minister similarly argued that states seem preoccupied with minimum standards; Christian schools, on the other hand, get their standards 'from the word of God.... We have maximum standards.'[39]

Some fundamentalist schools accept a degree of state regulation and believe that this does not compromise their religious principles. A Christian school leader in Lake Oswego, Oregon, is one of many fundamentalists who demand that teachers have state certificates.[40] But this is a minority viewpoint within the Christian school movement. State interference invariably leads to state control, many fundamentalists fear, and the camel must never be allowed to get its nose under the tent. In Kentucky, where the state association of Christian schools warded off attempts at increased state control, one prominent private school spokesperson raised the central issue in 1977: 'If the state tells us what kind of textbook to have, what do we have? A glorified public school.'[41] Many fellow activists concur, believing with the Albany, New York, minister and school founder that accreditation would mean working 'under state education auspices and curriculum and finances. We fear state control.'[42]

When policemen padlocked the Baptist church of the Revd Edward Sileven in Louisville, Nebraska, the action only confirmed the worst fears of many conservative fundamentalists. Rodney Clapp, writing about the controversy for *Christianity Today* in 1982, explained how Sileven and his congregation viewed the situation: 'With their private, religious school, they believe they have built a thought-tight submarine, uncontaminated by the secular humanism they think floods public schools. Now that the school is built, they believe seeking state licensure would make as much sense as drilling holes in the submarine: state licensing opens the way to state control, and control means slavery to humanism.'[43] In the insular world of Christian schools, bound together into a community of believers linking parents with the chutch, the state has no legitimate place.

The outcome in Nebraska — the conviction of a Baptist minister and the padlocking of a church — was hardly a typical state response, even though it has often been viewed that way by the opposition. Christian legal associations have successfully defeated state regulation in landmark decisions, particularly in Kentucky and Ohio. Rallies and political lobbying have squashed efforts at more stringent state regulation that was proposed elsewhere, and lawsuits now pending in several states may well build upon the Ohio and Kentucky precedents. Many states, like Alaska, Kansas, and Oklahoma, have almost no provisions for the regulation of private schools.[44] Far from being a persecuted minority, Christian school reformers have enjoyed many legal victories, a testimony to their political savvy and the support the courts have given to First Amendment freedoms.

From this perspective, even the recent rulings by the US Supreme Court in cases concerning Bob Jones University and the Goldsboro, South Carolina, Christian schools, upholding the denial of tax exemptions for schools that practise racial discrimination, cannot be seen as part of some godless plot by the state. Considering the fact that in the 1960s hundreds of Christian schools were formed in the south to avoid racial integration, it is instructive that in the 1970s only approximately one hundred of them had lost their tax-exempt status. When the Internal Revenue Service tried to impose racial quotas on Christian schools under newly proposed guidelines in 1978, only Health, Education, and Welfare and a few civil rights organisations endorsed the plan. Major nonfundamentalist religious groups joined with the Christian schools to condemn the IRS proposals, and many fundamentalists testified at public hearings in Washington that true racists were only a tiny minority within the Christian school movement. The principle of separation of church and state — leaving church-based schools free from quotas or other interventionist policies — was deemed more important than trying to punish a few racists by punishing everyone.[45]

Controversies over state regulation will continue in different states far into the future, as new policies toward private education evolve in response to changing educational issues. One thing is certain: Christian schools appear to be a permanent part of the American educational landscape. In response to a host of cultural and educational changes in the 1960s, conservative fundamentalist Christians have fashioned an alternative to the public schools monopoly. The Christian schools are the result of multiple factors, not a single cause, and they have been reasonably successful in avoiding excessive state entanglement. In a nation dominated by corporate influences, fundamentalist parents and their ministers have tried to build a haven from the world and its often sinful ways. With the godless state, there can be no compromise, for as one enthusiast from Maryland told the *Washington Post*, 'We will not keep abandoning the ship to the cancerous liberal element that wants to contaminate everything.'[46] One would not expect less from a soldier for Christ.

## The Character of Christian day schools

'I pledge allegiance to the Christian flag and to the Saviour, for whose kingdom it stands. Our Saviour, crucified, risen and coming again, with life and liberty for all who believe.'[47] With these words, piously pronounced, many children begin their school day in the the thousands of independent Christian day schools that have appeared in America since the early 1960s. Saluting first the Christian flag and then the American flag, children thus set the moral tone at the beginning of each new day. A great deal has been written about the origins of these private sectarian schools, their alleged racist qualities, and their numerous battles with state education officials. Much less has been written on the internal life of these schools. Who sends his children to Christian schools? Who teaches in these schools? What constitutes the formal and hidden curricula that await children as they march into the classroom? How different is this educational experience from that in the public schools? What can one generalise about the nature and characteristics of independent Christian schools?

Simply in terms of physical size, Christian day schools tend to be rather small. This is hardly surprising, since these institutions draw upon a fairly narrow local population of born-again Christians, often members of a particular denomination, but not exclusively so.[48] Parents alienated from the bureaucratic red tape of many public school systems, which only seem concerned with parents when bonds are presented to the electorate, naturally desire a small-scale institution to gain influence upon the daily life of the school. Christian schools vary in size from a handful of children to the several thousand students enrolled in a few institutions. Paul Kienel of the Association of Christian Schools International determined in 1979 that, of the 1,042 schools represented in this organisation, the average school enrolled 218 pupils.[49] Many Christian schools only accommodate as many children as can fit in the church basement or in a small building adjoining the sponsoring church.

Since they frequently operate on a tight financial plan, Christian schools usually minimise expenditures on facilities. A few schools are magnificently furnished and compare easily with an elaborate public school facility; however, more typically they are quite modest. Studies conducted by different Christian school associations indicate that 80 to 95 percent of all independent Christian schools are church sponsored; the remainder are parent sponsored, without ties to any particular religious institution.'[50] In the majority of church-sponsored schools, 'almost without exception, the pastor of the church is the superintendent of the school.'[51] This helps reduce educational expenses. Hence these schools tend to be small, modest, and church affiliated, whether they are located in rural Kentucky or urban Ohio.

Exactly who sends their children to the nation's five to six thousand Christian day schools? There is no satisfactory study of the subject. The circumstance that these schools are often fiercely independent and refuse to share such data with the state makes absolute judgments impossible. Social commentators in America, while often discounting the existence of true and distinct class divisions in our society, nevertheless revert to the use of class descriptions. In 1981 the Executive Director of the Council for Private Education referred to Christian schools as 'lower-middle-class.'[52] During the previous year, a writer in Virginia claimed that Norfolk's schools appealed 'primarily to solidly middle-class families:'[53] A fine study of North Carolina's fundamentalist schools found 'working and lower-middle class families' and parents 'of modest means' generally patronising these schools.[54] While addressing a senate committee on the issue of tuition tax credits, Jerry Falwell described Christian school parents as 'rank and file Americans, middle income and down.'[55]

To send children to any private school requires surplus capital, and clearly the majority of Christian schools are supported by families who, while hardly wealthy, have attained middle-class standing or are desperately trying to reach that position from the ranks of working people. The very wealthy and the very poor are not the mainstay of most Christian day schools. There are, however, assuredly many schools in which working-class children predominate. But David Nevin and Robert E Bills, in their study of southern Christian schools in 1976, concluded that most parents attracted to these private schools were from the middling ranks of society. 'Most of the students come from unbroken homes and live in houses that stand half-paid-for in undistinguished suburbs with a second car or a pickup outside or a small boat in the yard. Many of these families have moved from relative poverty to relative comfort by very hard work and are not yet secure in their standing.'[56] Most of the fundamentalist Christians attracted to independent day schools seem to be middle- or lower-middle-class.

Just as the social backgrounds of the parents may vary somewhat from church to church, so too do the expenses associated with attending Christian schools. Some churches require their members to tithe in order to defray the expenses of operating a local school and to lessen the burden of tuition on individual parents. Tuition can vary greatly for Christian schools, even within a single geographical area. A recent study of the schools of Cleveland, Ohio, for example, revealed that tuition varied from $650 to $2,000 per year, depending upon the institution and the level of instruction.[57] Many schools have sliding tuition scales to enable poorer children to attend at reduced rates; other schools cannot offer that opportunity to the disadvantaged. The very existence of special financial packages for lower-income students, of course, illuminates the essentially middle-class character of most Christian schools. As in many other spheres of consumer society, everyone is welcome to participate in theory, but not everyone has the financial ability to do so.[58]

If Christian schools are mainly for the middle and lower-middle classes, they are also basically white. That does not mean that there are no racially integrated Christian schools, that the Christian school movement is 'racist,' or that this sphere of private education will not become more racially integrated sometime in the future. American blacks, however, are not well integrated into the population pools upon which Christian schools ordinarily draw, since churches, like other institutions in society, are hardly ever well integrated racially. Blacks frequently have their own Baptist churches (among others), and overall they have supported public education throughout American history. Unlike Catholic immigrants, blacks did not create their own separate school system, though now they are present in significant numbers in Catholic schools in many large cities. Since the 1950s, a major thrust of the civil rights movement has been directed at public school integration. Many blacks remember that early southern Christian schools were formed explicitly to frustrate civil rights reformers, and they are naturally offended by those private school leaders who continue to endorse apartheid policies.[59]

Because of these factors, even well-intentioned Christian school leaders have been unable to draw many blacks into their institutions. In contrast to the still lingering racist image of their movement, many fundamentalists have refused to accept white students whose parents are simply trying to avoid public school desegregation but who do not really share the educational philosophy of the particular Christian school.[60] Many church administrators sadly note that they had to place ceilings on enrolments when local public schools began busing plans; others are frustrated by their inability to change the movement's continuing racist image. W Wayne Allen of the Briarcrest School System in Memphis, Tennessee, operates a system with 3,800 pupils. In 1979 he told a House Committee studying the issue of tax-exempt status for private schools that nothing seemed to lure blacks into his system. He tried to build alliances with black ministers, and he advertised in newspapers and used other forms of the media. But, after six years' effort, he had attracted a grand total of two students.[61] Many Christian schools have attracted some black pupils over the years, but the image of these mostly all-white institutions will change slowly in some parts of the nation.

Given the politically conservative backgrounds of most individuals in the Christian school movement, it is not surprising that teachers employed in fundamentalist schools differ noticeably from their public school counterparts. Although teachers throughout history have been screened for their moral and political, as well as academic, qualifications, Christian schools are especially concerned with a prospective employee's religious and moral background. Often suspicious of teachers trained in secular state or private colleges or universities, fundamentalist school administrators often prefer teachers trained at Bible colleges and other religiously oriented institutions of higher learning; many former public school teachers, of course, have found their way into the private school sector as well. Since many independent schools are unaccredited and school leaders remain critical of state regulation, Christian school teachers often lack state accreditation and would be unable to teach in the public school system.

'Certification means nothing at all to us,' argues Dewayne Payne, administrator of the East Park Christian School in Anchorage, Alaska. 'Certification is just something the state does.'[62] Many Christian schools employ teachers trained at state colleges and universities, but this is hardly viewed as a prerequisite for employment and is sometimes viewed with suspicion. Instead of hiring a teacher trained in a school of education with a 'secular' or 'humanist' orientation, Christian schools usually prefer a different type of BA: a Born-Again Degree.[63] Moreover, teachers are often screened carefully for evidence of sound moral character and religious conviction. 'We do not hire a teacher who smokes, drinks, curses, or goes to public dances,' asserts the Revd Floyd H Jones, an administrator of the First Christian Assembly Academy in Memphis, Tennessee.[64] The Thrifthaven School, located in the same city, in the early 1970s used an application form for prospective teachers that asked: 'Are you now ... or have you ever been a communist or socialist? A homosexual or pervert of any kind?'[65]

With a national surplus of trained teachers and a revival of popular interest in private schools, Christian schools have been able to operate their schools without huge costs associated with teacher salaries or fringe benefits. Many Christian school teachers earn only one-half of the salary of a comparable public school employee and often do not have fringe benefits or retirement plans. Insiders remark that 'the pay isn't great, but the retirement benefits are out of this world.'[66] In this world, however, fundamentalist teachers are paid low salaries, lack job security, and yet fill an essential role in the Christian school movement. Since many private schools struggle mightily to remain economically solvent, these teachers not only form a moral link between home, church, and school, but also enable many schools to survive through economic hard times.[67]

Christian school teachers, therefore, differ from public school teachers in their preparation for their work, their religious orientation, and their financial benefits. But even more so than public school teachers, they have been greatly affected by modern efforts to create a teacher-proof formal curriculum. In the twentieth century many schemes of teacher management have been devised for public schools, from scientific management methods of the early twentieth century to the recent behavioural objectives craze.[68] Christian schools often deskill teaching. Because many fundamentalist schools operate on a tight budget, they have been especially attracted to a curriculum that is not overly dependent on a large or even particularly well-trained teaching staff. Many small schools teach children of all ages in a single room through the use of curriculum packages, especially a favorite series of programs called Accelerated Christian Education (ACE). The program is affordable, efficient, and widely used.

Begun in 1970, Accelerated Christian Education was used in approximately 3,500 Christian day schools by 1981. The curriculum is based on four broad areas of instruction: mathematics, language arts, social studies, and science. Children plough through workbooks for each grade level, take standardised tests at the end of particular lessons, and move forward at their individual pace. For most schools using Accelerated Christian Education, therefore, social promotion has been eliminated. Teachers are available to help answer questions students may have as they work each day in their study carrels, and the education is oriented toward reading and individual mastery of materials. Heavily laced with religious teachings and reflecting conservative political, economic, and social viewpoints, Accelerated Christian Education fits the economic and religious orientations of fundamentalist schools well.[69] Like some other critics, the principal of the Portland, Oregon, Christian High School recently complained that 'the kids get sick of sitting for a whole year in their cubicles doing their booklets. It's deadly.'[70] Still, prepackaged curricular materials have been an essential part of the Christian school movement.

While helping students master their basic subject matter, Christian school teachers simultaneously inculcate religious values in their charges. Both the formal curriculum of the fundamentalist schools and their general atmosphere are infused with religious sentiment. The central goal of Christian education is not simply to master a particular curriculum, but to learn a way of life in accordance with the Bible. Fundamentalist activists, of course, believe that the Bible is the literal word of God and that its message must have direct application in one's life on earth. Prayer and Bible reading are crucial in fundamentalist schooling, and teachers and pastors view academic and religious training as closely related if not identical activities. This is a logical extension of the belief that Sunday school and Monday school are one and the same thing.

To Christian school activists, the Bible is the most important text that children will ever encounter. As one Colorado minister has asserted. 'A Christian education is created around God's word – the Bible. It is a commandment of scripture to teach the word of God to our children and that involves a Christian school.'[71] The aim of Christian schools, which often provide a nondenominational, pan-Protestant training, is therefore often seen as different from the objectives of traditional parochial schools. 'Their goal is to make more Catholics or Lutherans,' one Nebraskan has argued. 'Ours is to teach the Bible.'[72] Since knowledge of God is the beginning of wisdom, as revealed in the Bible, Christian schools try to create an academic and religious climate to help save children's souls. 'We want our boys and girls to be saved and go to heaven,' a Nashville, Tennessee, school principal recently asserted, and the hope is that Bible and religious training can contribute to this outcome.[73]

Whether or not they utilise prepackaged curriculum materials, or employ teachers as monitors or in traditional roles, Christian schools link most of their formal instruction to the Bible. Children learn (or fail to learn) more than is formally taught, but they are in an environment in which many believe that 'if you're not taught the Bible, there's nothing to teach. The Lord gave us mathematics, science. He gave us all our subjects.'[74] 'Our study materials are loaded with the scripture, and the Bible is our main textbook,' argues a partisan from the Charles City Baptist School in Iowa.[75] Over and over again, fundamentalists active in Christian schools across the nation highlight the inseparability of religion and education. 'No education has any foundation other than the Lord Jesus Christ,' according to the principal of the Temple Christian School in Newark, Delaware. 'We teach all subjects in relation to the Creator, who in his mind created mathematics, syntax, social studies; history is his story.'[76]

Not every Christian school teacher and administrator believes that all subjects are easily taught from a fundamentalist perspective. Trudy Hathaway, principal of the Faith Heritage School in Syracuse, New York, recently commented on the problem: 'Some subjects are harder to relate to the Bible than others. Science is easier, mathematics is harder. Social studies – we teach them to be responsible as Christian citizens. English – he wants us to speak clearly, to understand and to get our ideas across.'[77] Other school people literally see God's design in every academic subject. History is God's unfolding of his plan for mankind, and even mathematics has its religious side, a sign of God's plan for an orderly universe. 'It's not just happenstance that numbers fit together as they do,' observes one fundamentalists.[78] When a conflict arises between a textbook and biblical teaching, some fundamentalists quickly dispose of the dilemma. As one fundamentalist has argued, 'If the Bible and a textbook differ, we know the textbook is wrong, and we teach children that.'[79]

Through the conscious molding of a Bible-based curriculum, Christian school administrators and teachers have created a genuinely alternative form of education. Academic subjects, like mathematics, history, and literature, are imbued with a religious orientation clearly absent in public school teaching. Subjects like science, especially the study of evolution, create special problems in some Christian schools, but they are not insurmountable ones. 'Evolution is not taught here,' one fundamentalist from Iowa has announced, and his position is not unusual.[80] Many schools either do not teach evolution or else simply teach that Genesis is correct and Darwin is wrong: 'We believe and we teach that man was created by God, and not derived from a monkey or any other source.'[81] A few schools do apparently teach pupils that God created the world but that evolution also shaped man's destiny, no doubt in accordance with a divine plan.

Even 'science' classes, therefore, do not escape from the overall religious values that permeate Christian schools. And when one looks beyond the formal curriculum to the climate of fundamentalist classrooms, one discovers an attempt to recapture a perhaps lost or mythical educational past, when all children presumably respected authority, had faith in God and nation, and were moulded into God-fearing and literate adults. Children learn much more than the materials contained in their Christian workbooks, which they pore over daily in their cubicles. In addition, they learn attitudes about power and authority, propriety and decorum. If, as with public school children, they do not learn these lessons well, it is not due to lack of effort on the part of their teachers.

Like all schools, Christian academies teach values as well as academic subjects, admittedly from a conservative fundamentalist perspective. Christian school activists continually lambast the public schools for their liberal student dress and behaviour codes, lack of attention to teacher authority, and overall moral decline. An Atlanta minister, writing in *Christianity Today* in 1981, conveniently summed up the fundamentalist position by asserting that 'parents could once assume that when they sent their children to school, the traditional Judeo-Christian values they held would at least be respected by the schools, if not reinforced. But no longer can parents make that assumption.'[82] A high school senior in the Midwest, who similarly stereotyped public schools, made the identical point when she compared public school and Christian school discipline: 'Here they teach us character and to have morals. In the public schools, they just let you go.'[83]

Respect for authority, an aim that has never been lost in public schools, is a central concern of fundamentalist education. Dress codes and rules for personal behaviour are standard at Christian day schools. For example, students often wear uniforms, appropriately available in red, white, and blue. 'If kids dress sharp, they're going to act sharp,' according to a Wichita, Kansas, private school activist.[84] And it is expected that children learn early that obedience and patriotism are closely connected at school as well as later in life. 'If they (the students) don't salute the flag, they're out the door,' proclaimed one enthusiast from Illinois in 1977.[85] Taking this sentiment one step further, the principal of the North Coast Christian School in Seaside, Oregon, told the *Portland Oregonian* in 1981 that 'I would like to be able to say that every boy who leaves this school would be willing to die for his country.'[86]

Obedience to authority is reinforced in countless ways during the school day. Children working in their cubicles raise Christian or American flags when they need to ask a teacher a question. Students at the Dade Christian School in Miami, Florida, are required to take an oath: 'As a student of Dade Christian School, I will not cheat, swear, smoke, gamble, dance, drink alcoholic beverages, use indecent language, use or even talk about narcotics, and will act in a very orderly and respectful manner.' Moreover, students must promise 'not to draw, wear, or display in any way the "peace" symbol.'[87] One Christian school in Providence, Rhode Island, dispenses demerits for humming or singing without permission, and another one prohibits children from getting closer than six inches from each other 'to keep teenagers from necking and younger children from fighting.'[88] These are not isolated examples; they are indicative of Christian school practices throughout the country. Because students often need time to adjust to the traditional dress codes and discipline at these schools, the Kent Christian School in Delaware places all new students on a six-week probationary status to weed out habitual offenders.[89]

To challenge authority (except for godless forms of state authority) is a sin in the eyes of many Christian fundamentalists. A pamphlet for the Capital City Baptist School in Lansing, Michigan, states: 'The challenge to the authority of a parent or teacher is a challenge to God's authority.'[90] A Baptist preacher from Montgomery, Alabama, claims that 'we will not put up with any disobedience, disrespect to teachers or anything else. We try to build character as well as stress academics.'[91] For that reason, parents whose children attend fundamentalist schools often must approve of the use of corporal punishment when needed at school. One inventive pedagogue entered the phrase 'Board of Education' on the school paddle.[92] 'The Lord God made the butt for sitting on and for spanking,' asserts one fundamentalist from Texas, and one national leader allegedly claims that a genuine spanking leaves 'marks' on the child.[93] That attitude has led to practices resulting in law suits on child battery when teachers or principals had used excessive force in particular situations. These are extreme cases, and fundamentalist parents continue to endorse corporal punishment when reasonably dispensed in Christian schools.

With an emphasis on respect for God, parents, and nation, Christian schools have tried to reconstruct an educational environment that many fundamentalists believe once existed in most public schools. Unfortunately, in their opinion, creeping secularism and liberalism undermined the true mission of education: to produce children who obeyed authority, were outwardly patriotic, and decidedly Christian. Unlike public schools, which are forced to accept and deal with a wide variety of children, Christian schools have the luxury enjoyed by all forms of private education. They can select their pupils, expel those who violate existing rules, and therefore eliminate anyone who would disrupt the educational process. Christian school pupils caught smoking, drinking, or dancing are routinely expelled from some schools without receiving a second chance, which highlights a real difference between public- and private-sector education.[94]

Christian schools are commonly criticised for being all-white and racially restrictive, and especially for isolating youth from the modern world. All private schools, whether secular or sectarian, have historically been selective in some ways, whether by race, class, religion, or geography. But the charge of isolation from modernism either infuriates or amuses Christian school partisans. Clearly, many fundamentalist parents openly desire to protect their children from the evil values they perceive in public education. They believe that isolation from low academic training, drugs, secular textbooks, and the like is a requirement for Christian nurture. A Christian school leader in North Carolina, recognising the selective quality of religiously based schools, has argued that 'if anyone is isolated from ideas, it is the public schools. They are deprived of the Christian philosophy. They are a captive audience in the atheistic-humanistic culture.'[95]

Oriented around the Bible, determined to link spiritual training with sound academics, and led by individuals who have not been afraid to contest state power, Christian schools testify to the diversity of educational life in contemporary America. Americans will never agree upon the single best way to educate youth, and in a nation with deep Protestant roots, many fundamentalists will continue to espouse values that liberals dismiss as 'racist,' blindly patriotic, and narrow-minded. What has made Christian fundamentalist schooling distinctive has been the willingness of conservative evangelical Protestants to provide another option to public education and to do it without the use of direct public funds. As more and more Christian school leaders flirt with tuition tax credit reforms or school voucher plans, this basis for distinctiveness may disappear.

The issue of state aid to fundamentalist institutions by any means remains a controversial subject within the Christian school movement. While increasing numbers of private school activists now support vouchers or tuition tax credits, most fundamentalists and evangelical Christians remain properly sceptical of the state.

When tuition tax credits were discussed in Congressional hearings in Washington, DC, groups like the Alabama Christian Education Association and the North Carolina Association of Christian Schools adamantly opposed state aid.[96] At the grass-roots level, many individuals believe that state control was what caused the deterioration of mass education in the first place. As the principal of the Salem Academy in Oregon put it, 'We don't want some of that humanism imposed on us.'[97]

It is both inconsistent and possibly dangerous for many private school activists to refuse to accept state regulation of their institutions, based on First Amendment rights, and then to lobby for various forms of direct and indirect aid for their schools. Christian schools cannot have it both ways. Many Christian schools are unalterably opposed to any form of state subsidy for their institutions. They literally believe in the separation of church and state and realise that state grants almost always lead to state regulations. A Pentecostal minister from Kentucky reflected this position well in 1978 when he warned private schools of state entanglement: 'We don't want any state money.... We don't want their nose in our business all the time.'[98] A Baptist minister from Buffalo, New York, evoked the sentiments of many fellow activists recently when he denounced the idea of tuition tax credits. 'We feel Christian education should not be subsidised from other people's pocketbooks. Besides, anytime there is a subsidy, it opens the door to interference.'[99]

Despite these warnings, certain Christian school associations and fundamentalist leaders have publicly supported state aid. When the Packwood-Moynihan tuition tax credit proposal was debated in Washington in the late 1970s, *Christianity Today* observed that the bill had various types of supporters, including 'many evangelicals who support private schools.'[100] Jerry Falwell and other television evangelists, who represented groups that had historically opposed state aid because they believed it violated the First Amendment, had done an 'about face' on this policy question. While Catholics, Lutherans, and traditional parochial schools had often fought in the past for state support, the magazine continued, the 'strongest support' for the bill 'may be coming from backers of fundamentalist schools.'[101]

There is no small measure of historical irony in the rise of vocal evangelical support for public aid to sectarian schools. After all, evangelical Protestants were central political agents in the creation of our public school system in the nineteenth century. Now representatives of religious groups that once zealously defended the public schools and assailed private alternatives have championed marketplace competition as a cure for modern educational ills. What was once predominantly a Catholic issue, public aid for private schools, enjoys wider support than ever before in American history. Whereas Catholics were always expected to pay their taxes and their tuition as well, some fundamentalist leaders curry state favor to protect their schools from genuine competition in the marketplace.

Whether Christian schools are actually the hope of the American republic or a solution to the many problems that face modern school systems, fundamentalists in small towns and large cities, suburbs and rural retreats, have tried over the last two decades to spread this idea of Christian day schools across the nation. Once found almost exclusively in the South, where they were scorned for undermining efforts at public school desegregation, Christian schools are now found in every state and attract adherents for a wide range of reasons. Wherever Christian day schools appear, parents and sympathetic religious leaders have attempted to recreate a world they believe once existed and which they would like to preserve for their children. It is a world of moral absolutes, of literate children who mature into productive, God-fearing, patriotic adults. It is a world where moral and religious training infuse school life along with traditional academic subjects. It is a world of certainty, of shared moral values. And, most of all, it is a world where youth realise that they must be soldiers for Christ in the army of God.[102]

**Notes**

1.  See, for example, the much publicised report of the National Commission on Excellence in Education, *A Nation at Risk: the imperative for educational reform*, Washington, DC, US Department of Education, 1983.

2.  Joan Richardson, 'ACE fundamentalists' alternative to "pagan" public school systems,' *Indianapolis Star*, 17 December, 1978, A12. Donald Howard continued: 'The Pilgrims were just like you. They were fundamentalists. They were separatists. They believed in educating their own children.'

3.  James C Carper, 'The *Whisner* decision: a case study in state regulation of Christian Day Schools,' *Journal of Church and State*, 24, Spring, 1982, 281, no. 1. Also see Carper's other essays on the subject, 'The Christian day school in the American social order, 1960–1980,' in Thomas C Hunt and Marityn M Maxson (eds), *Religion and Morality in American Schooling*,' Washington, DC, University Press of America, 1981, pp. 79–101; 'The Christian day school movement,' *Educational Forum*, 47, 1983, pp. 135–49: and 'The Christian day school,' in James Carper and Thomas C Hunt (eds), *Religious Schooling in America: historical insights and contemporary concerns*, Birmingham, Alabama, Religious Education Press, 1984, chapter 5. The classic critique of the Christian school movement in the south is by David Nevin and Robert E Bills, *The Schools That Fear Built: segregationist academies in the South*, Washington, DC, Acropolis Books, 1976.

4.  Quoted by Adell Crowe and Saundra Ivey, 'Church schools flourish here over decade,' *Nashville Tennessean*, 4 August, 1980, A2. Also see Jerry Falwell, *Listen, America*! New York, Bantam Books, 1980; and Ed Dobson and Ed Hindson, *The Fundamentalist Phenomenon: the resurgence of conservative Christianity*, Garden City, New York, Doubleday, 1981.

5.  Compare Peter Skerry, 'Christian schools versus the IRS,' *The Public Interest*, 61, Fax, 1980, pp. 18–41, with Nevin and Bills, *The Schools That Fear Built*.

6.  Quoted by Jonathan Roos: 'Students stand firm in fight against order closing school,' *Des Moines Register*, 11 November, 1981, B4. The struggles over regulation in Iowa can be traced in the following articles in the *Register*, all written by Jonathan Roos: 'More Christian schools resist Iowa's rules,' 4 April, 1980, C2–3; 'Baptist school chief, parents face charges,' 6 November, 1980, A8–9; 'Church rally assails states' school laws,' 27 October, 1981, B7; 'Churches file suit to block school laws,' 10 November, 1981, B2–3; and 'Fellowship asks for meeting with Governor Ray,' 12 November, 1981, B6.

7. Contemporary criticisms of public schools are based on many different political and educational philosophies. Some critics want higher academic standards and weaker teacher unions; others want the reintroduction of 'voluntary' school prayer and equal time for creationism; and still others have faith in the 'back to the basics' movement. To gain a sense of this diversity, compare the perspectives contained in *A Nation at Risk*; James S. Coleman, Thomas Hofler and Sally Kilgore, *High School Achievement*, New York, Basic Books, 1982; and Burton Yale Pines, *Back to Basics: the traditionalist movement that is sweeping grass-roots America*, New York, William Morrow, 1982, chapter 4.

8. The historical literature on public education and Protestantism in America is vast and is summarised by William J Reese in 'The public schools and the great gates of Hell,' *Educational Theory*, 32, 1982, pp. 9–17. Two very important articles by David B Tyack should be consulted: 'The kingdom of God and the common school: Protestant ministers and the educational awakening in the west,' *Harvard Educational Review*, 36, 1966, pp. 447–69; and 'Onward Christian soldiers: religion in the American common school,' in Paul Nash (ed.), *History and Education*, New York, Random House, 1970, pp. 212–55.

9. Henry A Buchanan and Bob W Brown, 'Will Protestant church schools become a third force?' *Christianity Today*, 11, 12 May, 1967, p. 5. Also see William H Fischer, 'Wanted: Protestant schools,' *Christianity Today*, 9, 7 May, 1965, pp. 11–12; and Frank E Gaebelein, 'American Education,' *Christianity Today*, 11, 20 January, 1967, p. 4.

10. Many local Christian school leaders admit that the desegregation of public schools contributes to higher Christian school enrolments. At the same time they repeatedly argue that desegregation is only one of the many stimuli influencing private school growth. For a sampling of useful sources, examine Helen Huntley, 'In Christian schools, the Bible enters all classrooms,' *St. Petersburg Times*, 2 September, 1981, B10–11; Deena Mirow, 'Religion: the big R,' *Cleveland Plain Dealer*, 8 November, 1981. G2–4; Pat T Patterson, 'Six families explain switch,' *Little Rock Gazette*, 18 October, 1981, B9–12; Isabel Spencer, 'Christian schools growing,' *Washington Evening Journal*, 28 February, 1978, D4–5; Randy McClain and Richard Wright, 'Private parochial school enrolments here soaring,' *Baton Rouge Morning Advocate*, 24 August, 1981, C3–4; 'Two church groups will open schools,' *St. Louis Post-Dispatch*, 10 August, 1980, G14; and 'Public schools: in need of prayer?' *Christianity Today*, 18, 26 October, 1973, p. 67. Even Nevin and Bills assert that racism alone poorly explains the rise of Christian schools in the south in the 1960s. See *The Schools That Fear Built*, p. 11: 'The question is more complicated than the simple racism that marked the 1960s but obviously race is a big ingredient in the new schools.'

11. East Side Baptist Pastor Rick Henry, quoted in Terry Monahan, 'City parochial school bucks state's accreditation system,' *Sioux Falls Argus Leader*, 2 December, 1979, E8.

12. Quoted in Michael Disend, 'Have you whipped your child today?' *Penthouse*, 13, February, 1982, p. 60. For a full-blown critique of public education by one of the founders of Moral Majority read Tim LaHaye, *The Battle for the Public Schools*, Old Tappan, New Jersey, Fleming H Reveil, 1983.

13. 'Preacher fights to control school,' *Cleveland Plain Dealer*, 6 July, 1975, D4.

14. Quoted in Sharon M Bertsch, 'Lansing Christian, growing new school system in city,' *Lansing State Journal*, 16 September, 1979, G1.

15. *Tax-Exempt Status of Private Schools*, Hearings before the Subcommittee on Oversight of the Committee on Ways and Means, House of Representatives, Ninety-Sixth Congress, 1979, Washington, DC, United States Government Printing Office, 1979, part 2, p. 949.

16. John Thoburn, quoted in 'The Christian schools come marching on,' *Louisville Courier-Journal*, 26 October, 1975, F2.

17. Quoted in Danny Lewis, 'Christian schools drawing greater number of students,' *Montgomery Advertiser*, 21 February, 1981, E10. See LaHaye, *The Battle for the Public Schools*; and Falwell, *Listen, America!*

18. Pastor Clyde Winegar, quoted in Joan Richardson, 'Education – according to the gospels,' *Peoria Journal Star*, 30 October, 1977, C1. Reverend Leland Kennedy, pastor of the New Castle Baptist Church in Delaware, claims that 'the public schools are offering a secular education which is anti-God.' Quoted in Isabel

Spencer, 'Christian schools growing,' *Wilmington Evening Journal*, 28 February, 1978. D4.

19. Dick Ulmer, 'Christian schools buck trend,' *Omaha World Herald*, 16 August, 1981, B9.

20. *Ibid.*, B10.

21. See Carper's essays 'The Christian day school in the American social order, 1960–1980,' and 'The Christian day school movement.' Like many evangelicals, Carl F Henry has criticised the influence of Dewey in the schools in 'Religion in the schools,' *Christianity Today, 17,* 14 September, 1973, p. 38. Until the twentieth century, most American education presupposed a supernatural God as its ultimate explanatory principle and as the cohesive and integrative factor in learning.' Dewey's instrumentalist philosophy, conservative critics contend, led to the erosion of absolute standards of morality and academic training.

22. Rick Osborne, quoted in Huntley Collins, 'Christian schools gain resurrection,' *Portland Oregonian*, 12 July, 1981, D8.

23. Very M Haley, secretary of Christian Academy, cited in Harley R Bierce, 'Faith-oriented schooling shows rapid growth among Protestants,' *Indianapolis Star*, 11 July, 1975, D9. Pastor Dean Goddard of the Calvary Baptist School in Casper, Wyoming, similarly notes: 'Our school is a traditional classroom-structured school. I'm trying to make the school just like they went to 20 years ago.' Quoted in John Wheaton, 'Each parochial school different,' *Caspar Star-Tribune*, May, 1979, D1.

24. On the national level, the primacy of the family in education has been well publicised by Jerry Falwell in *Listen, America!* and by Tim LaHaye in *The Battle for the Public Schools.*

25. Quoted in Joan Roesgen, 'Will state put brakes on church schools?' *Billings Gazette*, 17 September, 1978, B2. An activist in Arnold, Maryland, has asserted that 'God in his word has given the responsibility of training children to parents primarily.' In Nancy Jane Adams, 'Stress on values a chief attraction,' *Annapolis Evening Capital*, 3 March, 1981, G12. Also see Denise Melinsky, 'Sooners protest church school closing,' *Daily Oklahoman*, 21 October, 1982, C2; Art Toalston, 'Jackson schools grow with fundamentalist movement,' *Jackson Clarion Ledger*, Mississippi, 20 August, 1978, D5; and 'What about the Becker amendment?' *Christianity Today*, p. 8, 19 June, 1964, p. 22.

26. Ron Brooks, an adminstrator in the Southside Christian School in South Carolina, was speaking to interested listeners in Keene, *New Hampshire*, as reported by Bert Latamore, 'Private school growth boom,' *Manchester Union Leader*, 10 May, 1979, D9.

27. Gloria Wright quotes David Grey, who enrolled three of his children at Faith Heritage School, in 'Christian schools prospering,' *Syracuse Herald American*, 22 March, 1981, G3.

28. Robert K Gorbon, 'Academy for born-again Christians going strong,' *Trenton Times*, 28 June, 1981, G3. Parents are often screened very carefully by Christian school administrators, since they want to attract families that share a common religious orientation. Some activists boast that, while public schools admit children, they admit entire families to their schools.

29. *Tuition Tax Credit Proposals*, Hearing Before the Committee on Finance, US Senate, Ninety-Seventh Congress, Second Session, Washington, DC, US Government Printing Office, 1982, p. 258.

30. 'The Christian schools come marching on,' *Louisville Courier Journal*, 26 October, 1975, F2. The standard case study of this conflict is by George Hillocks, Jr, 'Books and bombs: ideological conflict and the schools – a case study of the Kanawha County book protest,' *School Review*, 86, 1978, pp. 632–54.

31. Excellent research and analysis of the issue of state regulation of private education has already been completed by several scholars, mostly defending Christian school independence. See, for example, Carper, 'The *Whisner* Decision;' Skerry, 'Christian schools versus the IRS'; and Jeremy Rabkin, 'Behind the tax-exempt schools debate,' *The Public Interest*, 68, 1982, pp. 21–36.

32. Quoted by Joe Simmons, 'Battle lines drawn over registering of schools,' *Montgomery Advertiser*, 15 October, 1981, E4.

33. William Stewart, Indiana Director for Accelerated Christian Education, cited

in 'All private schools face taking problems,' *Indianapolis Star*, 17 December, 1978, G10.

34. Falwell was quoted by L Kent Wolgamott, 'Falwell predicting Nebraska will sanction Christian schools,' *Lincoln Journal and Star*, 25 October, 1981, A14. Fundamentalists from across the nation take a similar position. For a sampling of fundamentalist opposition to state regulation, see Marsha Rhea, 'Christian educators to fight encroachment,' *Montgomery Advertiser*, Alabama, 13 October, 1978, G3; Joe Simmons, 'Battle lines drawn over registering of schools,' *Montgomery Advertiser*, 25 October, 1981, E4; Barbara T Roessner, 'Enfield church school case targeted for Supreme Court,' *Hartford Courant*, Connecticut, 18 February, 1979, D12; Megan Rosenfeld, 'Fundamentalists challenge state licensing of their schools,' *Washington Post*, 24 July, 1978. E9–10; Joan Richardson, '1,500 protest state involvement in operation of church schools,' *Indianapolis Star*, 17 January, 1979, E13; Jonathan Roos, 'More Christian schools resist Iowa's rules,' *Des Moines Register*, 27 April, 1980, C2–3; Jerry Moskal, 'Rise in church-run schools confounds state,' *Lansing State Journal*, Michigan, 11 October, 1979, A9–10; Joan Roesgen, 'Will state put brakes on church schools?' *Billings Gazette*, Montana, 17 September, 1978, B2–3; Maureen Boyle, 'Church school defies state,' *Manchester Union Leader*, New Hampshire, 13 April, 1979, D12–13; and Chuck Raasch, 'Control of schools up to court,' *Sioux Falls Argus Leader*, South Dakota, 1 February, 1980, C14.

35. Carper, 'The *Whisner* decision,' pp. 281–302. My understanding of conflicts over the public regulation of Christian schools has been based largely on a comprehensive examination of newspaper coverage of the various states cited in the text. Also see, 'Christian schools: learning in the courtroom,' *Christianity Today*, 22, 22 September, 1978, pp. 36–37; and Edward E Plowman, 'Alarmed at government intrusion, religious groups close ranks,' *Christianity Today*, 25, 13 March, 1981, pp. 72–74.

36. Rodney Clapp, 'The police lock a Baptist church,' *Christianity Today*, 26, 12 November, 1982, pp. 52–55, 58.

37. Pastor Clyde Winegar, quoted in Richardson, 'Education – according to the gospels,' C4.

38. Quoted in Roos, 'Students stand firm,' B5.

39. Revd George Logan, administrator of the Calvary Baptist Christian School in Keokuk, Iowa, cited in Roos, 'More Christian schools resist Iowa's rules,' C2.

40. Huntley Collins, 'New students flock to Christian schools,' *Portland Oregonian*, 12 July, 1981, D5.

41. Revd T Eugene Holmes, quoted in Doug Perry, 'Christian school would rather operate without accreditation from state board,' *Louisville Courier-Journal*, 26 September, 1977, D5. The *Courier-Journal* gave considerable attention to the conflict between fundamentalists and the state of Kentucky. For a quick introduction to the issues, examine the following: Richard Wilson, 'Carroll sees school suit as a threat,' 24 March, 1978, F6; Anne Pardue, '2 Christian school officials testify they can't follow state standards,' 15 June, 1978, F6; Ann Pardue, 'Non-accredited Christian schools legal, judge rules,' 5 October, 1978, G5–6; and 'Christian schools applaud ruling that limits state control,' 10 October, 1979, B4–5.

42. Revd Gerald Metcalf, founder of the Glenmont Christian School, quoted in Frederick P Szydlik, 'Private school rolls soar,' *Albany Times-Union*, 6 September, 1982, G4.

43. Clapp, 'The police lock a Baptist church,' 54. The *Omaha World Herald* and the *Lincoln Journal and Star* were consulted to follow the history of the conflict in Louisville, which continues to rage. See Jack Kelley, 'Pastor vows to keep church school open,' *USA Today*, 31 August, 1983.

44. Bob Miller, 'Certification: is it necessary?' *Anchorage Daily Times*, 7 December, 1981, G11; Janice Rombeck, 'Schools that blend Christianity, ABCs flourishing,' *Wichita Eagle*, 11 May, 1980, G13–14; and Kurt Hechenauer, 'Religious schools pop up in state as escape from public education,' *Daily Oklahoman*, 29 March, 1982, C13–14.

45. See especially the congressional reports on the IRS and Christian Schools: *Tax-Exempt Status of Private Schools*, Hearings before the Subcommittee on Oversight of the Committee on Ways and Means, House of Representatives, Ninety-Sixth Congress, Washington, DC, United States Government Printing Office, 1979, parts

1 and 2. Also see 'The IRS pins "badge of doubt" on tax-exempt private schools,' *Christianity Today*, 23, 5 January, 1979, p. 42; 'Private schools Get IRS procedure suspended,' *Christianity Today*, 23, 5 October, 1979, pp. 58–59; and Tom Minnery, 'Religious schools rev up for new round with IRS,' *Christianity Today*, 24, 21 November, 1980, p. 50.

46. Revd John C Macon, administrator of the Clinton Christian School in Prince George's County, Maryland, and an activist in the Eastern Association of Christian Schools, quoted in Rosenfeld, 'Fundamentalists challenge state licensing of their schools,' E9. Macon sensed that fundamentalists in the recent past failed to shape history property: 'Historically, we've sat by while things we originally agreed with were taken over. For example, when the public school system was founded in the 1850s, it had a strong emphasis on morals. Gradually it was torn down and replaced with John Dewey and secular humanism, and we built our own schools.'

47. Adams, 'Stress on values a chief attraction,' G12.

48. Individual Christian schools often attract pupils whose parents attend a fundamentalist or evangelical church other than the sponsoring institution. For example, a Christian school in Ewing Township in greater Trenton, New Jersey, enrolls pupils who are 'Baptists, Methodists, Catholics, and members of the Assembly of God and the Church of the Nazarene.' See Gordon, 'Academy for born-again Christians going strong,' G4.

49. *Tax-Exempt Status of Private Schools*, 1979, part 1, 555. James Carper estimates in 'The Christian day school movement' that 'the average number of students per school is probably between 100 and 200 ...' (137).

50. *Tax-Exempt Status of Private Schools*, 1979, part 1, 555; and *Tuition Tax Relief Bills*, Hearings before the Subcommittee on Taxation and Debt Management Generally of the Committee on Finance, United States Senate, Ninety-Fifth Congress, Second Session Washington, DC, United States Government Printing Office, 1978, part 2, p. 702.

51. Arno G Weniger Jr, Executive Vice-President, American Association of Christian Schools, testifying before Congress and cited in *Tax-Exempt Status of Private Schools*, 1979, 117; and Skerry, 'Christian schools versus the IRS,' 20.

52. 'Fundamentalist schools multiply,' *Chicago Tribune*, 21 September, 1981, C7.

53. Stacey Burling, 'Private schools doing well despite costs,' *Norfolk Virginian-Pilot*, 8 September, 1980, D4.

54. Skerry, 'Christian schools versus the IRS,' 26, 32.

55. *Tuition Tax Credits*, Hearings before the Subcommittee on Taxation and Debt Management of the Committee on Finance, United States Senate, Ninety-Seventh Congress, first session Washington, DC, US Government Printing Office, 1981, part 2, 63. Joseph Bayty has a different perspective in 'Why I'm for Christian schools,' *Christianity Today*, 24, 25 January, 1980, pp. 92–95. 'There is a tendency in Christian schools, after they have become established and accepted, to draw their students from an increasingly narrow portion of the socio-economic spectrum' (p. 92).

56. Nevin and Bills, *The Schools That Fear Built*, p. 40. The authors continue: 'They tend to relate to monetary success, to be impatient of those less successful and to see change as a threat. Few of the new school patrons are rich; some are still quite poor and the tuition represents a sacrifice.'

57. Mirow, 'Religion: the big R,' G2.

58. The issue of tuition is well described in the following: Tom Rademacher, 'Public schools lose while private gain,' *Grand Rapids Press*, Michigan, 11 October, 1981, C1; Jeanne Pugh, 'Parents plan concert to raise funds for Christian schools,' *St. Petersburg Times*, Florida, 29 October, 1977, A12; Sharon J. Selyer, 'Private schools are doing well despite the high cost of tuition,' *Atlanta Journal*, 9 August, 1982, C13–14; John Furey, 'Private schools in Salem bucking hard times trend,' *Oregon Statesman*, 1 November, 1981, C4–5; Jon Walker, 'SF private schools doing fine despite tough economic times,' *Sioux Falls Argus Leader*, 28 October, 1982, E4–5; and Jimmie Covington, 'Inflation ups private school costs, but parents willingly pay,' *Commercial Appeal*, Memphis, Tennessee, 27 April, 1980, C5–6.

59. On school integration and the civil rights movement, see at least Richard Kluger, *Simple Justice: The History of Brown v. Board of Education and Black America's Struggle for Equality*, New York, Vintage Books, 1975, and J Harvie Wilkinson III,

*From Brown to Bakke: The Supreme Court and School Integration, 1954–1978*, New York, Oxford University Press, 1979.

60. See, for example, Peggy Peterman, 'Private schools: a growing alternative,' *St Petersburg Times*, 29 August, 1976, G8–9; and Spencer, 'Christian schools growing, D4–5. Deena Mirow, 'Religion: the big R,' G2, quotes Revd Roy Thompson, whose Cleveland Baptist Church sponsors Heritage Christian School: 'We could have 1,000 more students if we would take them simply to avoid busing. We feel sorry for them, but we can't take them for that reason because our religious convictions are so strong.'

61. *Tax-Exempt Status of Private Schools*, 1979, part 1, 385–93.

62. Quoted in Miller, 'Certification: is it necessary?' G11; Nevin and Bills, *The Schools That Fear Built*, chapter 8.

63. Richardson, 'Education – according to the gospels,' C1–4.

64. Quoted in Jimmie Covington, 'Private schools gear for rise in fall enrolment of students,' *Commercial Appeal*, 29 April, 1974, G8.

65. Cited in Nevin and Bills, *The Schools That Fear Built*, 57. The application form also asked the applicants to reveal their thoughts on capitalism, progressive education, the Jesus Movement, creation, and Billy Graham's cooperative evangelism.

66. Ulmer, 'Christian schools buck trend,' B10.

67. Nevin and Bills, *The Schools That Fear Built*, chapter 8.

68. The classic historical study is by Raymond E Callahan, *Education and the Cult of Efficiency*, Chicago, University of Chicago Press, 1962. Also see Michael Apple, 'Interpreting teaching: persons, politics, and culture,' *Educational Studies*, 14, 1983, pp. 112–35.

69. Detailed descriptions of ACE are available in the following: Bob Miller, 'Jesus supplies incentive in Christian study,' *Anchorage Daily Times*, 7 December, 1981, G2–3; Richardson, 'ACE fundamentalists' alternative to "pagan" public school systems,' A11–12; Sharon M Bertsch, 'Do-it-yourself package works for fundamentalist schools,' *Lansing State Journal*, 15 October, 1978, F8–10; Lisa Hammersly, 'Church schools purchase Christian education plan,' *Charlotte Observer*, North Carolina, 28 February, 1981, G4.

70. David Dubose, quoted by Huntley Collins, 'Christian school centers on strict, individual effort,' *Portland Oregonian*, 13 July, 1981, A12.

71. Ken Parsley, pastor of the Covenant Christian Fellowship and administrator of its school, quoted by Deborah Frazier, 'Bible is the answer for grand junction schools,' *Rocky Mountain News*, 18 October, 1981, C14. Bob Winebarger, principal of the Park West School in Lincoln, Nebraska, has stated: 'We base everything on the Bible, the only source of absolute truth and knowledge. We centre our teachings on Christ rather than the child or the academic content.' See Anita Fussell, 'Standards split launches Bible schools,' *Journal and Star*, 14 September, 1980, A2.

72. Unidentified Christian school administrator, cited in Ulmer, 'Christian schools buck trend,' B9.

73. Principal Joe Haas of the Woodbine Christian Academy, cited in Saundra Ivey and Adell Crowe, 'Parents seek something special in private school,' *Nashville Tennessean*, 3 August, 1980, B8.

74. Josie Zachary, a high school senior cited at the beginning of this essay, whose remarks appear in Roos, 'Students stand firm in fight against order closing school,' BA.

75. Rick Rutherford, quoted by John Carlson, 'Boom in religious schools: threat to public education?' *Des Moines Register*, 14 September, 1980, A11.

76. Donald Jesse, cited in Spencer, 'Christian schools growing,' D5.

77. Quoted in Wright, 'Christian schools prospering,' G3.

78. Rosemary Hatcher, principal of Shively Christian School, Louisville, Kentucky, quoted in Nevin and Bills, *The Schools That Fear Built*, 62. Tom Schultz, principal of the New Hope Christian School in Grants Pass, Oregon, has asserted that 'in mathematics, we see reflected the order of God's universe. Two plus two equals four. It's that way yesterday, today, and tomorrow.' See Huntley Collins, 'New students flock to Christian schools,' *Portland Oregonian*, 12 July, 1981, D6.

79. An unidentified principal, admittedly representative of an extremist position within the Christian school movement, quoted in Nevin and Bills, *The Schools That Fear Built*, 61.

80. Rick Rutherford, of the Charles City Baptist School, cited in Carlson, 'Boom in religious schools: threat to public education?' A11.
81. An unidentified principal, cited in Nevin and Bills, *The Schools That Fear Built*, 63. The subject 'scientific' creationism is too vast to be explored here.
82. Timothy D Crater, 'The unproclaimed priests of public education,' *Christianity Today*, 25, 10 April, 1981, p. 45.
83. Heidi Christner, a senior from Kalona, Iowa, cited in Roos, 'Students stand firm in fight against order closing school,' B4.
84. Quoted in Rombeck, 'Schools that blend Christianity, ABCs flourishing,' G14.
85. Revd Ray Borah of Jacksonville, Illinois, state representative for Accelerated Christian Education, cited in Richardson, 'Education – according to the gospels,' C2.
86. Ken Newman, quoted in Collins, 'New students flock to Christian schools,' D5.
87. Frank Beacham, 'A ruling is near on Dade School's refusal to admit black students,' *Miami Herald*, 19 May, 1975. E5. Conservative dress codes for both males and females are common at fundamentalist schools.
88. See 'Ask Jesus to help you,' *Providence Journal*, 13 April, 1980, A1: and Ward Pimley, 'Church classes alter approach to education,' *Providence Journal*, 18 November, 1979, F4.
89. Fran Krzywicki, 'Church schools find acceptance,' *Delaware State News*, 25 February, 1978, C9.
90. Bertsch, 'Do-it-yourself package works for fundamentalist schools,' F9. The manual continues: 'Whether or not a rule seems unreasonable or reasonable is not important! What is important is that the student learn to submit to human authority so that he can better submit to God's authority.'
91. Dr George Nulph, pastor of the Perry Hill Road Baptist church and administrator of the Landmarks Christian school, quoted in Danny Lewis, 'Christian schools drawing greater number of students,' *Montgomery Advertiser*, 21 February, 1981, E11.
92. Pamela Mendels, 'Basics, Bible, and a "Board of Education,"' *Providence Journal*, Rhode Island, 25 October, 1981, D6.
93. Quoted in Bob Banta, 'Bibles and blacksides,' *Austin American Statesman*, 1 August, 1982, B1: and Disend, 'Have you whipped your child today?'
94. Christian school leaders often take pride in the moral characteristics of their pupils. Short hair on boys and modest dress for girls, they believe, are part of the larger respect for authority children need as they progress toward adulthood. Robert Billings of Christian School Action Inc. has asserted that Christian school activists 'are for the most part highly patriotic, God-fearing, law-abiding, and productive citizens.' His comments appear in *Tuition Tax Relief Bills*, 702.
95. Revd Daniel D Carr, Executive Director of the Organised Christian Schools of North Carolina, cited in John Robinson, 'Christian schools add discipline, doctrine to learning routines,' *News and Observer*, Raleigh, 29 November, 1981, F13.
96. Kate Harris, 'Public school officials fear proposed tuition tax credits,' *Birmingham News*, 24 May, 1981, A8–9; and Sherry Johnson, NC officials fear tax plan would destroy public schools,' *News and Observer*, 16 April, 1982, D10–11.
97. Paul Blikstad, quoted in John Furey, 'New debate over private school costs,' *Oregon Statesman*, 2 May, 1981, C14.
98. Senator Gene Huff, cited in Livingston Taylor, 'Senate passes private-school textbooks aid,' *Louisville Courier-Journal*, 18 March, 1978, E13.
99. Revd Curtis Porter, pastor of Amherst Baptist Church, in Anthony Cardinale, 'Tuition tax credit gets mixed reviews,' *Buffalo Evening News*, 17 April, 1982, D6.
100. 'Private education: a tax break?' *Christianity Today*, 22, 21 April, 1978, p. 43.
101. 'School tax credits: making new converts,' *Christianity Today*, 22, 22 September, 1978, pp. 37–38. Also see the testimony of various Christian school representatives in *Tuition Tax Proposals*, 1982.
102. The Spencer Foundation and the National Academy of Education generously supported my research on the Christian school movement. I alone am responsible for all facts and interpretations.

# 8.2 Fundamentalist Christian schools: should they be regulated?

*Alan Peshkin*

## Introduction

Fundamentalist Christian schools – or Christian schools, to use their own designation – are a diverse lot. They stretch along a continuum that has the public school model at one end and the full-blown, scripture-permeated model at the other. The school I use for illustrative purposes in this paper is located at the scripture-permeated end of the continuum. Hereafter, I will characterise this school and in light of this characterisation consider the policy question: should the states regulate such schools?

Regulation, clearly, is not limited to a particular, single definition. Its many possible forms vary in the extent to which they place control of a school in the hands of centralised agencies, a state's office of instruction or its legislature. A state's interest in regulating any of its K-12 schools falls within three general areas. First, states generally want to know where its school-aged children are receiving their schooling. Simple registration establishes the location and type (public or private) of school. Second, states are concerned with the physical well-being of these children. Such concern brings the state into a school since it necessitates on-site inspectors whose findings have financial implications. Third, states have an obligation to insure the appropriateness of children's schooling in academic, moral, and vocational terms. The issue of appropriateness carries implications for who is teaching and what is taught and leads to state standards, edicts, and periodic visitations. By these intentions and means, states can reach into those ordinary, ongoing affairs of a school that are at the core of its nature.

From the perspective of Christian schools, any regulation deemed unwarranted will lead the schools to infer undue control from the state. Thus, some schools refuse to accede to any state prerogative *vis-à-vis* themselves. They base their case on the principle of separation of church and state and on the belief that once the state is granted the least prerogative, further prerogatives inevitably follow. Other Christian schools, albeit uncomfortably, are willing to accept registration and health and safety inspections, but then draw a sharp line beyond which the state's involvement must not extend.

My research of Christian schools was conducted at Bethany Baptist Academy (BBA), a K-12 school of 350 students located in a small

Illinois city. The academy belongs to the 1000-member national organisation called the American Association of Christian Schools, most of whose schools are attached to the doctrinally conservative Independent Baptist Church. Christian education leaders consider BBA an exemplary school, as indicated by the quality of its administrators and by its success in creating a curriculum dominated, as they would say, by the Word of God. In schools such as BBA, the glorification of God is the ultimate goal; no other concern can compete with it. The God they glorify is spelled out in scripture, in both the Old and New Testament, according to the King James version of the Bible. They take scripture literally as God's Word.

We all are given to inadvertent overgeneralisation, often finding it bothersome to present the necessary qualifications that would make our characterisations accurate. Fundamentalist Christian schools suffer from such overgeneralisation. To outsiders, such schools may appear strikingly more like than unlike each other, but up close (which is where I believe researching outsiders should look) they include distinguishably different types. For the purpose of this paper, I refer to just one type, a school whose view of and commitment to scripture as the foundation of education places it a significant distance away from the public school.

## Fundamentalist Christian schools

Taken as a single group, fundamentalist Christian schools (hereafter referred to as Christian schools) contain approximately one million students, less than half the number in Catholic schools, and a small fraction of the nation's overall total of forty-eight million or so school children.[1] Should warrant for the regulation of Christian schools be affected by their relatively small numbers? This is the first of many questions I raise, without yet answering them, as I pursue the matter of the regulation of Christian schools.

As a group, Christian schools are in the class designated 'nonpublic school,' lumped together with all other private schools of both the religious and independent type. As a nonpublic, religious school the Christian school is an alternative to the public school and, because of its unusual nature, to other nonpublic schools, as well.

Given the several designations so far considered, does the issue of regulation arise? Does it arise, for example, as a result of the Christian school's status as a nonpublic school? No, because states do not actively consider schools so labeled as serious candidates for regulation. Does it arise because of the school's religious nature? No, we hear little to nothing about regulating Lutheran, Seventh Day Adventist, or Jewish day schools. Finally, Christian schools are not targeted for regulation as alternative schools. We must conclude, therefore, that there is something about this subtype of nonpublic school that raises hackles, stirs passions, and animates policymakers and others to entertain them as grist for their policy mills.

What could this something be? I will begin by noting what I think is not true about Christian schools and should thus not raise hackles. Notwithstanding the popular media image of red, white, and blue-uniformed Christian students waving American flags to be called on to recite or to receive permission for a trip to the toilet, such students belong only to the national group called Accelerated Christian Education, a franchise-like enterprise that expedites the establishment of shoestring schools in a Christian mode. To the contrary, the students I attended school with for eighteen months are not automata who have been regimented beyond recognition as American adolescents. The Christian students I know are spontaneous, fun-loving, friendly, accepting, and warm human beings, who − like the rest of American students − romance, cheer on their teams, and cheat on exams. Which is to say, that in terms of the categories that subsume their students' activities, Christian schools are recognisably like most public schools: in the categories, for example, of subjects taught, topics covered, games played, examinations taken, rules broken and punishments awarded. In Christian schools, bells ring to punctuate the day; students and teachers watch the clock, which is to say that much is reassuringly familiar in the American Christian school, much of the time.

Since the Christian school strives to be, as the sign on the lawn outside BBA proclaims, 'A school with a difference,' the operation of the Christian school also varies in each of the above-mentioned categories. But is the difference in name only? Or, possibly, are there jolting distinctions that mark those schools located at God's end of the continuum? I believe there are: as evident in the trim, never blue-jeaned appearance of all students − the boys with their short hair, the girls with only their modesty displayed; as evident also in the compulsory thrice-weekly chapel sessions, daily Bible class, and speech class with its rationale that developing fluent use of language will help spread the word of God; as evident in the optional soul-winning class and preacher-boy's class for aspiring ministers, evangelists, and missionaries; and, finally, as evident in the teachers, all of whom are certain that God has called them to be Christian school teachers and are willing to sign a pledge as a condition of employment that reads in part:

> I affirm that I am a born-again Christian believing the Bible to be the inspired word of God without contradiction or error in its original languages. I believe that every Christian should be separated from worldly habits.

There are further jolting distinctions from public schools. I see them in the Christian school's commitment to integrate scripture into *everything* that is taught; in the belief that the school has failed if its college-bound graduates do not attend one of a select few Christian colleges; in the school's overall vocational orientation favoring careers known collectively as full-time Christian service; in the librarian's censorship of all materials that fail the doctrinal test; in the school's prohibition of artistic or literary experiences that fail this same test; and in the extraordinarily consistent effort BBA directs to the total control of students whatever the time or place, as long as they remain BBA students. The headmaster called this control his 'twenty-four hour umbrella' policy. It is a serious policy, more than a matter of mere words spouted for the benefit of parents and visiting researchers.

Does the issue of regulation arise because this just-mentioned array of distinctions truly establishes 'a school with a difference'? Does this set of qualities mark Christian schools as an academic beast run amok and in need of control? If hyperbolic language serves to haul one back to more moderate views, it also directs attention to the kernels of truth in the objections of critics who are disturbed by the above characteristics of Christian schools. These critics perceive the Christian school as enmeshed in a broader network of Christian undertakings:

a.   with fellow fundamentalists who attack the public schools on matters of prayer, choice of textbooks, and the teaching of creationism;
b.   with organisers of right-wing political-action groups, who defeat 'preferred' candidates for elective office;
c.   with the organisers of dynamic churches whose growth is correlated with the decline of mainline Protestant churches; and
d.   with television evangelists, whose mastery of the electronic media has raised public money raising to a standard well beyond the imagination of the Elmer Gantrys of the past.

If the rapid expansion of Christian schools, once reputed to be at the rate of four new schools per day, does not inspire fear for the future of the commonwealth, fear can be generated by linking the Christian schools to this network of four undertakings, for a network implies that a movement is afoot, an organised collectivity. Does the impression of a movement establish firm warrant for nipping Christian schools in the bud?

I return to further consideration of Christian schools in order to reflect on what else about them may invite regulation. What exactly do they offer parents and their children? Among other things, their students achieve above-average scores on national tests; they receive good instruction in english; and they are taught by hardworking, dedicated teachers. Christian schools create a safe environment in physical and moral terms; they emphasise character training; they promote a sense of community; and, according to my data, their students are noted for their low alienation and also for personal qualities that make them attractive to local employers. Plainly, not a bad record.

On the 'negative' side, Christian schools are apt to provide poor instruction in science and the social studies. By virtue of their monolithic doctrinal orientation, they try to confine students to a narrow range of social and sensory experiences. Personal growth, as judged by external standards, is circumscribed. The Christian school is closed to experience that will compete, it is believed, with the ways of their singular truth. Thus, marked as taboo is much of the world's art, literature, music, and dance. Plainly, not a good record.

## The case for regulation

By internal standards, Christian schools do fine. Should anyone else's standards prevail? Should the definition of an acceptable education reside with parents? Whom, that is what constituencies, should we presume our schools must serve?

I began answering this latter question in Mansfield, the rural community in Illinois I studied in the early seventies.[2] I was responding to an argument I have continued to hear ever since, which runs as follows: though local people may know what they want their schools to achieve and also what they find pleasing, they do not necessarily know what is best for their children in school, nor do local educators, let alone school board members, necessarily know what is best. Who, then, does know? The answer must, of course, be: those who are informed and enlightened, who hold standards consistent with a view of schooling that maximizes growth, opens opportunities, and extends horizons, to use the cliché phrases, which their propounders mean to be taken seriously.

A school that fits the norms and values of its host community, it is argued, may well offer an education so limited that it prepares students only for that community. It is further argued that there must be some warranted basis by means of which critics can validly evaluate the quality of schooling. Otherwise, anything goes, and it should not. Surely the numerous blue-ribbon national, state, and privately supported commissions, which in recent years have deluged us with their critiques and blueprints for reform, assumed they had a basis for saying, in effect: even though we are not members of your community and we do not send our children to your schools, we can identify what is good for you and your children. Surely the judgment of experts should not be excluded from reform and policymaking. Therefore, if the effects of local control are limiting and if external critics are justifiable interventionists, do we not have at least logical grounds for regulation, in order to ensure that Christian children are not placed at risk?

In fact, states have managed varying degrees of regulation of Christian schools, ranging, as previously described, from the minimal – no more than simple registration – to somewhat more than the minimal – enforcing health and safety codes and guidelines related to length of school day and school year. These are relatively uncontroversial items of procedural control. Controversy enters the picture with substantive control; for example, in the matters of teacher certification and directives about curriculum, such as what subjects to teach, what course content to stress, how many years of a subject to require for graduation, and (in states that control textbooks) what textbooks to use.

The state's case for regulating the procedural matters of health and safety in all schools, matters that are far from the central goals of a Christian school, seems relatively easy to make. We can use the same arguments that are made in favor of compulsory vaccination and for the use of seat belts in cars and safety helmets by cyclists. Should states have less of a right to control and monitor substantive matters, those that bear on what can deeply affect the minds of youth? Traditionally, we accede less readily to regulations that touch the sensitive realms of beliefs and values. Yet, are not all of us affected by the insularity of a Christian education that is based on Truth with a capital T, an education that literally shuts doors to worlds of learning and experience ruled invalid by application of a yardstick of orthodoxy? Should the state have any less interest in children because they attend a school that is driven by religious doctrine? Are Christian school children somehow less a part of our communities, less a part of our national life because their elders mean to place them beyond the impact of the world rejected as Satan's? If by non-Christian school standards these children are cognitively handicapped, do we not have a responsibility to intervene on their behalf? Should the fact, as mentioned earlier, that Christian schools are so few in number affect our deliberation as to whether they belong within the purview of the state? Do small numbers confer a privileged, protected status?

## The nature of Christian schools further elaborated

The many questions I have raised have to do with educational policy as it pertains to state regulation of both procedural and substantive aspects of Christian schools. Before further consideration of this issue, I would like to return to a characterisation of the Christian school in even stronger terms than I have thus far used.

I take as my text for this elaboration an observation by Naomi Bliven: 'Whenever men and women take belief seriously, orthodoxy and heresy emerge struggling, like Jacob and Esau, and spiritual disagreement becomes physical conflict.'[3]

In fundamentalist Christian terms, to take belief seriously is to clothe it in garments of orthodoxy. In such garb, belief becomes sacred and thereby inviolable. To be inviolable is to be placed safely beyond doubt and question, save for the purpose of clarification and reassurance. Orthodox belief derives from him whom Christians cast as God. Such belief, because of its authority, is absolute and eternally true. Some groups, the Amish for example, are also orthodox in belief, but they do not read their texts to say that all of humanity must march down their scriptural road. As a result, such groups do not have an outreaching evangelism, they do not recruit missionaries to purvey their orthodoxies among nonbelievers, and they do not see their true belief as charging them to change their society so that it is congruent with, not just congenial to, their sacred truth. To the contrary, fundamentalist Christians do have this sense of mission, and they integrate such ideas into their instructional program. They weave their particular garment of orthodoxy with the thread of universalism and, accordingly, they are doctrinal imperialists with the concomitant arrogance, however unwitting, of the proselytising true believer.

Furthermore, the very act of creating true believers simultaneously makes heretics of all those who hold divergent views. Fundamentalists, by their own unyielding opposition to nonbelievers, as they define belief, may possibly even provoke nonbelievers toward adopting orthodox-like stances themselves, whereas they might have held none before.

Finally, the fundamentalist's opposition to nonbelievers is not confined to conventional matters of religion; they apply their doctrine to the full range of human affairs. In this respect, I heard the pastor of Bethany Baptist Church say:

> We never will be in control of this or any other society until the Lord establishes his kingdom ... I can think of Christians taking over political life and pockets of power in certain communities ... It can be done where there is a thriving church. If on the city council of my town the majority were members of Bethany Baptist Church and committed Christians, well, what would we do about liquor and liquor ordinances? I'd vote against them all the way. We'd be a dry town if I could control it. I guess I wonder if I'd be very tolerant of a non-Christian position. I would hope to believe that I'd be very understanding, but when my Christianity affects my whole life, it has to affect my politics. It has to affect what I'd do Monday night at a city council meeting.

The pastor's logical extension of his sacred belief into secular public affairs, similar to fundamentalist Christian resistance to the Equal Rights Amendment and abortion, relates to Bliven's final point, in which she spoke of spiritual disagreement becoming physical conflict. To be sure, this requires a large leap, but we have seen signs of this in the 1970s textbook controversy in Kanawha County, West Virginia, and, more recently, in the bombing by Christians of abortion clinics. Larger signs are available in history (in the inquisition, for example) and currently in the Iran of the ayatollahs.

Given this picture, what do I see as the possible consequences of Christian schools for American society? Their truth-driven curriculum creates true believers of children who are taught to see the world in the dichotomised terms of us and them, with the clear-cut good guys – the born-again brethren – learning to stay separate on principle from the clear-cut bad-guys – the rest of us. Labeling is a powerful practice of the Christian school; children readily acquire the terms for stereotyping: secular humanist, Satan and the world, on the one hand, and believer, born-again and Christian, on the other. These terms receive the repeated emphasis that Bethany Baptist Academy gives to all important matters it intends to inculcate. For fundamentalist Christians, their truth creates positions of support and opposition on public issues backed by the force of the Lord. Their truth creates censorship of that which lies beyond what is defined as the realm of legitimate learning. And their truth creates divisiveness, inevitable if its rightful, uncontestable imperatives are to be upheld. 'Be in the world not of it,' is an injunction Christian students learn throughout their school days, along with 'Be ye separate, saith the Lord' and 'Be ye not unequally yoked together with unbelievers' (2 Corinthians 6:14).

Given a commitment to such truth, can we doubt that the Christian school's success must be seen in zero-sum terms: insofar as they win, we, outside their born-again boundaries, must lose.

## The case for regulation

In light of this picture, I return to considering the policy of regulating Christian schools. To begin with, are such schools legal? The answer: absolutely yes. Legality of religious schools in general has not been an issue since a 1925 Supreme Court decision declared, in effect, that if it is legal to be a Roman Catholic, it is legal to establish and operate schools that socialise children to live as a Roman Catholic. The actual language of this court decision is instructive: 'The child is not the mere creature of the state.'[4] This does not say that children are exclusively the creatures of their parents. Nor does it say that children are never creatures of the state; compulsory education and the mandatory teaching of physical education and US history indicate otherwise. But in the 1925 case of a Roman Catholic school in Oregon, the Court saw the states' interests neither as preeminent nor in jeopardy.

Furthermore, the 1925 ruling cannot be interpreted to say that if a certain type of school, for example one fully established and operated under church auspices, is legal in structure, then anything goes with regard to its content. In other words, the court did not forever protect religious schools from all state regulation. The judgment point for concluding that a school has gone beyond allowable limits was stated by the Ohio Supreme Court in a 1976 decision. The court ruled against Ohio's regulation of Christian schools on the grounds that the state's evidence was not persuasive that its case for regulation had passed the 'compelling interest' test.[5] What, in fact, compelling interest amounts to is debatable: *you* may feel a hot, threatening breath blowing on your head, while *I* feel no more than a cool, soothing breeze. Historically, our supreme courts have been conservative about extending the scope of state control.

Compelling interest – in this terse expression 'unpopular' institutions find the protection they need for their perpetuation. Such principled protection of aberrant institutions is not commonly found elsewhere in the world, but it is bred in the bones of our society. Moreover, it is integral to the particular form we give pluralism. It is peculiarly American to ascribe so much weight to the prerogatives of parents and local communities in the education of their children. Centralised, state-run schools are significantly more the norm throughout the world. The result of our tradition of local control is a patchwork of schools characterised by standards so variable as often to make a mockery of the concept of equal access. What virtue can equal access have if the access is to academically undernourished schools? Yet, while we may easily agree at the extreme as to what constitutes undernourishment, we may come to blows over its remedy – as we know from James Madison's outlook on factions. Madison wrote, to wit, that curing a problem may be worse than the problem itself. In short, the fact that highly variable academic standards prevail in the United States has not yet persuaded either state or federal legislators of the necessity for uniform regulation.

In deciding whether a state's compelling interests are at stake, it is more to the point to ask if, in the normal course of pursuing their doctrinal dictates, Christian schools actually engender harmful divisiveness. The case for Christian schools contributing to the fragmentation of American society is one I take seriously. I cannot be comfortable with a school about whose goals I can say, 'the more successfully they are attained, the more the democratic society I esteem is threatened.' I make this strong assertion because fundamentalist Christians' strict interpretation of scripture leaves no legitimate place for their presumed antagonists. In the secure, legal haven of Bethany Baptist Academy, I never heard a word of support for the pluralism that undergirds its existence. To the contrary, I heard them exalt their own beliefs and denigrate those of all others not identifiable as born-again Christians. 'Is it good that we have so many different churches and religions in America?' I asked students, teachers, and parents. Nearly two-thirds of each group disagreed or strongly disagreed.

## Conclusion

I fear those who couch their beliefs in absolute terms and thereby turn causes into crusades. I fear those whose beliefs provide no place for compromise, for bargaining, for the live- and-let-live attitude that makes life possible in our crowded, communication-shrunk world. That Christian schools are factions that bite the societal hand that feeds them, I have no doubt. That they should be able to continue to do so with no regulation beyond registration and meeting health and safety standards, I also have no doubt. On this point, turn to James Madison's Paper 'No. X':[6]

> There are two methods of curing the mischiefs of faction: the one by removing its causes; the other, by controlling its effects. There are again two methods of removing the causes of faction: the one, by destroying the liberty which is essential to its existence; the other, by giving to each citizen the same opinions, the same passions, the same interests. It could never be more truly said than of the first remedy, that it was worse than the disease. Liberty is to faction what air is to fire ... The second expedient is as impracticable as the first would be unwise ... The inference to which we are brought is, that the *causes* of faction cannot be removed, and that relief is only to be sought in the means of controlling its *effects*.

By focusing on controlling the effects of Christian schools, I do not mean to exempt them from applicable federal law, for example laws relating to racial discrimination, or to leave them totally beyond the purview of the state. State regulation relating to procedural matters, such as health and safety, does not infringe upon the prerogatives Christian schools feel they need in order to shape their students' experiences in scriptural terms. Moreover, state standards relating to substantive matters, such as curriculum and teacher certification, can be nonprescriptive for Christian schools as to the specific means they use to meet the standards.[7] In this way, Christian schools can remain unregulated in substantive matters while still observing the standards a state holds for its public schools.

I am persuaded that controlling the effects of the faction known as the fundamentalist Christian school is the proper response to them, with control of effects taking various forms, for example:

- Public schools could be made a competitively attractive alternative − of course, in secular terms − and thereby preempt the Christian school's appeal in all but the two areas, in which public schools cannot and should not compete: offering the presence of God (this is the monopoly of the Christian school) and insuring the presence of a single racial group. On most other grounds − academic merit, physical and emotional safety, character development − the public school should be able to be competitive.[8]

- The Constitution, especially the Bill of Rights, needs to become the centre-piece of vibrant, robust social studies instruction in the public schools.
- Support could be given to those agencies that promote and reinforce the principle of pluralism and resist the claims of those who see in diversity and dissent danger to our national unity.

I endorse controlling the effects rather than the institutions because this is congruent with the principle of pluralism, which permits the institutions to exist. I do not interpret this principle to mean, however, that any institution that is formed should thrive.

The three points I suggest above for controlling effects would be no less meaningful if Christian schools did not exist. They are, in a sense, homilies drawn from a certain view of maintaining a democratic society. They do not exhaust the possibilities for control, nor does the brief discussion that follows begin to settle the matter of how to achieve this control. The intent of this article has been to explore the basic issue of whether states should regulate Christian schools, not what they should do if and when they decide that full procedural and substantive regulation is a misguided policy.

Controlling the effects of schooling by direct action in the schools is exceptionally hard. For public schools are designed and used essentially for individual rather than collective or national needs. To be sure, collective needs are served when an individual's personal academic and economic needs are met but, relatively speaking, schools give short shrift to the civic requirements of society. Thus they sidestep the thorny, controversial issues incorporated in the particulars of the Bill of Rights. In the end, the control of effects derives more from the functions of organisations such as the American Civil Liberties Union and from a free press and an independent Department of Justice and judiciary system, which relates to my third point of supporting those agencies that are the bulwark of pluralism. At the level of words, these functions pass as the rhetoric of discourse on democracy in the United States. At the level of practice, they are regularly contested whenever a new administration takes over in Washington and proceeds to place its stamp on the national instruments of power and authority.

Controlling the effects of Christian schools in situ is even more unlikely, if not unreasonable. For example, Christian schools cannot be compelled to make consideration of the Bill of Rights the keystone of their social studies instruction; such compulsion would not work meaningfully even in the public schools, and they are subject to state edicts. Christian schools cannot promulgate ideas that would fail the test of their doctrinal orthodoxy. Accordingly, the control of effects cannot be charged to the Christian schools themselves, that is, either by constraining them from something they do or by compelling them to do something they do not do − unless their action or inaction is, by clear legal and moral standards, injurious to children. Barring the latter case, the control of effects remains essentially a political matter: whom we vote into office from the local to the national level. Beyond the political arena, I would be cheered if students left their public and private schools with such a clear understanding of the Bill of Rights that they could ringingly endorse the diversity of thought and behavior that the Bill of Rights enables. I do not expect to see this happen soon.

Perhaps the day will come when states must conclude that Christian schools should be regulated so their effects, verified as noxious, are stopped at their source − in classrooms and in chapels. It has been said that sometimes 'the defense of tolerance requires intolerance.'[9] Not seeing that disagreeable day as either here or imminent, I conclude with the words abolitionist Wendell Phillips spoke in 1852 about the affairs of another era:[10]

> Eternal vigilance is the price of liberty ... Never look ... for an age when the people can be quiet and safe. At such times despotism, like a shrouding mist, steals over the mirror of Freedom.

Our open society invites a diversity that is manifest in an abundance of organisations, interest groups, and ethnic associations. A concomitant of this polyvalent multitude is risk to the very openness that engenders the multitude, because openness begets diversity and diversity may beget organisations that oppose openness. I prefer running this risk to establishing any preemptive, horse-flight-barn-door-closing regulatory policies based on the presumed certainty of danger, when there is only potential threat. Should non-Christians be content with Christians' contentment with their own schools, and should non-Christians pay a price for Christian students' supposed cognitive handicaps? These, and other questions raised above, imply the desirability of state regulation. Nonetheless, my straight answer is 'hands-off,' for the most part. There is indeed ample space in a pluralistic society for insular truth to operate. I do not worry when truth's organisations, fundamentalist Christian schools, operate as total institutions. I worry when they prevail. Until that dreadful day comes, I worry when they are denied the right to try to prevail. In between the two extremes of complete hands off and complete regulation is where paradoxes proliferate and where, in a democratic society, we always should prefer to live[11].

### Notes

1.  Corrine Glesne and Alan Peshkin, 'Christian day schools: the Bible and the state,' in Patricia A Bauch (ed.), *Private Schools and the Public Interest*, Westport, Connecticut, Greenwood Press, forthcoming.

2. Alan Peshkin, *Growing Up American: Schooling and the Survival of Community*, Chicago, University of Chicago Press, 1978.

3. Naomi Bliven, 'Living at this hour,' *New Yorker*, February 1979, pp. 116–18.

4. David Fellman, *The Supreme Court and Education*, New York, Teachers College Press, 1969, p. 5.

5. James C Carper, 'The Whisner decision: a case study in state regulation of Christian day schools,' *Journal of Church and State*, Spring 1982, pp. 281–302.

6. A T Mason, (ed.), *Free Government in the Making*, 2nd ed., New York, Oxford University Press, 1956, pp. 286–87.

7. I am indebted to Professor Perry Johnston, University of Vermont, for the point about standards.

8. See also B B Seiferth, 'The new Christian schools,' *The High School Journal*, December 1984-January 1985, pp. 70–74.

9. J L Sullivan, J Pierson, and G F Marcus, *Political Tolerance and American Democracy*, Chicago, University of Chicago Press, 1982, p. 9.

10. Wendell Phillips, 'Address delivered before the Massachusetts anti-slavery society,' 28 January 1852.

11. The Spencer Foundation and the University of Illinois' College of Education and Research Board supported the research on which this article is based.

# 9. Canadian perspectives

This chapter turns attention to the debate in Canada regarding public funding for private schools.

In the first article, Dr Bernard J Shapiro focuses on the situation in Ontario where the government decided to extend it's funding to Catholic schools in 1984. He rehearses the arguments and counter-arguments put forward to the Commission on Private Schools in Ontario, and reported more fully in *The Report of the Commission on Private Schools in Ontario*, published in 1985.

Bernard J Shapiro was Commissioner for the Commission on Private Schools in Ontario. He is currently Deputy Minister of Colleges and Universities for the Province of Ontario. This article was first published in *Canadian Journal of Education* in 1986.

In the second article, Professor Ralph M Miller argues that, in spite of Canada's long history of public education and considerable effort to distinguish *religious* from *public* education, it is now more than ever difficult to determine whether to include religious alternative schools within the public system. He identifies the legal and practical limits on such funding as based on fear of division in society, fear that the curriculum of such schools may be too narrow, and shortages of sufficient pupils and funding.

Ralph Miller is Professor of Education at the University of Calgary. This article was first published in *Canadian Journal of Education* in 1986.

# 9.1 The public funding of private schools in Ontario: the setting, some arguments, and some matters of belief

*Bernard J Shapiro*

## The setting

There are two publicly funded school systems in Ontario, both responsible to locally elected Boards of Trustees. These are the board of education schools (frequently referred to as *the* public schools) and, at least through Grade 10, the Roman Catholic separate schools. In addition, in 1984–85, there were in Ontario 535 private elementary and secondary schools serving 87,126 students. Of the 535 schools, approximately 48% and 24% were elementary and secondary schools respectively while the balance offered programs at both levels. Analysed from another perspective, 70% of the Ontario private schools enrolling 80% of the private school students were private schools with religious definition. Finally, enrolment data reveal growth in the Ontario private sector in recent years. Thus, in the period 1973–83, elementary and secondary private school enrolment increased by 60% and 90% respectively. In 1973, private school students represented 2.3% of the total number of elementary and secondary students in Ontario. In 1984, the comparable percentage was 4.7%.

Although Ontario private schools do not have access to either local education taxes or direct provincial grants for operating or capital expenses, it would not be correct to conclude that these private schools receive no public assistance. Most of the direct aid programs (for example access to the ministry of education's book purchase plan) are, however, quite minor in scale. Of greater importance is the indirect aid to private schools in the form of exemption from property taxes on non-profit schools, income tax deductions for tuition attributable to religious instruction, and income tax deductions for charitable purposes. The annual cost to the public treasury of these indirect programs – at the local, the provincial, and the federal levels – is not known. In fact, this cost is very difficult to estimate, for such an estimate would depend on currently untested assumptions such as the market value of private school properties, the marginal tax rates of parents receiving tuition tax receipts and parents or other contributors receiving tax receipts for charitable donations, and the proportion of tuition attributable to religious instruction. Moreover, in each area there would be wide differences among individual private schools although the aid programs clearly favour those schools with a religious orientation. In a paper prepared for the Commission on Private Schools in Ontario, Lawton suggests that the actual level of aid 'amounts to about one-sixth of the average total in cost per pupil enrolled in a private school' (Lawton, 1985, appendix D). This seems a conservative estimate, and there are certainly some individual private schools where the aid level is at least twice Lawton's average estimate.

There is, of course, no absolute answer to how much public monies should be used to support the education of persons attending elementary and secondary schools not owned or operated by government bodies. In a democratic and heterogeneous society, any existing policy in this area is the result of the interaction of many factors, and the current arrangements can and should be expected to alter over time. Further, in considering what, if any, change or changes would be appropriate currently for Ontario, one cannot look to other jurisdictions or the available research results for easy guidance. With regard to other jurisdictions, their experience, although often informative, is always conditioned by their special social and cultural history. Therefore, extrapolation to Ontario, even from other Canadian provinces, can never be either single or straightforward. With regard to the available research, there are two problems. First, although the pace of inquiry has quickened recently, research in the area of private schooling has not, in fact, been extensive. Thus the results of the research tend to be fragmentary and suggestive rather than cumulative and definitive. Second, the *facts* yielded by research studies cannot in themselves respond to the public *policy* question of whether to provide more public funds to private schools. The response to such a question is not so much a matter of facts as it is a matter of *values*.

Nevertheless, the decision of the Ontario government (in June, 1984) to fund Grades 11 to 13 of the Roman Catholic separate schools refocussed public attention on the funding of private schools, at very least those private schools which were religiously defined. The Commission on Private Schools in Ontario was established by the provincial government and, during the course of its work, the commission received 514 written briefs. In terms of public policy preferences, the writers of these briefs represented a very wide range of options, all the way from the full funding of all private schools to the withdrawal of public funds from all schools, public or private. What were the most common arguments put forward to the commission for these various views?

## The arguments

The most common arguments put forward in support of the public funding of private schools were:

a. not only should parents be able to choose school environments that affirm and extend their own values, but they also have a prior right to select the kind of education they believe appropriate for their children. The function of the state is (within recognised limits of costs and standards) to enable parents to choose, free from the financial constraints which now threaten, through the economics of schooling, the right of many parents to choose a private school;

b. it is discriminatory and, therefore, inappropriate for Ontario to continue to offer to its Roman Catholic community an educational option not offered to all other Ontario communities, at least to all other Ontario communities that are religiously defined;

c. parents who choose to send their children to private schools should not have to bear the 'double taxation' of paying both private school tuition fees and their share of the education taxes in support of the publicly funded schools.

These arguments were urged not only on the grounds of justice but also with repeated reference to the view that public goals can be realised in many ways. It must, therefore, be recognised that diverse communities have, within them, different preferences for educational goods and services, thereby creating a need for different models of school organisation. Thus, while education should be public in its finance and opportunity structure, it need not be public, or at least exclusively public, in its organisation. Finally, it was suggested that the current near-monopoly of the state in elementary and secondary schooling reduces competition, raises costs, lowers efficiency, and degrades the quality of the product delivered while, at the same time, imposing majoritarian ideologies and life-styles and making dissent less legitimate. By contrast, the commission was assured that the provincial funding of private schools would ensure the diversity appropriate to a pluralistic society (compulsory education never implied that all children be schooled in the same way); reconcile individual freedom with majority rule, the very difficulty that has so bedevilled efforts of boards of education to act as a socially cohesive force; stimulate competition and, therefore, quality; rid parents of double taxation; and allow the free exercise of conscience and religion within all income levels. Moreover, the existing public school system would not be threatened by this policy change since those making the argument envisioned no large-scale enrolment shifts from public to private schools as a result of any decision to provide new and provincial funding support to the latter.

Forceful counter-arguments were also presented. The three most common of these arguments were:

a.  Whatever one's view in principle, the current financial con-
    straint on the Ontario treasury and, consequently, on
    the funding of public schools makes any extension of
    public finding to private schools inappropriate, at least at
    this time;

b.  allowing the use of public funds to support and create private
    schools, many of which by their own admission would be seg-
    regated along lines of, for example religion or class, would
    be unwise since it would sanction the isolation of students
    in homogeneous groups and thereby not only abandon the
    advantages of a common acculturation experience but also
    foster a tendency among the students to think of other people
    as outsiders, an invitation to prejudice and intolerance:

c.  support of private schools erodes the financial and ideological
    support for public schooling and this, in turn, denies equality
    of educational opportunity to large groups of students by fos-
    tering a two-tier system of schooling inimical to the democratic
    traditions that public schools are intended to serve.

In support of these arguments, reference was made not only to the
various financial restraint programs of the provincial government
but, more importantly, to the experience of other jurisdictions, most
frequently of Australia and Great Britain, where private schools are
seen to have played a major role in keeping alive and legitimising
the ideology of class and, therefore, in exacerbating the divisions in
society. Overriding all these concerns, however, was a commitment
to the public schools as a source of common (not in the sense of *low*
but in the sense of *shared*) experiences and common opportunities
and, therefore, at least potentially, of a socially integrating sense of
purpose. This view stressed the great extent to which private schools
were seen as catering to individual needs rather than the social ends
of public policy. No claim was made that the rights of individual
students and their parents were irrelevant. What was, however,
emphasised was the likelihood that only in the public schools and
through the public schools could social decisions be funded and
reinforced. Those who argued against the public funding of private
schools also suggested – since the custom-tailored can be expected
to fit better than the ready-made – that such public funding would
result in substantial shifts in enrolment away from the public schools,
probably removing from the public constituency the most articulate
parents, those most likely to champion change, development, and
improvement in the public schools themselves.

   In terms of the three most common arguments advanced by the proponents of public funding for the private schools (i.e. parents rights,
discrimination *vis-à-vis* the province's Roman Catholic community,
and double taxation), the double taxation argument, although psy-
chologically strong (a private school parent is, in fact, paying both

a tuition bill and education taxes in support of the publicly funded schools), is nevertheless without real merit. First, the argument arises at least partly as an unintended consequence of a tax system which happens to itemise certain education levies but not other objects of public tax expenditure. Second, the argument confuses an education tax with a tuition bill, which is not the case. What the education tax represents is a general levy in support of what society has identified as a common good, a public school system. The raising of this or any other tax does not entitle a citizen to an opting-out process. Decisions concerning the raising and alloction of tax revenues are political decisions, and legal redress is available to individual citizens only through the periodic election process and the courts. Finally, the double taxation argument would seem to imply that: citizens without children (and, perhaps, citizens without children currently of school age) would not be expected to pay education taxes; that citizens with more than one residence are, or at least might be, not only double-taxed, but triple-taxed, quadruple-taxed, etc.; and that citizens education taxes should be in proportion to the number of their children. Each option is, of course, a potential public policy but not one is supported by any individual or group proposing the double taxation argument itself.

The argument arising from parents rights is, it seems, somewhat stronger. Parents are the first educators of their children and their continued active involvement in their children's schooling can contribute mightily to its success. Further, it is reasonable to suppose that providing parents with a greater range of choice and, therefore, increasing the chances that they will identify closely with the option selected will, in turn, increase the likelihood of active engagement in their children's schooling. Finally, in a democratic society individual choice is valuable for its own sake. On the other hand, although the idea of choice is important, it does not in itself define self-government or democracy as there are, for example, some things, such as slavery, which a democratic society cannot reasonably choose. Thus, I would *favour* the enhancement of parental choice without regarding such a choice as a *prior right*. Rather, parental choice is a desirable objective but one whose claims must be measured against the competing claims of other social policies and goals.

In contrast to this rejection of the double taxation argument and only partial support for the argument from prior parental rights, the argument against the status quo on grounds of discrimination against non-Roman Catholics is very strong. On moral grounds, limiting public support to Roman Catholic schools seems indefensible, for the constitutional provisions usually advanced to justify the special status of such schools serve only to describe its history. They do nothing to inform us about what we *ought* to do. In terms of this moral choice, it does seem inappropriate for Ontario to continue to offer to its Roman Catholic community an educational option not offered to other communities as well. It is true that a strict application of equity in this matter *might* limit any extension of this option to other religious communities, but the public good will not be served by involving the provincial government in decisions as to whether or not particular communities are to be considered as religiously defined.

On legal/constitutional as well as on moral grounds, the special status of the Roman Catholic schools is discriminatory. The relatively permissive nature of s.93 of The British North America Act − it specified only which schools must be funded and not which others could or could not be funded − when read together with the anti-discrimination provisions of the Canadian *Charter of Rights and Freedoms* provides a strong argument for the extension of public funding to private schools. The strength of this argument is increased by the recent extension of public funding to the secondary Roman Catholic schools since this appears more clearly an act of political will than fulfillment of a constitutional obligation. The government is, of course, clearly entitled to exercise this political will but not on a discriminatory basis. On the other hand, the arguments for maintaining the unique status of the Roman Catholic separate schools do not seem convincing. Thus, for example, the argument from the large size of the Roman Catholic community, while of some political and, perhaps, economic interest, is not convincing on either moral or legal grounds. Similarly, the argument from historical and constitutional status is, as suggested above, unconvincing morally. Further, its legal basis seems firm only if one suggests that a publicly supported denominational school system was an unfortunate historical mistake, one which may have to be supported or tolerated but which certainly should not be repeated. Given, however, the recent Canadian constitutional exercise during which the historical policy with regard to denominational schools was reaffirmed, the historical-mistake argument seems unconvincing with regard to the development of public policy. Since Ontario appears much more than casually determined to maintain and fund publicly the Roman Catholic schools, only very strong arguments about other public benefits could justify a continued policy of discrimination against private schools from other than Roman Catholic communities.

In terms of the three most common arguments advanced against public funding of private schools − social cohesion and tolerance, equality of educational opportunity, and spending priority − the spending priority argument is of little merit. Interestingly, the two most common premises of this argument are acceptable − that the public schools should be the priority public investment in education and that, at present, the public schools are underfunded. Nevertheless, it cannot be concluded that as a matter of public policy there should, therefore, be no extension of public funding to private schools − funding estimated at no more than $200 million annually, compared to the $6.5 billion per annum already being expended on the public elementary and secondary schools in the province. Further, since educators are fully engaged in maximising the funds to be made available to their work and then fully expending these funds in the interest of their students, it is hard to imagine a funding context in which the public school community, or any other school community, would see itself as having sufficient financial support to enable the funding of other systems to assume a first priority. The spending priority argument must therefore be rejected.

The social cohesion argument is on stronger ground. The argument has two facets. First, it posits the need, in a heterogeneous society, for more rather than fewer common cultural touchstones, arguing that the public schools (rather especially the board of education schools) represent the only institutional vehicle for providing a common but non-commercial experience for young Ontarians of, at least potentially, widely different personal and family backgrounds. While sympathetic with this view, I recognise that in many actual settings (for example the neighbourhood school or the separate school) the student body of a particular public school may be quite homogeneous. Nevertheless, a society should strive to realise some common socialisation experience, and public schools represent the most likely setting for this effort. It is not easy to imagine that largely segmented schools will lead to a cohesive social environment, though one cannot totally dismiss the alternative minority group argument that common settings can hurt their distinctive needs.

The second aspect of the social cohesion argument relates to tolerance. It is argued that in a multicultural society, tolerance is among the supreme civic virtues. It is, however, the unfortunate experience that, with some exceptions, schools, whether public or private, do not actually take this matter seriously in developing their own programs. Public schools too easily assume that the mere physical presence of various groups within their student bodies somehow, of its own accord, breeds tolerance and understanding. On the other hand private schools, most of which are religiously defined, rather too easily assume that piety produces good citizenship without taking into account that, for at least a number of religious groups, the claim to universality often means the spiritual repression of other religions and cultures. It must, however, be admitted that no one knows just which schooling experiences will produce understanding and tolerant adult citizens and that, from the point of view of minority groups, large-scale common settings are often repressive settings. One cannot help but recall, for example, Ryerson's own opposition to cultural diversity when he wrote in 1846 about the arrival of the Irish Catholic victims of famine (Ryerson, 1984, p. 300):

> It is therefore of ... importance that every possible effort should be employed to bring the facilities of education within the reach of the families of these unfortunate people that they may grow up in ...

industry and intelligence ... and not in the idleness and pauperism, not to say the mendicity and vices of their forefathers.

Nevertheless, in the absence of sure knowledge, it does seem plausible that tolerance and understanding will more likely arise from settings in which various groups are interacting rather than segmented and segregated – whether voluntarily or otherwise. Indeed, if the opposite is true, that is, if familiarity breeds contempt or, what is worse, contamination, then the very concept of a multicultural and pluralistic society becomes a contradiction in terms. Thus, I would argue that the context of the public school represents, whatever its past failures, the most promising potential for realising a more fully tolerant society.

With regard to the equality of educational opportunity, I agree with those advising against the funding of private schools. One of the historic missions of the public school has been to act as a kind of social mobility ladder for young people who do not bring to schooling special advantages of background, experience, and/or wealth. It cannot be claimed that this mission has always been achieved and that the public schools have always risen to Thomas Jefferson's historic call for an 'education to enable every man to judge for himself what will secure or endanger his freedom.' Indeed, it is often observed that the public schools help reinforce and maintain the high status of the exchange rather than the utility of credentials. This inevitably results in a hidden curriculum that favours the middle class and harms working-class children and values. Further, on occasion the public schools actively prevent citizenship and promote the stifling of government. Nevertheless, there have also been many successes and, more to the point, the alternatives seem even more unattractive. The great advantage of the private school is that it can focus its priorities and its programs to fit particular students (and their families). It is hardly surprising, therefore, that those for whom the school is designed find that it suits their needs more admirably than the public school which must, perforce, provide a program of much broader and less focussed dimensions. Thus, readily recognised individual advantage is provided by the private school – at least for those for whom the school is designed and who can afford its cost. The funding of these schools might make such advantages available without regard to parental income, and this could result in an increased interest in attending such schools although the actual extent of this new demand is difficult to forecast. The resulting benefits would be individual but their cost a social one encountered in the growing realisation that the seemingly legitimate parental desire to gain advantages for their children is something to be fully accomplished only at the expense of others. In any case, if such funding should result in any large transfer of either the higher achieving or the more affluent students from the public to the private schools, public schools (as the schools of second choice) could no longer offer equal educational opportunity. It is, of course, by no means certain that this outcome would occur. It would be, however, a rather large risk to take.

## Some matters of belief

In reviewing the various arguments and my response to them as outlined above, the emerging difficulty was how to envision future schooling arrangements for Ontario that would increase parental choice and address discrimination while not only maintaining but also enhancing – in the name of social cohesion, tolerance, and the quality of educational opportunity – the integrity of Ontario's public schools. In considering this matter, the language of rights tends to be rather absolutist and not, therefore, helpful when conflicting rights emerge. Second, in the matter of schooling, children's rights would be important, and, relative to these rights, it is difficult to determine whether it was society's (or the government's) vision of these rights or the parents' visions that should take precedence. Nevertheless, the question of values could not be entirely circumvented. Social viability is always based on a shared system of values, for it is only with common values that a truly shared existence (as opposed to mere coexistence) is possible. Thus, for example, in multicultural societies such as Ontario, among the common or shared values must be a conception of tolerance which demands respect for others and alternative points of view. This, in turn, is based on a commitment to such values as the minimal order required for dialogue, a respect for truth, the need sometimes to act for the sake of others, and so on. Of course, in any society there are conflicts of value and, therefore, alternative visions of what constitutes justice and appropriate social policy. In fact, such conflicts have historically shaped Ontario's policies in education. Thus, commitments to common schools and private schools start with values not subject to empirical demonstration and with beliefs about what sort of society Ontario should become – that is, with a vision of a preferred future expressed as a particular kind of schooling for the young. Policy making in education is, therefore, primarily political. As such, it must be seen – within a democracy – as a question to be settled, in the final analysis, not by social scientists but by elected officials or the courts.

Thus, the importance of values and the implications of different values and value systems for public policy with regard to schooling would be difficult to overestimate. Education is a dominant social concern and, although schooling is only part of society's much wider arrangements for education, the more complex and dynamic the society, the greater its need to clarify the function of its schools and their role in realising a better society. In this context and without any claim to a complete and comprehensive view, I believe that:

a.  elementary and secondary schools are important institutions whose goal is to develop, nurture, and enhance the intellectual and moral autonomy of the young; this goal and attendant responsibilities are shared with parents and other societal agencies;

b.  in a democratic society, this goal (i.e. intellectual and moral autonomy) is a social and individual good of sufficient importance to justify the compulsory schooling of children;

c.  such schooling should be made available so as to: (i) maximise the equality of educational opportunity, that is, the likelihood that persons will be prepared to realise their potential and to make informed and independent choices as to their future; (ii) provide for the shared responsibility of government and family – the family exercising its natural interest in and responsibility for the welfare of the child and the government acting on behalf of the interests of the wider society and as a protector of the rights of individual children; and (iii) ensure that, in a pluralistic and multicultural society, schools can contribute to strengthening the social fabric by providing a common acculturation experience for children.

It is clearly not logically necessary for governments both to finance and to provide educational services, but I do believe that the requirements of accessibility and accountability make such a double role entirely appropriate. Further, such a double role provides, in way that no other policy can, a context in which publicly funded schools are tied not only to the private purposes of self-interest and individual mobility – principles heavily weighted in favour of those already advantaged – but also to the provision of public service committed to improving collective and democratic traditions. Further, discussion and action about public and common schools presents at least a potential opportunity for citizens to become concerned about what is good for themselves or their children and what is necessary to bring about a more just and efficient society for others. Finally, to the extent that the public and common schools are chosen by most families, these schools can respect group differences while helping their students to perceive the common concerns that transcend such differences. Schools are better able to teach common understanding and shared values if they are less homogeneous and can, at least potentially, bring children of different backgrounds together. That is, I believe that:

d.  it is appropriate for the government to finance and provide an effective system of common public elementary and secondary schools that meet society's educational requirements for schooling; are accessible and open to all; are tuition-free; provide substantial opportunity for parental and community participation; represent the priority, but not necessarily the exclusive, public investment in education; and are the schools of choice for most young people and their families;

e.    *relevant constitutional issues aside*, no further obligation for the public funding of elementary and secondary schools exists.

Constitutional issues must, of course, actually be considered. In addition, none of the above denies the value of private schools. Thus, for example, in a heterogeneous society, the arguments for a common acculturation experience can be overstated so that dissent and variation are suppressed in favour of some single, necessarily imperfect vision; and, unfortunately, the public school community has not always avoided this pitfall. Past failures should not, however, rule out the present potential of the public schools in which it should, in principle, be possible both to widen and to deepen the existing social consensus by capitalising on our differences without unnecessarily institutionalising them. I, however, believe that:

f.    there should be no legal public monopoly in education, and private schools that meet the minimum standards specified by the government in terms of obligation to society and individual children should have a clear status in recognition both of the rights of citizens to make alternative choices and of the general value of diversity;

g.    moreover, diversity within the public school system should also be encouraged.

Finally, although — again, constitutional issues aside — no obligation for the public funding of private schools may exist, some public assistance to private schools might, nevertheless, be a feature of a creative public policy. Thus, I believe that:

h.    as a matter of public policy, and so long as the public policy objectives outlined above are not substantially eroded, new initiatives both in public support of private schools and in the relationship of these to the public schools should be actively developed and tested.

Given both this framework of belief and the importance of dealing more equitably with the constitutional issues of discrimination raised by the funding of the Roman Catholic separate schools, Ontario should modify its current arrangements with regard to private schools. The particular recommendations of the Commission on Private Schools in Ontario can be found in its report but, although these recommendations were regarded by the commission as appropriate, I cannot argue that they are the uniquely correct way to proceed. Whatever policy route Ontario elects to take, it is, however, likely to succeed only if all of those involved are prepared to summon up their resources for cooperative, perhaps even conscionable, behaviour. Interestingly, Green (1984) has described a variety of aspects of conscience among which are the conscience of membership (i.e., the recognition that we must sometimes act for the sake of others) and the conscience of sacrifice (i.e., the willingness to override the pursuit of self-interest and act beyond the limits of mere duty). The success of any proposed program will, in fact, depend to no small degree on the extent to which these aspects of conscience are exhibited by the government, by the boards of education schools, by the private schools, by the separate schools, and by the many communities and individuals to which each relates and responds.

**References**

Green, Thomas (1984) *The Formation of Conscience in an Age of Technology*, San Antonio, The John Dewey Society.

Lawton, S (1985) 'Alternative methods of financing private schools in Ontario,' in *The Report of the Commission on Private Schools in Ontario*, Toronto, The Government of Ontario, pp. 81–108.

Ryerson, Egerton (1984) *Journal of Education for Upper Canada* (Vol. 1), Toronto, J H Lawrence.

## 9.2 Should there be religious alternative schools within the public school system?
*Ralph M Miller*

### The problems

Arguments over possible religious alternative schools within public school systems are typically conducted in a tone of certainty unjustified by the principles and information on which particular conclusions, for or against such placement, are based. The arguments over religious alternative schools are frequently dogmatic in that some participants claim to know or speak as if they know that it is simply wrong to have a religious alternative school within the public school system while others evince equal conviction in maintaining that religious alternative schools can properly be included within public school systems. This paper will show that the argument is most uncertain and that, in spite of our long history of public education and considerable effort to distinguish *religious* from *public* education, it is now more than ever difficult to determine whether to include religious alternative schools within the public system.

By *religious alternative school* I mean a school which exhibits some or all of the following characteristics:

a. it provides an optional program of religious instruction;
b. religious exercises such as prayer or reading from scripture are regularly conducted but again optional;
c. interest in working in a religiously oriented school and personal religious convictions are considered when assigning staff;
d. there is an attempt to maintain a religious ethos in the school.

Some of these characteristics may be puzzling. For example, why should religious instruction be optional in a religious alternative school? If such a school is to be included within the public school system it must operate within the provincial regulations (in Canada) governing public schools; in the Province of Alberta, for example, the School Act (s. 160) stipulates that 'a board may (1) prescribe religious exercises for pupils in its schools and (2) permit religious instruction for pupils in a school.' However, the School Act (s. 163) also states:

> On receipt by a teacher of a written statement signed by a parent requesting that a pupil be excluded from religious or patriotic

exercises or instruction, or both, the pupil shall be permitted to leave the classroom or may be permitted to remain without taking part.

This mixture of legislation allowing religious exercises and instruction with exemptions exists in every province of Canada except Quebec and Nova Scotia.[1] What is missing in Quebec and Nova Scotia is the right of the pupil to be exempted from religious exercises or instruction; however, that right has been resolved beyond question by a legal judgment in Quebec in 1975 (*Chabot* v. *Les Commissaires d'écoles de Lamorandière*, 1957, p. 796). Thus there is no constitutional prohibition of religion in *public* schools in Canada, and legislation allowing religious exercises and instruction would not be subject to challenge under s. 7 (Legal Rights) of the *Charter of Rights and Freedoms*. Indeed, s. 29 of the *Charter*, consistent with Canadian legislation since 1867, recognises the paramount rights of Protestant and Catholic minorities in Canada:

> Nothing in this Charter abrogates or derogates from any rights or privileges guaranteed by or under the Constitution of Canada in respect of denominational, separate, or dissentient schools.

If religion is permitted in public schools and if the rights of Protestants and Catholics (when they are the minority) to tax-supported denominational schools are widely recognised, is there not discrimination in favour of Catholics and Protestants in respect of religion in public (tax-supported) schools? Further, does not the promulgation of legislation asserting individual rights, particularly the *Charter of Rights and Freedoms*, strengthen the case of non-Christians for recognition of their religious concerns within the public (tax-supported) schools?

As a final twist to the perplexities of religion in public schools, is it possible that a case can be made for the rights of non-Christians *without* equally making a case for the rights of various Protestant denominations?

## Protestant, Catholic, and non-Christian schools

It may seem that these questions are pertinent only in jurisdictions which, as in Canada, permit religious exercises or instruction. However, with the growing support for voucher systems and the increasing readiness to allow for cultural distinctiveness of pupils, some jurisdictions which think the issue of religious schools has been laid to rest by such events as the US Supreme Court decision against prayer in schools may find it resurrected in a new guise.

The increasing emphasis on individual rights opens the way to questions about the appropriateness, or even the justice, of maintaining public school programs which are presumed to serve all students irrespective of religious affiliation or lack thereof. In Canada, where publicly supported schools have been identified as Protestant and Catholic since before Confederation and have been protected in legislation since then, the question is: Why should only two classes of persons, identified on the basis of religion, be recognised and provided for in legislation pertaining to schools?

This question was addressed in the case of *Hirsch* v. *the Protestant School Commission of Montreal* (1928), a case which was carried to the Privy Council, then the highest court of appeal. The Council's judgment on the protection afforded to denominational schools by the British North America Act and subsequent legislation is most significant. (1928, 202, p. 213)

> The statute protects the rights which at the union belong to the Roman Catholic population as a class, as well as those belonging to the Protestant population as a class; but to treat both members of both denominations, who substantially made up the whole population of the province at the time of the union, as forming together a 'class of persons' with a right to object to the establishment of any school not under Christian control, would be to give a meaning to the statute which its words will not bear. It appears to their lordships that it would be possible to frame legislation for establishing separate schools for non-Christians without infringing the rights of the two Christian communities in their denominational schools; and they agree with the Supreme Court that legislation confined within those lines would be valid.

If legislation permitting separate schools for non-Christians would be valid in any jurisdiction which permits Protestant and Catholic (or public and separate) schools, thus allowing non-religious schools, Hindu schools, Moslem schools, and so on, then the possibility of specific Protestant denominations having religiously distinctive schools may also have to be allowed. Put the case that the public schools (as in Calgary) are nominally secular, that there are no religious exercises nor any religious instruction, and that in their work teachers cannot favour any religious group. Suppose that such a secular school climate is particularly pleasing to the non-religious, agnostic, or atheistic. Could not any and every Protestant then argue that their legal rights as a class of persons to have denominational schools have been infringed, that the public schools, having become non-religious, the creation of a non-Christian school system, as allowed for in the judgments of the Supreme Court and the Privy Council, had in fact been accomplished, and that the purposes of the existing legislation can then only be realised through the creation of a new Protestant school system?

The issue recently arising in Alberta is whether alternative Christian schools may rightfully be established within a public school board in a jurisdiction in which the public schools are *not* Catholic. One legal opinion provided to the Edmonton Public School Board holds that such schools would be 'constitutionally unobjectionable' if established so as not to infringe the rights of the Roman Catholic minority to have a separate school system to educate their children and not to infringe the restrictions on religious instruction.

To recapitulate, schools supported by taxes and freely accessible to the public were organised in Canada on a denominational basis, and their existence has been confirmed by statute. For many years, the practice of treating the population as largely Roman Catholic and Protestant and of organising tax-supported schools on that basis was unquestioned. When questioned, it was held that the educational rights afforded to Protestants and Catholics could properly be afforded to non-Christians. Now that we are more mindful and more respectful of the religious diversity of our society, and with the non-Catholic tax-supported schools accommodating this diversity by becoming more secular, it can be questioned whether Protestants have not effectively lost some of their religious rights in education. Equally, it may be argued that religious groups other than Christian *may* have educational rights which have not been enacted.

## Secular public schools

Other questions of religion in education were raised in Alberta in the case of *Regina* v. *Wiebe* and, although this case concerned the right of parents to remove their children from the public schools and educate them in private religious schools, the judgment had ramifications for public education. What led Judge Oliver to find in favour of the parent (Wiebe) was that: 'The law of Alberta would, *without first permitting him recourse to the courts*, penalise him for this (removing his child from the public school) on the basis of absolute liability' (*Regina* v. *Wiebe*, 1978, p. 36). The grounds of judgment are very narrow for, as was pointed out earlier by Judge Oliver, 'What is important is the possibility of discrimination inherent in a system where public officials and *not the courts* have the final say.' In his ruling, Judge Oliver held that the Department of Education Act, which reserved final decision to public officials, was on that account 'rendered inoperative by reason of the Alberta Bill of Rights ... because it denies to the accused, Elmer Wiebe, freedom of religion guaranteed by Section 2 of the Alberta Bill of Rights.'

The significance of the judgment is in what followed, namely, the Minister of Education announced in the legislature that the regulations of the Alberta Department of Education would be revised to allow a fourth category of private schools (*Communications*, 1978, p. 1):

> ... which receive no government funds. Such schools will be required to follow either the Alberta curriculum or a course of studies approved by the minister, but will not be required to employ certified teachers. High school programs in such schools will not be accredited.

Under this regulation there would be no basis for action against Wiebe as his child would have been in a Category 4 private school.

In preparing to approve the programs of schools employing uncertified teachers, the Department of Education seemed to be accepting the position urged by the defence in *Regina* v. *Wiebe*: namely, 'Character and quality is required in teachers as a child will imitate its teachers, and thus parents at home should have the final say concerning the selection of teachers' (testimony of Mr. Hiebert).

The wider significance of the judgment is also indicated in Judge Oliver's comment:

> A close study of the citations from Drybones, Robertson and Rosetanni, Adelaide, and Yoder[2] does however lead me to the conclusion that, where it can be shown in a particular case that religious beliefs are irrefutably and irrevocably linked to education, a foundation has been laid for the application of the Alberta Bill of Rights where freedom to educate children in conformity with those beliefs is infringed upon.

It is also important to note Judge Oliver's observation:

> The accused ... has not refused to send his child to school, only to a particular school where, among other factors that are abhorent to his religious beliefs, he says that the teachers are indoctrinated in a liberal value system unacceptable to him or his church.

Should other judges be of like mind, objections to the doctrines of the secular school, related to the argument that secular humanism is a kind of religion, will carry weight when parents argue for the appropriateness of different educational dispensations. Recognition of a parent's right to seek a particular religious emphasis in education, combined with the willingness of the Department of Education to approve schools not employing certified teachers, give the Wiebe case emphasis beyond the question of private schools.

Suppose that the public schools in a district are effectively secular: would it not then be the case that parents wishing a Protestant emphasis in the education of their children could argue that their children are subjected to an abhorrent doctrine? Protestant parents with this view have recently (in Calgary) argued to establish religious alternative schools within the public school system. They established such a school under school board regulations which had originally allowed the establishment of two Jewish alternative schools. As of June, 1984, the school board majority, elected in 1983 on the platform, 'Save public education,' refused to renew the contracts of the three alternative schools operated, thus excluding them from the public school system.

While the public school board has the legal right to refuse to renew these contracts, it is not clear whether legal action could successfully establish that parents have a right to have their religious convictions accommodated by means of special arrangements such as designated alternative schools. Such action might be taken under s.15 (equality rights) of the *Charter of Rights and Freedoms*, which provides 'equal protection and equal benefit of the law without discrimination and, in particular, without discrimination based on race, national or ethnic origin, colour, *religion* ...' (emphasis added). The legal force of the *Charter*, in combination with the scope for claims of discrimination may well afford grounds for action.

## Separation of church and state

What I have tried to demonstrate, to this point, is that in Canada there is considerable ambiguity concerning religious rights in education because of the denominational basis of Canadian systems of tax-supported education. There is also more ambiguity than commonly thought concerning religious rights in education in the United States, and I wish to comment, in particular, on the point that the principle of separation of church and state (SCS) is not a well-defined principle and its application requires judgment.

So long as church and state exist within the same society, there will be some form and degree of connection between them, and therefore to know what SCS means it is necessary to know in what respects and to what extent the state is deemed to be separate from the church or churches. More specifically, such declarations of principle as that embodied in the First Amendment to the United States Constitution, 'Congress shall make no law respecting an establishment of religion, or prohibiting the free exercise thereof,' do not define SCS, for the granting of tax exemptions to churches means that the state encourages churches by giving them advantages not given other organisations. Some sense of religious impartiality is conveyed by the fact that tax exemptions are granted to all churches, but even if no church is favoured more than others or no church is established as a national church, the churches are still not completely separate from the state.

It is important to remember that the point at issue when the idea of SCS is invoked is to determine actions which public legislative bodies may or may not take with respect to churches or to matters respecting religion. A tax exemption is clearly an action. While SCS may be greater now than in the days when the church could invoke the secular arm to enforce ecclesiastical judgments, even a long list of changes in interaction between church and state is not necessarily the same as effecting a complete separation. So long as there is *not* complete separation (and I reiterate that complete separation is not possible in the lived world), then SCS requires definition. This definition can only be in terms of the practices of a particular society, and, once we embark upon such a process of definition, we define the limits of practical action rather than delineate a principle.

Nor will it serve to argue that the differences in access to tax funding for denominational schools mean there is SCS in the United States but not in Canada. If such a claim is advanced, the argument has become circular, for the meaning of SCS is now taken to be the very tax support or lack thereof which the principle of SCS is used to justify.

Whatever SCS means, it must mean something more or something other than that there be no public funding of religious schools. As demonstrated previously, what this something more or other may be is far from clear. To cite a few further examples of the connection of church and state, the use of oaths taken on the Bible in courts of law, the assignment of chaplains to legislative bodies, the recognition of religious ceremonies of marriage as legally binding, and the recognition of clergymen as persons who can attest to declarations on some civil documents all constitute state recognition of the powers of the church or its representatives with respect to some state functions. Such recognition establishes some relations between church and state.

We might further note that as recently as 1968 the US Supreme Court upheld a New York state law requiring local public school authorities to lend textbooks free of charge to all secondary students whether in private or public schools. The comment in the court opinion that 'the line between state neutrality to religion and state support of religion is not easy to locate' (Feldman, 1976, p. 103) is most apt to the present discussion. When we come to separate church and state in the daily affairs of our society, it is manifestly not easy to locate that line of separation.

In the United States, the issue is confused further by the growth of the Christian school movement which, in the main, strenuously resists state regulation of education and hence state funding. However, some fundamentalist groups are more inclined to argue for state aid for religiously oriented schools. The two viewpoints are cited by Reese (1985, p. 193):

A Baptist minister from Buffalo . . . denounced the idea of tax credits. 'We feel Christian education should not be subsidised from other people's pocketbooks. Besides, anytime there is a subsidy, it opens the door to interference.' . . . When the Packwood-Moynihan tuition tax credit proposal was debated in Washington in the late 1970s, *Christianity Today* observed that the bill had various types of supporters, including 'many evangelicals who support private schools.' Jerry Falwell and other television evangelists, who represented groups that had historically opposed state aid because they believed it violated the First Amendment, had done an 'about face' on this policy question.

Should a coalition of Catholics, Lutherans, and traditional parochial school supporters who have long argued for state funding be joined by the fundamentalists and by some supporters of individual rights, there might be sufficient political support to effect change in legislation. Even if such an effort would have to be carried to the level of constitutional amendment, it must be remembered that under democratic processes majority opinion can change any legislated state of affairs such as the denial of public support for religiously distinctive schools. Ultimately, the question of public support for religious education is political, and arguments over SCS or any other issue, such as right of choice, are essentially arguments for or against possible political decisions.

Thus to recognise the role of various issues, including issues of principle, in the political process gives added point to the meaning and weight assigned to the so-called principle of separation of church and state. The discussion, to this point, has shown that SCS is more like the expression of the confused practices of various societies with respect to the relation of church and state than the expression of a principle which serves to clarify those practices.

## Practical reasons

Given the difficulty of arguing from the SCS, questions about the propriety of religious alternative schools within public school systems should be settled on practical grounds by considering the possible consequences of establishing such schools. It is, for example, contended that the creation of religiously based schools may result in misunderstanding and intolerance if pupils are hived off into separate schools and associate only with their religious brethren. If we accept that religious toleration is desirable, then a practical question is whether religiously distinctive schools are detrimental to religious toleration. If we cannot demonstrate that religiously distinctive schools result in more intolerance, then this argument against them fails. It is at least suggestive that in Canada, where publicly supported schools identified as Protestant and Catholic have existed since before Confederation, there has never been any problem in electing and accepting a Catholic prime minister, whereas religion was still an issue in the election of John F Kennedy.

### *Viability*

A practical argument against religiously distinctive schools within the public system is that given the variety of religious groups in large modern societies — particularly, we might say, in North America — we must consider whether the school system could, in practical terms, accommodate all the groups who might wish such schools. No school board could undertake to choose among religious groups. So long as a religious group was within the law and had a sufficient number of adherents (for a school board could specify the minimum number of students needed to establish a school), there would be no reason for the school board to deny that group's request while allowing any other religious group a school. In brief, if any religiously distinctive schools are to be allowed, then they must all be allowed. This argument is fraught with all the dangers of extreme arguments, for it is highly unlikely that each religious group would want its own school. However, school boards must consider the possible consequences of the fact that one religiously distinctive school establishes the precedent which will then justify any other such school.

A further consideration is important to the school board, and this was evident in the Wiebe case cited. The school board resisted declaring that the children, though not in the public school, were under effective instruction because the viability of the public school was threatened by the loss of the pupils in question. The greater part of public school funding comes from provincial grants paid on a per-pupil basis.

The possible loss of pupils and of grant funding is also an argument for religious alternative schools within the public system for, should such schools be developed privately, any migration of pupils to them will reduce grant funding to the public schools. The viability of individual schools is more dramatically affected by the development of alternative programs. When the first Logos Christian School was opened in Calgary, for example, a public school with declining enrolment, a prime candidate for closure, rapidly became a full school with almost 400 students. People in the community — with prior access to the school as their neighbourhood school and not subscribing to its religious emphasis — were glad to have a viable school in their district. Moreover, the school was able to offer all the program benefits of a large elementary school and attracted families with children into the area.

Public schools losing students to private or independent religious schools may therefore suffer on two accounts: first, the loss of per-pupil grants and, second, the loss of enrolment which make it difficult to maintain programs in specific schools. On this point, it is interesting to consider events consequent on the termination of the alternative school contracts by the public school board in Calgary in the case discussed above. The Jewish and Hebrew alternative schools now operate under the auspices of the Calgary Catholic Board of Education, and a recent repoit estimates a transfer of $1.4 million of annual tax revenue to the Catholic system during 1985 (Public board fears, 1986, p. B-1). Thus, there is increased potential for financial pressure when, as in most provinces and territories of Canada, there exists *more than one* tax-supported system of education. For if either system is then willing to accommodate alternative schools, the transfer of local asessment which may result combined with provincial funding for the number of pupils involved can lead to a significant shift of resources.

## Selectivity

A second practical argument concerns the selective nature of any distinctive school. Those parents organising a distinctive school and facing the possible added cost and effort of getting their children to such a school (for presumably there will not be such a school in every neighbourhood) care about their children's education. They must make an extra commitment, serve on the committees, and support the fund-raising needed to keep a special school in operation. They provide that support from the home which makes the work of the school go better. By banding together in their own school, they concentrate their supportive influence, and the good effects of their concern for education are lost to other schools in the system.

We must seriously question whether the public school system can provide a sound education for all children if groups of parents who care the most withdraw into distinctive schools or even into alternative schools contained within the public school system. It may be argued, in turn, that alternative schools can result in centres of interest which arouse the support of parents who would otherwise not be committed or so extensively committed to the support of a regular school. Further, it may be argued that parents always support a specific school, that is, the school which their child attends, and that there is little or no parental support for the system as distinct from support for 'their' school. Goodlad has recently commented on the specificity of parental attitudes towards schools (1984, p. 36):

> The quality of schools and schooling is not very good, but the school down the street to which our own children go isn't bad − in fact, it's quite good. At least this kind of mixed vision is what is suggested by some Gallup Polls of the late 1970s and supported by the responses of the parents in our sample.

If this is true, does the school system lose because parents support an alternative school? There is no research information to settle such practical questions, and there is at least the possibility that total public involvement in and support for the public schools may increase with a variety of alternative public schools appealing to the interests of various groups.

Religiously distinctive schools may become select schools in another way. A group of parents supporting a distinctive school and joined by adherence to a common faith may be inclined to raise money to provide extras for their school. In this regard, it must be pointed out that fund raising is a part of life for virtually every public school and is carried on through spellathons, bottle drives, sales of chocolate bars, and so on. Short of banning such activities completely, there is no way of setting limits to fund raising, for who can establish what would be a *reasonable* level of fund raising? Can the mothers who operate the school lunch program help it if they earned $20,000? (This figure was one part of the funds raised in one Calgary public school.) Therefore, if the parents supporting a distinctive school extend themselves to provide funds for books, computers, and science equipment, who is to say they should not?

This requires further elaboration. If alternative schools are allowed, can they be restricted only to religious alternative schools? Consider a group of parents in an area of a city forming an educational improvement association or some other praiseworthy association and wishing to support the development of an alternative school with an academic emphasis. If religious groups can raise funds to support their preferred schools, who is to say that other parents may not do the same? Such an extension of the alternative school concept seems to strike more directly at the concept of a public school system, for parental input and effort focussed on particular schools can result in some having more resources than others. Such a process would increase the socio-economic differences already existing among various public schools.

I do not use such terms as *selective schools* or *advantaged schools* lightly, and it is clear that alternative schools will be select and advantaged to some degree. It is difficult to determine how much selection and advantage are to be allowed within public education. On the one hand, we do not wish to fall prey to the simplistic dogma that all schools must be equal. On the other, we must be careful not to exacerbate inevitable differences. Creating inequities is *not* the same as failing to achieve equality.

## The common school

Since large public school systems already offer different programs ranging from those for the learning handicapped to those for the gifted, programs differentiated as vocational and academic, and a wide variety of options, it may well be asked why hesitation exists in introducing further variety into the public schools. Are programs which are related to learning needs, career expectations, or individual interests different in principle from programs organised on the basis of religious need or religious interest? I believe they are and insist that, irrespective of pupils' religious backgrounds or interests, a school must try to address their learning needs and, if that requires a different program, such a program then be available for all who may benefit from it without regard to their religious affiliation.

Goodlad is worth noting on this point for it pertains to his defence of the common school. In his chapter, 'Access to knowledge,' he argues strenuously for a common curriculum for 70 to 80% of school time and contends (1984, p. 161)

> ... if the school is to be anything other than a perpetuator of whatever exists in society, states and local school districts must set − if they have a mind to − school policies that to some degree transcend and minimise the role of the classroom as reproducer of the culture.

Thus, to defend the public school as a major common experience for all students (with particular emphasis on its responsibility to give students, as much as possible, equal opportunity to qualify for employment and advancement) is directly to challenge the arguments for all forms of alternative education or parental choice in education except insofar as those choices are founded upon identified individual differences such as physical disabilities or learning handicaps.

Translating this into the language of individual rights, do parents have absolute rights in choosing education for their children such that the state cannot enforce minimum standards or effect control of the curriculum? While the issue may not often reach this pitch, there are schools, for example those of the Hutterites in Western Canada, which offer a very limited curriculum and in which few students advance beyond the level of junior high school. Because children in Hutterite colonies can find a place and become respected and productive within the colony on the basis of such education, and particularly because they never require social assistance from the larger society, it is easy to overlook the limitations of this education. Nonetheless, the claim to parental choice cannot be absolute and unlimited unless we conclude that children have no rights or that the state is not properly acting in the common good when it regulates education.

I return, finally, to the question of toleration, for surely much of the effort to develop the public schools is motivated by the concern that children of the entire community learn common values and learn to live with and respect each other. Even if this goal is an ideal, the means for achieving it can be assessed in practical terms. Unfortunately, the information is far from decisive, so we cannot prove that children attending schools differentiated on the basis of religion are less tolerant of people of other faiths than those who attend public schools. Can we even demonstrate that racial prejudice has been reduced by the desegregation of schools?

However, research limitations do not make the issue any less practical. If toleration and some community of values are desired, it seems highly likely that such outcomes will be advanced more by some school arrangements than by others. Rather than simply declaring religiously distinctive schools to be a cause of intolerance, we must understand the actual effects of such schools. Should we discover that such schools do foster intolerance, then there is an argument against allowing the schools.

This short excursion through three practical arguments is, I hope, sufficient to indicate a major difficulty. We have little or no evidence with which to settle such arguments. Perhaps that is why we tend to fall back upon dubious arguments of principle. As I have previously argued, the principle of SCS may be most uncertain, but those who embrace it 'know' that religious alternative schools must not be allowed within the public school system. Furthermore, persons who have come to that conclusion need not be troubled by any lack of evidence of the consequences of the existence of such schools.

In a society which gives more prominence to individual rights and in which various interest groups make more diverse claims upon social institutions, particularly the public schools, it will not be easy to demonstrate that the ideal of the common school should be maintained. Perhaps a careful regard for the practical consequences of religious alternative schools within public school systems may inform and moderate the debate and the resultant decisions. The quality of education and the upbringing of youth are far too important to be left as matters of doctrinaire dispute.

### Notes

1.  The variety of accommodations for religion in tax-supported schools in Canada is as follows: British Columbia, single non-denominational public system but with some provision for textbooks, health care, and transportation for independent schools; Nova Scotia, New Brunswick, Prince Edward Island, and Manitoba, informal arrangements for funding denominational schools; Ontario, Saskatchewan, Alberta, Northwest Territories, and Yukon Territories, separate school systems; Quebec, dual confessional system; Newfoundland, denominational system (Wilson, 1981, pp. 102–103).
2.  The judgments in *Regina* v. *Drybones* (*Supreme Court Reports*, 1970, p. 282) and *Robertson and Rosetanni* v. *The Queen* (*Supreme Court Report*, 1963, p. 651) deal with 'particular religious practice' and 'discrimination.' In 1963, the Supreme Court held that the Lord's Day Act, restricting the operation of businesses on Sundays, did not constitute the imposition of particular religious practices on persons of a differing faith or none. The court held that Sunday closing was a long-established custom marking Sunday as a day of rest rather than a particular religious observance. In 1970, the Supreme Court held that Drybones, an Indian who had been convicted for a liquor violation under the Indian Act, should be acquitted because the Canadian Bill of Rights took precedence over a law which discriminated against a particular group.

    The case of *Wisconsin* v. *Yoder* in 1972 was the instance in which the US Supreme Court upheld the right of the Amish to keep their children from public school and to provide their own schooling, usually terminating at Grade 8. The case involving the Adelaide (Australia) Company of Jehovah's Witnesses centred more on the validity of powers given to the governor-general to act in the interest of national security than on religious rights.

## References

*Chabot* v. *Les commissaires d'écoles de Lamorandière* (1957) *Dominion Law Reports*, 12, 2d.

*Charter of Rights and Freedoms* (1982) Ottawa, Publications Canada.

*Communications* (Information bulletin, 14) (1978) Edmonton, Alberta Education.

Feldman, David (ed.) (1976) *The Supreme Court and Education* (3rd ed.), New York, Teachers College Press.

Goodlad, John I (1984) *A Place Called School: prospects for the future*, New York, McGraw-Hill.

*Hirsch* v. *The Protestant School Commission of Montreal* (1928) *Appeal Cases, The Law Reports*.

Public board fears shrinking tax base (1986) *The Calgary Herald*, January 23. p. B-1.

Reese, William J (1985) 'Soldiers for Christ in the army of God: the Christian school movement in America,' *Educational Theory*, 35(2), pp. 175–194.

*Regina* v. *Wiebe* (1978) *Western Weekly Reports* (vol. 3).

*Supreme court reports* (1963) Ottawa, Registrar of the Court, Supreme Court of Canada.

*Supreme court reports* (1970) Ottawa, Registrar of the Court, Supreme Court of Canada.

Wilson, J Donald (1981) 'Religion and education: the other side of pluralism,' in J Donald Wilson (ed.), *Canadian Education in the 1980s*, Calgary, Detselig Enterprises, pp. 102–103.

# 10. Empirical perspectives on distinctiveness

This chapter provides three examples of different research strategies which have attempted to identify and qualify the distinctiveness of church schools, both within the state maintained and independent sectors.

In the first article, Brenda M Gay analyses the public statements made by independent schools in England about themselves in two major school yearbooks. She utilises this information to profile independent schools associated with the Church of England, giving particular attention to the involvement of clergy, religious education and school worship.

At the time of writing Brenda Gay was an Honorary Research Associate of the Culham College Institute for Church-Related Education. A fuller version of this article, including more tables, was first published as chapter 4 in her monograph, *The Church of England and the Independent Schools*, published by the Culham College Institute in 1985.

In the second article, the Revd Professor Leslie J Francis analyses the attitudes of 338 teachers working within the state maintained church schools in Suffolk. He is concerned to assess their attitudes towards the church school system, towards the distinctiveness of church schools, and towards traditional and progressive educational methods. He concludes that younger teachers are less likely to be churchgoers and that teachers who are not churchgoers are less likely to be favourably disposed towards the church school system.

In the third article, the Revd Professor Leslie J Francis compares the presence of church-related educational perspectives in county schools, Church of England voluntary aided schools, Church of England voluntary controlled schools and Catholic voluntary aided schools throughout Gloucestershire. He concludes that there is greater evidence of church-related perspectives in church schools, but that the religious beliefs of head teachers are also significant in determining the church-related character of both Anglican and county schools.

Leslie Francis is D J James Professor of Pastoral Theology at Trinity College, Carmarthen, and St David's University College, Lampeter. The study of teachers in Suffolk was first printed as chapter 8 in his book, *Partnership in Rural Education*, published by Collins in 1986. The study of schools in Gloucestershire was first printed as chapter 12 in his book, *Religion in the Primary School*, published by Collins in 1987.

# 10.1 The Church of England and the Independent Schools: a Survey

*Brenda M Gay*

## The scope of the survey

This survey focuses on the 458 independent senior schools in England which were listed in either the *Public and Preparatory Schools Yearbook* or the *Girls School Yearbook* for 1983. The schools listed in these yearbooks form the very large majority of what would be recognised as the major independent secondary schools in the country, and together they educate nearly two-thirds of all the secondary pupils in this sector. As the study is concerned with the Church of England's role in independent education, schools in Scotland, Wales and Northern Ireland have been excluded.

### Research method

Various alternative research strategies were examined at an early stage. An attractive option would have been to send a detailed questionnaire to each of the 1,300 or so senior schools listed in the Independent Schools Information Service (ISIS) publications but that option was ruled out for this first study on the grounds of political complexity and cost. Instead it was decided to make use of one readily accessible source of information, namely the public statements made by the schools about themselves in the two year-books. Although this information was not presented in completely standard form, nevertheless there was sufficient consistency for it to form a useful source of basic information about each of the schools. It is very much hoped that subsequent work will be able to follow up many of the issues raised here in much more detail and with more sophisticated research methods. This would inevitably require the full co-operation of the schools and would best be done on a collaborative basis.

From an initial reading of the yearbooks it was possible to derive a set of questions which could be answered from the information provided. These questions included the style of the school in terms of whether it was single sex or co-educational, boarding or day; the size of the school; its religious foundation; clerical representation on the governing body; staffing; religious education and worship. A questionnaire was devised which was then used to obtain information from each of the school entries. The information was computer coded and then analysed using the SPSS routines. What follows is based on the numerical evidence provided from this study.

The question arose as to how far this particular group of schools is representative of the independent secondary sector as a whole. There are a few large and/or prestigious schools, for example Millfield, which do not appear in the yearbooks but they are sufficiently small in number not to distort the overall findings. Conversely many of the very small schools are omitted, but precisely because they are small they are not a major influential factor in the independent sector. One group of schools which is significantly under-represented in the yearbooks is the Roman Catholic schools. Figures derived from *The Parents' Guide to Independent Education* (1984) indicate that there are 33 Roman Catholic schools, each with more than 300 pupils, which are not included in the yearbooks. However, as the major part of this survey is concerned with the Church of England schools this is not a major problem. Only a relatively small number of Anglican schools are not included in the yearbooks and these tend to be those with small pupil numbers.

To what extent can one rely upon the information provided in the yearbooks? The information is provided by the schools themselves and so is arguably not 'hard' factual information but rather information that the schools wish the readers to see. Clearly some of the statements, particularly those relating to the school's aims, may refer more to pious hope than actual reality, but even in these instances the fact that schools wish to convey particular impressions is in itself significant. There is, of course, a problem over the interpretation of silence on a particular issue. For example, the lack of comment about Sunday communion services may simply mean that the school assumes that readers would take it for granted that such services are provided and therefore not mention them in the yearbook entry. A significant amount of the information used is, however, straightforward factual information about which there can be relatively little ambiguity.

## The size of the independent secondary sector

The Department of Education and Science (DES) lists 2,338 independent schools in England in January 1982. Unfortunately the list does not distinguish between type of school and so there is no way of knowing the proportion of preparatory, secondary and all-through schools. However the schools are listed according to pupil size, and of the total number of schools 78% have under 300 pupils. In all, the DES identifies 513 schools with over 300 pupils and this compares with 336 schools with over 300 pupils identified in the yearbooks. In terms of reasons for the difference between these two totals, three issues go a long way towards an explanation. Firstly, a number of preparatory schools will have more than 300 pupils.

Secondly, as the DES list covers all-age schools, there will be some schools which have under 300 pupils in their secondary departments but which exceed 300 when their junior or preparatory departments are included. Finally, a number of secondary schools with over 300 pupils have not been included in the yearbooks.

The DES also lists the total number of pupils in independent schools for each year group and according to regions. In January 1982 there was a total of 311,198 pupils between the ages of 11 and 19 in independent schools. Of this total 172,295 (55%) were boys and 138,903 (45%) were girls. Overall 6.2% of the total pupil population in England is being independently educated. The north-south divide comes through very clearly with three times the proportion of pupils being independently educated in the south-east (9.3%) as in the north (2.8%).

The 458 schools covered by this survey educate approximately 204,000 pupils between the ages of 11 and 19, representing approximately 66% of all the independent school pupils of this age range.

## Characteristics of the survey schools

The first section of the analysis involved collecting data about each school in terms of school size; whether the school was a member of the Head Masters Conference (HMC), the Girls Schools Association (GSA) or the Society of Head Masters of Independent Schools (SHMIS); whether the school was single sex or co-educational; whether the school was day or boarding; and the religious affiliation claimed by the school.

In terms of size only a small number of the schools had fewer than 200 pupils (11.6%) or more than 800 (8.1%). Almost half (48%) fell within the middle range of 300 to 600 pupils. The girls schools were on average smaller and the boys schools larger.

By virtue of their inclusion in the yearbooks, the schools were members of either one of the three associations or were girls schools not belonging to GSA. 84% of the boys schools were members of HMC while the remaining 14% were in SHMIS. 87% of the girls schools were members of GSA and the remaining 13%, while listed in the yearbooks, were not members of any formal group.

In terms of the single sex/co-educational dimension, 50% of all the schools in the survey were single sex girls schools, 40% single sex boys schools and the remaining 10% were co-educational. Although a number of boys schools admitted girls in the sixth form, schools were only coded as co-educational if girls and boys were admitted throughout the school. In terms of school numbers it can be seen that the girls schools form a slightly higher percentage of the total yearbook schools than boys, and co-educational schools are in a small minority.

In terms of the residential dimension, four measures were used to determine school style on the day/boarding continuum. Schools were categorised as mainly boarding if they had fewer than one-third of their intake as day pupils. Those schools which had between a third and two-thirds of their pupils on a non-residential basis were categorised as mixed boarding and day schools and those with less than a third of their pupils as boarders were categorised as mainly day. Those schools which had no boarding provision whatsoever were categorised as total day schools. Boarding figures included pupils who were resident on a weekly basis. Approximately half the schools are day (29%) or mainly day schools (19%) and the other half boarding schools (33%) or those with a major boarding element (18%).

In order to compile the religious affiliation of the schools, in those cases where yearbook entries did not state the religious affiliation of the school the ISIS booklets were used. Only 5.7% of all the schools failed to state their religious affiliation. Of the 458 schools, 79% claimed some religious affiliation. Church of England schools accounted for 56.3%, educating approximately the same percentage of the total pupil numbers. Undoubtedly the Roman Catholic proportion is understated due to the exclusion, already noted, of a significant number of Roman Catholic schools. Only 15% of all the schools explicitly disclaim any religious affiliation but even these schools, and also those which omit mention of any religious affiliation, may in practice have some of the outward symbols of Anglicanism such as chaplains, clerical governors and Church of England patterns of worship.

Although there may well be a significant difference between what a particular school says is its religious affiliation and the attitude it adopts to religion within the school context, the fact that a school claims a religious affiliation is in itself significant and an important starting point for an examination of the religious dimension within schools.

## The Church of England schools

The 258 schools which see themselves as being Anglican either by foundation or by tradition do not themselves form a homogeneous group. Some were monastic foundations which were refounded after the reformation as church schools; others were charitable foundations provided by individual benefactors or companies in the sixteenth and seventeenth centuries and have in their statutes explicit references to the teaching of religion.

In the nineteenth and early twentieth centuries there was a rapid expansion of independent schooling and many of the schools founded during this period established close links with the Church of England. 30 girls schools were founded by religious orders; 11

schools were the result of the initiative of the Woodard Corporation, 33 were established by the Church Schools Company, 18 schools were under the aegis of the County Schools Movement and 14 were set up by the Allied Schools Movement. Furthermore, leading churchmen were active in raising money to found individual schools which, although seen as firmly Anglican, had no formal structural links with other schools. Some of the nineteenth century foundations were established in response to the perceived threat from Roman Catholic, nonconformist or non-denominational schools and others were explicitly to provide education for children of Anglican clergy.

During the twentieth century there have been some closures, mergers and additions to schools within these different categories. Today although there are some distinctive groups, the majority of Anglican schools do not specify a particular category of foundation.

## Some institutional characteristics of the schools

Of the 56% of all schools which claim some allegiance to the Church of England, a higher proportion (65%) are boys schools, whereas the figure is lower for co-educational schools (53%) and even lower for girls schools (50%).

When the balance between the various types of school is compared on a Church of England basis and on a total basis, some interesting differences emerge. Whereas girls schools form 50% of all the schools in the study, they only account for 45% of the Church of England schools. This difference may partly be explained by the 22 Girls Public Day School Trust schools which were established on an explicitly non-denominational basis. By contrast the boys schools form a smaller proportion (40%) of all the schools, but they account for 46% of those claiming Anglican allegiance. The co-educational schools are roughly equally represented in both categories. The explanation for the greater likelihood of boys than girls schools being Church of England is largely an historical one.

In terms of the residential dimension, 62% of all the Church of England schools are either boarding or mainly boarding schools. The percentage is slightly higher for boys schools (62%) than for girls schools (56%). Overall the Church of England schools form a larger percentage of all the boarding schools in the two yearbooks than they do of day schools. 70% of all the mainly boarding schools, 66% of the mixed boarding and day schools, 57% of the mainly day schools and 37% of the total day schools claim Church of England affiliation.

Anglican schools are proportionally over-represented on HMC and under-represented on GSA. Out of all the HMC schools in the yearbooks, 65% of them claim Anglican allegiance whereas of the 207 GSA schools only 50% are Anglican.

In terms of school size as measured by pupil numbers, the Church of England schools account for roughly a similar percentage in each size category and there is certainly no evidence to suggest that Church of England schools are over-represented amongst smaller schools. However when one looks at the schools on the single sex/co-educational dimension, it is found that the girls schools tend to be smaller than the boys' schools.

## The governing bodies

One of the formal structural links between the independent schools and the Church of England is through the governing bodies of schools. While it is extremely difficult to determine how much influence individual governors have on school policies or indeed how much time individual governors spend in schools, it is possible to look at the number of clerics on governing bodies as their very presence is a potential source of influence. Obviously there will be many lay governors who are also Anglicans, but this information is not easily accessible in objective form from the yearbooks and indeed it can also be argued that clerics represent at a more formal level the structural links with the Church of England. Therefore it was decided to enumerate the number of clergy who are members of governing bodies. From the data, a picture emerges of a considerable involvement by clergy, including the two archbishops, a high proportion of bishops and many other senior clerics.

At the top of the formal management structure of most schools is the visitor. Very often the role and duties of the visitor are shrouded in mystery and indeed a very useful piece of work could be undertaken on the constitutional and practical aspects of the office of visitor. Whatever else the visitor may be, he or she almost invariably appears in a prominent place in the school prospectus and has an important symbolic role in underwriting the overall style of the school. An examination of the visitors of the Church of England schools reveals that of the 119 Anglican schools which list a visitor, 17% have an archbishop, 53% a diocesan bishop, 7% a suffragan or other bishop and 1% a dean. Thus of all the schools which list a visitor, 77% have a senior cleric. Interestingly, with one exception, a mitre seems an essential qualification for an ecclesiastical visitor.

One stage down from the visitor in hierarchical terms, although much more important in practical terms and a crucial figure in the overall management of the school, is the chairman of the governors. Here senior clerics, perhaps because of the workload, are in evidence in much smaller numbers.

Of the 227 schools which list their chairman, only 30 have a clerical chairman (13%). While a mitre seems necessary for a visitor, other clerics, and particularly deans, come more into their own as chairmen.

From the 211 schools which listed their governors it was possible to examine the role of the episcopate within governing bodies generally. The two archbishops are between them governors of five schools, and 20 diocesan bishops between them hold 27 school governorships, of which only seven are in girls schools. 11 retired and 20 suffragan bishops between them hold 53 school governorships.

When these governorships are examined according to the style of school, it is found that 72% of the governorships held by diocesan bishops (including the two archbishops) and 77% of those held by suffragan and other bishops are in boarding schools. Furthermore, 59% of the governorships held by diocesan bishops and 58% of those held by suffragan and other bishops are in boys schools, whereas only 28% held by diocesans and 34% by other bishops are in girls schools (the remainder being in co-educational schools). This suggests that the episcopal involvement as governors is biased towards boys schools and the boarding sector.

A further analysis using the names of the bishops from the yearbooks was undertaken and it was found that both archbishops and 35 of the 41 diocesan bishops are involved as visitors or governors. Only 8 diocesan bishops have no formal structural involvement with the independent sector and there are only 4 dioceses in which there is no involvement on the part of either the diocesan or a suffragan bishop as a visitor or governor of an independent school.

Not all the bishops are governors or visitors of schools in their own diocese and indeed one of the features of the independent sector is the way in which bishops regularly cross diocesan boundaries to attend governors meetings. Even when the school is in a bishop's own diocese, he is frequently on the governing body in a personal capacity rather than as a formal representative of the diocese.

Because of the importance of the structural links between the independent sector and the Church of England as represented by the bishops, it was decided to do a supplementary examination of the educational background of those bishops involved in the independent schools. *Who's Who* gives the educational background of the large majority of bishops. Among those for whom information was available, over half the diocesan bishops and archbishops were educated at independent schools (56%). This was then related to the holding of governorships to see whether those who had attended independent schools were significantly over-represented as governors or visitors of independent schools. It was found that bishops who have themselves been educated at independent schools are not more or less likely to hold governorships in the independent sector or to be visitors of schools than those who have been educated at state schools.

At the governing body level, non-episcopal clerics are well represented. Twenty-three school governorships are held by deans, 19 by
archdeacons, six by members of religious orders and 148 by other
clerics. In terms of the type of school there is no significant sex bias
here. Deans are more likely to be found on the governing bodies
of boys schools and archdeacons on the governing bodies of girls
schools, but the overall balance of clerics is roughly equal.

In addition to ecclesiastical involvement at the governing body
level, clergy are also involved in the management of independent
schools through their membership of the Council of the Church
Schools Company and the Divisional Chapters of the Woodard
Corporation.

The total picture presented is one of a significant potential
influence by clerics on the policies of the schools through the governing bodies. Just what this potential influence is in practical terms
is a crucial question and one that requires further investigation.

## Clergy in the staffroom

Recently, there has been some considerable discussion about the
possibility of the independent sector making inappropriate demands
on the ordained manpower of the Church of England. An attempt
has been made therefore, using the staff lists in the two yearbooks,
to ascertain the number of clergy on the staffs of the independent
schools.

At the beginning of the twentieth century the headmastership of
a public school was a recognised route to ecclesiastical preferment
and 'if you looked up a copy of *Crockford*'s for 1920 you would
probably find at least a dozen serving bishops who were formerly
headmasters of public schools. Today you will find none' (Nott,
1984). Only four of the Church of England schools in the yearbooks have ordained headteachers and a further four have ordained
deputy heads who also act as chaplains. Unlike the Roman Catholic
schools where there are eleven heads who are members of religious
orders, none of the Church of England schools have such heads.
There is, however, one girls school, maintained by a religious order
but not listed in the yearbooks, whose headteacher is a member of
the order.

Today the formal institutional presence of religion in the schools
is largely mediated through the school chaplains. Information about
the school chaplains was collected from the yearbooks under three
main headings: whether a chaplain was listed or implied in the staff
list; whether his appointment was full-time, shared with a parish, or
a largely parish appointment; and whether the chaplain was resident
on the school site. Of the 258 schools, 163 (63%) list a chaplain; 10
imply that there is a chaplain; 10 do not give any staff list; and the
remaining 75 list the staff without mentioning a chaplain.

In some cases it was difficult to determine whether the chaplain is full or part-time, resident or non-resident. Only 14 schools specify that the chaplain is resident but many boarding schools with a full-time chaplain would have taken residence for granted and so not thought to mention it. In all, 108 schools state that they have a full-time chaplain of which 76 are boys schools, 15 girls schools and 17 co-educational schools. Two boys, three girls and one co-educational school state that their chaplain is part-time and a further two girls and one co-educational school explain that the local parish priest acts as chaplain. The remaining 46 schools which say they have chaplains do not mention the nature of his appointment.

In general there is a much greater likelihood of there being a chaplain in boys than in girls schools and in boarding than in day schools. Frequently the chaplain in boys schools also teaches religious education, whereas in many girls schools the chaplaincy is separated from teaching and so there is a much greater likelihood of chaplaincy duties being performed by a local parish priest. Furthermore in girls schools the practice of female lay chaplaincy is gaining ground.

The position of the chaplain in the staff list may give a useful clue as to his status in the school. In four schools the chaplain is listed as the deputy head; in 48 schools, including the Woodard schools, he is listed as second or third in the hierarchy; in seven schools he is listed with the housestaff; in two instances as a head of department and in 72 cases he is included generally among the list of staff. In a further 33 instances the chaplain is listed with the support staff such as the administrative officer and the matrons. However, one problem in assessing how far the position in the hierarchy of the staff lists reflects a chaplain's influence with the school's official structure is that a number of chaplains are part-time, especially in the girls schools. What is really needed is a substantial and detailed study of the role of the chaplain in the school. This study can only provide some pointers.

It is also possible to identify from the staff lists the number of other ordained staff in the schools. Fifteen schools specify an assistant chaplain, one school has two assistant chaplains and Eton has four assistant chaplains. Fifty-seven other ordained clergy are mentioned in the staff lists although not all of these would necessarily be Anglicans as there has been a long tradition of Free Church clergy teaching religious education in schools.

In the 248 Anglican schools in the yearbooks which gave staff lists, the total ordained manpower actually mentioned is 255, consisting of four ordained heads, four ordained deputies who also act as chaplains, 159 chaplains, 21 assistant chaplains, 57 other ordained clergy and there are 10 instances where a chaplain is implied but not specifically named. In addition to these 255 clergy specifically identified, there will be a significant number of others who come into the schools either as part-time chaplains or teachers.

## The religious commitment of the school

The information contained in the previous sections was relatively objective and easy to quantify from the yearbooks. This next section deals with data that was less easy to define with such exactness. Schools vary considerably in the amount of information they provide about themselves, with some giving little information, perhaps on the grounds that their reputations are sufficient to attract prospective parents or because they consider that it is only by a visit to the school that parents can gain a satisfactory impression. However, many schools do provide quite detailed information about their curriculum and aims. Of particular interest was the information they gave about religious education, worship, confirmation and the relationship between Christian principles and various aspects of their corporate life.

Clearly considerable care has to be taken in interpreting the material. Information in the yearbook is designed to attract prospective customers and so is frequently couched in very general and perhaps somewhat optimistic terms. Furthermore the fact that a school omits any reference to a particular aspect of the religious dimension does not necessarily mean that this aspect is absent in the school. Of the 258 schools claiming an Anglican allegiance, 34% (27 boys schools, 55 girls schools and 5 co-educational schools) gave little information about themselves and so have been excluded from all numerical calculations in this section.

In terms of **religious education**, each school's yearbook entry was studied to see whether it mentioned religious education in the curriculum list for the lower school, as a general subject at fifth and sixth form level, as an optional or compulsory O level and as an option at A level. Statements about religious education were also examined for any indication of denominational or Christian weighting.

Naturally there are some difficulties in interpreting such data. A school may have assumed that parents would take it for granted that the curriculum would include religious education and so not feel it necessary to mention it. Many schools, in discussing the range of O level subjects, frequently say 'The usual O levels are taken and in addition ...' In these cases it is not immediately clear as to whether religious education is counted as a 'usual subject.' In some instances schools clearly state that religious education is taught according to a denominational or Christian emphasis, whereas others may well feel that this would be automatically assumed and therefore make no specific mention of it.

When Church of England schools were compared with other types, it was found that roughly the same percentage (36%) of Roman Catholic and Church of England schools state that they give specific denominational teaching. The Roman Catholic schools had the highest percentage (66%) which state that religious education is taught with a Christian emphasis (this category includes those schools mentioned above which say they give a denominational emphasis to their religious education teaching). This compares with the Church of England (50%), inter-denominational schools (40%), Quaker schools (20%), Free Church schools (14%) and Methodist schools (7%). Interestingly 5% of the non-denominational schools state that their religious education has a Christian emphasis and indeed some of these schools make very positive statements about their Christian commitment.

In terms of religious studies as a compulsory O level subject, 7% of the Church of England schools and 8% of the Roman Catholic schools specifically state that all pupils will take the subject. The highest proportion of schools mentioning religious studies as an optional O level are the Free Church ones (71%), followed by the Methodist schools (30%), Roman Catholic schools (29%) and the Anglican schools (20%). A similar position emerges over statements about religious studies as an A level option, mention being made as follows: Free Church schools (42%), Methodist schools (31%), Roman Catholic schools (29%) and Church of England schools (21%). The percentage of Anglican schools stating that they teach fifth form general religious education was only 36%, being lower than the Roman Catholic (41%), Quaker (40%), and Free Church (42%) schools. At the sixth form level 29% of Roman Catholic schools, 26% of the Church of England schools and 15% of the Methodist schools make specific mention of some religious education being taught at this level. In terms of the general inclusion of religious education in the curriculum list, it is found in the entries of 85% of the Free Church schools, 77% of the Anglican ones, 76% of the non-denominational schools, 70% of the Roman Catholic schools, 69% of the Methodist schools.

A subsequent analysis then divided the Anglican schools according to whether they are mainly boarding or mainly day schools (see table 1). It was found that there was little difference between boarding and day schools in the percentage which say they teach religious education with a denominational or Christian emphasis. A higher percentage of day schools state that religious education is an O level option, whereas all but one of the schools which teach this as a compulsory O level are boarding schools. There is relatively little difference between the type of schools and the percentage which say they offer A level or make specific mention of religious education at fifth and sixth form level. However a far larger percentage of day schools include it in the curriculum list.

*Table 1: Religious education in Church of England schools[1]*

| Style of school | | Total N of schools | 1 Denominational emphasis % | 2 Christian emphasis % | 3 Optional 'O' level % | 4 Compulsory 'O' level % | 5 Optional 'A' level % | 6 Fifth year % | 7 Sixth year % | 8[2] Curriculum list % |
|---|---|---|---|---|---|---|---|---|---|---|
| boys: | boarding | 56 | 30 | 43 | 21 | 16 | 21 | 55 | 39 | 75 |
| | day | 36 | 19 | 39 | 36 | 3 | 28 | 56 | 36 | 86 |
| | total | 92 | 26 | 41 | 27 | 11 | 24 | 55 | 38 | 79 |
| girls: | boarding | 36 | 36 | 50 | 14 | 3 | 14 | 3 | 6 | 61 |
| | day | 24 | 71 | 79 | 17 | 0 | 17 | 13 | 13 | 100 |
| | total | 60 | 50 | 62 | 15 | 2 | 15 | 7 | 8 | 77 |
| co-educational: | boarding | 17 | 35 | 47 | 6 | 6 | 24 | 24 | 12 | 59 |
| | day | 2 | 50 | 100 | 0 | 0 | 50 | 100 | 100 | 100 |
| | total | 19 | 37 | 53 | 5 | 5 | 26 | 32 | 21 | 63 |
| all schools: | boarding | 109 | 33 | 46 | 17 | 10 | 19 | 33 | 24 | 68 |
| | day | 62 | 40 | 56 | 27 | 2 | 24 | 40 | 29 | 92 |
| | total | 171 | 36 | 50 | 20 | 7 | 21 | 36 | 26 | 77 |

Note:   1.   This table is based on the 171 Church of England schools which provide reasonable or full information about themselves in the yearbooks. It excludes the 87 schools (27 boys schools, 55 girls schools and 5 co-educational schools) which give little information about themselves in the yearbooks.

2.   Columns 1 to 8 are as follows – schools say:

1 – Religious education is taught with a denominational emphasis.
2 – Religious education is taught with a Christian emphasis: this subsumes those schools which are listed in column 1.
3 – Religious education is taught as an optional 'O' level.
4 – All pupils take religious education as an 'O' level.
5 – Religious education is available as an optional 'A' level.
6 – Religious education is taught in the 5th Year.
7 – Religious education is taught in the 6th Year.
8 – Religious education is specifically mentioned in the curriculum list.

When boys, girls and co-educational schools are compared (see table 1) a higher percentage of girls schools state that religious education is taught with either a denominational or Christian emphasis. Compulsory religious studies is most frequently referred to in the boys boarding schools. In only one boys day school and in no girls day schools was religious studies mentioned as a compulsory O level. A very low percentage of girls schools specifically mention religious education as a general fifth or sixth form subject. This may be because a large number of boys schools divide their curriculum entries into lower, middle and upper sections whereas the girls schools tend not to do this and perhaps feel that it is sufficient to mention religious studies once in the curriculum list. The difference between schools on O and A level provision may reflect the fact that there are more small girls schools than boys schools with the result that some girls schools are likely to carry fewer O and A level courses.

Information about **school worship** was derived from the yearbooks under a number of separate headings (see table 2). There are clear cautions over interpretation; the fact that a school does not mention a particular aspect of worship, for example Sunday services, could mean one of several things. It might be that the school does not have Sunday services; equally the school may have Sunday services but does not feel that this is a sufficiently significant aspect of the school's life to mention in the yearbook; or it could equally mean that the school assumes that parents will take it for granted that because there is a chapel Sunday services are held.

In general terms, as can be seen from table 2, on all but two of the indices connected with worship the greatest proportion of schools making positive statements are the co-educational boarding schools. Looking at all the schools in table 2, 64% of them mention the existence of a chapel, nearly half make mention of weekday and some denominational services, 44% hold Sunday services and slightly over a third explicitly refer to school confirmation services. In general, on all the indices connected with worship, positive statements are made more frequently by boys than girls schools and by boarding than day schools. Recognising that many of the co-educational schools are in practice boys schools which have diversified, then undoubtedly the strongest emphasis on school worship is to be found in the boys boarding schools, a reflection perhaps of the clerical schoolmaster tradition.

Regarding **confirmation,** information was collected from the yearbooks as to whether a school mentioned confirmation services or preparation. The Public Schools Commission of 1968 had noted that there was a change in direction towards voluntary attendance at services and that in many Church of England schools confirmation had become a matter of personal choice. As a result of this, the Commission predicted that there would be a drop in numbers

*Table 2: School worship in Church of England schools[1]*

| Style of school | Total N of schools | 1 Denominational services % | 2 Weekday services % | 3 Sunday services % | 4 School chapel % | 5 Use parish church % | 6 School communion services % | 7 Confirmation mentioned % | 8 Provision for other groups % | 9[2] Chapel choir % |
|---|---|---|---|---|---|---|---|---|---|---|
| boys: | | | | | | | | | | |
| boarding | 56 | 64 | 64 | 66 | 88 | 16 | 18 | 48 | 7 | 32 |
| day | 36 | 33 | 42 | 25 | 47 | 22 | 3 | 33 | 0 | 14 |
| total | 92 | 52 | 55 | 50 | 72 | 18 | 12 | 42 | 4 | 25 |
| girls: | | | | | | | | | | |
| boarding | 36 | 36 | 31 | 39 | 53 | 22 | 3 | 31 | 14 | 3 |
| day | 24 | 21 | 25 | 8 | 25 | 17 | 8 | 12 | 4 | 17 |
| total | 60 | 30 | 28 | 27 | 42 | 20 | 5 | 23 | 10 | 8 |
| co-educational: | | | | | | | | | | |
| boarding | 17 | 76 | 71 | 76 | 94 | 24 | 12 | 59 | 24 | 35 |
| day | 2 | 50 | 100 | 50 | 100 | 0 | 0 | 100 | 0 | 0 |
| total | 19 | 74 | 74 | 74 | 95 | 21 | 11 | 63 | 21 | 32 |
| all schools: | | | | | | | | | | |
| boarding | 109 | 57 | 54 | 59 | 77 | 19 | 12 | 44 | 12 | 23 |
| day | 62 | 29 | 37 | 19 | 40 | 19 | 5 | 27 | 2 | 15 |
| total | 171 | 47 | 48 | 44 | 64 | 19 | 9 | 38 | 8 | 20 |

Note: 1.  As with table 18, this table is based on the 171 Church of England schools which provide reasonable or full information about themselves.
2.  Columns 1 to 8 are as follows – schools say:

1 – Some services are of a denominational character.
2 – Pupils attend weekday services.
3 – Pupils attend Sunday services.
4 – The school has a chapel.
5 – The school uses a local parish church for some school services.
6 – Communion services are held in school.
7 – Opportunities are provided for pupils to be confirmed.
8 – Members of other religious groups have some provision made for them in terms of worship.
9 – The school has a chapel choir.

being confirmed. However, Ellis (1984) argued that 'a large number of them (i.e. pupils) – the majority at Marlborough and no doubt at most other traditional boarding schools – are confirmed.' The present survey shows that just over a third of the schools which gave more detailed information about themselves in the yearbooks specifically mention confirmation preparation and confirmation services at school and in a number of such schools confirmation preparation is in the hands of the head and the chaplain. There is an apparent discrepancy between Ellis' statement and the statements which the schools themselves make about confirmation. It may well be that more schools provide confirmation opportunities than the statements in the yearbook suggest and also that pupils are already being confirmed elsewhere before they come to their secondary school or are confirmed in their home parishes. If, as it appears, confirmation is not regarded by the majority of the schools as a strong selling point, it would be interesting to know from current trends within schools just how long Ellis' statement is likely to remain valid.

Regarding **the relationship between Christian principles and the corporate life of a school,** one might expect that Church of England schools would reflect their Christian tradition in the general aims of the school, their corporate life and in the curriculum. Therefore each school's entry in the yearbook was examined to see whether the school makes statements about these aspects. Some schools, particularly the Woodard schools, lay great emphasis on these aspects. One co-educational school, King Edward's Witley, states 'the school was founded as a result of Christian concern and it still aims to provide a full education that has a Christian setting within a caring community.' Felixstowe College, one of the Allied schools, aims 'to provide a sound education based on the Christian faith.'

Of the 171 Anglican schools which gave detailed or average information about themselves, 37 reported that their general aims were related to Christianity, 27 that Christian principles were present in the corporate life of the school and only nine that Christian principles were specifically related to the curriculum. Given the small numbers overall, caution should be exercised in any further subdivision, but it does appear that boarding schools made more of a feature of their Christians aims and principles than day schools, and co-educational schools more than single sex schools. This hypothesis would, however, need testing out by a more detailed study.

## Conclusions

It has clearly emerged from the survey that the Church of England has a very considerable stake in the independent sector. Of the 458 schools used in the survey, 56% of them educating some 114,000 pupils claim Anglican allegiance. These schools represent some two-thirds of all the independent schools in the country and therefore on a very conservative grossing-up basis it is reasonable to assume that at least 150,000 pupils nationally are educated in schools which would claim some association with the Church of England. By contrast, in the maintained sector of education only 4% of all secondary schools are either voluntary aided or controlled Church of England schools and they educate some 125,000 pupils. Thus it would appear that there are more pupils in Anglican schools in the independent sector than in the maintained sector.

For historical reasons a higher proportion of boys schools than girls, and boarding than day schools, are Anglican by either foundation or tradition.

The survey has also highlighted the potential influence of the clergy on the policy and ethos of Church of England schools through their role as governors or visitors. However, many clerical governors sit on governing bodies in a personal rather than a mandated capacity and although they may have a strong influence on a school's decision making they are not necessarily expressing Church of England policy. The episcopal link with independent schools is strengthened by the amount of time many bishops spend visiting such schools for confirmation and other services. The survey has also produced evidence of the considerable input into independent schools from other clergy acting in chaplaincy and teaching capacities.

Despite the difficulty in quantifying information about the religious commitment of the schools, there are some indicators such as the statements made by the schools about religious education, worship, opportunities for confirmation and the inclusion of Christian aims in the curriculum and corporate life of the schools. It does seem that a significant proportion of the Anglican schools continue to make positive statements about their religious commitment and affiliation. Undoubtedly in practice a much higher proportion of schools have a positive religious affiliation and what has been revealed in this section respresents a base line. It is hoped that subsequent work might reveal just how far above the base line this affiliation and commitment is in reality.

Finally, while this survey has revealed some important general pointers to the relationship between the Church of England and the independent schools, much more detailed investigation is needed to elucidate the full subtlety and complexity of the interrelations between religion and education in the independent sector. The next stage in the research process is reported in Gay (1993).

### References
*Crockford's Clerical Directory 1980–2*, London, Oxford University Press.
Department of Education and Science, *School Statistics for January 1982*, London, HMSO.

Ellis, R (1984) 'The head, the chaplain and school religion,' published paper from the Bloxham Conference.

Gay, B M (1993) 'Religion in the girls' independent schools,' in G Walford (ed.), *The Private Schooling of Girls: past and present*, pp. 187–206, London, Woburn Press.

*Girls School Yearbook* (1984) London, Adam and Charles Black.

Nott, P (1984) 'Towards a theology of leadership,' published paper from the Bloxham Conference.

*The Parents' Guide to Independent Education: 4th Edition* (1984) Maidenhead, SFIA Educational Trust.

*Public and Preparatory Schools Yearbook* (1983) London, Adam and Charles Black.

Public Schools Commission (1968) *Report of the Public Schools Commission*, London, HMSO.

# 10.2 Partnership in rural education: teacher attitudes

*Leslie J Francis*

## Introduction

Francis (1986) describes a detailed survey into the attitudes of teachers working in church of England voluntary aided and voluntary controlled schools throughout the diocese of St Edmundsbury and Ipswich. The research was conducted by a self-completion questionnaire, using multiple choice and Likert type attitude items (Likert, 1932). These items had been developed and refined in close consultation with teachers, clergy and governors and carefully piloted before the survey.

During the course of one term each school was visited and the purpose of the questionnaire was explained to the headteacher. Wherever possible, the individual teachers were also seen personally. All told, questionnaires were distributed to 519 teachers; 338 of them returned their questionnaire thoroughly and carefully completed, making a response rate of 65%.

Examination of the teachers' responses to the individual attitude questions by means of correlational techniques and factor analysis identified three key attitudinal dimensions underlying the individual teachers responses to their work in church schools. I will attempt to define these three key attitudes briefly and then return to examine them in greater detail.

The first key attitude represents an overall response to the church school system. Teachers vary greatly in their overall acceptance of the church school system. At one end of this attitudinal continuum are those who are favourably disposed to the church school system and at the other end are those who are unfavourably disposed to the system.

The second key attitude represents the way in which the teachers view the relationship between church schools and county schools. Again, teachers vary greatly in the way in which they understand this relationship. At one end of this attitudinal continuum are those who argue that church schools should be identical with county schools in their ethos and practice, while at the other end are those who assert strongly the distinctiveness of church schools. The point is that those who are most in favour of the church school system are not necessarily those who also wish to assert the greatest distinctiveness of church schools.

The third key attitude represents the way in which the teachers understand their actual role in the classroom. At one end of this attitudinal continuum are those who see their work in terms of what we have already styled traditional educational methods, while at the other end are those who favour progressive educational methods. Having suggested that many of the differences between the individual teachers can be summarised in terms of these three key attitudinal continua, I now need to take the argument two stages further. First, I need to demonstrate precisely what I mean by these three attitudinal continua: how, in practice, can we recognise them? Second, I need to demonstrate how this extra information about the teachers attitudinal structure can be of practical use: are we any closer to being able to understand why individual teachers hold the views they do? For example, put in more concrete terms, is it likely that the men and women who teach in church schools see their functions differently? Do the older teachers differ much in their views from the younger teachers? Do those who practise the Christian faith tend to have a different view on the value of church schools from those who are not practising believers?

## For or against church schools

The first attitude scale sets out to identify the issues which are best able to distinguish between those teachers who are in favour of the church school system and those who are not in favour of it. The statistical procedures of item analysis selected the sixteen items which most satisfactorily satisfy this question. These items are set out in table 1, together with an indication of the way in which they cohere to produce a unidimensional scale. The internal consistency of these items produces an alpha coefficient of .8523, which demonstrates that the items cluster together very satisfactorily to form a cumulative scale.

These sixteen items demonstrate that those who are most in favour of the church school system tend to say things like 'I applied for my present post specifically because it was in a Church of England school,' 'Anglican parents should be encouraged to send their children to a Church of England school,' and 'the Church of England should develop more secondary/middle/upper schools.' Those who are most hostile to the church school system say things like, 'the Church of England school system has outlived its usefulness,' 'Church of England schools should be given over to the state' and 'the Church of England has too many schools.' Closely associated with the individual teachers stand on these polarising issues are their views on the relationship between

*Table 1: Scale of attitude towards the church school system*

| Scale item | Corrected item-total correlation |
|---|---|
| I applied for my present post specifically because it was in a Church of England school | + .5069 |
| The Church of England has too many schools | − .5400 |
| There is no such thing as a specifically Christian view of education | − .3833 |
| The Church of England should develop more secondary/middle/upper schools | + .5819 |
| Church of England schools should teach their pupils about the communion service | + .5184 |
| The Church of England school system has outlived its usefulness | − .6212 |
| Christian education is the job of parents and the church, not schools | − .4033 |
| It is not the task of Church of England schools to initiate children into a religious faith | − .2915 |
| Church of England schools should be given over to the state | − .6069 |
| Church of England schools should encourage pupils to accept the Christian faith | + .4939 |
| The diocese should foster links between Church of England schools and local churches | + .5239 |
| It is educationally unsound for Church of England schools to try to teach the Christian faith | − .4453 |
| Church of England schools are racially divisive | − .3448 |
| The idea of 'worshipping' God in school assembly should be abandoned | − .4376 |
| Anglican parents should be encouraged to send their children to a Church of England school | + .5434 |
| The Church of England spends too much money on church schools | − .4591 |

church and school and the relationship between religion and education. Those in favour of church schools tend to believe that the school system should teach about the church and encourage pupils to accept and practise the Christian faith, while those against church schools tend to believe that the task of Christian education should rest with the churches and with parents rather than with the school system and that it is inappropriate for schools to ask pupils to participate in signs of religious commitment like worship and prayer.

Since the teachers have responded to each of these items on a five point scale, ranging from five for the most favourable response through one for the most unfavourable response, it is now possible to calculate a cumulative scale score for each teacher by adding together their responses for each of the sixteen items. The sixteen item scale thus produces a range of scores from sixteen through eighty.

Elsewhere in the questionnaire, the teachers were asked to specify the kind of school in which they would actually prefer to teach. If this scale successfully distinguishes between those who are favourable to the church school system and those who are unfavourable towards it, there should be a high correlation between the scores on the scale and stated school preference. This is a way of checking that the scale actually measures what it sets out to measure, and is technically known as a method of confirming 'construct validity.' The results are very satisfactory: those who state their preference as teaching in a Church of England aided school score 65.4 points on the scale; those who opt for a Church of England controlled school score 57.6 points; those who opt for a county school score 49.5 points. Those who say that they have no real preference between a church and county school score 53.8 points, a score higher than those who opt for a county school, but lower than those who opt for a controlled school.

The next stage is to examine how much the individual teachers attitudes for or against the church school system are related to other factors. The factors I shall take into consideration are age, sex, present teaching grade, pattern of church attendance, the differences between those who teach in aided and in controlled schools, the differences between middle schools and the first or primary schools, and the admissions policy of the school. The statistical procedure used to explore these relationships is known as path analysis (Keeves, 1988). The results are shown in path model one.

Path diagrams show relationships in terms of straight lines and arrow heads. I have followed the convention of locating the outcome variable in which we are interested, the attitude score, at the bottom of the page, while the variables which are likely to influence the attitude score are listed from the top of the page in the order in which they were entered into the equation. For example, sex and age appear at the top of the page because they are logically prior to all the other factors and not subject to any influence from them. Church attendance comes next as a personal characteristic, and the more specifically job related characteristics follow on from that. This convention means that all the arrow heads logically point down the page. Where downward progressing arrows are not drawn into the diagram, it means that statistically significant relationships do not exist; for example, in path model one no lines appear between age and attitude or between teaching grade and attitude.

We will begin the interpretation of the path diagram by looking at the heading 'teaching grade.' The arrow between age and teaching grade (+.13) confirms the expected outcome that those in more

Path model one
Attitude towards the church school system

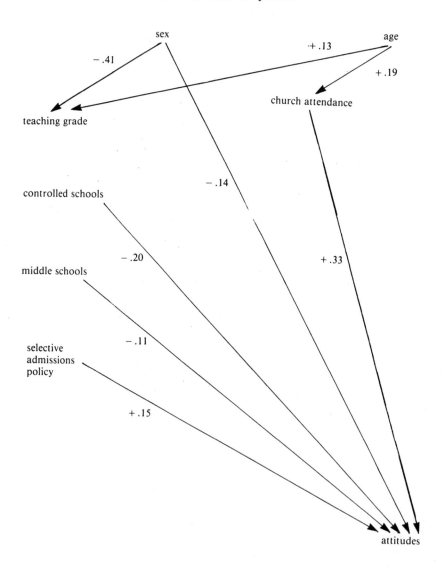

senior posts tend to be older. The arrow between sex and teaching grade ($+.41$) indicates that the senior posts in church schools tend to go to men.

Church attendance is also positively related to age ($+.19$). The older teachers in church schools are more inclined to attend church than the younger teachers. No line emerges between sex and church attendence. This is a very interesting point since, in the population as a whole, women are much more inclined to be church-goers than men. The path model indicates that the men who teach in church schools have the same pattern of church attendance as the women who teach in church schools. In other words, in terms of their religious behaviour, the male teachers in church schools are more likely to be different from the population at large than the female teachers.

The line between church attendance and attitude ($+.33$) indicates that the teachers who go to church are more likely to be in favour of the church school system than those who do not go to church. Although age influences church attendance and church attendance influences the attitude towards church schools, age itself does not have a direct bearing on attitude towards church schools. This means, for example, that the church-going older teachers will hold a more favourable attitude towards church schools than the non-church-going teachers of the same age, but that there is not necessarily going to be any difference between the attitudes of non-church-going older teachers and of non-church-going younger teachers.

The lack of a line between teaching grade and attitude is also very revealing. This means that those who hold senior posts in church schools are not more likely to have a favourable attitude towards church schools than those of the same age and the same sex who hold junior posts. This indicates that, generally speaking, the allocation of senior posts has neither discriminated in favour of those who support the church school system, nor produced in those who have received promotion a greater degree of support for that system.

The other lines in the path diagram indicate that the female teachers ($-.14$) tend to be less in favour of the church school system than the male teachers; those who work in controlled schools ($-.20$) are less in favour of church schools than those who work in aided schools; those who work in middle schools ($-.11$) are less in favour of church schools than those who work in primary or first schools; those few teachers who work in aided schools which operate a selective admissions policy on religious criteria tend to be more in favour of the church school system than those in the other schools.

One of the strengths of path analysis is the way in which it is able to take all the factors discussed above into account simultaneously.

This reduces the risks of error through contaminating influences.

On the basis of the above discussion, it is now possible to draw a profile of those who are most likely and those who are least likely to be in favour of the church school system. Those most in favour of the church school system are male teachers who attend church weekly and who work in aided primary or first schools which operate a selective admissions policy. Those least in favour of the church school system are female teachers who never attend church and who work in controlled middle schools operating an exclusively neighbourhood admissions policy.

## Distinctive or not

The second attitude scale sets out to identify the characteristics of church schools which are most likely to be emphasised by those who wish to assert the distinctiveness of the church school. Again, the statistical procedures of item analysis selected the sixteen items which most satisfactorily distinguish between those teachers who say that church schools are or should be different from county schools and those who say that church schools and county schools should be doing exactly the same sort of job, with the same kind of priorities.

Those who wish to emphasise the distinctiveness of church schools tend to talk in terms of the specifically religious characteristics of the school. Right at the top of their list they tend to place the ideas of providing a regular Christian assembly and teaching about Christianity, God and Jesus. They also consider it important to teach about the bible and the church. They feel that church schools should have committed Christians on the staff and develop close contacts with the local clergy. They believe that prayer has a place in the classroom. They argue that the church school should be a place for putting Christian values into practice and for providing an atmosphere of Christian community.

When these sixteen items are aggregated they also produce a unidimensional scale (see table 2) with a range of scores from sixteen through eighty. The internal consistency of these items produces an alpha coefficient of .9445.

The validity of this scale can also be tested against what the individual teachers claim to be their preferred type of school. We might expect those who want to emphasise the distinctiveness of church schools to wish to teach in aided schools, while those who want to stress that church schools should not be distinctive might well see little point in being in a church school. Those who state their preference as teaching in a Church of England aided school score 73.8 points on the scale; those who opt for Church of England controlled schools score 66.3 points; those who opt for a county school score 52.7 points. Those who say that they have no real preference

*Table 2: Scale of attitude towards the distinctiveness of church schools*

| Scale item | Corrected item-total correlation |
| --- | --- |
| Teaching about Jesus | + .8282 |
| Putting into practice Christian values | + .6448 |
| Having RE taught by a committed Christian | + .6652 |
| Providing an atmosphere of Christian community | + .7390 |
| Saying classroom prayers | + .6426 |
| Developing close contacts with clergy | + .6699 |
| Integrating religious and secular studies | + .5333 |
| Teaching about God | + .8065 |
| Teaching about Christianity | + .8115 |
| Encouraging regular visits from clergy | + .6704 |
| Providing a daily Christian assembly | + .7373 |
| Teaching about the Bible | + .7490 |
| Providing a regular Christian assembly | + .8322 |
| Having committed Christians on the staff | + .6866 |
| Teaching RE | + .7133 |
| Teaching about the church | + .6040 |

between a church school and a county school score 63.9 points, a score higher than those who opt for a county school, but lower than those who opt for a controlled school.

Path model two, which explores the teachers attitude towards the distinctiveness of church schools, assumes a somewhat different shape from path model one. This helps to confirm our notion that attitudes towards the distinctiveness of church schools function independently from attitudes towards the church school system itself. The paths leading to teaching grades and church attendance are, of course, identical in both path models because they are working on the same sets of data.

The first major difference between the two path models is that, in the case of attitudes towards the distinctiveness of church schools, there is a direct path between age and attitude, while this path did not exist in the case of attitudes towards the church school system. While older teachers are not more inclined to be in favour of the church school system, they are more inclined to consider that church schools are or should be different from county schools. Looking more closely at the data, it is the teachers in their fifties or sixties who are most inclined to feel that church schools should be distinctive. This is likely to be a function of the fact that they were trained and served their apprenticeship in a context which was more conscious of the distinctiveness of church schools than has been the case in more recent years. These are men and women who will

Path model two
Attitude towards the distinctiveness of church schools

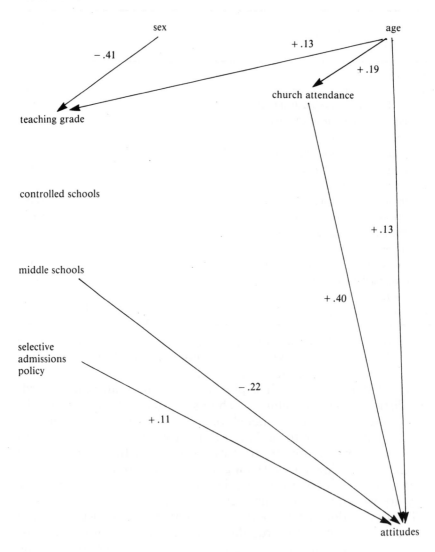

remember more clearly the controversy of the religious factor surrounding the 1944 Education Act.

The second major difference is that, in the case of the distinctiveness of church schools, no direct path exists between sex and attitude. While the male teachers were more inclined to be in favour of the church school system, they are not more inclined than the female teachers to wish to emphasise the distinctiveness of church schools.

The third major difference is that no path exists between the controlled schools and attitude towards the distinctiveness of church schools. Although those who work in controlled schools are less likely to be in favour of the church school system than those of the same age and sex who work in aided schools, they are not less likely to support the distinctiveness of church schools.

In three other ways the two path models assume a similar shape. The church attendance of the individual teachers is the strongest predictor of their attitude in both cases. Those who go to church regularly are more likely both to be in favour of the church school system and to emphasise the distinctiveness of church schools. Those who teach in middle schools are less likely to emphasise the distinctiveness of church schools, while those who teach in the aided schools which operate a selective admissions policy on religious grounds are more likely to emphasise the distinctiveness of church schools.

On the basis of the above discussion, it is now possible to draw a profile of those who are most likely and those who are least likely to emphasise the distinctiveness of church schools. Those most likely to emphasise the distinctiveness of church schools are the older men and women who attend church weekly and who work in the kind of aided primary school which operates an admissions policy based on religious criteria. Those least likely to emphasise the distinctiveness of church schools are the younger men and women who never attend church and who work in the middle schools which do not operate an admissions policy based on religious criteria.

## Traditional or progressive

The third attitude scale sets out to identify the teaching preferences of those who would characterise themselves as favouring traditional teaching methods, rather than progressive teaching methods. Again, the statistical procedures of item analysis selected sixteen items which most satisfactorily distinguished between those in favour of traditional teaching methods and those in favour of progressive teaching methods. These items are set out in table 3, together with an indication of the way in which they cohere to produce a unidimensional scale. The internal consistency of these sixteen items produced an alpha coefficient of .8820 which, once

*Table 3: Scale of attitude towards traditional teaching methods*

| Scale item | Corrected item-total correlation |
|---|---|
| Promoting a high level of academic attainment | + .4433 |
| Giving stars or credits for good work | + .3953 |
| Punishing chidren for persistent disruptive behaviour | + .5208 |
| Training children in hard work | + .5517 |
| Giving regular maths tests | + .6119 |
| Bringing the best out of bright pupils | + .5201 |
| Teaching children to read | + .4817 |
| Teaching children to know their multiplication tables by heart | + .6579 |
| Teaching children to be tidy | + .5936 |
| Teaching children to write clearly | + .5473 |
| Following a regular timetable for different lessons | + .4599 |
| Adopting strict discipline | + .4943 |
| Correcting most spelling and grammatical errors | + .6059 |
| Giving regular spelling tests | + .6461 |
| Expecting children to seek permission before leaving the classroom | + .5573 |
| Adopting firm discipline | + .5777 |

again, is a highly satisfactory index of the scale's reliability and unidimensionality. The cumulative scale scores again range. from sixteen through eighty.

Those who value traditional teaching methods place a high priority on teaching children to know their multiplication tables by heart, giving regular maths tests and giving regular spelling tests. They believe in training children in hard work, teaching children to be tidy and adopting firm discipline. They like to follow a regular timetable for different lessons. They emphasise the importance of bringing the best out of bright pupils and of rewarding good work by giving stars and other credit marks. They expect children to seek permission before leaving the classroom, and they expect children to be punished for persistent disruptive behaviour.

The key question now concerns the way in which a preference for traditional teaching methods is likely to be associated with other factors. Are men more or less likely to favour traditional teaching methods than women? Are older teachers more likely to favour traditional teaching methods than younger teachers? Are those who attend church regularly more or less likely to be traditionalists in their approach to teaching? Are those in aided schools any more traditional in their approach than those in controlled schools? Are teachers in middle schools any more traditional in their teaching methods than those in primary or first schools?

Path model three answers each of these questions in the negative. None of these factors is significantly related to the individual's

## Path model three
## Attitude towards teaching style

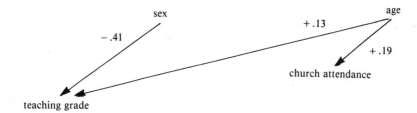

controlled schools

middle schools

selective
admissions
policy

teaching
style

attitude towards traditional teaching methods. Women are just as likely to favour traditional teaching methods as men. Young teachers are just as likely to favour traditional teaching methods as older teachers. Those in first schools are just as likely to favour traditional teaching methods as those in middle schools. Regular church-goers are just as likely to favour traditional teaching methods as those who never go to church. Traditionalists are just as likely to be found in controlled schools as in aided schools and in posts of senior responsibility as in scale one posts.

Having seen that preferences for and against traditional teaching methods are totally unrelated to these other factors, the final question is to examine whether a preference for traditional teaching methods is related to the teacher's attitudes either towards the church school system or towards the distinctiveness of church schools. Are the teachers who favour traditional teaching methods also likely to favour the church school system or to emphasise the distinctiveness of church schools? This is a very straightforward statistical question for correlational analysis.

The first point to emerge from the correlational analysis is that there is a statistically significant, but very weak relationship between preferences for teaching style and attitude towards the church school system ($r = +.1172$, $P < .05$). Those who favour traditional teaching methods are also slightly more in favour of the church school system.

The second point to emerge is that the relationship between preference for teaching style and attitude towards the distinctiveness of church schools is considerably stronger ($r = +.3246$, $P < .001$). Those who favour traditional teaching methods are also much more in favour of emphasising the distinctiveness of church schools. This suggests that the image of church schools as an environment in which it remains appropriate to emphasise the religious dimension of Christianity is closely associated with a more general tendency to favour traditional teaching methods. At the same time, a relatively independent set of values is operating in determining the teachers attitudes towards the church school system itself.

While ideas about the religious distinctiveness of church schools may well involve a projection of conservative teaching values onto the church schools issue, these values in no way seriously interact with the individual teachers arguments for or against the church school system itself. From the teachers point of view, there is little truth in the notion that church schools are favoured as a final bastion of traditional teaching methods.

## Implications

The detailed statistical analysis of this article offers some significant pointers regarding the likely future of the church school system in rural areas. If it is true that the character of church schools depends very much upon the attitudes and policies of those who actually teach in them, the church needs to be taking very seriously the views of today's teachers. The church also needs to begin to predict the climate of opinion among the teachers of tomorrow, as the senior members of staff retire, as a new generation of teachers is promoted into headships and as young men and women are recruited into teaching in their first church schools.

The first pointer is provided by the scale of 'attitude towards the church school system' itself. Already we are aware that today only a small proportion of those who teach in church schools specifically chose to be working in the church school system, just 10% of the teachers in controlled schools and 37% of the teachers in aided schools. While the majority of the teachers who find themselves working in the church school system still show considerable goodwill towards that system, their goodwill towards church schools is also clearly associated with their goodwill towards the church in general.

The statistical model suggests that the younger teachers are less likely to be church-goers and that the teachers who are not church-goers are less likely to be favourably disposed towards the church school system. This model could imply that the next generation of teachers in church schools is likely to be less favourably disposed towards the church school system than the present generation. My earlier study, *Rural Anglicanism: a future for young Christians?*, demonstrates the decline in membership of rural churches and highlights the increasing inability of rural churches to attract children, young people and young families into membership (Francis, 1985). My prediction is that, as young teachers in rural church schools become more alienated from their local churches, so their sympathy for the church school system itself will decline. The puzzle with which the rural churches will be left is making sense of retaining an investment in school sites after the commitment of the teaching staff to the church's involvement in education has worn thin. The signs are that the rural church will have to face this problem soonest in its controlled middle schools.

The second pointer is provided by the scale of 'attitude towards the distinctiveness of church schools.' At present the main emphasis of the teachers who argue in favour of the distinctiveness of church schools specifically concerns the Christian character of these schools. For example, half of the teachers in controlled schools and two-thirds of the teachers in aided schools currently argue that church schools should give more emphasis than county schools to providing a regular Christian assembly. The statistical model clearly suggests that this notion of distinctiveness is not only related to the individual teachers attitudes towards the church, but also to their age.

In the case of their attitude towards the church school system, younger church-going teachers are just as likely to be favourably disposed to the church's involvement in education as older church-going teachers. It is simply the case that fewer young teachers go to church. In the case of their attitude towards the distinctiveness of church schools, younger church-going teachers are less likely to support the Christian distinctiveness of church schools than older church-going teachers.

This model implies that the belief among teachers in church schools that church schools should be different is likely to disappear more rapidly, as the next generation of church school teachers emerges, than their general goodwill towards the church's continued involvement in education. My prediction is that, as younger teachers replace the more senior members of staff in rural church schools, so the desire to assert the distinctiveness of church schools will decline. The puzzle with which the rural churches will be left is making sense of operating schools which are indistinguishable from comparable neighbourhood county schools. The signs are that the rural church will have to face this problem soonest in its middle schools.

**References**

Francis, L J (1985) *Rural Anglicanism: a future for young Christians?*, London, Collins Liturgical Publications.

Francis, L J (1986) *Partnership in Rural Education: church schools and teacher attitudes*, London, Collins Liturgical Publications.

Keeves, J P (1988) 'Path analysis,' in J P Keeves (ed.) *Educational Research, Methodology, and Measurement: an international handbook*, pp. 723–731, Oxford, Pergamon Press.

Likert, R A (1932) 'A technique for the measurement of attitudes,' *Archives of Psychology*, 140, pp. 1–55.

## 10.3 Measuring differences in church-related perspectives in education

*Leslie J Francis*

### Introduction

Francis (1987) describes a detailed survey conducted throughout the primary schools of Gloucestershire. The survey included a questionnaire sent to the headteachers and designed to profile the religious life and curriculum of the schools. This questionnaire concentrated on seven main areas: religious education, assemblies, worship, church contact, resources, staff, and the head teachers' personal religious commitment. Replies were received from 111 county schools, 41 Church of England aided schools, 73 Church of England controlled schools, 8 Catholic aided schools and one other voluntary school, making a response rate of 96%.

Preliminary analyses of the data made it clear that some schools understand themselves to be working in a much closer partnership with the churches than others. Some act as if they consider it appropriate for state maintained schools to function as an extension of the Christian churches, while others do not.

At first glance, however, it is not easy to specify the range of characteristics which most clearly distinguishes schools which pursue a church-related approach to education from those which do not. For example, is a daily assembly for the whole school a clear indication of a church-related approach, or can it simply mean that the school sees social and educational advantages in a daily assembly, and not necessarily explicit religious significance? Does the regular singing of hymns in assemblies indicate a clear church-related intention, or can it simply mean that hymn singing has musical and social meaning rather than explicit religious connotations? Is the imaginative use of resources in religious education indicative of a close relationship with the churches, or can it simply mean that religious education is taken seriously in the school on educational grounds, rather than on religious grounds?

### Measuring differences

In order to answer this kind of question and to form a clear idea how schools which follow a church-related approach to education differ from those which do not, the information gathered by the headteachers questionnaires was subjected to a series of factor

analyses and other exploratory correlational techniques. The idea
of these techniques is to identify the various patterns implicit in
the questionnaire data and to summarise the main trends underlying these patterns. The end result of this process was to identify
twenty-two pieces of information which most clearly differentiate
between schools which adopt a church-related approach and those
which do not.

The twenty-two pieces of information which produce this scale
of church-related education are listed in table 1, together with their
statistical properties. These statistics show that, within the available
indicators in the questionnaire, contact with clergy emerges as the
most central feature distinguishing the schools which adopt a church-
related approach to education.

This scale demonstrates that schools which encourage contact with
clergy also emphasise other aspects of the religious life of the school
differently from schools which do not encourage contact with clergy.
Schools which encourage contact with clergy also have more contact
with local churches; they hold more explicitly Christian assemblies
and relate these assemblies more explicitly to the life of the church;
they give more emphasis to the church-related aspects of religious
education.

According to this scale, the most church-related schools receive
regular visits from clergy. They invite clergy to contribute to assemblies and religious education. They arrange for pupils to visit and
study the local church and to talk with the clergy during this visit.
They hold a school service in church from time to time and encourage
the pupils to contribute to a weekday or Sunday service. When the
pupils attend a church service, these schools prepare well in advance
so that the pupils can display their work in the church and have something to contribute to the service itself, in the form of music, dance or
drama. Assemblies set out to be explicitly Christian acts of worship
and reflect closely the shape of the church's year. They regularly
make use of readings from the Bible and stories from a Christian
background. The pupils regularly recite the Lord's Prayer and are
given the opportunity to write and use their own prayers. The hymns
sung in assemblies bear a close relationship with those used in local
churches and the pupils also sometimes sing the psalms and canticles used in church. Religious education makes regular use of the
Bible and studies church-related topics. These schools are likely to
possess class sets of one or more modern translation of the Bible.

According to this scale, the least church-related schools do not
receive visits from clergy, nor invite clergy to contribute to religious education or assemblies. They do not make use of the local
church as a resource in religious education. They do not arrange for
the pupils to visit the local church to look at the building, to meet
the clergy or to study the purpose of the church. They neither hold
a school service in church, nor involve the pupils in a weekday or

## Table 1: Scale of church-related education

| Scale item | Corrected item total correlation |
|---|---|
| Frequency of clergy contribution to assemblies | .4254 |
| Frequency of clergy contribution to RE lessons | .5076 |
| Frequency of clergy visits to school | .5808 |
| Relationship between assemblies and church's year | .2826 |
| Relationship between hymns in assemblies and local churches | .2362 |
| Religious emphases of assemblies | .2854 |
| Class sets of modern Bibles | .1982 |
| Visit church to look at the building | .2608 |
| Visit church to talk with the clergy | .3810 |
| Visit church to study the purpose of the church | .2545 |
| Take part in a weekday church service | .3545 |
| Take part in a Sunday church service | .2405 |
| Hold a school service | .3826 |
| Make a display of pupils work in church | .2381 |
| Present music, dance or drama in church | .3940 |
| Use copies of the Bible in RE lessons | .3448 |
| Visit Christian churches as part of RE | .4572 |
| Pupils read their own prayers in assemblies | .3304 |
| Pupils say the Lord's Prayer in assemblies | .3423 |
| Pupils sing psalms or canticles in assemblies | .3285 |
| Pupils hear passages from the Bible in assemblies | .4124 |
| Pupils hear Christian stories in assemblies | .3603 |

Note:  The scale items list the issues which most clearly distinguish between the schools which adopt a church-related approach and those which do not.
The corrected item total correlations show the strength of the relationship between the individual items and the product of the rest of the items.
The internal consistency and unidimensionality of this scale are indicated by an alpha coefficient of .7777.

Sunday service. Assemblies do not set out to be explicitly or implicitly Christian in character. They do not have a close relationship with the shape of the church's year. While the pupils sing hymns, these hymns do not reflect the usage in local churches. The pupils do not join in saying the Lord's Prayer. They do not sing psalms or canticles. Passages are not read from the Bible and stories are chosen from secular rather than Christian backgrounds. The pupils are not encouraged to write their own prayers to use in assemblies. Religious education does not make much use of the Bible, nor study church-related topics. These schools are unlikely to possess class sets of a modern translation of the Bible.

While the items attracted into this scale draw a clear profile of the distinguishing characteristics of church-related schools, it is equally important to learn from some of the items which do not form part of this cluster. The number of days the whole school meets for an assembly every week is not indicative of the extent to which the school adopts a church-related approach; it is the content, not the frequency of assemblies which counts. The number of days on which the pupils sing hymns each week is not indicative of the extent to which the school adopts a church-related approach; it is the relationship between hymns sung in school and church which counts. The fact that prayers are used in assemblies does not distinguish between church-related and non-churchrelated approaches; it is the specific use of the Lord's Prayer which counts. The range of resources used in religious education does not distinguish between church-related and non-churchrelated approaches, but the use of the Bible in religious education does distinguish between the two approaches. The possession of a set of Bibles in school does not distinguish between church-related and non-churchrelated approaches, but the possession of a set of Bibles in a modern translation does distinguish between the two approaches.

Having identified the indicators which help to distinguish schools which adopt a church-related approach to education from those which do not, it is now possible to add up these pieces of information and create a score for each individual school on a scale of church-related education.

## Accounting for differences

Having calculated each school's unique score on the scale of church related education, it is now possible to explore in greater detail the factors which influence where individual schools are placed on this continuum, from being very church-related at one end to being completely non-churchrelated at the other end. Two key factors emerge as crucial in influencing the church-related character of individual schools. These are the nature of the foundation of the school and the personal religious disposition of the headteacher. The importance of these factors is summarised in table 2.

As far as the foundation of the school is concerned, the mean scores on the scale of church-related education confirm that Catholic schools are clearly the most church-related and county schools the least church-related. Church of England controlled schools show more signs of being church-related than county schools, but less signs than Church of England aided schools. In their turn, Church of England aided schools show less signs of being church-related than Catholic schools.

As far as the personal religious disposition of the headteachers is concerned, three issues raised in the questionnaire show clear relationships with the level of church-relatedness demonstrated by their schools. First, the headteachers were asked to state the kind

## Table 2: Mean scores on scale of church-related education

| Groups | Mean | SD | N |
|---|---|---|---|
| *Foundation of school* | | | |
| County | 50.7 | 8.3 | 107 |
| C of E controlled | 57.5 | 6.1 | 68 |
| C of E aided | 64.0 | 6.6 | 41 |
| Catholic | 73.0 | 7.9 | 8 |
| *Headteachers preferred type of school* | | | |
| County | 51.2 | 8.6 | 85 |
| no preference | 56.8 | 7.7 | 67 |
| C of E controlled | 57.0 | 6.2 | 24 |
| C of E aided | 62.5 | 8.3 | 31 |
| Catholic | 74.6 | 7.1 | 7 |
| *Headteachers religious affiliation* | | | |
| Humanist or Agnostic | 48.4 | 7.7 | 22 |
| Free Church | 54.4 | 6.1 | 40 |
| Church of England | 57.1 | 9.2 | 141 |
| Catholic | 65.7 | 14.8 | 11 |
| *Headteachers church attendance* | | | |
| Never or once a year | 48.2 | 7.5 | 39 |
| Major festivals | 54.6 | 8.0 | 31 |
| At least once a month | 58.7 | 8.9 | 144 |

Note: Potential scores on this scale range between 21 and 90.

Some headteachers did not divulge personal information.

*N*    indicates the number of schools within each category.

*SD*    indicates the standard deviation

of school they would prefer to be working in. Their personal preference is clearly mirrored in the extent to which their present schools demonstrate a church-related policy. Headteachers who say that they prefer to be in the county sector show least signs of church-relatedness in their schools, while those who say that they prefer to be in the Catholic sector show most signs of church-relatedness in their schools. Those who say that they prefer to be in the Church of England aided sector show more signs of church-relatedness in their schools than those who say that they prefer to be in the Church of England controlled sector. Those who say that they have no particular preference between the church or county sectors are working in schools where the church-related profile is similar to that of Church of England controlled schools.

Second, the headteachers denominational affiliation is a clear predictor of the church-relatedness of their present schools. Humanist or agnostic headteachers show the least signs of church-relatedness in their schools, while Catholic headteachers show the most signs of church-relatedness in their schools. Headteachers who are members of the Church of England show less signs of church-relatedness in their schools than the Catholics, but more than the members of the Free Churches.

Third, the headteachers personal pattern of church attendance is a clear predictor of the church-relatedness of their present schools. Headteachers who never go to church or go only once a year show fewer signs of church-relatedness in their schools than those who go to church for the major festivals. In their turn, headteachers who go to church only for the major festivals show fewer signs of church-relatedness in their schools than those who go to church at least once a month.

## Differences in neighbourhood schools

In the above analysis, Catholic schools and Catholic headteachers have both emerged as the most distinctively church-related. This is consistent with the fact that most of the Catholic headteachers work in Catholic schools and that Catholic schools clearly operate a church-related admissions policy. On the other hand Church of England aided, Church of England controlled and county schools all operate primarily to serve specific neighbourhoods, rather than specific religious communities. The rest of this article, therefore, proposes to concentrate on trying to understand the relative significance of the foundation, the location and the headteachers personal religious practices in determining the level of church-relatedness displayed by neighbourhood schools. In other words, Catholic schools are excluded from the following analyses.

The statistical procedure employed to explore the church-relatedness of neighbourhood schools is path analysis (Keeves, 1988). The results of this analysis are shown in path model one. This path model sets out to answer a series of interrelated questions.

First, how do the headteachers personal religious practices interact with the foundation of the schools? For example, is the apparent relationship between headteachers personal religious practices and the church-relatedness of the school really an artifact of the way in which church schools tend to appoint church-going headteachers? Or do the headteachers personal religious practices really have an influence on the church-relatedness of schools, irrespective of the nature of the foundation?

Second, does the foundation have an impact on the schools church-relatedness independent of the headteachers own personal religiosity? For example, do church schools where there is a headteacher who attends church weekly show any more signs of being church-related than county schools where the headteacher also attends church weekly?

## Path model one
## Church-related education

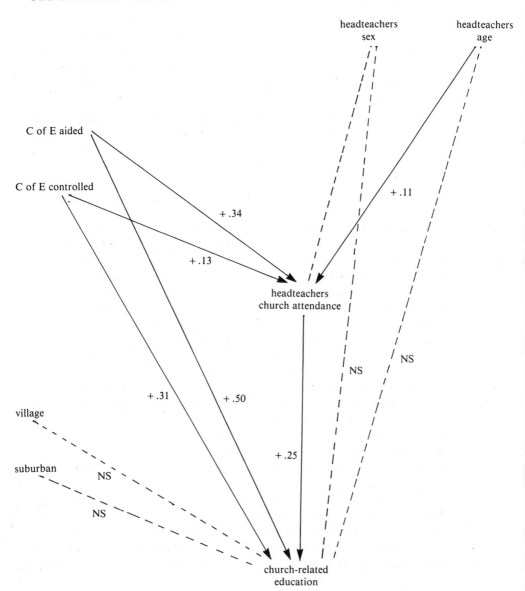

Third, does the location of the school affect its church-relatedness, irrespective of the foundation and the headteachers personal religiosity? For example, according to present data suburban schools emerge as less church-related than village or town schools. Can this be accounted for entirely by the fact that there are fewer church schools in suburban areas and that headteachers of suburban schools are less likely to be church-goers, or is there an additional factor which can be described as the suburban environment itself?

Fourth, is the age or sex of headteachers influential in determining the church-relatedness of their schools? For example, are schools with women headteachers likely to be more or less church-related? Are schools with younger headteachers likely to be more or less church-related?

Path models show the hypothesised direction of relationships in terms of straight lines and arrowheads. The strength and direction of these relationships are indicated by the path coefficients or standardised regression weights and the preceding signs. The convention in path models is to locate the outcome variable, in this case the score of church-related education, at the bottom of the page, while the variables which are likely to influence this outcome are listed from the top of the page in the order in which they are entered into the equation.

According to this convention, sex and age appear at the top of the page because they are logically prior to the other factors. The foundation of the school appears next since we are interested in discovering the extent to which church schools are likely to choose church-going headteachers. Church of England aided and Church of England controlled schools are entered into the equation as 'dummy variables,' with county schools serving as the reference point. Similarly, village and suburban schools are entered into the equation as 'dummy variables,' with town schools serving as the reference point.

This convention means that all the arrowheads logically point down the page. Where downward progressing arrows are now drawn into the diagram, it means that statistically significant relationships do not exist. The fact that the possibility of these relationships has been taken into account in computing the equations is demonstrated in path model 1 by dotted lines.

The interpretation of the path diagram begins by looking at the first equation leading to headteachers church attendance. The arrow between age and church attendance means that older headteachers are significantly more inclined to attend church than younger headteachers. On the other hand, no line emerges between sex and church attendance. This is a very interesting point since, in the population as a whole, women are much more inclined to be church-goers than men. The path model indicates that men headteachers have the same pattern of church attendance as women headteachers. In other words, in terms of their pattern of church attendance, men headteachers are likely to be more different from the population at large than women headteachers.

The arrows from Church of England aided and Church of England controlled to church attendance mean that headteachers of Church of England schools are significantly more inclined to attend church than headteachers of county schools. Comparison of the two coefficients shows that headteachers of Church of England aided schools are more inclined to be frequent church attenders than headteachers of Church of England controlled schools.

The second equation now includes the headteachers pattern of church attendance as a predictor of the church-relatedness of schools, along with their sex and age, foundation of the school and geographical location (see table 3). The arrow between church attendance and church-related education means that schools where headteachers attend church regularly also display more signs of church-related education. The absence of an arrow between sex and church-related education means that the church-relatedness of schools does not depend on whether the headteacher is a man or a woman.

The absence of an arrow between age and church-related education means that the influence of the headteachers age on the church-relatedness of schools is mediated entirely through the headteachers pattern of church attendance. Older headteachers are more inclined to attend church and church-going headteachers are more inclined to influence schools in a church-related way, but the headteachers age does not have an additional direct influence on the church-relatedness of schools.

The arrows from Church of England aided and Church of England controlled to church-related education mean that the foundation has a direct influence on the church-relatedness of schools in addition to the influence exerted by headteachers. Comparison of the two coefficients shows that aided status has a greater influence on the church-relatedness of schools than controlled status. Moreover, Church of England aided status and Church of England controlled status exert both an indirect influence on the church-relatedness of schools by favouring the appointment of church-going headteachers and a direct influence as well.

The absence of arrows leading from villages and suburbs means that location does not have an impact on the church-relatedness of schools, after the foundation and the religious practices of headteachers have been taken into account. In other words, the fact that suburban schools tend to be less church-related than town schools (Francis 1987, chapter 11) can be explained by the lower proportion of church schools in suburban areas and the appointment of fewer church-going headteachers to suburban schools.

*Table 3: Multiple regression significance tests for path model 1*

| Criterion variable | Predictor variables | $R^2$ | Increase in $R^2$ | F increase | P< increase | Beta |
|---|---|---|---|---|---|---|
| Church-related education | church attendance | .1534 | .1534 | 36.97 | .001 | + .2546 |
| | age | .1541 | .0006 | 0.15 | NS | + .0072 |
| | sex | .1566 | .0026 | 0.62 | NS | − .0391 |
| | controlled status | .1775 | .0208 | 5.09 | .05 | + .3080 |
| | aided status | .3821 | .2046 | 66.22 | .001 | + .4985 |
| | village area | .3823 | .0002 | 0.08 | NS | + .0283 |
| | suburban area | .3826 | .0003 | 0.09 | NS | + .0206 |

Two particular pointers emerge from this path model which deserve closer scrutiny. The first indicates that headteachers personal religious practices have a significant influence on the extent to which schools display characteristics of a church-related approach to education. The second indicates that younger headteachers are less likely to show signs of religious commitment than more senior headteachers and that this is directly reflected in their schools displaying fewer characteristics of church-related education. The practical significance of these two pointers will now be examined in greater detail.

## Headteachers religious practice

In order to look more closely at the relationship between the headteachers personal religious practices and the church-related characteristics of their schools, it is necessary to deal with county and church schools separately for two reasons. Church schools tend to appoint more church-going headteachers and the clergy have a more direct relationship with church schools, irrespective of the religious disposition of the headteachers. While it would also be interesting to look at the differences between controlled and aided schools, the size of the sample does not really permit this kind of detailed analysis. The following analyses are, therefore, based on 107 county schools and 108 church schools. The cross tabulations reported are based on two groups of headteachers: those who attend church less frequently than the major festivals and those who attend church at least monthly. For convenience in the following discussion, these two groups will be styled the non-churchgoers and the regular church-goers.

The impact of the headteachers personal religious practices on the church-related character of county schools is considerable and affects nearly all the indicators identified by the scale of church-related education.

The headteachers personal religious practices influence the amount of contact clergy have with county schools. Where the headteacher is a regular church-goer, 74% of the county schools are visited by clergy at least once a term; 70% invite clergy to lead assemblies at least once a term; 16% invite clergy to contribute to religious education at least once a term. Where the headteacher is not a church-goer, 54% of the county schools are visited by clergy at least once a term; 54% invite clergy to lead assemblies at least once a term; 7% invite clergy to contribute to religious education at least once a term.

Similarly, the headteachers personal religious practices influence the amount of contact county schools have with local churches. Where the headteacher is a regular church-goer, 72% of the county schools visited a local church within the past year to look at the buildings; 58% arranged to meet the clergy in church and 41% studied the purpose of the church. Where the headteacher is not a church-goer, 64% of the county schools visited a local church within the past year to look at the buildings; 43% arranged to meet the clergy in church and 32% studied the purpose of the church.

Where the headteacher is a regular church-goer, 56% of the county schools held a school service in church during the past year and 12% took part in a Sunday service. Where the headteacher is not a church-goer, 39% of the county schools held a school service during the past year and 7% took part in a Sunday service. Where the headteacher is a regular church-goer, 28% of the county schools arranged a display of the pupils work in a local church during the past year and 44% gave the pupils an opportunity to present music, dance or drama in the church. Where the headteacher is not a church-goer, 21% of the county schools arranged a display of the pupils work in a local church during the past year and 18% gave the pupils an opportunity to present music, dance or drama in church.

County schools where the headteacher is a regular church-goer are much more likely to experience church-related assemblies. Thus, 37% of the regular church-goers describe the majority of their assemblies as explicitly Christian, compared with 18% of the non-churchgoers. Where the headteacher is a regular church-goer, the fourth year junior pupils hear the Bible read in assemblies at least once a week in 47% of the county schools, compared with 7% where the headteacher is not a church-goer. Where the headteacher is a regular church-goer, the fourth year junior pupils hear religious stories from a Christian background in assemblies at least once a week in 84% of the county schools, compared with 64% where the headteacher is not a church-goer. There is a close relationship between assemblies and the church's year in 65% of the county schools where the headteacher is a regular church-goer, compared with 43% where the headteacher is not a church-goer.

Where the headteacher is a regular church-goer, 60% of the county schools possess a set of a modern translation of the Bible, compared with 29% where the headteacher is not a church-goer. The fourth year junior pupils often use copies of the Bible in religious education in 21% of the county schools where the headteacher is a regular church-goer and in none of the county schools where the headteacher is not a church-goer.

The impact of the headteachers personal religious practices on the church-related nature of church schools is less considerable than in the case of county schools, but still very real.

In the case of church schools, the headteacher's personal religious commitment does not influence whether or not the school visits the local church to study the buildings; nor does it influence whether or not the school holds a school service in church. On the other hand, the headteacher's personal religious commitment does influence the extent to which the pupils become actively involved in these occasions. While 65% of the church schools where the headteacher is a regular church-goer give the pupils an opportunity to share their music, dance or drama in church, only 45% where the headteacher is not a church-goer do so. While 37% of the church schools where the headteacher is a regular church-goer make a display of the pupils work in church, only 18% where the headteacher is not a regular church-goer do so. Headteachers who do not attend church themselves are less likely to involve their church schools in Sunday church services: 27% of the regular church-goers have involved their church school in a Sunday church service within the past year, compared with 18% of the non-churchgoing headteachers.

In the case of church schools, the headteacher's personal religious commitment does not influence whether or not the school possesses a set of modern Bibles. It does, however, influence whether or not these Bibles are used. The fourth year junior pupils often use copies of the Bible in religious education in 38% of the church schools where the headteacher is a regular church-goer, but in none of the church schools where the headteacher is not a church-goer. The fourth year junior pupils hear passages from the Bible read in assemblies at least once a week in 62% of the church schools where the headteacher is a regular church-goer, but in only 36% where the headteacher is not a church-goer.

There is also a range of other ways in which the headteachers personal religious practices influence assemblies in church schools. Thus, 54% of the regular church-going headteachers describe the majority of their assemblies as explicitly Christian, compared with 36% of the non-churchgoers; 42% of the regular church-going headteachers say that there is a close relationship between hymns sung in assemblies and in the local church, compared with 18% of the non-churchgoers.

The frequency and degree of contact which the clergy have with church schools is also related to the religious commitment of the headteachers. Where the headteacher is a regular church-goer, 89% of the church schools are visited by the clergy at least once a term;

80% have clergy leading assemblies at least once a term; 56% have clergy contributing to religious education at least once a term. Where the headteacher is not a church-goer, 73% of the church schools are visited by the clergy at least once a term; 63% have clergy leading assemblies at least once a term; 36% have clergy contributing to religious education at least once a term.

## Headteachers age

The path model suggests that younger headteachers are less likely to be practising church-goers than more senior headteachers. In order to understand what this means in practice, the religious behaviour of the headteachers of county and Church of England schools was analysed according to age categories. From this analysis it emerges that at least monthly church attendance is practised by 58% of the headteachers under the age of forty, 68% of the headteachers in their forties or fifties and 77% of those in their sixties.

This relationship between church attendance and age can be explained in two ways: either headteachers tend to increase their church attendance as they grow older, or the younger generation of headteachers is less religious than their predecessors. While both trends may in fact contribute to the differences found in the data, the general trend in society towards lower levels of church attendance favours the theory that the present generation of headteachers may be less religious than their predecessors. At the same time, it needs to be emphasised that even the younger headteachers are much more likely to attend church regularly than the adult population as a whole.

The path model goes on to suggest that there is no direct influence between headteachers age and the church-related character of schools, but that there is an indirect influence mediated via the impact of age on church attendance and the impact of church attendance on the churchrelated character of schools. Cross tabulation between headteachers ages and the items identified by the scale of church-related education confirms that there is a relationship between the church-related character of schools and headteachers ages. The real difference emerges between headteachers who are now in their thirties and the rest.

The majority of headteachers over the age of forty will have completed their initial teacher training before the end of the 1960s when new thinking began to emerge in educational philosophy and religious education. The headteachers who are not yet in their forties will have had greater chance of exposure to this new thinking. For convenience in the following discussion, those under the age of forty will be styled the 'younger headteachers,' while those over the age of forty will be styled the 'older headteacher.'

It is particularly in county schools that the younger headteachers are moving away from the characteristics of church-related education. For example, 38% of the younger headteachers in county schools describe the majority of their assemblies as largely secular and social, compared with only 9% of the older headteachers. Fourth year junior pupils hear passages read from the Bible in assemblies at least once a week in 12% of the county schools where the headteacher is under forty, compared with 40% where the headteacher is over forty. Fourth year junior pupils hear religious stories of a Christian background at least once a week in 69% of the county schools where the headteacher is under forty, compared with 80% where the headteacher is over forty. There is a close relationship between assemblies and the church's year in 37% of the county schools where the headteacher is under forty, but in 67% where the headteacher is over forty.

Similarly, the Bible is less likely to be used in religious education in county schools where the headteacher is under forty. Thus, the fourth year junior pupils rarely or never use the Bible in religious education in 63% of the county schools in the charge of a younger headteacher, compared with 30% in the charge of an older headteacher.

While clergy are just as likely to make informal visits to county schools where the headteacher is under forty, the younger headteachers are less likely to invite clergy to take part in assemblies at religious education. Thus, clergy are invited to take assemblies at least once a term in 56% of the county schools where the headteacher is under the age of forty, compared with 66% where the headteacher is over the age of forty.

The younger headteachers in county schools are less likely to make use of the local church as an educational resource. Thus, only 50% of the county schools where the headteacher is under forty arranged for pupils to visit a local church within the past year to look at the building, compared with 71% where the headteacher is over forty; 31% of the county schools where the headteacher is under forty arranged for pupils to meet and talk with the clergy in the local church, compared with 55% where the headteacher is over forty; 44% of the county schools where the headteacher is under forty held a school service within the past year, compared with 51% where the headteacher is over forty.

In the case of church schools, the relationship between headteachers age and the church-related character of schools is less clear, but still evident in some specific ways. For example, only 40% of the younger headteachers of church schools describe the majority of their assemblies as explicitly Christian, compared with 51% of the older headteachers; only 43% of the younger headteachers of church schools arranged for their pupils to visit the local church to meet with the clergy during the past year, compared with 58% of the older headteachers.

## Implications

These detailed statistical analyses of factors which influence the church-related character of neighbourhood schools have some clear and important implications for the Church of England's assessment of its partnership in the state maintained system of education. In particular, ten points demonstrated by this analysis are worth highlighting.

First, the church still has considerable influence to determine the church-related character of neighbourhood schools. It can do so both directly through its involvement in aided and controlled schools, and indirectly through the Christian commitment of headteachers. These two channels of influence constitute a powerful presence in the state maintained system of schools. Christian people may rejoice that the church's influence can still be so strong in a secular educational system. Secular educationalists may be suspicious of such pervasive religious influence.

Second, church schools are distinctive in the sense of displaying more characteristics of church-related education than county schools. Controlled schools are significantly more church-related than county schools; aided schools are significantly more church-related than controlled schools. Christian people may be pleased that the church is still able to utilise aided and controlled status to promote neighbourhood schools which are more church-related than county schools. Secular educationalists may accuse the church of using its theology of service to the nation to cloak confessional aims in education.

Third, headteachers hold a key position in determining the church-related character of neighbourhood schools. Primary headteachers are much more church-going than the population at large and they use their Christian commitment to influence the church-relatedness of their schools, irrespective of whether the pupils come from religious or secular backgrounds. Christian people may be happy to know that the headships of many church and county schools are held by their fellow believers who are in a key position to influence the religious development of children. Secular educationalists may raise questions about the right of headteachers to allow their personal beliefs to influence their professional practice in a state maintained system of schools.

Fourth, church schools, both aided and controlled, are more likely to appoint church-goers to the position of headships than county schools. Those in favour of church schools may applaud this as good stewardship of the church's investment in the state maintained system of education. Those not in favour of church schools may see this as further evidence of the inequality and professional divisiveness fostered by voluntary schools.

Fifth, the religious foundation of a school has a direct impact on the church-related character of the school in addition to the indirect influence exerted through the tendency to appoint church-going headteachers. At the time of the 1944 Education Act, the Free Churches tended to argue that church influence was best brought to bear on state maintained schools through the training of Christian teachers rather than through the maintenance of voluntary schools. The present study shows that, from the church's point of view, while Christian teachers are important, the foundation of the school is also important in promoting church-related education.

Sixth, aided status is a more significant influence than controlled status in promoting the church-related character of a school. At the time of the 1944 Education Act, the Church of England adopted two different views on the relative advantages of aided and controlled status. Some voices argued that aided status was essential for preserving the church-related character of church schools; other voices argued that, provided the teachers were Christian men and women, aided status offered no positive advantages over controlled status. The present study shows that, while controlled status is able to promote greater church-relatedness than county schools, aided status is considerably more powerful in achieving this end than controlled status.

Seventh, the lower level of church-relatedness in suburban schools, compared with town and village schools, can be explained in terms of the lower proportion of church schools in suburban areas and the appointment of more secular headteachers to the headships of suburban schools. This is a reflection on the church's historic inability to extend its educational influence into the more recent areas of development. Having failed to take the initiative to build new church schools in suburban areas, the church now witnesses the accelerated secularisation of educational provision in these areas.

Eighth, church aided schools differ in their church-relatedness from county schools, both in the Christian commitment of the headteachers and in the range of church-related phenomena in the life of the school. At the same time, these schools set out to serve a neighbourhood function in the same way as county schools. The church needs to ask whether it still ought to have the right to determine so radically the church-related character of some neighbourhood schools.

Ninth, some county schools are far removed from offering the same kind of church-related education as aided schools. The headteacher may not be a practising church-goer and the range of church-related contacts offered by the school may be minimal. Nevertheless, some of the pupils attending such secular neighbourhood schools may be practising church-goers from practising church-going families. The church needs to ask whether it should be content to direct the children of its practising members to predominantly secular schools.

Tenth, the younger headteachers are less likely to be regular church-goers than the more senior headteachers. They are also less likely to promote church-related education in their schools. If this trend between headteacher's age and the church-related character of schools persists, it is likely that the Christian character of schools will decrease as the older headteachers are replaced by a younger, more secular generation of headteachers. This could have important implications for the churches, especially given the conclusion of related research studies that there is already a growing gap between the churches and successive generations of young people. Secular educationalists may rejoice that the changes which have occurred in educational theory over the past two decades are now being reflected in school practice. The churches, however, need to be alert to the possibility of accelerated secularisation within state maintained schools, even in the shire counties. If the churches need to recognise that the secular educational system is unlikely to continue to make a significant contribution to church-related education, they need also to redirect their work among children in ways appropriate within an increasingly secular society.

**References**

Francis, L J (1987) *Religion in the Primary School: partnership between church and state?*, London, Collins Liturgical Publications.

Keeves, J P (1988) 'Path analysis,' in J P Keeves (ed.) *Educational Research, Methodology and Measurement: an international handbook*, pp. 723–731, Oxford, Pergamon Press.

# 11. Empirical perspectives on curriculum

This chapter begins with two examples of empirical research into the extent to which church schools promote multi-cultural education.

In the first article, Wendy Ball and Dr Barry Troyna report the findings of two surveys. In one survey 71 head teachers were asked whether their school was involved in multi-cultural education. In the other survey 121 departmental or faculty heads were asked whether they considered multi-cultural education to be relevant to their school. The authors conclude that church schools have lagged behind county schools in promoting multi-cultural education.

Both Wendy Ball and Barry Troyna currently serve in the Department of Education at the University of Warwick. This article was first published in *Journal of Educational Policy* in 1987.

The second article by the Revd Dr Edwin Cox and Dr Martin Skinner reports an early stage of a curriculum development project based in five church aided primary schools in a north Warwickshire town. It sets out to uncover the attitudes of the teachers to multi-faith religious education and to assess the impact of in-service training. The authors conclude that the teachers have welcomed and responded favourably to a multi-faith approach to religious education, and they found the change less difficult than they had expected.

At the time of writing Edwin Cox was Associate Fellow in the Department of Arts Education at the University of Warwick, and Emeritus Reader in Education at the University of London. Dr Martin Skinner is Lecturer in the Department of Psychology at the University of Warwick. This article was first published in *British Journal of Religious Education* in 1990.

In the third article, the Revd John L Higgins analyses the ways in which the syllabuses of religious education developed for use in Church of England voluntary aided schools treat the role of women in the context of the current social and ecclesiastical debate. He finds the syllabuses uninformed by these contemporary perspectives.

John Higgins is an Anglican parish priest, currently serving the small market town of Longton, Cumbria. This article was first published in *British Journal of Religious Education* in 1989.

# 11.1 Resistance, rights and rituals: denominational schools and multicultural education

*Wendy Ball and Barry Troyna*

## Introduction

In 1981, in an article for *Multiracial Education* (journal of the then named National Association for Multiracial Education) Rick Rogers made the important point that, 'One consequence of the declining school population has been a renewed interest in and criticism of the dual system of schooling in England and Wales' (1981, p. 27). Rogers' concern focused particularly on those schools with voluntary aided status and the extent of autonomy from the local education authority (LEA) which this allowed. As Rogers noted, aided schools have the potential to pursue policies and practices not only different from but antithetical to those adopted by the LEA. To demonstrate his argument, Rogers considered how the admissions policies of aided schools could, and in certain cases did, undermine the principle of comprehensive education subscribed to by the LEA. Similarly, the operation of these policies by certain schools constituted *de facto* discrimination against black students. As he put it, 'the procedures of selection by religion and ability *have* slid quietly into a social and racial selection as well' (Rogers 1981, p. 30 emphasis in original). Nor was Rogers alone in articulating these concerns. As early as 1975 a survey carried out by the Catholic Commission for Racial Justice had revealed how the admissions policies of some Catholic schools had disadvantaged black students, including those from Catholic families (CRJBCEW, 1975, p. 37). Further corroboration for this pattern was provided in 1981 by Ann Dummett and Julia McNeal. In their booklet for the Runnymede Trust they showed how the control over admissions policies exercised by aided schools in the voluntary sector provided the room to pursue a selective and elitist procedure in which racist judgments and assumptions were allowed to operate with impunity.

These contributions draw our attention to the failure of (some) church schools to provide equality of access to black students.[1] Our own research into the relationship between LEA policy and school practices in multicultural education builds on this by indicating the extent to which these schools resist calls for the infusion of this new educational orthodoxy into their procedural values and pedagogic and organisational routines. Our research was carried out in an LEA which we shall call 'Milltown,' and details of some of the major findings are already available (Troyna and Ball, 1983, 1985a, 1985b).[2] Here we want to concentrate particularly on the differential responses of county and voluntary schools to the Authority's policy on multicultural education as part of a general discussion about the dual system of education in the UK. This seems to us a timely contribution given the resurgence of interest in this issue generated by the publication in 1985 of *Faith in the City* (the report of the Archbishop of Canterbury's commission on urban areas), *Education for All*, the final report from the Swann Committee, and growing pressure from certain members of the Muslim communities in the UK for their own denominational schools (Troyna and Ball, 1986). In all cases, the role of denominational schools in the promotion of cultural diversity and in combatting racial inequalities in education has been carefully scrutinised. According to the authors of *Faith in the City*, for instance, 'The problems and opportunities of a multicultural society have many implications for our schools' (GSCE, 1985, p. 303). However, as we will illustrate here, reality does not correspond with this rhetoric, as schools in the voluntary sector show a dogged resistance to be implicated in local trends toward the legitimation of multicultural education. Before moving on to this, we want to spend a little time specifying more clearly the status and ascribed responsibilities of church schools in the UK's dual system of education.

## The voluntary education sector: who governs?

Discussion about policy and practice in church schools inevitably draws attention to issues of government within and over those schools. Here, we are concerned primarily with church schools with voluntary aided status; it is these schools, after all, which enjoy the greatest level of independence. In accordance with the 1944 Education Act religious bodies are able to establish voluntary aided schools which can select their pupils on religious criteria and in which denominational religious education can be provided. Whilst the voluntary body provides premises for the school and is responsible for external maintenance, repairs and major capital expenditure (for which it is eligible for a DES grant of up to 85%) the LEAs pay all of the running costs. However, as Pat Williams and Terry Murphy point out (1979, p. 3):

> Despite bearing the cost, local authorities do not get the real control. The law allows voluntary school governors to take many important decisions which county schools governors do not take, and yet the authorities appoint only one-third of these governors. Two-thirds are appointed by the voluntary body itself — the foundation or the church.

Voluntary aided schools evidently enjoy a considerable degree of autonomy in that they exercise control over staff appointments, curriculum and pupil admission (O'Keeffe 1983). In other words, some religious bodies have the right to determine who shall have access to a substantial proportion of state schools and to decide the content and nature of the educational provision offered by those schools. According to Rick Rogers (1981, p. 27):

> Around a third of all state schools are run in part by religious bodies. These are in the main the voluntary schools. Two thirds of those schools are Church of England — the rest are Catholic, Jewish or Methodist. Of every five children, one is being taught in a denominational or church school.

In recent years a substantial number of LEAs have introduced policies concerned with the promotion of cultural diversity and/or the eradication of racial inequality in education. The implications of the dual system of schooling for the implementation of these policies invites consideration. Our research in 'Milltown' schools exemplifies this issue and underlines the problem which faces those LEAs committed to the principle of equality of educational opportunity for all children.

## LEA policy and school practices in 'Milltown'

'Milltown' LEA was one of the first authorities to make a public commitment to the principle of multiculturalism by issuing a policy statement in 1980. During 1983 and 1984 we carried out two surveys into the relationship between policy and practice in multicultural education in this LEA. Our main objective was to establish how far the policy had influenced the organisational, administrative and pedagogic orientation of local schools. As we have already pointed out, the general research findings have been discussed elsewhere (Troyna and Ball 1983, 1985a, 1985b) and do not need to be reiterated. At the broadest level, however, we found that the policy had made a limited and patchy impact on the routine practices and procedures of the schools visited. One particular and recurrent feature of our survey findings was the relatively greater reductance of the voluntary aided schools in our sample to recognise the relevance of multicultural education to their situation. In our first survey[3] of 71 primary and secondary headteachers across the authority we asked, 'Would you say your school was involved in multicultural education?' Responses to this question alone, which tapped only the question of *perceived* involvement, revealed important differences between the schools in the country and voluntary sectors (see table 1).

*Table 1: Responses of county and voluntary school headteachers*
*to: 'Would you say your school was involved in*
*multicultural education?'*

| Responses | County | Voluntary[3] | N |
|---|---|---|---|
| Yes | 33 (76.7%) | 14 (50.0%) | 47 (66.2%) |
| No | 10 (23.3%) | 14 (50.0%) | 24 (33.8%) |
| *Total* | 43 (100%) | 28 (100%) | 71 (100%) |

According to these data 24 headteachers (33.8%) across the
authority freely admitted that their school was not involved in
multicultural education. The most obvious and common characteristic of these 'non-involved' schools was that they were situated
in areas of the authority with little or no black settlement, a demographic feature reflected in their student populations. In fact, 18 of
these headteachers said that the low number of black students in
their school was the principal reason for their disengagement from
the LEA policy on multicultural education (Troyna and Ball, 1983).
At the same time our data suggest that the status of the school (i.e.
voluntary or county) and its associated ethos, as described by the
headteacher, also has explanatory power.

In our second survey of 121 senior teachers (i.e. departmental
or faculty heads) in secondary schools[4] we were able to pursue
many of the themes thrown up in the first stage of the research.
We asked individual teachers, 'Do you consider the current debates
about multicultural education to be relevant to this school?' Here
we were aware that the additional variable of departmental and
faculty bias might influence teachers views on multicultural education. Our statistical analysis, however, confirmed the trends of
the previous survey in showing that teachers in county secondary
schools, irrespective of the geographical location of their schools
and their student intake, and independently of their subject or curriculum responsibilities were far more likely to see multicultural
education as relevant to their school than were those staff in
voluntary secondary schools. Thus, in those schools which contained 10% black students or less, 77.4% ($n$ = 24) of county
teachers compared with 45.8% ($n$ = 22) of voluntary teachers
regarded multicultural education to be relevant to their institution
(see table 2).

We found the same pattern when we controlled for departmen-
tal/faculty responsibilities. That is to say, the type of school rather
than subject specialism exerted the greater influence on teachers'
orientation towards multicultural education (see tables 3 and 4).

This pattern of responses was not confined simply to answers from
one question, but was sustained throughout the study. For instance, a
far higher proportion of the 73 county school teachers (78.1%) com-

Table 2: *Responses of county and voluntary secondary school teachers to: 'Do you consider the current debates about multicultural education to be relevant to this school?' by percentage of black students in school*

| Responses | Up to and including 10% black students | | More than 10% black students | | Total |
|---|---|---|---|---|---|
| | County | Voluntary | County | Voluntary | |
| Yes | 24 (77.4%) | 22 (45.8%) | 38 (90.5%) | 0 (0%) | 84 (69.4%) |
| No | 5 (16.1%) | 23 (47.9%) | 2 (4.8%) | 0 (0%) | 30 (24.8%) |
| Don't know/no | 2 (6.5%) | 3 (6.3%) | 2 (4.8%) | 0 (0%) | 7 (5.8%) |
| Total | 31 (100%) | 48 (100%) | 42 (100%) | 0 (0%) | 121 (100%) |

Table 3: *Responses of county school teachers to: 'Do you consider the current debates about multicultural education to be relevant to this school?' by department*

| Responses | Arts | Sciences | Creative arts | Other | Total |
|---|---|---|---|---|---|
| Yes | 28 (84.9%) | 18 (90.0%) | 8 (66.7%) | 8 (100%) | 62 (84.9%) |
| No | 2 (6.1%) | 1 (5.0%) | 4 (33.3%) | 0 (0%) | 7 (9.6%) |
| Don't know/ no answer | 3 (9.1%) | 1 (5.0%) | 0 (0%) | 0 (0%) | 4 (5.5%) |
| Total | 33 (100%) | 20 (100%) | 12 (100%) | 9 (100%) | 73 (100%) |

Table 4: *Responses of voluntary school teachers to: 'Do you consider the current debates about multicultural education to be relevant to this school?' by department*

| Responses | Arts | Sciences | Creative arts | Other | Total |
|---|---|---|---|---|---|
| Yes | 9 (50.0%) | 6 (50.0%) | 5 (41.7%) | 2 (33.3%) | 22 (45.8%) |
| No | 9 (50.0%) | 5 (41.7%) | 5 (41.7%) | 4 (66.7%) | 23 (47.9%) |
| Don't know/ no answer | 0 (0%) | 1 (8.3%) | 2 (16.7%) | 0 (0%) | 3 (6.3%) |
| Total | 18 (100%) | 12 (100%) | 12 (100%) | 6 (100%) | 48 (100%) |

pared with the 48 voluntary school teachers (47.9%) were in favour of the LEA's policy on multicultural education. The county school teachers (57.5%) were more likely to encourage multicultural perspectives to be taken into account by their departmental faculty staff than those in the voluntary schools (35.5%). They also were more likely to have been in contact with the LEA specialist services for multicultural education (that is, the Multicultural Education Resource Centre, the Adviser for Multicultural Education, and the provision for in-service education in this field) than their voluntary school counterparts. Although takeup of these initiatives was low in both sectors, 31.5% of county teachers compared with 14.6% of voluntary teachers said they made use of these initiatives.

In all, it was possible to establish two incontrovertible and highly significant findings from these research surveys. First, there was a disappointing response of local schools in general to the LEA policy on multicultural education. This is a pattern of responses which we have referred to and interpreted elsewhere (see, in particular, Troyna and Ball 1983, 1985a). Second, as we have shown here, there was a significant disparity between the county and voluntary sectors in an interest in and institutional response to multicultural education. Nor is this disparity confined to 'Milltown.'

In 1984 a Working Party on Catholic Education in a Multi-racial/Multicultural Society reported on its visits to 50 Roman Catholic Schools in different parts of England and Wales. These schools included (1984, p. 39):

> both primary and secondary schools, as well as sixth-form colleges in urban, suburban and rural areas were visited. Voluntary aided, independent, day and boarding schools were included, as were those run by religious orders and those with entirely lay staffs.

On the basis of these visits, the working party reported that most headteachers and their staffs understood multicultural education to be relevant only to black students. What is more, when multicultural perspectives were adopted they were confined to a narrow range of subjects (for example religious education, social studies). However, the working party also argued (1984, p. 45):

> One of the strongest impressions gained from our visits was the influence of a policy, whether this was formulated by the school or the local authority, on the life of the school ... the schools in local authorities which had strong policies on this subject had also been stimulated to a higher level of activity.

Our own research findings call this claim into question. It seems to us that the *general* problems of implementing LEA policies on multicultural education are particularly acute in relation to voluntary schools because of their greater autonomy from their LEA and the particular educational and religious ethos and practices which they promote. Let us elaborate on these points.

We have pointed out elsewhere that there is always likely to be a gap between multicultural education policy as intended by an LEA and its implementation because of the decentralised nature of the UK education system, at the very least (Troyna and Ball, 1985b). The long-running saga involving the opposition of Raymond Honeyford, headteacher of Drummond Middle School in Bradford to his LEA's policy on multicultural education provides a classic example of this dilemma; as Troyna points out, it highlights, amongst other things, the debate about ' ... who ultimately controls what goes on in individual schools: is it the head, the professional teacher unions, school governors, the LEA or the DES?' (1986a p. 20). This lack of clarity, some might say struggle for control, is exacerbated in the voluntary school sector where the religious bodies feature as an additional and powerful interest group influencing educational provision and practice.[5] The permissive approach taken by 'Milltown' LEA and others to the implementation of multicultural education ensures that the role of the church in the determination of school ethos and priorities in the voluntary sector has not been addressed seriously.

It is generally recognised that there is no commonly agreed definition of multicultural education. In 'Milltown' LEA's 1980 policy statement two major and related themes were stressed: first the notion of cultural pluralism/diversity; and second the relevance and appropriateness of this notion in all educational milieux irrespective of location or the proportion of black students in the school. As we have shown, voluntary school staff seem particularly reluctant to recognise the legitimacy of these principles. Our qualitative research data provide some clues to the reasons for this which relate to teachers perceptions of the ethos and values which they believe should be promoted by church controlled schools. On the one hand were those teachers who felt that the celebration of cultural diversity contradicted the notion of religious unity which constituted the *raison d'être* of the school. Consider the following remarks, for example, made respectively by a teacher of religious education and a headteacher in Roman Catholic secondary schools:

> We have only a small number of non-European pupils in school. As these are of the Catholic religion, they identify strongly with the majority.

> West Indians are not regarded as any different from anyone else ... we have few ethnic minorities in the school and as a Roman Catholic school there is a common base.

On the other hand there were those teachers who felt that the promotion of tolerance and understanding for all cultures was best tackled through the established religious, Christian ethos of the school and not by the introduction of multicultural education, as shown in these statements made respectively by a head of History department and a head of English department in Roman Catholic secondary schools:

> As this is a denominational school one hopes to impact Christian values which should include tolerance and consideration for others.
>
> Our Catholic school accommodates all nationalities easily.

It seems that the diffuse nature of the notion of multicultural education has enabled voluntary school teachers to circumvent the possible clash between the traditional aims of church schools (to promote Christianity) and their responsibilities to develop an education appropriate for a multicultural society, as specified by the LEA, at least. For teachers in these schools, faced with an unclear definition of multicultural education, Christianity becomes the vehicle on which the values of cultural diversity, tolerance and harmony can apparently best be transmitted. Put another way, these teachers do not see a conflict between what and how they teach routinely and the approach the LEA now expects them to adopt.

The evidence from this research and corroborating data from other studies suggests that the relative autonomy of the voluntary sector in controlling both admissions and the school curriculum generally may act as a powerful constraint on the effective diffusion and institutionalisation of LEA policies on multicultural education/antiracist education. Voluntary schools need to consider how their established policies and procedures may deny black and white students equal access to, and appropriate educational experiences in school. Those LEAs which are ostensibly concerned to promote cultural diversity and to combat racial inequality in education also need to consider how the dual system may inhibit their espoused aims. Paradoxically, the failure of the mainstream education system to recognise the wishes of the black communities and to provide their children with an appropriate education has led some members from these communities to appeal to their legal entitlement to set up their own separate schools. As the authors of *Faith in the City* acknowledge, by insisting on 'a narrow view of the school as a place for Christian instruction' some clergy provide 'strength to the wish by members of the Muslim community to have their own separate schools' (GSCE 1985, p. 307). Let us look at this issue in more detail.

## The debate on 'separate' schools

The request by some black groups to be allowed to set up their own separate schools has been considered in some detail by the Swann

Committee (1985). The committee pointed out that 'separate provision' may be used as an umbrella term for a variety of alternatives to existing mainstream provision. For the purposes of this article we are concerned primarily with the pressure to establish schools for certain black groups as voluntary aided schools within the maintained system, for as the committee acknowledged, 'the right of the ethnic minority communities to seek to establish their own voluntary aided schools is firmly enshrined in law' (1985, p. 499). The established churches in the UK have taken full advantage of this legal entitlement (specified under the provisions of the 1944 Education Act) but central government and most LEAs are clearly hostile to the idea of Sikh, Hindu, and Muslim groups establishing schools along religious lines. Because of this, these groups have tended to initiate their own schools in the private sector (Rogers, 1981). However, it is unlikely that the pressure to be granted a place in the maintained sector will cease. In the London Borough of Brent an independent Muslim primary school has been campaigning for some time now, for voluntary aided status. It was recently reported in the *Times Educational Supplement* (Lodge, 1986, p. 1) that:

A London Muslim school's bid to get voluntary aided status took another step forward this week. Brent Education Committee agreed to support the school, which has been run independently in the borough for the last two years

This decision has now been ratified by the full council, despite the opposition of Labour members, and the council will now make a recommendation to the Secretary of State for Education to grant the school voluntary aided status. This is likely to establish a precedent for other groups. Interestingly it appears that Conservative groups in some local authorities are moving towards a policy of support for allowing certain black community groups to set up their own schools with voluntary aided status. This may be understood as part of their overall commitment to the perpetuation of the dual system. In the Conservative manifesto for the ILEA Elections of May 1986, *Pupils Before Politics*, for example, the party's commitment to voluntary schools is recorded and justified on the grounds that (CP, 1986, p. 8):

These schools exercise a proper measure of independence within the maintained system, in their management, admissions, and internal school policies. This creates a greater diversity within the schools available in London, a variety of provision which is clearly welcomed by the parents.

It is also pointed out that the local Conservative Party is 'very willing to discuss the special educational needs of other communities and would be willing to discuss with them the establishment of voluntary aided schools' (1986, p. 9). However, the case for 'separate' schools has been rejected firmly by the Swann Committee on the grounds that these would not be in the long-term interests of the black communities. What is more, the committee insisted that such schools would militate against the adoption of policies for 'Education for All' within the mainstream education system (1985, p. 510):

> In view of our overall aim of schools offering a full education for all our children it is hardly surprising that we find we cannot favour a 'solution' to the supposed 'problems' which ethnic minority communities face, which tacitly seems to accept that these 'problems' are beyond the capacity and imagination of existing schools to meet and that the only answer is therefore to provide 'alternative' schools for ethnic minority pupils thus in effect absolving existing schools from even making the attempt to reappraise and review their practices.

We do not wish to argue in support of the establishment of separate schools. With the Swann Committee we believe that existing state schools should be the site of change. However, we are critical of the reformist proposals offered by the Swann Committe. These do not go far enough in specifying how schools can promote cultural diversity and combat racial inequality in education. As Troyna (1986b, p. 179) has pointed out, the Swann Committee:

> succeeded in denying the legitimacy of certain demands from the UK's black communities, obfuscated the thrust of the debate by failing to consider how racism might operate in the education system and eschewed responsibility for reformulating the education system so that it might cater more effectively and appropriately for its ethnically diverse clientele.

Moreover the prospects for the implementation of the committee's limited proposals are bleak. Multicultural education grew initially as a grassroots initiative over a decade ago in response to the wide-ranging grievances of the black communities over educational provision. Even before the publication of the Swann Report a substantial number of LEAs had introduced policies on multicultural education. These include many of the proposals included in the report and, in the case of a minority of LEAs, progress beyond the ideological framework of 'education for all' to a more explicit concern with the issue of racism (Williams, 1984). As we reported earlier, our research in 'Milltown' showed that this LEA's policy had made only a partial impact on local schools. The general problems of policy implementation which we identified undoubtedly apply to other LEAs which have introduced similar initiatives. In this context it is unlikely that the Swann Committee's proposals will win the consent of the black communities and deflect the demands of some groups for the establishment of their own separate schools.

## Conclusion

The evidence we have adduced in this article calls into question the fairness of the present dual system of schooling in which only the established or traditional western european churches are allowed *in practice* to provide denominational education. It seems to us that the maintenance of this divisive system of schooling provision and treatment, *de facto*, undermines the espoused commitment of the state to equality of educational opportunity. There are two dimensions of our argument which we want to emphasise. First, the resistance shown by schools in the voluntary sector, particularly, in recognising the wishes of the black communities by failing to offer them equality of access and by refusing to reappraise educational provision. Second, the minority religions have not been afforded the same treatment as the established churches which have successfully and traditionally gained the right to set up their own denominational schools. In all, we have a scenario in which equality of access and equality of treatment is denied systematically to black students and their communities. The Swann Committee did at least recognise this paradox and states that (1985, p. 514):

> we feel it is important to acknowledge the real and far-reaching changes which have taken place in the nature of British society particularly in recent years. We believe therefore that the time has come for the DES, in consultation with religious and educational bodies, to consider the relevant provisions of the 1944 Act to see whether or not alterations are required in a society that is now very different.

In fact a review of the dual system is to be carried out by the Association of Metropolitan Authorities as the *Times Educational Supplement* reported in November 1985. 'All 48 member LEAs will be asked for their views on this tricky question which has become more acute recently because of Muslim demands for separate schools' (Anon, 1985, p. 10). It seems unlikely, however that the DES will respond to the recommendation of either of these bodies. In its recent White Paper, *Better Schools* (1985), the DES makes it clear it intends to allow voluntary aided (and special agreement) schools to retain their favoured status in relation to the county sector (1985, p. 75, para 256–257, emphasis added):

> The government does not intend to change the composition of the governing bodies of aided and special agreement schools or to alter their functions except in minor respects ... The minor changes are on the lines proposed in the Green Paper and are designed to reflect the changes which will be made in the functions of county, controlled

and maintained special schools *without altering the distinctive status of aided and special agreement schools.*

Indeed it would appear that the government is seeking to *strengthen* the dual system. It will do this indirectly through the proposals included in the 1986 Education Bill to give new powers and responsibilities to governing bodies in both county and voluntary sectors. This will obviously enhance the already considerable influence of the voluntary bodies, given their majority representation on the governing bodies of voluntary schools. However, this situation could be used to encourage the participation of the black communities in school decision-making if the recommendation of the authors of *Faith in the City* is taken on board: 'the governors and managers of church schools should consider whether the composition of their foundation governors adequately reflects the ethnic constituency of the catchment area' (GSCE, 1985, p. 315, para 13.911 [ii]). However, even this would not, indeed could not, resolve the problem of the failure of voluntary schools in areas of minimal black settlement to promote multicultural and antiracist education.

In the light of our observations it seems to us that it is the responsibility of those LEAs with a stated commitment to multicultural/antiracist education to consider, as part of the process of policy development and implementation, the role and place of voluntary schools. Particular attention should be paid to gaining the support of the controlling church bodies in addressing the issue of racial inequality. In relation to this, the authors of *Faith in the City* have made a useful recommendation (GCSE, 1985, p.315, para 13.91 [iv]):

> a review of the Diocesan Education Committee measures should be undertaken, to allow the formulation of diocesan policies for church schools on admissions criteria and other issues such as religious education and worship, equal opportunities and community education. We do not believe that this would lead to a damaging erosion of the freedom of the individual church school.

In the long term, however, we agree with the Swann Committee that the place of the dual system of schooling in contemporary society must be reconsidered if processes of racial inequality in education are to be mitigated.

**Notes**
1. We use the term 'black' to refer to people of Afro-Caribbean and South Asia origin.
2. We have used the pseudonym 'Milltown,' to ensure the anonymity of the LEA, individual schools and teachers.
3. In the first survey our voluntary school sample comprised 19 Roman Catholic, eight Church of England and one Jewish school. The interested reader should refer to Troyna and Ball (1985a) for an explanation of our sampling framework and research methodology.

4.  Our sample included teachers drawn from 12 county secondary schools, nine voluntary secondary schools (seven Roman Catholic, one Church of England, one Jewish), two county sixth-form colleges and one Roman Catholic sixth-form college.

5.  The 1986 Education Bill attempts to clarify the powers and responsibilities of those involved in the running of schools. However, it is not clear that it has succeeded in this respect. Indeed the proposals for a new system of governing bodies including the intention to increase parental involvement in those for county schools seem likely to exacerbate the confusion over who controls. What is more, these proposals will ensure that some of the powers of governing bodies which are confined, at present, to those in the voluntary sector will be conferred on those in the county sector, hence reducing the relatively greater influence of an LEA over this sector. This may act as a further constraint on the implementation of LEA policies on multicultural education.

## References

Anon. (1985) 'Dual systems to be reviewed,' *Times Educational Supplement*, 15 November, p. 10.

Commission for Racial Justice of the Bishop's Conference of England and Wales (1975) *Where Creed and Colour Matter: A Survey on Black Children and Catholic Schools*, London, National Catholic Commission for Racial Justice.

Committee of Enquiry into the Education of Children from Ethnic Minority Groups (Swann) (1985) *Education for All*, Cmnd 9453, London, HMSO.

Conservative Party, (1986) *Pupils Before Politics*, The Conservative Manifesto for the ILEA Elections, London, Greater London Conservatives.

Department of Education and Science (1985) *Better Schools*, Cmnd 9469, London, HMSO.

Dummett, A and McNeal, J (1981) *Race and Church Schools*, London, Runnymede Trust.

General Synod of the Church of England (1985) *Faith in the City*, The Report of the Archbishop of Canterbury's Commission on Urban Priority Areas, London, Church House Publishing Company.

Lodge, B (1986) 'Muslim plan moves a step nearer,' *Times Educational Supplement*, 7 March, p. 1.

O'Keeffe, B (1983) 'Schools for all faiths,' *The Tablet*, 237, pp. 482–483.

Rogers (1981) 'Denominational schooling,' *Multiracial Education*, 10 (1), pp. 27–33.

Troyna, B (1986a) 'The controversy surrounding Raymond Honeyford,' *Social Studies Review*, 1 (4), pp. 19–22.

Troyna, B (1986b) '"Swann's song": the origins, ideology and implications of *Education for All*,' *Journal of Educational Policy*, 1, pp. 171–181.

Troyna, B and Ball, W (1983) 'Multicultural education policies: are they worth the paper they're written on?' *Times Educational Supplement*, 9 December, p. 20.

Troyna, B and Ball, W (1985a) *Views from the Chalk Face: School Responses to an LEA's Multicultural Educational Policy*, Warwick University Policy Papers in Ethnic Relations No. 1, Coventry, University of Warwick.

Troyna, B and Ball, W (1985b) 'Education decision-making and issues of "Race": a study of policy and practice on multicultural education in a local education authority,' *The Quarterly Journal of Science Affairs*, 4, pp. 322–325.

Troyna, B and Ball, W (1986) 'Partnerships, consultation and influence: state rhetoric in the struggle for racial equality,' in A Hartnett and M Naish (eds), *Education and Society Today*, Lewes, The Falmer Press.

Williams, J (1984) 'From institutional racism to anti-racism: the relationship between theories, policies and practices,' unpublished MSc dissertation, University of Aston.

Williams, P and Murphy, T (1979) 'Dual system, end it or mend it,' *Teaching London Kids*, 14, pp. 3–7.

Working Party on Catholic Education in a Multiracial/Multicultural Society (1984) *Learning from Diversity: A Challenge for Catholic Education*, London, Catholic Media Office.

# 11.2 Multi-Faith Religious Education in Church Primary Schools

*Edwin Cox and Martin Skinner*

## Introduction

The coming to Britain of religious pluralism has caused religious education in schools to widen its perspective. Whereas formerly it was almost entirely the teaching of Christianity it now has to take a multi-faith view and teach about all the major world faiths. Recent agreed syllabuses have, on the whole, accepted and encouraged this wider outlook. The change, however, has not been wholly painless, and has caused heart-searching among those teachers who are personally deeply committed to Christianity. It would be natural to suppose that this would be most acute in church schools, whose trust deeds require them to provide an education based on Christian principles.

The issue of multi-faith education in church primary schools has received little direct research although church bodies have discussed schools and multi-cultural education and some educationalists have written on religious education in the multi-cultural community.

Taking a world-wide perspective the World Council of Churches, in conjunction with the Sacred Trinity Centre, have produced a paper, *Christians and Education in a Multi-faith World*,[1] in which they draw attention to ' ... the concerns expressed by many Christians in different parts of the world about their role in education in multifaith environments.' The General Synod of the Church of England Board of Education has produced a discussion paper with the title *Schools and Multi-cultural Education*,[2] which discusses religious education in maintained schools in a multi-cultural United Kingdom. In this paper the issue of multi-cultural education is identified as a complex and important one, facing not only the Church of England but all those involved in education. It sets out the view that the Church of England, with its institutionalised involvement in schools, should be concerned with that issue, and that all Christian teachers will have to address the tensions between their felt obligations to their church and to the multi-cultural society in which they live and teach. The discussion also makes it clear that this is not a matter only for areas with relatively high proportions of ethnic minorities, but that it has implications for all children in all schools if they are to be given an adequate understanding of the nature of the society in which they are to live and the world into which this particular society fits.

The Board's paper is broadly about multi-cultural education in schools but addresses, too, religious education in the maintained system, seeing religious education as having perhaps the greatest contribution to make to multi-cultural education, and it notes the attention given, and the attendant difficulties, in revising agreed syllabuses to incorporate other world religions. The paper concludes with a caveat to its overall positive regard for the issue of multi-cultural education by noting that, although most teachers are in principle favourable to it, their support can sometimes be expressed without adequately having considered the possibly painful, testing and frustrating nature of steps towards a harmonious and truly multi-cultural society.

From within the field of education Aspin has discussed the relationship between church schools, religious education and the multi-ethnic community.[3] Aspin sees religious education in a multi-ethnic community as raising important questions of cultural relativism and absolutism. Broadening the argument concerning the place of church schools to any schools serving what he terms sectional interests he points out difficulties both in the position of schools claiming most of their funding from public sources while imposing specific qualifications relating to those sectional interests on staff in the schools, and in making decisions about what special interests should be deemed suitable and which unsuitable for receiving 'aided' status. In reply to Aspin, Blake points to the fine line between cultural imperialism and the duties of a state to treat all its members with respect, though not necessarily to hold them in esteem.[4]

Bernadette O'Keeffe's enquiry, published in *Faith, Culture and the Dual System*[5] suggested concern, uncertainty about how to accommodate to cultural changes, and a certain amount of resistance on the part of teachers who were keenly committed to Christianity. Church primary schools tend to think of themselves as neighbourhood schools, catering for all the young children in the vicinity, whatever their family religious background but, at the same time, the majority of them think of themselves as attempting to teach the Christian faith, and governing bodies are inclined to appoint practising Christians to the staff whenever possible.

A survey of all primary schools in Gloucestershire was undertaken by Leslie J Francis and the results published in 1987 in *Religion in the Primary School*.[6] Among other things Francis discovered that church schools do not have greater influence on pupils' religious attitudes than do state schools, and that whereas Roman Catholic schools see their function as giving positive Christian attitudes Anglican schools think of themselves as neighbourhood schools providing education with a religious tinge. He asks the pointed questions of what is the reason for them continuing as church schools if they are not offering anything distinctive from county schools, and if they are intended to be neighbourhood schools, what is the justification in a multi-culture for their Christian distinctiveness.

## Purpose of the study

The present study was undertaken to ascertain how church primary schools in a specific area were responding to the challenge of multi-faith religious education. It involved all five church primary schools in a town in North Warwickshire, six miles from the multi-cultural city of Coventry, and with a population of forty-one thousand. It was conducted at the time when the new Warwickshire Agreed Syllabus of Religious Education was being introduced. The syllabus required that a greater degree of attention be paid to the pluralistic religious situation than formerly and the five teachers with special responsibility for religious education, together with other representatives of the staff of the schools, were undergoing a course of in-service training, based in one of the schools, to increase their expertise. The course, which was organised by Warwick University Arts Education Department, consisted of ten sessions of one and a half hours each, some of them led by religious educators (lecturers and advisers in religious education) and others by members of faith communities (for example a Rabbi and a Buddhist monk). The purpose of the study was threefold:

   a.  to uncover the attitudes of the teachers to multi-faith religious education in church schools;
   b.  to see if the in-service course modified that attitude;
   c.  to find out how the teachers reacted to the new Warwickshire Agreed Syllabus.

## Method of collecting data

At the beginning of the school year, and at the time when the course of in-service training was about to begin, each school was visited and the teacher with special responsibility for religious education was interviewed, with the interviewer asking a number of predetermined questions and noting the answers. At the same time the teachers were asked to complete a questionnaire, which is described in the next paragraph. That questionnaire was submitted to them again on two further occasions, the second time being at the end of the term in which the in-service course finished, and the third time being six months after the course had concluded.

The questionnaire was divided into two parts. The first part was intended to assess changes in goals, or aims, in teaching religious education. It was composed of eight statements, all but one taken from the 1986 Warwickshire Agreed Syllabus of Religious Education, which the teachers were asked to rank in terms of their subjective importance. The statements were these.

1. Religious education helps pupils to understand more fully their cultural heritage.
2. Religious education helps pupils appreciate the variety of beliefs and customs of people living around them.
3. Religious education provides an insight into the role of religion in international affairs.
4. Religious education shows how men and women of different nations have been inspired by their beliefs.
5. Religious education contributes to moral and social education.
6. Religious education promotes an understanding of standards of fairness and justice.
7. Religious education promotes personal growth by adding a spiritual dimension.
8. Religious education helps to generate and promote religious faith.

The second part of the questionnaire was an attempt to assess changes in the teachers attitudes to the subject. It contained twelve statements, each accompanied by a seven-point scale for indicating degrees of agreement or disagreement in a Likert format (although this was not a true Likert scale with item analysis; all statements were presented in such a way that agreement was positive). The statements, which were chosen to cover the possible functions which positive and negative attitudes towards religious education and its teaching might have, were as follows.

1. Teaching religious education is an important part of the curriculum because any view of the world without a religious dimension would be incomplete.
2. I have taken on special responsibility for religious education because it has given me extra salary increments.
3. Teaching religious education enables me to share my religious faith with pupils.
4. Religious faith is important for personal security and stability.
5. Religious education involves the learning of important facts and knowledge like any other school subject.
6. Taking on special responsibility for religious education is, for me, part of my career development.
7. Teaching religious education allows me to nurture religious faith in pupils.

8.  I feel a strong commitment to teach religious education which cannot easily be put into words.
9.  Religious education provides explanations of events in this world which are just as important as any other explanations.
10. For me, responsibility for religious education is just the same as any other responsibilities which I hold in the school.
11. It is important to express the values and beliefs contained within religion and religious education facilitates this.
12. There is nothing more important in this world than religious faith.

## Results of the questionnaire

### *Teachers goals in religious education*

Though the sample of five schools was not large and one of them, because of change of staff, contributed only to the first interview and questionnaire, a number of interesting and thought-provoking findings emerged. The responses to the first part of the questionnaire, on the goals of religious education, are contained in table 1.

The first column of each school represents the responses to the first administration of the questionnaire, the middle column the responses to the second administration and the third column those of the final administration. The lower the figure the more highly was the stated goal rated.

In interpreting the table one has to ask firstly to what extent are the schools agreed about the goals of religious education, secondly what goals do they see religious education as trying to achieve, and thirdly did the in-service course cause any modification of their assessment of those goals.

The first thing that strikes the reader on inspection of the figures in table 1 is the comparative lack of uniformity in the rating of the eight goals. For instance, the first statement is ranked at one time or another in every position except first; and statement 5 is variously ranked from first to sixth. This would seem to suggest a degree of divergence among church primary school teachers as to the purpose of religious education. Nevertheless, certain trends can be noticed. The responses to statement 7 indicate that the promotion of personal growth by the addition of a spiritual dimension seems to be consistently the outstanding aim, with perhaps its moral and social influence (statement 5) coming next in all schools except school C, which seems to prefer helping its pupils to appreciate the beliefs and customs of people living near. The idea of religious education giving an insight into the role of religions in international affairs (statement 3) is a somewhat mature notion for children of primary school age, which may account for its consistently low rating. More

*Table 1: Rankings of eight goals of religious education on three occasions*

|  | School A | School B | School C | School D | School E |
|---|---|---|---|---|---|
| statement 1 | 4 5 3 | 8 6 7 | 3 2 3 | 6 5 2 | 4 |
| statement 2 | 5 3 1 | 4 3 4 | 2 3 2 | 7 4 4 | 6 |
| statement 3 | 8 7 8 | 7 8 8 | 8 5 4 | 8 8 8 | 8 |
| statement 4 | 6 6 4 | 5 7 5 | 4 4 8 | 3 6 7 | 7 |
| statement 5 | 2 4 2 | 3 4 2 | 6 6 5 | 5 3 3 | 1 |
| statement 6 | 3 2 6 | 2 2 3 | 7 7 7 | 4 2 6 | 2 |
| statement 7 | 1 1 5 | 1 1 1 | 1 1 1 | 1 1 1 | 3 |
| statement 8 | 7 8 7 | 6 5 6 | 5 8 6 | 2 7 5 | 5 |

surprising is that church schools should place so far down the scale the objective of generating and promoting religious faith; statement 8 is generally placed in fifth to eighth place, and the school that initially ranked it second seems to have modified its view considerably after experiencing the in-service course. It may be that these teachers regard nurture as the responsibility of the home and the church, with the school providing the sort of religious education that will complement rather than initiate that nurture.

All this would seem to imply that teachers in church primary schools are beginning to be aware of the need for a multi-cultural religious education, that they do not see their task as principally inducting their pupils into a specific religious faith, but that they are concerned with personal, social and moral growth for which they think an awareness of a spiritual dimension to experience is necessary. It may reflect the religious uncertainty of the times that they feel justified in trying to give their pupils a spiritual or religious view of life, which will permit a variety of interpretations, but not in trying to give them a particular religion.

As regards the effect of the in-service course on attitudes to multicultural education one can detect a certain amount of influence. Schools A and D seem to have become more aware of the need for religious education to lead pupils to appreciate the variety of beliefs and customs in people living near, and School C modified its view about the subject giving insight into the role of religion in international affairs. One could also think that the demoting of School D of the importance of transmitting religious faith is a sign of increased awareness of the multi-cultural situation. The effect of the course is perhaps more clearly shown in table 2 which gives the average rankings for the three administrations of this part of the questionnaire.

The significance of table 2 is that the first two statements, both of which refer to the relation of religious education to the prevailing culture, are ranked higher with each succeeding administration of

*Table 2: Average rankings of goals of religious education*

|             | Pre-course | Post-course | Final |
|-------------|:----------:|:-----------:|:-----:|
| statement 1 | 5.3        | 4.5         | 3.8   |
| statement 2 | 4.5        | 3.3         | 2.8   |
| statement 3 | 7.8        | 7.8         | 7.0   |
| statement 4 | 4.5        | 5.5         | 6.0   |
| statement 5 | 4.0        | 4.3         | 3.3   |
| statement 6 | 4.0        | 3.3         | 5.5   |
| statement 7 | 1.0        | 1.0         | 3.0   |
| statement 8 | 5.0        | 7.0         | 6.0   |

the questionnaire. It is perhaps too much to claim that this change is directly related to the course, but the respondents seem to have become more aware of the need for a multi-cultural goal during the time in which they were attending the course.

## Teachers attitudes to religious education

Several psychologists writing on attitudes have chosen to discuss the importance of the functions of attitudes.[7,8] It seemed likely, therefore, that teachers would display not just a variety of attitudes towards the teaching of religious education but a variety of reasons for holding those that they do hold. To probe a little into this we grouped our statements of attitudes in the second part of the questionnaire in terms of their assumed indication of function in the following way:

a.  those that might be regarded as instrumental in bringing some good or advantage beyond the content of the teaching (statements 2, 6 and 10);

b.  those which permitted expression of values (statements 3, 7 and 11);

c.  those concerned with personal security and peace of mind, which we have called ego-defensive (statements 4, 8 and 12);

d.  those which are related to an interest primarily in transmission of knowledge (statements 1, 5 and 9).

The ratings of the twelve attitudes are set out in the following table where, as in table 1, the three columns refer to completions of the questionnaire before and after the course and six months afterwards, and the lower the figure the more strongly the attitude statement was approved.

Inspection of this table provokes several intriguing speculations. In the first instance the responses to statement 2 show that teachers do not undertake their religious education responsibilities in order to gain more salary. This may be because they are altruistic or because religious education is not generally rated sufficiently important to carry a salary increment, which may well be the case in primary schools, where increments are not usually linked to subject expertise. Secondly, the relatively high scoring in the ego-defensive and knowledge sections would seem to imply that teachers see their task as giving information about religions and the need to give pupils a religious view which will minister to their own and the pupils sense of personal security and stability. This reinforces the findings connected with table 1 which dealt with goals of teaching religious education. Thirdly, the responses to question 8 may mean that teachers are not totally conscious of why they teach the subject. They feel it is important, possibly because of their own commitment, but find it difficult to put into words what precisely its importance is. This may imply a certain emotional attachment to the subject, rather than a clear conception of what it is intended to do. Fourthly, the responses to statement 7 show a reluctance, in at least two of the schools, to the nurturing of a religious faith in pupils, which again links with the responses in table 1. Consequently it may be true to say that the teachers rating of the twelve offered attitudes shows that they are concerned with giving pupils an awareness of a spiritual dimension to experience in order to encourage a stability and a sense of security, that they feel this is important without being able to say exactly why, but that they do not think this involves the promotion or nurture of any specific religious system.

## Attitude change due to the course

The ranking of the attitudes does not greatly change during the three administrations of the questionnaire. Indeed in thirty instances of the forty-eight in table 3 they either remain constant or change by only one point, which suggests that the in-service course had practically no influence on teacher attitudes. The two instances of progressive change are in the response of school A to statement 10 (which may indicate that the respondent came to see religious education in a more educational light as a result of the course), and in the response of school D to statement 2. One can hardly suppose that it was the course which had affected a teacher's attitude to salary increments and this change must be due to other influences.

## Teachers views of multi-faith religious education

Six months after the termination of the in-service course, as well as being asked to complete for the third time the questionnaire discussed above, the teachers were given certain open-ended questions about multi-faith religious education and their answers reveal

*Table 3: Rankings of attitudes to religious education on three occasions*

| | School A | School B | School C | School D | School E |
|---|---|---|---|---|---|
| **Instrumental** | | | | | |
| statement 2 | 7 7 7 | 7 7 7 | 7 7 7 | 7 3 2 | 7 |
| statement 6 | 5 7 7 | 7 7 7 | 2 1 2 | 3 2 2 | 1 |
| statement 10 | 7 3 2 | 6 6 6 | 1 1 1 | 2 2 6 | 3 |
| **Value expressive** | | | | | |
| statement 3 | 1 3 1 | 4 3 3 | 1 3 2 | 6 6 5 | 1 |
| statement 7 | 1 7 4 | 4 3 3 | 6 7 7 | 6 7 7 | 1 |
| statement 11 | 2 4 2 | 1 1 2 | 1 1 1 | 3 3 2 | 1 |
| **Ego-defensive** | | | | | |
| statement 4 | 1 5 1 | 1 1 1 | 1 3 2 | 2 2 4 | 1 |
| statement 8 | 1 1 1 | 2 2 2 | 4 4 7 | 1 2 1 | 2 |
| statement 12 | 1 1 4 | 1 1 1 | 1 1 1 | 2 4 4* | 1 |
| **Knowledge** | | | | | |
| statement 1 | 2 1 1 | 1 1 1 | 1 1 1 | 1 1 1 | 2 |
| statement 5 | 1 5 6 | 3 4 5 | 3 3 4 | 2 3 1 | 3 |
| statement 9 | 3 1 1 | 3 2 2 | 1 1 1 | 4 4 4 | 2 |

* denotes scale middle point inserted where response was omitted by respondent.

more clearly their attitude to it. The questions asked whether their attitude to it had changed, what they had done to promote it, in what ways they had been successful and what ways unsuccessful, what resistance they had encountered, and what advice they would give to other teachers embarking upon a similar program.

Without exception they thought that in the present world multi-faith religious education was necessary, and even inevitable. After an initial reluctance because of felt incompetence they had found that their competence had increased once they had set about trying it. Doubts about whether multi-faith religious education was appropriate before secondary school level had been allayed; the increased knowledge that they had obtained of diverse faith — possibly as a result of the in-service course — had augmented their confidence, though there was a feeling that they did not yet know enough to develop the subject to its fullest extent.

Work undertaken had mostly consisted of visits to places of worship and examination of the major religious festivals, such as Passover, Divali and Christmas, both of which had been found engrossing and profitable. In one school Hindu and Sikh parents had come to the school to talk of their religions, and in another Asian parents had helped with the loan of artefacts. The children had been pleased, and in one school enthusiastic, about what had been done; parents had not been opposed, though there had been

queries from some of them which had been answered satisfactorily. Colleagues in one school had shown a little unease and were
reluctant to undertake it, but were now 'coming round.' More sur-
prisingly perhaps, the religious leaders in the district had made no
objection, with the exception of one who, while trying to understand, 'doesn't want to compromise his own beliefs but sees which
way education is going.'

Advice to others trying to introduce multi-faith religious education was to 'have a go' because it is not as difficult as it appears
from outside, to expect a certain amount of opposition, to try to
build up knowledge and confidence, to make as much use as possible
of visits and visitors, but to introduce the new studies gradually,
and not to attempt too much or 'to cover too many faiths and too
many cultures at a time.' The general impression of these answers
is that the schools being studied are moving into multi-faith religious education with a strong degree of success, that the teachers
are not finding it as difficult as they had anticipated because they
had more relevant knowledge than they had realised, that their confidence had grown with experience so that they felt able to extend
the work, that there had been wide sympathy for what they were
trying, and that the only setback had been when they had tried too
much too soon.

## Teachers reactions to the Agreed Syllabus

In the initial interview teachers were asked for their reactions to
the newly published Warwickshire Agreed Syllabus. The overall
impression is that they welcomed it because it would open up
the subject to a new range of studies of a wider and multi-faith
nature. It would move from nurture to a more genuine education in
religion and give children 'a meaningful understanding of the nature
of religion.' One thought it would provide 'a chance for a religious
quest to be explored on a broader, deeper level.' By embracing other
faith systems, there would be 'a heightened awareness of a universal set of approaches to this quest, leading to greater empathy
and understanding with and of others.' Another opinion was that its
influence on the pupils would allow them to think more deeply, and
lead to 'an awareness of differences and a deeper understanding of
what religion is about for them and for others of different faiths.'

At the same time there was little *detailed* awareness of what the
adoption of the syllabus would mean in practice for the schools. On
the negative side fears were expressed that it might be misinterpreted
by parents who still saw religious education as Christian instruction
and that some teachers might feel threatened by it. There was a general unease about the theoretical nature of the syllabus ('The theory
was fine but the practice is lacking') and that it appeared to give less
guidance than they would have wished about the content to be used

to implement the theory. One said 'It can be difficult to translate its aims and objectives, being without illustrations, in the main, into practical classroom material.' Using the syllabus properly would demand of teachers much work, soul-searching and rethinking. This might inhibit some, but there was an underlying confidence that they felt the exercise worthwhile and would be prepared to undertake it with both interest and enthusiasm.

## Conclusion

The sample on which this study is based is a small one and it might be unwise to extrapolate from it too widely. All the same, it seems to indicate that the teachers in this particular group of church schools are aware of the pressures for a fresh approach to religious education which has been occasioned by the change from a Christian based to a multi-cultural situation. Their previous view of religious education, being more concerned with the personal and spiritual development of their pupils than with propagating a specific faith, has enabled them to welcome and respond favourably to a new approach, and they have found the change less difficult than they had expected. Resistance from parents, church leaders and colleagues has been minimal. It would be interesting to investigate whether this pattern is reproduced in church primary schools of other denominations and in other places, and how far similar rethinking is taking place in church secondary schools.[9]

**Notes**
1.   World Council of Churches and the Sacred Trinity Centre, *Christians and Education in a Multi-faith World*, 1982.
2.   Board of Education of the General Synod of the Church of England, *Schools and Multicultural Education: a Discussion Paper*, (Memorandum 2/84), 1984.
3.   D N Aspin 'Church schools, Religious Education and the multi-ethnic community,' *Journal of Philosophy of Education*, 17, 1983, pp. 229–240.
4.   Nigel Blake, 'Church schools, religious education and the multi-ethnic community: a reply to David Aspin,' *Journal of Philosophy of Education*, 17, 1983, pp. 241–250.
5.   Bernadette O'Keeffe *Faith, Culture and the Dual System*, Lewes, The Falmer Press, 1986.
6.   Leslie J Francis *Religion in the Primary School*, London, Collins, 1987.
7.   D Katz 'The functional approach to the study of attitudes,' *Public Opinion Quarterly*, 24, 1960, pp. 163–204.
8.   M B Smith, J S Bruner and R W White, *Opinions and Personality*, New York, Wiley, 1956.
9.   This article reports an early stage of a curriculum development project based in five church aided primary schools in a north Warwickshire town, funded by Nicholas Chamberlaine's Charity School Foundation and directed by Robert Jackson, Department of Arts Education, University of Warwick.

# 11.3 Gender and Church of England diocesan syllabuses of religious education

*John L Higgins*

The syllabuses in question are those addressed to day-schools within the state maintained system of education where some schools with historic and financial ties to the church are substantially maintained by the state but with the church retaining the right to determine certain aspects of their distinctive character. One of the most important of these is the nature and quality of the religious education as expressed in the classroom setting. About half the dioceses of the Church of England offer their own syllabus of religious education for the schools within their area that are designated 'Church of England Voluntary Aided Schools.' These schools are free either to use such a syllabus or to develop one of their own. Some schools and some dioceses choose to use the religious education syllabus of the Local Authority of the county concerned. Content and practice is therefore varied as a result of competing philosophies. Some dioceses and some church-schools emphasise the 'distinctiveness' of their situation, while others emphasise the close partnership and inter-relatedness of their schools with the rest of the state system. This article seeks to analyse how the syllabuses treat the role of women in the context of the current social and ecclesiastical debate.

Given the concern within the Church of England in recent years with the issue of the ordination of women first to the diaconate and more recently to the priesthood, one might perhaps suspect that it would have received an appropriate level of interest in the diocesan syllabuses of religious education, so allowing a new generation of children to move towards informed views on the issues of gender and ministry touched on by the debate. For the most part the reality would appear to be somewhat different from this. Finding even a mention of this whole area of concern is somewhat difficult and even where there is direct reference to it, underlying assumptions and perhaps even prejudices speak powerfully through what is not said. For instance, in the Canterbury and Rochester scheme it is stated quite categorically that the full-time priesthood in some branches of the Christian church, including the Anglican, is made up of men, not women.[1] Even passing over the culturally imperialistic notion that the Church of England equals the Anglican church, which of course it does not, and the fact that some branches of the Anglican church have been ordaining women to the priesthood for some years, no attempt is made to qualify the statement or set it into its rapidly evolving English context, and that in a year which saw the Ordination of Women to the Diaconate Measure passed by the General Synod. This is the more remarkable because this syllabus is one of the few recent ones which seeks to address the needs of the secondary age pupil. In the notes for the thirteen-sixteen age group in this same section of the syllabus the stated aim is that of building up a community in which all men share equally, contribute to totally with absolute generosity, and by which they are supported and sustained by each other.[2] The use of the term 'men' in this context, therefore, seems to carry the meaning of 'males.'

It almost goes without saying that the entire set of current syllabuses have language that some would see as having a thoroughly male orientation, but then that is true of almost all other literature. Feminist critiques of language are readily available and I do not propose to pursue this particular angle any further other than to suggest that if religious education is to do with meaning and value, then the meanings and values inherent in the language used will of themselves convey something about religious belief. If this is true about the more general use of language it is also true about the topics, illustrations, supportive evidence and references that provide the content of the syllabuses. The Canterbury and Rochester scheme to which we have already referred suggests under the heading 'The family and marriage' that teenage girls in particular like to learn about the practical and domestic aspects of housekeeping and child rearing. This is linked almost immediately to what it sees as an important focus for the religious educator, namely that the family is where we learn to be fully human and that marriage should be seen as a sacrament whereby God's presence can be entered.[3] When these are put together the overall impression that is conveyed is one in which girls are to concern themselves with housekeeping and babies and are to see these as a divine vocation within marriage and the home. Clearly, a sizeable number of people today, including many with deep religious commitment, would challenge this view. This alternative view, and the possible theological underpinnings of it, receive no mention. Without this alternative perspective one is entitled to ask whether it really justifies itself as religious education in today's world, or whether it is really confessional catechesis that belongs somewhere other than in the classroom of a largely state-financed day school.

A number of other diocesean syllabuses also include sections on a similar theme. The Manchester scheme uses the word 'parent' rather than mother or father, and this is true of others too, though this may be an attempt to register sensitivity to the increasing number of one-parent families rather than to address the gender issue in an abstract sense.[4] The Bath and Wells scheme for juniors has a similar section which seems to be more concerned with domestic architecture. Additional project notes later in the syllabus deal with life in biblical times. Of the five paragraphs on the family two deal with women, of which the second and longer one is given over to the working of a Jewish well and the women's role in fetching water.[5] This material is taken over and reworked in the Chester syllabus,[6] while the Derby syllabus contains flow-charts on birth, the family and the community with pages of supportive material, but although multi-faith and multi-cultural aspects receive considerable mention there is nothing in any of this to suggest that gender issues are a matter of contemporary concern.[7]

Another way of reflecting on the gender issue might be through the introduction provided by Mothering Sunday. The Sheffield scheme speaks of the joys of family life, the church family and Mother Church, but the child's picture which accompanies this theme shows a large family all seated with what is clearly the mother standing at the sink doing the washing-up.[8] The Hereford scheme tackles the same theme but here traditional notions associated with Mothering Sunday are expanded to embrace not just mothers but 'parents and others who care for children.'[9] There is little to indicate the reasoning behind this expansion and nothing to suggest that it is motivated out of concern for sexual stereotyping.

Choice of biblical material also seems to be illustrative of underlying attitudes and assumptions. The Canterbury and Rochester scheme actually opens up the subject of male and female stereotypes in its secondary school material, yet in seventy-six pages of notes and comments on the teaching of the Bible only two women are mentioned, Eve and Bathsheba, the first traditionally seen as the cause of the fall of Adam and the second associated with the fall of David.[10] The Chichester scheme[11] and the Durham scheme[12] both make mention of the *Book of Ruth*. The first of these claims that it is rarely understood but is best seen as an attack on racism and exclusivism. The second prefers to explore such things as caring and sharing and invites examination of family ties, family provision and the acceptance of responsibility for others. In both cases the dignity, decisiveness and inner nobility of Ruth go unmentioned. Similar perspectives carry through to the New Testament. That singularly important visit by Jesus to the home of Martha and Mary in which the latter's attentiveness to the gospel is commended and encouraged by Jesus is reduced to 'homes Jesus went to' in the Guildford scheme[13] and 'meals Jesus shared' in the Carlisle scheme.[14] No woman is mentioned in the list of people whose lives Jesus changed in the Wakefield scheme,[15] while the Hereford scheme for young children invites the telling of the annunciation narrative with reference to how Mary was chosen for her joyful obedience and then immediately launches into a discussion on getting ready for a new baby.[16] In this particular instance it may be that the Church of England's dilemma over the place of Mary has much to answer for and it could be that sensitivity to past theological problems is hindering discussion on contemporary sociological and theological ones.

The position with respect to church history is little better and again we find that women are marginalised or even ignored altogether. In the Winchester scheme for the theme outline 'The Church of England', twenty-three men are mentioned plus 'the Pilgrim Fathers,' but only one woman, Florence Nightingale.[17] The Manchester scheme has reference to twelve men under the same heading but no women.[18] The Southwark scheme, however, has a greater degree of balance though does not achieve parity. Under the heading 'People of Courage' three women are included out of a total of nine specific names,[19] but having said that, no other scheme currently available addresses the women in history issue at all and the only references to be found in the two dozen or so syllabuses currently in use are the ones referred to above. The marginalisation and undervaluing of women in society and the church is not new, though it may seem surprising to some that it is as evident in contemporary syllabuses as it clearly is. In one sense one cannot rewrite history, and that includes the social context of the Bible. On the other hand, there is a sense in which history does need to be rewritten so that pupils can reflect on the gender bias. While biblical and subsequent history has much to confirm established social orders of male domination there can also be found substantial challenges to such things.

The point has already been made about Ruth and how easy it seems to be to minimise the integrity and decisiveness of her actions. Elsewhere in the Old Testament we find Miriam the prophetess ministering to the women of Israel, and Deborah and Huldah acting as judges over the entire population, both men and women. In the New Testament we find Simon the Pharisee scandalised by Jesus' grateful acceptance of the anointing with tears by a woman described as sinful, while elsewhere he talks to a Samaritan woman despite normal racial and social conventions of the day, as well as touching a ritually unclean woman to offer healing when accepted wisdom would have made him unclean too. He had a number of women who were his followers and it was from amongst these that first reports of the resurrection came. Paul, it is true, reflected more the social conventions of his day, and for that matter much of the rest of the Bible, but even he can be touched by authentic and radical alternatives. So Galations 3.28 speaks about there being neither Jew nor Greek, slave nor free, male nor female, 'for you are all one in Christ' (NIV). The same points can be made about almost the entire range of church history. Conventions of the day, together with the focus of the recording process down the centuries, have tended to marginalise the role of women who were active in their own right and not just as the wives and mothers of their menfolk. Even then it is the exception for even this to happen, more frequently their lot was to be ignored or entirely forgotten. The general impression emerging from the current Church of England diocesan syllabuses of education is that this continues to be the situation, though perhaps more by default than because there has been a conscious espousal of the generally accepted Pauline perspective. However, whether the stance is adopted by accident or intention, it does not justify ignoring an alternative perspective that is both ancient and authentic. If this was not sufficient reason then the contemporary concern for gender issues and the church's own debate about ordination ought to merit an awareness of this whole area, but the reality is somewhat different. The result is that both materials and ideas are presented that are partial and incomplete and that in turn leads to the accusation that the syllabuses are educationally unsound.

A little over a decade ago the Church of England syllabuses began to come to terms with multi-faith religious education. There is no doubt that today almost all of them addresses the issue with genuine commitment to the educational value of such an approach in church schools, as in county schools. Whole sections are devoted to the rationale of multi-faith education in a church school and many syllabuses have either specific sections on the subject or have adapted many themes and outlines to take account of this perspective. Indeed, the Derby syllabus which was originally produced in 1983 was almost completely reprinted in order to take this perspective on board in the second edition of 1987.[20] The Carlisle syllabus, produced for an area with relatively little experience of ethnic minorities and faiths other than Christianity, has a resource section for multi-faith books that extends to some twenty-five items, many of which are general headings for a whole series of books.[21] Perhaps in time the gender issue will be approached in a similar way. At the moment there is not a single reference to any book in any resource section of any diocesan syllabus of education, and that at a time when the issue is so controversial for the church and relevant in society as a whole. It is not the task of the religious education teacher in a maintained school to either support or oppose the ordination of women any more than it is the intention of this article. It is, however, an appropriate task to bring a valid and authentic tradition to the notice of all pupils in ways which will assist them to understand the church's current debate and which will also inform their stance on gender issues in the wider social arena.[22]

**Notes**
1.  *Canturbury and Rochester Diocese: Handbook of Christian Religious Education*, 1986, p. 71.
2.  *Ibid.*, p. 77.
3.  *Ibid.*, p. 117. The paragraph in question is headed 'Pitfalls.' The precise point being made seems to be that the religious educator must now allow the educational program to remain at the level of marriage rites and domestic practicalities but go on to what is suggested as 'a more important focus, namely, the notion

of the family as the most accessible place in which we learn to be fully human and marriage itself as a sacrement whereby God's presence can be entered.' An opening reference to 'teenage girls' creates the impression that traditional social patterns are being endorsed by Christian doctrine. Two pages later under the heading 'Secondary school approaches 13–16 years – contemporary challenge' we find, ' ... to introduce them to the notion of Christian marriage as marked by the willingness of each partner to take total responsibility for the other in a relationship of equality,' which restores some balance, but almost immediately we are back to traditional assumptions; on p. 120 'mothers' are the ones responsible for cooking and shopping.

4.  Diocese of Manchester, *Guidelines for Religious Education in Church Primary Schools*, 1983, pp. 17f, theme entitled 'Families.'
5.  Diocese of Bath and Wells, A *Syllabus of Religious Education for use in Church of England Voluntary Aided Primary Schools*, 1980. In particular the theme for 7–9 year olds entitled 'Homes' p. 50 and the article entitled 'Life in biblical times,' p. 79f especially paragraph headed 'The family' on p. 81.
6.  Diocese of Chester, *Religious Education*, 1987. See theme 'Homes and Families' p. 62f, and article entitled 'Life in biblical times,' sub-heading 'Homes and schools' p. 110f, especially the paragraph headed 'The family' p. 112.
7.  *Derby Diocesan Religious Education Syllabus*, 1987, pages 24–28.
8.  Diocese of Sheffield, *A Handbook of Suggestions for Church Schools*, 1985, p. B48.
9.  Diocese of Hereford, *Journey for Life*, 1982, p. 77.
10. *Op. cit.*, pp. 143–214.
11. Diocese of Chichester, *Guide Lines in Religious Education*, pp. 1985. This is essentially a collection of articles, some of which have page numbers but there is no page numbering running through the entire scheme.
12. Diocese of Durham, *Religious Education for Church Primary Schools*, 1977, 'Syllabus supplement,' p. 5.
13. Diocese of Guildford, *Diocesan Syllabus Guidelines for Religious Education*, p. 14.
14. Diocese of Carlisle, *Guidelines for Religious Education in Primary Schools*, 1982, p. 38.
15. Diocese of Wakefield, *A Handbook of Suggestions for Religious Education in Church Schools* (first published in 1988), p. 44.
16. Diocese of Hereford, *Signposts for a Journey*, 1980, p. 113.
17. Diocese of Winchester, *Religious Education Guidelines*, 1977, p. 22.
18. Diocese of Manchester, *Op. cit.*, p. 30.
19. Diocese of Southwark, *Religious Education Guidelines*, 1988, p. 32.
20. Diocese of Derby, *Op. cit.* See 'Introduction to the second edition (1987).'
21. Diocese of Carlisle, *Op. cit.*, p. 72.
22. This article is based on the author's unpublished dissertation for the degree of Master of Education at the University of Birmingham, England, 1988, 'Aspects of distinctiveness: an analysis and comparison of some key aspects of current Church of England diocesan syllabuses of religious education.'

# 12. Empirical perspectives on pupils

This chapter turns attention away from the schools, the teachers and the curriculum, and focuses on the pupils themselves.

In the first article, the Revd Professor Leslie J Francis and Sister Josephine Egan, PhD, test the theoretical view of the Catholic school as a faith community against the empirical reality of the pupils' backgrounds, expectations and attitudes. This study utilises data from over twelve hundred pupils attending Catholic schools in the USA and confirms and extends the findings of the authors' earlier studies conducted in England, Wales and Australia. They argue that it is considerably more realistic to modify the theory underpinning the Catholic school system to take into account the presence of non-Catholic pupils, pupils from non-practising Catholic backgrounds, and non-practising Catholic pupils, than to attempt to redefine enrolment policies to ensure that Catholic schools more truly represent a community of faith.

Leslie Francis is D J James Professor of Pastoral Theology at Trinity College, Carmarthen, and St David's University College, Lampeter. Josephine Egan is a member of the Community of the Daughters of the Holy Spirit. Currently she teaches at a Catholic independent school at Lechlade in Gloucestershire. This article was first published in *Religious Education* in 1990.

Northern Ireland remains a country deeply divided between Catholic and Protestant communities. This division is clearly reflected in the existence of two separate systems of schools. In the second article, the Revd Dr John E Greer investigates how pupils attending these schools perceive those who belong to 'the other side.' He employs psychometric techniques to assess the effect of age, sex, denomination and attitude towards religion and openness to members of the other religious groups. The data demonstrated that the young people most favourably disposed towards religion were also most open to the other religious traditions.

John Greer is an Anglican priest. Currently he is Reader in Religious Education at the University of Ulster in Coleraine. This article was first published in *Journal for the Scientific Study of Religion* in 1985.

# 12.1 The Catholic school as 'faith community': an empirical enquiry

*Leslie J Francis and Josephine Egon*

## Introduction

Our earlier studies have examined the relationship between Catholic secondary schools and pupil attitudes in England,[1] Scotland,[2] Wales,[3] and Australia.[4] Because these studies have deliberately adopted a common methodology and focus, it has been possible to compare and integrate their findings. When the same pattern of relationships begins to emerge between Catholic schools and pupil attitudes in more than one country, there is greater reason to take seriously the practical implications of the empirical findings. A significant conclusion that has developed through the English, Welsh, and Australian studies concerns the disparity between the theoretical view of the Catholic school as a faith community and the empirical reality in terms of the pupils' backgrounds, expectations, and attitudes. The aim of the present study is to extend this research perspective to the United States. First, a review is made of the weight given by American Catholic educationalists to the theory of the Catholic school as a faith community. Then this theory is tested against the perceptions of 1,204 16-year-old students.

Quantitatively Catholic schools in the US reached their all-time high in 1965-66 when they provided places for 5.6 million elementary and secondary pupils, constituting 87% of non-public school enrollment. By this time, however, the Catholic school system was coming under a number of pressures from within the church itself,[5] while the research reports by Greeley and Rossi[6] and Neuwein[7] seemed to suggest that Catholic schools were not central to the church's survival. By 1981–82 the Catholic school population had declined to 3.1 million, accounting for 64% of non-public school enrollment.[8]

Alongside this period of quantitative decline, there developed a process of qualitative reassessment. The bishops' pronouncement in 1967, entitled 'Catholic schools are indispensable,' led to the restatement of the role of Catholic schools during 1972 in the pastoral letter 'To teach as Jesus did.'[9] The bishops argued that only in the 'unique setting' of a Catholic school could children and young people 'experience learning and living fully integrated in the life of faith.' This report set in motion a new quest after the distinctiveness of Catholic schools. At the same time, Greeley's more recent research had concluded that 'far from declining in effectiveness in the past decade, Catholic schools seem to have increased their impact.... In terms of the future of the organisation, Catholic schools seem more important for a church in time of traumatic transition than for one in a time of peaceful stability.'[10]

O'Neill[11] argues that recent emphasis on Catholic schools becoming 'more of an alternative, more unique' was being accomplished by a strong emphasis on the schools developing as a 'faith community' of students, teachers, and parents. According to O'Neill,[12] a faith community is characterised by a common intentionality:

> when people in a school share a certain intentionality, a certain pattern or complex of values, understandings, sentiments, hopes, and dreams that deeply condition everything else that goes on, including the maths class, the athletic activities ... everything.

A number of other recent documents on the development of the Catholic school system in the US through the 1980s and into the 1990s also talk in terms of developing aspects of the distinctive faith community. For example, Sullivan[13] argues that Catholic schools offer parents an atmosphere in which 'home and school share a common and explicitly religious understanding of the meaning of life;' McBride[14] identifies the 'most basic' challenge facing Catholic schools in the 1980s as keeping 'Catholic schools Catholic, institutionally, morally and spiritually;' the *National Catechetical Directory*, issued by the National Conference of Catholic Bishops,[15] speaks in terms of the acceptance and living 'of the Christian message' and the striving 'to instill a Christian spirit' in the students.

The faith community view of the Catholic school, especially in the strong form expressed above by Sullivan,[16] seems to imply support for a very separatist notion of the Catholic school providing an alternative educational environment primarily for the practising Catholic children of practising Catholic parents. In practice, however, there are usually three different groups of pupils attending Catholic schools: Catholic pupils from practising backgrounds, Catholic pupils from non-practising backgrounds, and non-Catholic pupils. According to O'Neill,[17] the Catholic school as faith community is not impaired by students who do not share the same beliefs; rather he believes that their presence 'in many cases' will stimulate the other persons in the school to deepen and broaden their own perspective. This view has helped Catholic schools to respond to issues of racial integration through the admission of minority students who are not themselves Catholic.[18] However, there remains a significant lack of empirical information about the impact of non-Catholic pupils and, indeed, non-practising Catholic pupils on the character of American Catholic schools as faith communities.

In a recent study in England, Francis[19] demonstrates that non-Catholic pupils attending Catholic schools record a less sympathetic attitude toward Christianity than Catholic pupils. About 17 percent of the pupils admitted to these schools were not baptised Catholics. He concludes that if one of the aims of the Catholic church in maintaining Catholic schools in England is to provide a faith community in which Catholic pupils are supported by positive attitudes toward Christianity among their peers, these findings place a caveat against the policy of recruiting a significant proportion of non-Catholic pupils, even from churchgoing backgrounds. He suggests that the lower attitudes toward Christianity among the churchgoing non-Catholic pupils might well be a function of the incompatibility between their own religious background and the doctrinal, liturgical, and cathechetical assumptions of the school.

In a recent study in Wales, Egan and Francis[20] demonstrate that the most serious disaffection with the Catholic school is attributable not so much to the non-Catholic pupils as to the non-practising Catholic pupils. This is a much larger problem for the Catholic church in Wales. While less than 9% of the Welsh sample was non-Catholic, less than half of the girls and only slightly more than two-fifths of the boys were weekly mass attenders, while only two fifths of both sexes were supported by weekly mass-attending mothers and only one-quarter by weekly mass-attending fathers. They suggest that if Catholic schools are to exercise an effective ministry among Catholic pupils from non-practising backgrounds, these schools need to consciously abandon the assumption that all pupils can be treated as if they are part of the faith community characterised by practising Catholics.

The present study sets out to examine the religious background and practice of pupils attending some Catholic schools in the US, to explore the relationship between religious background and practice and the pupils' attitude toward Catholic schools, and to assess the implications of the findings for an understanding of the Catholic school as a faith community.

## Method

Four Catholic schools from New Jersey, Connecticut, and New York participated in the study by administering a questionnaire to all their 16-year-old pupils. The questionnaire included three main indices. First, frequency of pupils' mass attendance, fathers' mass attendance, and mothers' mass attendance were recorded on a four-point scale: every week, once or twice a month, a few times a year, never. Second, an indication of pupils' religion, mothers' religion, and fathers' religion were recorded on a two-point scale: Catholic and non-Catholic. Third, a detailed 66-item Likert[21] type attitude inventory,[22] containing items concerned with the pupils' views of the purpose and practice of Catholic schools, were responded to on a five-point scale: agree strongly, agree, not certain, disagree, disagree strongly.

All questionnaires were administered by teachers within the schools, following a standardised procedure. Completed questionnaires were returned from 535 boys and 669 girls. The data were analysed by means of linear multiple regression and path analysis, with listwise deletion of missing cases, using the SPSS package.[23]

## Results

The replies to the questionnaire indicate that 13% of the boys and 13% of the girls attending the Catholic schools in the sample were not themselves baptised Catholics. This compares with 7% of the same age group in the English study and 9% in the Welsh study. Over three quarters of the pupils in the present sample have been recruited from homes in which both parents are Catholic. As far as the boys were concerned, 86% reported that their mothers were baptised Catholics, 81% that their fathers were baptised Catholics, and 77% that both their parents were baptised Catholics. As far as the girls were concerned, 83% reported that their mothers were baptised Catholics, 80% that their fathers were baptised Catholics, and 76% that both their parents were baptised Catholics. Both the English and Welsh studies show much greater evidence of pupils coming from religiously mixed homes.[24] In the English study, 62% and, in the Welsh study, 43% of the pupils report that both their parents are baptised Catholics.

While the majority of the pupils (87%) attending Catholic schools in the present sample are baptised Catholics, just half of the girls (50%) and considerably less than half the boys (43%) claim to be fully practising Catholics in the sense of attending mass most weeks. As is consistent with much previous research, the girls demonstrate more religious practice than the boys.[25]

Totally consistent with the Welsh and English data is the fact that both the boys and the girls receive more religious support, in terms of mass attendance, from their mothers than from their fathers. Half the mothers (51%) and two-fifths of the fathers (40%) are weekly mass attenders. The comparison with the English data deserves closer scrutiny. While in England more pupils are likely to come from religiously divided homes, those parents who are baptised Catholics are more likely to be mass attenders. In other words, while the American pupils are more likely to come from homes in which both parents are baptised Catholics, it is also more likely that the faith is not being practised in these homes.

Two key subscales of the 66-item Likert attitude inventory used in this study are particularly appropriate to testing the pupils' own attitudes toward the Catholic school as a faith community and to exploring the differences in the perceptions of pupils from practising Catholic, non-practising Catholic, and non-Catholic backgrounds. These two scales can be described as measuring attitude toward attending the Catholic school and attitude toward religious education in the Catholic school. The items composing these scales, together with their statistical properties, are presented in appendices 1 and 2.

The scale of attitude toward attending the Catholic school demonstrates that the pupils who are happiest in Catholic schools believe that their parents made the correct decision by sending them to a Catholic school. Given the choice all over again, they would still opt to attend a Catholic school. They believe that there is a friendly relationship between the Catholic teachers and pupils in their school, and they attribute this friendly and happy atmosphere to a shared community of faith in which 'teachers and pupils work together to live the Christian way of life.' They claim that attendance at Catholic schools has helped them to understand the real meaning of life. The six items of this scale produce an alpha coefficient of .81707.[26] Since individual scores can range between 6 and 30 on a six-item Likert scale, the fact that the overall sample produces a mean of 22.22 (SD = 4.58) indicates that the majority of the students lean toward the positive end of this attitudinal continuum.

The scale of attitude toward religious education in the Catholic school demonstrates that pupils who are most supportive of religious education in their schools claim that religious education lessons have helpd them both to know Christ more deeply and also to deal with the important problems of life. This is the kind of integration of faith and life envisaged within the faith community. The four items of this scale produce an alpha coefficient of .72868. Since individual scores can range between 4 and 20 on a four-item Likert scale, the fact that the overall sample produces a mean of 12.04 (SD = 3.07) indicates that the majority of the students tend to hold a position toward the middle of this attitudinal continuum.

The path diagram[27] in figure 1 sets out to explore the extent to which the variation in the pupils' attitudes toward attending the Catholic school and toward religious education in the Catholic school can be accounted for in terms of their sex, their personal baptismal status, their parents' baptismal status, their personal mass attendance, and their parents' mass attendance. The correlation matrix from which this path model is developed and the accompanying multiple regression significance tests are presented in appendices 3 and 4. Four main conclusions emerge from this path model.

First, it is the pupils' personal contact with the church, expressed

*Figure 1:*  Path Model

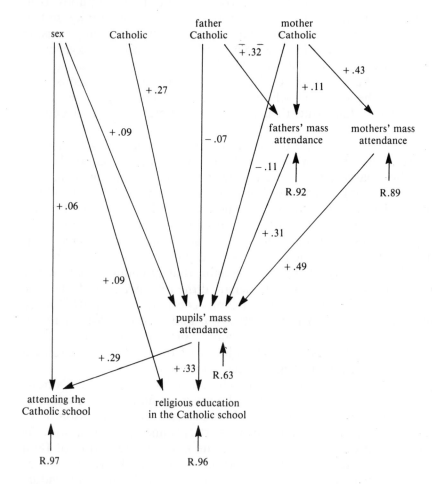

in terms of mass attendance, which is the key predictor of the pupils' attitude toward attending the Catholic school and toward religious education in the Catholic school. Pupils who attend mass more regularly also tend to feel more positively about attending the Catholic school and about the kind of religious education they receive in school. According to the beta weights, after the pupils' personal mass attendance has been taken into account, information about their personal baptismal status, their parents' baptismal status, and their parents' mass attendance contributes no additional predictive power to explaining variance in attitude scores.

Second, given the centrality of the pupils' personal pattern of mass attendance in predicting their attitudes, it is important next to examine the factors that help to predict the pupils' pattern of mass attendance. Here parental example and practice hold the key. If their parents attend mass regularly, the pupils are also much more likely to attend mass regularly. The path model also attributes greater significance to maternal influence than to paternal influence. This is consistent with Hornsby-Smith's findings.[28] What is extremely interesting at this point in the model is the direction of the influence from parental baptismal status. According to the correlation matrix, both fathers' and mothers' baptismal status is positively related to the pupils' mass attendance. According to the beta weights, when parental mass attendance has also been entered into the equation, both fathers' and mothers' baptismal status produces a negatives relationship with the pupils' mass attendance. This means, for example, that the pupils from a Catholic home where one or both parents have ceased to attend mass are less likely to attend mass themselves than the pupils from a religiously mixed home where one parent is a mass attending Catholic and the other parent is not a Catholic. In other words, parental disaffection has a stronger negative influence on the pupils than a partially non-Catholic background. This is consistent with Egan and Francis' findings in Wales.[29]

Third, given the centrality of parental mass attendance in predicting the pupils' pattern of mass attendance, it is important next to examine the factors which help to predict parental mass attendance. Here parental baptismal status holds the key. This, of course, is not surprising, since it is presumably the Catholic parents who go to mass. The path model does, however, enable us to go one step beyond this simple conclusion. Fathers' mass attendance is related not only to fathers' baptismal status but also to mothers'. This means that Catholic fathers tend to be more regular mass attenders when they are married to a Catholic wife. Mothers' mass attendance is not, however, related to the baptismal status of their husband. Catholic mothers are just as likely to be regular mass attenders whether or not their husbands are also Catholics.

Fourth, the pupils' sex is a significant predictor of their attitude toward attending the Catholic school and toward religious education in the Catholic school. This influence works in two ways: indirectly through the frequency of mass attendance and directly in addition to the influence mediated through mass attendance. This means, for example, that girls are more likely to attend mass regularly than boys and that regular mass-attending girls tend to hold more favorable attitudes toward attending the Catholic school and toward religious education in the Catholic school than regular mass attending boys. This is consistent with a range of research that reports higher levels of religiosity[30] and more favorable attitudes[31] toward religion among girls and women than among boys and men.

This path model would lead to the predictions that the pupils with the most positive attitudes toward attending the Catholic school and toward religious education in the Catholic school are the practising Catholics from homes where both parents are practising Catholics, and that the pupils with the least positive attitudes are the non-practising Catholics from homes where both parents are non-practising Catholics, while non-Catholic pupils from non-Catholic homes occupy a mid-way position between these two extreme groups. Table 1 compares the responses of these three groups to the individual items of the attitude scales, confirming the predictions made from the path model and providing further detail about the variation in attitudes between the three groups. For example, just 62% of the non-practising Catholics from non-practising Catholic homes agree that their parents made the correct decision by sending them to a Catholic school, compared with 75% of the non-Catholic pupils from non-Catholic homes and 88% of the practising Catholic pupils from practising Catholic homes.

## Conclusion

The above data analysis has set out to explore the sense in which Catholic schools in the US can be regarded as a faith community. Three key conclusions emerge from this analysis.

First, an examination of the baptismal status of the pupils attending these schools, together with the baptismal status of their parents, demonstrates that only 13% of the pupils are not themselves baptised Catholics, while 77% of the pupils come from homes where both parents are baptised Catholics. In the sense, therefore, of shared baptismal status and shared religious background, Catholic schools in the US show much evidence of potential for being a community of faith.

Second, an examination of the pattern of mass attendance of these pupils, together with the mass attendance of their parents, demonstrates that only half the girls and considerably less than half the boys are weekly mass attenders. At the same time, only half their mothers and two-fifths of their fathers are weekly mass attenders. In the sense, therefore, of Sullivan's[32] notion of home and school

*Table 1: Comparison between practising Catholic, non-practising Catholic, non-Catholic pupils*

|  | Practising Catholic % | Non-practising Catholic % | Non- Catholic % |
|---|---|---|---|
| **Attitude towards attending the Catholic school** | | | |
| My parents made the correct decision by sending me to a Catholic school | 88 | 62 | 75 |
| There is a friendly relationship between the Catholic teachers and pupils in my school | 77 | 52 | 71 |
| There is a happy atmosphere in my school because teachers and pupils work together to live the Christian way of life | 62 | 48 | 51 |
| Attendance at Catholic school has helped me to understand the real meaning of life | 53 | 16 | 44 |
| If I had the choice all over again, I should still wish to attend a Catholic school | 77 | 56 | 58 |
| I am happy to be a pupil in my school | 81 | 60 | 74 |
| **Attitude towards religious education in the Catholic school** | | | |
| Religious education is more important to me than any other subject that I study in my school | 10 | 0 | 12 |
| Religious education lessons have helped me to know Christ more deeply | 69 | 40 | 64 |
| Religious education lessons provide me with the principles with which to deal with the important problems of life | 65 | 44 | 60 |
| If attendance at religious education lessons were voluntary, I should still want to attend them | 46 | 20 | 41 |

*Note:* 'Practising Catholics' means weekly mass-attending pupils from homes where both parents are weekly mass-attenders.
'Non-practising Catholics' means baptised Catholic non-mass-attending pupils from homes where both parents are baptised Catholics but non-mass-attenders.
'Non-Catholics' means pupils who are not baptised Catholics from homes where neither parent is baptised Catholic.

sharing 'a common and explicitly religious understanding of the meaning of life,' there is considerably less evidence of Catholic schools being able to realise the potential for being a community of faith.

Third, an examination of the pupils' attitudes toward attending a Catholic school and toward religious education in a Catholic school demonstrates that a positive attitude among pupils toward the Catholic school as a faith community is clearly related to their own pattern of mass attendance. At the same time, the pupils' pattern of mass attendance is closely related to their parents' mass attendance. In short, Catholic pupils from non-practising homes are less likely to be regular mass attenders, while pupils who are not regular mass attenders are less likely to feel positively about either attending a Catholic school or the religious education they receive in the Catholic school. Similarly, non-Catholic pupils are also less likely to feel positively about the Catholic school than practising Catholic pupils. In the sense, therefore, of O'Neill's[33] notion of a common intentionality 'when people in a school share ... a certain pattern or complex of values, understanding, sentiments, hopes and dreams,' the evidence seems to suggest that by catering to pupils with three different backgrounds − practising Catholic, non-practising Catholic, and non-Catholic − the Catholic school vitiates the claim to be a faith community. As currently expressed, Catholic schools are most appreciated by practising Catholic pupils. The presence of non-Catholic and non-practising Catholic pupils in these schools increases the pool of those who are not supportive of the common intentionality of the school, who are not positively disposed toward attending a Catholic school, and who do not value the religious education provided within the school as an integrative factor.

While the student body embraces some pupils who are hostile toward the Catholic school system itself alongside many who are supportive of the system, it is difficult to maintain that these schools represent a true community of faith. Given the hard reality of adolescent attitudes toward religion and the church,[34] together with the many positive contributions the Catholic school system is able to make to the education of non-Catholic pupils,[35] it is considerably more realistic to modify the theory underpinning the Catholic school system to take into account the presence of non-Catholic pupils, pupils from non-practising Catholic backgrounds, and non-practising Catholic pupils, than to attempt to redefine enrollment policies to ensure that Catholic schools more truly represent a community of faith.

## *Appendix 1: Scale of attitude towards attending the Catholic school*

| | *Corrected item — total correlation* |
|---|---|
| My parents made the correct decision by sending me to a Catholic school | .62180 |
| There is a friendly relationship between the Catholic teachers and pupils in my school | .45428 |
| There is a happy atmosphere in my school because teachers and pupils work together to live the Christian way of life | .53536 |
| Attendance at Catholic school has helped me to understand the real meaning of life | .52333 |
| If I had the choice all over again, I should still wish to attend a Catholic school | .64986 |
| I am happy to be a pupil in my school | .70612 |

*Note:* alpha — .81707

## *Appendix 2: Scale of attitude towards religious education in the Catholic school*

| | *Corrected item — total correlation* |
|---|---|
| Religious education is more important to me than any other subject that I study in my school | .44470 |
| Religious education lessons have helped me to know Christ more deeply | .56229 |
| Religious education lessons provide me with the principles with which to deal with the important problems of life | .47529 |
| If attendance at religious education lessons were voluntary, I should still want to attend them | .59941 |

*Note:* alpha = .72868

*Appendix 3: Correlation Matrix*

| | Attending Catholic school | Religious education | Fathers' mass attendance | Mothers' mass attendance | Pupils' mass attendance | Father Catholic | Mother Catholic | Pupil Catholic |
|---|---|---|---|---|---|---|---|---|
| sex | +.0857<br>.001 | +.0857<br>.001 | −.0438<br>NS | −.0125<br>NS | +0.730<br>.01 | −.0113<br>NS | −.0386<br>NS | −.0010<br>NS |
| pupil Catholic | +.0821<br>.01 | +.0756<br>.01 | +.3127<br>.001 | +.3834<br>.001 | +.4209<br>.001 | +.6779<br>.001 | +.7696<br>.001 | |
| mother Catholic | +.0331<br>NS | +.0138<br>NS | +.2932<br>.001 | +.4443<br>.001 | +.3650<br>.001 | +.5963<br>.000 | | |
| father Catholic | +.0229<br>NS | +.0134<br>NS | +.3861<br>.001 | +.2982<br>.001 | +.3124<br>.001 | | | |
| pupils' mass attendance | +.2287<br>.001 | +.2450<br>.001 | +.6354<br>.001 | +.7158<br>.001 | | | | |
| mothers' mass attendance | +.1160<br>.001 | +.1137<br>.001 | +.6091<br>.001 | | | | | |
| fathers' mass attendance | +.1134<br>.001 | +.1057<br>.001 | | | | | | |
| religious education in the Catholic school | +.5446<br>.001 | | | | | | | |

*Appendix 4: Multiple regression significance tests*

| Criterion variables | Predictor variables | $R^2$ | Increase in $R^2$ | B | Beta | St error B | F ratio | df | P< |
|---|---|---|---|---|---|---|---|---|---|
| fathers' mass attendance | father Catholic | .14707 | .14707 | +1.06012 | +.32116 | 0.11039 | 92.22 | 1,1165 | .001 |
| | mother Catholic | .15426 | .00719 | +0.38298 | +.10522 | 0.12173 | 9.90 | 1,1165 | .01 |
| mothers' mass attendance | mother Catholic | .20554 | .20554 | +1.41653 | +.42726 | 0.10738 | 174.03 | 1,1165 | .001 |
| | father Catholic | .20680 | .00126 | +0.13251 | +.04407 | 0.09738 | 1.85 | 1,1165 | NS |
| pupils' mass attendance | sex | .00624 | .00624 | +0.19309 | +.08859 | 0.04023 | 23.03 | 1,1161 | .001 |
| | pupil Catholic | .18900 | .18275 | +0.89137 | +.27212 | 0.10379 | 73.76 | 1,1161 | .001 |
| | mother Catholic | .19340 | .00440 | -0.34347 | -.11262 | 0.09278 | 13.70 | 1,1161 | .001 |
| | father Catholic | .19406 | .00066 | -0.18643 | -.06740 | 0.07227 | 6.66 | 1,1161 | .01 |
| | mothers' mass attendance | .55128 | .35722 | +0.45228 | +.49166 | 0.02302 | 385.86 | 1,1161 | .001 |
| | fathers' mass attendance | .60692 | .05563 | +0.26023 | +.31057 | 0.02030 | 164.32 | 1,1161 | .001 |
| pupils' attitude towards attending the Catholic school | sex | .00809 | .00809 | +0.59009 | +.06408 | 0.26481 | 4.97 | 1,1160 | .05 |
| | pupil Catholic | .01501 | .00692 | +1.03191 | +.07455 | 0.69763 | 2.19 | 1,1160 | NS |
| | father Catholic | .01744 | .00243 | -0.78221 | -.06693 | 0.47237 | 2.74 | 1,1160 | NS |
| | mother Catholic | .01850 | .00106 | -0.65401 | -.05075 | 0.60828 | 1.16 | 1,1160 | NS |
| | fathers' mass attendance | .03083 | .01244 | -0.01243 | -.00351 | 0.14137 | 0.01 | 1,1160 | NS |
| | mothers' mass attendance | .03329 | .00236 | -0.29053 | -.07474 | 0.17322 | 2.81 | 1,1160 | NS |
| | pupils' mass attendance | .06553 | .03244 | +1.21013 | +.28639 | 0.19129 | 40.02 | 1,1160 | .001 |
| pupils' attitude towards religious education in the Catholic school | sex | .01362 | .01362 | +0.52886 | +.08579 | 0.17582 | 9.05 | 1,1160 | .01 |
| | pupil Catholic | .01862 | .00500 | +0.64632 | +.06975 | 0.46320 | 1.95 | 1,1160 | NS |
| | mother Catholic | .02173 | .00311 | -0.65115 | -.07548 | 0.40387 | 2.60 | 1,1160 | NS |
| | father Catholic | .02366 | .00193 | -0.48230 | -.06164 | 0.31363 | 2.37 | 1,1160 | NS |
| | mothers' mass attendance | .03583 | .01217 | -0.20568 | -.07904 | 0.11501 | 3.20 | 1,1160 | NS |
| | fathers' mass attendance | .03894 | .00311 | -0.06625 | -.02795 | 0.09386 | 0.50 | 1,1160 | NS |
| | pupils' mass attendance | .08080 | .04186 | +0.92312 | -.32634 | 0.12701 | 52.83 | 1,1160 | .001 |
| constants | attending the Catholic school | 19.28432 | | | | | | | |
| | religious education in the Catholic school | 10.09518 | | | | | | | |

**Notes**
1. L J Francis 'Are Catholic schools good for non-Catholics?' *The Tablet*, 240, 1986, pp. 170–172; L J Francis, 'Roman Catholic secondary schools: falling rolls and pupil attitudes', *Educational Studies*, 12, 1986, pp. 119–127.
2. J Rhymer, and L J Francis, 'Roman Catholic secondary schools in Scotland and pupil attitude towards religion,' *Lumen Vitae*, 40, 1985, pp. 103–110.
3. J Egan and L J Francis, 'School ethos in Wales: the impact of non-practicing Catholic and non-Catholic pupils on Catholic secondary schools,' *Lumen Vitae*, 41, 1986, pp. 159–173.
4. L J Francis and J Egan, 'Catholic schools and the communication of faith: an empirical inquiry,' *Catholic School Studies*, 60, 2, 1987, pp. 27–34.
5. M P Ryan, *Are Parochial Schools the Answer?* New York, Guild Press, 1964; J L Reedy and J F Andrews, *The Perplexed Catholic*, Notre Dame, Indiana, Ave Maria Press, 1966.
6. A M Greeley and P H Rossi, *The Education of Catholic Americans*, Chicago, Aldine Publishing Company, 1966.
7. R A Neuwien (ed.), *Catholic Schools in Action*, University of Notre Dame Press, 1966.
8. T C Hunt and N M Kunkel, 'Catholic schools: the nation's largest alternative school system,' in J C Carper and T C Hunt (eds) *Religious Schooling in America*, Birmingham, Alabama, Religious Education Press, 1984.
9. National Conference of Catholic Bishops, *To teach as Jesus did*, Washington DC, United States Catholic Conference, 1973.
10. A M Greeley, W C McCready and K McCourt, *Catholic Schools in a Declining Church*, Kansas City, Sheed and Ward, 1976.
11. M O'Neill, 'Catholic education: the largest alternative system,' *Thrust*, 7 (May), 1978, pp. 25–26.
12. M O'Neill, 'Toward a modern concept of permeation,' *Momentum*, 10 (May), 1979, pp. 48–49.
13. T F Sullivan, 'Catholic schools in a changing church,' in T C Hunt and M M Maxson (eds) *Religion and Morality in American Schooling*, Washington DC, University Press of America, 1981.
14. A McBride, 'Major challenges facing Catholic education in the 1980s,' *Momentum*, 13 (December), 1982, pp. 10–11.
15. National Conference of Catholic Bishops, *Sharing the Light of Faith, National Catechetical Directory for Catholics of the United States*, Washington DC, United States Catholic Conference, 1979.
16. See note 13 above.
17. See note 12 above.
18. A M Greeley, *Catholic High Schools and Minority Students*, New Brunswick, Transaction Books, 1982.
19. See note 1 above.
20. See note 3 above.
21. R A Likert, 'A technique for measurement of attitudes,' *Archives of Psychology*, 140, 1932.
22. J Egan, An evaluation of the implementation of the principles of Catholic education in the Catholic comprehensive schools in Wales. Unpublished PhD dissertation, University of Wales, Cardiff, 1985.
23. SPSS Inc, SPSSX *User's Guide* (second edition), New York, McGraw-Hill, 1986.
24. These differences in pupil background between the English, Welsh, and USA studies are reported here to help the reader compare the path models constructed on the basis of the different studies, not to imply that inferences can be drawn from the present sample of schools.
25. See for example, J J Boyle and L J Francis, 'The influence of differing church aided school systems on pupil attitude towards religion,' *Research in Education*, 35, 1986, pp. 7–12.
26. L J Cronbach, 'Coefficient-alpha and the internal structure of tests,' *Psychometrika*, 16, 1951, pp. 297–334.

27. See K I Macdonald, 'Path Analysis,' in C A O'Muircheartaigh and C Payne (eds), *The Analysis of Survey Data*, Vol. 2, chapter 3, New York, John Wiley and Sons, 1977.

28. M P Hornby-Smith, *Catholic Education: the unobtrusive partner*, London, Sheed and Ward, 1978.

29. See 3 above.

30. M Argyle and B Beit-Hallahmi, B *The Social Psychology of Religion*, London, Routledge and Kegan Paul, 1975.

31. L J Francis, 'The child's attitude towards religion and religious education: a review of research,' *Educational Research*, 21, 1979, pp. 103–108.

32. See 13 above.

33. See 12 above.

34. L J Francis, *Teenagers and the Church*, London, Collins Liturgical Publications, 1984.

35. See 18 above.

## 12.2 Viewing 'the other side' in Northern Ireland

*John E Greer*

### Introduction

Northern Ireland is one of the most deeply divided countries in the world and one of the most violent. According to historian J C Beckett, members of its two communities 'mingle with a consciousness of the differences between them,' differences reflected in and heightened by separate education, political parties, newspapers, leisure activities, housing and, of course, churches (See Darby, 1976, p. 140). Other countries with which Northern Ireland has been compared have divisions, but in this particular country, ethnic, religious and other cleavages appear to be congruent, and the lack of crosscutting cleavages has contributed to the polarisation of the two communities and led to continuing political instability (Aunger, 1981, p. 161). According to Deane (1984, p. 191), Northern Ireland is not only polarised but segregated into two communities which have drawn apart and hardly ever meet. The role of religion in the conflict is a matter of some debate, but there is abundant evidence to support O'Brien's claim that while it is not a theological war it is 'a conflict between groups defined by *religion*' (O'Brien, 1974, p. 286). Lyons (1979, p. 144) is one of a number of historians who have pointed out the religious dimensions in the conflict. In Ulster,

> different cultures have collided because each has a view of life which it deems to be threatened by its opponents and power is the means by which a particular view of life can be maintained against all rivals. These views of life are founded upon religion because this is a region where religion is still considered as a vital determinant of everything important in the human condition. And religion is vital because there have been in conflict three (latterly two) deeply conservative, strongly opinionated communities each of whose churches still expresses what the members of these churches believe to be the truth.

According to the sociologist John Hickey, Northern Ireland society has 'consisted of two groups of people divided by the consciousness of different historical and religious traditions and accustomed to confronting each other across a divide created by those traditions' (1984 p. 21).

## A review of research

How do the members of the two communities in Northern Ireland view each other? Are cross cultural perceptions dependent on variables such as religion, sex and age? While remarkably little work has been done to provide answers to these important questions, there is some relevant research. In one of the earliest studies, which was mostly carried out in 1952–53 in a rural community, Harris (1972, p. xi) found that all social relationships were 'pervaded by a consciousness of the religious dichotomy.' Social separation in 'Ballybeg' led to ignorance of the other tradition and it was 'not only religious instruction but also religious prejudice that was learned and in a sense had to be taught at the mother's knee' (p. 178). This work throws light on intergroup relationships in one anonymous rural community, but it leaves questions about other parts of Northern Ireland unanswered. In his study of a stratified random sample of the population of Northern Ireland, carried out in 1968 shortly before the outbreak of the present 'troubles,' Rose (1971) included several questions which had a direct bearing on intergroup relationships. Respondents were asked what sort of attitude their parents had towards mixing between Protestants and Catholics when the respondents were children. Rose reports: 'The replies showed a high degree of collected goodwill. A total of 40 per cent said their parents were actively friendly, and another 43 per cent said they had a live-and-let-live attitude; only 13 per cent said that parents were against mixing with the other religion. The views reported were slightly more friendly among Catholics' (pp. 329–30). Respondents were also asked how they would deal with the members of the other religion, and three possible answers were provided. 32 per cent of Protestants compared with 29 per cent of Catholics said they would stand up strongly for their own religion. 25 per cent of Protestants compared with 21 per cent of Catholics said they would ignore religious differences. 40 per cent of Protestants compared with 45 per cent of Catholics replied that in view of past troubles they would make a special effort to be friendly (pp. 481, 484). Thus, many of Rose's respondents expressed tolerant attitudes.

Salters (1970) noted that two earlier small-scale studies of prejudice in Northern Ireland had reached conflicting conclusions, so he constructed scales to measure general tolerance, religious tolerance and civic responsibility. Using these scales, he investigated the attitudes of nearly 1000 fourth form pupils at Belfast secondary schools. He found that pupils in Catholic schools were significantly more tolerant than pupils in Protestant schools. He also concluded that in the area of sex differences, 'the results are according to the expected pattern. Boys appear to be less tolerant and less civic-minded than girls, irrespective of religious denomination' (pp. 86–7). In 1973, Fairleigh carried out a pilot study designed to investigate the feelings of Protestants and Catholics towards each other using the Authoritarian (F) Scale. Unfortunately the group was not a random sample of the population but consisted of about 100 people from their late teens to early forties attending day release and further education classes, so his conclusions must be treated with caution. Fairleigh indicates that 'The main finding was that the Protestants felt significantly more social distance from Catholics than did the Catholics from Protestants' (Fairleigh, 1975, p. 11). For Protestants but not for Catholics, social distance correlated significantly with authoritarianism.

In 1975, O'Donnell (1977) used a word-list technique in his study of Northern Irish stereotypes with a sample of 1,680 subjects of age 15–55 from Enniskillen, Belfast and Londonderry. He found a degree of similarity of stereotypes across ages, socio-economic classes, sexes and geographical locations and concluded that these variables could be regarded as irrelevant and discounted when examining stereotypes. He found that Roman Catholics thought of Protestants as British and as powerholders, in the past and in the future, while Protestants saw Roman Catholics as having an unfortunate hankering after a united Ireland. According to O'Donnell, 'religion *per se* plays an insignificant role in the stereotypes of Northern Ireland. Power is the crucial factor' (p. 155). This study has thrown light upon the mental images which the people of Northern Ireland use to conceptualise 'the other side,' but it does not tell much about the depth of feeling between the sides, and O'Donnell draws attention to the need for research into the relationship between behavioral or attitudinal prejudice and the stereotypes which he found among his sample of Northern Ireland subjects. 'It might be found that these verbalised stereotypes might not communicate the emotional, unconscious or repressed elements typically involved in prejudice' (pp. 160–1).

Finally, in a recent study of inter group perceptions carried out in 1978–79, Murray (1982) used participant observation to investigate the culture and character of one controlled (i.e. Protestant) and one Roman Catholic primary school. He concluded that 'at an educational level, in keeping with other sections of society, both sides judge each other across a gulf of ignorance. Arising from this ignorance comes the negative responses of suspicion and antipathy' (p. 303). In a study of this kind it is doubtful if one can generalise with confidence from knowledge of two schools to schools throughout the country. It may, however, be noted that the schools which were studied served a relatively peaceful part of the country which has had a low level of sectarian violence and where such suspicion and antipathy might not have been expected.

These studies all throw some light on relationships between the two communities in Northern Ireland, relationships which have a long history in the past and which have resulted in the situation existing today. Some of the studies, such as those of Harris and Murray, give sensitive insight into a local community or particular schools, but it is difficult to generalise from them. Other studies such as those by Rose and Salters provide 'harder' information which is more generalisable, but perhaps less perceptive. Taken together, the overall picture of Catholic/Protestant relationships is one of ignorance and prejudice, though Rose reported the expression of tolerant attitudes and a high degree of recollected goodwill, and both Rose and Salters reported greater goodwill among Roman Catholics than Protestants. It is important to note that Harris and Rose carried out their research prior to 1969 while the other cited studies were made after that year. The present troubles began in 1969 with bombing by Protestant extremists and with rioting in Londonderry and Belfast. Research since 1969 has been carried out against the background of increasing polarisation between the two communities, most recently as a result of the hunger strikes in 1981.

Before concluding this review of research, references must be made to recent work on religious development during adolescence by Hyde (1965) and Francis (1978, 1979) which is conveniently summarised by Mark (1984, p. 5). During the period of adolescence,

> differences due to the effects of age and sex are clearly discernable. Attitudes to Christianity and involvement in the activities of the church become less positive as children get older. Where involvement in the church is maintained attitudes to religion remain positive. Girls consistently show more positive attitudes than boys and greater involvement, but a linear decline in attitude to religion and in religious involvement is associated with increase in age.

Mark also noted the coincidence of deterioration of positive attitudes to religion with the period of cognitive development when abstract thinking emerges. This coincidence has also been observed among pupils at school·in Belfast (Greer, 1981) and it is consistent with the results of a study of social attitudes in English children by Powell and Stewart (1978), who measured aspects of the personality and social attitudes of over eight hundred children aged 8–15 years, and found that scores of conservatism and religiosity declined with age while scores for 'sex/hedonism' increased. They concluded that 'by the age of 8, children have learned to hold society's traditional beliefs ... but thereafter proceed to *unlearn* orthodox social values and become gradually liberalised' (p. 309). They also found that 'girls are more religious, less punitive and less ethnocentric than boys' (p. 316). After considering different approaches to development which might explain this pattern of change, they concluded that modelling theory was the only one which could explain their results. Their synthesis was that (p. 315)

> children copy the authoritarian behavior and attitude of their adult

parents and are probably positively reinforced for doing so, but gradually become aware of alternate models, which some children will copy even in the face of continued positive reinforcement of orthodox behavior.

At a later point in this paper we shall return to this research into social and religious development during adolescence when we consider its relevance to cross cultural perspectives in the Northern Ireland situation.

## Rationale for the present study

The present study was carried out to discover if a psychometric measure could be devised to study the relationships between members of the two communities in Northern Ireland, and to see if such measurement might throw some light on the relationships. However, before describing the methodology employed, it is important to clarify what was being investigated. Allport (1954) regarded prejudice as an over-generalised prejudgment which may be pro or con an individual or a group, and which is made irrespective of the evidence. An important feature of a prejudice is that is is held without sufficient warrant, and Allport recognised that 'we can never hope to draw a hard and fast line between "sufficient" and "insufficient" warrant. For this reason we cannot always be sure whether we are dealing with a case of prejudice or non-prejudice' (p. 8). If the difficulty of distinguishing between prejudice and non-prejudice is too great to handle and if a convenient line cannot be drawn, then the value of the concept of prejudice is limited. This is a serious weakness in the concept, particularly because a prejudice would often seem to have a kernel of truth for many people, a root in the personal experience of those who hold it. This is certainly the case in Northern Ireland where people may hold hostile attitudes to members of the other community because of bad experiences. Negative attitudes to 'the other side' may be the result of discrimination in employment or housing, strained relationships in the family resulting from mixed marriage, or suffering caused by violence or physical intimidation. As Fairleigh has put it, 'Underlying what might simplistically be called prejudice can be real struggles for economic or political power.... It may be a response to objectively real economic, social or political conflict' (1975, p. 10–11).

In the present study it was decided to avoid the use of the term 'prejudice.' Instead a scale was designed to measure the openness of the pupils of one tradition in relation to those of the other tradition. This openness was not the concept used by Rokeach, for whom 'the relative openness or closedness of a mind cuts across specific content' (1960, p. 6), and whose Dogmatism Scale was 'designed to transcend specific ideological positions in order to penetrate the formal and structural characteristics of all positions'

(p. 72). By openness was meant the willingness of pupils to value members of the other tradition as neighbors, relatives, workers, and people worth knowing and understanding. Openness was conceived as a measure of acceptance, of non-discrimination against members of the other religious tradition. Thus the aims of the study were:

a. to construct and to test the reliability and validity of an openness scale appropriate to Northern Ireland;
b. to use the scale to measure the openness to the other tradition of a group of pupils living in Northern Ireland of secondary school age;
c. to investigate the importance of three variables in relation to openness, sex, age and religious affiliation;
d. to study the attitude to religion, as measured by the Francis scale, of the group of pupils in relation to sex, age and religious affiliation, and to investigate the relationship between openness and attitude to religion; and
e. to relate the results of the study to other research and to suggest some tentative conclusions.

## Research design

The openness scale was devised in 1981 by the present writer and was a six item Likert-type scale to which respondents replied on a five point scale from agree strongly − agree − not certain − disagree − disagree strongly. The six items, four positive and two negative, are indicated in table 1. Responses to the positive items were scored 5−1 and responses to the two negative items were scored 1−5. Responses were totalled, allowing for an openness score ranging from 30 (most open) to 6 (most closed). The same scale was used with pupils of the two traditions, with the following rubric, 'This question is concerned with the way you feel about people who differ from you in religion, i.e. how you feel about Protestants if you are a Roman Catholic, or how you feel about Roman Catholics if you are a Protestant.'

One of the difficulties facing researchers in Northern Ireland is travelling through troubled areas where they may be in danger. For example, O'Donnell spent six weeks in Northern Ireland carrying out field work and he commented that 'this was no simple task in a situation where every journey was risky and every house, public or private, a potential bomb target. For instance, the gentleman staying in the next room to the investigator, in a guest house, had six bullets put through his head one morning and died instantly' (O'Donnell, 1977, p. 70). Obtaining permission from school authorities for access to pupils in a suitable environment in order to raise controversial issues was another problem. In his study of two primary schools, Murray (1982) reported that 'the single constraint imposed by both principals was that I should not interview or converse with pupils on sensitive issues' (pp. 90–1). In the present study, some of the potential problems were overcome by making the study of openness part of a larger investigation of religious attitudes, beliefs, practice, experience and moral judgment, reports on some of which have already been published (Greer, 1982, 1984). Another way of avoiding problems involved the use of teachers known personally to the writer to administer the test instrument to classes in their own schools. It so happened that in 1981 a mixed group of teachers was involved in a religious education curriculum development project based at the New University of Ulster (Greer and McElhinney, 1984). These teachers agreed to administer the questionnaire to classes in their schools *not* involved in the project. By this means the openness scale was administered to 2133 pupils from form 1 to form 5 in 19 secondary schools. It must be explained that pupils in Northern Ireland undergo a selection procedure at 11 years, prior to entry to secondary education, as a result of which roughly one quarter move to grammar schools where they receive a more academic form of education and three quarters to secondary (intermediate) schools. Unfortunately, there was an imbalance in the type of schools which participated in the present study, the importance of which it was not possible to determine. Two Roman Catholic schools were grammar schools and 7 secondary (intermediate), 6 Protestant voluntary/controlled schools were grammar schools and 4 secondary (intermediate).

The schools were located in different parts of Northern Ireland and included 3 city and 6 country Roman Catholic schools and 3 city and 7 country Protestant schools. The sample of pupils included 940 Catholics (517 boys; 423 girls) and 1193 Protestants (719 boys; 474 girls). It included the following numbers of pupils in each class: form 1 (12 years), 472; form 2 (13 years), 454; form 3 (14 years), 450; form 4 (15 years), 414; and form 5 (16 years), 343. This group of 2133 pupils was clearly not a random sample of all secondary pupils in Northern Ireland. It will also be seen that a small number of respondents did not give answers to all the questions, with the result that the number of replies was sometimes slightly lower than the total expected in a group or sub-group. Despite these limitations it was felt that given the dangers and difficulties involved in research into cross-cultural perceptions in this country, the results would be of some value and interest to social scientists and educators.

## Results

### *The reliability and validity of the scale*

To investigate the reliability of the openness scale, an item analysis was carried out. Each item in the scale was correlated with the total score from which that item was deleted. The corrected item-total correlation for each item was found to range from .45 to .75 and the alpha reliability coefficient for the whole scale was .85. The same coefficient was also calculated for each age group, each religious tradition and each sex, and it was found that the alpha reliability coefficient varied from .80 to .87. The coefficients of these sub-groups may be seen in appendix 1. It was concluded that the items in the openness scale were measuring substantially the same thing and that the scale functioned satisfactorily with sub-groups in the sample of pupils.

There was no other independent data relating to pupils openness with which the results of the openness scale could be correlated, and it was not possible to study the concurrent validity of the scale. However, it was possible to test the content validity of the items in the scale. The six items in the scale were mixed up with 12 other items relating to religious belief and practice, and to relationships between the two traditions in Northern Ireland. Eleven university lecturers in education or a related field agreed to classify each of the 18 items in one of 4 categories: very relevant, relevant, and irrelevant to the measurement of openness/closedness, and don't know. 40 out of a total of 66 judgments on the six items in the openness scale were 'very relevant' and 23 were 'relevant' to the measurement of openness. It was concluded that this result provided adequate evidence for the content validity of the scale.

## Results from openness scale

The results of the openness scale were analysed and are reported in two ways. Responses to the scale were expressed as percentages of respondents who indicated agreement with each category of response from 'strongly agree' to 'strongly disagree.' This made it possible to study the pattern of response to each statement. In addition, mean scores for the whole scale ranging from 30 to 6 were calculated for each pupil, which allowed a study to be made of openness in relation to different variables, including sex, religious affiliation and age as measured by form in school from form $1-5$. This represented an age range of approximately $12-16$ years. The percentage results in table 1 indicate that overall the pupils tended to show openness to those of 'the other side.' For example, 71% of Roman Catholic pupils and 57% of Protestant pupils agree strongly or agreed that there should be greater opportunities for pupils of different religious traditions to mix and meet. 63% of Roman Catholic pupils and 61% of Protestant pupils agreed strongly or agreed that they would be happy if someone of the other religion moved next door. But only 47% of Roman Catholic pupils and 42% of Protestant pupils welcomed the chance of learning more about the belief and worship of the other religious tradition. When pupils responses to the six items were analysed according to religion, it was found that (with one exception) Roman Catholic pupils were more open to 'the other side' than

*Table 1: Percentage responses to the attitude statements in the openness scale*

| Items | | Strongly agree % | Agree % | Not certain % | Disagree % | Strongly disagree % |
|---|---|---|---|---|---|---|
| 1. I would be quite happy if someone of the other religion moved in next door tomorrow. | RC | 30.7 | 32.6 | 21.8 | 6.4 | 8.4 |
| | Prot. | 28.2 | 32.6 | 18.1 | 8.6 | 12.4 |
| 2. I would be strongly opposed to a brother or sister or other close relative marrying a member of the other religion | RC | 9.8 | 10.6 | 22.9 | 28.5 | 28.2 |
| | Prot. | 18.3 | 14.4 | 20.7 | 22.1 | 24.5 |
| 3. I would be quite happy to have someone of the other religion as my boss. | RC | 18.5 | 37.3 | 24.0 | 10.2 | 10.1 |
| | Prot. | 21.9 | 35.2 | 19.1 | 11.0 | 12.8 |
| 4. I believe that in Northern Ireland members of the two religions are best kept apart. | RC | 12.7 | 15.2 | 21.4 | 25.0 | 25.7 |
| | Prot. | 19.0 | 16.6 | 19.4 | 21.7 | 23.3 |
| 5. I would welcome the chance of learning more about the beliefs and worship of people of the other religion. | RC | 16.5 | 30.6 | 26.0 | 15.2 | 11.8 |
| | Prot. | 14.8 | 27.1 | 23.3 | 16.4 | 18.3 |
| 6. Pupils in Protestant and Catholic schools in Northern Ireland should have greater opportunities to meet and mix. | RC | 40.7 | 30.5 | 11.8 | 6.7 | 10.3 |
| | Prot. | 28.6 | 28.3 | 15.9 | 10.8 | 16.4 |

were Protestants, and chi-square tests showed that these differences between pupils of the two traditions were significant at the .01 level (see appendix 2). The one exception to Roman Catholics being more open was the item expressing happiness at having someone of the other religion as one's boss. In the case of this item, 21.9% of Protestants compared with 18.5% of Roman Catholics expressed strong agreement, while almost the same prcentage of Protestants (57.1%) as of Roman Catholics (55.8%) expressed strong agreement or agreement.

This difference between pupils from the two traditions was also apparent when oppenness scale scores derived from all six items were analysed. The mean openness score for the whole group of 2133 respondents was 20.27, but it can be seen in table 2 that the mean score for Roman Catholic pupils was significantly higher than that for Protestant pupils. The mean score for Roman Catholic girls was significantly higher than that for Protestant girls, while the mean score for Roman Catholic boys was slightly but not significantly higher than that for Protestant boys.

Openness scores were found to increase with increasing age. Form

*Table 2: Openness scores analysed by religious affiliation and sex*

|  | Mean | SD | N | t | df | P |
|---|---|---|---|---|---|---|
| Roman Catholics | 21.0277 | 5.578 | 940 | 5.11 | 2131 | 0.000 |
| Protestants | 19.6647 | 6.518 | 1193 |  |  |  |
| Boys | 18.7581 | 6.214 | 1236 | − 13.85 | 2131 | 0.000 |
| Girls | 22.3423 | 5.436 | 897 |  |  |  |
| RC Boys | 19.1219 | 5.704 | 517 | − 12.50 | 938 | 0.000 |
| RC Girls | 23.357 | 4.424 | 423 |  |  |  |
| Prot. Boys | 18.4965 | 6.547 | 719 | − 7.81 | 1191 | 0.000 |
| Prot. Girls | 21.4367 | 6.064 | 474 |  |  |  |
| RC Boys | 19.1219 | 5.704 | 517 | 1.75 | 1234 | 0.081 |
| Prot. Boys | 18.4965 | 6.547 | 719 |  |  |  |
| RC Girls | 23.3570 | 4.424 | 423 | 5.36 | 895 | 0.000 |
| Prot. Girls | 21.4367 | 6.064 | 474 |  |  |  |

1 pupils scored 18.80; form 2, 19.29; form 3, 20.65; form 4, 20.9; and form 5, 22.29. An analysis of variance carried out on openness scores in relation to form yielded a significant linear trend (see table 3). Since the F ratio associated with the linear trend was highly significant it was concluded that there was a significant difference among the forms.

This regular increase in openness scores was also found when boys and girls, Roman Catholics and Protestants, were studied separately. As a group girls were significantly more open than were boys, and this was also true when girls in each age group were compared with boys in the same age group. This variation in openness scores with form, sex and religious tradition may be seen in figure 1.

While figure 1 clearly suggests that openness scores increased with age, it must be remembered that this research was a cross-sectional study of pupils aged 12−16 years and any suggested age trends must be treated with caution. Before one could reach firm conclusions about the development of children's openness in a particular society, a longitudinal study would be necessary.

## Attitude to religion

The attitude to religion of pupils was measured using the Francis attitude to religion scale, and attitude scores were studied in relation to three variables, age, sex and religious affiliation. Attitude scores were found to decrease with increasing age, and an analysis of variance carried out in relation to form yielded a significant linear trend. (See table 4). Since the F ratio associated with the linear

*Table 3: Analysis of variance of openness scores by year group*

| Source | df | ss | MS | F |
|---|---|---|---|---|
| between groups | 4 | 3093.03 | 773.26 | 21.17 |
| linearity | 1 | 2965.43 | 2965.43 | 81.17* |
| deviation from linearity | 3 | 127.60 | 42.53 | 1.16+ |
| within groups | 2128 | 77740.78 | 36.53 | |

*p<.0001
+n.s.

*Table 4: Analysis of variance of attitude to religion scores by year group*

| Source | df | ss | MS | F |
|---|---|---|---|---|
| between groups | 4 | 29049.62 | 7262.41 | 21.29 |
| linearity | 1 | 27051.53 | 27051.53 | 79.29* |
| deviation from linearity | 3 | 1998.09 | 666.03 | 1.95+ |
| within groups | 2128 | 725999.83 | 341.17 | |

*p<.0001
+n.s.

trend was highly significant it was concluded that there was a significant difference among the forms. Girls were found to have higher scores than boys, and Roman Catholics were found to have higher scores than Protestants.

This variation in attitude to religion scores with form, sex and religious tradition may be seen in figure 2.

## Openness and attitude to religion

At first glance, the comparisons between figures 1 and 2 may tend to suggest that there was a negative relationship between openness and attitude towards religion. As children grew older they became both more open and less favorably disposed towards religion. The relationship was not, however, as simple as this, since the graphs in figures 1 and 2 disguised the important interrelationships between age, sex, denominational affiliation, openness and attitude. In order to unscramble this set of intricate relationships, multiple regression techniques were employed (see table 5).

*Figure 1:*   Openness scores by year group in school

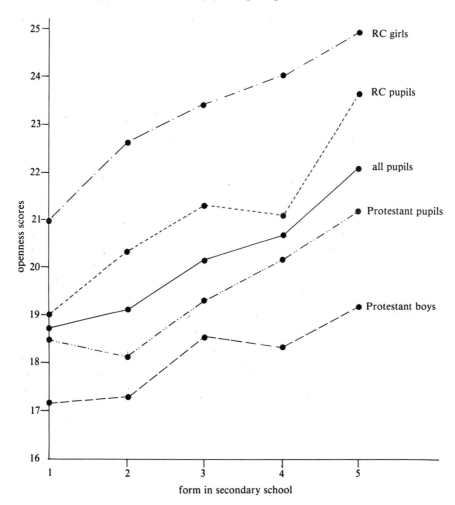

*Figure 2:*   Attitude to religion scores by year group in school

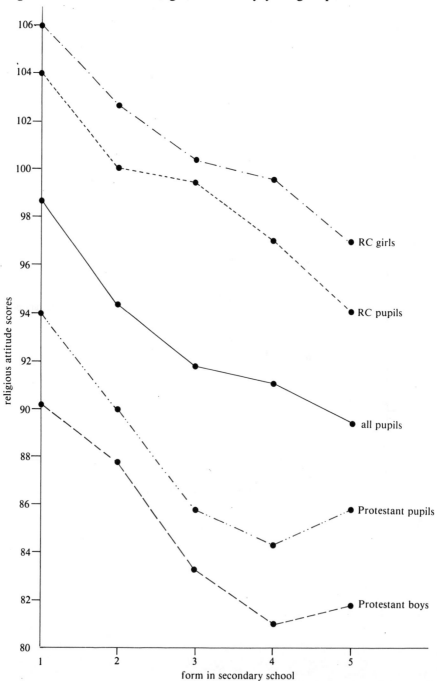

*Table 5: Multiple regression significance tests using openness as criterion variable*

| Predictor variables | Multiple R | $R^2$ | Increase in $R^2$ | Beta | F ratio | df | P< |
|---|---|---|---|---|---|---|---|
| **model 1** | | | | | | | |
| attitude | .15164 | .02299 | .02299 | + .1516 | 49.9 | 1,2121 | .001 |
| **model 2** | | | | | | | |
| sex | .28766 | .08275 | .08275 | + .2702 | 193.6 | 1,2120 | .001 |
| attitude | .30674 | .09409 | .01134 | + .1079 | 26.5 | 1,2120 | .001 |
| **model 3** | | | | | | | |
| form | .19239 | .03702 | .03702 | + .2289 | 84.7 | 1,2120 | .001 |
| attitude | .27121 | .07355 | .03654 | + .1946 | 83.6 | 1,2120 | .001 |
| **model 4** | | | | | | | |
| school type | .11194 | .01253 | .01253 | − .0746 | 27.3 | 1,2120 | .001 |
| attitude | .16765 | .02811 | .01558 | + .1303 | 34.0 | 1,2120 | .001 |
| **model 5** | | | | | | | |
| sex | .28766 | .08275 | .08275 | + .2591 | 204.4 | 1,2118 | .001 |
| form | .34338 | .11791 | .03516 | + .2143 | 86.9 | 1,2118 | .001 |
| school type | .35791 | .12810 | .01019 | − .0613 | 25.2 | 1,2118 | .001 |
| attitude | .37810 | .14296 | .01486 | + .1312 | 36.7 | 1,2118 | .001 |
| **model 6** | | | | | | | |
| sex | .28766 | .08275 | .08275 | | | | |
| form | .34338 | .11791 | .03516 | | | | |
| school type | .35791 | .12810 | .01019 | | | | |
| attitude | .37810 | .14296 | .01486 | | | | |
| 6 two-way interactions | .38933 | .15158 | .00862 | | 3.6 | 6,2112 | NS |

Model 1 shows that, in the data as a whole, there was a significant positive correlation between openness and attitude towards religion (Beta = +.1516), indicating that those who held more favorable attitudes towards religion were also more open. When model 2 controlled for sex differences, the relationship between openness and attitude towards religion remained significant and positive, but was less strong; the beta was reduced from +.1516 to +.1079. This was because girls tended to score more highly than boys on both the openness scale and the attitude scale. Model 3 goes one stage further by controlling for form. Now a much stronger positive relationship emerged between attitude and openness, producing a beta of +.1946. This was because older pupils both scored higher on the openness scale and lower on the attitude scale. Model 4 controls for the third contaminating variable, denominational differences. Now the beta between attitude towards religion and openness was +.1303. This slight reduction in the beta weight was accounted for by the fact that Roman Catholic pupils scored more highly on the openness scale and also on the attitude scale. Model 5 takes all three of these contaminating variables into account simultaneously in order to give a complete picture of the relationship between attitude towards religion and openness. After the effects of sex, form and denomination were simultaneously controlled for, there emerged a clear positive correlation between attitude toward religion and openness, producing a beta coefficient of $+.1312$. Finally, model 6 demonstrates that there were no significant interaction terms in the equation, implying that this relationship was basically the same for both sexes and for both denominational groups throughout the entire age range.

These results, therefore, indicate that throughout the age range for both sexes and both denominational groups, there was a positive relationship between attitude towards religion and openness. The young people most favorably disposed towards religion were also most open to members of the other religious group. This is an important finding, contradicting the notion that in Northern Ireland increased religiosity increases closedness to 'the other side.'

## Discussion

The mean openness score was found to be 20.27, which was slightly above the mid point of the scale, 18. This result suggests that despite the years of violence and bloodshed since 1969, pupils of secondary school age were inclined to be open rather than closed towards 'the other side' of the Northern Ireland community. Something of the tolerance and recollected goodwill found by Rose appeared to have persisted despite all that has happened in this country. Thus Moore (1972) is correct when he claims that 'it would be a mistake to present a picture of Northern Ireland as a scene of continual hostility' (p. 54). Moore does, however, qualify this statement by adding that social distance was maintained and intolerance was always latent and likely to express itself in conflict and violence. The truth of this qualification has been evident in events since 1972 when Moore published his paper.

The present study also found that Catholics were significantly more open than Protestants, and that this was true at different age levels and for boys and girls separately. This is consistent with the conclusions of Rose (1971) who found Catholics to be slightly more friendly, and with the conclusions of Fairleigh (1975) who, working with a non-random sample, found that Catholics felt less social distance than Protestants. It is also in agreement with the conclusions of Salters who found 15 year old Catholics to be more tolerant than Protestants and girls to be more tolerant than boys, irrespective of religion.

Why are Catholics significantly more open than Protestants? Perhaps we may find a partial explanation in the concept of 'the double minority' first put forward in 1971 by a journalist, Jackson, and subsequently used by other writers about the Irish problem. According to Jackson (1971, p. 4),

> Within their own enclave the Protestants of Ulster, one million strong, out-numbered their Catholic brethren by two to one. But in the wider context of Ireland they themselves are easily out-numbered three to one. The inevitable result has been the disastrous advent of a ruling establishment with the reins of power irremovably in its hands but acting under the stresses of a beseiged minority.
>
> For its entire fifty years Northern Ireland has been ruled by the Unionist Party and for most of them there has only been one issue, the preservation of the border with the Catholic Republic. Any real attempt at social, political and economic advance has hit this barrier and bounced back from it. And what has emerged has been a society suffering a deep psychosis in which rational thought and action are invariably overtaken by emotional spasms the moment it comes under stress.... Fifty years of failing to get any real say in the government of the province – have left the Catholics with a burning sense of grievance, reinforced by both institutionalised and informal discrimination.

Other writers have made use of the double minority model, and Whyte (1978, p. 276) points out its advantages of simplicity, accuracy and its capacity to illuminate the stress found in both communities. For him, it is the most satisfactory of the models so far developed.

While fear has affected both traditions, the Protestant majority in the north is more clearly affected by the events of the past 14 years, and it is now characterised by 'a profound sense of insecurity,' a 'sense of beleaguerment,' 'a sense of embattlement' (Hickey, 1984, pp. 46–8). This has been well expressed by Dr Cahal Daly, Roman Catholic bishop of Down and Connor, who has emphasised the need both for Catholic grievances and sensitivities to be met and also for the fears and suspicions of Protestants to be overcome. He recognised the significance for Protestants of the dissolution of Stormont and the imposition of direct rule in 1972, which he argued 'has caused a great and unprecedented insecurity and uncertainty among Unionists. It has led to distrust of Britain, fear of the Irish Republic, suspicion of Roman Catholics and Nationalists, a sense of being alone and threatened' (Daly, 1983, p. 13). In relation to the present research, it is argued that the same fear, insecurity and lack of trust on the part of Protestants were reflected in the lower openness scores which were recorded among Protestant secondary school pupils.

It is unnecessary to make further comment on the significant differences between the sexes which were found in the present research, with girls consistently more positive in their attitude to religion and more open to the other side. This difference between the sexes was consistent with the findings of Salters and of Powell and Stewart and also fits in with Argyle and Beit-Hallahmi's summary of research into sex differences in which they reported women to be more religious than men on every criterion (Argyle and Beit-Hallahmi, 1975, p. 71). Also, it is unnecessary to comment on the importance of the age factor in respect to attitude to religion, since the results of the present study clearly confirm the conclusion of much other research that as pupils get older, their attitude to religion becomes less positive. What is important, the results suggest strongly that pupils become more open as they get older, and that after controlling for the effects of sex, age and religious affiliation, there was a positive correlation between attitude to religion and openness. A possible explanation for this increase in openness with age may be that pupils in Northern Ireland begin life as members of a close-knit family circle characterised by a strong attachment to a particular church. With this close relationship may go a sense of antipathy to those outside their church who, in Northern Ireland terms, belong to 'the other side.' The years of adolescence bring increasing independence and the emergence of 'a sense of inner identity' (Erikson, 1968, p. 87). They also bring increasing ability to think hypothetically, abstractly and in terms of propositions which can be tested. The results of this study suggest that part of the process of growing up in Northern Ireland involves declining acceptance of family religion and increasing openness to those people who belong to the other religious tradition. From the point of view of the family grouping, this loosening of religious ties may be viewed with regret. From the point of view of good community relations, the growth of openness may be regarded as a sign of hope, an indication that young people are able to break out of narrow sectarian patterns of thinking and behavior. Unfortunately, there is no evidence available about what happens beyond school when young people move into the adult world of scarce employment, economic hardship and other social responsibilities which are open to explanation in a sectarian way. We do not know what will happen when the present younger generation become the parents of the next generation, though O'Donnell's study does suggest that cross-cultural stereotypes remain similar from age 15 to age 55.

The results of the present study are consistent with the conclusions reached by Powell and Stewart (1978) in England about the way in which adolescents unlearn the religion and the orthodox values of their parents and gradually become liberalised. The modelling theory which Powell and Stewart put forward is a plausible explanation of the way in which positive attitudes to religion and traditional values are influenced by 'alternate models' found outside the home, in the peer group, at school, in places of work and recreation, and through the media. However, the modelling theory remains a theory which would need to be tested in practice among young people in Northern Ireland.

# Conclusion

It is not the social scientist's role to make value judgments about the results of a given study or to make recommendations about their significance. But the scientist is also a citizen, and the present writer finds himself recognising certain signs of hope in the results of this study, particularly in the evidence that openness was greater among the older pupils. From this evidence there are clearly lessons to be learned and opportunities to be grasped by teachers of religion and social studies who are willing to contribute to the building of a more tolerant and harmonious society in Northern Ireland. Already there are several curriculum projects underway in schools in this country, one which focuses on social studies (Robinson, 1980) and another which focuses on religious education (Greer and McElhinney, 1984). Both projects are based on a reconstructionist concept of education as propounded by Skilbeck (1973). They are relatively small attempts to encourage educators to deal with the controversial religious, social and political issues which divide Northern Ireland in such a way that openness is developed in pupils at school. Those involved in the projects are, however, aware that neither social scientists nor educators can create by themselves the conditions in society that nurture the relationships between individuals and communities which make for the kind of openness reported here.

**References**

Allport, G W (1954) *The Nature of Prejudice*, Cambridge, Massachusetts, Addison-Wesley.

Argyle, M and B Beit-Hallahmi (1975) *The Social Psychology of Religion*, London, Routledge and Kegan Paul.

Aunger, E A (1981) *In Search of Political Stability*, Montreal, McGill – Queen's University Press.

Daly, C B (1983) *Building Bridges in a Divided Community*, Belfast, Chapel of Unity Study Centre, St Anne's Cathedral.

Darby J (1976) *Conflict in Northern Ireland*, Dublin, Gill and MacMillan.

Deane D (1984) 'Northern Ireland and Ecumenism,' *Doctrine and Life*, 34, pp. 190–96.

Erikson, E H (1986) *Identity: Youth and Crisis*, London, Faber.

Fairleigh, J (1975) 'Personality and social factors in religious prejudice,' in P Burke (ed.), *Sectarianism: roads to reconciliation*, Dublin, The Three Candles Limited, pp. 3–13.

Francis, L J (1978) 'Attitude and longitude: a study in measurement,' *Character Potential*, 8, pp. 119–30.

Francis, L (1979) 'The child's attitude towards religion,' *Educational Research*, 21, pp. 103–8.

Greer, J R (1980) 'The persistence of religion: a study of adolescents in Northern Ireland,' *Character Potential*, 9, pp. 139–49.

Greer, J R (1982) 'The religious experience of Northern Irish pupils,' *The Irish Catechist*, 6, pp. 49–58.

Greer, J R (1984) 'Moral cultures in Northern Ireland,' *The Journal of Social Psychology*, 123, pp. 63–70.

Greer, J E and E McElhinney (1984) 'The project on religion in Ireland: an experiment in reconstruction,' *Lumen Vitae*, 39, pp. 331–42.

Harris, R (1972) *Prejudice and Tolerance in Ulster*, Manchester, Manchester University Press.

Hickey, J (1984) *Religion and the Northern Ireland Problem*, Dublin, Gill and MacMillan.

Hyde, K E (1965) *Religious Learning in Adolescence*, Edinburgh, Oliver and Boyd.

Jackson, H (1971) *The Two Irelands*, London, Minority Rights Group Report no. 2.

Lyons, F S L (1979) *Culture and Anarchy in Ireland 1839–1939*, Oxford, Clarendon Press.

Mark, T (1984) 'Adolescence,' in J M Sutcliffe (ed.), *A Dictionary of Religious Education*, London, SCM Press, pp. 4–7.

Miller, R (1978) 'Opinions on school desegregation in Northern Ireland,' in A E C W Spencer and H Torey (eds), Sociological Association of Ireland: *Proceedings of First and Fourth Annual Conference*, Belfast, Queen's University.

Moore, R (1973) 'Race relations in the six countries: colonialism, industrialisation and stratification in Ireland,' *Race*, 14, pp. 21–42.

Murray, D (1982) 'A comparative study of the culture and character of Protestant and Roman Catholic primary schools in Northern Ireland,' unpublished DPhil dissertation, The New University of Ulster.

O'Brien, C C (1974) *States of Ireland*, St Albans, Panther.

O'Donnell, E E (1977) *Northern Irish Stereotypes*, Dublin, College of Industrial Relations.

Powell, G E and R A Stewart (1978) 'The relationship of age, sex and personality to social attitudes in children aged 8–15 years,' *British Journal of Social and Clinical Psychology*, 17, pp. 307–317.

Rokeach, M (1960) *The Open and Closed Mind*, New York, Basic Books.

Rose, R (1971) *Governing without Consensus*, London, Faber.

Salters, J (1970) 'Attitudes towards society in Protestant and Roman Catholic school children in Belfast,' unpublished MA dissertation, Queen's University, Belfast.

Skilbeck, M (1973) 'The school and cultural development,' *The Northern Teacher*, pp. 13–18.

*Appendix 1: Alpha reliability coefficients for the openness scale*

|  | Number of cases | Alpha coefficient |
|---|---|---|
| Form 1 | 468 | 0.82 |
| 2 | 450 | 0.85 |
| 3 | 446 | 0.85 |
| 4 | 414 | 0.84 |
| 5 | 341 | 0.85 |
| boys | 1229 | 0.83 |
| girls | 890 | 0.84 |
| Roman Catholics | 933 | 0.80 |
| Protestants | 1186 | 0.87 |
| total population | 2119 | 0.85 |

*Appendix 2: The results of chi-square tests on the responses of Roman Catholic and Protestant pupils to the six items in the openness scale*

| Item | Chi-square | df | P |
|---|---|---|---|
| 1 | 15.57 | 4 | 0.0036 |
| 2 | 44.75 | 4 | 0.0000 |
| 3 | 13.42 | 4 | 0.0094 |
| 4 | 18.26 | 4 | 0.0011 |
| 5 | 19.52 | 4 | 0.0006 |
| 6 | 54.15 | 4 | 0.0000 |

# 13. Empirical perspectives on effectiveness

This chapter presents two studies which have set out to evaluate the effectiveness of church schools from rather different theoretical and empirical perspectives.

In the first article, Dr Joseph Rhymer and the Revd Professor Leslie J Francis assess the impact of Catholic educational provision in Scotland on the attitudes of 1,113 Catholic adolescents. In Scotland the Catholic church is able both to provide church schools wholly maintained by the state and to offer Catholic religious education in non-denominational schools in areas where it is not feasible to support a separate school system. The authors conclude that both provisions contribute significantly to a more favourable pupil attitude towards Christianity among Catholic pupils than non-denominational schools in which Catholic religious education is not provided.

At the time of writing Joseph Rhymer was on the staff of St Andrew's College of Education in Glasgow. This article was first published in *Lumen Vitae* in 1985.

In the second article, the Revd Professor Leslie J Francis and David W Lankshear assess the impact of Church of England voluntary primary schools on village church life in England in a sample of 1,637 communities ranging in size from 250 to 1,250 inhabitants. The authors conclude that the presence of a church school augments slightly the village church's usual Sunday contact with 6–9-year-olds and with adults, the number of infant baptisms, the number of 6–13-year-olds in the choir and the number of young confirmands under the age of 14 years.

David Lankshear is Deputy Secretary of the National Society and Schools Officer of the General Synod Board of Education. This article was first published in *Educational Studies* in 1990.

# 13.1 Roman Catholic secondary schools in Scotland and pupil attitude towards religion

*Joseph Rhymer and Leslie J Francis*

## Introduction

Historically the Roman Catholic church has worked to implement the aim, 'every Catholic child from a Catholic home to be taught by Catholic teachers in a Catholic school.'[1] Seventy-five years ago, in 1929, Pope Pius XI's encyclical letter *Divini Illius Magistri* reaffirmed 'the prescriptions of canon law which forbid Catholic children on any pretext whatsoever to attend ... schools open indiscriminately to Catholics and non-Catholics alike.' The *Declaration on Christian Education* issued from the second Vatican Council in the mid 1960s was couched in softer terms, but continued to remind Catholic parents of 'their duty to entrust their children to Catholic schools, when and where this is possible, to support such schools to the extent of their ability, and to work along with them for the welfare of their children.'[2] At the same time a range of Roman Catholic opinion was beginning to raise questions about the contribution of the separate school system,[3] while some were marshalling very articulate criticisms against it.[4]

In Scotland the Roman Catholic church has developed separate primary and secondary schools within the state maintained system of education.[5] In some ways the Scottish system is similar to the English system, while in other important respects it differs considerably.[6] The English system of state maintained church schools, derived from the English 1944 Education Act, has committed the Roman Catholic church in England to a considerable financial investment in the building of voluntary aided schools,[7] while the Scottish system of church schools, derived from the Scottish 1918 Education Act, enabled the Roman Catholic church in Scotland to develop distinctive denominational state maintained schools without any cost to the church itself.[8] In addition, the Scottish act permits the church to provide distinctive denominational religious education within non-denominational state maintained schools in areas in which it has not been feasible to develop separate denominational schools, for example in areas of low population density. It is, therefore, comparatively simple for the parents who wish to do so to obtain distinctive Roman Catholic religious education for their children in one of these two forms within the state maintained system.

466

During the past two decades a growing body of empirical research has begun to emerge on the effectiveness of the Catholic school system, for example in England by Hornsby-Smith,[9] Hornsby-Smith and Lee,[10] Francis[11] and Francis and Carter;[12] in America by Greeley and Rossi,[13] Neuwein[14] and Greeley, McCready and McCourt;[15] and in Australia by Flynn[16] and Fahy.[17] Because of the differences in the Scottish situation the direct relevance of these studies is not clear.

The aim of the present study is to examine whether the Roman Catholic educational provision within the Scottish state maintained sector of secondary schools has any measurable impact on the attitudes of Roman Catholic pupils towards Christianity. This study builds upon the method employed in the English context by Francis and Francis and Carter[18] in order to compare the attitudes of three groups of pupils, namely Roman Catholic pupils in Roman Catholic schools, Roman Catholic pupils in non-denominational schools receiving Roman Catholic religious education, and Roman Catholic pupils in non-denominational schools not receiving Roman Catholic religious education.

Before comparing the attitude scores of pupils in different types of school, it is necessary to take into account other variables which are known to be significant predictors of the child's attitude. The key variables in this context are sex and age,[19] religious behaviour[20] and social class.[21] Although parental religious behaviour is also known to be a strong predictor of the child's attitude towards religion,[22] Francis demonstrates that this influence on attitude is mediated entirely through the child's own religious practice.[23] In other words, after the child's own religious practice has been taken into account, parental religious practice appears to have no further predictive power in relationship to the child's attitude.

## The research project

### Sample

A stratified sample is constituted, representing the distribution of Scottish Roman Catholic pupils between Roman Catholic and non-denominational secondary schools, and drawn from areas of Strathclyde Region typical of geographical and economic conditions in Scotland as a whole.[24] 1,113 Roman Catholic pupils completed the attitude inventory; of which 882 were drawn from Roman Catholic schools, 121 from non-denominational schools receiving Roman Catholic religious education and 110 from non-denominational schools not receiving Roman Catholic religious education.

## Measures

a. scale of attitude towards religion, Form ASC4B: the scale contains items concerned with the child's attitude towards God, Jesus, the Bible, prayer, the church and religion in school.[25] The scale is known to function reliably and validly throughout the secondary age range;[26]

b. frequency of pupil's church attendance, gauged on a four point scale ranging from weekly to never;

c. socio-economic groups: the five point scale proposed by the Office of Populations, Censuses and Surveys[27] is used in association with information about the trade or profession of father or guardian.

## Procedure and data analysis

The questionnaires were all administered by teachers within the schools following a standardised procedure. The data was analysed by means of linear multiple regression and path analysis, using the SPSS package.[28]

## Results

The inter-relationships between the predictor variables were explored through a developing sequence of path models analogous to the sequence proposed by Francis.[29] The present paper presents in table 1 and figure 1 only the final stage of this sequence as sufficient to demonstrate the relationship between type of school attended and pupil attitude towards religion.

Table 1 demonstrates that sex and social class are both significant predictors of religious practice among Roman Catholic pupils of secondary school age. Girls are more inclined to engage in religious practice than boys. Pupils from lower social class backgrounds are less inclined to engage in religious practice than pupils from higher social class backgrounds. Age, however, is not a significant predictor of religious practice among Roman Catholic pupils of secondary school age.

On the other hand, both age and sex are significant predictors of the attitude towards religion of Roman Catholic pupils of secondary school age. Girls are more favourably disposed towards religion than boys. Younger pupils are more favourably disposed towards religion than older pupils. Social class, however, does not have a direct influence on the pupil's attitude towards religion. The influence of social class on the pupil's attitude towards religion is wholly mediated through the pupil's religious practice.

The strongest predictor of the pupil's attitude towards religion is the pupil's own level of religious practice. In evaluating the path

Table 1: *Multiple regression significance test*

| Criterion variables | Predictor variables | $R^2$ | Increase in $R^2$ | B | Beta | St error B | F ratio | df | P< |
|---|---|---|---|---|---|---|---|---|---|
| religious practice | sex | .02293 | .02293 | +0.25861 | +.1442 | 0.05810 | 19.817 | 1,916 | .001 |
| | age | .03020 | .00726 | +0.03002 | +.0570 | 0.01743 | 2.974 | 1,916 | NS |
| | social class | .04975 | .01955 | -0.26733 | -.1427 | 0.06157 | 18.847 | 1,916 | .001 |
| attitude towards religion | sex | .02969 | .02969 | +4.98164 | +.1430 | 1.07960 | 21.292 | 1,913 | .001 |
| | age | .05449 | .02481 | -2.03066 | -.1983 | 1.03268 | 38.617 | 1,913 | .001 |
| | social class | .06241 | .00792 | -1.57140 | -.0432 | 1.14775 | 1.874 | 1,913 | NS |
| | religious practice | .14723 | .08482 | +5.81053 | +.2993 | 0.60897 | 91.043 | 1,913 | .001 |
| | non-denom school with RC RE | .14998 | .00272 | +2.44006 | +.0438 | 1.73763 | 1.972 | 1,913 | NS |
| | non-denom school with RC RE | .15427 | .00429 | -3.94578 | -.0672 | 1.83364 | 4.631 | 1,913 | .05 |
| constant | | | | 70.00090 | | | | | |

*Figure 1:*  Path model

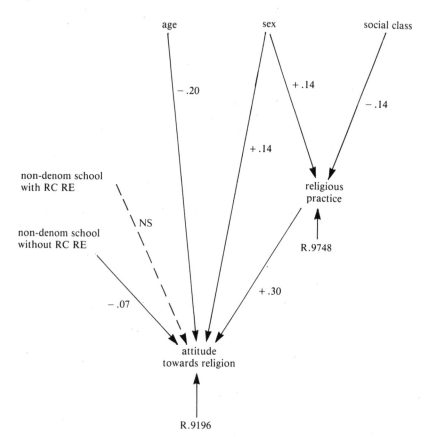

model it needs to be appreciated that the relationship between attitude and practice is interactive. By designing the model in such a way that the variance in attitude scores accounted for by practice scores is considered before examining the relationship between school type and attitude scores the most stringent criterion is being applied to assure that variance is not erroneously attributed to school influence. In other words, if school type is found to be significantly related to the pupil's attitude towards religion, after controlling for the relationship between practice and attitude, it can be confidently assumed that the school itself is having a real impact on the child's attitude.

The final stage in the development of the path models introduced the type of school attended by the pupils into the multiple regression equation through the creation of a set of dummy variables.[30] In this system of dummy variables the Roman Catholic pupils attending Roman Catholic schools function as the reference category. This choice was made because they represent the largest group in the data base. The implication of this decision is that the dummy variables are exploring the extent to which the attitude scores of Roman Catholic pupils (1) in non-denominational schools receiving Roman Catholic religious education, and (2) in non-denominational schools not receiving Roman Catholic religious education, differ from those in Roman Catholic schools, after differences attributable to age, sex and religious practice have been taken into account.

Table 1 demonstrates two important conclusions regarding the influence of the school on the attitudes towards religion of Roman Catholic pupils. First, there is no significant difference in the attitude scores of Roman Catholic pupils in Roman Catholic schools and Roman Catholic pupils in non-denominational schools receiving Roman Catholic religious education. Second, the attitude scores of Roman Catholic pupils in non-denominational schools not receiving Roman Catholic religious education are significantly lower than either Roman Catholic pupils in Roman Catholic schools or Roman Catholic pupils in non-denominational schools receiving Roman Catholic religious education. The regression co-efficient indicates that the predicted attitude scores of Roman Catholic pupils in non-denominational schools not receiving Roman Catholic religious education would be about four points lower on the 96 points attitude scale than for comparable pupils of the same age, sex and social class who engage in the same level of religious practice but who attend a Roman Catholic secondary school.

## Conclusion

If one of the aims of the Roman Catholic church is to promote favourable attitudes towards religion in Roman Catholic pupils, these findings support the importance for the Roman Catholic church in Scotland of continuing both to support separate Roman Catholic secondary schools and to provide Roman Catholic religious education in non-denominational schools where it is not possible to provide a separate school system. There is no evidence to suggest from these data that the provision of a separate school system achieves anything more than does the provision of Roman Catholic religious education in non-denominational schools.

**Notes**
1.   Catholic Education Council, *The Case for Catholic Schools* (2nd ed.), London, Catholic Education, 1955.
2.   Abott, W H (ed.), *The Documents of Vatican II*, London, Chapman, 1966.
3.   For example, P Jebb (ed.), *Religious Education: drift or decision?*, London, Darton, Longman and Todd, 1968; and B Tucker (ed.), *Catholic Education*, London, Sheed and Ward, 1968.
4.   For example, A E C W Spencer, *The Future of Catholic Education in England and Wales*, London, Catholic Renewal Movement, 1971.
5.   Brother Kenneth, *Catholic Schools in Scotland*, Glasgow, Catholic Education Commission, 1972.
6.   M Cruickshank, *Church and State in English Education*, London, Macmillan, 1963; J Murphy, *Church, State and Schools in Britain, 1800–1970*, London, Routledge and Kegan Paul, 1971.
7.   H C Dent, *The Education Act 1944: provisions, possibilities and some Problems* (3rd ed.), London, University of London Press, 1947.
8.   J Scotland, *The History of Scottish Education*, London, University of London Press, 1969.
9.   M P Hornsby-Smith, *Catholic Education: the unobtrusive partner*, London, Sheed and Ward, 1978.
10.   M P Hornsby-Smith, and R M Lee, *Roman Catholic Opinion: a study of Roman Catholics in England and Wales in the 1970s*, Guildford, University of Surrey, Department of Sociology, 1979.
11.   L J Francis 'School influence and pupil attitude towards religion', *British Journal of Educational Psychology*, 49, 1979, pp. 107–123; L J Francis, 'Roman Catholic Schools and pupil attitudes in England,' *Lumen Vitae*, 39, 1984, pp. 99–108.
12.   L J Francis and M Carter, 'Church aided secondary schools, religious education as an examination subject and pupil attitude towards religion,' *British Journal of Educational Psychology*, 50, 1980, pp. 297–300.
13.   A M Greeley and P H Rossi, *The Education of Catholic Americans*, Chicago, Aldine Publishing Company, 1966.
14.   R A Neuwein (ed.), *Catholic Schools in Action*, Notre Dame, Indiana, University of Notre Dame Press, 1966.
15.   A M Greeley W C McCready and K McCourt, *Catholic Schools in a Declining Church*, Kansas City, Sheed and Ward Inc. 1976.
16.   M F Flynn, *Some Catholic Schools in Action*, Sydney, Catholic Education Office, 1975.
17.   P S Fahy, 'The effectiveness on Christian criteria of 17 Australian Catholic High Schools,' unpublished MEd dissertation, Boston College, Massachusetts, USA, 1980; P S Fahy, 'The religious effectiveness of some Australian Catholic High Schools,' *Word in Life*, 28, 1980, pp. 86–98.
18.   See notes 11 and 12 above.
19.   For example, C H Povall, 'Some factors affecting pupil's attitudes to religious education,' unpublished MEd dissertation, University of Manchester, 1971; T J Mark, 'A study of cognitive and affective elements in the religious development of adolescents,' unpublished PhD dissertation, University of Leeds, 1979.
20.   For example, K E Hyde, *Religious Learning in Adolescence*, University of Birmingham Institute of Education Monograph No. 7, London, Oliver and Boyd, 1965; W P C Johnson, 'The religious attitudes of secondary modern county school pupils,' unpublished MEd dissertation, University of Manchester.

21. J A Jones, 'An investigation into the responses of boys and girls to scripture as a school subject in certain co-educational grammar schools in industrial South Wales,' unpublished MA dissertation, University of Wales, Swansea, 1962.
22. J E Greer, 'Religious belief and church attendance of sixth form pupils and their parents,' *Irish Journal of Education*, 7, 1971, pp. 98–106.
23. L J Francis, 'School Influence and pupil attitude towards religion,' *British Journal of Educational Psychology*, 49, 1979, pp. 107–123.
24. A full description of the sample is given in J Rhymer, 'Religious attitudes of Roman Catholic secondary school pupils in Strathclyde Region,' unpublished PhD dissertation, University of Edinburgh, 1983.
25. The scale is printed in L J Francis, 'Roman Catholic Schools and pupil attitudes in England,' *Lumen Vitae*, 39, 1984; for full details of the process of scale construction see L J Francis, 'Attitude and longitude: a study in measurement,' *Character Potential*, 8, 1978, pp. 119–300.
26. Details of reliability and validity for age groups separately are available in L J Francis, 'An enquiry into the concept "Readiness for Religion",' unpublished PhD dissertation, University of Cambridge, 1976.
27. Office of Population, Censuses and Surveys, *Classification of Occupations*, London, HMSO, 1970.
28. N H Nie, C H Hull, J G Jenkins, K Steinbrenner and D H Bent, *Statistical Package for the Social Sciences*, New York, McGraw-Hill, 1975; C H Hull and N H Nie, *SPSS Update 7–9*, New York, McGraw-Hill, 1981.
29. See note 23 above.
30. J Cohen, 'Multiple regression as a general data analytic system,' *Psychological Bulletin*, 70, 1968, pp. 426–443.

# 13.2 The impact of church schools on village church life

*Leslie J Francis and David W Lankshear*

## Introduction

Through the founding of the National Society in 1811 (Burgess, 1958) the Church of England played a crucial role in the established of a national network of schools in England and Wales (Cruickshank, 1963; Murphy, 1971) long before the 1870 Education Act established the machinery for building non-denominational schools (Murphy, 1972). The 1944 Education Act continued to safeguard the partnership between church and state in the provision of a national networks of schools and proposed the present system of voluntary aided and voluntary controlled status (Dent, 1947). According to the 1944 Education Act, voluntary controlled status absolved the church from on-going financial responsibility for the maintenance of the school, although the church retained the right to appoint a minority of governors, provide denominational worship throughout the school, offer denominational religious education on parental request, and in schools of more than two teachers appoint 'reserved teachers' competent to give denominational religious instruction. Voluntary aided status gave the churches additional rights, including the appointment of the majority of governors and the provisions of denominational instruction as well as worship throughout the school, but also involved them in continued financial liability for certain capital expenditures (Brooksbank *et al.*, 1982).

The Church of England's investment in schools has been placed mainly in the primary sector (Cruickshank, 1972; Kelly, 1978). As the school population rose between 1949 and 1974 the proportion of the state maintained primary places provided by Anglican schools in England and Wales fell steadily from 22.5% to 16.3%. After 1974, in a situation of falling primary rolls, the Anglican church's contribution gradually crept up again to 16.9% in 1985 and currently stands in 1988 at 16.8% (information supplied by Department of Education and Science and the Welsh Office). In his analysis of the size of Anglican primary schools today, Gay (1985a) draws attention to the fact that the church's main investment is in small schools, while Francis's (1986a) analysis of the geographical distribution of church schools points to their concentration in the more rural shire counties. For example, while in England as a whole the Church of

England provided 25% of primary schools in 1983, including the middle schools deemed primary by the Department of Education and Science, the proportion rose to 51% in Oxfordshire, and to 50% in Shropshire, Somerset and Wiltshire.

A more detailed analysis of the geographical distribution of Church of England schools within one shire county, Gloucestershire, indicated that 65% of the village schools were Church of England voluntary aided or voluntary controlled, compared with 43% in the towns and 25% in the suburban areas (Francis, 1987). Clearly, from the Church of England's point of view, the functioning of the rural primary school should be a matter of considerable interest.

According to Cruickshank (1963) 'perhaps nothing in the educational controversies of the nineteenth century did more to influence denominational bitterness than the Anglican refusal to concede rights of conscience' in single school areas where the Church of England owned the only school. During the twentieth century the Church of England became increasingly sensitive to the responsibilities and constraints of operating church schools in single school areas and in an increasingly secular and pluralist society. The key statement on the Anglican philosophy of church schools, *The Fourth R* (Ramsey, 1970), sharpens the distinction between the Church of England's *domestic* and *general* functions in education. The domestic function characterises the inward-looking concern to 'equip the children of the church to take their place in the Christian community,' while the general function characterises the outward-looking concern 'to serve the nation through its children.' This report recognises that while historically the two roles were 'indistinguishable, for nation and church were, theoretically, one, and the domestic task was seen as including the general,' in today's environment 'no one would pretend to claim that nation and church are coextensive.' In the light of this observation *The Fourth R* recommends that the church should see its church schools 'principally as a way of expressing its concern for the general education of all children,' that 'religious education, even in a church aided school, should not be seen in domestic terms' and that especially in single school areas church schools should be 'looked on as a service provided by the church, rather than something provided for the church.' The more recent green paper, *A Future in Partnership* (Waddington, 1984), reaffirms that the *voluntary* aspects of Church of England schools should be stressed in preference to their denominationalism. In two important essays on the future of Church of England schools within the state maintained sector, the deputy secretary and schools officer of the National Society and schools secretary of the General Synod Board of Education develops the case further for the role of 'church schools in service to the community' (Duncan, 1986, 1988).

Church schools are not, however, without their critics, from within the church as well as from without. The British Humanist Association (1967) argues that the state should not be involved in financing and recognising denominational teaching and accuses the churches of abusing their privileged position by indoctrination. The Socialist Education Association (1981, 1986) suggests that denominational schools frustrate true equality of opportunity in education. Professor Paul Hirst (1972, 1981) argues that Christian belief and educational principles are logically incompatible; the logic of education precludes the churches from influencing the educational curriculum and from operating distinctive educational institutions. Dummett and McNeal's (1981) study on race and church schools argues that the Christian reference of church schools can hamper the development of multi-racial institutions in some areas. The Swann Report, *Education for All* (1985), in its majority recommendation, advises against the extension of voluntary aided status to other faith communities and on this basis seriously calls into question 'the role of the churches in the provision of education.' In his analysis of the implications of the Swann report for religious education, Cole (1988) argues that 'denominational schools become increasingly anachronistic and less desirable.' From within the church, the report of the Church of England's Partners in Mission Consultation (1981), *To a Rebellious House*, questions the place of church schools on the grounds that the church has put too much of its resources into church schools during the past hundred years without achieving sufficient benefit in terms of mission and nurture. The Archbishop's Commission on Urban Priority Areas (1985), *Faith in the City*, warns that 'a segregated or sectarian education can increase tensions and misunderstanding.' Against such a background of criticism, it is important to establish a secure research basis on which to assess and to evaluate the current functioning of church schools.

The international literature on the effectiveness and distinctiveness of Roman Catholic schools is becoming well established, as evidenced by studies in: America (Greeley and Rossi, 1966; Neuwein, 1966; Greeley et al., 1976; Greeley, 1982; Jensen, 1986; Francis and Egan, 1990); Australia (Mol, 1968; McSweeney, 1971; Anderson, 1971; Anderson and Western, 1972; Leavey, 1972; Flynn, 1975, 1985; Fahy, 1976, 1978, 1980a, 1980b; de Vaus, 1981; Francis and Egan, 1987); Canada (McLaren, 1986); Eire (Breslin, 1982); England (Brothers, 1964; Hornsby-Smith, 1978; Burgess, 1983; Francis, 1984, 1986b; Boyle and Francis, 1986; Dent, 1988); Northern Ireland (Turner et al., 1980; Greer, 1981, 1985; Murray, 1985); Scotland (Rhymer, 1983; Rhymer and Francis, 1985) and Wales (Egan, 1985, 1988; Egan and Francis, 1986). There is also a developing research literature on the effectiveness and distinctiveness of Anglican secondary schools within the state maintained sector in England, including their role in a multicultural society (O'Keeffe, 1986), teacher attitudes (Gay, 1985b), influence on pupil attitudes towards religion (Taylor, 1970; Francis and Carter, 1980) and influence on pupil attitudinal predisposition to prayer (Francis and Brown, 1991).

Within the past decade a research literature has also begun to emerge on the distinctiveness and effectiveness of Church of England primary schools within the state maintained sector, and this research has been based largely within the more rural shire counties. Francis (1986a) reports on the attitudes of teachers in Church of England voluntary aided and voluntary controlled schools in Suffolk. These data demonstrate that the attitudes of teachers in church schools are related both to their age and to their personal practice of church-going. Older teachers and church-going teachers hold a more favourable attitude towards the church school system and tend to give more emphasis to the distinctiveness of church schools. Francis (1987) reports on the church-relatedness of state maintained primary schools in Gloucestershire and the influence of different types of school on pupil attitude towards Christianity. These data demonstrate both that church schools display more signs of being church related than county schools, and that the personal religious convictions of the headteachers are crucial in determining the church relatedness of both church schools and county schools. According to this study it is possible to identify the influence of church schools on shaping the attitude of their eleven year old pupils towards Christianity. Francis (1986c) reports on three studies conducted in East Anglia in 1974, 1978 and 1982 to assess the comparative influence of Church of England, Roman Catholic and county schools on the religious development of their pupils. These data also confirm the influence of church schools on shaping pupil attitudes towards Christianity. Finally, Kay *et al.* (1988) report on the attitudes of the governors of voluntary aided church schools in the diocese of Oxford. These data demonstrate that the foundation governors are committed 'to preserve the ethos of the voluntary aided school,' while 'in contrast parents of children in the school tend to value the Christian ethos of the schools less.' The authors conclude that: 'since this is a group that we can expect to see increasing in numbers and influence, this is potentially a worrying situation for those who value the distinctiveness of the church school.'

While the focus of the above studies concerned with Church of England primary schools has been on the curriculum, governors, pupils or teachers, Francis (1983) sets out to explore the impact of church schools on the life of the local church. Using data provided by one anonymous rural diocese, he employed path analysis to assess whether the presence of a church school in a benefice increased the number of 6–9-year-olds who come into contact with the local church during the course of a· week. The results of this analysis indicate that, while the presence of a church school makes no difference to the number of 6–9-year-olds who attend church services or children's groups on a Sunday, it does increase the likelihood of the local clergy having contact with this age group during the week, usually by visiting the school.

Although Francis (1983) provides an interesting example of data analysis, there are five significant limitations with the study. The survey is based on data from just one diocese. The path analysis is conducted on benefice units, understood as the total group of churches within the care of a clergyman, rather than on individual parishes. Although the data is based on a 92.4% response rate, it is limited to the replies of 171 benefices. While the diocese studied is predominantly rural, the sample includes church schools in town and urban areas as well as in single school areas. The outcome variables included in the study are limited simply to Sunday and weekday contact with 6–9-year-olds.

The aim of the present study is to explore the impact of church schools on village church life by specifying the context of the analysis with much greater precision than Francis's earlier study and by including a much wider range of outcome variables. This is made possible by the potential for re-analysis of a large data base of information on Anglican church life.

## Method

As part of a large national survey of the Church of England's contact with children and young people (Francis and Lankshear, 1988) a detailed questionnaire was distributed to every Anglican place of worship within 24 dioceses and one additional archdeaconry, a total of 9909 centres. The questionnaire, based on the instrument originally designed for the survey *Rural Anglicanism* (Francis, 1985), asked each church to make a detailed profile of its activities over two Sundays and the intervening weekdays, carefully listing contact with the numbers of people in each age category. The questionnaire also requested key information about each church's activity throughout the year, including numbers of baptisms, confirmations, children on Sunday school roll, parent and toddler groups, electoral roll, Easter and Christmas communicants, church choirs, house groups and other activities. Currently 7129 questionnaires have been returned, making an overall response rate of 72%. The response rate varies from 100% on the Isle of Wight and 97% in the diocese of Worcester to 50% in the diocese of Hereford.

The present analysis is conducted on the villages and small market towns with populations between 250 and 1250 people within the original nationally based survey. In the data base there are 1637 communities within this category and for which there is a complete set of information. This subset of data was selected so as to exclude both the very small villages and hamlets at one end and the larger villages and market towns at the other end, where there might conceivably be more than one school. In other words, the study focuses on a carefully specified subset of single school communities.

As potential indicators of village church life the questionnaire contains a wide range of numerical measures, like baptisms, confirmations, Sunday schools and Sunday church attendance. Before being able to explore the relationship between such numerical measures and the presence of a church school within the village, it is necessary to take into account other factors which may also affect these outcomes (Francis, 1985), like the number of people who live in the village, the number of people who regard themselves as members of the village church in terms of registering their names on the electoral roll, the number of churches joined together within a single benefice, the age of the incumbent and whether or not the clergyman resides within the village. Statistical techniques which are able to take such factors into account and to screen out their influence before testing for the impact of the presence of a church school in the village are multiple regression and path analysis (Duncan, 1966; MacDonald, 1977; Keeves, 1988). These techniques are made available through the SPSSX statistical package (SPSS Inc., 1986).

## Results

The clergy or lay people who completed questionnaires for these 1637 churches or worship centres indicated whether there was a Church of England voluntary aided or voluntary controlled school within the parish served by the church in question. Their replies identify 321 aided and 466 controlled schools.

Inspection of the spread of communities within the sample indicates that 47% of them have populations between 250 and 499, 25% between 500 and 749, 15% between 750 and 999, and 15% between 1000 and 1250. The number of names on the electoral rolls of these churches ranges from eight to 470, with 44% being under 50 and a further 41% being between 50 and 99. The majority (91%) of the churches are within multi-church benefices. A larger proportion (58%) of the churches do not have a resident clergyman than those which retain an occupied parsonage house (42%). In an earlier study Francis (1985) indicated that, in a rural diocese, clergy around the age of sixty begin to have significantly smaller congregations and significantly less contact with children and young people than younger clergy working in parishes of similar size and potential. In the present sample, 28% of the churches were served by clergy aged sixty years and over.

Preliminary inspection of the range of potential outcome variables included within the questionnaire indicated that some, like play groups, parent and toddler groups, church sponsored uniformed organisations, youth clubs and regular contact with cubs, brownies, scouts and guides, were evidenced by such a small proportion of churches in communities of between 250 and 1250 inhabitants, that it was not sensible to employ path analysis to explore the impact of the presence of a church school on such measures. The following outcome variables were, however, considered to be represented in sufficient churches to sustain careful analysis (the percentages refer to the proportions of churches reporting each form of contact): total contact over two Sundays with under 2-year-olds (29%), with 2−5-year-olds (57%), with 6−9-year-olds (69%), with 10−13-year-olds (68%), with 14−17-year-olds (55%), with 18−21-year-olds (35%) and with adults over the age of 21 (99%); 6−9-year-olds attending Sunday schools or CPAS groups (45%); church choir membership of 6−9-year-olds (16%), 10−13-year-olds (27%) and 14−21-year-olds (20%); confirmation candidates under the age of 14 (27%), between the ages of 14−17 (21%) and adolescents and adults over the age of 17 (23%); and infant baptisms under the age of 2 (78%). Preliminary analysis of the data also indicated that no clear differences emerged between the impact of church voluntary aided and church voluntary controlled schools on the outcome variables. For this reason the following regression equations do not differentiate between these two types of church schools.

Table 1 presents the multiple regression significance tests designed to explore the impact of the presence of a church school within the area served by a church on each of these fifteen outcome variables, after taking into account differences in population sizes, the number of names on the electoral roll, multi-parish benefices, the presence of a vicarage and the age of the clergyman. The presence of a church school adds significant additional predictive information in respect of six of the outcome variables, but not in relationship to the other nine. These six variables influenced by the presence of a church school are the number of 6−9-year-olds who come into contact with the local church on a Sunday, the number of adults who come into contact with the local church on a Sunday, the number of 6−9-year-olds who belong to the church choir, the number of 10−13-year-olds who belong to the church choir, the number of infants baptised under two years of age, and the number of under 14-year-olds who come to be confirmed.

While table 1 presents the final conclusion of the regression analyses, it fails to make explicit the assumed causal paths being taken into account. Table 2 and Figure 1, therefore, make these paths explicit in relationship to just three of the outcome variables, namely Sunday contact with 2−5-year-olds, with 6−9-year-olds and with adults. In this path model, electoral roll is first explored as a function of population, number of parishes in the benefice,

*Table 1: Multiple regression significance tests*

| Dependent variables | | Total R2 | Incr. R2 | F | P< |
|---|---|---|---|---|---|
| Sunday contact, | under 2 years | 0.0559 | 0.0004 | 0.7 | NS |
| Sunday contact, | 2−5 years | 0.1504 | 0.0019 | 3.4 | NS |
| Sunday contact, | 6−9 years | 0.1071 | 0.0048 | 8.3 | 0.01 |
| Sunday contact, | 10−13 years | 0.1241 | 0.0021 | 3.7 | NS |
| Sunday contact, | 14−17 years | 0.0272 | 0.0016 | 2.5 | NS |
| Sunday contact, | 18−21 years | 0.1126 | 0.0003 | 0.6 | NS |
| Sunday contact, | over 21 years | 0.4413 | 0.0027 | 7.4 | 0.01 |
| Sunday school, | 6−9 years | 0.1301 | 0.0020 | 3.6 | NS |
| church choir, | 6−9 years | 0.0387 | 0.0046 | 7.3 | 0.01 |
| church choir, | 10−13 years | 0.0922 | 0.0062 | 10.6 | 0.001 |
| church choir, | 14−21 years | 0.0886 | 0.0018 | 3.1 | NS |
| infant baptisms, | under 2 years | 0.1928 | 0.0066 | 12.6 | 0.001 |
| confirmands, | under 14 years | 0.0896 | 0.0025 | 4.3 | 0.05 |
| confirmands, | 14−17 years | 0.0325 | 0.0005 | 0.8 | NS |
| confirmands, | over 17 years | 0.0544 | 0.0002 | 0.4 | NS |

presence of a vicarage and age of the clergyman. Then the three outcome variables are explored as a function of population, electoral roll, number of parishes in the benefice, presence of a vicarage, age of the clergyman and presence of a church school. When these relationships are found to be statiscally significant they are indicated in the path diagram by straight arrows.

Considerable additional information is conveyed by this path model which helps to explore the complex factors at work in predicting the village church's contact with these three age groups. First, the number of people living in the parish is shown to have an important influence on the number of names on the electoral roll and on the number of individuals within each of the three age groups who come into contact with the local church on a Sunday. Second, churches with larger electoral rolls tend to have more Sunday contact with all three age groups than churches in communities of the same size with smaller electoral rolls. Third, churches in multi-parish benefices have smaller electoral rolls than churches which serve the same size population but do not share their clergyman with other parishes. Churches in multi-parish benefices also have contact with fewer people in each of the three age groups than churches which serve the same populations and have the same number of names on the electoral roll but do not share their clergyman with other parishes. Fourth, parishes in which the clergyman resides tend to have more names on the electoral roll and more Sunday contact with adults and with preschoolers than parishes of the same size where there is no resident clergyman. In relationship to contact with 6−9-year-olds, however, it is the

*Table 2: Multiple regression significance tests for path model 1*

| Dependent variables | Independent variables | R2 | Increase in R2 | F | P< | Beta | T | P< |
|---|---|---|---|---|---|---|---|---|
| electoral roll | population | 0.1385 | 0.1385 | 248.9 | 0.001 | +0.2544 | +10.6 | 0.001 |
| | multi-parish benefice | 0.2031 | 0.0645 | 125.3 | 0.001 | -0.2145 | -9.0 | 0.001 |
| | vicarage in area | 0.2344 | 0.0313 | 63.2 | 0.001 | +0.1925 | +7.9 | 0.001 |
| | clergy aged 60+ | 0.2344 | 0.0003 | 0.6 | NS | +0.0174 | +0.8 | NS |
| 2–5-year-old Sunday contact | population | 0.1063 | 0.1063 | 184.1 | 0.001 | +0.2218 | +8.4 | 0.001 |
| | electoral roll | 0.1287 | 0.0224 | 39.8 | 0.001 | +0.1181 | +4.4 | 0.001 |
| | multi-parish benefice | 0.1329 | 0.0042 | 7.6 | 0.01 | -0.0598 | -2.3 | 0.05 |
| | vicarage in area | 0.1419 | 0.0090 | 16.2 | 0.001 | +0.1063 | +4.0 | 0.001 |
| | clergy aged 60+ | 0.1485 | 0.0066 | 12.0 | 0.001 | -0.0809 | -3.4 | 0.001 |
| | church school | 0.1504 | 0.0019 | 3.4 | NS | +0.0441 | +1.8 | NS |
| 6–9-year-old Sunday contact | population | 0.0700 | 0.0700 | 116.5 | 0.001 | +0.1808 | +6.7 | 0.001 |
| | electoral roll | 0.0882 | 0.0182 | 30.8 | 0.001 | +0.1081 | +3.9 | 0.001 |
| | multi-parish benefice | 0.0977 | 0.0095 | 16.3 | 0.001 | -0.1106 | -4.2 | 0.001 |
| | vicarage in area | 0.0979 | 0.0002 | 0.3 | NS | +0.0106 | +0.4 | NS |
| | clergy aged 60+ | 0.1023 | 0.0045 | 7.7 | 0.01 | -0.0656 | -2.7 | 0.01 |
| | church school | 0.1071 | 0.0048 | 8.3 | 0.01 | +0.0708 | +2.9 | 0.01 |
| adult over 21 Sunday contact | population | 0.2086 | 0.2086 | 408.0 | 0.001 | +0.2226 | +10.4 | 0.001 |
| | electoral roll | 0.4072 | 0.1986 | 518.4 | 0.001 | +0.4147 | +19.0 | 0.001 |
| | multi-parish benefice | 0.4228 | 0.0156 | 41.8 | 0.001 | -0.1198 | -5.7 | 0.001 |
| | vicarage in area | 0.4344 | 0.0116 | 31.7 | 0.001 | +0.1184 | +5.5 | 0.001 |
| | clergy aged 60+ | 0.4386 | 0.0042 | 11.5 | 0.001 | -0.0640 | -3.3 | 0.001 |
| | church school | 0.4413 | 0.0027 | 7.4 | 0.01 | +0.0527 | +2.7 | 0.01 |

*Figure 1:* Path model

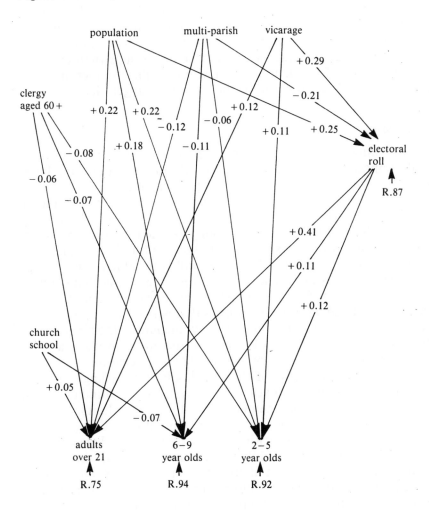

presence of a church school rather than the presence of a vicarage within the parish which really counts. Fifth, while the clergyman's age has no effect on the number of names on the electoral roll, churches within the care of clergy aged 60 and over have significantly less Sunday contact with all three age groups than churches in communities of the same size and with the same number of names on the electoral roll but within the care of younger clergy.

## Discussion

These findings indicate that church schools do have a significant, if small, impact on certain key measures of village church life. Three aspects of this impact are worthy of closer scrutiny and comment.

First, while the presence of a church school has no additional impact on the local church's Sunday contact with children under the age of 6 or with children and young people between the ages of 10 and 21, it does increase the local church's Sunday contact with children between the ages of 6 and 9 and with adults over the age of 21. These trends are consistent with the observation that children between the ages of 6 and 9 are those most likely to attend the local church school and with the hypothesis that when children in this age group attend church on a Sunday they encourage their parents to attend as well. Church schools are seen, therefore, to make a small contribution to the growth of the Sunday congregation.

Second, the main impact of church schools on the village church's Sunday contact with 6–9-year-olds is seen not in Sunday school attendance, but in the membership of church choirs. Church schools do not recruit more 6–9-year-olds into attending Sunday schools. This is consistent with the view that some village churches regard their contact with children through the local church voluntary primary school as an alternative to providing Sunday school classes. On the other hand, church schools do help to recruit more 6–9-year-olds into church choirs and this influence continues to be seen among the 10–13-year-age group. This is consistent with the view that village church choirs provide a major way of involving children in church services when there is no special Sunday school or junior youth activities available for them. Church schools are seen, therefore, to help shape the village church's ministry among children and young people.

Third, the presence of a church school has a small additional impact on certain membership statistics, in terms of infant baptisms and confirmations under the age of 14. The small increase in infant baptism is consistent with the view that church schools help to bring more young parents into contact with the life of the local church. Some of the additional infant baptisms may well be the younger siblings of children attending the church school. The small increase in young confirmands is consistent with the influence identified above of church schools on pre-teenage church-going in general and membership of church choirs in particular. Church schools are seen, therefore, to help bring additional individuals into baptised or confirmed membership of the church.

While Francis (1983) demonstrated that church schools may exert a positive influence on the contact between the clergy and 6–9-year-olds during the week, the present data, on a larger and more clearly specified sample of rural parishes, clearly indicate that church schools also exert a beneficial influence on church membership and Sunday church attendance.

## Acknowledgements

We are grateful to the Sarum St Michael Educational Charity who sponsored the analysis undertaken in this paper; to the Department of Education and Science and to the Welsh Office for statistics on church schools; to the many churches who cooperated in the present study; to the All Saints Educational Trust, the Foundation of St Mathias, the Hockerill Educational Foundation, St Gabriel's Trust, the Sarum St Michael Educational Charity, St Christopher's Trust, the Central Church Fund of the Church of England and the Culham Trustees who provided funding for the original survey; to members of the children, young people and the church management committee who commented on drafts of this paper.

### References

Anderson, D S (1971) 'Do Catholic schools cause people to go to church?', *Australia and New Zealand Journal of Sociology*, 7, pp. 65–67.

Anderson, D S and Western, J S (1972) 'Denominational schooling and religious behaviour,' *Australian and New Zealand Journal of Sociology*, 8, pp. 19–31.

Archbishop's Commission on Urban Priority Areas (1985) *Faith in the City*, London, Church House Publishing.

Boyle, J J and Francis, L J (1986) 'The influence of differing church aided school systems on pupil attitudes towards religion,' *Research in Education*, 35, pp. 7–12.

Breslin, A (1982) 'Some correlates of tolerance among adolescents in Ireland,' *Journal of Moral Education*, 11, pp. 112–127.

British Humanist Association (1967) *Religion in Schools*, London, British Humanist Association.

Brooksbank, K, Revell, J, Ackstine, E and Bailey, K (1982) *County and Voluntary Schools*, 6th edn, Harlow, Longman.

Brothers, J (1964) *Church and School: a study of the impact of education on religion*, Liverpool, University of Liverpool Press.

Burgess, H J (1958) *Enterprise in Education*, London, National Society and SPCK.

Burgess, R G (1983) *Experiencing Comprehensive Education: a study of Bishop McGregor School*, London, Methuen.

Cole, W (1988) 'Religious education after Swann,' in B O'Keeffe (ed.), *Schools for Tomorrow*, Barcombe, Falmer Press, pp. 125–144.

Cruickshank, M (1963) *Church and State in English Education*, London, Macmillan.

Cruickshank, M (1972) 'The denominational schools issue in the twentieth century,' *History of Education*, 1, pp. 200–213.

Dent, H C (1947) *The Education Act 1944: provisions, possibilities and some problems*, London, University of London Press.

Dent, R (1988) *Faith of Our Fathers: Roman Catholic schools in a multifaith society*, Coventry, City of Coventry Education Department.

De Vaus, D A (1981) 'The impact of Catholic schools on the religious orientation of boys and girls,' *Journal of Christian Education*, 71, pp. 44–51.

Dummett, A and McNeal, J (1981) *Race and Church Schools*, London, Runnymede Trust.

Duncan, G (1986) 'Church schools: present and future,' in G. Leonard (ed.), *Faith for the Future*, London, National Society and Church House Publishing, pp. 67–78.

Duncan, G (1988) 'Church schools in service to the community,' in B O'Keeffe (ed.), *Schools for Tomorrow*, Barcombe, Falmer Press, pp. 145–161.

Duncan, O D (1966) 'Path analysis: sociological examples,' *American Journal of Sociology*, 72, pp. 1–16.

Egan, J (1985) 'An evaluation of the implementation of the principles of Catholic education in the Catholic comprehensive schools in Wales,' unpublished Ph.D. dissertation, University of Wales, Cardiff.

Egan, J (1988) *Opting Out: Catholic schools today,* Leominster, Fowler Wright.

Egan, J and Francis, L J (1986) 'School ethos in Wales: the impact of non-practising Catholic and non-Catholic pupils on Catholic secondary schools,' *Lumen Vitae*, 41, pp. 159–173.

Fahy, P S (1976) 'Religious beliefs of 15,900 youths,' *Word in Life*, 26, pp. 66–72.

Fahy, P S (1980a) 'The effectiveness on Christian criteria of 17 Australian Catholic high schools,' unpublished doctoral dissertation, Boston College, MA, USA.

Fahy, P S (1980b) 'The religious effectiveness of some Australian Catholic high schools,' *Word in Life*, 28. pp. 86–98.

Flynn, M (1975) *Some Catholic Schools in Action*, Sydney, Catholic Education Office.

Flynn, M (1985) *The Effectiveness of Catholic Schools*, Homebush NSW, Saint Paul Publications.

Francis, L J (1983) 'Anglican voluntary primary schools and child church attendance,' *Research in Education*, 30, pp. 1–9.

Francis, L J (1984) 'Roman Catholic schools and pupil attitudes in England,' *Lumen Vitae*, 39, pp. 99–108.

Francis, L J (1985) *Rural Anglicanism: a future for young Christians?* London, Collins Liturgical Publications.

Francis, L J (1986a) *Partnership in Rural Education*, London, Collins Liturgical Publications.

Francis, L J (1986b) 'Roman Catholic secondary schools: falling rolls and pupil attitudes,' *Educational Studies,*' 12, pp. 119–127.

Francis, L J (1986c) 'Denominational schools and pupil attitude towards Christianity,' *British Educational Research Journal*, 12, pp. 145–152.

Francis, L J (1987) *Religion in the Primary School*, London, Collins Liturgical Publications.

Francis, L J and Brown, L B (1991) 'The influence of home, church and school on prayer among sixteen-year-old adolescents in England,' *Review of Religious Research*, 33, pp. 112–122.

Francis, L J and Carter, M (1980) 'Church-aided secondary schools, religious education as an examination subject and pupil attitudes towards religion,' *British Journal of Educational Psychology*, 50, pp. 297–300.

Francis, L J and Egan, J (1987) 'Catholic schools and the communication of faith,' *Catholic School Studies*, 60, 2, pp. 27–34.

Francis, L J and Egan, J (1990) 'The Catholic school as "faith community": an empirical enquiry,' *Religious Education*, 85, pp. 588–603.

Francis, L J and Lankshear, D W (1988) 'The survey,' in *Children in the Way*, chapter 7, London, National Society and Church House Publishing.

Gay, J (1985a) *The Size of Anglican Primary Schools*, Occasional Paper 7, Abingdon, Culham College Institute.

Gay, J (1985b) *Between Church and Chalkface: the views of teachers in Church of England aided secondary schools in the Oxford diocese*, Occasional Paper 6, Abingdon, Culham College Institute.

Greeley, A M (1982) *Catholic High Schools and Minority Students*, New Brunswick, Transaction Books.

Greeley, A M, McCready, W C and McCourt, K (1976) *Catholic Schools in a Declining Church*, Kansas City, Sheed and Ward.

Greeley, A M and Rossi, P H (1966) *The Education of Catholic Americans*, Chicago, Aldine Publishing Company.

Greer, J E (1981) 'Religious attitudes and thinking in Belfast pupils,' *Educational Research*, 23, pp. 177–189.

Greer, J E (1985) 'Viewing "the other side" in Northern Ireland: openness and attitudes to religion among Catholic and Protestant adolescents,' *Journal for the Scientific Study of Religion*, 24, pp. 275–292.

Hirst, P H (1972) 'Christian education: a contradiction in terms?', *Learning for Living*, 11, 4, pp. 6–11.

Hirst, P H (1981) 'Education, catechesis and the church school,' *Learning for Living*, 15, pp. 155–157.

Hornsby-Smith, M P (1978) *Catholic Education: the unobtrusive partner*, London, Sheed and Ward.

Jensen, G F (1986) 'Explaining differences in academic behaviour between public-school and Catholic-school students: a quantitative case study,' *Sociology of Education*, 59, pp. 32–41.

Kay, B W, Piper, H S and Gay, J D (1988) *Managing the Church Schools: a study of the governing bodies of Church of England aided primary schools in the Oxford diocese*, Occasional Paper 10, Abingdon, Culham College Institute.

Keeves, J P (1988) 'Path analysis,' in J P Keeves (ed.) *Educational Research, Methodology, and Measurement: an international handbook*, Oxford, Pergamon Press, pp. 723–731.

Kelly, S E (1978) 'The schools of the established church in England: a study of diocesan involvement since 1944,' unpublished Ph.D. dissertation, University of Keele.

Leavey, M C (1972) 'Religious education, school climate and achievement: a study of nine Catholic sixth form girls schools,' unpublished Ph.D. dissertation, Australian National University, Canberra.

MacDonald, K I (1977) 'Path analysis,' in C A O'Muircheartaigh and C Payne (eds) *The Analysis of Survey Data*, vol. 2, New York, John Wiley and Sons, ch. 3.

McLaren, P (1986) *Schooling as a Ritual Performance*, London, Routledge and Kegan Paul.

McSweeney, R V (1971) 'Values of Queensland students from different types of school,' *Journal of Christian Education*, 14, pp. 132–139.

Mol, J J (1968) 'The effects of the denominational schools in Australia,' *Australian and New Zealand Journal of Sociology*, 4, pp. 18–35.

Murphy, J (1971) *Church, State and Schools in Britain 1800–1970*, London, Routledge and Kegan Paul.

Murphy, J (1972) *The Education Act 1870*, Newton Abbot, David and Charles.

Murray, D (1985) *Worlds Apart: segregated schools in Northern Ireland*, Belfast, Appletree Press.

Neuwien, R A (ed.) (1966) *Catholic Schools in Action*, Notre Dame, Indiana, University of Notre Dame Press.

O'Keeffe, B (1986) *Faith, Culture and the Dual System: a comparative study of church and county schools*, Barcombe, Falmer Press.

Partners In Mission Consultation (1981) *To a Rebellious House?* London, CIO Publishing.

Ramsey, I (1930) *The Fourth R*, London, National Society and SPCK.

Rhymer, J (1983) 'Religious attitudes of Roman Catholic secondary school pupils in Strathclyde region,' unpublished Ph.D. dissertation, University of Edinburgh.

Rhymer, J and Francis, L J (1985) 'Roman Catholic secondary schools in Scotland and pupil attitude towards religion,' *Lumen Vitae*, 40, pp. 103–110.

Socialist Education Association (1981) *The Dual System of Voluntary and County Schools*, London, Socialist Education Association.

Socialist Education Association (1986) *All Faiths in All Schools*, London, Socialist Education Association.

SPSS Inc. (1986) *SPSSX User's Guide*, New York, McGraw-Hill.

Swann Report (1985) *Education for All*, London, Her Majesty's Stationery Office.

Taylor, H P (1970) 'A comparative study of the religious attitudes, beliefs and practices of sixth formers in Anglican, state and Roman Catholic schools and an assessment of religious opinion upon them asserted by home and school,' unpublished M.Phil. dissertation, University of London.

Turner, E B, Turner, I F and Reid, A (1980) 'Religious attitudes in two types of urban secondary school: a decade of change,' *Irish Journal of Education*, 14, pp. 43–52.

Waddington, R (1984) *A Future in Partnership*, London, National Society.

# Acknowledgements

The publisher and editors would like to acknowledge the following permissions to reproduce copyright material. All possible attempts have been made to contact copyright holders and to acknowledge their copyright correctly. We are grateful to: *British Journal of Educational Studies*, for L J Francis, 'Theology of education,' 38, 349–364, 1990; *British Journal of Religious Education*, for J Arthur, 'Catholic responses to the 1988 Education Reform Act: problems of authority and ethos,' 13, 181–189, 1991, for D G Attfield, 'Presenting the eucharist in a primary school,' 12, 167–171, 1990, for D G Attfield, 'The challenge of the Education Reform Act to church schools,' 13, 136–142, 1991, for E Cox, and M Skinner, 'Multifaith religious education in church primary schools,' 12, 102–109, 1990, for J L Higgins, 'Gender and Church of England diocesan syllabuses of religious education,' 12, 58–62, 1989, for P H Hirst, 'Education, catechesis and the church school,' 3, 85–93, 1981 and for P Malone, 'The language of religious education curriculum in Australian Catholic schools,' 9, 138–147, 1987; *Canadian Journal of Education*, for R M Miller, 'Should there be religious alternative schools within the public school system?' 11, 278–292, 1986, and for B J Shapiro, 'The public funding of private schools in Ontario: the setting, some arguments, and some matters of belief,' 11, 264–277, 1986; *Common Ground*, for A Brown, 'Aided Schools: help, hindrance, anachronism or trailblazer,' 3, 5–9, 1988; *Compare*, for O Boyd-Barrett, 'State and Church in Spanish Education,' 21, 179–197, 1991; *Educational Policy* and Corwin Press, Inc., for A Peshkin, 'Fundamentalist Christian schools: should they be regulated?,' 3, 45–56, 1989; *Educational Studies*, for L J Francis and D W Lankshear, 'The impact of church schools on village church life,' 16, 117–129, 1990; *Educational Theory*, for W J Reese, 'Soldiers for Christ in the army of God: the Christian school movement in America,' 35, 175–194, 1985; *European Journal of Education*, for M De Kwaasteniet, 'Denominational education and contemporary education policy in the Netherlands,' 20, 371–383, 1985, and for S Ó Buachalla, 'Church and State in Irish Education in this Century,' 20, 351–359, 1985; *Journal for the Scientific Study of Religion*, for J E Greer, 'Viewing "the other side" in Northern Ireland: openness and attitude to religion among Catholic and Protestant Adolescents,' 24, 275–292, 1985; *Journal of Christian Education*, for B V Hill, 'Christian schools: issues to be resolved,' 75, 5–17, 1982; *Journal of Educational Policy*, for W Ball and B

Troyna, 'Resistance, rights and rituals: denominational schools and multicultural education,' 2, 15–25, 1987; *Journal of Philosophy of Education*, for D N Aspin, 'Church Schools, religious education and the multi-ethnic community,' 17, 229–240, 1983, for N Blake, 'Church schools, religious education and the multi-ethnic community: a reply to David Aspin,' 17, 241–250, 1983, and for E J Thiessen, 'Two concepts or two phases of liberal education,' 21, 223–234, 1987; *Lumen Vitae*, for J Rhymer and L J Francis, 'Roman Catholic secondary schools in Scotland and pupil attitude towards religion,' 40, 103–110, 1985; *One in Christ*, for P Marr, 'Denominational schools: some implications from ARCIC-I,' 25, 333–346, 1989; *Religious Education*, for L J Francis and J Egan, 'The Catholic school as "faith community": an empirical enquiry,' 85, 588–603, 1990 (*Religious Education* is published by the Religious Education Association, 409 Prospect Street, New Haven, CT 06511–2177 USA, Membership information available upon request); *Westminster Studies in Education*, for D H Webster, 'Being Aflame: spirituality in county and church schools,' 10, 3–11, 1987; Harper Collins Religious, an imprint of Harper Collins Publishers Limited, for extracts from L J Francis, *Partnership in Rural Education: church schools and teacher attitudes*, London, Collins Liturgical Publications, 1986, and for extracts from L J Francis, *Religion in the Primary School: partnership between church and state?*, London, Collins Liturgical Publications, 1987; Culham Educational Foundation, for extracts from B M Gay, *The Church of England and the Independent Schools*, Abingdon, Culham College Institute, 1985; InterEuropean Commission on Church and School, for G S Duncan, 'The School: commitment and openness, in 'Commitment and Neutrality: a useful opposition,' 1989; National Society, for extracts from R M Waddington, *A Future in Partnership*, 1984.

# Index of subjects

# Index of names